# WILDERNESS PROTECTION IN EUROPE

Europe still retains large areas which play host to numerous native and free-functioning ecosystems and lack roads, buildings, bridges, cables and other permanent manifestations of modern society. In the past, such areas were considered wastelands, whose value lay only in their potential for cultivation and economic exploitation. Today, these wilderness areas are increasingly cherished as places for rest and recreation and as important areas for scientific research, biodiversity conservation and the mitigation of and adaptation to certain climate change effects. This book provides the first major appraisal of the role of international, European and domestic law in protecting the remaining wilderness areas and their distinguishing qualities in Europe. It also highlights the lessons that can be learned from the various international, regional and national approaches, identifies obstacles to wilderness protection in Europe and considers whether and how the legal protection of wilderness can be further advanced.

KEES BASTMEIJER is Professor of Nature Conservation and Water Law at Tilburg University, The Netherlands, and a visiting professor at the School of Business, Economics and Law at the University of Gothenburg, Sweden. His research focuses on the role of international, European and domestic law in protecting nature, with a particular interest in nature conservation in the polar regions, relationships between law and philosophical human–nature attitudes, property rights and nature and the role of law in protecting wilderness.

# WILDERNESS PROTECTION IN EUROPE

## The Role of International, European and National Law

Edited by
KEES BASTMEIJER
*Tilburg University, The Netherlands*

CAMBRIDGE
UNIVERSITY PRESS

**CAMBRIDGE**
**UNIVERSITY PRESS**

University Printing House, Cambridge CB2 8BS, United Kingdom

Cambridge University Press is part of the University of Cambridge.

It furthers the University's mission by disseminating knowledge in the pursuit of education, learning and research at the highest international levels of excellence.

www.cambridge.org
Information on this title: www.cambridge.org/9781107057890



First published 2016

*A catalogue record for this publication is available from the British Library*

*Library of Congress Cataloguing in Publication data*
Bastmeijer, C. J., 1966– editor.
Wilderness protection in Europe : the role of international, European and national law / edited by Kees Bastmeije.
Cambridge, United Kingdom : Cambridge University Press, 2016. | Includes bibliographical references and index.
LCCN 2016004899 | ISBN 9781107057890 (hardback : alk. paper)
LCSH: Wilderness areas – Law and legislation – Europe. | Nature conservation – Law and legislation – Europe.
LCC KJC6255 .W55 2016 | DDC 346.404/6782–dc23
LC record available at http://lccn.loc.gov/2016004899

ISBN 978-1-107-05789-0 Hardback

# CONTENTS

# CONTRIBUTORS

**Kees Bastmeijer** is Professor of Nature Conservation and Water Law at Tilburg University, The Netherlands, and a visiting professor at the School of Business, Economics and Law at the University of Gothenburg, Sweden. His research focuses on the role of international, European and domestic law in protecting nature, with a particular interest in nature conservation in the polar regions, relationships between law and philosophical human–nature attitudes, property rights and nature and the role of law in protecting wilderness.

**Nicole Bauer** holds a PhD in environmental psychology from the Technical University of Berlin, Germany. She is a research scientist at the Research Institute for Forest, Snow and Landscape Research WSL in Birmensdorf, Switzerland. She is interested in the attitudes towards different types of landscapes and landscape changes (including wilderness and re-wilding) and in the impact of natural environments on human health and well-being. Since 2012 she has been co-editor of the journal *Umweltpsychologie*.

**Simon Boyle** is a solicitor who has specialized in environmental law since 1990, including ten years in the manufacturing industry. He is Environmental Law Director of Landmark Information Group. Since 2005 he has been the Convenor of the Wild Law Special Interest Group of the UK Environmental Law Association. A keen climber, he spends much of his free time in the Scottish Highlands and the English Lake District and enjoys wild camping.

**Richard Caddell** is a Nippon Foundation Senior Nereus Fellow and a Senior Research Associate at the Netherlands Institute for the Law of the Sea, Utrecht University, having previously held a series of academic posts in the UK and Estonia. His main research interests engage international and EU environmental law, the law of the sea, biodiversity conservation, fisheries, Polar law and environmental regulation in the former Soviet Union, with a particular focus on the Baltic States. Dr Caddell is also an academic member of Francis Taylor Building, Inner Temple, London, the UK's foremost environmental and planning law barristers.

**Steve Carver** is a senior lecturer in Geography at the University of Leeds and Director of the Wildland Research Institute. He has a wide ranging interest in wilderness and wild lands but his research focuses on the application of Geographical Information Systems (GIS) and participatory approaches in mapping and modelling the spatial patterns in wilderness quality. He is largely responsible for the methods and approaches used in the Scottish wild land policy maps.

**Natalia Danilina** is the Director of the Russian NGO Zapovedniks Centre (since 1996). She has worked as a researcher in the field of Protected Areas (PA) design and was from 1993 to 1995 the Head of the Department of PA Management of the Ministry of the Environment. She is one of the authors of the Russian Federal Law on Specially Protected Nature Areas and of various PA policy documents, including policies on visitation and environmental education. From 1993 to 2008, Natalia was the Regional Vice-chair of IUCN's World Commission on Protected Areas (1993–2008).

**Harald Egerer** is the Head of the UNEP Vienna SCC Office and has acted as the Secretary of the Carpathian Convention on behalf of the United Nations Environment Programme (UNEP) since the year 2004. He graduated in Law at the University of Vienna and worked as an environmental reporter for the Austrian Press Agency. In 1996, Mr Egerer joined UNEP's Secretariat of the Basel Convention on the Control of Transboundary Movements of Hazardous Wastes and their Disposal. With UNEP's European Office as of 2001, Mr Egerer supported the seven Carpathian countries in the development of the Framework Convention on the Protection and Sustainable Development of the Carpathians.

**Ole Kristian Fauchald** is research professor at the Fridtjof Nansen Institute. His chapter was part of the research project 'Managing Protected Areas in a Time of Internationalization', funded by the Norwegian Research Council. Fauchald is also professor at the Department of Public and International Law at the University of Oslo. His main research interests are national and international environmental law, international investment law and international trade law.

**Mark Fisher** is an Honorary Research Fellow of the Wildland Research Institute at the University of Leeds. His work for the Institute has included a report to the Scottish Government on the national protected area systems of Europe, their legislative basis and ability to protect wild land, and a European wilderness register and indicator for the European Commission. Fascinated with the self-assembly of wilderness, he explores that ecology on his advocacy website Self-willed land.

**Sandor Fulop** is the chair of Environmental Management and Law Association (EMLA) Hungary, a scientific research, education and public interest litigation organization. He has a degree in law (1982) and a degree in psychology (1997). He achieved his PhD degree from the Debrecen University (2010) with a thesis on comparative environmental procedural law. Dr Fulop was the first Parliamentary Commissioner for Future Generations of Hungary, a position he held from 2008 till 2012.

**Ewald Galle** graduated in Law (Vienna) with a focus on International Environmental Law. Since 1990 he has been an officer in the Division for International Environmental Affairs of the former Austrian Ministry for Environment, nowadays the Federal Ministry for Agriculture, Forestry, Environment and Water Management. From the very beginning of his career, he has been responsible for all international aspects of the Alpine Convention and later on for the national implications of the Convention in Austria. He is a member of the International Council of Environmental Law.

**Agustín García-Ureta** is currently full-time Professor of Law at the University of the Basque Country (Bilbao, Spain). He has written more than 140 chapters, articles and case commentaries on European environmental and biodiversity legislation (in particular the wild birds and habitats directives). His books include *Derecho Europeo de la Biodiversidad* (2010) and he has coordinated *La Directiva de Hábitats de la Unión Europea: balance de 20 años* (2012) and *Estudios de Derecho Ambiental Europeo* (2006).

**Cai Lin Gwee** is an environmental engineer and consultant who worked on the Carpathian Convention and climate change-related areas at the UNEP Vienna Secretariat of the Carpathian Convention Office. She holds a double Master's degree in Environmental Sciences from the University of Natural Resources and Life Sciences, Austria, and the University of Copenhagen, Denmark, and a Bachelor's degree in Environmental Engineering from the National University of Singapore. Cai Lin has international experience in

Singapore, Germany and Austria, with a focus on sustainable development and environmental research and management.

**Bernd Hansjürgens** is professor of Economics, especially Environmental Economics, at Martin Luther-University Halle-Wittenberg and is head of the Department of Economics at the Helmholtz Centre for Environmental Research – UFZ. He has been involved in the international research initiative 'The Economics of Ecosystems and Biodiversity' (TEEB) and is associated editor of the journal 'Ecosystem Services' (Elsevier). His research interests encompass market-based instruments of environment and nature protection policy, economic valuation as well as institutional economic analyses of the implementation of environmental policies.

**Aðalheiður Jóhannsdóttir** (LL.D. UU Sweden) is a professor of Environmental and Natural Resources Law (International, EU and National) at the Faculty of Law, University of Iceland, and a former vice Dean of the Faculty. She has published more than thirty articles and book chapters on environmental and natural resources-related issues, both nationally and internationally. Her main research activities include international publications in the field of environmental law methodology, biodiversity law and Arctic-related topics.

**Mathilde Köck** worked as a consultant for the UNEP Vienna Secretariat of the Carpathian Convention in the fields of Biodiversity and Climate Change Adaptation. She was responsible for the management of the South East Europe BioREGIO Carpathians project, on biodiversity and ecological connectivity in the Carpathians. Ms. Köck now works for the International Disaster Management Department of the Austrian Red Cross. She holds an MSc in Water Conflict Management from UNESCO-IHE in Delft, Netherlands, and a Bakk. Tech. in Environmental Management from the University for Life Sciences in Vienna, Austria.

**Kai T. Kokko** (LL.D.) is Professor of Environmental Law at the Faculty of Law, University of Helsinki, and a former professor at the University of Lapland. He has written a book on legal principles and mechanisms for safeguarding biodiversity (2003) and is the author of several scientific articles on nature protection and forestry law. In 2005 and 2006, Kai Kokko worked on nature conservation cases as a judicial secretary of the Supreme Administrative Court. In 2009, he led an assessment of possible implications of legally binding European forestry agreements on selected other international agreements and the EU/EC competence.

**Zdeňka Křenová** was a deputy director of the Šumava NP, CZ, and together with colleagues from the Bavarian Forest NP established the Wild Europe's Heart, the first transboundary wilderness area in Central Europe. Currently, she works in the Global Change Research Centre, AS CR, and participates in research projects focusing on population dynamics and stability of ecological communities. The results of this research are applied in the protection of biodiversity and nature conservation. She also teaches several nature conservation courses at Charles University in Prague and in České Budějovice.

**Nele Lienhoop** is a senior researcher in the Economics Department at the Helmholtz-Centre for Environmental Research – UFZ in Leipzig, Germany. She obtained a BSc degree in geography from the University of Iceland and completed her MSc and PhD in Environmental Economics at the University of Aberdeen. Her main research interests include the economic valuation of the environment with various applications related to water resources, wilderness, biodiversity, ecosystem services and renewable energies.

**Simon Marsden** is a professor at Flinders Law School. Simon has research interests in environmental law and policy, environmental planning and management, and the relationship between legal systems. These relate to domestic law in federal, unitary and mixed systems (Australia, England, Hong Kong), and international and EU law. Simon has published in many journals, including *ICLQ* and *Nordic JIL*. He has recently completed a book on the UNECE agreements in Asia and has begun another on the Third Pole.

**Volker Mauerhofer** received his Master and doctorate degree in Law (University of Graz/Austria – 1993/1998 with Honours) and his Master's degree in Natural Sciences (University of Vienna/Austria – 1999). After practising law at courts and law firms he passed the bar exam in Austria and obtained a post-graduate MA in Ecological Economics (University of Leeds/UK – 2003). Currently he is a lecturer at the University of Vienna in the Master program Nature Conservation & Biodiversity Management. He holds different visiting positions, such as Visiting Professor at UN University, Institute for the Advanced Study of Sustainability/Japan.

**Eleonora Musco** works as consultant for the European Academy of Bolzano (EURAC Research) at the UNEP Vienna Secretariat of the Carpathian Convention in Vienna. She is responsible for the Secretariat daily activities, its cooperation with the EU Bodies and research networks and for project development. She holds a Master's degree in International Relations from the LUISS University in Rome, Italy, and a Bachelor's degree in Political Science from the University of Perugia, Italy. Previously, she has worked at UNESCO in Paris, for the Italian Ministry of Foreign Affairs in Vienna and for the Italian Ministry of the Environment in Rome.

**Antje Neumann** is a legal researcher with a specialization in Polar Law. She is affiliated with the University of Tilburg, the Netherlands, where she currently conducts her PhD research on wilderness protection in Antarctica using case studies from the Arctic. Additional research interests include the recognition of indigenous peoples' rights in the context of area protection and management in the Arctic region.

**Markku Oksanen** is Senior Lecturer in Philosophy at University of Eastern Finland. He has co-edited *Philosophy and Biodiversity* (Cambridge University Press, 2004) and *Ethics of Animal Re-creation and Modification* and published articles on green political theory and environmental ethics.

**Marco Onida**, LLM in international and comparative law, is an official of the European Commission, specializing in environmental protection and international cooperation. From 2007 to 2013 he was the Secretary General of the Alpine Convention. He is the author of several publications in the field of European and International environmental law and policy.

**Arie Trouwborst** is associate professor of environmental law at Tilburg Law School's Department of European and International Law. Most of his research is in the field of international and European wildlife law. Currently, the principal focus of his research is on the conservation and management of large carnivores.

**Sergiusz Urban,** PhD (Institute of Law Studies of Polish Academy of Sciences), is an environmental lawyer, and he heads environmental law practice at WKB Wierciński Kwieciński Baehr law firm, Poland. Through an internship he has worked for the European Commission's Environment Directorate-General. Sergiusz has received a scholarship from the European Environment Agency and from American University College of Law in Washington and has received an individual recommendation from Chambers Europe in 2013, 2014 and 2015.

**Filippo Valguarnera** is an Italian-Swedish legal scholar. His main field of studies is comparative law, with a special interest in property law, civil procedure, access to nature and access to justice. He earned his law degree and PhD at the University of Florence (Italy) and has worked as a visiting fellow at Uppsala University and New York University. From 2009 to 2013, Filippo worked as senior lecturer at Örebro University and currently he is a member of the Law Faculty at Gothenburg University, Sweden.

**Nicola Wheeler** specializes in the environmental impacts sector, with a particular focus on climate change, flooding, natural capital and ecosystem services, and wild land. Since completing an MSc at the University of Sussex in Climate Change and Policy, Nicola works at the environmental think tank Green Alliance where she specializes in policy to protect and improve the natural environment. Prior to this, Nicola worked as an environmental consultant at Argyll Environmental Ltd, specializing in flood risk, contaminated land, climate change, and wilderness protection. Nicola also regularly speaks at public events and universities on issues associated with climate change and environmental protection.

**Jiří Zicha** worked at the Ministry of Environment of the Czech Republic in Prague from 2003 to 2011. Since 2011 he has been a lecturer at Tomas Bata University in Zlin. His main interest of research is environmental law with an emphasis on the role of law in biodiversity conservation.

# ACKNOWLEDGEMENTS

This book aims to contribute to the broader inter-disciplinary debate on nature protection in Europe by providing a comprehensive appraisal of the role of international, European and domestic law in protecting wilderness areas and their distinguishing qualities. As the wilderness concept has received relatively little attention in legal circles in Europe, the thirty experts involved in this project had to undertake extensive and innovative research in order to develop their chapters. As editor, I am deeply impressed by the willingness of each of the contributors to invest a substantial amount of time and effort in their research for this book. I am most grateful for the strong collaboration with and between all of these contributors, which has ensured that this book has become far more than a mere collection of chapters. These joint efforts made it possible to develop comprehensive and insightful answers to the central questions posed in this book.

This collaborative effort was greatly assisted by means of a workshop convened in Tilburg from 27 to 29 October 2013, where the first drafts of the chapters were discussed. I would like to thank the Tilburg Sustainability Centre (TLS), the Netherlands Polar Programme, the Netherlands Organisation for Scientific Research (NWO) and Tilburg Law School for jointly funding this workshop.

A special word of appreciation goes to Richard Caddell, who, as well as writing one of the chapters, also undertook a thorough language check of almost all other contributions to this volume, which substantially improved the overall quality of this book.

I am also very grateful to Toby Aykroyd, coordinator of the Wild Europe Initiative, and Zoltan Kun, former director of Pan Parks Foundation and Chairman of the European Wilderness Society, who have encouraged me to start this project.

I would also like to express my sincere thanks to my colleagues at Tilburg Law School, in particular Jennifer Dubrulle, Floor Fleurke, Melissa Lewis, Antje Neumann, Tim van der Putten, Jesse Reynolds,

Han Somsen, Arie Trouwborst, Jonathan Verschuuren and Anne de Vries. Some of them supported me in this book project through interesting discussions, proof-reading and by making valuable substantive comments or stylistic corrections; each of them have been instrumental in facilitating a supportive and inspirational working environment within which multi-year research initiatives, like this book project, are possible.

Special thanks go to Cambridge University Press, in particular Elizabeth Spicer (Commissioning Editor, Law), Richard Woodham (Editor, Law), Adam Hooper (production editor), Karthik Orukaimani (production project manager) and Chloé Harries (Content Manager). Through her positive and valuable advice and patience, Elizabeth Spicer has played a very stimulating role and I greatly appreciate her collaboration. Through their thorough editing work and advice on the full and final version of the manuscript, Richard Woodham, Adam Hooper, Karthik Orukaimani and Chloé Harries have further improved the quality of the book, for which I am very grateful. I would also like to thank Robert and Cynthia Swanson for developing the comprehensive index.

Finally, I would like to thank my family. I must admit this project has required far more time and effort than planned. I sincerely appreciate their patience and understanding, which made it possible to make this book project one of the most rewarding and enjoyable projects of my academic career.

*Kees Bastmeijer*

# PART I

# Introduction: wilderness in Europe

1

# Introduction

## *An international history of wilderness protection and the central aim of this book*

KEES BASTMEIJER

### 1 Western legal philosophical roots: stimuli for altering the earth's surface

From a historical perspective, a book on the role of the law in protecting 'wilderness' might appear remarkable. Wilderness protection is about protecting large, relatively undisturbed natural areas that are free from buildings, roads and other human-made artefacts and 'where natural forces and processes predominate';[1] however, in the past the Western human–nature relationship and broadly acknowledged legal principles on State sovereignty and private property were strong stimuli for humans to use and alter the natural world.[2] For many centuries there has been a broadly shared conviction that nature originally constituted the common property of all humankind[3] and was accordingly meant to benefit humans. Aristotle (384–322 BCE) has stated:

The author would like to thank each of the contributors to this book for their helpful comments on an earlier draft of this chapter. It is acknowledged that this chapter, as well as the book itself, adopts a Western perspective and should therefore not be considered an exhaustive account of all approaches to wilderness conservation worldwide.

1 Nigel Dudley (ed.), *Guidelines for Applying Protected Area Management Categories* (Gland: World Conservation Union/IUCN, 2008), http://cmsdata.iucn.org/downloads/iucn_assignment_1.pdf, at 14. For the definition of wilderness for the purposes of this book, see Subsection 5.2.

2 See Kees Bastmeijer, 'Addressing Weak Legal Protection of Wilderness: Deliberate Choices and Drawing Lines on the Map', in Steffen Fritz and Steve Carver (eds.), *Mapping Wilderness: Concepts, Techniques and Applications of GIS* (Dordrecht: Springer, 2016).

3 See, e.g., Hugo de Groot, *Mare Liberum* (Leiden: Elzevier, 1609), at 14, www.kb.nl/galerie/mareliberum/browse/index_1.html, English translation by Ralph Van Deman Magoffin: *The Freedom of the Seas or the Right Which Belongs to the Dutch to Take Part in the East Indian Trade* (Oxford/New York: Oxford University Press, 1916), http://oll.libertyfund.org/index.php?option=com_staticxt&staticfile=show.php%3Ftitle=552&layout=html. Grotius refers in Chapter V to Cicero: 'As Cicero says: "But nothing is by nature private property".'

> It is evident that we may conclude of those things that are, that plants are created for the sake of animals, and animals for the sake of men; the tame for our use and provision; the wild, at least the greater part, for our provision also, or for some other advantageous purpose, as furnishing us with clothes, and the like.[4]

Hallebeek researched the work of Thomas Aquinas (1225–1274) and explains that in Thomas Aquinas's vision 'God has the *dominium* over all of creation' and that, because humans are rational creatures since they were created in His image, 'man also has a certain dominion over other creatures.'[5] According to John Locke (1632–1704), '[t]he earth and all that is therein is given to men for the support and comfort of their being'.[6] The Swiss lawyer Emmerich de Vattel (1714–1767) expressed a similar view: 'The earth belongs to mankind in general; destined by the Creator to be their common habitation, and to supply them with food, they all possess a natural right to inhabit it, and to derive from it whatever is necessary for their subsistence, and suitable to their wants.'[7]

According to John Locke, the fact that nature was meant to benefit mankind implied that humans were justified in appropriating it as private property by physically using and adding value to it. With regard to the 'fruits and beasts of the earth' he stated: 'being given for the use of men, there must of necessity be a means to appropriate them some way or other before they can be of any use, or at all beneficial, to any particular men.'[8]

[4] Aristotle, *The Politics, A Treatise on Government*, translation from the original Greek by William Ellis (London & Toronto: J.M. Dent & Sons Ltd./New York: E.P. Duton & Co., first issue in 1912, reprinted in 1919, 1923, 1928), www.gutenberg.org/files/6762/6763-h/6762-h.htm, Chapter VIII of the first book. See Paul Cliteur, 'De filosofie van de dierenrechten', in Johan Braeckman, Bert de Reuver and Thomas Vervisch (eds.), *Ethiek van DNA tot 9/11*, (Amsterdam: Amsterdam University Press, 2005), pp. 135–159, http://libertyonline.hypermall.com/Locke/second/second-frame.html, Chapter 5, para. 25.

[5] Jan Hallebeek, *Quia Natura Nichil Privatum, Aspecten van de eigendomsvraag in het werk van Thomas van Aquino (1225–1274)* (Nijmegen: Gerard Noodt Instituut, 1986), at 37. Thomas Aquinas also refers to Psalm 8:8 and Aristotle's *Politica* to emphasize that the imperfect objects (for example animals) are there for the sake of the perfect objects (humans).

[6] See also John Locke, *Two Second Treatise of Government*, published in 1690, http://libertyonline.hypermall.com/Locke/second/second-frame.html, Chapter 5, para. 25.

[7] Emmerich de Vattel, *Le Droit des gens*, 1758, English translation by Joseph Chitty: *The Law of Nations* (Philadelphia: Johnson & Co., 1844), www.loc.gov/rr/frd/Military_Law/Lieber_Collection/pdf/DeVattel_LawOfNations.pdf, Ch. XVIII, para. 203.

[8] Locke, *The Second Treatise of Government, supra* note 6, Chapter 5, para. 25. See also David C. Snyder, 'Locke on Natural Law and Property Rights', in *Thom Brooks Locke and Law,* Philosophers and Law series (Hampshire: Ashgate 2007), pp. 3–30, at 15.

The actual use or cultivation of nature was also a condition for appropriation of nature as private property to be justified: claiming something from nature without actually using it would prevent others from benefitting from it and this would be in violation of Natural Law. In the words of Locke:

> But how far has [God] given [all things in nature] to us? To enjoy. As much as any one can make use of to any advantage of life before it spoils; so much he may by his labour fix a Property in. Whatever is beyond this, is more than his share, and belongs to others. Nothing was made by God for Man to spoil or destroy.[9]

Similar views can be recognized regarding the relationship between state governments and nature. According to De Vattel, governments of nations even had a positive obligation to cultivate the land:

> The cultivation of the soil deserves the attention of the government, not only on account of the invaluable advantages that flow from it, but from its being an obligation imposed by nature on mankind. The whole earth is destined to feed its inhabitants; but this it would be incapable of doing, if it were uncultivated. Every nation is then obliged by the law of nature to cultivate the land that has fallen to its share.[10]

Actual occupation and cultivation of land was also considered a condition for lawful sovereignty claims of States over land that was otherwise considered *terra nullius*:[11]

> But it is questioned whether a nation can, by the bare act of taking possession, appropriate to itself countries which it does not really occupy, and thus engross a much greater extent of territory than it is able to people or cultivate. It is not difficult to determine that such a pretension would be an absolute infringement of the natural rights of men, and repugnant to

[9] Locke, *The Second Treatise of Government, supra* note 6. See also Thom Brooks, *Locke and Law*, Philosophers and Law series (Hampshire: Ashgate, 2007), at xvi. Brooks summarizes the views of John Locke as follows: 'We can only have as much property as we can enjoy.' It should be noted that this is not the same as not using more than a person needs for his/her survival. If a person takes more from nature than he/she needs in order to trade this for silver or gold, this would according to Locke not be spoilage. See C.B. MacPherson, *The Political Theory of Possessive Individualism – Hobbes to Locke* (Oxford University Press, 1962), at 204.

[10] De Vattel, *The Law of Nations, supra* note 7, Chapter VII, para. 81, at 35.

[11] On the legal historical background of the concept of *terra nullius*, see Randall Lesaffer, 'Argument from Roman Law in Current International Law', *European Journal of International Law* 16, 1 (2005), 25–58; Lesaffer points out that the term *terra nullius* was not part of classic Roman law, but was based on the term *res nullius* to create a legal basis for territorial land claims during the Age of Discovery.

> the views of nature, which, having destined the whole earth to supply the wants of mankind in general, gives no nation a right to appropriate to itself a country, except for the purpose of making use of it, and not of hindering others from deriving advantage from it. The law of nations, will, therefore, not acknowledge the property and sovereignty of a nation over any uninhabited countries, except those of which it has really taken actual possession, in which it has formed settlements, or of which it makes actual use.[12]

Thomas Willing Balch discussed these principles in more detail in 1910, using the above quotation from De Vattel as well as the views of several other lawyers of the eighteenth and nineteenth centuries.[13] These theories were also used to justify the occupation of homelands of indigenous peoples (see Section 3.2).

These roots in Western legal thinking were stimuli for the active transformation of the 'wilderness' into cultivated lands, and rendered the protection of wilderness against human impacts illogical. Humankind in the Western world had positioned itself above nature and 'wilderness' was available to be exploited and 'civilized'.[14] Aldo Leopold stated in 1925: 'From the earliest times one of the principal criteria of civilization has been the ability to conquer the wilderness and convert it to economic use.'[15] As many of the above quotations make clear, this dominant human–nature attitude was strongly influenced by the Judeo-Christian tradition. Based on sources from the age of American pioneers, Roderick F. Nash states: 'Transforming the wild into the rural had Scriptural precedents which the New England pioneers knew well. Genesis 1:28, the first commandment of God to man, stated that mankind should increase, conquer the earth, and have dominion over all living things. This made the fate of wilderness plain.'[16]

During the last few centuries in particular, these convictions have been paralleled by processes of labour division, industrialization, international trade, a strong belief in a liberal market economy, and – strongly

[12] De Vattel, *The Law of Nations, supra* note 7, at 99.

[13] Thomas Willing Balch, 'The Arctic and Antarctic Regions and the Law of Nations', *American Journal of International Law* 4 (1910), 265–275.

[14] See also Chapters 2 and 12.

[15] Aldo Leopold, 'Wilderness as a Form of Land Use', *The Journal of Land & Public Utility Economics* 1, 4 (1925), 398–404, at 398.

[16] R.F. Nash, *Wilderness & the American Mind*, (4th edn.) (New Haven: Yale University Press, 2001), at 31. See also Lynn White Jr., 'The Historical Roots of Our Ecological Crisis', 155 *Science* (1967), 1203–1207. White expressed the view that the Judeo-Christian tradition predominantly underpins the dominant attitude of humans over nature.

interconnected with these developments – a substantial increase in the human population[17] and of the exploitation of the world's natural resources. This combination of factors has resulted in a continuing process of human cultivation of nature.[18] As explained by Crispin Tickell 'unlike other animals, we made a jump from being successful to being a runaway success [. . .] because of our ability to adapt environments for our own uses in ways that no other animal can match'.[19]

As a consequence of these 'adaptation processes', the number of wilderness areas has decreased substantially in almost every region of the world.[20] The Polar Regions are still characterized by large wilderness areas; however, these regions are also under pressure. Current discussions about the use of Arctic resources indicate that the legal philosophical roots noted above still exercise a strong influence at both levels of the human 'appropriation' of nature, namely private property and state sovereignty. In Greenland, for example, one of the very few places on Earth in which, based on Inuit traditions, formal private land-ownership is still anathema, private investment in the land (adding value to it) is being increasingly acknowledged as a justification for issuing more exclusive concessions for mining and tourism projects.[21] And, when announcing the construction of offshore patrol ships and a deep water port for the High Arctic on 9 July 2007, Canada's Prime Minister Stephen

[17] See, e.g., Jacobus A. Du Pisani, 'Sustainable Development – Historic Roots of the concept', *Environmental Sciences* 3, 2 (2006), 83–96, at 87: 'In the period between 1800 and 1970, when the world's population tripled from around 978 million to 3632 million, seemingly unslackened economic growth occurred and the quantity of manufacturing production in the world increased about 1730 times.' Du Pisani refers to W.W. Rostow, *The World Economy. History and Prospect* (London: Macmillan, 1978), at 47–48.

[18] See N. Roberts, 'The Human Transformation of the Earth's Surface' *International Social Science Journal* 150 (1996), 493–510.

[19] Crispin Tickell, 'The Human Species: A Suicidal Success?' *The Geographical Journal* 159, 2 (1993), 219–226, www.jstor.org/stable/3451413, at 219. See also Roberts, 'The Human Transformation of the Earth's Surface', *supra* note 18.

[20] See Cyril F. Kormos and Harvey Locke, 'Introduction', in Cyril F. Kormos (ed.), *A Handbook on International Wilderness Law and Policy* (Golden: Fulcrum Publishing 2008), at 16: '[V]ery roughly one-third of the planet remains undisturbed in large areas of wilderness.'

[21] Personal communication between the author and representatives of the Greenlandic Ministry of Infrastructure (Nuuk), the Ministry of Industry (Nuuk), Greenlandic advisors on tourism (Nuuk), agricultural advisers (Qaqortoq) and the mayor of the South Greenlandic municipality of Kujalleq (Qaqortoq), 8–20 September 2014 (research sponsored by the INTERACT program). In the conversations it was stressed that these rights may become more exclusive in favour of other commercial operators, but should not in principle exclude local people from conducting traditional activities, such as fishing, hunting and gathering.

Harper stated: 'Canada has a choice when it comes to defending our sovereignty over the Arctic. We either use it or lose it. And make no mistake, this Government intends to use it.'[22]

## 2 Acknowledgement of the downside of civilization and the increase of wilderness appreciation

During the nineteenth century in particular, people in Western societies became increasingly aware of the downside of the intensive human use of nature. As Jepson and Whittaker explain, by the end of the nineteenth century, the Passenger Pigeon had established 'the concept of human-induced extinction [. . .] in the public mind' and 'concepts of nature as a robust preordained system of checks and balances had been replaced by the notion of delicate and intricate systems sensitive to human interference'.[23] A shift in the human–nature relationship may also have been influenced by an increased appreciation for wildlife: 'Doubts and hesitations had arisen about man's place in nature and his relationship to other species. [. . .] A closer sense of affinity with the animal creation had weakened old assumptions about human uniqueness.'[24] In this context, the works of Charles Darwin (1809–1882)[25] and his contemporaries such as Thomas Henry Huxley (1825–1895)[26] are of great importance.[27] A more positive attitude towards nature was also stimulated by the downside of 'modern life' in large cities: increasing air pollution, crime and disease. Keith Thomas offers considerable evidence to show that the

22 News Release of Canada's Prime Minister of 9 July 2007, www.pm.gc.ca/eng/news/2007/07/09/prime-minister-stephen-harper-announces-new-arctic-offshore-patrol-ships.

23 Paul Jepson and Robert J. Whittaker, 'Histories of Protected Areas: Internationalisation of Conservationist Values and their Adoption in the Netherlands Indies (Indonesia)', *Environment and History* 8 (2002), 129–172, at 133.

24 Keith Thomas, *Man and the Natural World, Changing Attitudes in England (1500–1800)*, (Harmondsworth, Middlesex: Allen Lane/Penguin Books Ltd., 1983), at 243. See also Jepson and Whittaker, 'Histories of Protected Areas', *supra* note 23, 132: 'The image of humans as divinely created beings was replaced with the realisation (or possibility) of kinship with animals.'

25 Darwin's classic treatise *On the Origin of Species* [. . .], in which he does not really discuss the descent of humans is not his only text of relevance in this respect, but also especially his later works such as *The Descent of man, and Selection in Relation to Sex* (London: John Murray, 1871). See Paul Cliteur, *Darwin, Dier en Recht* (Den Haag: Boom, 2001), http://media.leidenuniv.nl/legacy/Darwin%20%20dier%20en%20recht.pdf, at 6.

26 Thomas H. Huxley, *Evidence as to Man's Place in Nature*, 1863, www.gutenberg.org/files/2931/2931-h/2931-h.htm.

27 See Cliteur, *Darwin, Dier en Recht, supra* note 25, at 6.

idealization of cities of earlier times in Europe had to give way to an increasing appreciation for country life and nature.[28]

The changing appreciation of nature also applied more specifically to relatively untouched natural areas: 'Mountains and wilderness which once were landscapes of fear now became panoramas of awe and admiration.'[29] The strong advocacy in North America by Thoreau, Muir, Marsh and others to set aside untouched nature is well-known, although, as Steve Carver explains in the next chapter, this advocacy also had European roots.[30] In Europe, wild nature had become scarce and received increasing appreciation from the second half of the eighteenth century. This is reflected for instance in the public perception of mountains in England: prior to the romantic period 'the dominant tendency in England and many other parts of Europe was to regard mountains as inconvenient, aesthetically repellent, and dangerous not just to one's body but to one's soul', while in the late eighteenth century 'English attitudes toward mountain landscape underwent nearly a 180-degrees reversal.'[31] Mark Fisher explains that in Germany in the 1850s, the German journalist, writer and historian Wilhelm Heinrich Riehl (1823–1897) was arguing against the process of turning every piece of forest into field, and cites Riehl from the English translation of his book *Die Pfälzer. Ein rheinisches Volksbild* (1857):

> For centuries it was fitting that progress should advocate exclusively the rights of the field; now, however, it is fitting that progress should advocate the rights of the wilderness together with the rights of the cultivated land.[32]

[28] Thomas, *Man and the Natural World, supra* note 24, pp. 242–254.

[29] C. Michael Hall, 'The Changing Cultural Geography of the Frontier: National Parks and Wilderness As Frontier Remnant', in S. Krakover and Y. Gradus (eds.), *Tourism in Frontier Areas* (Lanham: Lexington Books, 2002), pp. 283–298, at 286. For a comprehensive discussion of this shift in attitude, see Nash, *Wilderness & the American Mind, supra* note 16, Chapters 2 and 3.

[30] See Chapter 2. See also C. Michael Hall, 'The Changing Cultural Geography of the Frontier: National Parks and Wilderness As Frontier Remnant', *supra* note 29, at 286: 'To the Romantics, the New World was perceived as a new Eden in which man could draw close to wild nature.' For a rich debate on the history of international nature conservation, see also Martin Holdgate, *The Green Web. A Union for World Conservation* (Abingdon: Earthscan, 2009).

[31] William Cronon, 'Foreword', in Marjorie Hope Nicolson, *Mountain Gloom and Mountain Glory: The Development of the Aeshetics of the Infinite* (Washington: University of Washington Press, 1957 (reprint of original, published by Cornell University in 1959), pp. vii–xii, at viii.

[32] Wilhelm Heinrich Riehl, *Die Pfälzer. Ein rheinisches Volksbild* (Stuttgart: Cotta'scher Verlag, 1857), https://archive.org/stream/diepflzereinrhe00riehgoog#page/n7/mode/2up; English translation: Kuno Francke and William Guild Howard (eds.), *The German Classics of the Nineteenth and Twentieth Centuries: Masterpieces of German Literature,*

With reference to Frederik Willem van Eeden Sr. (1829–1901), the Dutch nature conservationist H.P. Gorter describes a similar awareness in the Netherlands during the second half of the nineteenth century:

> It was at that time, that they, who looked further into the future, saw the signs that the wilderness, which at one time covered our land as far as the eye could see, would become a scarcity, and that it would become necessary to defend the 'right of the wilderness'.[33]

Such statements should not however be 'over-romanticised': the general attitude towards nature remained strongly anthropocentric. 'Though Muir like other romantics denied that the earth was made for man, it was for men's spiritual salvation that they sought to save wild nature [. . .].'[34] This is illustrated by the Act that designated Yellowstone as the first National Park of the US: According to the Act, the natural area was 'set apart as a public park or pleasuring-ground for the benefit and enjoyment of the people'.[35]

The above discussions also illustrate that the concept of wilderness may to a large extent be considered an 'invention' of Western society: Increasing scarcity is often paralleled by increasing appreciation and the conviction that protection is needed.[36]

Some go one step further by taking the view that the appreciation of wilderness is a luxury: 'A general appreciation of the positive virtues of nature and of the wilderness could only be developed after the conversion of some of the wild lands into a cultivated or semi-cultivated landscape

Volume VIII (New York: The German Publication Society, 1914), pp. 404–477, at 427, https://archive.org/details/germanclassicsof08franuoft. See Mark Fisher, 'The Natural Vegetation of England', electronic publication, 28 August 2014, www.self-willed-land.org.uk/articles/natural_veg_england.htm.

33 H.P. Gorter, 'Vijftig jaar natuurmonumenten' (fifty years nature monuments), in *Vijftig jaar natuurbescherming in Nederland* (Amsterdam: Drukkerij De Volharding, 1956), pp. 11–66, at 11. In the eighteenth and early nineteenth century, in other parts of Europe too the special value of wilderness was emphasized in literature, works of art, as well as in legal and policy debates. See Chapter 3 and Part III.

34 David Lowenthal, 'Nature and Morality from George Perkins Marsh to the Millennium', *Journal of Historical Geography* 26, 1 (2000), 3–27, http://geography.fullerton.edu/taylor/ENST595T/Lowenthal_JHG.pdf.

35 'An Act to set apart a certain tract of land lying near the headwaters of the Yellowstone river as a public park', approved 1 March 1872, 17 Stat. 32/ U.S.C., title 16, sec. 21 and 22), www.cr.nps.gov/history/online_books/anps/anps_1c.htm.

36 For North America, see, e.g., Michael McCloskey, 'The Wilderness Act of 1964: Its Background and Meaning', *Oregon Law Review* 45, 288 (1965–1966), 288–321, at 288: 'A pronounced scarcity of wilderness was needed to change the attitudes of a nation long preoccupied with taming wilderness.'

and until this stage was reached, the pioneer was more concerned with survival than with appreciation.'[37] One may question whether indigenous people would agree with this: while the term 'wilderness' will have been unknown to them, their 'general appreciation of the positive virtues of nature' certainly did not depend on cultivation of the land. However, as will be discussed later, in the relationship with indigenous people we find one of the most fundamental arguments against the concept of wilderness.

## 3 Law and policy making to protect wilderness: an international historical perspective

### *3.1 Establishment of the first national parks: wild nature 'withdrawn from settlement'*

Over the past few centuries, many regulations have been established to protect certain species and natural areas. Until the mid-nineteenth century, many of these regulations aimed to protect the hunting privileges and other interests of the elites. For instance, Fuks and Van der Windt explain that, according to Danish laws of the sixteenth century, the illegal taking of gyrfalcons in Iceland was punishable by death, because the species (particularly the relatively rare white phase) was 'reserved' for falconry by European sovereigns.[38] At the end of the nineteenth century, the increasing appreciation of nature and recognition of over-exploitation of certain resources (e.g., species that were popular hunting trophies in the African colonies) intensified the development of nature protection legislation at the domestic as well as the international level.[39] Jepson and Whittaker explain in detail how 'elite lobby groups' in the US and Europe promoted this development.[40]

> Big-game hunters of North America and Britain [promoted] a moral limit to human exploitation of nature, expressed as sanctuaries and game law; and [. . .] the learned naturalists and scientists of Europe [promoted] the

[37] Hall, 'The Changing Cultural Geography of the Frontier: National Parks and Wilderness As Frontier Remnant', *supra* note 29.

[38] Simon Fuks, with a contribution of Henry J. van der Windt, 'De IJslandse Giervalk, een Koninklijke vogel', in *Jaarboek voor ecologische geschiedenis 2004. Mensen en dieren in het verleden* (Gent: Vereniging voor Ecologische Geschiedenis, 2004), pp. 137–152, at 144. See also David Evans, *A History of Nature Conservation in Britain* (London: Routledge, 1996).

[39] For a comprehensive discussion on the history of international conservation law, see Michael Bowman, Peter Davies and Catherine Redgwell, *Lyster's International Wildlife Law* (Cambridge University Press, 2010; 2nd edn.), Chapter 1, and P. van Heijnsbergen, *International Legal Protection of Flora and Fauna* (Amsterdam: IOS Press, 1997).

[40] Jepson and Whittaker, 'Histories of Protected Areas', *supra* note 23, at 133.

> protection of *Naturdenkmal* as objects for the contemplative side of human identity.[41]

In this time period, in parallel to the emergence of regulations to protect species, the designation and protection of natural areas became an increasingly important pillar of nature conservation. At the domestic level, the designation of Yellowstone National Park in 1872 is internationally recognized as the first national park. In the aims reflected in the 'Yellowstone Act 1872'[42] several characteristics of the modern wilderness concept may be recognized, although the idea of setting aside areas for the enjoyment of the people was the central consideration. According to the Act, the area is

> reserved and withdrawn from settlement, occupancy, or sale under the laws of the United States, and dedicated and set apart as a public park or pleasuring-ground for the benefit and enjoyment of the people.[43]

Furthermore, the Act states that the Secretary of the Interior must 'make and publish [. . .] rules and regulations' that 'shall provide for the preservation, from injury or spoliation, of all timber, mineral deposits, natural curiosities, or wonders within said park, and their retention in their natural condition'.[44]

Many designations of National Parks in the US followed and the instrument of National Park was also introduced in many other parts of the world. Examples include Royal National Park near Sydney, Australia (1879), Tongariro National Park in New Zealand (1894) and Banff National Park in Canada (1898).[45] The arguments made for

41 *Ibid.*, at 137.

42 'An Act to set apart a certain tract of land lying near the headwaters of the Yellowstone river as a public park', 1 March 1872, 17 Stat. 32, U.S.C., title 16, sec. 21 and 22, www.cr.nps.gov/history/online_books/anps/anps_1c.htm.

43 *Ibid.* Section 1. In the light of the above discussions on appropriation of private property, it is interesting to note that one of the aims of the Yellowstone designation was to prevent persons from appropriating certain valuable components of the area, such as springs and geysers. See House Report No. 26, The Yellowstone Park. The Reports of Committees of the House of Representatives for the Second Session of the Forty-Second Congress, www.loc.gov/manuscripts/?fa=partof%3Ageneral+collections&c=50, at 1871–1872: 'Persons are now waiting for the spring to open to enter in and take possession of these remarkable curiosities [. . .].'

44 *Ibid.* Section 2.

45 Stuart Chape, Mark Spalding and Martin Jenkins (eds.), *The World's Protected Areas* (Berkeley/Los Angeles/London: University of California Press, 2008), at 4. In relation to the time period since these first designations of National Parks, Martin Holdgate explains: 'Arguments over what constituted a "real" national park have run through succeeding decades, including the whole history of IUCN, but for many years it was the unpeopled

establishing these parks were similar to those in the US:[46] Based on the increasing awareness of the downsides of cultivation and city life, natural areas were set aside for enjoyment by the general public. The broad conviction that nature was meant to be cultivated by humankind led to the germination of the converse idea that nature could be of value in 'cultivating' city people. For instance, Geoff Mosley quotes a *Sydney Morning Herald* report of 7 September 1878, according to which the Premier of New South Wales (Australia) Sir Henry Parkes had stated that the establishment of Ashfield Park was:

> most desirable not only because of its natural beauty – because it afforded the means of public enjoyment and refined pleasure, but also because it would give scope for physical culture, and it was important to develope [sic] the physical energy of the people, as well as to cultivate their mental faculties [. . .].[47]

### 3.2 *The downside of setting aside protected areas: forced relocation of indigenous people*

While wilderness appreciation was a response to the increasing awareness of the downsides of civilization, in many countries the designation of the first national parks had a serious shortcoming too: the forced removal of indigenous people from their homelands. While this important topic is discussed in more detail elsewhere,[48] the developments regarding Yellowstone may function as an example. Section 2 of the Yellowstone Act 1872 states that 'the Secretary of the Interior [. . .] shall also cause all persons trespassing upon the same after the passage of this act to be

"Yellowstone model" that most nations aspired to copy.' See Holdgate, *The Green Web. A Union for World Conservation, supra* note 30, at 7.

46 See Sahotra Sarkar, 'Wilderness Preservation and Biodiversity Conservation. Keeping Divergent Goals Distinct', *BioScience* 49, 5 (1999), 405–412, at 406. In relation to the establishment of national parks in the US during the early decades of the twentieth century, Sarkar states: 'The immediate target was the creation of national parks for recreational use. [. . .] Concern for biological diversity played no role in the selection of US national parks [. . .].'

47 Geoff Mosley, *The First National Park. A Natural for World Heritage* (Sutherland: Sutherland Shire Environment Centre, 2012), at 25.

48 See, e.g., Mark David Spence, *Dispossessing the Wilderness. Indian Removal and the Making of the National Parks* (Oxford: Oxford University Press, 1999) and Marcus Colchester, 'Salvaging Nature: Indigenous Peoples and Protected Areas', in Krishna B. Ghimire and Michel P. Pimbert (eds.), *Social Change and Conservation* (London: Earthscan Publications, 1997 (reprint 2000)), 97–130.

removed therefrom'.[49] John Ise explains that the Secretary of the Interior (Carl Schurz) published rules in 1877 on hunting and to ensure that '[n]o person was allowed to reside permanently in the park, and those living there at the time were to vacate within thirty days after being served notice'.[50] The consequence was that several Indian tribes were excluded from using Yellowstone during summer as their hunting grounds. It has even been stated that the Shoshone ('Sheepeaters'), permanent residents who 'lived by hunting bighorn sheep in the loftiest and most remote areas',[51] were removed from the area. This has been denied by Susan Hughes, who concludes that 'the Sheepeaters is predominantly a myth passed down from the mid-nineteenth century and rooted in Victorian romanticism and colonial stereotypes of Native Americans';[52] however, this assertion has been criticized by several other ethnographers and archaeologists.[53] Merchant explains that a treaty with the Shoshone had been negotiated in 1868 (prior to the designation of the park), 'which insured their right to hunt in Yellowstone in return for ceding their lands';[54] however, 'once they were gone, the government refused to ratify the treaty'.[55] In 1961, Ise explained: 'As usual in our treatment of the Indians, whenever the whites wanted a given area the government would "negotiate" a "treaty" with the Indians the general purport of which was "Get the hell out of here!".'[56]

[49] An Act to set apart a certain tract of land lying near the headwaters of the Yellowstone river as a public park, approved 1 March 1872, 17 stat. 32, www.cr.nps.gov/history/online_books/anps/anps_1c.htm.

[50] John Ise, *Our National Park Policy. A Critical History* (New York: Earthscan 2011; reprint of the first edn., Baltimore: Johns Hopkins University Press 1961), at 19.

[51] Carolyn Merchant, *The Columbia Guide to American Environmental History* (New York: Columbia University Press, 2002), at 148.

[52] Susan Hughes, 'The Sheepeater Myth of Northwestern Wyoming', *Plains Anthropologist* 45, 171 (2000), 63–83, www.nps.gov/yell/naturescience/upload/part1.pdf.

[53] See, for instance, Lawrence L. Loendorf and Nancy Medaris Stone, *Mountain Spirit. The Sheep Eater Indians of Yellowstone* (Salt Lake City: The University of Utah Press, 2006), pp. 163–175, at 170–172. See also Laura L. Scheiber and Judson Byrd Finley, 'Obsidian source use in the Greater Yellowstone area, Wyoming Basin, and Central Rocky Mountains', *American Antiquity* 76, 2 (2011), 372–394. The authors refer to Susan Hughes, but conclude (at 375): 'Most ethnographers and archaeologists do, however, recognize a unique Mountain Shoshone presence in the region, with a subsistence economy that revolved around bighorn sheep [. . .] and this study lends credibility to this claim.'

[54] Merchant, *The Columbia Guide to American Environmental History, supra* note 51, at 148.

[55] *Ibid.*

[56] Ise, *Our National Park Policy. A Critical History, supra* note 50, at 22.

Similar practices have been described in relation to other regions of the world. For instance, Marcus Colchester observes:

> Bernard Grzimek, whose campaigns to conserve wildlife in East Africa made the Serengeti Plains into one of the most well-known protected areas on the planet, was single-mindedly dedicated to excluding the indigenous Massai cattle herders from their lands.[57]

To a large extent, the occupation of the homelands of indigenous peoples were based on the conviction discussed above of the eighteenth and nineteenth centuries that nature was meant to be civilized, that wastage was against Natural Law and that therefore lawful appropriation of land required active use and cultivation of that land. In this view, hunter-gathering societies occupied excessive portions of land. De Vattel stated in relation to the North American Indians: 'We do not, therefore, deviate from the views of nature, in confining the Indians in narrower limits.'[58] Cultivation of the land was considered a necessity, particularly in view of the growth of the human population:

> But when the human race became extremely multiplied, the earth was no longer capable of furnishing spontaneously, and without culture, sufficient support for its inhabitants; neither could it have received proper cultivation from wandering tribes of men continuing to possess it in common. It therefore became necessary that those tribes should fix themselves somewhere and appropriate to themselves portions of land, in order that they might, without being disturbed in their labour, or disappointed of the fruits of their industry, apply themselves to render those lands fertile, and thence derive their subsistence. Such must have been the origin of the rights of property and dominion: and it was a sufficient ground to justify their establishment.[59]

This view can, for instance, be recognized in the aims of the Homestead Act of 1862 and the General Allotment Act (the Dawes Act) of 1887 in the US.[60] To implement the Federal government's policy 'to encourage Indians to become farmers', the Dawes Act 'empowered the president of the United

[57] Colchester, 'Salvaging Nature: Indigenous Peoples and Protected Areas', *supra* note 48, p. 99. See also Rachelle Adam, *Elephant Treaties. The Colonial Legacy of the Biodiversity Crisis*, (Lebanon: University Press of New England, 2014), p. 34: 'Signifying a global trend, the exclusion of indigenous populations from national parks was manifest in European conservation policy in Africa.'

[58] De Vattel, *The Law of Nations, supra* note 7, at 100.

[59] *Ibid.*, Ch. XVIII, para. 203.

[60] See Anna Khomina, 'The Homestead Act of 1862: Dreams and Realities', a US History Scene, (no date), www.ushistoryscene.com/uncategorized/1862homesteadact/.

States to authorize the division of reservations into 160-acre allotments, assign one to each family, and open the remaining lands to white settlers'.[61]

### 3.3 *The development of international nature conservation law: limited attention for wilderness protection*

#### Early nature conservation conventions: the first half of the twentieth century

While national parks were established in various countries around the globe, at the international level the protection of natural values in the colonized countries of Africa received attention through the 'Convention for the Protection of Wild Animals, Birds and Fish in Africa',[62] signed in 1900 in London by the colonial authorities of Africa. Although this convention (in a similar manner to the domestic developments and other early conventions),[63] also took a strong anthropocentric approach and was 'concerned predominantly with direct and immediate human interests rather than motivated by any more elevated or altruistic ideals',[64] it nevertheless already included the notion of 'areas which may be established as reserves'.[65] This convention never entered into force and was replaced by the London Convention of 1933,[66] in which the policy of designating 'national parks' and 'strict natural reserves' was worked out in more detail. Certain qualities of the modern concept of wilderness are particularly recognizable in the 1933 convention's definition of the term 'strict natural reserve' in Article 2(2):

[61] Leonard A. Carlson, 'Learning to Farm: Indian Land Tenure and Farming before the Dawes Act', in Terry L. Anderson (ed.), *Property Rights and Indian Economies* (Lanham: Rowman & Littlefield Publishers, 1992), pp. 67–83.

[62] Convention for the Protection of Wild Animals, Birds and Fish in Africa, London, 10 May 1900, 188 *Parry's Consolidated Treaty Series* 418. See M.J. Bowland, 'The Protection of Animals under International Law', *Connecticut Journal of International Law* 4 (1988–1989), 487–499. See also P. Sands, *Principles of International Environmental Law* (Manchester: Manchester University Press, 1995), at 27.

[63] See, e.g., the Convention to Protect Birds Useful to Agriculture, Paris, 19 March 1902, 191 *Parry's Consolidated Treaty Series*, 91.

[64] M.J. Bowland, 'The Protection of Animals under International Law', *supra* note 62, at 487. See also Daniel Bodansky, *The Art and Craft of International Environmental Law*, (Harvard University Press, 2010), at 24.

[65] Convention for the Protection of Wild Animals, Birds and Fish in Africa, *supra* note 62, Art. III.

[66] Convention Relative to the Preservation of Fauna and Flora in the Natural State, London, 8 November 1933, 172 LNTS 241, http://treaties.fco.gov.uk/docs/pdf/1936/TS0027.pdf. See Philippe Sands and Jacqueline Peel, *Principles of International Environmental Law*, (Cambridge: Cambridge University Press, 2012), at 480.

> The term 'strict natural reserve' shall denote an area placed under public control, throughout which any form of hunting or fishing, any undertakings connected with forestry, agriculture, or mining, any excavations or prospecting, drilling, levelling of the ground, or construction, any work involving the alteration of the configuration of the soil or the character of the vegetation, any act likely to harm or disturb the fauna and flora, and the introduction of any species of fauna and flora whether indigenous or imported, wild or domesticated, shall be strictly forbidden; which it shall be forbidden to enter, traverse, or camp in without a special written permit from the competent authorities; and in which scientific investigations may only be undertaken by permission of those authorities.

Richard Ladle, Paul Jepson and Lindsey Gillson explain that '[t]his category of reserve was invented [...] to accommodate Belgian and French views that tourism (as promoted by the British and US) was incompatible with preserving nature in a natural state'.[67] As expounded further by Jepson and Whittaker:

> The British conceived of a 'national park' as borrowed from the US – namely a piece of public land to which public entry for recreation and observation was facilitated, but wherein fauna and flora were preserved in a near natural state. The French and Portuguese conceived a park as a place with lawns and flower beds and saw a contradiction between free public access and the preservation of anything in its natural state. [...] As a compromise the Belgians proposed a 'strict nature reserve' category denoting an area immune to any sort of human exploitation or alteration where entry was permitted by special permit only.[68]

As noted in the literature, this concept of 'strict natural reserves' in the 1933 Convention 'is clearly closely related to the underlying philosophy of wilderness reserves as they were originally conceived',[69] and this probably has a logical explanation. The 1933 Convention constituted an important foundation for the discussions on nature conservation in Pan-America, particularly through the work of John C. Phillips and Harold J. Coolidge.[70] Phillips and

[67] Richard J. Ladle, Paul Jepson and Lindsey Gillson, 'Social Values and Conservation Biogeography', in Richard J. Ladle and Robert J. Whittaker, *Conservation Biogeography*, (Chichester: Wiley-Blackwell, 2011), pp. 13–30, at 21.

[68] Jepson and Whittaker, 'Histories of Protected Areas: Internationalisation of Conservationist Values and their Adoption in the Netherlands Indies (Indonesia)', *supra* note 23, at 142–143.

[69] Ladle et al., 'Social Values and Conservation Biogeography', *supra* note 67, at 21.

[70] See John Sheail, *Nature's Spectacle. The World's First National Parks and Protected Places*, (Abingdon: Earthscan, 2010), at 268; Adam, *Elephant Treaties, supra* note 57, at 154 (footnote 179), and Mark Cioc, *The Game of Conservation. International Treaties to Protect the World's Migratory Animals*, (Athens: Ohio University Press, 2009), at 95.

Coolidge, co-founders of the American Committee for International Wild Life Protection in 1930, had been present at the 1933 Convention as observers and in the following years actively advocated the development of a Pan-American nature conservation convention.[71] Following a resolution adopted at the eighth International Conference of American States (Lima, 1938),[72] the 'Convention on Nature Protection and Wild Life Preservation in the Western Hemisphere' was adopted and opened for signature in 1940.[73] This convention 'was modeled [sic] almost entirely on the 1933 London Convention';[74] however, the Western Hemisphere Convention advanced the possibility of designating 'strict wilderness reserves' as a separate category of protected reserve. It appears that this category was based on the 'strict natural reserve' considered under the 1933 Convention, a category that was not included in the Western Hemisphere Convention.

According to Article II of the 1940 Convention, '[t]he Contracting Governments will explore at once the possibility of establishing in their territories national parks, national reserves, nature monuments, and strict wilderness reserves as defined in the preceding article'.[75] Article IV states that:

> [t]he Contracting Governments agree to maintain the strict wilderness reserves inviolate, as far as practicable, except for duly authorized scientific investigations or government inspection, or such uses as are consistent with the purposes for which the area was established.

It has been considered that the convention 'failed to provide for regular meetings of the parties or any other institutional follow-up' and 'became a "sleeping beauty" – its excellent substantive provisions virtually devoid

[71] *Ibid.* See also Mark V. Barrow, *Nature's Ghosts: Confronting Extinction from the Age of Jefferson to the Age of Ecology* (Chicago/London: University of Chicago Press, 2009), Chapter 5.

[72] *Ibid.*

[73] Convention on Nature Protection and Wild Life Preservation in the Western Hemisphere, 12 October 1940, 161 U.N.T.S. 193, into force 30 April 1942. See Kathleen Rogers and James A. Moore, 'Revitalizing the Convention on Nature Protection and Wild Life reservation in the Western Hemisphere: Might Awakening a Visionary but "Sleeping" Treaty Be the Key to Preserving Biodiversity and Threatened Natural Areas in the Americas?', *Harvard International Law Journal* 36, 2 (1995), 465–508.

[74] See Mark Cioc, *The Game of Conservation. International Treaties to Protect the World's Migratory Animals, supra* note 70, at 95.

[75] Art. 1(4) defines 'strict wilderness reserves' as: 'A region under public control characterized by primitive conditions of flora, fauna, transportation and habitation wherein there is no provision for the passage of motorized transportation and all commercial developments are excluded.'

of influence'.[76] However, in the past, Simon Lyster has concluded that 'correspondence with bureaucrats in national parks departments in party countries indicates that the Convention has been of considerable value both in the conceptual development of habitat protection since 1940 as a leverage to support their efforts to establish protected areas'.[77]

## The post-World War II period and the 'non-use' of nature as a non-issue

After World War II, international discussions on the availability of natural resources for economic development intensified. At the UN 'Conference on the Conservation and Utilisation of Resources', convened in 1949 (17 August–6 September 1949, Lake Success, New York)[78] '[d]-iscussions focused on the world resource situation, including the issues of resource depletion, critical shortages, use and conservation, and resource exploitation techniques suitable for less developed countries'.[79] Concurrently, there was increasing public awareness that the use of technology and higher welfare standards for a growing world population could have negative impacts on natural values. For instance, in 1952 the third General Assembly of the IUCN (established in 1948) adopted Resolution 1, to draw 'the attention of the Governments concerned to the danger which threatens National Parks and strict nature reserves, as defined by the Conventions of London (1933) and Washington (1940)'.[80] Although the term 'wilderness' was not used explicitly,[81] these concerns clearly related to protecting the integrity and inviolability of natural areas from large public works:

> As a result of public works, and particularly hydroelectric dams which are capable of seriously altering the integrity of these reserve areas, the

[76] Daniel Bodansky, *The Art and Craft of International Environmental Law*, *supra* note 64.

[77] Bowman, Davies and Redgwell, *Lyster's International Wildlife Law*, *supra* note 39, at 247. In footnote 28, the authors refer to the research by Lyster for the first edition of the book.

[78] Sands, *Principles of International Environmental Law*, *supra* note 62, at 31–32. For an extensive discussion of this conference, see C. Goodrich, 'The United Nations Conference on Resources', *International Organization* 5, 1 (1951), 48–60.

[79] Nico Schrijver, *Sovereignty Over Natural Resources: Balancing Rights and Duties in an Interdependent World* (Groningen: Rijksuniversiteit Groningen, 1995), at 35. See also Nico Schrijver, *The Evolution of Sustainable Development in International Law: Inception, Meaning and Status, Pocketbook of The Hague Academy of International Law* (Leiden/Boston: Martinus Nijhoff Publishers 2008), at 37–38. Schrijver refers to the report of the Conference, UN doc. E/CONF.7/7 (1950), at xvi.

[80] IUCN, Third General Assembly, Resolution 1, http://cmsdata.iucn.org/downloads/resolutions_recommendation_en.pdf.

[81] The term 'wilderness' was used in Resolution 23.

> Assembly considers itself authorized to remind the Governments of countries concerned that they are pledged to guarantee not only the safekeeping but the inviolability of the areas they have taken the initiative to delimit and to protect.[82]

However, during the immediate post-war years, inviolable natural areas, wilderness, undisturbed or pristine nature, or similar concepts received very little attention in multilateral debates. States were more concerned with securing the availability of natural resources for their own economic development, and to gain access to such resources outside their own territories: '[i]n the aftermath of the world economic crisis of the 1930s and of the devastating Second World War, industrialized States – especially the USA – became aware of their dependence on overseas raw materials and of the vulnerability of their supply lines'.[83] In the United Nations General Assembly (UNGA), the permanent sovereignty of States over natural resources within their territory was intensively debated and became the subject of various resolutions.[84] Special attention was devoted to the position of developing States. Economic development in these countries could support world peace and was therefore in the interests of Western States too, not only to ensure supplies, but also to strengthen international trade: 'High international economic growth rates could only be maintained if wealth could be distributed more evenly on a global scale, which would lead to the continued expansion of world markets.'[85]

Consequently, the 'non-use' of natural resources to preserve wilderness was not an issue; in fact, the UNGA Resolutions stressed the importance of the actual use of these resources 'in the interest of their national development and of the well-being of the people of the State concerned'.[86] The international law principles on the justification of sovereignty over *terra nullius* may be clearly recognized: 'Reiterating also that an intrinsic condition of the exercise of the sovereignty of

[82] IUCN, Third General Assembly. Resolution 1, *supra* note 80.

[83] Schrijver, *Sovereignty Over Natural Resources, supra* note 79, at 33.

[84] See, e.g., UNGA, Resolution 626 on the 'Right to Exploit Freely Natural Wealth and Resources', A/RES/626(VII), approved during the 411th plenary assembly, 21 December 1952, and UNGA, Resolution 1803 'Permanent sovereignty over natural resources', A/RES/1803(XVII), approved during the 1194th plenary assembly, 14 December 1962. For a detailed discussion, see Schrijver, *Sovereignty Over Natural Resources, supra* note 79, Chapter 2.

[85] Du Pisani, 'Sustainable Development – Historic Roots of the Concept', *supra* note 17, at 88.

[86] See, e.g., UNGA, Resolution 2692 on 'Permanent sovereignty over natural resources of developing countries and expansion of domestic sources of accumulation for economic development', A/RES/2692(XXV), approved during the 1926th plenary assembly, 11 December 1970.

every State is that it be exercised fully and effectively over all the natural resources of the State, whether found on land or in the sea.'[87] Nature conservation received less explicit attention and *if* the topic was indeed discussed, it was done so in the context of finding the right balance between economic development and the exploitation of natural resources. For instance, the 1962 UNGA Resolution on 'Economic Development and the Conservation of Nature' aimed for 'preservation' of natural resources, but also for 'rational use' of such resources and the elimination of 'wasteful exploitation of soil, rivers and flora and fauna'.[88]

### Focus on sustainability and biodiversity conservation

The importance of balancing human interests with environmental protection (including nature conservation) was also a central message of the outcomes of the UN Stockholm Conference on the Human Environment in 1972. This conference resulted in the adoption of the Stockholm Declaration[89] with twenty-six principles, an action plan (Action Plan for the Human Environment) with 109 recommendations for concrete action, and the foundation of the UN Environment Programme (UNEP).[90] On the one hand the Declaration continued to reflect human dominance over nature: 'It is the people that propel social progress, create social wealth, develop science and technology and, through their hard work, continuously transform the human environment.'[91] On the other hand, the Declaration recognized the increasing human influence on the Earth – partly because of technological developments and population growth: 'A point has been reached in history when we must shape our actions throughout the world with a more prudent care for their environmental consequences.'[92] Both sides must be balanced through wise management: 'Man has a special responsibility to safeguard and wisely manage the heritage of wildlife and

[87] UNGA, Resolution 'Permanent Sovereignty over Natural Resources', A/RES/1371 (XXVIII), approved during the 2203rd plenary assembly, 17 December 1973. See Schrijver, *The Evolution of Sustainable Development in International Law, supra* note 79, see note 137, at 41.

[88] UNGA, Resolution 'Economic Development and the Conservation of Nature', A/RES/1831 (XVII), approved during the 1197th plenary assembly, 18 December 1962. See Schrijver, *The Evolution of Sustainable Development in International Law, supra* note 79, at 41.

[89] Declaration of the United Nations Conference on the Human Environment, Stockholm, 1972, www.unep.org.

[90] See Essam El-Hinnawi, 'UNEP: Two Decades of Achievement and Challenge. 20 Years', UNEP report, www.eric.ed.gov, at 10.

[91] Stockholm Declaration, *supra* note 89, preamble, paragraph 5.

[92] *Ibid.*, preamble, paragraph 6, see also paragraph 1 of the preamble.

its habitat, which are now gravely imperilled by a combination of adverse factors.'[93]

This global awareness of a special responsibility of humankind for wildlife and habitats resulted in much international law making, particularly during the 1970s. Important conventions that were adopted in the wake of the Stockholm Conference include: the Convention on Wetlands of International Importance Especially as Waterfowl Habitat (Ramsar Convention, 1971),[94] the Convention Concerning the Protection of the World Cultural and Natural Heritage (Paris Convention, 1972),[95] the Convention on International Trade in Endangered Species of Wild Fauna and Flora (CITES, Washington Convention, 1973)[96] and the Convention on the Conservation of Migratory Species of Wild Animals (Bonn Convention, 1979).[97] Today's broad international support for these treaties is reflected by the impressive number of Contracting Parties. This also applies to the 1992 Convention on Biological Diversity (Rio Convention, 1992),[98] to which over 190 States are now Contracting Parties. Apart from these global conventions, a considerable volume of regional nature conservation legislation has been developed. Important examples include the African Convention on the Conservation of Nature and Natural Resources, signed in 1968,[99] and, for Europe, the Convention on the Conservation of European Wildlife and Natural Habitats (Bern Convention) of 1979[100] the latter of which inspired the European Union's Wild Birds Directive (1979)[101] and Habitats Directive (1992).[102]

93 Stockholm Declaration, *supra* note 89, Principle 4.

94 Convention on Wetlands of International Importance (Ramsar Convention or Wetland Convention), Ramsar, 2 February 1971, www.ramsar.org.

95 Convention concerning the protection of the world cultural and natural heritage, Paris, 16 November 1972, http://whc.unesco.org/archive/convention-en.pdf.

96 Convention on International Trade in Endangered Species of Wild Fauna and FLora, (CITES, Convention of Washington), Washington, 3 March 1973, www.cites.org/eng/disc/text.shtml#texttop.

97 Convention on the Conservation of Migratory Species of Wild Animals (Convention of Bonn), Bonn, 23 June 1979, www.cms.int/documents/convtxt/cms_convtxt_english.pfd.

98 Convention on Biological Diversity, June 5, 1992, U.N. Doc. DPI/1307 (reprinted in 31 I. L.M. 818; hereinafter CBD).

99 African Convention on the Conservation of Nature and Natural Resources, Algiers, 15 September 1968, effective since 16 June 1969, www.africa.union.org.

100 Convention on the Conservation of European Wildlife and Natural Habitats (Convention of Bern), Bern, 1979, http://conventions.coe.int/Treaty/en/Html/104.htm.

101 Birds Directive, Directive 79/409/EEC on the Conservation of Wild Birds, 1979, OJ L 103/1; consolidated version: Directive 2009/147/EC, OJ L 20, 26 January 2010.

102 Habitats Directive, Directive 92/43 on the Conservation of Natural Habitats and Wild Fauna and FLora, 1992, OJ L 206/7.

Although some of these legal instruments are relevant to wilderness protection,[103] there is no direct reference to the term 'wilderness' or similar terminology in the main text of any of the conventions. Instead, they focus strongly on the conservation of 'biological diversity' (biodiversity)[104] and/or the sustainable or wise use of biodiversity. In part this may be explained by developments discussed above, such as the increasing awareness of the over-exploitation of certain species and a shift in human societies towards a more positive human–nature attitude in respect of wild animals.[105] As Kalamandeen and Gillson explain:

> Over time, the conservation rationale for PA [protected areas] designation and management shifted from landscape, scenery and natural resources, to preservation of wildlife and biodiversity. This change in focus resulted from an interest in protecting animals for their own sakes, and for preserving species for science and for the potential and actual benefits in terms of genetic resources and ecosystem services.[106]

Furthermore, the focus on sustainability and biodiversity conservation may also be explained by the fact that these concepts leave more scope for social and economic human interests (particularly those related to human exploitation of natural resources) than the concept of wilderness. Setting aside relatively untouched natural places is simply more difficult in a global society in which human interests have the central focus. It has been stated that '[b]iodiversity conservation can avoid contentious political issues while simultaneously promoting long-term conservation by maintaining independence and distance from wilderness preservation'.[107] Likewise, an increased awareness of the importance of biodiversity for humankind may have influenced this focus. As Michael has put it:

> The greatest push for conserving protected areas has come with the recognition that biodiversity is also crucial for human survival. [. . .] Along with

[103] See Part II.

[104] Article 2 of the Convention on Biological Diversity defines 'Biological diversity' as: 'the variability among living organisms from all sources including, inter alia, terrestrial, marine and other aquatic ecosystems and the ecological complexes of which they are part; this includes diversity within species, between species and of ecosystems.' See Patricia Birnie, Alan Boyle and Catherine Redgwell, *International Law & the Environment* (Oxford: Oxford University Press, 2009), at 588. 'Wilderness' is mentioned in Annex I to the CBD as a relevant component of 'ecosystems and habitats'.

[105] See Section 2 and Subsection 3.1.

[106] Michelle Kalamandeen and Lindsey Gillson, *Biodiversity Conservation* 16 (2007), 165–182, at 170–171.

[107] Sahotra Sarkar, 'Wilderness Preservation and Biodiversity Conservation. Keeping Divergent Goals Distinct', *BioScience* 49, 5 (1999), 405–412, at 410.

this concept came a change in the view of what should comprise a protected area. Instead of untouched wilderness, current protected areas are frequently made up of areas of supervised human activity.[108]

## IUCN's continued efforts for wilderness protection

Despite the focus on sustainability and biodiversity conservation in international nature protection conventions, the concept of wilderness protection was not entirely absent from the global agenda. At the international level, the IUCN continued to ask attention for the importance of wilderness protection.[109] In 1981, the General Assembly of the IUCN noted 'that the opportunities to establish protected areas in the last remaining pristine areas are fast disappearing in many countries'.[110] The same General Assembly adopted Resolution 15/20, '[r]ecognizing [. . .] the paramount importance to mankind of [Antarctica's] great wilderness qualities for science, education and inspiration'. As discussed elsewhere,[111] wilderness protection has indeed played a significant role in the shaping of the international agreements that constitute the Antarctic Treaty system.

In 1984 the General Assembly of the IUCN adopted Resolution 16/34, entitled 'Protection of Wilderness Resources and Values'. Here, the IUCN recognized 'the role that wilderness can play in protecting the diversity of both flora and fauna and thus assuring the conservation of biological diversity *in situ*'.[112] The resolution also states that 'the growing human populations of the world increasingly will need the values of

[108] I.J. Michael, 'An International Legal Regime for Protected Areas', in IUCN, *International Environmental Governance: an International Regime for Protected Areas*, IUCN Environmental Policy and Law Paper No. 49 (Gland: World Conservation Union (IUCN), 2004), pp. 9–40, at 14. See also R.H.G. Jongman, 'Nature Conservation Planning in Europe: Developing Ecological Networks', *Landscape and Urban Planning* 32 (1995), 169–183, at 170. Jongman explains that after World War II, '[c]onservation Was More and More Focused on the Preservation of Values within Semi-natural Landscapes.'

[109] For an overview of all IUCN Recommendations and Resolutions, see the searchable 'IUCN Resolutions and Recommendations Platform', https://portals.iucn.org/library/resrec.

[110] IUCN, Fifteenth General Assembly, Resolution 15/12, 'Protection of Mangrove Ecosystems', 1981.

[111] Kees Bastmeijer, 'Protecting Polar Wilderness: Just a Western Philosophical Idea or a Useful Concept for Regulating Human Activities in the Polar Regions?', in Gudmundur Alfredsson, Timo Koivurova (eds in chief) and David Leary (special ed. Volume 1), 1 *The Yearbook of Polar Law* (Boston/Leiden: Brill/Martinus Nijhoff Publishers 2009), pp. 73–99.

[112] IUCN, 16th Session of the General Assembly, Resolution 16/34, 1984, https://portals.iucn.org/library/sites/library/files/resrecfiles/GA_16_RES_034_Protection_of_ Wilderness_Resources_a.pdf.

wilderness' and the General Assembly of IUCN 'recommends that all nations identify, designate and protect their wilderness areas on both public and private lands'.[113]

In 1988, IUCN adopted Resolution 17/36 to congratulate the 'World Commission on Protected Areas' (WCPA) for developing the proposal 'to adopt wilderness within its system for classifying protected areas'.[114] In 1975, the WCPA had started to work on a categorization of protected areas on the basis of their management purposes, resulting in a preliminary list of ten categories in 1978.[115] In 1992, the system was reviewed, and since then wilderness areas have been one of the six formal management categories of protected areas. In 2008, the revised version of the guidelines on protected areas management categories, including a definition, set of objectives and a clear description of 'distinguishing features' of wilderness areas (category Ib) was adopted.[116] In 2003, the US WILD Foundation[117] took the initiative of establishing a 'Wilderness Task Group' 'under the auspices of' IUCN's WCPA,[118] which subsequently received the status of IUCN 'Wilderness Specialist Group' in 2009.[119]

The IUCN resolutions also paid attention to the development of domestic wilderness legislation. The 1984 resolution stated 'that the passage of United States wilderness legislation in 1964 has contributed significantly to the protection of natural areas in that country', and the 1988 resolution recognized 'that a growing number of nations are setting aside wilderness areas as important components of their systems of protected areas'.[120]

### 3.4 *The development of domestic wilderness legislation*

In comparison to the international law and policy developments discussed above, wilderness has received more explicit attention at the domestic

[113] *Ibid.*

[114] IUCN, 17th Session of the General Assembly, Resolution 17.36, 1988, https://portals.iucn.org/library/efiles/documents/GA-17th-011.pdf.

[115] IUCN, *50 Years of Working for Protected Areas. A Brief History of IUCN World Commission on Protected Areas* (WCPA) (Gland: IUCN, 2010), http://cmsdata.iucn.org/downloads/history_wcpa_15july_web_version_1.pdf, at 17–18.

[116] Dudley (ed.), *Guidelines for Applying Protected Area Management Categories*, *supra* note 1.

[117] See www.wild.org/.

[118] See www.wild.org/main/how-wild-works/policy-research/wilderness-task-force-iucn/. See also IUCN, Wilderness Specialist Group, www.iucn.org/about/work/programmes/gpap_home/gpap_biodiversity/gpap_wcpabiodiv/gpap_wilderness/.

[119] *Ibid.*

[120] Resolution 17.36, 1988, *supra* note 114.

level. Kormos provides an overview of 'laws and policies that create an explicit wilderness protected area classification corresponding to Category Ib-Wilderness in the World Conservation Union's (IUCN) protected areas classification system'.[121] Without doubt the most prominent example of domestic wilderness legislation is the US Wilderness Act of 1964.[122] In the spirit of the Convention of London (1933) and the Western Hemisphere Convention (1940) and based on the long-standing practice of designating protected areas to safeguard their natural character,[123] this Act constitutes the legal basis for the US Congress to designate and protect Federally owned wilderness areas as part of the 'National Wilderness Preservation System'. The objectives are explicitly reflected in Section 2(a) of the Act:

> In order to assure that an increasing population, accompanied by expanding settlement and growing mechanization, does not occupy and modify all areas within the United States and its possessions, leaving no lands designated for preservation and protection in their natural condition, it is hereby declared to be the policy of the Congress to secure for the American people of present and future generations the benefits of an enduring resource of wilderness.

At the time at which the Act entered into force, some 9.1 million acres of wilderness received legal protection. Fifty years later over 750 areas, covering a total of almost 110 million acres of Federal land in forty-four States of the US, have received the status of protected wilderness under the Act (which corresponds to about five per cent of the entire US landmass).[124] This Act is generally considered as an important example of wilderness legislation, which – in conjunction with IUCN's guidelines on protected areas management categories - may have stimulated other governments to develop similar legislation. Kormos concluded in 2008 that, 'there are nine countries with laws, at least nine more with wilderness policies or zoning mechanisms, and two countries with laws pending [. . .]'.[125]

[121] Kormos (ed.), *A Handbook on International Wilderness Law and Policy, supra* note 20; citation from the first chapter, Kormos and Locke, 'Introduction', *supra* note 20, at 3.

[122] Wilderness Act 1964, Public Law 88–577 (16 U.S. C. 1131–1136), 88th Congress, Second Session, September 3, 1964, http://wilderness.nps.gov/document/wildernessAct.pdf. For the speech by President Lyndon B. Johnson at the occasion of signing the Act, see http://wilderness-society.org/wilderness-act-50th-anniversary/.

[123] McCloskey, 'The Wilderness Act of 1964: Its Background and Meaning', *supra* note 36.

[124] Katie Hoover, 'Wilderness: Overview and Statistics' (Washington: Congressional Research Service, 2010), http://nationalaglawcenter.org/wp-content/uploads/assets/crs/RL31447.pdf. For a popular overview, see www.youtube.com/watch?v=XD0g2ILIz50.

[125] Cyril F. Kormos, 'Conclusion', in Kormos (ed.), *A Handbook on International Wilderness Law and Policy, supra* note 20, pp. 355–359, at 358.

## 4 Europe: Focus on biological diversity and the recent wilderness debate

The focus on biodiversity conservation, discussed in Subsection 3.3, is a particular characteristic of the main European nature conservation instruments: the Bern Convention[126] and the European Union's Wild Birds Directive (1979)[127] and Habitats Directive (1992).[128] This is, for instance, reflected in the aim of the Habitats Directive: 'to contribute towards ensuring bio-diversity through the conservation of natural habitats and of wild fauna and flora in the [EU]',[129] in which the description 'conservation' should be read as 'a series of measures required to maintain or restore the natural habitats and the populations of species of wild fauna and flora at a favourable status [...]'.[130] Since the 1990s, the concept of wilderness has received explicit protection under the domestic laws of some European countries;[131] however, it is only since 2006 that wilderness has become the subject of a European-wide debate. Various non-governmental organizations were particularly active in stimulating this debate through the organization of conferences and lobbying activities.[132] The European Commission also played a clear role in putting wilderness on the political agenda, particularly through the strong involvement of the Director of Directorate B (Nature) of the European Commission, Ladislav Miko.[133] At the First European Congress of Conservation Biology in 2006, Miko stated: 'A wider European approach to allowing natural processes to work in favour of biodiversity and ecosystem services, including e.g. the need for definition of wilderness areas in some habitats close to climax stage, will need to be addressed.'[134]

[126] See note 100 and Chapter 7.

[127] Birds Directive, *supra* note 101.

[128] Habitats Directive, *supra* note 102.

[129] *Ibid.*, Article 2.

[130] *Ibid.*, Article 1(a).

[131] See Part III of this Volume.

[132] E.g., the Wild Europe Initiative, the Europarc Federation and the Pan Parks Foundation. Key-persons in this lobby work include Toby Aykroyd, coordinator of the Wild Europe Initiative, Zoltan Kun, deputy chairman of the European Wilderness Society (established in 2013), and Vlado Vancura, director wilderness development of the European Wilderness Society.

[133] Ladislav Miko was Director of Directorate B (Nature) in the Directorate-General Environment from 1 May 2005 to 07 May 2009 and from 1 December 2009 to 15 January 2011.

[134] First European Congress of Conservation Biology, Eger, Hungary, 22–26 August, 2006, 'Abstracts', www.carnivoreconservation.org/files/meetings/eccb_2006_eger_full.pdf, at 7.

A year later, at the Europarc Federation's General Assembly and Conference, he expressed the view that '[t]here is a need to make a strong case for wilderness in Europe'.[135]

The European wilderness debate received further impetus with the adoption of a Resolution on 'Wilderness in Europe' by the European Parliament on 3 February 2009.[136] In this Resolution, the Parliament '[e]xpresses its strong support for the strengthening of wilderness-related policies and measures'.[137] In the light of the above discussion, it is particularly noteworthy that the Parliament explicitly connects the concepts of wilderness and biodiversity by stressing that 'the effective protection and, where necessary, restoration of Europe's last wilderness areas are vital to halting the loss of biodiversity by 2010'.[138] In the Resolution, the European Parliament '[c]alls on the Commission and Member States to devote special attention to the effective protection of wilderness areas'[139] and requests the Commission more specifically 'to give a special status to and stricter protection for wilderness zones in the Natura 2000 network'.[140]

As a follow-up to this Resolution, the 'Conference on Wilderness and Large Natural Habitat Areas in Europe' was held in Prague on 27 and 28 May 2009, hosted by the Czech EU Presidency and the European Commission.[141] This conference resulted in the 'Message from Prague, an Agenda for Europe's Wild Areas',[142] which provides twenty-four recommendations for strengthening wilderness protection in Europe.[143]

In its 2011 *Communication on a Biodiversity Strategy 2020*,[144] the European Commission explicitly refers to wilderness protection. Action 12

[135] Federation General Assembly and Conference 'Nature – Bridging Borders', 26–30 September 2007, Cesky Krumlov, Czech Republic (Grafenau: Europarc Federation, 2007), www.europarc.cz/download/conf2007/conference_report.pdf, at 24.

[136] European Parliament Resolution of 3 February 2009 on Wilderness in Europe (Resolution 2008/2210(INI)), www.europarl.europa.eu/sides/getDoc.do?type=TA&reference=P6-TA-2009-0034&language=EN.

[137] *Ibid*, under 25).

[138] *Ibid*, under A) and 4).

[139] *Ibid.*, under 10).

[140] *Ibid.*, under 18).

[141] 'Conference on Wilderness and Large Natural Habitat Areas in Europe', 27–28 May 2009, see www.wildeurope.org.

[142] 'Message from Prague, An Agenda for Europe's Wild Areas', 28 May 2009, www.wildeurope.org/images/pdf/agenda_for_wilderness.pdf.

[143] The Resolution, the recommendations from the Message from Prague, as well as other follow-up initiatives of this European debate are discussed in more detail by Steve Carver in Chapter 2.

[144] Communication from the European Commission, 'Our life insurance, our natural capital: an EU biodiversity strategy to 2020,' COM(2011) 244 final, (Brussels:

('Integrate biodiversity measures in forest management plans') lists measures that Member States should seek to include in 'forest management plans or equivalent instruments', and one such measure is the preservation of wilderness areas.[145]

As a component of this European debate, the legal protection of wilderness in Europe has received particular attention. It is, for instance, a central component of the 'Message from Prague': 'The remaining pristine areas in Europe should be regarded as a unique asset and benefit from the highest level of protection. They should not be diminished or degraded.'[146] For this purpose, one of the recommendations in the 'Message from Prague', directed at the European Commission and the EU Member States, is to 'provide guidance on how wilderness qualities could receive legal protection both under the Natura 2000 regime and outside the EU, without compromising concrete protection of species and habitats in Europe'.[147] In 2013, this recommendation was implemented through the publication of the European Commission's *Guidelines on Wilderness in Natura 2000.*[148] The Guidelines also include two pages on legal wilderness protection at the domestic level.

Despite this general importance attributed to legal wilderness protection, a comprehensive academic analysis of the extent to which wilderness receives legal protection in Europe – through international conventions, European Union legislation and domestic law – is still absent. This is the central aim of this book.

## 5 Central aim, research questions and scope of this book

### *5.1 Central aim and research questions*

This book aims to contribute to the broader multi disciplinary European wilderness debate by providing a comprehensive appraisal of the role of international, European and domestic law in protecting wilderness areas

European Commission, 2011), http://ec.europa.eu/environment/nature/biodiversity/comm2006/pdf/2020/1_EN_ACT_part1_v7[1].pdf.

145 *Ibid.*, p.14.

146 'Message from Prague', *supra* note 142, Section III.

147 *Ibid.*, paragraph III(A)(1).

148 European Commission, 'Guidelines on Wilderness in Natura 2000. Management of terrestrial wilderness and wild areas within the Natura 2000 Network', (Brussels: European Union, 2013; prepared with the assistance of Alterra, PAN Parks Foundation and Eurosite), http://ec.europa.eu/environment/nature/natura2000/wilderness/pdf/WildernessGuidelines.pdf.

and their distinguishing qualities in Europe. For the purpose of this book, 'Europe' includes Western Europe, Central and Eastern European countries,[149] and European Russia.[150] More specifically, the book aims to address the following questions:

I What does 'wilderness' mean in a European context, where may wilderness areas in Europe be found, and what values do these areas represent?

II What is the role of international, European and domestic law in protecting wilderness areas and their distinguishing qualities in Europe?:

  a To what extent are European wilderness areas subject to protection under international and regional conventions and European law?

  b To what extent are European wilderness areas subject to protection under domestic law?

III Taking into account the outcomes of the analysis of questions I and II (including best practices and lessons learnt), is there a need to strengthen the legal protection of wilderness areas in Europe, and if so, what are the options to do so?

## *5.2 Working definition of wilderness in Europe*

### Defining wilderness

In defining wilderness,[151] some authors have emphasized the subjective element of wilderness. Taking the 'perspective of the people'[152] as a starting point, wilderness might be defined as a 'state of mind':[153]

> There is no specific material object that is wilderness. The term designates a quality [. . .] that produces a certain mood or feeling in a given individual

[149] For a definition of the Central and Eastern European countries (CEEC), see http://stats.oecd.org/glossary/detail.asp?ID=303.

[150] European Russia is generally referred to as the part of Russia West of the Ural mountains. See, e.g., Andrew Hamilton, Europe's Continental Boundaries, posted online, online source, posted 5 August 2011, www.counter-currents.com/2011/08/europes-continental-boundaries/.

[151] See Kees Bastmeijer, 'Protecting Polar Wilderness', *supra* note 111.

[152] See S. Fritz, S. Carver and L. See, 'New GIS Approaches to Wild Land Mapping in Europe,' *USDA Forest Service Proceedings* RMRS-P-15, Vol.2 (2000): 120–121, www.fs.fed.us/rm/pubs/rmrs_p015_2/rmrs_p015_2_120_127.pdf

[153] See Nash, *Wilderness & the American Mind, supra* note 16, at 5.

> and, as a consequence, may be assigned by that person to a specific place.[154]

This approach is sometimes used to demonstrate why it is problematic to protect 'wilderness' through law.[155] How can something be protected when it is unclear what it actually is? There is, however, another approach in defining wilderness: describing wilderness as a 'real place' by identifying the main physical characteristics (or wilderness qualities) that qualify a natural area as 'wilderness'. This approach has been followed in the US Wilderness Act 1964,[156] in several other domestic jurisdictions,[157] as well as in the aforementioned IUCN 'Guidelines for Applying Protected Area Management Categories'.[158] As the Guidelines were adopted on the basis of a comprehensive worldwide consultation process and taking into account that the IUCN has about 1300 member organizations (NGOs and governments), one could argue that the IUCN's definition is the most broadly accepted wilderness definition available:

> Category Ib protected areas are usually large unmodified or slightly modified areas, retaining their natural character and influence, without permanent or significant human habitation, which are protected and managed so as to preserve their natural condition.[159]

According to the IUCN the primary objective of such a wilderness area is therefore '[t]o protect the long-term ecological integrity of natural areas that are undisturbed by significant human activity, free of modern infra-structure and where natural forces and processes predominate, so that current and future generations have the opportunity to experience such

[154] *Ibid*, at 1. See also David R. Klein, 'Perspectives on Wilderness in the Arctic,' in *Wilderness in the Circumpolar North: Searching for Compatibility in Ecological, Traditional, and Ecotourism Values*, proceedings of a workshop, 15–16 May 2001, eds. Alan E. Watson, Lilian Alessa and Janet Sproull (Anchorage: USDA Forest Service Proceedings, 2002), pp. 1–6. Klein states (p. 1) that '[t]he concept of wilderness dwells in the mind's eye' and that 'the concept of wilderness [...], like all products of human perspective, is unique to each individual'.

[155] This argument is for instance used in discussions within the Antarctic Treaty System. See Kees Bastmeijer, 'Protecting Polar Wilderness', *supra* note 111.

[156] See Section 2 (c), of the U.S. Wilderness Act 1964, 'An Act to establish a National Wilderness Preservation System for the permanent good of the whole people, and for other purposes,' *supra* note 122.

[157] Kormos (ed.), *A Handbook on International Wilderness Law and Policy, supra* note 20.

[158] Dudley (ed.), *Guidelines for Applying Protected Area Management Categories, supra* note 1.

[159] *Ibid*, at 14.

areas'.[160] Thus, while the IUCN takes the approach of defining wilderness as a 'real place', the last part of the definition explicitly acknowledges the social value of wilderness.

As will be discussed further in Chapter 2, the IUCN definition constituted the starting point for defining wilderness in a European context. The Guidelines of the European Commission and the Wilderness Working Group of the Wild Europe Initiative adopted the following 'Working Definition' for wilderness:

> A wilderness is an area governed by natural processes. It is composed of native habitats and species, and large enough for the effective ecological functioning of natural processes. It is unmodified or only slightly modified and without intrusive or extractive human activity, settlements, infrastructure or visual disturbance.[161]

The Guidelines explain that this definition 'includes four qualities of wilderness: (a) naturalness, (b) undisturbedness, (c) undevelopedness and (d) scale'.[162] The definition – as well as the discussion of the four qualities – appears to particularly emphasize the ecological relevance of wilderness. This is, for instance, reflected by the explanation of the quality of 'undevelopedness': 'Habitation, settlements or other human artefacts such as power lines, roads, railways, fences may hinder ecological processes directly or by promoting the likelihood of human interference.'[163] For the purpose of the Guidelines, this may be a logical approach; however, this quality is also of importance from other perspectives, such as the socio-economic value of wilderness. Nonetheless, the above definition constitutes a strong foundation for researching the role of law in protecting wilderness in Europe.

It should however be emphasized that the discussions in this book are not limited to legislation that expressly aims to protect wilderness areas as described above. This would result in the exclusion of a considerable volume of legislation from the discussions. To ensure an in-depth analysis of the role of law regarding wilderness protection, the scope of the research also includes legislation that does not focus explicitly on areas that fully meet the above definition, but that still is of value for protecting one or more of the characteristic qualities of wilderness. Consequently, these main qualities of wilderness are as important as the definition itself.

[160] *Ibid.*

[161] European Commission, 'Guidelines on Wilderness in Natura 2000', *supra* note 148, at 10; Wild Europe Initiative (prepared by the Wilderness Working Group), 'A Working Definition of European Wilderness and Wild Areas', 10 September 2013, at 2.

[162] European Commission, *Guidelines on Wilderness in Natura 2000, supra* note 148, at 10.

[163] *Ibid.*, at 12.

### Main qualities of wilderness

To ensure a strong connection with the broader European wilderness debate, the following three main wilderness qualities identified in the European Commission's Guidelines will receive special attention in the discussions. These qualities are also recognized in the IUCN's wilderness definition, as well as those advanced in domestic laws, and the work of the University of Leeds[164] in the mapping of wilderness:

- *Naturalness*: native species and ecosystems and free-functioning natural processes;
- *Undevelopedness*: The absence of roads, buildings, bridges, tracks, cables or other evidence of modern human society, as well as a minimum distance from such facilities and development;
- *Relatively large size (scale)*: often indicated by means of acres or hectares, the time needed to cross the area, or related to effective ecological functioning.[165]

### A flexible concept

As the term 'working definition' implies, the overarching definition and the three main wilderness qualities elaborated above provide a uniform starting point for the discussions in each of the chapters; however, in conducting the research, authors have been aware of the possibility that this working definition may not provide an appropriate template for a particular region or jurisdiction in Europe, for instance because the concept of 'wilderness' in a certain country may have certain special historic, social or legal connotations. Consequently, the definition of wilderness in Europe is not rigidly expressed: this issue receives attention in the chapters on legal systems in Part II and Part III and is also one of the components of the concluding chapter.

## 5.3 *How 'wild' should an area be to qualify as 'wilderness'?*

An important question is 'how wild a region must be to qualify as wilderness, or conversely, how much of the influence of civilization

[164] See Chapter 2.

[165] To prevent unnecessary complexity, the quality of 'undisturbedness' is not adopted as a separate wilderness quality for the purpose of this book. Insofar as this quality relates to the concept that 'nature is essentially unhindered and free from modern human control or manipulation' (see the European Commission, 'Guidelines on Wilderness in Natura 2000, *supra* note 148, at 12) for the purpose of this book, it is assumed that this quality falls within the quality of 'naturalness'.

can be admitted'.[166] For instance, if the feature of naturalness or ecological intactness is applied strictly, we may not have any genuine wilderness left on Earth, taking into consideration the various forms of global environmental impacts caused by human activities.[167] Nash explains that a possible solution of the definitional problem is 'the conception of a spectrum of conditions or environments ranging from the purely wild on the one end to the purely civilized on the other – from the primeval to the paved.'[168] With this approach, 'the necessity of finding the watershed where wild becomes civilized is made less pressing'[169] and, more importantly, a discussion on protecting remaining existing wilderness qualities in natural areas is not impeded by definitional issues. This approach is considered useful in the European context as well and is also the approach followed by the University of Leeds in developing 'maps of the wilderness continuum', which show the degree of 'wildness' of Europe.[170] This book also adopts this approach: instead of focusing only on the last few per cent of the 'pure wilderness' that still exists, attention is also devoted to the legal protection of natural areas with a relatively high 'degree' of wilderness qualities that remain within Europe.

### 5.4 *Structure and limitations of the discussions*

#### Structure

The introductory **Part I** of the book focuses on *research question I*: This introductory chapter will be followed by a chapter by Steve Carver discussing the fundamentals of 'mapping wilderness', and to outline

166 See Nash, *Wilderness & the American Mind, supra* note 16, at 4.

167 See, among others, E. Ritter, 'Forests in Landscapes – The Myth of Untouched Wilderness', in E. Ritter and D. Daukstra (eds.), *New Perspectives on People and Forests* (Dordrecht: Springer, 2011), pp. 11–27. Ritter concludes (at 24): 'Intensive and extensive forest use in much of Europe has affected forest ecosystems so much that today's forests have to be understood in the context of past and present patterns of forest use. Even ecosystems that may have escaped direct impact by human use are nowadays threatened by man-made influences such as increased nutrient input through atmospheric deposition or acidification. Hence, "natural" ecosystems untouched by human beings can hardly be found in Europe.'

168 Nash, Wilderness & the American Mind, *supra* note 16, at 6.

169 *Ibid.*

170 M. Fisher, S. Carver, Z. Kun, R. McMorran, K. Arrell and G. Mitchell, 'Review of Status and Conservation of Wild Land in Europe', Project commissioned by the Scottish Government (Edinburgh, Scottish Government, 2010), www.scotland.gov.uk/Resource/Doc/1051/0109251.pdf.

where remaining wilderness quality land in Europe may be found (Steve Carver – Chapter 2). The following three chapters discuss the values of wilderness in Europe, taking an ecological (Mark Fisher – Chapter 3), social (Nicole Bauer – Chapter 4) and economic perspective (Nele Lienhoop and Bernd Hansjürgens – Chapter 5).

Based on this comprehensive introduction, *research question II* will receive attention in Part II and Part III. Part II discusses the extent to which European wilderness receives protection under global and regional treaties: The World Heritage Convention (Simon Marsden – Chapter 6), the Bern Convention (Arie Trouwborst – Chapter 7), the Alps Convention (Volker Mauerhofer, Ewald Galle and Marco Onida – Chapter 9) and the Carpathian Convention (Harald Egerer, Cai Lin Gwee, Eleonora Musco and Mathilde Koeck – Chapter 10). The extent to which wilderness receives legal protection under the European Union's Natura 2000 system, established under the EU Wild Birds Directive and Habitats Directive, is also discussed in this Part (Kees Bastmeijer – Chapter 8).

Part III analyses wilderness protection under the domestic legal systems of selected European countries: Austria (Volker Mauerhofer – Chapter 11), the Czech Republic (Zdeňka Křenová and Jiří Zicha – Chapter 12), Estonia (Richard Caddell – Chapter 13), Finland (Kai T. Kokko and Markku Oksanen – Chapter 14), Hungary (Sandor Fulop – Chapter 15), Iceland (Aðalheiður Jóhannsdóttir – Chapter 16), Norway (Ole Kristian Fauchald – Chapter 17), Poland (Sergiusz Urban – Chapter 18), Russia (Natalia Danilina, Antje Neumann and Kees Bastmeijer – Chapter 19), Spain (Agustín García Ureta – Chapter 20), Sweden (Filippo Valguarnera – Chapter 21) and the United Kingdom (Simon Boyle and Nicola Wheeler – Chapter 22).

The discussions in Part II and Part III are not limited to legislation that explicitly incorporates the term 'wilderness' in its title or main text. Wilderness may receive legal protection even if the term is not explicitly used in the relevant legislation. Conversely, the use of the term wilderness in legislation is not always a guarantee of legal protection for each of the characteristic qualities of wilderness. Therefore the discussions in Parts II and III pay detailed attention to the extent to which the relevant convention (Part II) or domestic legislation (Part III) provides legal protection to the main qualities of wilderness areas identified above. This approach also brings legislation on national parks and other categories of protected areas, as well as spatial planning law, within the scope of the Part III discussion.

Furthermore, the discussions in Parts II and III will also pay attention to the practical implementation and enforcement of wilderness law.

Part IV aims to answer *research question III*: it examines the lessons learned from these international, regional and national approaches and discusses the future of legal protection of wilderness areas in Europe (Kees Bastmeijer – Chapter 23).

### Limitations

The maximum size of the book as well as the feasibility of the project required clear choices regarding the scope. These choices resulted in a number of limitations. To start with, the focus is on terrestrial wilderness and not on marine wilderness. The concept of wilderness certainly also applies to the marine environment, but discussing the extent of marine wilderness protection would have required a different focus, with substantial attention to international marine law.

Furthermore, for Part II and Part III not all conventions and countries of relevance to the central aim of the book could be selected. For instance, in relation to Part II, some conventions, such as the European Landscape Convention of the Council of Europe,[171] were not selected, as a preliminary study by the editor indicated that the chosen conventions of Part II were more important for wilderness protection in Europe. The selection of the countries in Part III of the book has been based on a number of criteria: (a) the extent to which wilderness areas may be found in a country (based on previous research on the mapping of wilderness), (b) the geographical location of the country in Europe (to have all parts of Europe represented), (c) EU Membership (EU Member States as well as non-EU Member States [e.g., Iceland, Norway and Russia] have been selected), (d) the availability of an academic expert with a high level of knowledge on the theory and practice of nature conservation law in the relevant country and (e) a maximum number of twelve countries for Part III (to respect the maximum size of the book). Regrettably, the application of these criteria resulted in the exclusion of a number of countries that are relevant to the discussion on the legal protection of wilderness in Europe. For instance, several Eastern European countries, such as Romania and Bulgaria, could not be discussed due to criterion (d).

[171] European Landscape Convention, Council of Europe, Florence, 20 July 2000, ETS No. 176, http://conventions.coe.int/Treaty/en/Treaties/Html/176.htm. For an introduction to the convention, see Maguelonne Déjeant-Pons, 'The European Landscape Convention', *Landscape Research* 31, 4 (2006), 363–384, www.tandfonline.com/doi/pdf/10.1080/01426390601004343.

Finally, the concept of 're-wilding' through the restoration of wilderness (e.g., removal of non-native species, removal of permanent infrastructure) or the establishment of 'new wilderness areas' (in combination with long-term non-intervention management) is an important component of the European wilderness debate, but is not a central topic of this book. The discussions in this book focus on the extent to which existing areas with relatively high wilderness qualities receive legal protection. However, it is clear that both topics are inter-related. For instance, for re-wilding projects it is important to consider what instruments are available to ensure the legal protection of the wilderness qualities of 'rewilded' areas.

These limitations make it possible to focus the full attention of the chapters that follow on the central research questions. As these questions have yet received little attention in the literature, the authors have made great research efforts, resulting in comprehensive chapters that are full of new information and knowledge. It is hoped that these discussions may contribute to the wider multi disciplinary debate on the protection of wilderness in Europe.

2

# Mapping wilderness in Europe

STEVE CARVER

## 1 Introduction

*HC SVNT DRACONES*: 'Here be dragons'

The word 'wilderness' has its origins in the early Norse/Teutonic languages (literally meaning 'place of wild beasts'), and has been used since in a biblical concept to mean a desert. However, it was during the Age of Discovery in the sixteenth, seventeenth and eighteenth centuries that the concept was to find its best expression in the new lands of Africa, the Americas, Asia and Oceania.[1] Although these were in the main already inhabited and managed by native peoples when 'discovered' during this time, Europeans often bestowed upon them the idea, or at least the perception, of them being ungodly places – the home of wild animals that needed to be tamed and the land made otherwise fruitful. Maps of this period were often illustrated with dragons and other fanciful creatures, suggesting wild and dangerous beasts inhabited the uncharted corners of the world. Some maps contain the Latin phrase 'HC SVNT DRACONES' or 'here be dragons', further indicating that these lands were yet to be civilized.[2] Such an opinion widely persisted until the Romantic period towards the end of the eighteenth century, when wilderness began to take on a more positive tone associated with the state of nature and the sublime.

Today while we still appreciate and value wilderness for its aesthetic and heroic qualities, we additionally understand and value the true and original ecological condition: as the state of pristine nature where human influence on ecosystems and natural processes is absent or minimal. Even this concept of wilderness has its critics, however, with many suggesting that all lands have been modified and managed by humans to some

[1] See R. Nash, *Wilderness and the American Mind* (New Haven: Yale University Press, 2001), Chapter 1.

[2] For examples, see http://2.bp.blogspot.com/_p2KqxkFzn6A/S_ul-EIE8UI/AAAAAAAAAI0/nXc0GLsqSkA/s1600/old-world-map.jpg; and http://en.wikipedia.org/wiki/Here_be_dragons.

degree such that the true state of nature no longer exists and was, in any case, only a human construct in the first place.[3] Putting aside these critiques, and by accepting the multiple meanings and understandings of the word, wilderness has returned to find a new home within Europe. After hundreds of years of exploring the wilderness in foreign continents, Europe is now looking inward upon itself and beginning to both recognize and appreciate the wildernesses we have in our own lands and on our own doorsteps. In many ways, the concept has matured way beyond the naive colonial view. In today's scientific and rational world we understand that 'wilderness' is just a word in the English language and that while its meanings and embodied histories are as varied as the landscapes it tries to describe, it is in essence a reference point of ecological purity against which we can judge our impact on ecosystem form and function.

Knowing what wilderness is, or refers to, is only the start of the problem. Deriving a universally acceptable definition and applying it to identify and map remaining wilderness such that it might be best protected is another. It is to this problem that this chapter of the book is addressed. The chapter is split into two sections: the first providing further background information on the definition of wilderness in Europe supporting the discussion in Chapter 1, the second on mapping wilderness globally, but with a special emphasis on Europe. A conclusion provides an indication of the current status quo within Europe and what this means for the rest of the world.

## 2 Wilderness definition in Europe

### *2.1 Defining wilderness: an international perspective*

The United States Wilderness Act 1964 was the first significant piece of modern wilderness legislation that laid a legal foundation for its definition and protection.[4] The definition used within the Act was written by Howard Zahniser and took over fifteen years and more than sixty drafts to get accepted, which illustrates the difficulty of defining wilderness.[5]

[3] See, for example, W. Cronon, 'The Trouble with Wilderness: Or, Getting Back to the Wrong Nature', *Environmental History* 1, 1 (2000), 7–28, and N. Castree, 'The Production of Nature,' in E. Sheppard and T. Barnes (eds.), *A Companion to Economic Geography* (Oxford and New York: Blackwell, 2000), pp. 269–275.

[4] The Wilderness Act, *Public Law* 88–577 (16 U.S. C. 1131–1136) 88th Congress, Second Session, 3 September 1964.

[5] M.W.T. Harvey, *Wilderness Forever: Howard Zahniser and the Path to the Wilderness Act* (Seattle: University of Washington Press, 2005).

The final wording of the Act, signed on 3 September 1964 by President Lyndon B. Johnson, states in Sec. 2(c):

> A wilderness, in contrast with those areas where man and his own works dominate the landscape, is hereby recognized as an area where the earth and its community of life are untrammeled by man, where man himself is a visitor who does not remain. An area of wilderness is further defined to mean in this Act an area of undeveloped Federal land retaining its primeval character and influence, without permanent improvements or human habitation, which is protected and managed so as to preserve its natural conditions and which (1) generally appears to have been affected primarily by the forces of nature, with the imprint of man's work substantially unnoticeable; (2) has outstanding opportunities for solitude or a primitive and unconfined type of recreation; (3) has at least five thousand acres of land or is of sufficient size as to make practicable its preservation and use in an unimpaired condition; and (4) may also contain ecological, geological, or other features of scientific, educational, scenic, or historical value.

Upon signing the Act, President Johnson is quoted in his speech as saying:

> If future generations are to remember us with gratitude rather than contempt, we must leave them something more than the miracles of technology. We must leave them a glimpse of the world as it was in the beginning, not just after we got through with it.[6]

The Act lays the foundations of the US National Wilderness Preservation System, which at the time covered 9.1 million acres of federal land but which has since been expanded to cover nearly 110 million acres.[7]

The Act has been influential in expanding wilderness definition and protection worldwide. The IUCN now defines wilderness[8] under Category 1 either as Category 1a (Strict Nature Reserve), which are areas set aside primarily for research, or as Category 1b (Wilderness), the definition of which was cited in Chapter 1. Looking at this definition and comparing it to the text from the US Wilderness Act (1964), it is easy to see where the inspiration for the IUCN definition comes from. The

[6] Lyndon B. Johnson, 'Remarks Upon Signing the Wilderness Bill and the Land and Water Conservation Fund Bill', 3 September 1964, published online by Gerhard Peters and John T. Woolley, The American Presidency Project: www.presidency.ucsb.edu/ws/?pid=26481.

[7] This is a constantly changing figure but the most recent figure given by www.wilderness.net is 109,511,966 acres.

[8] IUCN, *Guidelines for Applying Protected Area Management Categories* (Gland: Switzerland, 2008).

language and wording may be different but the message and meaning are the same.

### 2.2 *Re-importing the wilderness idea back into Europe*

As described in the opening paragraphs, Europe is now the focus of attention in recognizing its own wilderness resource. Notwithstanding the remnants of great ancient civilizations, the New World frontier was during the seventeenth and eighteenth centuries seen very much as wilderness and the edge of Western civilization. Only with the Romantic Period in the nineteenth century did Europeans begin to value wilderness as a source of artistic inspiration and spiritual refreshment rather than purely as a source of material resources and of land to be tamed.[9] As formulated by Muir in respect of the United States:

> Thousands of tired, nerve-shaken, over-civilized people are beginning to find out that going to the mountains is going home; that wildness is a necessity; and that mountain parks and reservations are useful not only as fountains of timber and irrigating rivers, but as fountains of life.[10]

As Europe started to look inward to its own remaining wild landscapes, we re-imported the wilderness ideal.

More recently, as indicated in Chapter 1, the European wilderness debate has intensified and broadened to law and policy development, learning from developments in wilderness protection and legislation in North American, Africa and former colonies elsewhere in the world, including South Africa, Canada, New Zealand and Australia, all of which have their own wilderness definitions, and all of which owe much to the original wording defined by Howard Zahniser in the US Wilderness Act.[11]

There are a number of possible reasons why Europe has begun to take this more inward perspective. One reason clearly stems from the original desire to explore and experience wilderness first seen in the Age of Discovery. Despite the quest for land, wealth and resources, there is still the primeval need within even the most modern societies to

[9] See Chapter 1.

[10] J. Muir, *Our National Parks* (Cambridge: The Riverside Press, 1901), p. 1

[11] See, e.g., C.P. Dawson and J.C. Hendee, *Wilderness Management: Stewardship and Protection of Resources and Values* (Golden: Fulcrum Publishing, 2009) and C.F. Kormos, *A Handbook on International Wilderness Law and Policy* (Golden: Fulcrum Publishing, 2008).

experience and be part of nature. It comes as a surprise to many Europeans who are long used to living in heavily modified landscapes that significant wilderness landscapes remain within their otherwise crowded continent.

Another reason for the rise in interest in a European wilderness movement has been the over-exploitation of resources elsewhere in the world. Globally, wilderness is under threat from numerous quarters, partly driven by the demand for resources (oil, gas, minerals, food, timber, etc.) generated from within Europe itself to sustain our high standard of living. Saving our own backyard wildernesses might therefore serve two purposes: (a) it demonstrates to developing nations that developed nations are protecting their wilderness areas (and associated biodiversity) and so are leading by example and encouraging developing nations to do the same, and (b) it helps preserve and maintain natural processes that provide valuable ecosystem services.[12] Thus, the European focus on wilderness preservation can be classified as both an ethical/moral duty and as a self-serving anthropocentric one. The latter is generating a great deal of interest among governments and agencies keen to push the sustainability message, or as another of the great Romanticists Henry David Thoreau succinctly put it: '[. . .] in wildness is the preservation of the world'.[13]

The value of wilderness has long been realized in terms of protected watersheds for the supply of clean drinking water to nearby cities. The Catskill Mountains have supplied the city of New York with drinking water for nearly 200 years, but only relatively recently has the city begun to purchase land to protect its watersheds from human land use and pollution. De Groot et al. identify four main groups or categories of ecosystem services:[14] provisioning, regulating, supporting and cultural services. Examples are given in Table 1.

The ecological, economic and social values of wilderness in Europe will be discussed in more detail in the next chapters, but it is easy to see from Table 1 how wilderness areas might be best placed to supply these services to nearby, and in some cases, distant urban populations.[15] Human-modified

[12] The concept of ecosystem service values derived from use and non-use of wilderness areas is covered in Chapters 4 and 5 of this volume.

[13] Henry David Thoreau, 'Walking', *Atlantic Monthly* 9 (1862), 657–674, http://thoreau.eserver.org/walking2.html, Part 2, para. 18.

[14] R.S. De Groot, M.A. Wilson and R.M. Boumans, 'A Typology for the Classification, Description and Valuation of Ecosystem Functions, Goods and Services', *Ecological Economics* 41, 3 (2002), 393–408.

[15] See Chapters 4 and 5.

Table 1 *Ecosystem services*

| Category of service | Examples |
|---|---|
| Provisioning | Water supply, carbon storage, wildlife habitat |
| Regulating | Runoff and river flow regimes (flood protection), groundwater recharge, erosion control, nutrient stripping, carbon sequestration, etc. |
| Supporting | Hydrological cycle, carbon cycle, nitrogen cycle, etc. |
| Cultural | Recreational environments, aesthetic landscapes, human health and well-being, sense-of-place, etc. |

landscapes on the other hand can reduce or even compromise these services entirely. It is well known, for example, how deforestation, drainage and over-grazing of watersheds lead to more rapid runoff, soil erosion, biodiversity losses, flooding and poor water quality.[16]

### 2.3 *Poselství from Prague and developing a European definition of wilderness*

After several years of lobbying by the Wild Europe Initiative and other interested parties, in 2009 the European Parliament passed a resolution recognizing the value of wilderness in Europe by a majority of 538 votes in favour to just 19 against.[17] With the resolution (under A)(4)), the European Parliament:

> emphasises the importance of protecting Europe's last remaining wilderness areas and [...] calls on the European Institutions to develop appropriate guidance to EU Member States on the best approaches to ensure the protection of these natural habitats as an important contribution to halting the loss of biodiversity.

The resolution and the 'Conference on Wilderness and Large Natural Habitat Areas', held in Prague in May 2009, both called on the European Commission and EU Member States, having regard for the Habitats

[16] S.E. Gergel, M.G. Turner, J.R. Miller, J.M. Melack and E.H. Stanley, 'Landscape Indicators of Human Impacts to Riverine Systems', *Aquatic Sciences* 64, 2 (2002), 118–128.

[17] European Parliament Resolution of 3 February 2009 on Wilderness in Europe (Resolution 2008/2210(INI)), www.europarl.europa.eu/sides/getDoc.do?type=TA&reference=P6-TA-2009-0034&language=EN. See also Chapter 1.

Directive, the Natura 2000 network, the Convention on Biodiversity and the European Environmental Agency sustainable forests report, to define European wilderness, map the remaining wilderness areas, study the value and benefits of wilderness protection, develop management guidelines and protect wilderness areas. The Poselství (message) from Prague documents these in full (see Box 1 for a summary of the key recommendations) and served to kick start a wider debate on wilderness in Europe and paved the way for strategic thinking and policy development on wilderness.[18]

A number of significant developments have occurred in Europe on the topic of wilderness and wild lands since the Prague conference in 2009. The first of these occurred within Scotland, where there has long been a recognition and appreciation of the importance of wild land, particularly in the Highland region. The 2009 resolution and the Prague conference both provided impetus for the Scottish Government to forge ahead and produce two key outputs: a comprehensive review of the status and conservation of wild land in Europe[19] and a detailed national wildness map produced using a robust and repeatable methodology adapted from work for the Scottish National Parks.[20] The report on wild land was the first of its kind to cover the whole of Europe in detail and as such has been widely cited in subsequent work. The mapping of Scotland's wild land remains the most detailed and comprehensive programme of its kind for any country in Europe and possibly the world.

The resolution of the European Parliament and the Poselství both call for the development of guidelines on managing wilderness within Natura 2000, a unified European definition of wilderness and a register of remaining areas. These three issues have all received substantial attention since 2009. The required guidance on wilderness was published in the document *Guidelines on Wilderness in Natura 2000: Management of*

[18] *POSELSTVÍ FROM PRAGUE: An Agenda for Europe's Wild Areas. Summary of the Conference on Wilderness and Large Natural Habitat Areas*, Prague, Czech Republic, 27–28 May 2009. See also Chapter 1.

[19] M. Fisher, S. Carver, Z. Kun, R. McMorran, K. Arrell and G. Mitchell, *Review of Status and Conservation of Wild Land in Europe*, Project commissioned by the Scottish Government (Leeds: Wildland Research Institute, 2010).

[20] See work by S.J. Carver, A. Comber, R. McMorran and S. Nutter, 'A GIS Model for Mapping Spatial Patterns and Distribution of Wild Land in Scotland', *Landscape and Urban Planning* 104, 3–4 (2012), 395–409, and Scottish National Heritage, *Mapping Scotland's wildness and wild land* (Inverness: Scottish National Heritage, 2012), www.snh.gov.uk/protecting-scotlands-nature/looking-after-landscapes/landscape-policy-and-guidance/wild-land/mapping/.

BOX 1 THE POSELSTVÍ FROM PRAGUE

The following four sets of recommendations have been identified, calling in particular for action by the European Commission and EU Member States with the support of other stakeholders:

A. *Policy development:*
   1. Provide guidance on how wilderness qualities could receive legal protection both under the Natura 2000 regime and outside the EU, without compromising concrete protection of species and habitats in Europe.
   2. The management of the Natura 2000 network should take account of the need to protect ecological processes as well as habitats and species.
   3. Guidance should be developed concerning the protection of wilderness areas in the context of the EU nature legislation, addressing issues such as natural changes to sites, response to climate change, the maintenance of specific succession states and non-intervention.
   4. [. . .]
   5. In the light of a clearer definition of wilderness and wild land in different parts of Europe, and the extent to which this is protected by existing legislation and policy, consider and promote the action needed to ensure existing legislation protecting wilderness and wildlands is monitored and enforced effectively by all responsible authorities and steps are taken to fill the gaps in protective cover that are identified.
   6. [. . .], 7. [. . .]

B. *Awareness building:*
   8. In the short run, to incorporate recommendations from the Conference into relevant reports (including TEEB), government meetings (upcoming EU Presidencies), international conferences (CBD/Nagoya, UNFCCC/Copenhagen) and other events –facilitated by compilation of a relevant schedule and production of appropriate policy documents.
   9. To further develop awareness in the conservation sector of the contribution wilderness and wildland areas can make to halting biodiversity loss and supporting Natura 2000 and the Emerald Network.
   10. [. . .], 11. [. . .]

C. *Further work and information needs:*
   12. Finalization of a definition of wilderness and wild areas, taking into account the globally agreed definitions, criteria and characteristics and the continuum of natural habitats and ecological processes, the range of ecological and cultural interpretations of these terms and their application in different parts of Europe.
   13. Compilation of a Register of Wilderness using existing databases, such as the EEA and WDPA, identifying in tandem with appropriate interested parties the remaining areas of wilderness and wildlands, the threats and opportunities related to these, and their economic values, with practical recommendations for action.

BOX 1 (CONT.)

14. Completion of mapping wilderness and wildland areas in Europe, involving appropriate definitional and habitat criteria and level of scale to effectively support plans for protecting and monitoring such areas.
15. Identification of key opportunities for prospective restoration of wild natural habitats and processes, involving mapping, biodiversity design and benefit assessment for relevant parties including local landholders and communities.
16. […], 17. […]
18. Identification and promotion of how ecosystem services such as carbon sequestration, flood mitigation, water purification, erosion control, and pollution alleviation can be linked to specific payment mechanisms, via landholders, communities and other beneficiaries, for protection and restoration of wilderness and wildland. The public goods benefits of wilderness will require public funding.
19. […]

D. *Supporting capacity*

20. […], 21. […]
22. Develop examples, based on best practice, of how local communities and landholders can secure value from recreation, tourism and other initiatives.
23. Undertake a full assessment of government, institutional and private sector funding opportunities for protection and restoration, as part of broader conservation programmes.
24. Build inter-sector consensus and support by developing initiatives for joint approaches based on common ground with other sectors including: landholders, forestry, agriculture, business.

*terrestrial wilderness and wild areas within the Natura 2000 network.*[21] This document also includes a definition of wilderness, which was cited in Chapter 1. Furthermore, the guidelines document highlights the position of wilderness within the Birds and Habitats Directives and Natura 2000 together with approaches essential for the maintenance or re-establishment of natural habitat types and species in wilderness areas.[22] Ecosystem service benefits from wilderness and best practice examples with an emphasis on potential conflicts between non-intervention

[21] European Commission, *Guidelines on Wilderness in Natura 2000: Management of Terrestrial Wilderness and Wild Areas within the Natura 2000 Network* (Brussels: EU, 2013), http://ec.europa.eu/environment/nature/natura2000/wilderness/pdf/WildernessGuidelines.pdf.

[22] See Chapter 8 on wilderness protection and Natura 2000.

management and natural hazards are presented and the role of stakeholder dialogue is promoted.

A European wilderness register for all EEA member countries has been developed. This provides improved data on wilderness at the level of countries all over Europe, and makes it possible for countries to set their own priorities for maintenance and improvement of wilderness quality within their national territory. This register pays specific attention to trans-boundary areas since, like biodiversity, wilderness is no respecter of political boundaries. In the long run the wilderness register should give support on prioritizing areas for protection within the Natura 2000 and Emerald networks across Europe. The register has been produced through a process of joint consideration of the Common Database on Designated Areas (CDDA)[23] to extract IUCN Category 1a/b, 2 and 6 (Finland and Estonia) protected areas greater than 2,500 ha in size and a two-stage filtering process initially via consultation with nature NGOs and site managers of protected areas but then followed up by a verification stage using national contact points to develop the wilderness register.

For the purpose of the register, two categories of wilderness are defined: Category A and Category B. Four main criteria were used to differentiate between these wilderness categories, namely size, extractive use, subsistence use and infrastructure. These are summarized in Table 2. At the same time, a European spatial wilderness index has been developed (see Subsection 4.2.).

## 3 Mapping wilderness quality: how and why?

Geographers have been mapping wilderness and wilderness quality for around twenty-five years now since the first global reconnaissance of remaining wilderness was developed by Mike McCloskey and Heather Spalding for the 4th World Wilderness Congress.[24] However, we have been mapping wilderness for millennia, not by dint of what we have mapped, but rather by what we haven't. Maps and navigation charts have until the last few hundred years been depicting wilderness by default, as the blank bits (i.e. the 'parts unknown' sometimes inscribed on ancient maps as 'HC SVNT DRACONES' or 'Here be dragons' as referred to at the start of

[23] See www.eea.europa.eu/themes/biodiversity/document-library/nationally-designated-areas-cdda.

[24] M.J. McCloskey and H. Spalding, 'A Reconnaissance-level Inventory of the Amount of Wilderness Remaining in the World', *Ambio* 18, 4 (1989), 221–227.

Table 2 *Main criteria used to distinguish between category A and B wilderness for the wilderness register*

| Issue | Category A | Category B |
|---|---|---|
| Size | Minimum 3,000 ha | Less than 3,000 ha (but with potential to expand) |
| Extractive use | None | Yes<br>For example, extensive hunting, fishing, collecting berries and grazing (but with potential to reduce or remove these uses) |
| Subsistence use | None | Yes<br>For example, subsistence hunting, fishing, collecting berries and grazing (but with potential to reduce or remove these subsistence uses) |
| Infrastructure | None* (certain compromises are necessary, e.g. existing/ old gravel road used for safety, fire control, management, etc.) | Yes<br>For example, existing roads (but with potential to reduce or remove them) |

Notes:
*Wilderness category A:* meets all criteria. For example, at least 3,000 ha, no habitation/settlement, no habitat and wildlife management, no extractive use of resources, no motorized access, no road building, etc.
*Wilderness category B:* does not fulfil all the criteria of the working definition, but in many cases gives a good 'sense of wilderness'. For example, some parts of the Carpathians or Alps will not qualify as category A due to livestock grazing or hunting. However, people visiting these areas would likely feel being in a wilderness. Another example is related to parts of Fenno-Scandinavian countries (especially Sami territories), which would not qualify as category A due to subsistence use. Again, however, people visiting these areas would likely feel that they were in a wilderness.

this chapter). These were the wildernesses or unknown regions as understood by those that mapped the world – its lands, rivers, oceans and seas – over the years until relatively recently when the entire planet has become mapped from the ground and photographed from satellites and therefore 'known' or at least spatially speaking in regard to its location, form and land cover. They were of course 'known' and understood by those that inhabited them long before the surveyors arrived.

> We did not think of the great open plains, the beautiful rolling hills, the winding streams with tangled growth, as 'wild'. Only to the white man was nature a 'wilderness' and only to him was it 'infested' with 'wild' animals and 'savage' people. To us it was tame. Earth was bountiful and we were surrounded with the blessings of the Great Mystery.[25]

Nonetheless, the emphasis on data, information and mapping technology has in the twentieth and twenty-first centuries enabled better and more detailed understandings of patterns of wilderness quality and the threats facing wilderness in the modern world. Although the difficulties in mapping a concept as vague and varied as wilderness are legion, these are no reason not to try. Although some might countenance that to map it is to know it, and therefore it may lose some of its wild qualities,[26] the alternatives are unthinkable. Without a rigorous and repeatable approach to mapping wilderness we are in grave danger of losing it, physically, from pressures of development (land take), pollution, resource extraction and so on, since without a defensible approach to the spatial definition of wilderness we are very much handicapped in our abilities to map that which we seek to defend.

## *3.1 Where is the wild?*

There have been numerous campaigns to map patterns of wilderness at a global scale. The first was the McCloskey and Spalding map. This was a rule-based map in which the authors used a set of simple Boolean criteria – areas greater than 400,000 ha in size and more than 6 km from any recorded human feature – which they applied to Jet Navigation Charts at a scale of 1:2 million to arrive at the map reproduced in Figure 1; a remarkable feat given all the work was done by hand with paper maps.

The key finding of this early map was that roughly thirty-seven per cent of the world's land surface can be classified as wilderness, although forty-one per cent of this total is disproportionately found in the Arctic or Antarctic. Subsequent maps have all used Geographical Information

[25] Chief Luther Standing Bear, of the Oglala/Lakota tribe cited in J.B. Callicott and M.P. Nelson (eds.), *The Great New Wilderness Debate* (Athens: University of Georgia Press, 1998), p. 201.

[26] J. Griffiths, *Wild: An Elemental Journey* (London: Penguin, 2007).

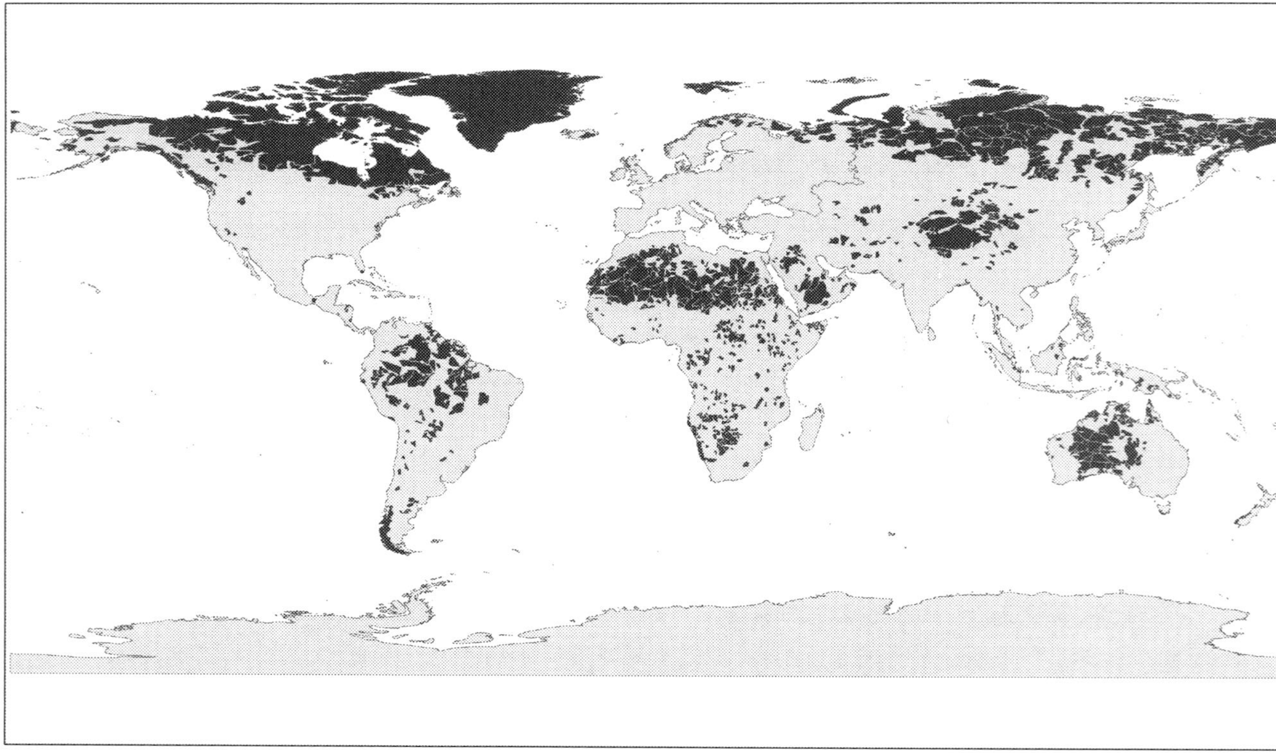

**Figure 1:** A global reconnaissance of the amount of wilderness remaining in the world (After McCloskey and Spalding, 1989). The grey areas show wilderness areas greater than 400,000 ha in size with no roads or human structures.

Systems (GIS) with digital map and satellite data. Many of these build on the basic principles established by Rob Lesslie and co-workers in developing the Australian National Wilderness Inventory (NWI). They mapped wilderness quality across the whole of Australia based around the wilderness continuum concept described by Roderick Nash in his book *Wilderness and the American Mind*, first published in 1967. Here wilderness is assumed to exist at one end of a continuum of human modification of natural ecosystems, while built and urban environments exist at the other.

The Australian NWI uses four basic spatial attributes to describe wilderness quality. These are: remoteness from human settlement, remoteness from mechanized access, apparent naturalness (distance from modern human artefacts) and biophysical (ecological) naturalness; all of which can be easily modelled and mapped from readily available digital map data sources such as population density, road networks, land cover and so on. These attributes have largely been adopted in one form or another by most subsequent mapping work. Lesslie et al. (1993)[27] mapped these four attributes and combined them in a simple raster-based cartographic model to map the wilderness continuum.

Similar wilderness models have been developed elsewhere, including the United States,[28] Austria,[29] the Barents region[30] and the UK,[31] and have been applied at a global scale by Sanderson et al. (2002) and Halpern et al. (2008).[32] Local scale models have also been developed for National

[27] R. Lesslie, D. Taylor and M. Maslen, *National Wilderness Inventory, Handbook of Principles, Procedures and Usage* (Canberra: Australian Heritage Commission, 1993).

[28] G. Aplet, J. Thomson and M. Wilbert, 'Indicators of Wildness: Using Attributes of the Land to Assess the Context of Wilderness', in Proceedings RMRS-P-15-VOL-2, *Wilderness Science in a Time of Change Conference-Volume 2: Wilderness within the Context of Larger Systems* (Ogden, UT: USDA Forest Service, 2000).

[29] C. Plutzar, F. Hejjas, M. Zika and B. Kohler, 'Linking the Wilderness Continuum Concept to Protected Areas', *Proc. 5th Symposium Research in Protected Areas* (Mittersill: 2013), pp. 587–590.

[30] D. Henry and E. Husby, *Wilderness Quality Mapping in the Euro-Arctic Barents Region: A Potential Management Tool* (Trondheim: Direktoratet for Naturforvaltning, 1994), www.esri.com/recourses/userconf/proc95/to150/p113.html.

[31] S. Carver, 'Mapping the Wilderness Continuum Using Raster GIS', in S. Morain and S. Lopez-Baros (eds.), *Raster Imagery in Geographic Information Systems* (New Mexico: OnWord Press 1996), pp. 283–288.

[32] See E.W. Sanderson, M. Jaiteh, M.A. Levy, K.H. Redford, A.V. Wannebo and G. Woolmer, 'The Human Footprint and the Last of the Wild', *Bioscience* 52, 10 (2002), 891–904 and B.S. Halpern, S. Walbridge, K.A. Selkoe, C.V. Kappel, F. Micheli, C. D'Agrosa and R. Watson, 'A Global Map of Human Impact on Marine Ecosystems', *Science* 319, 5865 (2008), 948–952.

Parks.[33] Although these differ in scale from the local to the global, they all essentially apply the same approach of combining wilderness attributes in a spatial model to identify areas with high wilderness quality or value.

### *3.2 Scaling issues: from global to local*

While the basic underlying model of the wilderness continuum remains the same even when mapping wilderness quality across all spatial scales, its implementation creates some interesting issues for the way we apply it.

Data availability varies across scales. At a global or continental scale we are reliant on global datasets, otherwise we have to try to patch together country-level datasets with associated difficulties of trans-boundary compatibility. Coordinated global datasets exist for many attributes, such as roads and railways, national boundaries, coastlines and land cover. These include the Digital Chart of the World, a digital version of the USAF Tactical Pilotage Charts or Jet Navigation Charts used by McCloskey and Spalding. Other datasets, such as population density, are often reported at the country level using different standards and so can show up as obvious trans-boundary differences when mapped at the global or continental scale. Such discontinuities are then propagated through the wilderness quality model into the final map and often appear as marked differences across national boundaries. This can be seen by careful scrutiny of the Human Footprint map produced by Sanderson et al. (2002) shown in Figure 2. At country or local level these issues are less of a problem and more detailed data sources become available.

Resolution of the data used has a marked effect on the detail of the map outputs, due to its effects on both data quality and the ability to apply more realistic modelling approaches at more local scales. Generally speaking, the more local the study, the higher the resolution data that is available, with associated gains in quality (precision and accuracy) and the more advanced modelling techniques that can be applied. At the global scale, datasets tend to be limited in resolution and so

[33] See for example Carver et al., 'A GIS model for mapping spatial patterns and distribution of wild land in Scotland', *supra* note 20, and S. Carver, J. Tricker and P. Landres, 'Keeping It Wild: Mapping Wilderness Character in the United States', *Journal of Environmental Management* 131 (2013), 239–255 and F. Orsi, D. Geneletti and A. Borsdorf, 'Mapping Wildness for Protected Area Management: A Methodological Approach and Application to the Dolomites UNESCO World Heritage Site (Italy)', *Landscape and Urban Planning* 120 (2013), 1–15.

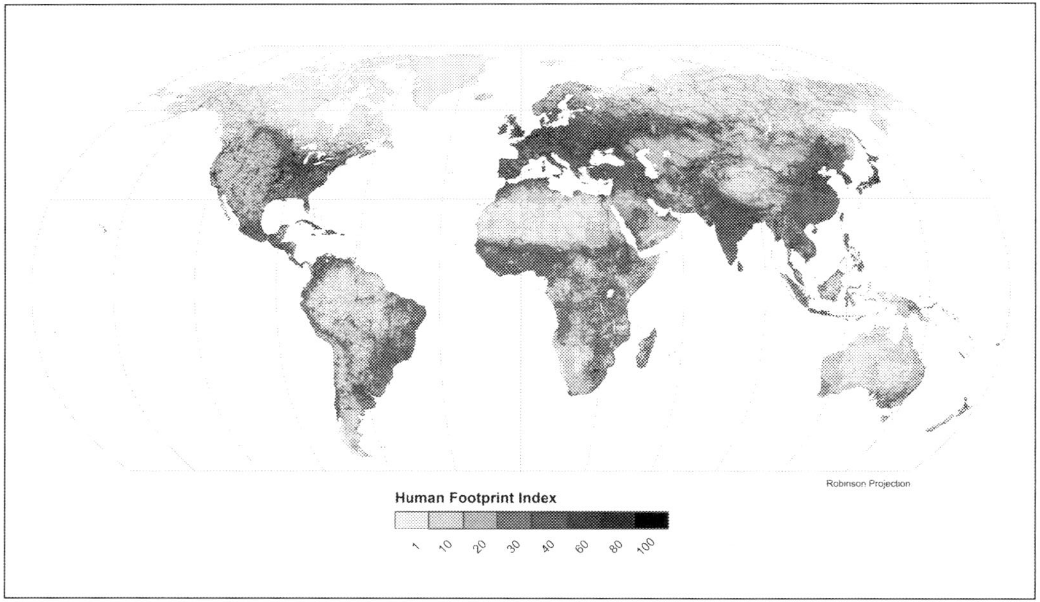


**Figure 2:** The Human Footprint (after Sanderson et al., 2002).[34] The Human Footprint Index (HF) expresses as a percentage the relative human interference in each terrestrial biome. HF values range from 0 to 100. A value of zero represents the least influences (the most wild part of the biome) with a value of 100 representing the most influenced (least wild) part of the biome.

generalization becomes an issue in both the quality of the data and the ability to apply spatial models. For example, most global level assessments of wilderness quality use data at a 1 $km^2$ resolution and simple models of human impact such as straight line distance from the nearest road. Indeed, one recent product relating to global wilderness potential is the Roadless Areas map developed from Google Maps road data and launched at Rio+20, which shows areas of the world more than 10 km from the nearest road. Here the assumption is a simple one; roads are related to human impact (roads are always present where there is human settlement and agriculture) and where roads penetrate undeveloped areas, they fragment the wilderness and development often follows shortly thereafter.

More detailed and sophisticated models of wilderness attributes can only be practically applied at more local scales where detailed, high resolution datasets are available and the study areas are small enough for the computational overheads are reasonable. Some of the most detailed modelling of wilderness quality to date has been carried out in Scotland for the two national parks: the Cairngorm National Park and the Loch Lomond and The Trossachs National Park.[35] Here wildness has been modelled and mapped using baseline national cadastre at a nominal scale and resolution of 1:10,000 and 20 m respectively. These high resolution datasets have enabled more realistic models of wilderness attributes to be applied. For example, remoteness from mechanized access is modelled as walking time from the nearest road or track rather than simple straight-line distance, which is used in most global models.

Another example is the advanced modelling of what Lesslie et al. (1993) called 'apparent naturalness'. This refers to the visual impact within the landscape from obvious human structures and artefacts such as roads, pylons, dams and buildings. At a global scale this is usually estimated using simple straight-line distance, but this is an obvious simplification as visual impact is strongly influenced by line of sight. While it is impossible to reliably estimate line of sight at global scales using 1 $km^2$ terrain data due to the effects of generalization, it is possible at local scales where detailed and highly accurate digital surface models

[35] See Carver et al., 'A GIS model for mapping spatial patterns and distribution of wild land in Scotland', *supra* note 20, and A. Comber, S. Carver, S. Fritz, R. McMorran, J. Washtell and P. Fisher, 'Evaluating Alternative Mappings of Wildness Using Fuzzy MCE and Dempster-Shafer in Support of Decision Making', *Computers, Environment and Urban Systems* 34, 2 (2010), 142–152.

including surface features (buildings and tree cover) are generally available. In the Scottish national parks example, visual impact of all modern human artefacts, including roads, tracks, railways, plantation forest, buildings and other structures, was calculated at 20 m resolution taking distance decay effects into account using a bespoke visual assessment tool.

The other attributes included in the mapping of wildness in the Scottish National Parks were perceived naturalness of the land cover (i.e. how natural the vegetation looks to the casual observer) and rugged and challenging nature of the terrain. These two attributes were modelled using detailed land cover data from satellite imagery, map surveys and aerial photographs, and from high resolution terrain data, respectively.

Finally, these four attributes are combined using a simple weighted linear summation model to create an overall wildness map. An example for the Cairngorm National Park is shown in Figure 3.

This work was accompanied by a national wild land public perception survey from which attribute weights were drawn. This has enabled the national parks to better explore the value and spatial patterns of core wild land areas within the parks for strategic planning and decision support purposes. The maps are able to show the core, buffer and periphery zones in the Cairngorm National Park based on the equally weighted attributes adopted by the park planners versus weights drawn from the national perception survey. While there is commonality in the overall geographical pattern, there are significant and noticeable differences at the boundaries of these zones.

Herein lays an interesting problem with potentially far-reaching legal implications for the mapping of wilderness. In those nations where wilderness is designated as a legal entity, policy-makers have to make a decision as to where 'wilderness' begins and ends by drawing a line on the map which is then used in applying wilderness laws and legislation. Wilderness quality maps are useful for exploring the patterns of wilderness quality across various spatial scales but they are in reality just spatial visualizations of what is in essence a fuzzy concept that will vary from one person to the next depending of previous experience, education, interests and so on (i.e. Nash's contention that 'one man's wilderness is another's roadside picnic ground'[36]). In local and national applications the implication is that these maps will be used to inform

[36] Nash, *Wilderness and the American Mind*, *supra* note 1, at 1.

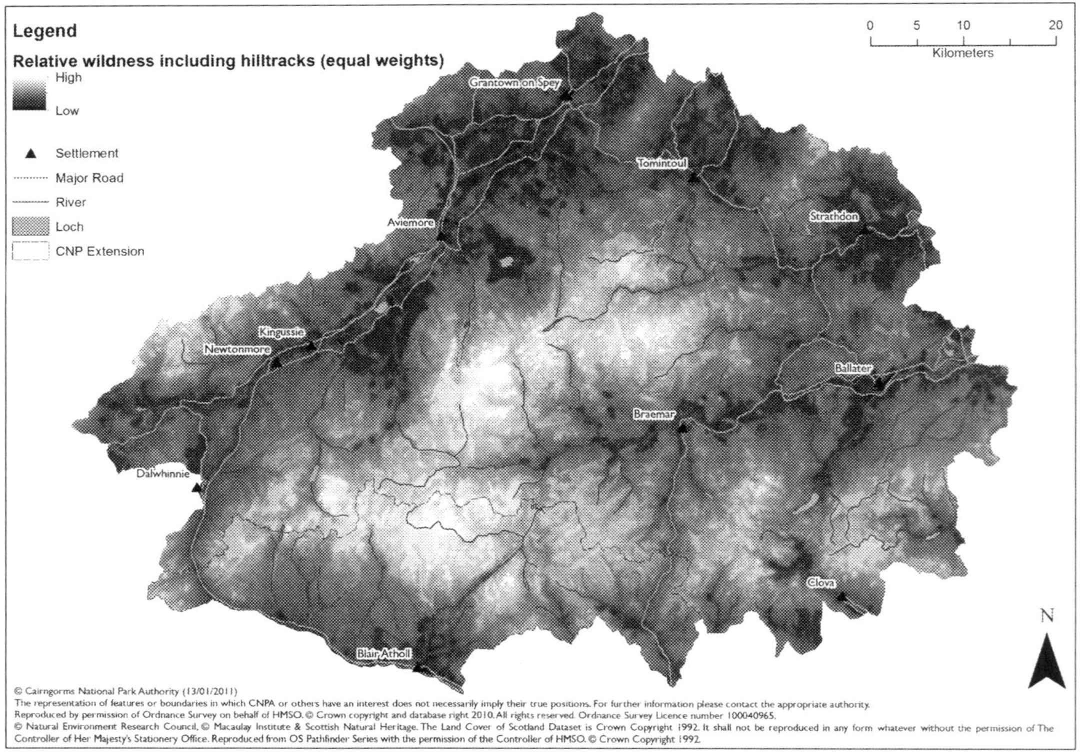


**Figure 3:** Wildness in the Cairngorm National Park (After Carver et al., 2012).

decisions regarding the designation of wilderness areas (i.e. assisting policy-makers in drawing lines on the map that dictate where *de jure* wilderness begins and ends). The approach and methods developed for the two Scottish national parks has been adopted by Scottish Natural Heritage and applied at a national scale at a nominal resolution of 50 m. The wilderness continuum map was launched in March 2012 (Phase 1) and a series of core wild land areas drawn from this (Phases 2 and 3) were launched in June 2014 as part of the Scottish Government's official planning policy review and after a period of consultation.[37] This included considerable political and legal representation together with objections as to the exact boundaries of these core areas on the grounds that they will be used to make decisions about planning applications for developments in the future, even though there is (as yet) no official wild land designation in Scotland.[38]

## 4 Mapping European wilderness

### *4.1 Early maps*

There have been a few attempts at drawing up a wilderness continuum for Europe. An early draft was produced for the Prague conference in May 2009 and this was subsequently adapted for an EEA publication on the mountain regions of Europe.[39] Both of these used the multiple wilderness criteria model described in Section 2.3 based on globally available data including population density, road and rail networks, land cover and terrain at a 1 $km^2$ resolution. Work recently completed as part of an EU/EEA contract on developing a Wilderness Register for Europe has produced a new spatial Wilderness Index for Europe. Although not officially published at the time of writing, the register and index were launched at the 10th World Wilderness Congress in October 2013.[40] Although the register was created by merging information from the

[37] Scottish Planning Policy (June 2014) http://www.scotland.gov.uk/Resource/0045/00453827.pdf and National Planning Framework 3 (June 2014) http://www.scotland.gov.uk/Resource/0045/00453683.pdf

[38] Although wild land is not a statutory designation, Paragraph 200 of the SPP states: 'Wild land character is displayed in some of Scotland's remoter upland, mountain and coastal areas, which are very sensitive to any form of intrusive human activity and have little or no capacity to accept new development. Plans should identify and safeguard the character of areas of wild land as identified on the 2014 SNH map of wild land areas.'

[39] European Environment Agency, *Europe's Ecological Backbone: Recognising the True Value of our Mountains* (Copenhagen: EEA, 2010), report 6/2010.

[40] www.wild10.org.

CDDA and national contact points to filter out *de jure* protected areas meeting the criteria identified in the European wilderness definition (see section 2.3 and Chapter 1) it was felt that additional information on the spatial patterns of *de facto* wilderness areas (i.e. those areas meeting all the criteria of wilderness in Europe but not formally designated) was required.

### *4.2 The EU Wilderness Indicator: a map for Europe*

The wilderness index has been created by combining coordinated European datasets on land cover, potential natural vegetation, grazing intensity, population density, roads, railways and navigable rivers and using these to map the variations in the three main qualities of wilderness as described in chapter 1 from the EU guidelines; namely those qualities of naturalness, undevelopedness and size.[41] Naturalness of the existing vegetation patterns in Europe is complicated by the degree of human modification through forestry, agriculture, urbanization and grazing. The CORINE land cover classes are compared to the Potential Vegetation (PNV) map showing the type of vegetation that would exist at a particular location under current climatic conditions in the absence of human modification.[42] These data are then combined with FAO information on grazing density to identify likely modification of natural vegetation through grazing pressure. One land cover dataset that was not available at a pan European scale was forest management. This means that the resulting maps should be used with care in areas known to have a long history of commercial forestry, such as southern Sweden, since although these areas may look like natural forest cover from satellite imagery they are often second or even third growth after clear felling for timber production, and so not wholly natural. Remoteness from road networks is calculated using a time-cost access surface describing the time-distance to the nearest road, including terrain ruggedness as a friction surface (i.e. the more rugged the intervening terrain the longer the travel times). Remoteness from population and absence from human artefacts is calculated based on distance from small towns/settlements (<50,000 people), medium (<50,000–200,000 people) and large cities (>200,000 people) together with the urban night lights dataset to correct

[41] European Commission, *Guidelines on Wilderness in Natura 2000: Management of Terrestrial Wilderness and Wild Areas within the Natura 2000 Network*, *supra* note 21.

[42] U. Böhn, G. Gollub, C. Hettwer, Z. Neuhauslova, H. Schlueter and H. Weber, *Karte der natürlichen Vegetation Europas* (Münster: Landwirtschaftsverlag, 2000).

for local disturbance around isolated settlements. Remoteness from roads and settlement together are indicative of the underdevelopedness quality of wilderness. The overall indicator is created by simply multiplying the three wilderness attributes of naturalness, remoteness from roads and remoteness from settlements. Using a multiplication-based approach means that any inputs with a value of zero denoting completely non-natural conditions will propagate through the model as zero and will therefore not be classified as wild, as might be a problem for farmland in very remote locations. The European wilderness map generated by this method is shown in Figure 4.

This map shows a series of clear and obvious patterns. First, there is a clear latitudinal gradient to wilderness quality in Europe with by far the majority of wilder landscapes being found in northern latitudes within the Scandinavian countries of Iceland, Norway, Sweden and Finland. Second, there is an additional underlying trend based on altitude, whereby mountainous regions are well represented across Europe, including the Alps, the Pyrenees, the Highlands of Scotland and the Carpathians as well as those in Scandinavia. One or two locations buck this trend with key lowland and coastal landscapes standing out, including the Danube delta, Doñana National Park and the island, lake/forest/bog communities of southern Finland and Estonia. A third, barely perceptible, trend may also be present with greater wilderness quality seen around the periphery as compared to the core regions of central Europe. Here the margins of the northwest Atlantic, the southeast Mediterranean and Eastern Europe seem well represented. Much of these patterns are driven by climate and topography with the most extreme and least readily farmed landscapes appearing the wildest in these maps.

By creating this European wilderness indicator in coordination with a European Wilderness Register, direct and meaningful comparisons can be made between protected area status and wilderness quality. The map in Figure 5 shows the protection status of the wildest areas in European (>seventy per cent wilderness value from Figure 4) which are greater than 3,000 ha in size when compared to information from Natura 2000 and CDDA. This shows that while significant areas of Europe have a legally protected status, many areas of *de facto* wilderness are still going without protection and might therefore form the basis for future expansion of existing protected area networks on the basis of landscape and/or biodiversity values. Furthermore, the question is to what extent the protected areas are indeed also protected because of their wilderness qualities, or are

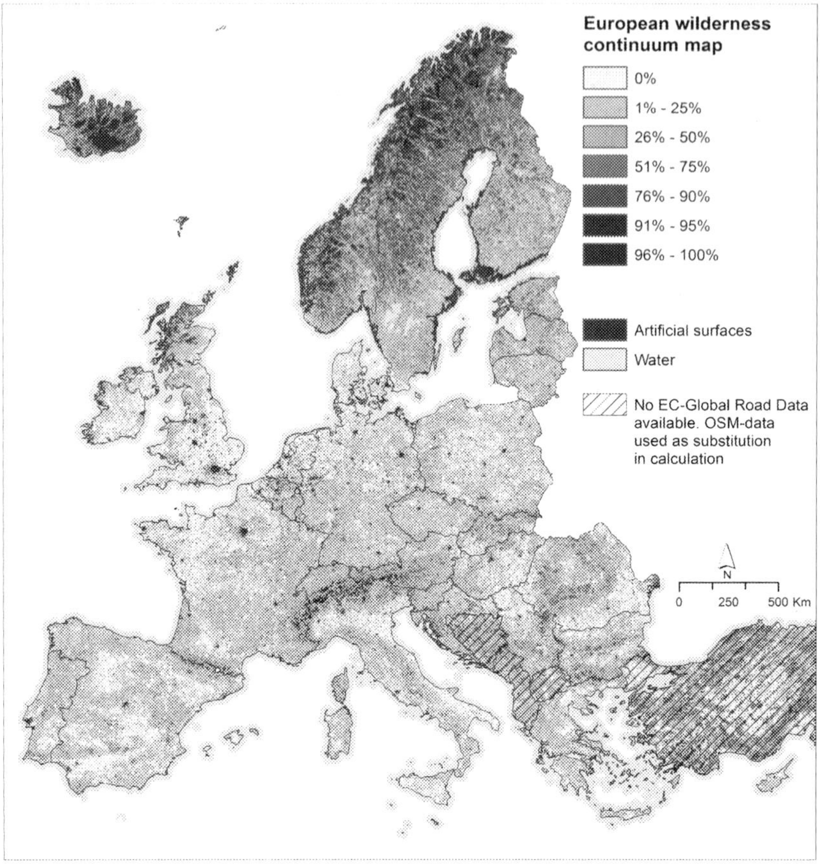


**Figure 4:** Wilderness indicator for Europe (After A.T. Kuiters, M. van Eupen, S. Carver, M. Fisher, Z. Kun and V. Vancura, *Wilderness Register and Indicator for Europe* [Wageningen/Leeds: Alterra/Wildland Research Institute, Pan Parks, 2013]).

there other reasons, a central question of this book. Figure 5 notwithstanding, it should be noted that the information contained in the CDDA is not one hundred per cent complete and with the missing information on forest management, the picture is incomplete.

## 5 Conclusions

This chapter has outlined the basis of wilderness definitions within Europe using lessons learnt from abroad, and described how, with such

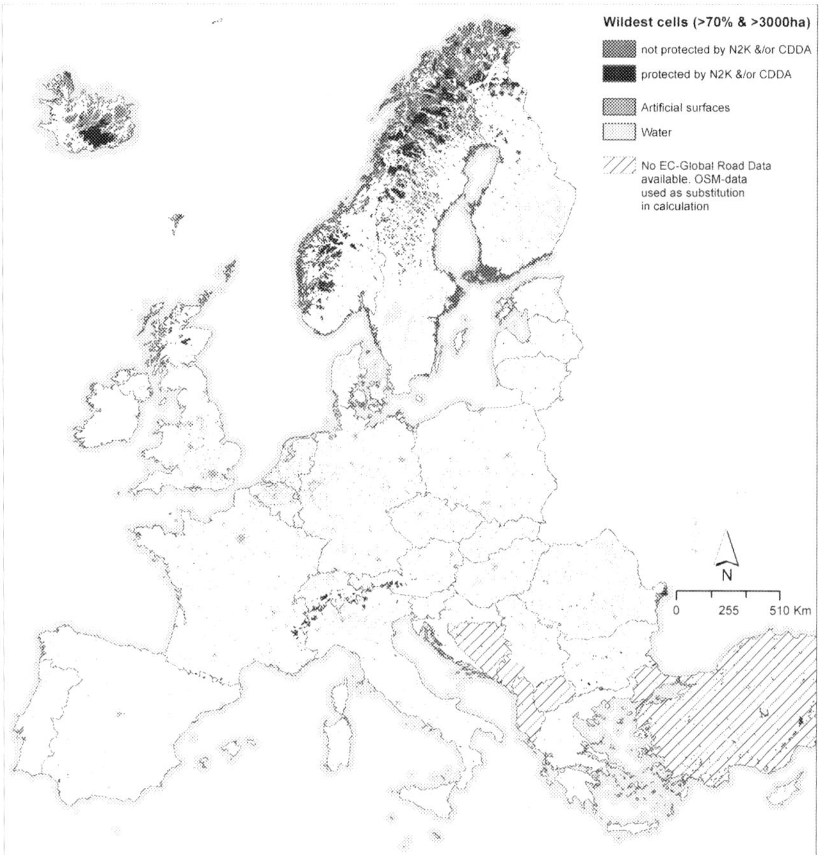


**Figure 5:** Protected and unprotected wilderness in Europe (After Kuiters et al., 2013).

definitions in mind, patterns of wilderness quality can be modelled and mapped at various spatial scales. Europe is now at something of a cross-roads as regards wilderness. As has been described here, Europe has been largely responsible for exporting the idea of wilderness across the world and has recently begun to re-import this concept of landscape and nature conservation into its own lands, hearts and minds. At the same time Europe has a long history of nature conservation (e.g. the Swiss National Park is 100 years old) and, through the EU's Birds and Habitats Directives, the Natura 2000 network and the Council of Europe's Emerald Network, presents the world's most well-developed nature and protected areas network. However, the question is to what extent these policies and legal regimes also aim to protect the qualities that characterize natural areas as 'wilderness areas', a question that will be the central focus of Part II and Part III of this book.

Knowing the pattern of wilderness quality in relation to protected area designations and relevant policies gives us the information required to better understand the landscapes we inhabit within Europe and helps us see the opportunities afforded for improved protection of wilderness qualities and better connectedness of landscapes, wildlife and people. In the past, protected areas were seen as largely separate; as reserves for natural habitats and species in the areas not seen as suitable for settlement and economic land use (Figure 6a). Surrounded by human modified landscapes and threatened by gradual erosion at their margins and by global climate change, such areas and the species they contain are in danger from fragmentation, isolation and ecological extinction. This is widely recognized by today's conservation managers, giving rise to the Cores, Corridors and Carnivores (CCC) model,[43] which works to reconnect isolated core protected areas using wildlife corridors, smaller 'stepping stone' nature reserves and wildlife-permeable agri-landscapes such that wildlife and ecosystems are able to respond to external forcing by migrating and/or shifting positions (latitude and/or altitude) (Figure 6b).

The re-importation of the wilderness concept has led to two distinct, though linked, approaches to wilder landscapes in Europe. One has been to focus on preserving what is left of our remaining wilderness landscapes through national and regional policies for better protection and certification using the 'gold standard' of wilderness based on the three main wilderness qualities mentioned in Chapter 1: naturalness (no extractive land uses, including no agriculture, no forestry, no mining, no hunting and no fishing); undevelopedness (absence of permanent proof of modern civil society, such as no roads and no settlements) and large size. To date this has been best represented in the PAN Parks network and, since 2013, the European Wilderness Society, which coordinates the protection of core wilderness areas through national and regional systems of nature and landscape protection and aims to protect 1 million hectares of wilderness across Europe. The other approach has been to focus on opportunities for creating wilder landscapes (e.g. from abandonment of margin agricultural land) within the existing landscape matrix and creating more wilderness areas over time. This is known as 'rewilding' and occupies a

[43] See G.L. Worboys, *The Connectivity Conservation Imperative. Connectivity Conservation Management: A Global Guide* (Washington DC: Earthscan, 2010).

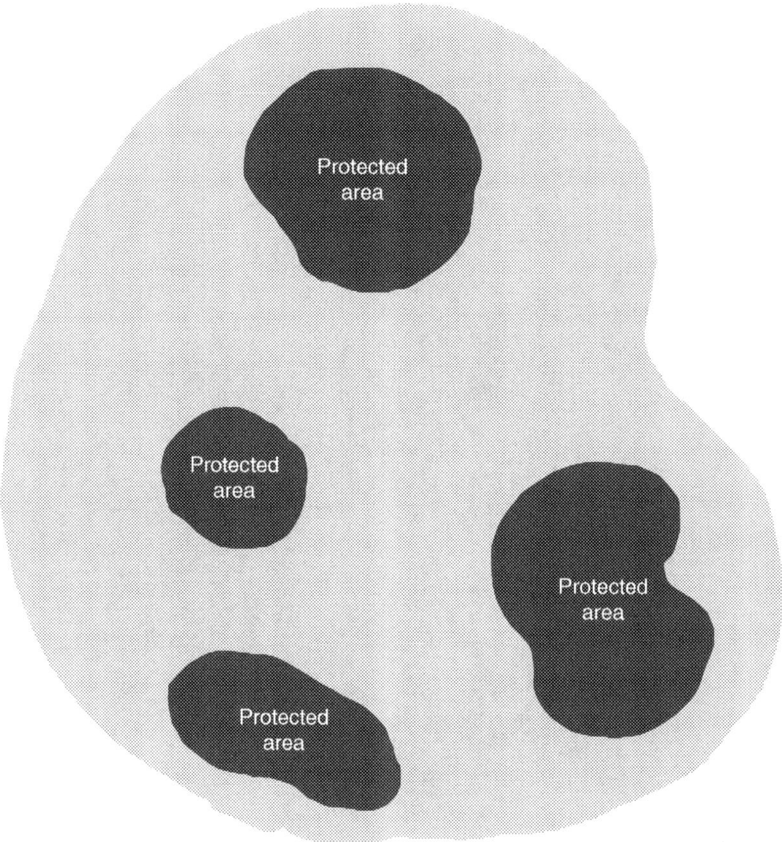


**Figure 6:** A model for the future of wilderness in Europe

place somewhere lower down the wilderness continuum, but together with core wilderness areas can add further value and coherence to the CCC model (Figure 6c). A number of individual rewilding projects exist across Europe, while the Rewilding Europe organization is aiming to develop a further ten large-scale projects totalling 1 million hectares. Ultimately, rewilded areas may, over time as they re-naturalize, contribute additional 'secondary' wilderness areas to the network of existing core areas by the process of donation, creating a fully integrated, coherent and connected system of landscape and nature protection with wilderness at its heart (Figure 6d). However, for both approaches, protecting what is left and rewilding, an important question is to what extent the

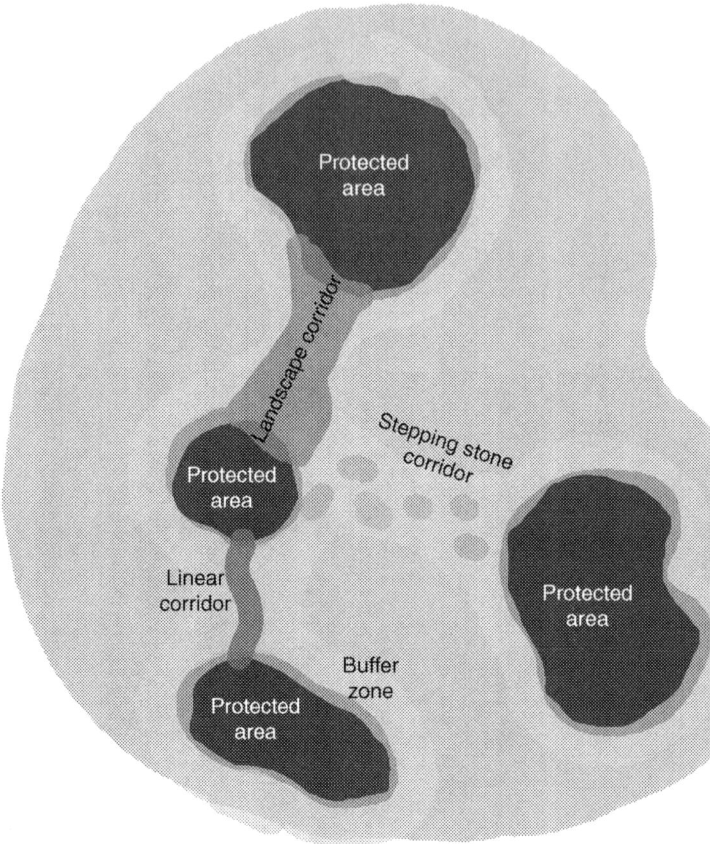


**Figure 6:** (cont.)

current legal systems at the international, European and domestic level in Europe do provide legal protection to those qualities that are characteristic to wilderness, which is the central question of Part II and Part III of this book.

Key to this process of protection, reconnection and rewilding is the availability of rigorous and robust mapping methods based on coordinated and high quality spatial information, such that the resulting maps are both repeatable (essential for monitoring purposes) and defensible (essential for legal reasons). How we choose to use this information is up to us, but as President Lyndon B. Johnston said in signing the 1964 Wilderness Act, we owe it to future generations of Europeans to seize

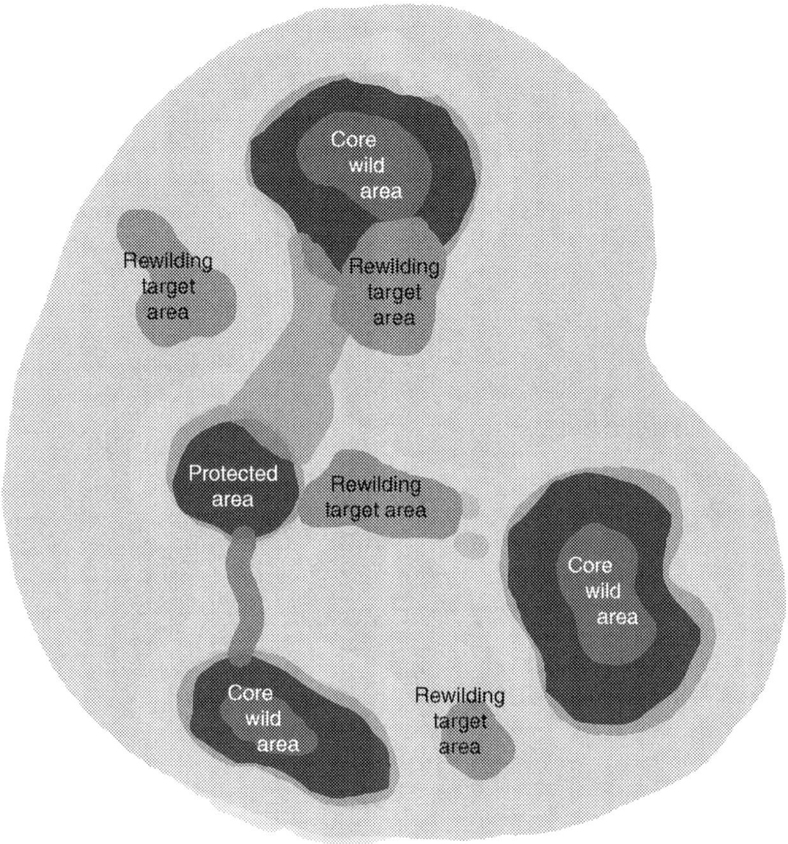


**Figure 6:** (cont.)

the moment and preserve what remains of our European wilderness. While approximately five per cent of our land surface is currently built on, only around two per cent of Europe's wilderness is formally protected through existing mechanisms. And as stated above, it is even unclear to what extent this existing legal protection indeed ensures wilderness protection. It seems reasonable that protected wilderness in Europe could be increased to five per cent; matching and offsetting the urbanized landscapes at the opposite end of the wilderness continuum. Exactly where the additional three per cent can be found, or created, is largely a problem of political will and associated public support, as well as the biophysical opportunities that remaining unprotected or *de facto* wilderness present.

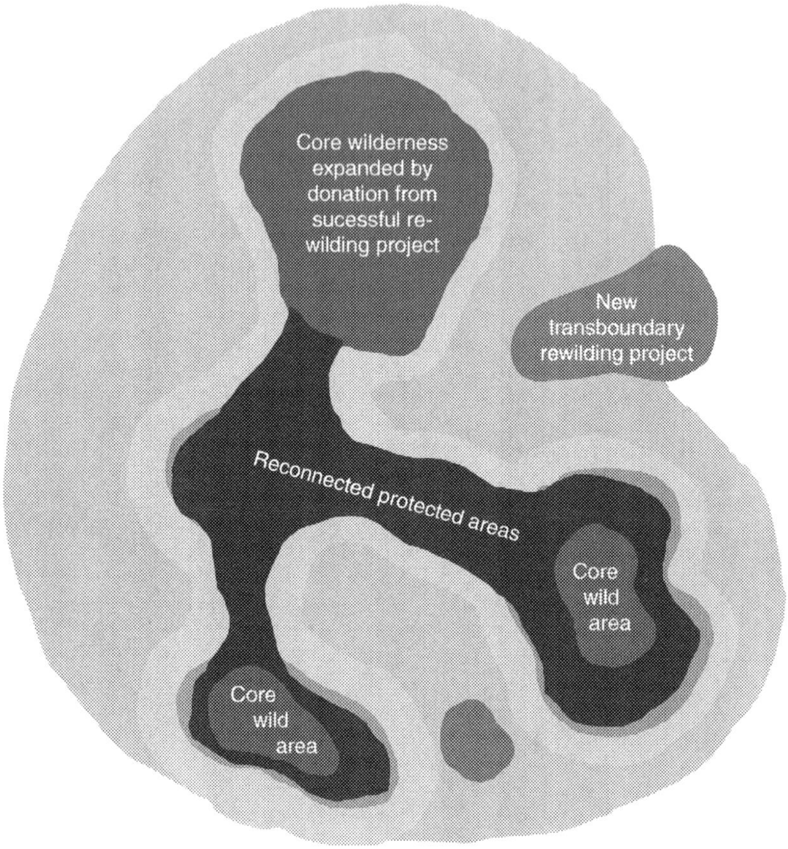


**Figure 6:** (cont.)

What is clear, however, is that maps will be central to making the case of strengthening wilderness protection in Europe.

Depending on the outcomes of this book on wilderness protection under current legal regimes, we may even think of creating a more coherent system of connected European wilderness areas underpinned by a strict system of protection under some pan-European equivalent of the US 1964 Wilderness Act, for instance, by establishing a European Convention on Wilderness. The editor of will return to this issue in the concluding part of this book.

3

# Ecological values of wilderness in Europe

MARK FISHER

## 1 Introduction

A history of wide-ranging landscape modification through having been at the forefront of human cultural exploitation and expansion over the last millennium may suggest that there is no wilderness in Europe.[1] The exportation of European agriculture around the world was the driver for accelerating landscape change where ever it took hold,[2] and economic development with consequent anthropogenic habitat modification remain major drivers of the ecological simplification of landscapes.[3] Given such a role in the advance of the Anthropocene[4] it is unsurprising that Europe is lacking a wilderness literature, and that many Europeans do not believe wilderness and wild nature fit in to European heritage.[5] It is perhaps this very reason that has held back an earlier and more significant recognition of a wilderness character in Europe.

It should be recognized that a contemporary understanding of the biophysical reality of wilderness, where freedom from human activity and habitation give rise to wilderness qualities, and where the processes of an undisturbed nature are an ecological condition, is the antithesis of

1 E.C. Ellis, 'Anthropogenic transformation of the terrestrial biosphere', *Proceedings of the Royal Society A: Mathematical, Physical and Engineering Science* 369 (2011), 1010–1035.

2 A.W. Crosby, *Ecological Imperialism: The Biological Expansion of Europe, 900–1900* (Cambridge: Cambridge University Press, 2004).

3 E.C. Ellis, J.O. Kaplan, D.Q. Fuller, S. Vavrus, K.K. Goldewijke and P.H. Verburg, 'Used Planet: A Global History', *Proceedings National Academy Science* 110 (2013), 7978–7985 and A. Skonhoft and S. Håvard, 'Economic Growth and Land-use Changes: the Declining Amount of Wilderness Land in Norway', *Ecological Economics* 37 (2001), 289–301.

4 W. Steffen, J. Grinevald, P. Crutzen and J. McNeill, 'The Anthropocene: Conceptual and Historical Perspectives', *Philosophical Transactions Royal Society A* 369 (2011), 842–867.

5 N. Bauer, A. Wallner and M. Hunziker, 'The Change of European Landscapes: Human-nature Relationships, Public Attitudes towards Rewilding, and the Implications for Landscape Management in Switzerland', *Journal of Environmental Management* 90 (2009), 2910–2920 and G. Lupp, F. Höchtl and W. Wende, '"Wilderness" – A Designation for Central European Landscapes?', *Land Use Policy* 28 (2011), 594–603.

the consequences of European cultural influence. If we are to seek out evidence of the presence of wilderness in contemporary Europe, so that its ecological values can be assessed, then it must be where the intensity and recent history of human intervention is at its least.

That there is recognition of wilderness now in Europe owes much to exponents of conserving wild nature in the nineteenth and early twentieth century, and the advocacy of protected areas in which to do so. While a coincidence in chronology may suggest a commonality in approach between America and Europe, there were clearly divergent paths of appreciation of wild nature. In nineteenth century America, wild land was viewed as a source of inspiration and recreational activity, having a spiritual, aesthetic and intrinsic beauty, whose species and natural systems had an inherent value that was not created by human beings, and nor was it dependent on human use or appreciation.[6] In Europe lay a scientific approach to conservation, less tempered by the aesthetic, and which sought the preservation of unique assemblages of species rather than necessarily of landscape values.[7]

The aim of this chapter is to demonstrate that the qualities of wilderness exist in Europe in areas governed by natural processes, and in which there are a diverse range of native species and natural habitats. It begins with tracing the history of nature protection in Europe to the emergence of the protected area (Section 2). The importance of large carnivores in natural processes is explained (Section 3) before exploring the dependency of European species on wilderness qualities (Section 4). Some indication is given of potentially the last ecologically intact areas in Europe (Section 5) and finally one of the contemporary opportunities for restoring wilderness qualities away from those areas is described (Section 6).

## 2 The emergence of the protected area in Europe

Hunting forests in Europe from time immemorial have defined a history of a protective element for wild nature, albeit as a resource for human consumption, and often in the interests of a privileged few.[8] Forest laws

[6] H. Zahniser, 'The need for wilderness areas', *The Living Wilderness* 21, 59 (1957), 37–43.

[7] H.M. Hall, 'European Reservations for the Protection of Natural Conditions', *Journal of Forestry* 27 (1929), 667–684.

[8] J.C. Welzholz and E. Johann, 'History of Protected Forest Areas in Europe', in G. Frank, J. Parviainen, K. Vandekerhove, J. Latham, A. Schuck and D. Little (eds.), *Protected Forest Areas in Europe – Analysis and Harmonisation (PROFOR): Results, Conclusions and*

were the forerunner in many countries to contemporary protected area legislation. Motivations varied for those laws, from regulating use to sustain a resource; in recognition that forests protected settlements against natural hazards; and in appreciation that nature protection is an intrinsic value of undisturbed forest function. It is perhaps surprising that areas of undisturbed forest in Europe have not been more generally acknowledged as having wilderness qualities. Thus, the recognition that remaining stands of virgin forest in the Czech Republic were essential to an understanding of natural processes uncontrolled by man led in the mid-nineteenth century to a number of strictly protected forest reserves, such as the Žofín and Boubín virgin forests.[9]

Wilderness can be understood on a visceral level, but its functional and ecological processes rely on an ecological literacy, an understanding of the autonomous self-assembly and day to day interaction of its components. The development of scientific concepts by Europeans in the nineteenth century, and into the twentieth century, such as ecology,[10] biocenosis,[11] phytosociology,[12] species abundance,[13] food webs[14] and ecosystems[15] paved the way for that understanding. These concepts guided the early strategies for identifying and safeguarding protected areas on the basis of scientific principles, but also through altruism towards wild nature, and which by their nature allow the ecological value of wilderness to be understood. The premises of this protection were thus areas of significant size that were largely undeveloped, and which were repositories of native species that were left undisturbed, areas that meet the working definition of wilderness as explained in Chapter 1. Two of the earliest examples in Europe are given here, and they establish

*Recommendations* (Vienna: Federal Research and Training Centre for Forests, Natural Hazards and Landscape, 2007).

[9] T. Vrŝka, D. Adam and L. Hort, 'Country Report - Czech Republic', in *Protected Forest Areas in Europe - Analysis and Harmonisation (PROFOR)*, (Vienna: Federal Research and Training Centre for Forests, Natural Hazards and Landscape, 2006).

[10] E. Haeckel, *Generelle Morphologie der Organismen: allgemeine Grundzüge der organischen Formen-Wissenschaft, mechanisch begründet durch die von Charles Darwin reformirte Descendenz-Theorie* (Berlin: Georg Reimer, 1866).

[11] K. Möbius, *Die Auster und die Austernwirthschaft* (Berlin: Verlag von Wiegandt, 1877).

[12] J. Paczoski, *Zycie gromadne roślin. Wszechświat: Tygodnik popularny, poświęcony naukom przyrodniczym* (T. 15, nr 26, Warsawa 1896).

[13] V. Volterra, 'Fluctuations in the abundance of a species considered mathematically', *Nature*, 118 (1926), 558–560.

[14] C. Elton, *Animal Ecology* (London: Sidgwick and Jackson, 1927).

[15] A.G. Tansley, 'The Use and Abuse of Vegetational Concepts and Terms', *Ecology* 16 (1935), 284–307.

a common principle of withdrawal of human influence so that there is free functioning of natural processes.

### 2.1 The Lagodekhi Gorge

The first legislative record for forest and nature protection in Georgia came in the twelfth century, when Queen Tamar issued a Royal Decree on the protection of certain territories.[16] In 1709, King Vakhtang VI substantially revised the legal code (*dasturlamali*[17]) including a reference to '*the place for hunting*' in what is now an area of protected floodplain forest on the banks of the Iori River to the east of Tbilisi.[18] Access to the forest was restricted, it was forbidden to cut trees, and the area was under guard to prevent disturbance. In addition, in the mountainous regions of Georgia, areas of '*Holy forest*' were subject to strict protection in the legal code, thus constituting the beginnings of a nature reserve system.[19]

It is likely that the forests of Lagodekhi on the southern slopes of the main ridge of the Greater Caucasus in the far northeast corner of Georgia were one of these protected areas. The abundant natural diversity of these steep forested slopes and valleys, with numerous streams, rivers and waterfalls, attracted the attention of botanists over the nineteenth century, including the Polish amateur naturalist Ludwig Mlokosiewicz. In 1875, Mlokosiewicz had discovered that the Black Grouse living in Lagodekhi differed from European Black Grouse, leading to it being recognized as a separate species, the Caucasian Black Grouse (*Tetrao mlokosiewiczi*).[20] As a Corresponding Member of the Russian Imperial Academy of Sciences, Mlokosiewicz collaborated with Nikoloz Kuznetsoff, Academy director and a professor at Tartu University, to organize a number of expeditions to explore the area further. Their studies revealed many rare species, including eight wild flower variants endemic to Lagodekhi.

[16] E. Devidze, 'The Purpose and Functions of Imereti Protected Areas', *Journal of Social Sciences* 1 (2012), 79–83.

[17] 'History of the Ministry', Ministry of Justice of Georgia, http://justice.gov.ge/Ministry/Department/392

[18] Korugi Managed Reserve, 'Mariamjvari Strict Nature Reserve Administration', Agency of Protected Areas, Ministry of Environment and Natural Resources Protection of Georgia, www.apa.gov.ge/en/protected-areas/cattestone/mariamdjvris-saxelmwifo-nakrdzalis-administracia

[19] Devidze, 'The Purpose and Functions of Imereti Protected Areas', *supra* note 16

[20] V. Pilāts and M. Laiviņš. 'Historical Parallels of Moricsala and Lagodekhi – Two 100-year Old Protected Nature Areas in Latvia and Georgia', *Acta Biologica Universitatis Daugavpiliensis* 13 (2013) 111–135.

In 1898, Mlokosiewicz made his first proposal to transform the Lagodekhi Gorge into a Nature Reserve. Unfortunately, in 1903 the Russian government instead leased the Lagodekhi Gorge and the neighbouring Shromi Gorge for recreational hunting to Demidov, a wealthy Russian industrialist. Demidov instituted a strict regime of protection against unauthorized hunting, fishing or logging. This had the fortunate outcome of allowing the wildlife to continue to flourish, the forests maintaining their natural state. In 1911, scientists presented a report on the protection of the Lagodekhi Gorge as a Monument of Nature at a meeting of the Caucasian Department of the Russian Geographic Society. A petition was drawn up by the Geographic Society and the Academy of Science, following which the Lagodekhi Gorge was declared a nature reserve in 1912. Tree felling, hunting and livestock grazing were banned at the outset on the reserve. These prohibitions were maintained when Lagodekhi joined with the *zapovedniki* system of strict reserves (see Chapter 19).

The original area of narrow river valleys forested with beech (*Fagus sylvatica*) and hornbeam (*Carpinus betulus*) have been added to since 1912, with the addition of sub-alpine woodland, alpine meadows and rocky mountainous terrain, so that today the Lagodekhi State Nature Reserve encompasses 244 $km^2$.[21] While it is not the oldest protected area in Europe, it has the distinction that it maintains the strict nature protection that it set out with, now being afforded under the nature protection legislation of Georgia from 1996.[22] Research at Lagodekhi has continued throughout, one of the aims of the *zapovedniki* being protected natural areas set aside for research in natural sciences.[23] Zoological studies became particularly intense during the Soviet period, a large part of this research dedicated to animal species, but there were also published studies on its soil, flora, invertebrates, forests and subalpine meadows.[24] The national legislation

[21] 'Lagodekhi Protected Areas Administration', Agency of Protected Areas, Ministry of Environment and Natural Resources Protection of Georgia, www.apa.gov.ge/en/protected-areas/cattestone/lagodexis-daculi-teritoriebis-administracia

[22] Law of Georgia on the System of Protected Areas, N003, 27.03.96 (Amended to 2014), https://matsne.gov.ge/index.php?option=com_ldmssearch&view=docView&id=32968&lang=en&Itemid=

[23] N. Danilina, 'The Zapovedniks of Russia', *The George Wright Forum* 18 (2001), 48–55. See also Chapters 13 and 19.

[24] 'Lagodekhis nakrdzalis da aghkvet'ilis menejmentis gegmis damtkits'ebis t'aobaze' (approval of the Lagodekhi Reserve Management Plan), Decree № 52, 1 February, 2006, Ministry of Environment and Natural Resources, Legislative Herald, Ministry of Justice, Georgia. Sakanonmdeblo Matsne, https://matsne.gov.ge/index.php?option=com_ldmssearch&view=docView&id=1421762.

for protected areas in Georgia embeds scientific research in its reserve areas, inviting state and public institutions to become involved in both the protection and research of various species and ecosystems in Lagodekhi through the setting up of a Scientific-Advisory Board.[25]

It is not surprising that the altitudinal range of the reserve of 3,000 m results in a wide range of habitats. Nearly a quarter of the Georgian flora, around 1,000 species, can be found in the reserve: 121 are endemic to the Caucasus, and nine endemic to this area.[26] The primary forests support system-directing large mammalian predators such as bear (*Ursus arctos*), lynx (*Lynx lynx*), wildcat (*Felix sylvestris*) and wolf (*Canis lupus*), as well as birds of prey such as the Golden Eagle (*Aquila chrysaetos*) and Eurasian Black Vulture (*Aegypius monachus*). Wild mammalian herbivores in the forested areas include red deer (*Cervus elaphus*), wild boar (*Sus scrofa*) and roe deer (*Capreolus capreolus*), whereas the sub-alpine and alpine areas have chamois (*Rupicapra rupicapra*) and East Caucasian Tur (*Capra cylindricornis*), an endemic goat species.

The restrictions on activity in this protected area, coupled with the presence of a diverse extant trophic assemblage of wild species, as well as a lack of built development, argues that Lagodekhi State Nature Reserve has strong claims to the wilderness qualities identified in Chapter 1. The maintenance of natural processes in a dynamic and undisturbed condition results in a high level of natural forest renewal that is supportive of a large part of that trophic assemblage, as well as having implications for the wider landscape. Snowfall, avalanches at height and heavy rains are frequent in the region, according the forests of this protected area with a particular role in the prevention of erosion and flooding in the southern villages.[27] It is perhaps unfortunate that the Georgian language does not have a specific word for wilderness – wild nature reserve (*nakrdzalis veluri bunebis*) is the nearest – or the modern-day Lagodekhi State Nature Reserve would likely appear described as such in the literature of the Agency of Protected Areas of Georgia.

## *2.2 Swiss National Park – the 100 year experiment*

Undisturbed nature as a long term, open air laboratory was also at the heart of a speech to the Swiss National Council, given in 1914 by Dr Walter

[25] Law of Georgia on the System of Protected Areas, *supra* note 22.
[26] Lagodekhi Reserve Management Plan, *supra* note 24.
[27] *Ibid.*

Bissegger in support of the resolution to establish the Swiss National Park.[28] This was the culmination of a decade of development of a vision of setting aside an area of land where nature could develop without human disturbance. Bissegger's speech opened by pointing to the power that humans had to modify landscapes to their own benefit. It had, however, come with a cost in Switzerland, Bissegger noting with regret the extinction of lynx, wildcat, bear, ibex (*Capra ibex*) and vulture (*Gypaetus barbatus*), species that were once the pride of the country. He also bemoaned the losses of songbirds, and the mass tearing out of wildflowers, such as Edelweiss (*Leontopodium alpinum*). Bissegger was persuaded that there was only one means to effectively counter the gradual destruction, which was through the creation of large natural parks, where everything that was originally indigenous would get permanent refuge.

Bissegger described the proposed location for a National Park, an area of 170 $km^2$ in the Eastern Alps composed of rugged, bare mountain peaks and ridges, alpine meadows, and deep river valleys forested with pine and other conifers, all with an abundant and characteristic flora. The choice of Ofen Pass lay in very practical reasons: the fact that the valleys were for the most part completely uninhabited, and that their use in forestry and farming was unimportant because of inaccessibility. He noted that the area had been commended for its botanical value by Prof. Carl Schröter, a Swiss phyto-geographer, providing a good opportunity for scientific study. Bissegger also pointed to the hope expressed by Prof. Freidrich Schokke, a Swiss Zoologist, that the mammals lost to the area would migrate back in, under the conditions of a strict reserve. The question Bissegger put to his fellow Council members was whether they wanted to:

> create such a sanctuary for animals and plants, as far as possible excluded from any human impact, an area in which for 100 years there would be no economic use, forestry, grazing and hunting, and where no axe, nor the sound of shooting would be heard [. . .]?[29]

The Council agreed, and the Federal Decree on the establishment of a Swiss National Park was enacted on 3 April 1914. The first article of the Decree stated that a Swiss National Park is established in which the entire animal and plant life would be left to its free and natural development,

[28] W. Bissegger, 'Über die Gründung des schweizerischen Nationalparkes. Die Rede Dr. Bisseggers vom 25. März 1914 im Nationalrat. Unser Nationalpark und die ausserschweizerischen alpinen Reservationen', *Neujahrsblatt Naturforschende Gesellschaft Zürich*, Stück 130 (1928), 3–8, http://www.ngzh.ch/media/njb/Neujahrsblatt_NGZH_1928.pdf.

[29] *Ibid.*, p. 7 (translation by the author).

protected from any human influence.[30] Importantly, the whole of the conservation area was to be placed under scientific observation. Thus a Scientific Review Commission was established in 1915, its goal to capture the diversity of species and to document their changes.[31] The first permanent observation plots were set up in 1917 by the Swiss botanist Josias Braun-Blanquet, who is recognized for establishing the importance of phytosociological studies as well as soil science through his developmental investigations of the soil and vegetation of the alpine meadows and forest succession in the subalpine areas of the Park.[32]

A strategy for the long-term research in the park was laid out by Carl Schröter in 1920, who noted that the Park would be invaluable for scientific study because of the absolute elimination of interference by humans.[33] He foresaw an ecological restoration taking place, where the effects of centuries of hunting, fishing, forestry, dunging, ploughing, mowing and grazing would disappear with time. He hoped to follow the reconquest by the original forest vegetation, and the associated change in mammal species, as well as observe in detail the reaction of the meadow flora to the cessation of mowing and grazing. He predicted that this naturalizing would provide important evidence on whether and to what extent the landscape would have been forested or were grasslands, which floral components were truly original and where the natural tree line would be.

Early evidence of that ecological restoration came within a few years when Schröter delivered the fourth Hooker lecture at the Linnaean

[30] *Ibid.*, p. 8, 'Bundesbeschluss betreffend die Errichtung eines Schweizerischen Nationalparkes im Unterengadin' (BS 4 259), Nationalrat 3, April 1914: 'Art. 1. Auf dem vertraglich näher bezeichneten Gebiete der Gemeinde Zernez wird ein Schweizerischer Nationalpark errichtet, in dem die gesamte Tier- und Pflanzenwelt ganz ihrer freien natürlichen Entwicklung überlassen und vor jedem nicht im Zweck des Nationalparkes liegenden menschlichen Einflusse geschützt wird.'

[31] C. Schröter, 'Der Werdegang des schweizerischen Nationalparks als Total-Reservation und die Organisation seiner wissenschaftlichen Untersuchung. Ergebnisse der wissenschaftlichen untersuchung des Schweizerischen Nationalparks', *Denkschriften der Schweizerischen Naturforschenden Gesellschaft* 55 (1920), 2–8.

[32] J. Braun-Blanquet and H. Jenny, 'Vegetations-Entwicklung und Bodenbildung in der alpinen Stufe der Zentralalpen' *Denkschriften der Schweizerischen Naturforschenden Gesellschaft. Schweiz. Naturforschende Gesellschaft* 53 (1926), 183–349 and J. Braun-Blanquet, H. Pallmann and R. Bach, 'Pflanzensoziologische und Bodenkundliche Untersuchungen im Schweizerischen Nationalpark und seinen Nachbargebieten. II. Vegetation und Böden der Wald- und Zwergstrauchgesellschaften (Vaccinio-Piceetalia)', *Ergebnisse der wissenschaftlichen Untersuchungen des schweizerischen Nationalparks*, Band IV (Neue Folge) (1954), 3–198.

[33] Schröter, 'Der Werdegang des schweizerischen Nationalparks als Total-Reservation und die Organisation seiner wissenschaftlichen Untersuchung', *supra* note 31.

Society.[34] He was able to report that the flora of the alpine pastures in the National Park had developed abundantly after removal of grazing. The removal of human activity across the whole of the National Park had also resulted in increases in a number of animals. Thus, between 1918 to 1925 red deer had increased from 12 to 90, ibex from 60 to 190, chamois from 1,000 to 1,250, capercaillie (*Tetrao urogallus*) from 10 to 60, black grouse (*Tetrao tetrix*) from 40 to 190, ptarmigan (*Lagopus muta)* from 120 to 310 and golden eagle from 15 to 40.

American botanist Harvey Hall visited the Swiss National Park in the company of Schröter in 1928, during a period spent investigating protected area approaches across Europe.[35] Unlike America, Hall observed that Europe no longer had any extensive unmodified natural areas, so that natural conditions had first to be re-created through long periods of protection, sometimes with re-instatement of lost vegetation cover and indigenous fauna. He noted that hunting, fishing, tree felling, agriculture, haying and grazing were prohibited in the Swiss National Park, and determined to take back the lessons of '*complete reserves*' for the National Parks and National Forests of America, and that a more scientific approach be taken as soon as an area was brought under protection in America.

The Swiss National Park set out on a course of developing a secondary wilderness over the 100 years since its foundation. Today, the Park describes the value of wilderness, and how it can be experienced in the Park by observation of natural cycles, the slow but expected return of undisturbed forest (*Urwald*) after the fellings of the nineteenth century and the accumulation of standing and lying deadwood in the forests providing habitat for insects, birds, and for germinating tree seedlings.[36] These are indications of the wilderness quality of free-functioning natural processes, identified in Chapter 1.

## 3 The importance of large carnivores in natural processes

The natural processes of a wilderness depend on the presence and abundance of organisms with particular functional traits. These traits or trophic functions are the interaction between animals and plants in a

[34] Anonymous, 'The Swiss National Park', *Nature* 117 (1926), 705–706.

[35] Hall, 'European Reservations for the Protection of Natural Conditions', *supra* note 7.

[36] 'Wert von Wildnis. Schweizerischer Nationalpark', www.nationalpark.ch/go/de/about/ueber-uns/wert-von-wildnis/.

food chain or web.[37] The greatest possible dynamic interaction in natural processes comes when the functional or trophic diversity is greatest, when species are present in all trophic levels of a natural system, such as top predators, middle (meso) predators, plant eaters, plants, carrion and detritus feeders. A trophic cascade occurs when the animals at the top of the food chain – the top predators – modify the numbers not just of their prey, but also of species with which they have no direct connection.[38] Their impacts cascade down the food chain, in some cases radically changing the ecosystem, such as maintaining the vegetation cover of a landscape in the face of herbivore pressure, and even enriching the composition of soil from decomposing carrion.

There is a lack of natural control mechanisms where carnivores have been removed. In the absence of carnivores, the numbers of wild herbivores across Europe, especially different deer species, have greatly increased in the modified landscapes of human use. The impact of increased herbivore pressure has affected ecosystems through reducing tree regeneration and tree species, the diversity of herbaceous vegetation, as well as decreasing songbird diversity.[39] This is the case in the Swiss National Park, where herbivore numbers continued to enlarge, especially red deer.[40] Considerable damage to forest regeneration is shown from repeat surveys of the forest of the Trupchun Valley within the Park, particularly when compared to the lesser extent seen in forest outside the Park where deer are still hunted.[41] Red deer are also an important factor in the alpine meadows, affecting the food resource of field mice and their abundance, which then reduces the prey for foxes and birds. Since 2009, a research project into the relationship structure and its dependencies was started by erecting fencing to specifically exclude

[37] M.W. Cadotte, K. Carscadden and N. Mirotchnic, 'Beyond Species: Functional Diversity and the Maintenance of Ecological Processes and Services', *Journal of Applied Ecology*, 48 (2011), 1079–1087.

[38] F. Sergio, T. Caro, D. Brown, B. Clucas, J. Hunter, J. Ketchum, K. McHugh and F. Hiraldo, 'Top Predators as Conservation Tools: Ecological Rationale, Assumptions, and Efficacy', *Annual Review of Ecology, Evolution, and Systematics* 39 (2008), 1–19.

[39] D.P.J. Kuijper, 'Lack of Natural Control Mechanisms Increases Wildlife–Forestry Conflict in Managed Temperate European Forest Systems', *European Journal of Forest Research* 130 (2011), 895–909, and Scott, D. Welch, M. Thurlow and D.A. Elston, 'Regeneration of *Pinus sylvestris* in a Natural Pinewood in NE Scotland Following Reduction in Grazing by Cervus Elaphus', *Forest Ecology and Management* 130 (2000), 199–211.

[40] Tiere. Natur. Schweizerischer Nationalpark, www.nationalpark.ch/go/de/flora-und-fauna/tiere/.

[41] Jungwaldinventur - Mehr wissen. Schweizerischer Nationalpark, www.nationalpark.ch/go/de/forschung/fachuebergreifende-forschung/huftiere/jungwaldinventur/.

various herbivorous animal groups (ungulates, marmots and hares, mice) and examine how the ecosystem responds to these exclusions.[42]

It is unfortunate for the natural ecology of the Swiss National Park that the hope that Bissegger had for the return of the lost predators under the conditions of a strict reserve has not yet materialized. The Park recognizes that Switzerland is a '*richly-laid table*' for the wolf, the number of red deer having risen to its highest level in recent centuries, suggesting that now is its chance to return.[43] The National Park has no plan for re-introduction of the bear, lynx or wolf into the Park area, but if any of these species do migrate into the Park (they are present in nearby Alpine countries) they will be afforded total protection within the Park's boundaries.[44]

The negative effect of herbivores in the Swiss National Park adds to the evidence from many studies that have demonstrated the effects of ungulate browsing on species composition, nutrient cycling and on the entire successional pathways of vegetation communities. Since top predators may in turn exert a strong influence on lower trophic levels, then they too function as system-directing species.[45] In addition, multiple predator effects on prey species and on ecosystems can be synergistic, the limiting effect of two co-occurring species of predators being stronger than that exerted by one species. Thus the densities of roe deer across Europe were found to be significantly lower in areas that had both wolf and lynx compared to areas with wolf alone, or areas without either predator.[46] The presence of bear alone appears to be insufficient to prevent a break

[42] Flurin Filli, 'Überwachung seltener Pfanzen in alpinen Schutzgebieten' (project number: CH-2203), Projects within the Swiss National Park. Database on research in European Mountain Areas, http://4dweb.proclim.ch/4dcgi/protareas/en/Detail_Project?ch-2203, 'Zaune auf Weiden. Schweizerischer Nationalpark', www.nationalpark.ch/tasks/sites/de/assets/File/Trophic_cascades_Infotafel.pdf, and Schweizerischer Nationalpark & Biosfera Val Müstair Forschungskonzept 2008–2018, Forschungskommission des Schweizerischen Nationalparks am 8. Dezember 2007, www.nationalpark.ch/tasks/sites/de/assets/File/Reihe_nationalparkforschung.pdf.

[43] 'Braunbär', Schweizerischer Nationalpark, www.nationalpark.ch/go/de/flora-und-fauna/tiere/braunbaer/.

[44] 'Wolf', Schweizerischer Nationalpark, www.nationalpark.ch/go/de/flora-und-fauna/tiere/wolf/.

[45] Sergio et al.,'Top Predators as Conservation Tools: Ecological Rationale, Assumptions, and Efficacy' *supra* note 38.

[46] C. Melis, Bogumiła Jędrzejewska, B.M. Apollonio, K.A. Bartoń, W. Jędrzejewski, J.D.C. Linnell, I. Kojola, J. Kusak, M. Adamic, S. Ciuti, I. Delehan, I. Dykyy, K. Krapinec, L. Mattioli, A. Sagaydak, N. Samchuk, K. Schmidt, M. Shkvyryal, V.E. Sidorovich, B. Zawadzka and S. Zhyla, 'Predation Has a Greater Impact in Less Productive Environments: Variation in Roe Deer, *Capreolus capreolus*, population density across Europe', *Global Ecology and Biogeography*, 18 (2009), 724–734.

out in cervid populations (deer and moose) in Northern European forest ecosystems, whereas the combination of wolf and bear predation, with or without human hunting, maintains cervid densities lower than without wolf and bear.[47]

There is evidence that the structuring force of top predators through trophic cascades promotes species diversity, or is spatio-temporally associated with it. At its simplest level, this could be due to top predators making available resources essential to other species that are otherwise unavailable, or scarcely available, such as carrion, a high quality detritus composed of dead animal material[48] or enhancing survival through suppression of middle (meso) predators.[49] Perhaps the key factor though is that top predators usually need large, undisturbed areas for foraging and breeding[50] and these areas can be expected to encompass the needs of many less demanding species.

Evidence for this species diversity comes from reports of a spatial occurrence between five raptor species that differ widely in their diet and habitat associations – goshawk (*Accipiter gentilis*), pygmy owl (*Glaucidium passerinum*), Tengmalm's owl (*Aegolius funereus*), tawny owl (*Strix aluco*) and scops owl (*Otus scops*) – with greater diversity of avian species, vulnerable avian species, butterfly species and tree species at various locations in the Italian Alps.[51] The alpine and forested landscapes of the Carpathian Mountains in Romania afford an example for synergy between mammalian predators, and where the presence of at least one or more of wolf, bear or lynx was co-located with fifty-five per cent of the birds and eighty per cent of the mammals of national

[47] W.J. Ripple and R.L. Beschta, 'Large Predators Limit Herbivore Densities in Northern Forest Ecosystems', *European Journal of Wildlife Research* 58 (2012), 733–742.

[48] E.E. Wilson and E.M. Wolkovich, 'Scavenging: How Carnivores and Carrion Structure Communities', *Trends in Ecology and Evolution* 26 (2011), 129–135.

[49] K.M. Berger, E.M. Gese and J. Berger, 'Indirect Effects and Traditional Trophic Cascades: a Test Involving Wolves, Coyotes, and Pronghorn', *Ecology* 8 (2008), 818–828 and E.G. Ritchie, B. Elmhagen, A.S. Glen, M. Letnic, G. Ludwig and R.A. McDonald, 'Ecosystem Restoration with Teeth: What Role for Predators?' *Trends in Ecology and Evolution* 27 (2012), 265–271.

[50] J. Linnell, V. Salvatori and L. Boitani (2008), *Guidelines for Population Level Management Plans for Large Carnivores in Europe*, A Large Carnivore Initiative for Europe report prepared for the European Commission (contract 070501/2005/424162/MAR/B2), http://ec.europa.eu/environment/nature/conservation/species/carnivores/pdf/guidelines_ for_population_level_management.pdf.

[51] F. Sergio, I. Newton, L. Marchesi and P. Pedrini, 'Ecologically Justified Charisma: Preservation of Top Predators Delivers Biodiversity Conservation', *Journal of Applied Ecology* 43 (2006), 1049–1055.

significance for Romania.[52] In reality, two thirds of the areas of occurrence in this study had the presence of all three carnivores.

The importance of the presence of the larger carnivores in contributing to and regulating natural processes worldwide is increasingly recognized: areas with the highest number of predator species and with intact large carnivore guilds are likely to be indicative of locations for exploring and conserving wilderness qualities. Compared to historical times, the contraction of the range of large carnivores has been most extensive in Europe. However, the contemporary overlap of large carnivore ranges shows the distribution of a three-species guild of wolf, lynx and bear stretching from Eastern Russia to Scandinavia and the edges of Central Europe, and including Finland, Sweden, the Baltic states, the Balkan states, and the Carpathian and Dinaric countries.[53] It is perhaps unsurprising that areas in these countries are well represented at the high end of the European wilderness continuum mapping, discussed in Chapter 2.

## 4 The dependency of European species on wilderness qualities

The contemporary species diversity of the Lagodekhi State Nature Reserve in Georgia described in Subsection 2.1 is compelling evidence that the wild nature of Europe is preserved in areas where there is a sustained period of restriction on human intervention. The presence of an extant trophic assemblage of mammalian predators and prey, coupled with the wide diversity of habitat niches argues that Lagodekhi is an important area for our understanding of the natural processes that contribute to wilderness qualities. It is from such locations that we learn why some species are more likely to thrive where there are these wilderness qualities compared to the modified and simplified ecologies of cultural landscapes. This is sometimes described as the wilderness dependency of species, but it very much depends on what aspect of natural processes is the key factor in survival and whether this is exclusively found in wilderness. It is therefore not a simple, binary relationship, but rather a relative dependency.

[52] L. Rozylowicz, V.D. Popescu, M. Pătroescu and G. Chişamera, 'The Potential of Large Carnivores as Conservation Surrogates in the Romanian Carpathians', *Biodiversity Conservation* 20 (2011), 561–579.

[53] W.J. Ripplel, J.A. Estes, R.L. Beschta, C.C. Wilmers, E.G. Ritchie, M. Hebblewhite, J. Berger, B. Elmhagen, M. Letnic, M.P. Nelson, O.J. Schmitz, D.W. Smith, A.D. Wallach and A.J. Wirsing, 'Status and Ecological Effects of the World's Largest Carnivores', *Science* 343, 6167 (2014), 1241484.

For the wilderness dependency of species in Europe a distinction has been drawn that separates between some whose survival has a strong linkage to specific natural processes, while others are only able to survive in areas with sufficient space and access to certain trophic functions of wild nature.[54] An example of the first group are those species dependant on the dead and decaying wood that is characteristic of ancient forests, such as lichens, fungi and invertebrates, as well as the forest specialist woodpeckers that prey on those invertebrates and which, along with some owls and bats, find nesting homes in that dead wood. The second group comprise the herbivores and carnivores in need of areas with sufficient home range and with elements of the trophic assemblies that are needed to support them.

### *4.1 The importance of dead wood in natural forests*

Dead wood in parts of the stems or branches of standing trees, as well as standing and fallen dead trees are indicators for naturalness in ancient forests, as are old trees (>200 years) with rough bark structures, severe crown damage, large cavities, clefts in the stem, open bark gaps and bark bags.[55] Standing and fallen dead wood is created by tree mortality, which in natural forests is caused by fire, wind, snow breakage, drought, competition, insects and pathogens.[56] Many species associated with dead wood do not live on the dead wood directly, but on other species that consume dead wood. A fungal community develops after tree death and a large number of beetle species feed on the fungal mycelium, or on the decaying wood. In turn, many parasitic insects live on wood living beetles.

Mould-filled bark bags arise from dead bark on dead or living trees, where the bark is partially lifted and filled up with mould between the bark and stem.[57] These mould-filled bark bags are variously used as nesting sites by tree creepers (*Certhia spp.*) and as breeding sites or roosts

[54] Edit Borza and Vlado Vancura, 'Last of the Wild: Overview of Status and Monitoring of Some Wilderness Related Species in the Natura 2000 Network', (Budapest: PAN Parks Foundation/ Kenguruprint, 2009; reprinted in 2011), www.europarc.org/uploaded/documents/1271.pdf.

[55] S. Winter, M. Flade, H. Schumacher, E. Kerstan and G. Möller, 'The Importance of Near-natural Stand Structures for the Biocoenosis of Lowland Beech Forests', *Forest Snow and Landscape Research* 79 (2005), 127–144.

[56] B.G. Jonsson, N. Kruys and T. Ranius, 'Ecology of Species Living on Dead Wood – Lessons for Dead Wood Management', *Silva Fennica*, 39 (2005), 289–309.

[57] Winter et al., 'The Importance of Near-natural Stand Structures for the Biocoenosis of Lowland Beech Forests', *supra* note 55.

for two rare and threatened bats, the Barbastelle[58] (*Barbastella barbastellus*) and Bechstein's Bat[59] (*Myotis bechsteinii*). They are also used by insects, both as hiding places and breeding nests, in particular by various species of beetle, such as skin (*Dermestidae spp.*) comb-claw (*Alleculidae spp.*) and Clown beetles *(Histeridae)*.[60] The foraging ecology of insectivorous woodpecker species is based on gleaning and probing for bark-dwelling and boring insects like the beetles.[61] The Middle Spotted Woodpecker (*Dendrocopos medius*) and the long-beaked white-backed woodpecker (*Dendrocopos leucotos*) are more often associated with the deadwood of deciduous forest, whereas throughout its range, the three-toed woodpecker (*Picoides tridactylus*) is found in old coniferous (spruce) forests,[62] but all three predatory woodpeckers use standing deadwood for roosting or nesting.[63]

The dependence of woodpecker species on large areas of long-lived forest with the characteristic properties of natural processes makes them indicator species for other species associated with unmanaged forests rich in older trees and dead wood.[64] Woodpeckers also play a keystone role in forests through the provision of cavities for a range of secondary cavity users, such as other birds and sometimes small mammals.[65] Their trophic function places them as a top predator, a positioning that in the case of the three-toed woodpecker exemplifies a contribution to the natural regulation of bark beetle populations in

[58] A.M. Hutson, S. Aulagnier and F. Spitzenberger, assessment of 2008, *Barbastella barbastellus*, in IUCN Red List of Threatened Species, version 2013.2 (2013), www.iucnredlist.org/details/full/2553/0.

[59] A.M. Hutson, F. Spitzenberger, K. Tsytsulina, S. Aulagnier, J. Juste, A. Karataş, J. Palmeirim and M. Paunović (2008), *Myotis bechsteinii*, in IUCN Red List of Threatened Species, version 2013.2 (2013), www.iucnredlist.org/details/full/14123/0.

[60] Winter et al., 'The Importance of Near-natural Stand Structures for the Biocoenosis of Lowland Beech Forests', *supra* note 55.

[61] Z. Kosński and A. Winiecki, 'Factors Affecting the Density of the Middle Spotted Woodpecker Dendrocopos Medius: A Macrohabitat Approach', *Journal of Ornithology* 146 (2005), 263–270.

[62] D. Czeszczewik, W. Walankiewicz, C. Mitrus, T. Tumiel, T. Stański, M. Sahel and G. Bednarczyk, 'Importance of Dead Wood Resources for Woodpeckers in Coniferous Stands of the Białowieża Forest', *Bird Conservation International* 23 (2013), 414–425.

[63] A. Lõhmus, R. Kinks and M. Soon, 'The Importance of Dead-Wood Supply for Woodpeckers in Estonia', *Baltic Forestry* 16 (2010), 76–86.

[64] J.-M. Roberge and P. Angelstam, 'Indicator Species among Resident Forest Birds – A Cross-regional Evaluation in Northern Europe', *Biological Conservation*, 130 (2006), 134–147.

[65] J.-M. Roberge, P. Agelstam and M.-A. Villard, 'Specalised Woodpeckers and Naturalness in Hemiboreal Forests – Deriving Quantitative Targets for Conservation Planning', *Biological Conservation* 141 (2008), 997–1012.

coniferous forests.[66] The European spruce bark beetle (*Ips typographus*) a conifer detrivore, can if unchecked periodically build up large populations, resulting in the death of many trees in a few years. In production forests, this is met with aggressive pest management programmes that involve either extensive harvesting of beetle-infested trees or chemical control. However, in natural unmanaged forests, predation of these beetles and their larvae by the three-toed woodpecker delays and lessens bark beetle outbreaks in spruce (*Picea spp).*

The Ural owl (*Strix uralensis*) is one of the largest cavity-nesting bird species in Europe, its presence is an indication of older forests that have a high availability of dead trees with natural holes, such as hollow trunks as well as wide cracks and large hollows created through wind damage breaking off branches and crowns.[67] The owl hunts from tree perches overlooking forest openings, like bogs and water courses, the main prey being small woodland mammals, such as bank voles[68] (*Myodes glareolus*). Although it may use deserted raptor nests made of sticks, the lack of large standing deadwood and tree cavities limits the numbers of Ural owls, which accept these structures for breeding more readily than stick nests.[69]

As resident bird species, owls and woodpeckers have higher vulnerability to habitat changes that decrease naturalness, such as the characteristics of managed forests where there is removal of deadwood, loss of mature deciduous trees and the introduction of coniferous trees.[70] Logging in the Białowieża Forest, Poland, leads to reduced volumes of deadwood, as well as reduced numbers of white-backed woodpecker[71] as well as three-toed woodpecker.[72] However, greater numbers of these

[66] P. Fayta, M.M. Machmerb and C. Steeger, 'Regulation of Spruce Bark Beetles by Literature Review', *Forest Ecology and Management* 206 (2005), 1–14.

[67] A. Lõhmus, 'Do Ural Owls (Strix uralensis) Suffer from the Lack Of Nest Sites in Managed Forests?', *Biological Conservation* 110 (2003), 1–9.

[68] J. Obuch, S. Danko, J. Mihók, D. Karaska and L. Šimák, 'Diet of the Ural Owl (Strix uralensis) in Slovakia', *Slovak Raptor Journal* 7 (2013), 59–71.

[69] Lõhmus, 'Do Ural Owls (Strix uralensis) Suffer from the Lack of Nest Sites in Managed Forests?', *supra* note 67.

[70] Borza and Vancura, 'Last of the Wild: Overview of Status and Monitoring of Some Wilderness Related Species in the Natura 2000 network', *supra* note 54.

[71] D. Czeszczewik and W. Walankiewicz, 'Logging Affects the White-backed Woodpecker Dendrocopos Leucotos in the Białowieża Forest', *Annales Zoologici Fennici* 43 (2006), 221–227.

[72] T. Wesołowski, D. Czeszczewik and P. Rowiński, 'Effects of Forest Management on Three-toed Woodpecker *Picoides tridactylus* Distribution in Białowieża Forest (NE Poland): Conservation Implications', *Acta Ornithologica* 40 (2005), 53–60.

woodpeckers are found in the unmanaged, strictly protected forest of the Białowieża National Park.[73] There is very little deciduous forest older than thirty years in parts of Sweden, particularly of aspen (*Populus tremula*) and birch (*Betula spp.*). and this has been accompanied by a gradual, natural overgrowth with spruce, resulting in a decline of the white-backed woodpecker by eighty per cent over the last twenty years, so that it has now become assessed as Critically Endangered.[74]

### 4.2 *Wild mammals have large home ranges*

It is in the behaviour of the large, free-living wild mammals and birds to have large territories or home ranges based on their feeding requirements, social characteristics and dispersal tendencies. The space available to these species to live freely and undisturbed substantially diminished as the extent of human habitation and landscape modification in Europe progressed. In the case of Europe's largest herbivore, the European bison (*Bison bonasus*), this loss of space eventually led to its temporary extinction in the wild.

The historical coverage of European bison included Western, Central and South-Eastern Europe, extending up to the Volga River and the Caucasus.[75] The home ranges of European bison vary from 80–150 $km^2$, although the central area of the range is most intensively used. Bison are active feeders during movement, spending sixty per cent of their day on feeding, and another ten per cent on roaming without feeding. As an intermediate feeder, which is able to digest lignin at a higher rate than cattle,[76] bison have the ability to vary between grazing in open areas of grass and browsing on trees and shrubs, depending on the season. This confers flexibility in habitat requirement that made bison a competing threat to the grasslands and crops of farmland. Relentlessly hunted, European bison ran out of space where they could live freely without conflict with humans over the nineteenth century, and then

[73] W. Walankiewicz, D. Czeszczewik, T. Tumiel and T. Stański, 'Woodpeckers Abundance in the Białowieża Forest – A Comparison between Deciduous, Strictly Protected and Managed Stands', *Ornis Polonica* 52 (2011), 161–168.

[74] Vitryggig Hackspett (*Dendrocopos leucotos*) Rödlistan, ArtDatabanken, Sveriges lantbruksuniversitet, www.artfakta.se/Artfaktablad/Dendrocopos_Leucotos_100046.pdf.

[75] Z. Pucek (ed.), *European Bison. Status Survey and Conservation Action Plan* (Gland: IUCN/SSC Bison Specialist Group, 2004).

[76] Z. Gębczyńska, J. Kowalczyk, M. Krasińska and A. Ziołecka, 'A Comparison of the Digestibility of Nutrients by European Bison and Cattle', *Acta Theriologica* 19 (1974), 283–289.

poaching from dwindling numbers protected in reserves led to their extinction in the wild during the first few decades of the twentieth century.[77]

Fortunately, a number of bison existed in zoological gardens, and it was from these captive animals that free-roaming populations were reinstated in nearly thirty locations in the second half of the twentieth century, in Poland, Belarus and the Ukraine. The choice of locations, while not necessarily having high wilderness qualities, were based on areas where human activity could not be disturbed by their presence, and were of sufficient extent that the free-ranging feeding strategies of bison could be accommodated, such as forests and national parks. Bison populations have a natural tendency to disperse into open habitats, as shown by nearly seventy per cent of the bison populations that were initially introduced into forest habitats expanding their distribution range to neighbouring open areas.[78] Thus, winter feeding strategies have been developed to discourage dispersal and limit encroachment into surrounding cultural landscapes. The most significant limit for the enlargement of European bison populations remains human population density, such that the population of this species is assessed as Vulnerable.[79]

The greater spotted eagle (*Aquila clanga*) is a migratory predator species that occupies a fragmented range in Central and Eastern Europe during the breeding season, and then over-winters in Southern Europe, Southern Asia and North-East Africa.[80] The eagle has suffered a rapid decline in most of its range, now breeding mainly in Belarus, Russia and Ukraine, but in small numbers also in Eastern Poland, Estonia and Moldova. It has become extinct or almost extinct in Finland, Latvia, Lithuania, Hungary and Romania, so that it is assessed as Vulnerable.[81] During the breeding season, the eagle needs extensive territories of large, wet deciduous forests in the lowlands that border wetlands, bogs and

[77] Pucek (ed.), *European Bison. Status Survey and Conservation Action Plan, supra* note 75.

[78] E. Hoffman-Kaminska and R. Kowalczyk, 'Farm Crops Depredation by European Bison (*Bison Bonasus*) in the Vicinity of Forest Habitats in Northeastern Poland', *Environmental Management* 50 (2012), 530–541.

[79] W. *Olech* (2008) IUCN SSC Bison Specialist Group, *Bison bonasus*, in IUCN Red List of Threatened Species, version 2013.2 (2013), www.iucnredlist.org/details/full/2814/0.

[80] B.-U. Meyburg, L. Haraszthy, M. Strazds and N. Schäffer, *European Species Action Plan for Greater Spotted Eagle* (*Aquila clanga*) (Brussels: European Commission, 1997, http://ec.europa.eu/environment/nature/conservation/wildbirds/action_plans/docs/aquila_clanga.pdf.

[81] BirdLife International, *Aquila clanga*, in IUCN Red List of Threatened Species, version 2013.2 (2013), www.iucnredlist.org/details/full/22696027/0.

marshes. It feeds mainly on water voles (*Arvicola amphibius*) but also other small mammals, birds, amphibians, lizards, snakes, small fish, carrion and sometimes insects. The eagle builds large stick nests under the canopy of deciduous trees. It is very intolerant of permanent human presence in its breeding area or hunting range and consequently birds abandon their territories once people start to live and work nearby. Pressures include habitat alteration and loss of nest sites caused by disturbance from forestry operations, loss of feeding habitat from disturbances to the groundwater systems and further disturbance through large scale building such as new roads, new powerlines and extension of towns. Poisoning has also reduced populations of their main prey of water vole, frequently considered a pest species in forestry, which is controlled by rodenticides that are fatal to the eagle. Poisoned bait put out to kill other carrion eaters is also fatal. Shooting during migration is an important factor as well.

Top mammalian predators, such as bear, wolf and lynx, have large area requirements, with home range sizes of individual large carnivores in Europe varying between 100 and 1,000 km$^2$ – depending on habitat characteristics and environmental productivity.[82] This implies that they never reach very high densities – typically ranging from 0.1 to 3 per 100 km$^2$. In addition to these characteristics of resident adult individuals, juvenile large carnivores often range widely during their dispersal phase, with some individuals moving over hundreds of kilometres.

Brown bear, in the absence of human disturbance would have occupied not just deciduous and coniferous forests of Europe, but also the steppes and northern and alpine tundra.[83] However, much of the former range of the bear is no longer suitable habitat due to human modification and habitation, and their presence now relies on large continuous areas of undisturbed habitat with sufficient food availability (ungulates, berries, fruit, bee colonies), cover for escape and good opportunities for denning. Bears occur at low densities, especially in northern populations (e.g., 0.5 bears/1,000 km$^2$ in South-Eastern Norway, compared to 100–200 bears/ 1,000 km$^2$ in Romania). Their home ranges vary depending on food availability, with male home ranges between 120 and 1,600 km$^2$, and female home ranges of 60 to 225 km$^2$. Dispersing young males may roam over areas of up to 12,000 km$^2$.

[82] Linnell et al., *Guidelines for population level management plans for large carnivores in Europe, supra* note 50.

[83] J.E. Swenson, N. Gerstl, B. Dahlea and A. Zedrosser, *Action Plan for the Conservation of the Brown Bear (Ursus arctos) in Europe* (Strasbourg: Council of Europe, 2000).

Insufficient suitable home range, coupled with persistent illegal killing, predominantly by hunters, has led to the bear population of the Central Apennines in Italy being assessed as Critically Endangered.[84] The Marsican bear population of perhaps forty bears has been small over a long time, and shows marked differences from other European populations, genetically, morphologically and behaviourally. It is confined mostly to the protection it receives in the National Park of Abruzzo, Lazio and Molise. However, overspill into the surrounding countryside creates conflict from livestock depredation and destruction of beehives. An EU Life-funded project over the last four years has provided a better understanding of the natural resources exploited by the bears, as well as planted up areas of Alpine buckthorn (*Rhamnus alpinus*), the berries of which are favoured by bear. The project resulted also in the installation of bear-proof waste bins in proximity of built-up areas, thus limiting access to the trophic resources that the bear might associate with man, and the installation of electric fences to protect livestock, apiaries and quality crops in critical areas. Furthermore, the project reduced vehicle access in critical areas for bear presence by closing a number of unpaved roads.[85]

Lynx are solitary animals, living in large deciduous, mixed and coniferous forests, their home range sizes varying considerably depending on habitat type and the composition and density of the prey community.[86] Studies based on telemetry have brought precise estimates of home range size of lynx in Europe: 180–2,780 $km^2$ for males and 98–759 $km^2$ for females. Mean distances travelled by lynx within their home ranges per night is between 1–45 km, and depends on age, sex, social status, prey density and hunting success. Half of the lynx populations in Europe stem from reintroductions carried out in the 1970s and 1980s, such as in Switzerland, Slovenia, Italy, Czech Republic, Austria, Germany and France, and which have been necessary because of the poor dispersal ability of this species.[87] Roe deer are their primary food, with other wild

[84] See 'Orso bruno marsicano (Ursus arctos ssp. marsicanus)', in *Liste Rosse italiane* (IUCN Comitato Italiano), www.iucn.it/scheda.php?id=539974414.

[85] For information on the 'Life Arctos project' (LIFE 09/NAT/IT/000160), see www.life-arctos.it/english/home.html.

[86] U. Breitenmoser, Ch. Breitenmoser-Würsten, H. Okarma, T.A.M. Kaphegyi, U.M. Müller and U. Kaphygyi-Wallmann, *Action Plan for the Conservation of the Eurasian Lynx in Europe (*Lynx lynx*)* (Strasbourg: Council of Europe, 2000).

[87] U. Breitenmoser, D.P. Mallon, M. von Arx and C. Breitenmoser-Wursten (2008), 'Lynx lynx', in *IUCN Red List of Threatened Species* (IUCN, 2013), version 2013.1, www.iucnredlist.org/details/full/12519/0.

species making up over ninety-eight per cent of their diet in the Jura[88] and Dinaric Mountains.[89] Even where roe deer densities are low, lynx still seek out roe deer in preference to domestic livestock.[90] Lynx also take red fox[91] (*Vulpes vulpes*), a middle predator that is persecuted in cultural landscapes as a pest species.[92]

Wolves are territorial, marking with urine and faeces in strategic sites and along boundaries, and defending their home range from wolves of neighbouring packs. Home ranges vary depending on wolf and prey densities, and on human disturbance, but are generally between 100 and 500 km$^2$.[93] The wilderness dependency of wolves will always be contested because of their great ability for dispersal through hostile terrain, and their seeming adaptability to habitat conditions and human presence. Wolf habitat has been described as everywhere humans do not kill the species and where there is something to eat. However, this is a function of their very nature, as territoriality, social behaviour and dispersal are the intrinsic mechanisms regulating wolf density. Moreover, while wolves are now establishing territories in areas that have less claim to wilderness qualities, they still seek out aspects of wild nature, as revealed by their dietary preference. Wild ungulates make up ninety-four to ninety-six per cent of the diet of wolves in Central and Western Poland[94] and Germany,[95] and eighty-nine to ninety-five per cent of the

[88] A. Jobin, P. Molinari and U. Breitenmoser, 'Prey Spectrum, Prey Preference and Consumption Rates of Eurasian Lynx in the Swiss Jura Mountains', *Acta Theriologica* 45 (2000), 243–252.

[89] M. Krofe, D. Huber and I. Kos, 'Diet of Eurasian Lynx (*Lynx lynx*) in the Northern Dinaric Mountains (Slovenia and Croatia)', *Acta Theriologica* 56 (2011), 315–322.

[90] J. Odden, J.D.C. Linnell and R. Andersen, 'Diet of Eurasian Lynx (*Lynx lynx*) in the Boreal Forest of Southeastern Norway: The Relative Importance of Livestock and Hares at Low Roe Deer Density', *European Journal of Wildlife Research*, 52 (2006), 237–244.

[91] Breitenmoser et al., 'Lynx lynx', *supra* note 87 and Jobin, 'Prey Spectrum, Prey Preference and Consumption Rates of Eurasian Lynx in the Swiss Jura Mountains', *supra* note 88.

[92] D.W. Macdonald and J. Reynolds, 'Red Fox (*Vulpes vulpes*)', in C. Sillero-Zubiri, M. Hoffmann, and D.W. Macdonald (eds.), *Canids: Foxes, Wolves, Jackals and Dogs. Status Survey and Conservation Action Plan* (Gland/Cambridge: IUCN/SSC Canid Specialist Group, 2004), www.carnivoreconservation.org/files/actionplans/canids.pdf, pp. 129–135.

[93] L. Boitani, 'Action Plan for the conservation of the wolves (Canis lupus) in Europe', (Strasbourg: Council of Europe, 2000).

[94] S. Nowaka, R.W. Mysłajeka, A. Kłosińska and G. Gabryś, 'Diet and Prey Selection of Wolves (*Canis lupus*) Recolonizing Western and Central Poland', *Mammalian Biology*, 76 (2011), 709–715.

[95] C. Wagner, M. Holzapfel, G. Kluth, I. Reinhardt and H. Ansorge, 'Wolf (*Canis lupus*) Feeding Habits during the First Eight Years of Its Occurrence in Germany', *Mammalian Biology* 77 (2012), 196–203.

diet of wolves in the Alpine, Apennine and Mediterranean ecosystems of Italy.[96]

Wolves are gradually moving west across Europe, with regular sightings in Denmark[97] and now in the Netherlands.[98] As will be shown in the next section, there is every reason to believe that areas recovering some wilderness qualities after removal of human influence do recover a wolf population. While the preservation of large mammals like the wolf and the bison may not have an absolute dependency on wilderness qualities, their existence is essential to those qualities through their trophic function (see Section 3.3). The issue then is that the areas of their home ranges outstrip the boundaries of most protected areas, and even some small countries. To maintain these animals living wild means a tolerance of their presence in the wider landscape, while at the same time a greater space is given over to wilderness so that they can live freely without conflict with humans.

## 5 The last ecologically intact areas in Europe?

The mapping of wilderness quality in Europe shows a preponderance of wilder areas in Iceland and the Scandinavian countries (see Chapter 2). It can also be found in mountainous regions, such as the Alps, Pyrenees and Carpathians, but there are smaller areas in the lowlands of Finland, Estonia, Latvia and Western Poland. The protection status of the wildest areas in Europe shows a partial overlap from nationally protected area designations, indicating that there is the potential for much more wilderness to be designated across Europe. Given the large home ranges of the bigger wild mammals and their unfavourable conservation status, there is an imperative to seek to have territories as large as possible, where there is a lack of humans and their agriculture.

Wildland in Europe is closely associated with protected areas classified under IUCN Categories I (strict reserve) and II (National Park).[99] As will be shown in Part III, the ability to designate protected areas in those

[96] C. Capitani, I. Bertelli, P. Varuzza, M. Scandura and M. Apollonio, 'A Comparative Analysis of Wolf (*Canis lupus*) Diet in Three Different Italian Ecosystems', *Mammalian Biology* 69 (2004), 1–10.

[97] Ulve i Danmark, Naturstyrelsen Miljøministeriet, www.naturstyrelsen.dk/Naturbeskyttelse/Artsleksikon/Dyr/Pattedyr/Rovdyr/Ulv/Fakta_om_ulv/ulve_i_danmark/.

[98] 'Wolf Plan for the Netherlands', *Alterra Wageningen UR News*, 9 July 2013, www.wageningenur.nl/en/show/Wolf-Plan-for-the-Netherlands.htm.

[99] M. Fisher, S. Carver, Z. Kun, R. McMorran, K. Arrell and G. Mitchell, '*Review of Status and Conservation of Wild Land in Europe*', Project commissioned by the Scottish

categories is widespread in the legislation for national protected area systems across Europe, and which lay down restrictions on extractive use, introduction of non-native species, as well as physical development as the means of protection. Much of this legislation is less than fifteen years old, but is often amending legislation from years earlier. It is not certain at what point this aspiration became a key aim in many European countries, and which was matched with sufficient restrictions on activity that would give rise to wilderness qualities. German forest ecologist Knut Sturm is credited with the development of a conservation strategy of non-intervention in the natural processes of ecosystems, allowing unhindered ecological restoration to take place, through his concept of Process Protection.[100] However, those with an historical perspective will see this as perhaps a timely re-iteration of the principle of withdrawal of human influence that a century ago was the basis of the foundation of the Swiss National Park and the Lagodekhi State Nature Reserve (see Section 2).

Wilderness quality mapping cannot necessarily distinguish between Primary, substantially unmodified habitats that are shaped by the natural processes of trophic cascades, soil conditions and climatic factors, natural disturbances, and Secondary habitats arising through human use and management of land. However, the lack of areas of high wilderness quality in many Western European countries, such as the Low Countries of the coastal region of North Western Europe, is likely an indication of an intensity of land use that far exceeds what would have been the demands of a wild trophic assembly, especially where the grazing of domestic livestock now far outstrips the capacity for primary production.[101] However, even in these agro-ecosystems, there is the potential to regain wilderness qualities if that human land use is removed.

## 6 The contemporary opportunities for restoring wilderness qualities

The Foundation for Natural Landscapes in Brandenburg has, since 2000, taken ownership of over 127 km$^2$ of former military training grounds in Saxony, with the aim of allowing them to restore their wilderness

Government (Edinburgh: Scottish Government, 2010), www.scotland.gov.uk/Resource/Doc/1051/0109251.pdf.

[100] K. Sturm, 'Prozeßschutz – ein Konzept für naturschutzgerechte Waldwirtschaft', *Zeitschrift für Ökologie und Naturschutz* 2 (1993), 181–192.

[101] V. Smil, 'Harvesting the Biosphere: The Human Impact', *Population and Development Review* 37 (2011), 613–636.

qualities.[102] The four areas of Jüterbog, Heidehof, Lieberose and Tangersdorf were relinquished by the military in 1994.[103] They are unique in Germany for their potential for development of wilderness qualities because of a military use going back 150 years that has left them without any roads or settlement, and without the recent modifying effects of agricultural use. This legacy manifests itself as a mosaic of diverse Primary and Secondary habitats, which includes sandy areas, heaths, conifer plantation, natural forests, lakes and fens, all now being shaped only by natural forces.[104] Over 120 species of birds have found a home, as well as reptiles, amphibians, otter (*Lutra lutra*), beaver (*Castor fiber*) and deer. There has been some thinning of the conifer plantation to open it to regeneration with native deciduous trees, but the overall aim of the Foundation is to allow this natural dynamic through a policy of non-intervention. The continuing successional changes in vegetation as well as the changes in species that make it their home will be monitored.[105] It is important to the Foundation that people get an opportunity to explore and experience the developing wilderness. The Foundation has constructed 30 km of hiking trails along which visitors can discover the landscape on their own or can take part in guided hikes into areas that are normally not accessible.[106]

Two wolves were photographed in Lieberose early in 2010, caught in an automatic camera trap[107] and these have since bred at least three wolf pups.[108] The first territorial settlement of a pair of wolves in Brandenburg took place in 2007, probably crossing over the border from Poland.[109]

[102] 'Wildnis konkret', Stiftung Naturlandschaften Brandenburg, www.stiftung-nlb.de/de/wildnis/wildnis-konkret.html.

[103] 'Geschichte', Stiftung Naturlandschaften Brandenburg, www.stiftung-nlb.de/de/stiftung/geschichte.html.

[104] 'Wildnis stiften', Stiftung Naturlandschaften Brandenburg, www.stiftung-nlb.de/de/wildnis.html

[105] 'Wildnis erforschen', Stiftung Naturlandschaften Brandenburg, www.stiftung-nlb.de/de/wildnis/wildnis-erforschen.html.

[106] 'Wildnis erleben', Stiftung Naturlandschaften Brandenburg, www.stiftung-nlb.de/de/wildnis/wildnis-erleben.html.

[107] 'Wolfsnachwuchs in der Lieberoser Heide', press release of the Stiftung Naturlandschaften Brandenburg, Lieberose, 2 July 2011, www.stiftung-nlb.de/de/presse/127-wolfsnachwuchs-in-der-lieberoser-heide.html.

[108] 'Wolfsnachwuchs in der Lieberoser Heide', joint press release of the *Stiftung Naturlandschaften Brandenburg, FORST Brandenburg, IFAW & Landesamt für Umwelt, Gesundheit und Verbraucherschutz*, Lieberose, 12 July 2011, www.stiftung-nlb.de/pdf/127_PM_Wolf_Lieberose_Jul2011_Endf.pdf.

[109] *Managementplan für den Wolf in Brandenburg 2013–2017* (Brandenburg: Ministerium für Umwelt, Gesundheit und Verbraucherschutz, 2012). www.lugv.brandenburg.de/cms/media.php/lbm1.a.3310.de/wmp_2013_2017.pdf.

Since then, the estimate is that there are nine packs in Brandenburg, with the packs in Lieberose and Jüterbog now assessed as permanently resident and breeding. Monitoring the return of the wolf, its behaviour and establishment of new settlements is another area of research of the Foundation. In wider context, the Foundation views their restoring wilderness areas as contributing to a national target of transforming two per cent of Germany's territory into wilderness by 2020.[110]

The returning presence of wolves fits with another aim: contributing to the habitat connectivity of a trans-European ecological network. In 2007, the Foundation launched a project to establish an ecological corridor that crosses the landscape of South Brandenburg to the border with Poland, linking nature parks, a biosphere reserve and forest habitat networks, and which encompasses the Foundation's land as core areas.[111] The Ecological Corridor of South Brandenburg will facilitate not only dispersal of wolves, but also the migration of deer, a property of the wild behaviour of this species that is restricted in Europe because of the fragmentation and insularity caused by human landscape modification.[112]

## 7 Conclusions

In recognizing the ecological values of wilderness, it is important to understand that humans do not create wild species, but we are very good at making them extinct. With the domestication of fire and the use of crafted tools, humans took themselves beyond being a natural influence. Then, through our agriculture, we have been simplifying ecologies ever since, as they are bent to our productive needs. Wild nature is therefore for the most part today in a forced co-existence with humans that limits its ability to thrive, and to distribute where it is not tolerated. We can identify and protect areas of high potential for wilderness qualities, but wild nature chooses where it wants to be – we cannot 'manage' wilderness for species. The importance is thus implicit, of

[110] *Nationale Strategie zur biologischen Vielfalt*, adopted by the Bundeskabinett on 7 November 2007 (Berlin: Bundesministerium für Umwelt, Naturschutz und Reaktorsicherheit, 2007), www.bmu.de/fileadmin/bmu-import/files/pdfs/allgemein/application/pdf/broschuere_biolog_vielfalt_strategie_bf.pdf.

[111] For information on the 'Ökologische Korridor Südbrandenburg', see the *Stiftung Naturlandschaften Brandenburg*, www.wildkorridor.de/.

[112] H. Herrmann and K. Scheurlen, 'Hirsch – Wolf – Otter – Biber. Zielarten für den Ökologischen Korridor Südbrandenburg', online publication, 2008, www.wildkorridor.de/pdf/077_Hirsch_Wolf_Otter_Biber_Leitarten.pdf.

adequately protected areas with wilderness qualities as safe refuges and references for natural systems, being repositories of trophic diversity, and especially for endangered native and endemic species. In both experimental and experiential terms, they are the reference areas for the effects of humans upon the natural environment.

Given the extent of human modification in Europe, it is the case that Secondary wilderness is the reality of contemporary wilderness in Europe, having arisen after a period of ecological restoration under strict protection. Its existence is indicated in those early protected areas, like the Swiss National Park and the Lagodekhi State Nature Reserve, which shared a common principle of withdrawal of human influence so that there is free functioning of natural processes. Thus those protected areas set out by prohibiting hunting, logging and livestock grazing, and this also led to withdrawal of the low level, if any, of human habitation, and prevention of any new, physical development, be it roads, powerlines or buildings. These protected areas and their wilderness qualities show their importance as absolute refuges for non-human species, a place where there is a right to an undisturbed existence that is not threatened by humans, and which is the best guarantee that natural systems are being protected.

Lack of human disturbance is crucial for natural processes. At a simple level, this is exemplified by the intolerance of the greater spotted eagle to remain and breed where there is permanent human presence or activity. In more complex scale, the occurrence of typical structures of the ageing phases in old, undisturbed forests, especially dead wood, is strongly linked to a whole cascade of species that ranges through fungi, insects, bats and birds. The natural processes of the breakage, death and subsequent decay of trees is lost from managed and production forests, where silvicultural practice and harvesting mean that the older age phases of forest ecology are rarely seen.

The greatest potential for the wilderness quality of undisturbed natural processes is where there is high existing trophic diversity, or where there is the potential for it to return. In natural systems, the abundance and behaviour of species is subject to natural control mechanisms. In the absence of top predators, negative impacts arise, such as on the state of natural vegetation, the lack of restraint being felt as well in our cultural landscapes. Thus, forestry production suffers from herbivore pressure through expanding populations of deer, water vole and bark beetle. Hunters and poultry producers suffer from predation of ground nesting game birds and free-range poultry by red foxes. In natural systems, these *pests* have natural predators in the wolf, the greater spotted eagle, the three-toed woodpecker and the lynx.

The large home ranges of the bigger, free-living wild mammals outstrip the extent of even the larger protected areas, even though their density may be greater in those protected areas because of the greater resource of prey arising from restrictions on hunting. What this means is that in accepting that these larger mammals are essential to wilderness qualities, we must also be accepting their presence in the wider cultural landscape. As the large carnivores redistribute, or are reintroduced, across Europe, they will be safe inside areas protected for wilderness qualities, like the Brandenburg Foundation areas, where the presence of wolves is welcomed and there are no cultural activities that are threatened. Outside of those areas, it must be recognized that once established the evidence is that the larger carnivores preferentially seek out wild prey rather than domestic livestock. It is in that establishing phase that the strategies to mitigate their effects, and which existed before their regional extirpation, must be re-learnt.[113]

Given the large home ranges of the bigger wild mammals and their unfavourable conservation status, it is an imperative to protect a greater proportion of the wildest areas in Europe by enlarging existing protected areas to give a larger territory where there is a lack of human habitation and agriculture. Areas with wilderness quality should, however, exist throughout Europe. Thus there should be recognition that even modified landscapes be given the opportunity to undergo ecological restoration, as is happening in the ex-military training areas of Brandenburg.

The protection of wilderness qualities in Europe can be seen as an ethical imperative. However, in purely anthropocentric terms, if humans continue to over-reach in their extractive activities, then species migrating out of wilderness areas do give a capability for our modified landscapes to self-renew, to wholly regenerate and recapture natural processes. It is to be hoped that we draw back from ever having reached the stage where we have to rely on that.

[113] Linnell et al., *Guidelines for Population Level Management Plans for Large Carnivores in Europe*, *supra* note 50.

4

# Social values of wilderness in Europe

NICOLE BAUER

## 1 Introduction: different concepts of 'value'

Understanding the social values of wilderness and the benefits of wilderness to the individual and to society is important for both the designation and management of these protected areas.[1] To enable a useful discussion on this issue, it is important to first have a closer look at the meaning of the term 'value'. Examining the meaning of this term is particularly important, since it is used differently in different research disciplines. Therefore, before formulating the key questions of this chapter, this introductory section discusses the main perspectives on the term 'value' in the existing wilderness literature:

(a) In (environmental) psychology, values are defined as the criteria people use to select and justify actions and to evaluate people and events.[2] Values are more general than attitudes and are known to influence ideologies, attitudes and actions in different domains (for instance, attitudes towards wilderness and the creation of protected areas). The theory of basic human values postulates that in all societies a distinction can be drawn between ten basic values (power, achievement, hedonism, stimulation, self-direction, universalism, benevolence, tradition, conformity and security).[3] Within the basic human value of 'universalism', Schwarz and Boehnke[4] identified the subtypes 'nature concern' and 'social concern'. The subtype 'nature concern' can be described as

[1] M. Lockwood, 'Values and Benefits', in M. Lockwood, G.L. Worboys and A. Kothari (eds.), *Managing Protected Areas. A Global Guide* (Sterling, VA: Earthscan, 2006), pp. 101–115.

[2] For example, S.H. Schwartz, 'Basic Human Values: Theory, Measurement, and Applications', *Revue Francaise de Sociologie*, 47:4 (2006), 929.

[3] S.H. Schwartz, 'Universals in the Content and Structure of Values: Theory and Empirical Tests in 20 Countries', in M.P. Zanna (ed.), *Advances in Experimental Social Psychology* (New York: Academic Press, 1992), pp. 1–65.

[4] S.H. Schwartz and K. Boehnke, 'Evaluating the Structure of Human Values with Confirmatory Factor Analysis', *Journal of Research in Personality*, 38:3 (2004), 230–255.

encompassing ideas concerning 'unity with nature', 'protecting the environment' and a 'world of beauty' and can be seen as a basic human value with different dimensions. In the empirical literature on wilderness and protected areas, different synonyms are used for this basic value, such as 'human–nature relationship'. The human–nature relationship, with its different dimensions (e.g. biocentric, ecocentric, biophobic), influences the more concrete attitudes towards wilderness and the qualities assigned to wilderness. In some parts of the wilderness literature, the term 'social value' can even be seen as a synonym for 'attitudes'.

(b) In other parts of the wilderness literature, the qualities that are assigned to wilderness are referred to as 'values'.[5] Similarly, Lockwood[6] defines values as those qualities that people attach to things such as goods, activities and services and that implicitly include the person's perception, their general human values, their preferences and the context of the valuation.

(c) Additionally, in the literature on wilderness and protected areas the terms 'value' and 'benefit' are often used interchangeably. However, the existence of a benefit means that there is a recipient who gains from the presence of a value, while a value can exist without a recipient.[7] A combination of these two uses of the term 'value' can be seen in the approach of van Riper et al.,[8] who define values as the perceived qualities carried by a natural environment that provides benefits (e. g., recreational, aesthetic, spiritual) to support human well-being.

Considering the social science literature on wilderness and the designation of wilderness areas, we can summarize that the term 'value' or 'social value' has a variety of meanings in the context of wilderness: we can talk about values as (a) ideals that provide reasons for setting aside land (e.g., ecocentric value orientation, respect for nature) and that can in many cases be considered as a synonym for 'attitudes'; or (b) as qualities assigned to a certain environment (i.e., to a wilderness area) or; (c) as the possible benefits that flow from wilderness protection and their value to society.

5 T.C. Brown, 'The Concept of Value in Resource Allocation', *Land Economics*, 60 (1984), 231–246.

6 M. Lockwood, 'Humans Valuing Nature: Synthesising Insights from Philosophy, Psychology and Economics', *Environmental Values*, 8:3 (1999), 381–401.

7 Lockwood, 'Values and Benefits', *supra* note 1.

8 C.J. van Riper, G.T. Kyle, S.G. Sutton, M. Barnes and B.C. Sherrouse, 'Mapping Outdoor Recreationists' Perceived Social Values for Ecosystem Services at Hinchinbrook Island National Park, Australia', *Applied Geography*, 35:1–2 (2012), 164–173.

From these different definitions and concepts of values we can derive two key questions that centre on the two meanings of values that are most common in the literature on protected areas and wilderness.

Key question A: What does wilderness mean to society?

This question will be answered in Section 2, where we will analyse the general human–nature relationship, which provides the basis for more concrete attitudes towards wilderness. Furthermore, we will consider the change of the human–nature relationship over time, since this change is indicative of a change in human attitudes towards wilderness. When discussing this first key question, we will focus on 'values' as ideals that provide reasons for setting aside land (e.g., respect for nature) and that can in many cases be considered as a synonym for 'attitudes'.

Key question B: What benefits does wilderness provide for the individual and/or for society?

This question will be answered in Section 3. In this section we will focus on the literature on wilderness and protected areas, where values are understood as possible benefits from wilderness protection and their value to society. This meaning of 'value' is mostly covered by studies originating in the US. Hence, we would not be able to discuss this question while restricting our focus to the European literature. In the last part of this section, we discuss the possibilities of applying the value taxonomies from the US to the situation in Europe.

Based on this better understanding of the values (attitudes) and social benefits of wilderness, Section 4 focuses on the third *key question* of this chapter: *How could the assessment of social values of wilderness benefit wilderness protection?* Section 5 summarizes the discussions by providing short answers to these three key questions.

## 2 What does wilderness mean to society?

In order to answer this question, we will analyse the literature on the basic human–nature relationship, which strongly influences attitudes towards wilderness and hence the willingness to protect wilderness and wilderness areas. The international literature, including publications from Western Europe and the US, will be considered in order to gain a better understanding of the general human–nature relationship (Section 2.1); while the European literature will be examined to establish a clearer picture of the more concrete attitudes towards wilderness and wilderness-related phenomena in Europe (Section 2.2). The regional focus of Section 2.3 (changes in the human–nature relationship over time) is on both Western Europe and the US.

### *2.1 Basic value orientations, the human–nature relationship and attitudes towards nature*

There are few studies that address the relationship between the general public and nature (described by Schwartz as 'nature concern'),[9] and these studies result in typologies of value orientations that differ in respect of types, focus (e.g., the feeling towards nature or the quality of the relationship) and content.

Wilson[10] defines two elementary value orientations that focus on the feelings of humans towards nature: biophilia – the love of all that lives[11] – and its antithesis, biophobia – the tendency for people to be afraid of nature. Grendstad and Wollebaek[12] reported that eighty per cent of their respondents in Norway and Sweden acknowledged an intrinsic value of nature, i.e., have a pronounced biophiliac attitude towards nature. Stern and Dietz[13] define three basic environmental value sets that describe the relationship: the egoistic, the altruistic and the biospheric value orientations; while Thompson and Barton[14] proposed an anthropocentric attitude type, an ecocentric attitude type and an environmentally apathetic type. Kaltenborn and Bjerke[15] found that the anthropocentric value orientation correlated positively with a preference for farmlands, while the ecocentric orientation correlated with a preference for wild lands.[16,17]

[9] Schwartz, 'Basic Human Values: Theory, Measurement, and Applications', *supra* note 2.

[10] E.O. Wilson, 'Biophilia and the Conservation Ethic', in S. Kellert and E.O. Wilson (eds.), *The Biophilia Hypothesis* (Washington: Island Press, 1993), pp. 31–41.

[11] *Ibid.*

[12] G. Grendstad and D. Wollebaek, 'Greener Still? An Empirical Examination of Eckersley's Ecocentric Approach', *Environment and Behavior*, 30:5 (1998), 653–675.

[13] P.C. Stern and T. Dietz, 'The Value Basis of Environmental Concern', *Journal of Social Issues*, 50:3 (1994), 65–84.

[14] S.C.G. Thompson and M.A. Barton, 'Ecocentric and Anthropocentric Attitudes toward the Environment', *Journal of Environmental Psychology*, 14:2 (1994), 149–157.

[15] B.P. Kaltenborn and T. Bjerke, 'The Relationship of General Life Values to Attitudes Toward Large Carnivores', *Human Ecology Review*, 9:1 (2002), 55–61.

[16] See P.W. Schultz, C. Shriver, J.J. Tabanico and A.M. Khazian, 'Implicit Connections with Nature', *Journal of Environmental Psychology*, 24:1 (2004), 31–42.

[17] See J.A.A. Swart and H.J. Van Der Windt, 'Visions of Nature and Environmental Sustainability: Shellfish Harvesting in the Dutch Wadden Sea', *Restoration Ecology*, 13:1 (2005), 183–192.

Stenmark[18] defined the non-anthropocentric values 'biocentric' and 'ecocentric' as follows: people endorsing the biocentric value orientation focus on the well-being and existence of individual animals and plants, while those with the ecocentric orientation have a more holistic view and focus on the well-being of ecosystems and species. Additionally, the different value orientations correlate with different beliefs (for instance, about the resilience and fragility of nature).

Some other studies propose a more differentiated value set. Especially relevant within our context is the typology of Kellert. On the basis of a questionnaire survey concerning attitudes towards wildlife,[19,20] Kellert makes assumptions concerning the general human–nature relationship and describes a human–nature relationship with nine dimensions: (1) the utilitarian dimension (the material value of nature is important); (2) the naturalistic dimension (nature is regarded with wonder and awe); (3) the ecological scientific dimension (nature is investigated systematically); (4) the aesthetic dimension (the beauty of nature is paramount); (5) the symbolic dimension (nature is a source of symbols); (6) the humanistic dimension (humans feel emotionally connected to nature); (7) the moralistic dimension (humans feel responsible for nature); (8) the dominating dimension (humans master the natural world); and (9) the negative dimension (humans view nature with fear and aversion).

In these dimensions, the concepts of biophilia and its converse, biophobia, are clearly apparent, although not all of Kellert's dimensions can be assigned to the two concepts. The dimensions reflect the tendency to consider specific values as being especially relevant and the human–nature relationship of a person can be described by more than one of the dimensions.

## 'Images of nature' and main concepts of the human–nature relationship

In the Netherlands there is a long tradition of analysing the 'images' or 'visions of nature', a concept that can be seen as indicative of the

[18] M. Stenmark, *Environmental Ethics and Policy-Making* (Uppsala: Uppsala University, Department of Theology, 2002).

[19] S.R. Kellert, 'Contemporary Values of Wildlife in American Society. Institutional Series Report Nr. 1' in W.W. Shaw and E.H. Zube (eds.), *Wildlife Values. Center for Assessment of Noncommodity Natural Resource Values* (Tucson: University of Arizona, 1980), pp. 241–267.

[20] S.R. Kellert, 'The Biological Basis for Human Values of Nature' in S.R. Kellert and O. Wilson (eds.), *The Biophilia Hypothesis* (Washington: Island Press, 1993), pp. 42–69.

properties and the condition of the human–nature relationship. In a study conducted by van den Born, Lenders, De Groot and Huijsman,[21] six different images of nature were identified and most respondents perceived the wild nature as being more natural than the Arcadian nature, which is strongly influenced by humans. De Groot and van den Born[22] found identical results in a similar study with another sample of respondents.

In the study of van den Born et al.,[23] seventy-two per cent of the respondents considered nature to have a value of its own, irrespective of its use for humans, a tendency that can be interpreted as indication of a clearly biophiliac attitude towards nature.

Studies of De Groot and van den Born,[24] De Groot, Drenthen and de Groot,[25] and Van den Born[26] revealed four major concepts of the human–nature relationship: (a) humans seen as adventurers and exploiters of nature, a concept with a clearly anthropocentric value orientation; (b) humans as responsible for nature, including the images of man as steward and guardian, and the image of man as partner, a concept with aspects of the anthropocentric as well as of the ecocentric value orientation; (c) humans as partners of nature; and (d) humans as participants in nature. The two latter concepts have a clear ecocentric value orientation. They differ, however, concerning freedom of choice: the partner acknowledges a free choice to collaborate with nature, while the participant considers himself part of nature and feels thereby obliged to respect the rules of nature. The level of adherence to the responsibility and the participant images was very high and can be seen as an indicator for the dominance of the ecocentric value orientation in the general population.

[21] R.J.G. van den Born, R.H.J. Lenders, W.T. de Groot and E. Huijsman, 'The New Biophilia: An Exploration of Visions of Nature in Western Countries', *Environmental Conservation*, 28:01 (2001), 65–75.

[22] W.T. de Groot and R.J.G. van den Born, 'Visions of Nature and Landscape Type Preferences: An exploration in The Netherlands', *Landscape and Urban Planning*, 63:3 (2003), 127–138.

[23] Van den Born et al., 'The New Biophilia: An Exploration of Visions of Nature in Western Countries', *supra* note 21.

[24] De Groot et al., 'Visions of Nature and Landscape Type Preferences: An Exploration in The Netherlands', *supra* note 22.

[25] M. de Groot, M. Drenthen and W.T. de Groot, 'Public Visions on the Human/Nature Relationship and Their Implications for Environmental Ethics', *Environmental Ethics*, 33:1 (2011), 25–44.

[26] R.J.G. van den Born, *Thinking Nature. Everyday Philosophy of Nature in the Netherlands*, dissertation (Nijmegen: Radboud Universiteit, 2007).

Another series of studies in the Netherlands by a different group of authors found similar images of nature. In a literature review in France and the Netherlands, Buijs, Pedroli and Luginbühl[27] found three main images of nature: the Arcadian image, the wilderness image and the functional image. The authors stressed that different functional ties to landscape were the most important reasons for differences in images between different social groups. In a study using a quantitative survey to investigate the human–nature relationship of immigrants from Islamic countries and native Dutch people, Buijs, Elands and Langers[28] identified a set of three slightly different nature images: (a) the wilderness image, focussing on ecocentric values and on the independence of nature; (b) the functional image, a concept with an anthropocentric value orientation, in line with the intensive management of nature; and (c) the inclusive image, with an ecocentric value orientation and defined by an intimate relationship between humans and nature. Interestingly, the majority of the native Dutch respondents supported the wilderness image, while forty-four per cent of the immigrant respondents endorsed the functional image.

In a qualitative study based on semi-structured interviews with fifty-nine individuals, Buijs[29] found five different images of nature: the wilderness image, the autonomy image, the inclusive image, the aesthetic image and the functional image. The ecocentric, biocentric and anthropocentric value orientations were found to be relevant for these five images.[30] The different nature images also correlated with the perception of nature as fragile or resilient, as well as with different levels of management (hands off, limited management, hands on) and different management goals. The wilderness image was characterized by an underlying ecocentric value orientation, combined with the perception of nature as being resilient and with adherence to the hands off approach to management.

[27] A.E. Buijs, B. Pedroli and Y. Luginbühl, 'From Hiking through Farmland to Farming in a Leisure Landscape: Changing Social Perceptions of the European Landscape', *Landscape Ecology*, 21:3 (2006), 375–389.

[28] A.E. Buijs, B.H.M. Elands and F. Langers, 'No Wilderness for Immigrants: Cultural Differences in Images of Nature and Landscape Preferences', *Landscape and Urban Planning*, 91:3 (2009), 113–123.

[29] A. Buijs, *Public Natures: Social Representations of Nature and Local Practices* (Wageningen: Wageningen University, 2009).

[30] See Stenmark, *Environmental Ethics and Policy-Making*, *supra* note 18.

### Nature lovers, nature sympathisers, nature connected users and nature controllers

Outside of the Netherlands, there have been few European studies on the human–nature relationship. One such study took place in Switzerland, where Bauer, Wallner and Hunziker[31] analysed general attitudes towards nature. Through a cluster analysis of survey data, these authors produced a typology which describes four general attitudes towards nature: (a) nature lovers; (b) nature sympathizers; (c) nature connected users; and (d) nature controllers. The majority of respondents in this study showed clear biophiliac tendencies, with nature lovers accounting for thirty-one per cent of the sample and nature connected users accounting for twenty-seven per cent. Nature sympathizers, who have an emotionally distanced attitude towards nature, show aspects of a biophiliac tendency as well as aspects of biophobia, while nature controllers have a pronounced biophobic attitude towards nature. Using Stenmark's terminology,[32] nature controllers can be considered to have an anthropocentric value orientation, nature lovers an ecocentric value orientation and nature connected users a biocentric value orientation with anthropocentric aspects. Nature sympathizers appear to display what Thompson and Barton[33] describe as 'environmental apathy', an attitude type that has not been further investigated until now.

### Overall picture: Nature-friendly relationship and prevalence of the wilderness image

In general we can say that, although the studies described above used different quantitative and qualitative methods, included different samples and took place in different regions (some having been conducted in Western Europe and others in the US), there is a surprising commonality in the nature images identified in this kind of research. We can consider the wilderness image, the Arcadian image and the functional image as key images, while the anthropocentric, ecocentric, biocentric/biophiliac and biophobic value orientations can be considered as the main underlying value orientations, which will also be of relevance for more concrete attitudes towards wilderness.

[31] N. Bauer, A. Wallner and M. Hunziker, 'The Change of European Landscapes: Human-Nature Relationships, Public Attitudes towards Rewilding, and the Implications for Landscape Management', *Journal of Environmental Management*, 90 (2009), 2910–2920.

[32] Stenmark, *Environmental Ethics and Policy-Making*, *supra* note 18.

[33] Thompson et al., 'Ecocentric and Anthropocentric Attitudes toward the Environment', *supra* note 14.

Most of the studies reveal that humans have a nature-friendly relationship, expressed either in an ecocentric, biocentric or biophiliac value orientation. Furthermore, many studies reveal the presence and strong endorsement of a wilderness image in the general population. This means that the idea of unmanaged nature is both present and appreciated amongst the general public.

This is a good starting point for wilderness protection, as the positive attitude towards nature (seen, for instance, in the biophiliac value orientation) and the positive evaluation of the wilderness image can be considered as preconditions for a positive relation to wilderness, as well as for wilderness protection.

### *2.2 Attitudes towards wilderness in Europe*

While Section 2.1 analysed the human–nature relationship in general, this section will summarize the most important publications on attitudes towards wilderness specifically. Among the different kinds of studies dealing with wilderness, those on landscape preferences and the attitudes towards wilderness and rewilding are especially important for this book. Due to differences between the physical conditions of the US and Europe (in particular, the size of wilderness areas and their remoteness in the US), results from the US cannot be compared and generalized to the situation in Europe. This section will consequently focus on the relatively few empirical studies which have been conducted within Europe.

#### Preferences for wild landscapes

Some studies have analysed the landscape preferences of laypeople, with such preferences being indicative of attitudes towards wilderness.

In a study in the Netherlands, De Groot and van den Born[34] found that the respondents differentiated between the following four landscape types: (1) landscape made for and by people; (2) Arcadian landscape (meaning a cultivated park-like landscape); (3) wild landscape; and (4) landscape in which one may experience 'the greatness and force of nature'. Surprisingly, fifty-one per cent of the respondents preferred the landscape in which they could experience the greatness and force of nature and thirty-one per cent preferred the wild, untamed landscape, while only thirteen per cent endorsed the park-like Arcadian landscape

[34] De Groot et al., 'Visions of Nature and Landscape Type Preferences: An exploration in The Netherlands', *supra* note 22.

and four per cent the man-made landscape. These results can be interpreted as indicating a certain open-mindedness in favour of wilderness and untamed landscapes.

The study of Buijs, Elands and Langers[35] indicates that there are differences between not only the nature images, but also the landscape preferences of immigrants and native Dutch. In contrast to the preference ratings of the native Dutch, the immigrants showed very low preferences for wild landscapes. While the native Dutch respondents considered natural landscapes to be beautiful, naturalness did not equate with beauty for the immigrants. A reason for these differences might be seen in the culturally determined differences in nature experiences. The study of Van den Born et al.[36] revealed that intensive nature experiences in childhood might lead one to perceive wild nature as being natural. Respondents who had no intensive nature experiences during childhood perceived Arcadian nature to be more natural.

Several investigations have found that landscape preferences are different for different social groups.[37] In the study of Hunziker, Felber, Gehring et al.,[38] four future landscape development scenarios in the Alps were assessed by locals, tourists, the general Swiss population and experts. The wilderness scenario (reforestation) was rated much more positively by the tourists and the general, unaffected public than by the local inhabitants. Van den Berg and Koole[39] found that the development of wild nature was assessed less positively in forested areas than in open, rural areas. Furthermore, the socio-demographic variables (such as age, place of residence, farming background and recreational motives) were important predictors of individuals' preferences for wild or managed nature.

From these studies we can conclude that people who are not affected by wilderness or rewilding in their professional or recreational activities

[35] Buijs et al., 'No Wilderness for Immigrants: Cultural Differences in Images of Nature and Landscape Preferences', *supra* note 28.

[36] Van den Born et al., 'The New Biophilia: An Exploration of Visions of Nature in Western Countries', *supra* note 21.

[37] See e.g., A.E. Stamps, 'Demographic Effects in Environmental Aesthetics: A Meta-analysis', *Journal of Planning Literature*, 14:2 (1999), 155–175.

[38] M. Hunziker, P. Felber, K. Gehring, M. Buchecker, N. Bauer and F. Kienast, 'Evaluation of Landscape Change by Different Social Groups. Results of Two Empirical Studies in Switzerland', *Mountain Research and Development*, 28:2 (2008), 140–147.

[39] A.E. Van den Berg and S.L. Koole, 'New Wilderness in the Netherlands: An Investigation of Visual Preferences for Nature Development Landscapes', *Landscape and Urban Planning*, 78:4 (2006), 362–372.

and those who do not consider wilderness as something new (as they grew up in another culture or are elderly and grew up with the ideal of an Arcadian nature) are more positive about it.

## Attitudes towards rewilding and wilderness

Although there are not many studies on attitudes towards formerly cultivated lands becoming wild, there are some studies analysing related phenomena, such as spontaneous regrowth of forest[40] and dead wood as an important attribute of unmanaged forests.[41]

In a study focussing on the perception of old-field succession, which took place in the central Alpine part of Switzerland (a region with an increasing amount of abandoned land), Hunziker[42] found that most people (locals as well as visiting tourists) experience spontaneous reforestation in an ambivalent way and prefer partially reforested landscapes with a high diversity. If the resulting forest patches become too big, a negative assessment can be expected.

Stelzig[43] analysed the attitudes towards dead wood in three German forest national parks and found that only fifteen per cent of the respondents were opposed to areas with dead wood in the forest, while eighty-eight per cent were in favour of leaving the dead wood in the forest. However, fifty-four per cent of respondents reported feelings of sadness when seeing a forest with a high amount of dead wood, as they (ignoring the ecological relevance of dead wood) considered this to be a damaged forest. Very similar results were found in the Swiss National Park.[44] Most of the visitors were in favour of dead wood. When dead wood was assessed in a negative way, the respondents considered dead wood as damage (such thinking being indicative of a lack of information) or as a waste of raw materials, or they expected that a National park should be managed and maintained. Some more recent studies also report on the

[40] See e.g. M. Hunziker, 'The Spontaneous Reafforestation in Abandoned Agricultural Lands: Perception and Aesthetic Assessment by Locals and Tourists', *Landscape and Urban Planning*, 31:1–3 (1995), 399–410.

[41] See e.g. I. Stelzig, 'Zur Akzeptanz von Totholz in deutschen Wald-Nationalparken', in G. Trommer and I. Stelzig (eds.), *Naturbildung und Naturakzeptanz. Beiträge zur biologischen Froschung* (Frankfurt: Shaker-Verlag, 2000), pp. 117–123.

[42] Hunziker 'The Spontaneous Reafforestation in Abandoned Agricultural Lands: Perception and Aesthetic Assessment by Locals and Tourists', *supra* note 40.

[43] Stelzig 'Zur Akzeptanz von Totholz in deutschen Wald-Nationalparken', *supra* note 41.

[44] M. Hunziker, 'Totholz in den Nationalparkwäldern: Störfaktor oder Attraktion? Ergebnisse einer sozialwissenschaftlichen Studie', *Cratschla*, 2 (1997), 2–8.

positive assessment of dead wood[45] and Lupp, Höchtl and Wende[46] stress that dead wood has even become an important feature of naturally managed forests. According to them, the negative perception of dead wood is limited to large segments of forest, such as the decaying forest stands in the Bavarian National Park, which have been affected by the bark beetle. Müller and Job[47] report that respondents with a low social status and higher age are especially associated with negative assessments of the non-interventionist forest management strategies that have resulted in the large decaying forest stands in this national park.

Höchtl, Lehringer and Konold[48] analysed attitudes towards both wilderness in Italy's Val Grande National Park, and the rewilding of the landscape in the Val Grande region outside the park. The respondents – locals from the region of the Val Grande Park – perceived the change of the landscape (the rewilding of formerly cultivated areas) as negative, but evaluated the wilderness in the National Park itself positively. The reason for the negative evaluation of the unintended landscape change outside the park was hypothesized to be the loss of the familiar landscape of former times, which was linked to the personal history of the respondents.

A more general study of attitudes towards wilderness was conducted in Switzerland.[49,50] In a quantitative survey of the Swiss population the authors found four different types of human–nature relationship (the 'nature-connected users', the 'nature controllers', the 'nature sympathizers' and the 'nature lovers'), with different attitudes towards wilderness

45 G. Lupp and W. Konold, 'Landscape Perceptions and Preferences of both Residents and Tourists: A Case Study in the Müritz National Park (Germany)', in D. Siegrist, C. Clivaz, M. Hunziker and S. Iten (eds.), *Visitor Management in Nature-based Tourism – Strategies and Success Factors for Parks and Recreational Areas* (Rapperswil: Series of the Institute of Landscape and Open Space. HSR University of Applied Sciences Rapperswil 2, 2008), pp. 47–58.

46 G. Lupp, F. Höchtl and W. Wende '"Wilderness" – A Designation for Central European Landscapes?', *Land Use Policy*, 28 (2011), 594–603.

47 M. Müller and H. Job 'Managing Natural Disturbance in Protected Areas: Toursists' Attitudes towards the Bark Beetle in a German National Park', *Biological Conservation*, 142 (2009), 375–383.

48 F. Höchtl, S. Lehringer and W. Konold, *Kulturlandschaft oder Wildnis in den Alpen? Fallstudien im Val Grande-Nationalpark und im Stronatal (Piemont/Italien)* (Zürich, Bern, Stuttgart, Wien: Haupt Verlag, 2005).

49 N. Bauer, *Für und wider Wildnis - Soziale Dimensionen einer aktuellen gesellschaftlichen Debatte* (Bern: Haupt, 2005).

50 Bauer et al., 'The Change of European Landscapes: Human-Nature Relationships, Public Attitudes towards Rewilding, and the Implications for Landscape Management', *supra* note 31.

and rewilding allowing a rough classification of the sample into wilderness opponents (fifty-one per cent) and wilderness proponents (forty-nine per cent). While the 'nature-connected users' (twenty-seven point three per cent of the sample) and the 'nature controllers' (twenty-two point eight per cent of the sample) evaluate wilderness in a negative way, the 'nature sympathizers' (eighteen point two per cent of the sample) and the 'nature lovers' (thirty-one point seven per cent of the sample) evaluate it positively. These four human–nature relationship types have different reasons for endorsing or being opposed to wilderness: the 'nature-connected users' feel threatened by the rewilding of nature and the 'nature controllers' regard the wilderness spread with contempt. However, both the opponents and the proponents agree on many of the rules and regulations that should apply in future wilderness areas.

The studies investigating public attitudes towards wilderness, rewilding and the phenomena that are linked to wilderness, such as dead wood and spontaneous reforestation, are not quite as positive as those dealing with the more general human–nature relationship. In many cases the assessment of wilderness is ambivalent and reasons for being opposed to wilderness are either aesthetic reasons,[51] feelings of fear and loss of control, or the lack of fascination for untamed nature.[52]

### 2.3 *Shift of the human–nature relationship over time*

In order to make reliable statements about the change of attitudes towards wilderness, a monitoring of wilderness attitudes would be needed. No such studies have yet been conducted in Europe. Therefore, we have to compare older studies on the human–nature relationship with more recent ones that have used similar methods. In the study by De Groot and van den Born,[53] the high level of adherence to the responsibility and participant images was interpreted as being indicative of a new biophilia – in other words, a new cultural phase of Western societies, succeeding the phases of nature's conquest and domestication.

[51] See e.g., Hunziker 'The Spontaneous Reafforestation in Abandoned Agricultural Lands: Perception and Aesthetic Assessment by Locals and Tourists', *supra* note 40.

[52] Bauer et al., 'The Change of European Landscapes: Human-Nature Relationships, Public Attitudes towards Rewilding, and the Implications for Landscape Management', *supra* note 31.

[53] De Groot et al., 'Visions of Nature and Landscape Type Preferences: An Exploration in The Netherlands', *supra* note 22.

A study in Switzerland monitored attitudes towards forests and forest development in 1997 and in 2010, respectively,[54] using the same questions for both questionnaires. Interestingly, the number of respondents opposed to protected forest areas which cannot be used economically dropped from twenty-nine per cent in 1997 to twenty-one per cent in 2010, while the number of respondents in favour of such areas dropped from sixty-seven per cent in 1997 to sixty per cent in 2010. However, the number of indifferent people (these being respondents who had no specific opinion concerning nature reserves) increased from four to nineteen per cent. This result could be interpreted as an indicator of a more pronounced environmental apathy, and future investigations will have to explore whether this is a persisting societal trend. Furthermore, the results showed that the majority of respondents were still in favour of protected forest areas which cannot be used economically. A study from the US comparing the wilderness values from 1994 with those from 2000 assumes that there have been some important changes in attitudes: wilderness was considered to be more important in 2000 than in 1994, and the authors observed a shift in emphasis from use values to non-use values.[55] These could be interpreted as indicators of a shift in the relevance of different values assigned to wilderness.

The results of the articles and studies analysing attitude changes over time seem to be mixed: on the one hand, there are some indications that wilderness is evaluated more positively, or perceived as more important, than used to be the case and that the human–nature relationship might have shifted slightly towards a more ecocentric value orientation. On the other hand, there are indications that the environmental apathy type[56] has increased in number. None of the cited studies found any indication that the human–nature relationship has moved towards a more anthropocentric value orientation and that wilderness is now evaluated more negatively than before. In general we can conclude from the few studies dealing with changes in the human–nature relationship that there is a high probability that attitudes towards nature, and especially towards

[54] M. Hunziker, E. von Lindern, N. Bauer and J. Frick, *Das Verhältnis der Schweizer Bevölkerung zum Wald. Waldmonitoring soziokulturell: Weiterentwicklung und zweite Erhebung – WaMos 2* (Birmensdorf: Eidg. Forschungsanstalt für Wald, Schnee und Landschaft WSL, 2012).

[55] H.K. Cordell, M.A. Tarrant and G.T. Green, 'Is the Public Viewpoint of Wilderness Shifting?', *International Journal of Wilderness*, 9 (2003), 27–32.

[56] Thompson et al., 'Ecocentric and Anthropocentric Attitudes toward the Environment', *supra* note 14.

wilderness or unmanaged landscapes, have improved slightly over the last two decades.

## 3 What benefits does wilderness provide for the individual or/and for society?

In this section we focus on 'values' defined as possible benefits that flow from wilderness and wilderness protection to the individual and to society. The values listed in the taxonomies below are very similar to those found in the literature about the economic value of wilderness. Due to this connection to the economic valuation of wilderness, we will refer to Figure 5.1 and will classify the social benefits described here by using the classifications of wilderness value that are common in ecological economics (see N. Lienhoop and B. Hansjürgens in this volume). From Figure 5.1 it is clear that not all of these values are use-related. Especially for wilderness, there are many non-use values. We can thus generally differentiate between (a) use values, which can be divided into direct use values, indirect use values and option values; and (b) non-use values, which include option values, bequest values and existence values. Some examples from these categories are listed below.

### Typologies of wilderness values

The European literature on wilderness usually does not analyse the different consequences of wilderness for the society or for the individual. However, in the US there are numerous articles and book chapters proposing different classifications of 'wilderness values', defined as benefits that wilderness provides for the individual and for society. The wilderness values are considered as a basis for sound decision-making regarding wilderness policy, and the explicit mention, listing and ranking of wilderness values during the designation process can be seen as a way to integrate these more intangible values into wilderness planning. As many of the taxonomies are based on surveys during the planning processes, they provide an overview of the values that are seen as relevant either by lay people or by managers.

According to the National Survey on Recreation and the Environment,[57,58] the most important benefits of wilderness are: (1) protecting

[57] H.K. Cordell, J.K. Bergstrom and J.M. Bowker, *The Multiple Values of Wilderness* (State College PA: Venture Publishing, 2005).

[58] H.K. Cordell, C.J. Beltz and G.T. Green, 'Nature-Based Outdoor Recreation Trends and Wilderness', *International Journal of Wilderness*, 14 (2008), 7–9.

air quality and (2) protecting water quality (both can be classified as indirect use values, see Figure 5.1); (3) protecting wildlife habitat (this can be classified as an option value or existence value and belongs to the non-use values); (4) protecting unique wild plant and animal species (option values or existence values); and (5) bequest to future generations – in other words, the belief that wilderness should be protected for future generations (the bequest value is part of the non-use values, see Figure 5.1). Most Americans considered six additional wilderness-related benefits as important:[59] (1) scenic beauty of wild landscapes (direct use value); (2) the knowledge that wilderness is being protected (existence value); (3) the option value, based on the possibility of visiting wilderness at some future time (use and non-use option value); (4) the opportunity for wilderness recreation experiences (direct-use value); and (5) preserving nature for research and spiritual inspiration (direct-use value). Schuster, Tarrant and Watson[60] present a taxonomy of fourteen social non-material values based on a literature review of the US wilderness literature. Their taxonomy of values is grouped into four different domains: (a) the self-centred values, which include character building, therapeutic means, personal well-being and self-enlightenment; (b) the societal values, including educational, spiritual, family and social values, citizenship, and historical and cultural values; (c) the human values, including aesthetic, artistic and epistemological values; and (d) the vehicles for acquiring values, including recreation, leisure and research. Using the terminology of ecological economics, these values can be classified as (non-consumptive) direct use values.

These lists of values originate in the US, where the history of wilderness protection (see Chapter 3 by Mark Fisher) as well as the size and remoteness of the wilderness areas are very different from the situation in Europe. The attitudes towards wilderness and wilderness areas are influenced by this history and these characteristics However, in contrast to the attitudes, the values that are defined as (non-material) benefits of wilderness to the individual and the society and that are listed in the taxonomies are rather general and seem to be widely independent from the size and remoteness of wilderness areas. Furthermore, these taxonomies of values are not meant to display a hierarchical order of values and make no assumptions concerning the relative or absolute weight or relevance of individual benefits. Therefore, it is possible to generalize the taxonomies of social

[59] Cordell et al., *The Multiple Values of Wilderness, supra* note 57.
[60] *Supra:* R.M. Schuster et al. (2003).

values of wilderness, i.e., a list of different values such as those mentioned above originating in the US to the situation in Europe. But it is of course not possible to generalize the results of empirical research in relation with these taxonomies of values (e.g., the assessment of the importance of the different values for the population) from the US to Europe. As there is no empirical research in Europe that assesses the social values of wilderness it is not possible, e.g., to make assumptions about the relevance of the different wilderness values. A taxonomy based on studies in the US could, however, be the starting point for similar research in Europe.

## 4 How could the assessment of social values of wilderness benefit wilderness protection?

While the former sections of this chapter provided an overview of the main attitudes towards wilderness and the various types of benefits of wilderness for the individual and society (as perceived by lay people and managers), this section focuses on the benefits of the assessment of wilderness attitudes and social benefits of wilderness during the process of designating wilderness areas. Generally, the feasibility of the designation of a wilderness area, as well as the effectiveness of the protection of a wilderness area, will increase if the attitudes towards wilderness within local society are positive and the social benefits of wilderness are being acknowledged. However, it should be noted that a case-by-case approach is important. Since the social values of wilderness and the attitudes towards wilderness differ between different countries, and even between different regions within countries, they have to be assessed in more detail and in a case-specific manner for every (prospective) wilderness area.

What could be done to actively influence attitudes towards wilderness (for instance, attitudes regarding the designation of areas as protected wilderness areas)? If, during the process of designating a wilderness area or another protected area, an assessment of attitudes and values showed a generally positive view towards wilderness, these positive attitudes could be strengthened through information campaigns (such as those often used by environmental NGOs), communicating the benefits of wilderness areas for individuals and society. In the case of negative attitudes, however, such a campaign would not be an appropriate way to influence the attitudes of people opposed to wilderness.[61] In order to change

[61] R.E. Petty and J.T. Cacioppo, *Communication and Persuasion – Central and Peripheral Routes to Attitude Change* (New York: Academic Press, 1986).

negative attitudes towards wilderness, it would instead be advisable to initialize campaigns using role models (well-known politicians, actors, sportsmen, etc.), who communicate their dedication to wilderness. This illustrates that a detailed assessment of attitudes and values regarding wilderness may prevent governments, park managers or NGOs from choosing an inappropriate campaign that might endanger the success of a wilderness area's designation.

In order to integrate the different attitudes towards wilderness into the process of designating wilderness areas, all stakeholders, and especially the inhabitants of the nearest communities, should be included in a participatory process.[62] At the start of the designation process, it is advisable to undertake a thorough assessment of the values and the more specific attitudes of all involved persons towards nature and rewilding. It is further advisable to use the available data to identify well-defined target groups – an approach that would also enable specific interventions and management actions to be customized to the characteristics of each of these groups. Furthermore, the results of a survey could also show possible commonalities between the opponents and proponents of a wilderness area. Such commonalities could be used as a starting point for the participatory designation of wilderness areas.[63]

Knowing and understanding the attitudes towards wilderness and the benefits that are expected from wilderness areas can also help to handle different views of stakeholders in relation to the management objectives and use of wilderness areas[64] and will help to minimize conflicts and maximize the use of wilderness areas in conformity with these objectives.[65] Of course, the management of existing wilderness areas may also profit from the assessment of attitudes towards wilderness and of the perceived benefits of wilderness. In existing wilderness areas, different groups of people may have competing demands, and such assessments may enable the manager to adapt his or her activities and communications to the needs and expectations of the public.

[62] A. Schenk, M. Hunziker and F. Kienast, 'Factors Influencing the Acceptance of Nature Conservation Measures – A Qualitative Study in Switzerland', *Journal of Environmental Management*, 83:1 (2007), 66–79.

[63] U. Wiesmann, K. Liechti and S. Rist, 'Between Conservation and Development: Concretizing the First World Natural Heritage Site in the Alps through Participatory Processes', *Mountain Research and Development*, 25:2 (2005), 128–138.

[64] Petty and Cacioppo, 'Communication and Persuasion – Central and Peripheral Routes to Attitude Change', *supra* note 61.

[65] I.R. Hunter, 'What Do People Want from Urban Forestry? The European Experience', *Urban Ecosystems*, 5:4 (2003), 277–284.

## 5 Conclusions

To conclude this chapter on the social values of wilderness in Europe, the key questions formulated in the chapter's introduction may receive the following answers:

What does wilderness mean to society?

From the literature review in Section 2, we may conclude that the general human–nature relationship is the basis for more concrete attitudes towards wilderness, which may be seen as a special type of nature. In general, Europeans are found to have a nature friendly attitude. Basic values, such as 'nature concern' or, more generally speaking, the human–nature relationship, provide the basic motivation to establish protected areas, such as wilderness areas, and give direction to their management. The more concrete attitudes towards wilderness are often more ambivalent. The reasons for a relatively negative evaluation of wilderness are often either aesthetic reasons or feelings of fear and loss of control, or a perceived loss of familiar landscapes. However, in Europe we notice indications of a change in the attitudes towards wilderness or wilderness-related phenomena, meaning that we can expect the attitudes towards wilderness to be more positive in the future.

What benefits does wilderness provide for the individual or/and for society?

Apart from the attitudes towards wilderness, there are possible benefits that flow from wilderness and wilderness protection to the individual and to society. As will be discussed in more detail in Chapter 5, the literature differentiates between a) use values, which can be divided into direct use values, indirect use values and option values; and b) non-use values, which include option values, bequest values and existence values. These taxonomies of values are based on surveys administered to lay people and authorities during wilderness planning processes in the US. As they are quite general and seem to be independent from the size and remoteness of wilderness areas, we can generalize them to the situation in Europe. An important advantage of these taxonomies is that the explicit listing of wilderness values during the designation process can be seen as a way to integrate these more intangible values of wilderness into wilderness planning.

### How could the assessment of attitudes and social values regarding wilderness benefit wilderness protection?

The general literature review on the attitudes towards wilderness and the perceived social benefits of wilderness is a valuable starting point, as it indicates the topics that may be important to consider in more detail during the designation of new wilderness areas or the management of existing ones. However, these general surveys cannot replace a more detailed and specific assessment of the human–nature relationship, the attitudes towards wilderness and the social benefits of wilderness in the regions with (prospective) wilderness areas. These more specific assessments are important for stimulating positive attitudes towards wilderness prior to designation, as well as for preventing conflicts in relation to the management of new and existing wilderness areas. The assessment of these attitudes and social benefits could well be combined with economic valuation – the central topic of the next chapter – in order to obtain an even more complete picture of the value of wilderness to society.

# 5

# Economic values of wilderness in Europe

NELE LIENHOOP AND BERND HANSJÜRGENS

## 1 Wilderness protection from an economic viewpoint

On first sight, wilderness protection and economics have nothing to do with each other. Here: nature, the diversity of species and remote areas; there: the economy, profit-maximizing behaviour, money and the financial crisis. Here: the beauty and the wilderness that people regard highly; there: the cold, artificial world of business and bankers, which many consider to be necessary because it guarantees our (economic) welfare, but is nevertheless unloved.

However, when one considers what economics is really about, this perspective cannot be sustained. Economics is not merely the business sector or the world of profits. According to the classical definition by Robbins (1932),[1] economics is the science of scarcity – it is based on the fact that there is less available than people want. All means of the world are scarce – not only the money in people's wallets and the goods that can be bought with it, but also other things, such as natural resources or beautiful landscapes. Scarcity is an all-compassing, ubiquitous and timeless problem.

It is important to note that both the environment and the services that it delivers to humans are becoming increasingly scarce: Species become extinct, their number and diversity are reduced, and wilderness is decreasing. Due to the increasing human footprint, there are hardly any resorts of pristine landscapes and wilderness areas left. The degradation and over-use of the environment is ongoing so that, ultimately, the basis for human well-being is affected.[2] With the decrease in wilderness

[1] L. Robbins, *An Essay on the Nature and Significance of Economic Science* (London: Macmillan, 1932).

[2] World Resource Institute, *Millennium Ecosystem Assessment*, 'Ecosystems and Human Well-being: Biodiversity Synthesis' (Washington: World Resources Institute, 2005).

areas, habitats, landscapes and (ecosystem) services that are beneficial for humans will be lost.[3]

While economic thinking and scarcity considerations are common in day-to-day decisions in the commercial realm, where goods and services are bought and sold on markets, such an approach is less common in decisions that concern nature or its (ecosystem) services. One reason is that people (at least in Western countries) are used to trade commodities on markets, and for nature no such markets exist.[4] Nature and its services are often public goods in the sense that there is non-rivalry in consumption (if A enjoys wilderness, B's benefits are not reduced) and non-excludability (it is impossible, or very expensive, to exclude a person from enjoying wilderness). However, if markets for these 'goods' do not exist, it follows that there is also no (market) mechanism that reflects scarcity, i.e., there is no price increase that signals an increase in scarcity. The consequence is that nature is neglected in decision-making and natural resources are over-exploited. Thus, the decline of wilderness areas can be explained economically: there are no markets, scarcity is not made explicit, and people use wilderness areas for free.[5]

The economic approach provides guidance on how best to handle such scarcity situations – its experiences and methods can be used to ensure a wise use of scarce resources. Economics places decisions – i.e., regarding the future use of wilderness areas – on systematic grounds by valuing and comparing all the advantages (benefits) and disadvantages (costs) of a certain option. Every option is characterized by so-called 'opportunity costs', meaning that, for every option we choose, we have to give something up. For example, the plan to build new roads or to undertake logging activities in a wilderness area would mean that the area would no longer provide the same level of wildlife habitat or other services, such as water regulation or micro-climate. On the other hand, strictly protecting wilderness would mean restricted access opportunities (e.g., for motorized vehicles or cyclists). The role of economics is to make the

[3] A.S. Mather and K. Chapman, *Environmental Resources* (Essex: Longman, 1995).

[4] In recent decades, markets have been established at various levels of governance to regulate the use of certain components of nature, based on a recognition of increased scarcity. These include, first of all, rights to release greenhouse gases into the atmosphere, but also water rights, habitat trading, etc.

[5] N. Hanley, J.F. Shogren and B. White, *Introduction to Environmental Economics* (Oxford: Oxford University Press, 2001); P. Morton, 'Wildland Economics: Theory and Practice', in F.S. McCool, D.N. Cole, W.T. Borrie and J. O'Loughlin (eds.), *Wilderness Science in a Time of Change Conference – Volume 2: Wilderness within the Context of Larger Systems* (Missoula: USDA Forest Service – RMRS, 2000), pp. 238–250.

inevitability of this dilemma explicit. It makes clear that nothing is for free. The economic perspective ensures that the costs of planned actions are not ignored in decision-making, and it thus counters one-sided and biased decisions.[6]

Economic thinking could be useful for wilderness protection because it encourages people to use wilderness resources sparingly and draws our attention to the fact that these resources are scarce. It further contributes to human well-being, because it attempts to safeguard and acknowledge wilderness aspects that might be of importance to society (see also Nicole Bauer, in this volume). The value that society attaches to wilderness provides an indication of its scarcity, and this information should be used to adjust private and public decisions. In order to prevent the decrease in wilderness areas, it is important to make the opportunity costs (i.e., reduction in aesthetic landscapes, habitats and recreation) of wilderness loss visible. It needs to be made explicit what the implications for society's well-being (note that this is an anthropocentric view) will be if wilderness areas are further degraded or disappear. In other words: the foremost role of economics in wilderness protection is to make the values of wilderness and the costs associated with protection measures explicit and incorporate them in decision-making.

## 2 Economic valuation of wilderness

### *2.1 Why is wilderness valuable?*

So far, it has been discussed that many goods and services provided by wilderness are public and are not traded in conventional markets, and therefore have no price. Hence, when developments are planned that have negative impacts on wilderness (e.g., building roads or using pristine areas for agriculture), the damage caused is of less importance to decision-makers, because they do not have to pay for it. At the same time, the general public can use wilderness in most cases for free (e.g., they do not have to pay for undertaking recreational activities in wilderness areas). This section explains why wilderness is valuable to society – despite the absence of prices – and how economics can contribute to the assessment of wilderness.

Different stakeholders and people consider wilderness valuable because they benefit from the different goods and services that wilderness provides. Since wilderness offers hardly any material or marketed goods

[6] *Ibid.* Hanley et al. (2001).

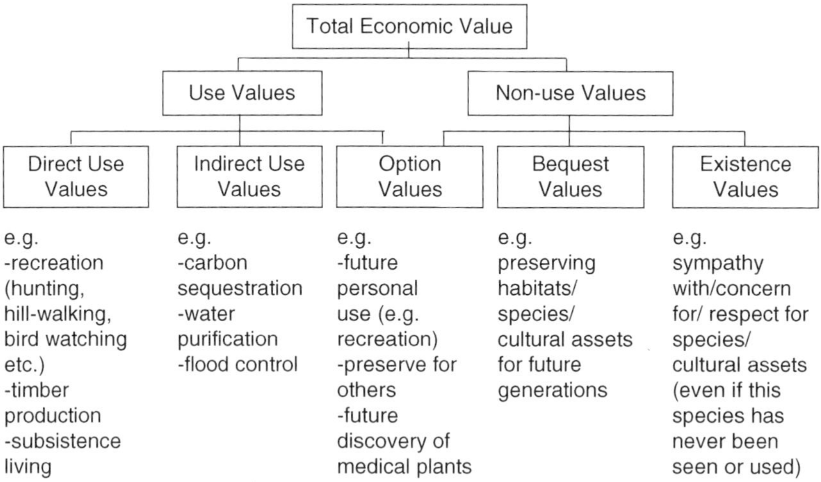


**Figure 1:** Total economic value of wilderness (source adapted).[7]

and services (e.g., timber production), its economic value is to a large extent generated by immaterial or non-market goods and services, such as landscape aesthetics or habitat provision. A further source of value that is often overlooked, but is of particular importance to wilderness valuation, arises when people derive a benefit from simply knowing of the existence of these services (e.g., they may have sympathy or concern for a certain species, habitat or landscape). Thus, the value of wilderness goods and services goes beyond the actual use of wilderness.[8] This distinction between use and non-use values, and the different value types associated with wilderness, are depicted in Figure 1.

*Use values* derive from all of the direct and indirect ways in which people make physical use of wilderness. Birdwatchers, hunters (if allowed in wilderness) and recreationists, for instance, use wilderness directly and benefit from it. These are *direct use values*. The use value class also has an

[7] TEEB (The Economics of Ecosystem and Biodiversity), *Ecological and Economic Foundations* (London: Earthscan, 2010), 410 p.; OECD, *The Economic Appraisal of Environmental Projects and Policies* (Paris: OECD Publishing, 1995).

[8] U. Pascual and R. Muradian et al., 'The Economics of Valuing Ecosystem Services and Biodiversity', in P. Kumar (ed.), *The Economics of Ecosystem Services and Biodiversity: Ecological and Economic Foundations* (London: Earthscan, 2010), pp. 183–256; H.K. Cordell, J.C. Bergstrom and J.M. Bowker, 'An Organizing Framework for Wilderness Values', in H.K. Cordell, J.C. Bergstrom and J.M. Bowker (eds.), *The Multiple Values of Wilderness* (Pennsylvania: Venture Publishing, 2005), pp. 47–55.

indirect dimension, which arises from the provision by wilderness of further benefits, such as water purification or carbon storage. In some cases, upstream wilderness areas offer benefits for residents downstream through water supply or water purification. A protected forest in the Alps might serve as a protection against stone-fall and avalanches. *Indirect use values* also arise when people enjoy reading books or watch TV programmes about wilderness and so value its preservation.[9] Weisbrod (1964)[10] first discussed what is now known as *option value*: even though people may not currently use the goods and services provided by wilderness, they may wish to keep an option open to use such goods and services sometime in the future, and this option in itself delivers a benefit to them. Option values of natural environments are frequently cited as important to their maintenance. Another type of option value relates to the yet unknown value that wilderness might have in the future. For example, yet undiscovered medical plants in tropical forests may, in the future, be crucial to people's health.[11] Furthermore, scientific information about highly valuable aspects of wilderness may not be revealed until a later date, and hence neither the costs of today's irreversible impacts nor the amount to be gained from protecting wilderness are currently known.[12] Thus, the significance of option value is enormous and implies that relying on present use values alone is not sufficient and will likely result in the future economic value of wilderness being underestimated.[13]

*Non-use values* make up a large part of the economic value associated with unique environmental assets that are irreplaceable and threatened with irreversible changes. People derive benefits from wilderness protection even though they do not obtain direct or indirect use from wilderness. Non-use benefits fall under two categories, vicarious consumption and stewardship, and exist due to both altruistic and selfish motives.[14]

[9] D.M. Hanink, 'Evaluation of Wilderness in a Spatial Context', *Growth and Change*, 26 (1995), 425–441.

[10] B.A. Weisbrod, 'Collective-Consumption Services of Individual-Consumption Goods', *Quarterly Journal of Economics*, 78 (1964), 471–478.

[11] Hanink, 'Evaluation of Wilderness in a Spatial Context', *supra* note 9; K.G. Willis, 'Option Value and Non User Benefits of Wildlife Conservation', *Journal of Rural Studies*, 5 (1989), 245–256.

[12] At the same time, humans can only value environmental amenities for which they expect a future value. If the future value of a wilderness area is unknown and even no option value is attributed to the area, there is no economic value.

[13] Willis, 'Option Value and Non User Benefits of Wildlife Conservation', *supra* note 11.

[14] R.K. Turner, 'The Place of Economic Values in Environmental Valuation', in I. Bateman and K.G. Willis (eds.), *Valuing Environmental Preferences* (Oxford: Oxford University Press, 1999), pp. 17–41.

The first category, vicarious consumption, represents the non-use side of *option value* because utility may also be gained from knowing that others benefit from using wilderness. People may support the preservation of wilderness because they feel obligated to provide its goods and services for others.[15] The dual character of option values, consisting of use values and non-use values is also shown in Figure 1.

The second category, stewardship values, is held by people because they think that environmental goods and services should be used in a responsible manner and because they want future generations to gain from them. There are two types of stewardship values: first, *existence values* include people's concern for, sympathy with and respect for rare environmental assets, such as free-flowing rivers or certain species in a wilderness area. This concept was first introduced by Krutilla in 1967,[16] when he suggested that non-users may be satisfied by knowing that natural environments exist and are protected, regardless of whether they will ever make use of them. Thus, an individual does not have to visit a wilderness area to gain utility from its maintenance or improvement. Second, *bequest value* is a similar phenomenon, with the only difference being the desire to preserve the environment and bequeath it to one's descendants. The motive for bequest value is a potential use or non-use value for future generations.[17]

Given that there is no strategic behaviour among individuals (i.e., individuals do not take a free-rider position), economic values reflect what individuals would be willing to trade-off to either sacrifice or preserve wilderness goods or services. Against the background of absent markets for many wilderness goods and services, conflicting use options and the need for more efficient resource allocation, it is necessary to have information about the marginal benefits or costs of wilderness goods and services that might arise when alternative uses are considered (e.g., what are the costs – or lost benefits – of building a road through a wilderness area or harnessing a free-flowing river for hydropower generation, or what are the benefits of increasing the protection status of a wilderness

[15] R.C. Mitchell and R.T. Carson, *Using Surveys to Value Public Goods: The Contingent Valuation Method*, Washington, DC: Resources for the Future, 1989); D. Pearce, A. Markandya and E. Barbier, *A Blueprint for a Green Economy* (London: Earthscan, 1999).

[16] J. Krutilla, 'Conservation Reconsidered', *The American Economic Review*, 57 (1967), 777–786.

[17] Mitchell and Carson, *Using Surveys to Value Public Goods: The Contingent Valuation Method, supra* note 15; Cordell et al., *An Organizing Framework for Wilderness Values, supra* note 8.

area and thus preventing other uses?) The economic value of wilderness is reflected by people's economic behaviour in the context of supply and demand. It is the maximum amount of goods and services – or money income – that an individual is willing to give up in order to obtain a positive environmental change that increases his or her welfare (e.g., protection of wilderness) or the minimum amount an individual is willing to receive in compensation to accept a negative environmental change that would decrease his or her welfare (e.g., timber harvesting in yet pristine forests). Individuals' maximum willingness to pay (WTP) or their minimum willingness to accept (WTA) in compensation for quantitative or qualitative changes to wilderness reflects the value of or peoples' preferences for wilderness goods and services and are therefore relevant measures in economic valuation.[18]

The economic concept of value is an anthropocentric one and differs from value concepts in other disciplines – for instance, the biocentric perspective, where a resource as such is assumed to be valuable independent of the goods and services it provides to humans (wilderness as 'ends', or intrinsic value). To economists, wilderness is not valuable as such, but due to its ability to generate benefits and meet peoples' needs (wilderness as 'means'). Economists cannot value wilderness itself – a common misbelief among non-economists – but they can value the extent to which changes in the provision of wilderness goods and services impact the welfare of society. This anthropocentric perspective means that the value of change in wilderness goods and services is subjective, because individuals have different needs, and therefore the benefits that they derive from these goods and services vary. The economic value of wilderness goods and services is therefore a reflection of subjective values based on individual preferences.[19]

[18] G. Garrod and K. Willis, *Economic Valuation of the Environment: Methods and Case Studies* (Cheltenham: Edward Elgar, 1999), p. 384; R. Brouwer, F.H. Oosterhuis, J.H. Ansink, D.N. Barton and N. Lienhoop, 'POLICYMIX WP 4: Guidelines for Estimating Costs and Benefits of Policy Instruments for Biodiversity Conservation', *Technical Brief*, Issue No. 6 (2011). http://policymix.nina.no/DesktopModules/Bring2mind/DMX/Download.aspx?Command=Core_Download&EntryId=876&PortalId=51 &TabId=3736.

[19] Wissenschaftlicher Beirat der Bundesregierung Globale Umweltveränderungen (WBGU), *Welt im Wandel: Umwelt und Ethik, Sondergutachten* (Marburg: Metropolis, 1999); *Millennium Ecosystem Assessment, supra* note 2; U. Eser, A.K. Neureuther and A. Müller, *Klugheit, Glück, Gerechtigkeit: Ethische Argumente in der Nationalen Strategie zur biologischen Vielfalt. Gutachten im Auftrag des Bundesamtes für Naturschutz* (Bonn: Bundesamt für Naturschutz, 2011); Brouwer et al., POLICYMIX WP 4, Ibid. note 18. B. Hansjürgens, *Bewertung von Wasser in Landschaften – Konzepte, Ansätze und Empfehlungen* (München: Acatech, 2011).

Step 1: Define the project/policy causing an environmental change, including its key characteristics, such as environmental objective, implementing agent, target group(s), geographical boundaries, time horizon and costs.
Step 2: Define the status quo in terms of level of wilderness goods and services.
Step 3: Determine the outcome of the project/policy in terms of level of wilderness goods and services and economic welfare implications. Identify all affected stakeholder groups (beneficiaries and burden-carriers).
Step 4: Estimation of the additional costs of implementation (e.g. fences for protecting the area, monitoring costs, opportunity costs) and the transaction costs (e.g. bargaining with farmers, political decision-making) of the project/policy.
Step 5: Valuation of the relevant welfare effects (benefits and costs) arising from a planned project/policy using market and non-market valuation methods (see below.)
Step 6: Comparison of costs (market and non-market) and benefits (market and non-market) and estimation of the net present value of the project/policy over the relevant geographical and temporal scale. (This includes the discounting of benefits and costs over time.)
Step 7: Sensitivity analysis of key uncertainties and assumptions underlying the estimation of the relevant welfare effects.

**Figure 2:** Steps to value the economic welfare implications of an environmental change in a wilderness area (Source: adapted).[20]

## *2.2 Economic valuation methods*

As mentioned above, economists assess value in terms of income equivalents (WTP or WTA) for positive or negative changes to wilderness goods and services. Thus, it is the aim of economic valuation techniques to express these values in monetary terms. In order to assess, quantify and value environmental changes and enable decisions that take such changes into account, several steps are necessary (see Figure 2).

These steps to valuation can be applied both for projects and policies that diminish the quality or quantity of a wilderness area and for those that improve wilderness (e.g., by increasing its protection status or restoring wilderness qualities).

In order to value changes to wilderness goods and services (Step 5) a number of economic valuation methods are available. The most important distinction is between market-based and non-market-based valuation techniques. Market-based valuation methods rely on information about market behaviour and transactions, and values are derived from market prices for inputs (production values) or outputs (consumption values). Since wilderness goods and services are usually untouched and are not harvested and sold on markets, only a fraction of economic value can be related to market

[20] Brouwer et al., POLICYMIX WP 4, *supra* note 18.

prices, and market-based valuation methods are therefore of little relevance to wilderness valuation. Wilderness values mainly refer to simply knowing that pristine and self-regulating ecosystems and habitats exist and will be available to one's descendants (non-use values). To a lesser extent, wilderness is valued for the recreational opportunities it offers.[21]

In order to capture the non-market and non-use values of wilderness, direct and indirect non-market valuation methods can be employed. Direct (or stated preference) methods use surveys to ask individuals about their preferences – expressed in the form of their WTP or WTA in compensation – for an environmental change. They bypass the need for actual markets by presenting survey respondents with a hypothetical market in which they have the opportunity to obtain an environmental good or service. The most common methods are contingent valuation (CV) and choice experiments (CE).

***Contingent valuation*** surveys consist of three parts: First, the wilderness good or service being valued and the changes expected to result from a planned project or policy are described. Second, people's preferences are elicited in terms of their WTP or WTA. Third, the survey asks socio-economic and attitudinal questions to be used as variables in validity testing. Once WTP/WTA bids have been acquired, mean values can be estimated and aggregated to the relevant population in order to obtain the economic value for the wilderness good or service in question.[22]

Instead of estimating one scenario of environmental change, ***choice experiments*** present respondents with different scenarios (e.g., different levels of protection status or different forest management strategies) from which they are asked to select the one that renders the highest personal utility. This method is particularly appropriate when the size of impact might vary due to the availability of different management options. Each scenario is described with the same predetermined attributes – including the price (WTP) or compensation (WTA) – which vary between the scenarios. The advantage of choice experiments over contingent

[21] Garrod and Willis, *Economic Valuation of the Environment: Methods and Case Studies, supra* note 18; J.B. Loomis, 'Economic Values of Wilderness Recreation and Passive Use: What We Think We Know at the Beginning of the 21st Century', in F.S. McCool, D.N. Cole, W.T. Borrie and J. O'Loughlin (eds.), *Wilderness Science in a Time of Change Conference – Volume 2: Wilderness Within the Context of Larger Systems* (Missoula: USDA Forest Service – RMRS, 2000), pp. 5–13.

[22] Mitchell and Carson, *Using Surveys to Value Public Goods: The Contingent Valuation Method, supra* note 15;

valuation is that they are more flexible since they facilitate the valuation of both individual attributes and the whole scenario, and hence collect a larger amount of data that can be useful for designing optimal wilderness management schemes.[23]

Indirect (or revealed preference) methods reveal WTP by observing people's behaviour on markets. Among these methods, the ***travel cost approach*** is the one most suited to value wilderness. The assumption behind the travel cost method is that the money people spend to travel to a wilderness area reflects its recreational value. Using surveys, the method elicits the travel costs of visitors living at different distances from the wilderness area under investigation. Both travel costs and the number of trips can be used to obtain a demand curve for recreation, and the demand curve serves as a basis to estimate net WTP for wilderness recreation. While the travel cost method has been widely applied to assess the value of recreation in nature parks or wilderness areas,[24] it is not capable of capturing the non-use values of wilderness.[25]

### *2.3 Challenges facing economic valuation*

Wilderness valuation is subject to a number of challenges related to the underlying economic assumptions and difficulties to predict biophysical changes. The most important issues are briefly discussed below.

Since wilderness value is to a large extent composed of non-use values,[26] benefits often accrue to people beyond the geographical boundaries of wilderness or to future generations. Non-use values are often difficult to grasp, because it is difficult to identify the stakeholder groups to which wilderness is valuable. Direct valuation techniques (contingent valuation and choice experiments) therefore need to spend considerable effort in locating the stakeholder groups affected by changes in the provision of wilderness goods and services, and surveys should be administered in a way that these people's views are taken into account. There is

[23] D.A. Hensher, J.M. Rose and W.H. Greene, *Applied Choice Analysis: A Primer* (Cambridge: Cambridge University Press, 2005).

[24] K. Veisten, P. Dybedal and B. Grue, 'Measuring the Economic Value of Nature and National Parks: Indirect Valuations from Travel Cost Method and Tourism Satellite Accounts', *International Journal of Tourism Policy*, 4 (2012), 317–335.

[25] Garrod and Willis, *Economic Valuation of the Environment: Methods and Case Studies, supra* note 18.

[26] K.A. Barrick and R.I. Beazley, 'Magnitude and Distribution of Option Value for the Washakie Wilderness, Northwest Wyoming, USA', *Environmental Management*, 14 (1990), 367–380. Morton, 'Wildland Economics: Theory and Practice', *supra* note 5.

no solution for considering wilderness values held by future generations, although this is of importance when changes to wilderness have long-term effects.[27] One means of addressing this issue could be to ask survey respondents to keep their children in mind when expressing their preferences.

It is often difficult to anticipate the environmental impacts of planned developments due to the complexity of ecosystems. Decisions are therefore often made under considerable uncertainty with little knowledge about expected changes and critical threshold levels.[28] Although the problem lies in the difficulty to predict biophysical changes – and not economic valuation methods – it is related to economic valuation, because information on accurate biophysical changes is the basis for valuation.[29] Furthermore, the fact that environmental changes may occur at a large-scale (e.g., global warming, extensive species extinction or the complete loss of wilderness areas) is not compatible with the marginal approach taken in economics. Economists can value small (marginal) changes (small percentage changes in supply and demand). Large changes have to be assessed very carefully and cannot simply be valued through extrapolation of costs and benefits from small changes for two reasons: (1) the magnitude of change is unlikely to be linear, particularly when threshold levels are exceeded (i.e., the functions and services of an ecosystem change entirely when a certain level is reached); and (2) the costs associated with the loss of a wilderness area are likely to be infinite and people may hold lexicographic preferences for wilderness.[30]

One of the fundamental assumptions in economics is that costs and benefits can be traded off against each other. For example, a decision to build a dam and inundate parts of wilderness for hydropower generation needs to be traded off against the costs of relinquishing other uses (e.g., recreational uses) or non-uses. In other words, a certain land use can be

[27] Pascual and Muradian, 'The Economics of Valuing Ecosystem Services and Biodiversity', *supra* note 8.

[28] I. Bateman, G.M. Mace, C. Fezzi, G. Atkinson and K. Turner, 'Economic Analysis for Ecosystem Service Assessments', *Environmental Resource Economics*, 48 (2011), 177–218.

[29] P. Rönnbäck, 'The Ecological Basis for Economic Value of Seafood Production Supported by Mangrove Ecosystems', *Ecological Economics*, 29 (1999), 235–252. Pascual and Muradian, 'The Economics of Valuing Ecosystem Services and Biodiversity', *supra* note 8.

[30] B. Hansjürgens, N. Lienhoop and S. Herkle, 'Grenzen und Reichweiten der ökonomischen Bewertung (Limits and scope of economic valuation)', Expert opinion report submitted to the Office of Technology Assessment at the German Bundestag (2012); N. Lienhoop and D. MacMillan, 'Contingent Valuation: Comparing Participant Performance in Group-based Approaches and Personal Interviews', *Environmental Values*, 16 (2007), 209–232.

preferred while another land use is dropped and regarded to be dispensable. This shows that economic valuation is based on a substitution paradigm and assumes that environmental goods and services can be substituted. However, substitution is only possible when adaptation opportunities are available to compensate environmental change. Such adaptation measures are usually only available for marginal changes and not for large ones. Economic valuation is therefore not applicable when no such adaptation measure exists and, following from this, when a certain land use is indispensable (i.e., essential).[31]

Each of the individual valuation methods, both direct and indirect, has its drawbacks, of which only a few shall be named here. Valuing the recreational value of a wilderness area by means of the travel cost method (TCM) can be tricky when respondents are on multi-purpose trips on which more sites – not only the wilderness area – are visited. Although TCM is suitable for inferring the recreational benefits that a site provides under current conditions, it is rather difficult to value marginal benefits or costs of environmental changes with this method. From a policy-making point of view, however, the valuation of marginal effects is highly relevant when changes to environmental quality/quantity or management rules at recreational sites are discussed. In order to address this shortcoming of TCM, it is possible to conduct surveys at multiple sites that differ with respect to a given quality/quantity (e.g., wilderness with roads and without roads). Such studies are often not suited for the ex-ante valuation of new projects or policy measures, because the environmental changes associated with future scenarios often do not exist today.[32]

Contingent valuation and choice experiments are criticized because respondents' WTP and WTA are expressed in a hypothetical market and might be less valid when people do not take the valuation exercise seriously. In order to counter this so-called hypothetical bias, follow-up

[31] R. de Groot, B. Fisher and M. Christie, 'Integrating the Ecological and Economic Dimension in Biodiversity and Ecosystem Service Valuation', in P. Kumar (ed.), *The Economics of Ecosystems and Biodiversity: Ecological and Economic Foundations* (London: Earthscan, 2010), pp. 9–40.; Beirat Umweltökonomische Gesamtrechnung, 'Umweltökonomische Gesamtrechnung – Zweite Stellungnahme des Beirats "Umweltökonomische Gesamtrechnung" beim Bundesminister für Umwelt, Naturschutz und Reaktorsicherheit zu den Umsetzungskonzepten des Statistischen Bundesamtes', *Zeitschrift für Angewandte Umweltforschung*, 8 (1995), 455–476.

[32] N. Lienhoop and T. Ansmann, 'Valuing Water Level Changes in Reservoirs Using Two Stated Preference Approaches: An Exploration of Validity', *Ecological Economics*, 70 (2011), 1250–1258.

questions can help to identify and remove invalid WTP and WTA bids from further analysis.[33]

A final drawback of economic valuation methods lies in the high costs of the described methods. Economic valuation is very time-consuming and requires experience in the application of social science methods (design of questionnaires, statistics, etc.) For many real-world problems, financial means to conduct a comprehensive economic analysis are not available. In order to overcome this problem, some economists recommend a 'benefit transfer' – i.e., transferring the results of an existing economic valuation study to other study sites. However, this method is highly controversial, as the conditions at the study site may vary considerably from the conditions at the site where the evaluation method has originally been applied.[34]

## 3 How economics can help to protect wilderness

It has been stated that economics can help to protect wilderness by providing guidance for the allocation of scarce resources, by sending signals (and incentives) about the scarcity of wilderness and by making suggestions for its wise use.[35] Economics can, in particular, deliver information about how much wilderness is enough or how strictly wilderness should be preserved. Thus, the economic perspective is not a 'yes-or-no-vote' (of having wilderness or not having wilderness); rather, it is about focussing on the adequate level of wilderness provision or the adequate management regime.[36]

Economic valuation faces considerable criticism, mainly by non-economists.[37] Some of the arguments are based on lack of knowledge or misperceptions regarding the economic approach; other arguments are valid and have to be taken into account. Many critics refer to the

[33] Mitchell and Carson, *Using Surveys to Value Public Goods: The Contingent Valuation Method, supra* note 15.

[34] Pascual and Muradian, 'The Economics of Valuing Ecosystem Services and Biodiversity', *supra* note 8.

[35] TEEB (2010) *supra* note 7.

[36] Loomis, 'Economic Values of Wilderness Recreation and Passive Use: What We Think We Know at the Beginning of the 21st Century', *supra* note 21.

[37] For an overview, see B. Hansjürgens, 'Economic Valuation through Cost-Benefit Analysis – Possibilities and Limitations', *Toxicology*, 205 (2004), 241–252; N. Lienhoop and B. Hansjürgens, 'Vom Nutzen der ökonomischen Bewertung in der Umweltpolitik (Why Is Economic Valuation Useful in Environmental Politics?)', *GAIA*, 19 (2010), 255–259; B. Hansjürgens and N. Lienhoop, 'Wider das Zerrbild von der ökonomischen Bewertung (Against the Distorted Picture of Economic Valuation)', *GAIA*, 20 (2011), 229–231.

aspect of monetization and regard economic valuation and monetization as identical. For others, economic valuation causes discomfort, because they fear that environmental concerns are neglected in decisions, especially those that cannot be monetized. While the costs of protecting wilderness areas are present and can often be calculated in monetary terms, this is not the case for the benefits, which are long-lasting, spatially and temporally widespread and often hard to capture. In the past, this has contributed to the decrease of wilderness areas.

Our position is a moderate one: we argue that economic valuation (and the underlying economic methods, such as contingent valuation, choice experiments, or the travel cost method) – if properly used – should be taken into account as an instrument providing additional arguments *for* – and not *against* – wilderness protection. The primary reason for this is that economic valuation is an important tool for awareness raising, especially when the non-market values of wilderness (see the different value categories in Figure 1) are taken into account, and helps to make the benefits of wilderness protection visible. Here, our position is in accordance with those of many environmental economists, who do not follow a (simplistic) approach of putting a price on nature ('What is the world worth?'), but instead seek to make society's values for nature visible in order to facilitate their consideration in decision-making.[38] Although an exact monetary value of wilderness protection cannot be provided in many (maybe most) cases, the process of economic valuation is highly important and extremely helpful because it supports the incorporation of wilderness values into decision-making. We would like to put forward four arguments that describe the importance of wilderness valuation:[39]

(1) Economic valuation can contribute to **awareness raising**. The quantification of benefits (if possible) makes the relevance of environmental impacts visible. In the field of wilderness protection, this is especially the case for non-use values – existence values and bequest values. Economic valuation for wilderness protection can thus help to identify and overcome blind spots in the landscape of public decision-making. In this understanding, economic valuation works against the powers

[38] WBGU, *Welt im Wandel: Umwelt und Ethik, Sondergutachten*; Marburg 1999; Naturkapital Deutschland – TEEB DE, *Der Wert der Natur für Wirtschaft und Gesellschaft: Eine Einführung* (Leipzig: Helmholtz Zentrum für Umweltforschung – UFZ, 2012).

[39] Lienhoop and Hansjürgens, 'Vom Nutzen der ökonomischen Bewertung in der Umweltpolitik (Why Is Economic Valuation Useful in Environmental Politics?)', *supra* note 37.

of markets that only refer to wilderness areas as being costless 'goods', which can thus be neglected in decisions about land use. Hence, economic valuation makes the general public, politicians and businesses sensible to wilderness protection by expressing its impacts (in the form of ecosystem services) in units that are understandable for these target groups and that could thus aggravate people's willingness to incorporate wilderness protection into their decisions.[40]

(2) At the same time, economic valuation can serve as a **feedback mechanism** to individuals and societies. This is especially the case for those societies that rely heavily on environmental resources, but are distant from environmental concerns and the impacts of their behaviour on the environment. Economic valuation confronts these damages of degraded land (losses of ecosystem services) with other economic interests that compete for the use of this land.[41] An important function of economic valuation can thus be seen in its potential to integrate the environment into the thinking and the underlying values of the Western world, where production, consumption and trading activities are so complex and seem so distant from the environment (although they are often based on it) that environmental changes are not traced back to them (as causing factors). By recognizing and measuring both economic interests and environmental services in the same unit (values and/or money), a behavioural change can be achieved. Thus, the economic perspective helps in particular to reach those stakeholders that do not belong to the groups of nature conservationists; it encourages them to re-think the relationship between humans and nature, and it makes explicit the impacts of their behaviour on nature. It can thus be seen as an instrument that (i) is suitable for self-reflection and (ii) 'mainstreams' the idea of nature protection beyond the field of nature conservation.[42]

(3) The recognition, demonstration and monetization of non-market values and their integration into private and public decisions can be seen as part of a **systematic process** of decision-making. This process ranges from the definition of environmental changes that a project

[40] U. Hampicke, *Naturschutz-Ökonomie* (Stuttgart: UTB, 1991).

[41] E.S. Brondízio, F.W. Gatzweiler et al., 'The Socio-Cultural Context of Ecosystem and Biodiversity Valuation', in P. Kumar (ed.), *The Economics of Ecosystem and Biodiversity: Ecological and Economic Foundations* (London: Earthscan, 2010), pp. 149–181.

[42] *Ibid.*, Brondízio and Gatzweiler (2010).

(or programme or measure) would cause in a wilderness area, to the identification of stakeholders (beneficiaries, cost-carriers), the analysis of project impacts on well-being, the monetization of benefits and costs, the validation and testing of results, and, finally the comparison of costs and benefits.[43] In this process, *all* relevant benefits and costs, *all* relevant alternatives, and *all* beneficiaries and cost-carriers have to be included. Economic valuation thus contributes to transparency and efficiency in decision-making. The entire 'process chain' requires information on (i) how certain decisions may change the environment and its values, (ii) how these changes can be expressed quantitatively and (iii) how they can be integrated into private and/or public decisions.[44] Thus, economic valuation can be seen as an important heuristic that exceeds the monetization of benefits and costs. The 'value' of such a heuristic for decision-making is high since it enables a more integrated approach.

(4) A further argument for economic valuation is the possibility to include, though to a limited degree, the public in decision-making. The economic approach is a preference-based one, where the underlying idea is the identification and quantification of (given) preferences. In European environmental policy there are several initiatives aimed at **public involvement** in decision-making. Interviews and questionnaires, in particular deliberative valuation methods, fulfil important societal functions with respect to participation and inclusion of stakeholders in decision-making.[45]

These arguments show that the economic approach is much broader and also more open than often stated by non-economists. This can also be fruitful for wilderness protection, whereas yet economic arguments do not seem to play a role. We will demonstrate this in the following section by focussing on a case study on the valuation of wilderness in Iceland.

[43] N. Hanley and C. Spash, *Cost-Benefit Analysis and the Environment* (Cheltenham: Edward Elgar, 1993).

[44] WBGU, *Welt im Wandel: Umwelt und Ethik, Sondergutachten*, *supra* note 38; Pascual and Muradian, 'The Economics of Valuing Ecosystem Services and Biodiversity', *supra* note 8.

[45] C. Spash, 'Deliberative Monetary Valuation (DMV): Issues in Combining Economic and Political Processes to Value Environmental Change', *Ecological Economics*, 63 (2007), 690–699; Lienhoop and MacMillian, 'Contingent Valuation: Comparing Participant Performance in Group-based Approaches and Personal Interviews', *supra* note 30.

## 4 Valuing wilderness in Iceland – how economic arguments could influence decision-making

Iceland has one of the last remaining wilderness areas in Europe. Prior to 2007, the island faced its greatest environmental dispute in history regarding the government's plan to develop a large-scale hydro scheme in a wilderness area in East Iceland, which would be the largest man-made construction in Iceland so far. Intense debates arose between those worried about the environmental impacts of the scheme and those pointing towards the benefits of diversifying the island's economy. The benefits of harnessing three rivers for hydropower generation included the provision of energy to a new aluminium smelter and the revenue generated from aluminium production, as well as related multiplier effects to remote communities in East Iceland. Costs included construction and maintenance costs, as well as the loss of wilderness goods and services. The large reservoir, dams and access roads would fragment and partly inundate rare breeding and moulting sites for Pink-footed Geese as well as the main grazing and calving grounds for reindeer, which areas enjoy protection as a reserve.[46] Further, a number of geological features would partly disappear, two of which are unique – Iceland's longest and deepest canyon and glacial ridge-like formations with a unique diversity of plants.[47]

The number of hydro scheme impacts on the wilderness area calls for decision-making methods that take these into account. Although Iceland has legislation on Environmental Impact Assessments (EIAs) that describe and quantify the physical change resulting from projects, it is difficult to integrate EIA outcomes (presented in the form of textual information) into the decision-making process, which is otherwise based on numerical benefit and cost estimates.[48] While an EIA assesses the complex environmental impacts, the decision-maker has the power to determine the extent to which the EIA should be considered in hydro scheme licencing. The outrage among the general public as well as people from outside Iceland has shown that people have views and preferences for keeping the wilderness area in East Iceland untouched. The potential value held by the general public – in other words, the extent to which a

46 K.H. Skarphéðinsson, 'Fuglar á Snæfellsöræfum', *Glettingur*, 2–3 (1998), 51–55; S. Þórisson, 'Hreindýr á Snæfellsöræfum', *Glettingur*, 2–3 (1998), 39–42.

47 G.P. Ólafsson, *Hálendið í náttúru Íslands* (Reykjavík: Mál og Menning, 2000).

48 Garrod and Willis, *Economic Valuation of the Environment: Methods and Case Studies*, *supra* note 18.

hydro scheme in the wilderness area would affect their welfare – is not reflected in an EIA and calls for environmental valuation. In order to ensure equal consideration of expected environmental changes with marketed costs and benefits, it is necessary to translate these non-market values into monetary units. In the following, we describe a research project that was set up to value the environmental costs of the hydro scheme development.[49]

Prior to the selection of an appropriate valuation method, focus groups with members of the general public were held in order to better understand why wilderness is valued. The findings revealed that most people hold non-use values (knowing that the wilderness area exists, keeping the option open to use it in the future and protecting it for their children were considered important) as well as recreational values. Since the wilderness area is remote and barren, it does not provide any direct market benefits.

Contingent valuation is the only economic method capable of measuring non-use values, and it was therefore applied to estimate the non-market costs of sacrificing parts of the wilderness area for the hydro scheme development. In order to obtain value, WTA in compensation to relinquish wilderness goods and services was used as a welfare measure. The CV study was conducted using two different survey methods: namely, personal interviews and a group-based approach, called 'Market Stall'. In both surveys, respondents received identical information and questionnaires. In order to enable respondents to value the expected change to the wilderness area due to the hydro scheme development they were given information in the form of a folder with textual information, pictures and maps. The information folder contained information on the positive impacts of hydro schemes on the rural economy, as well as non-market benefits (scenic driving on access roads, etc.). This was followed by a description of the negative impacts on flora, fauna, geological features and cultural heritage in the wilderness area. After wilderness goods and services and the expected change in their provision had been defined, the hypothetical market in which they were made available had to be explained. Respondents were told that the government's plan to utilize three rivers for hydropower generation would affect the wilderness area, but would also have impacts on the fiscal policy, the economy and, hence, Icelandic households. Thus, household finances

[49] N. Lienhoop, *Valuing Wilderness Preservation in Iceland using WTP and WTA: An Investigation into Data Collection Modes* (Leipzig: Helmholtz Centre for Environmental Research – UFZ, 2005).

could change (prices for consumer goods, value added tax, electricity rates, income tax, etc.) depending on the revenue generated by the hydro scheme. In order to elicit WTA, respondents were presented with different levels of savings to their annual household expenses to which respondents were asked to agree or disagree. Based on this data, it was possible to identify each individual's minimum amount of compensation required to tolerate the changes to the wilderness area. These estimates were then averaged and resulted in an average WTA of ISK 8,240–10,110 per year.[50] Due to the project's focus on methodological issues, a relatively small and unrepresentative sample was drawn. Hence, researchers decided not to aggregate mean WTA over all households in Iceland. This would be necessary if the total amount of wilderness costs related to the hydro scheme development were to be entered in a cost-benefit analysis. Nevertheless, the average household's compensation claims for the changes to the wilderness area clearly show that Icelanders hold non-use and recreational values for the wilderness area. Although a full-blown cost-benefit analysis was not attempted, the study served as an important awareness raising tool, as the Green Party used the results in parliamentary debates to stress the importance of protecting the wilderness area.

In the end, the lost wilderness assets were not considered in the decision-making process and the hydro scheme was constructed and has been in operation since 2007. The ignorance of environmental impacts in decision-making is common in many European countries, because legislation often exclusively requires EIAs, and not information on the preferences that the public holds for the expected environmental changes. Thus, decisions are commonly based on simple cost-benefit comparisons, including installation, operation and maintenance costs and revenue generated, and EIAs. It is important to note here that both cost-benefit estimates and EIAs provide an important basis for a holistic decision and can be interrelated through economic valuation. With EIAs predicting the environmental changes, there is only one further step needed – namely, the economic valuation of these changes – in order to be able to consider the impact these changes have on the well-being of society in the decision-making process.

[50] Two WTA estimates were calculated due to the two different survey methods used. The lower values were generated in the personal interviews, whereas the higher estimates were obtained in the Market Stall exercise. At the time of the study in 2003, these numbers were equivalent to EUR 97,000–120,000.

## 5 Concluding remarks

Wilderness protection in Europe is mainly associated with protected areas, with legal provisions defining whether and to what extent these areas can be used. In contrast, economic arguments on the benefits of wilderness protection are rarely considered in decision-making, and do not typically play a role in the regulation of wilderness areas. Instead, economic arguments are used in the context of short-term economic interests, such as logging and hydropower generation. It is this profit-oriented business perspective that improperly receives the label 'economics', and not a broader perspective that takes all societal benefits and costs and all types of costs and benefits into account.

In this chapter, we demonstrated that economic valuation can, nevertheless, be an important tool for wilderness protection. Economics makes transparent that every decision we take is inevitably connected with opportunity costs: if we choose an option, we lose other options. Economic valuation makes the benefits and costs of wilderness protection visible. This is not to say that economics is able to put a certain value on wilderness (i.e., 'Wilderness has the price of X'), but it can provide support for decisions if (gradual) changes of wilderness protection are considered. Thus, trade-offs can be made between the use of land for wilderness protection and other land uses, such as settlements or agriculture. The main result that can be derived from this chapter is that the concept of economic valuation is much broader than is often stated. It does not only include direct values or indirect values for humans (e.g., regulating services provided by wilderness areas), but also 'non-use values' (i.e., values derived from wilderness areas without using these areas directly or indirectly). Such non-use values are those derived from the existence of wilderness areas (existence value), or the benefits provided for other people of the same generation or future generations (altruistic value), or the benefits obtained from the possibility to use wilderness in the future (option value). Environmental economics has developed certain methods that are suitable for obtaining monetary estimates for these values.

The preference-based approach of economic valuation has several advantages: it (i) increases public awareness for wilderness protection, (ii) offers a feedback mechanism for society by demonstrating the impacts of individual and societal behaviour, (iii) helps to structure decision-making processes, and (iv) offers opportunities to increase stakeholder participation and the inclusion of the public in decision-making.

Nevertheless, the economic approach will not be the key for solving all problems associated with wilderness protection. It is not adequate when huge changes (like the extinction of species) are being analysed. Thus, it is not suitable for 'yes-or-no-decisions'. Therefore, it is of utmost importance to explicitly recognize the limits and constraints of economic valuation. Economic valuation has some drawbacks – it is neither a 'star', solving all problems of wilderness decrease (as it is considered to be by some nature conservationists, who think that problems of wilderness decrease can be overcome when they have economic numbers on their table), nor a 'devil' – causing one-sided, business-oriented action that is the major reason for wilderness decrease (as it is considered to be by other nature conservationists, who reject economic arguments without any attempt to follow the underlying arguments). If properly addressed, economic valuation can help to strengthen the idea of wilderness protection and support instrument design for protected area management.

# PART II

# The role of international treaties and European Union law in protecting wilderness in Europe

6

# Wilderness protection in Europe and the relevance of the World Heritage Convention

SIMON MARSDEN

> I shall attempt the vain task of conveying the feeling I experienced at the sight of this solitary harbour, placed at the ends of the earth, and enclosed so perfectly that one could think of it as separated from the rest of the universe. Here one meets at every step [. . .] trees of enormous height and corresponding width [. . .] crowned with foliage always green: some appear as old as the world; so interlaced and compacted as to be impenetrable [. . .]. Nature in all its vigour [. . .] seems to offer the imagination something more imposing and more vivid than the sight of the same nature embellished by industry and by civilised man; wanting to conserve only beauty, he has destroyed the charm; he has removed the unique character, that of being always ancient and always new.[1]

## 1 Introduction

Typical prosaic portrayal of wilderness, as identified by early European exploration of the New World (above), has been replaced by scientific description potentially capable of legal review. The World Heritage Convention (the Convention)[2] follows this path. What role does it play in the recognition and protection of wilderness in Europe? As a longstanding and much applied international treaty, it has been subject to considerable and significant scholarly and jurisprudential inquiry.[3] As it is equally

[1] Bruni D'Entrecasteaux of Van Dieman's Land (Tasmania), quoted in F. Horner, *Looking for La Pérouse: D'Entrecasteaux in Australia and the South Pacific, 1792–1793* (Melbourne: Melbourne University Press, 1995), at 54.

[2] Convention Concerning the Protection of the World Cultural and Natural Heritage, opened for signature 16 November 1972, 11 *ILM* 1358 (entered into force 17 December 1975; hereinafter 'The Convention').

[3] See generally, Francesco Francioni and Federico Lenzerini (eds.), *The 1972 World Heritage Convention: A Commentary* (Oxford: Oxford University Press, 2008).

concerned with cultural and natural properties its objective is not specifically the protection of wilderness; however the objective of this chapter is to show that it has undoubtedly made a contribution to it. Furthermore, with an approach based on 'outstanding universal value' (OUV) and an emphasis on the 'integrity' of listed sites, the chapter will show that it is also able to raise awareness of, and provide a framework for the protection of, some of the premier national and transboundary wilderness areas in Europe.

In order to answer the question fully, the chapter begins by providing an overview of the Convention (Section 2), before examining its relevance to wilderness protection with reference to the three wilderness qualities (Section 3). These demonstrate the approach to scientific description of wilderness which is outlined in Chapter 1, and which frames the legal analysis for this book. Two global examples of wilderness protection are then examined, one of which retains most of the prosaic qualities of place as enthused by the author above, as well as meeting the wilderness criteria, the objective of which is the primary focus (Section 4). The relevance of the Convention to wilderness protection in Europe will then be considered in depth (Section 5), and two European examples of the application of the Convention also examined (Section 6). Although the discussion is focused on the Convention, implementation by Parties' domestic law is considered to some extent as space allows. Conclusions then follow, summarizing the answer to the question raised above (Section 7).

## 2 The World Heritage Convention: an overview

### *2.1 Historical background*

The Convention was adopted in Paris in 1972 and came into force in 1975. It takes an anthropocentric approach, with OUV the underpinning concept for the definition of natural and cultural heritage. There is a twofold purpose: identifying heritage by Parties nominating properties that are part of their territory, ensuring their protection domestically and, where needed, through international cooperation. The relationship between domestic and international governance is, however, a close one once the obligations of the treaty have been accepted. Properties must be of sufficient size to ensure their integrity, although as one of the European case studies will show, this does not necessarily mean that they must be very large in geographical area. Isolation from human interference may be enough.

The Convention has been widely adopted globally, with 191 Parties, including all geographically European nations,[4] and European Union (EU) member states, but not the EU itself.[5] Parties are responsible for putting forward potential sites for incorporation onto the World Heritage List (the List),[6] and when approved by the World Heritage Committee (the Committee),[7] managing them in compliance with the Convention's provisions.[8]

### 2.2 *Legal obligations and policy requirements*

Legal obligations require Parties to: 'integrate the protection of that heritage into comprehensive planning programmes',[9] and 'take the appropriate legal . . . measures necessary for the . . . protection, conservation, preservation and rehabilitation of this heritage'.[10] Article 2 defines the components of natural heritage as follows:

> **natural features** consisting of physical and biological formations or groups of such formations, which are of outstanding universal value from the aesthetic or scientific point of view;
>
> **geological and physiographical formations** and precisely delineated areas which constitute the habitat of threatened species of animals and plants of outstanding universal value from the point of view of science or conservation;
>
> **natural sites** or precisely delineated natural areas of outstanding universal value from the point of view of science, conservation or natural beauty.[11]

4 The definition of Europe follows that of the book in general as defined in the Introduction. It therefore includes states beyond the EU, such as Iceland and Norway. With respect to the Convention, Contracting Parties are responsible for properties beyond this definition of Europe, such as Ilulissat Icefjord (Denmark), which is geographically part of North America, and the Gough and Inaccessible Islands (UK), which are in the South Atlantic Ocean. Because of their geographical location these properties are not considered in detail.

5 The EU is unable to be a Party because the treaty is not open to organizations such as it; see Art. 31 and Art. 32 of the Convention. It is in any event impractical since membership requires Parties to nominate properties on their national territory. The requirements of Natura 2000, discussed in Chapter 8 of this book, are however distinct.

6 The Convention, Art. 11(1).

7 The Convention, Art. 11(2).

8 For specific guidance, see UNESCO/ICCROM/ICOMOS/IUCN, *Managing Natural World Heritage*, Resource Manual (Gland/Paris/Rome: UNESCO/ICCROM/ICOMOS/IUCN, 2013).

9 The Convention, Art. 5(1).

10 The Convention, Art. 5(4).

11 Since the Convention allows mixed properties to be inscribed on the List on the basis of both natural and cultural criteria, it is important to note that the relevant cultural criteria of Art. 1 are usually **monuments**, defined as 'architectural works, works of monumental

Treaty obligations are supplemented by Operational Guidelines (the Guidelines), the latest version approved in 2013.[12] Parties are aided further by resource manuals in operationalizing obligations. The Guidelines emphasize that 'the *Convention* is not intended to ensure the protection of all properties of great interest, importance or value, but only for a select list of the most outstanding of these from an international viewpoint'.[13] They include the following requirements in relation to protection and management:

- regular review of the general state of conservation,[14]
- adequate long-term legislative, regulatory, institutional ... protection and management,[15]
- measures ... should assure ... its protection against development and change,[16]
- an adequate buffer zone should be provided,[17] and
- each nominated property should have an appropriate management plan.[18]

The Convention therefore requires Parties to introduce national legislation to implement international legal obligations. This has recently been expressed as follows, confirming that while the choice of joining the Convention is a sovereign one, once the treaty has been ratified, national sovereignty is constrained by international governance:

> [...] the actual functioning of the World Heritage Convention regime [...] suggests that global regulatory systems may realise a more complex

sculpture and painting, elements or structures of an archaeological nature, inscriptions, cave dwellings and combinations of features, which are of outstanding universal value from the point of view of history, art or science'; and **sites**, defined as 'works of man or the combined works of nature and man, and areas including archaeological sites which are of outstanding universal value from the historical, aesthetic, ethnological or anthropological point of view'. See the Guidelines, note 12, paras 46–47.

12 UNESCO Intergovernmental Committee for the Protection of the World Cultural and Natural Heritage, *Operational Guidelines for the Implementation of the World Heritage Convention* (Paris: UNESCO World Heritage Centre, 2013) ('the Guidelines').

13 The Guidelines, para. 52. This is intended to comply with the Global Strategy for a Balanced, Representative, and Credible World Heritage List, as adopted by the Committee in 1994 and discussed in the Guidelines. See Ben Boer, 'Article 3 Identification and Delineation of World Heritage Properties', in Francioni and Lenzerini, *The 1972 World Heritage Convention: A Commentary, supra* note 3, at 101–102.

14 The Guidelines, para. 96.

15 *Ibid.*, para. 97.

16 *Ibid.*, para. 98.

17 *Ibid.*, para. 103.

18 *Ibid.*, para. 108.

> path of integration, which is something in-between independent domestic regulation, on the one hand, and global regulation on the other [. . .]. It assigns to the domestic regulator the power to take decisions while entrusting to global bodies the function of introducing foreign and global interests into the decision-making processes preceding those decisions.[19]

### *2.3 Institutional mechanisms and governance*

The Committee is the main institutional mechanism, comprising twenty-one members of the Convention.[20] Meetings are regularly held to consider requests for new listings, ongoing conservation and management,[21] requests for financial assistance and, often related, potential 'in-danger' listings where the OUV of properties is threatened.[22] It is assisted by a secretariat, the World Heritage Centre.[23] The General Assembly of the Convention, comprising all Parties, is responsible for the election and activities of the Committee, from which it receives regular reports.[24]

There are in fact three lists under the Convention: a Tentative List of properties under consideration for listing,[25] the general List of inscribed properties, and a List of World Heritage in Danger (List in Danger),[26] where serious concerns about the state of conservation of existing properties have been raised and where practical assistance may be needed to

[19] Stefano Battini, 'The Procedural Side of Legal Globalisation: The Case of the World Heritage Convention', *International Journal of Constitutional Law*, 9 (2011), 340–368, at 350.

[20] The Convention, Arts 8–14.

[21] This includes periodic reporting based on completed questionnaires by Parties. See for example, UNESCO, *Exchange and Information Meeting, 2nd Cycle of the Periodic Reporting Exercise Europe and North America*, 37th session of the World Heritage Committee, Phnom Penh, 21 June 2013. This includes a report on the High Coast/Kvarken (Sweden/Finland) property.

[22] The Guidelines, para. 24, set out the main functions of the Committee.

[23] *Ibid.*, paras 27–29.

[24] *Ibid.*, paras 17 and 18.

[25] *Ibid.*, para. 62–76.

[26] At the end of 2014 two European properties were on the List in Danger, Liverpool – Maritime Mercantile City, and Medieval Monuments in Kosovo, neither of which are relevant to this chapter because they are cultural inscriptions. Neither are previous listings, Dresden Elbe Valley (delisted in 2009), and future listings, Palace of Westminster and Westminster Abbey (based on development concerns). In contrast, natural properties in Africa and Latin America are on the List in Danger, mainly due to war or civil unrest. The only natural properties in Western countries of relevance are the Everglades (USA), which is on the List in Danger, and the Great Barrier Reef (Australia), which is being considered for inscription.

return them to compliance.[27] At the time of inscription of a property on the List, the Committee adopts a 'Statement of OUV' which will be the key reference for the future protection and management of the property.[28] Interest in the property is undoubtedly raised by this, notably tourism, which in the context of wilderness listings may be counter-productive to environmental protection if not managed carefully.

Participation in the activities of the Convention by those other than Parties is actively encouraged.[29] A representative of the advisory body, the International Union for the Conservation of Nature (IUCN),[30] and, at the request of Parties representatives, IGOs and NGOs with similar conservation objectives may attend meetings of the Committee in an advisory capacity.[31] Public or private organizations or individuals are furthermore able to participate in some circumstances,[32] including providing information to the secretariat 'to denounce initiatives and decisions taken by the state authorities in violation of their international obligations [. . .]'.[33]

The IUCN in particular plays a very important role in the Committee's work,[34] contributing specialist research and guidance in relation to the original review of proposed natural sites, and providing other expertise concerning, among other matters, mission visits and related reports to consider and comment on the state of conservation of listed properties. It is made up of public and private institutions (including states under the former) as well as private individuals. Note, for example, the role played by the IUCN in connection with the reactive monitoring mission to the

[27] For a legal review of the obligations, see Philippe Sands and Jacqueline Peel, *Principles of International Environmental Law* (Cambridge: Cambridge University Press, 2012 (3rd edn)), pp. 509–511; David Hunter, James Salzman and Durwood Zaelke, *International Environmental Law and Policy* (New York: Foundation Press / Thomson West, 2007 (3rd edn)), pp. 1160–1169; and Patricia Birnie and Alan Boyle, *International Law and the Environment* (Oxford: Oxford University Press, 2002 (2nd edn)), at 620–622. The latter work makes valuable comparisons with related international treaties with similar conservation objectives.

[28] The Guidelines, paras 52 and 154.

[29] *Ibid.*, para. 12.

[30] For the mixed properties referred to in this chapter (and indeed the cultural properties), the advisory bodies are the International Centre for the Study of the Preservation and Restoration of Cultural Property (ICCROM) and the International Council on Monuments and Sites (ICOMOS). See The Guidelines, paras 30–37.

[31] The Convention, Art. 8(3).

[32] *Ibid.*, Art. 10(2).

[33] Battini, 'The Procedural Side of Legal Globalisation: The Case of the World Heritage Convention', *supra* note 19, at 353. In a world today shaped by global legal pluralism and public participation, this is how it should be.

[34] The Convention, Art. 13(7). For detailed roles, see The Guidelines, paras 31, 36 and 37.

Great Barrier Reef (Australia) in 2012 to consider whether the Reef should be added to the List in Danger.[35]

A notable absence in the governance of the Convention is a formal non-compliance procedure (NCP), which are common in modern environmental treaties. At present, state of conservation reports, reactive monitoring missions and 'in danger' listings provide the means to address compliance failures, together with international assistance.[36] Perhaps the time has come to explore a formal NCP along the lines of more recent treaties. The Helsinki Water Convention has recently introduced a NCP drawing on experience elsewhere.[37] If wilderness properties under the Convention are to be adequately protected, there should be an opportunity for other Parties to raise issues and for members of the public and other interested groups to express their concerns.

## 3 Relevance of the convention to wilderness protection

What exactly is the relevance of the Convention to wilderness protection? This section examines this question generally and with specific regard to the three wilderness qualities as described in Chapter 1. The protection of the OUV of natural properties, or mixed properties with both natural and cultural components is a useful starting point to answering the question. Further to the definition of natural heritage in Article 2 as set out above, which includes but does not define OUV, the primary way in which wilderness is addressed in the Convention is therefore through the concept of OUV, which the Guidelines explain in the following terms:

> Outstanding Universal Value means cultural and/or natural significance which is so exceptional as to transcend national boundaries and to be of common importance for present and future generations of all humanity. As such, the permanent protection of this heritage is of the highest importance to the international community as a whole. The Committee defines the criteria for the inscription of properties on the World Heritage List.[38]

[35] UNESCO, World Heritage Committee, 36th Session, Saint Petersburg, Russian Federation 24 June 6 July 2012, *Mission Report Great Barrier Reef (Australia) (N 154)*, 6–14 March 2012.

[36] Reactive monitoring and 'in danger' listings have been identified as key to a changed compliance approach of the Committee in the last decade. See Battini, 'The Procedural Side of Legal Globalisation: The Case of the World Heritage Convention', *supra* note 19, at 353–354.

[37] Convention on the Protection and Use of Transboundary Watercourses and Lakes (Helsinki, 17 March 1992), 31 *ILM* (1992) 1312, in force 6 October 1996.

[38] The Guidelines, para. 49.

The definitions of OUV, the natural properties and the criteria for listing them are, as will be seen below, similar to the definitions of the wilderness qualities canvassed in the Introduction of this book, as typified by the IUCN protected area categories of greatest relevance, especially the category 1b Wilderness area.[39] An example of the latter is the Tasmanian Wilderness, considered in the next section, which is a mixed property as a result of its cultural significance to Indigenous Australians, evidenced by a number of places of cultural importance.

### 3.1 *Naturalness (native species and ecosystem and free functioning natural processes)*

The first of the wilderness qualities is clearly identified in the Guidelines to the Convention. Each of the criteria for inscribing natural properties on the List quoted below therefore requires evidence to be submitted – in the form of a Statement of Integrity – that properties:

(vii) contain superlative natural phenomena or areas of exceptional natural beauty and aesthetic importance;
(viii) be outstanding examples representing major stages of earth's history, including the record of life, significant on going geological processes in the development of landforms, or significant geomorphic or physiographic features;
(ix) be outstanding examples representing significant on going ecological and biological processes in the evolution and development of terrestrial, fresh water, coastal and marine ecosystems and communities of plants and animals;
(x) contain the most important and significant natural habitats for in-situ conservation of biological diversity, including those containing threatened species of Outstanding Universal Value from the point of view of science or conservation.[40]

[39] See, for examples, Michael Lockwood, 'Global Protected Area Framework', in Michael Lockwood, Graeme L. Worboys and Ashish Kothari (eds.), *Managing Protected Areas: A Global Guide* (London: Earthscan, 2006), pp. 84–89.

[40] The Guidelines, para. 77. As noted in note 11, as mixed properties are inscribed on the basis of both natural and cultural criteria, it is important to be aware of the relevant criteria. These are likely to be (iii), (v) and (vi), or a combination, which are that properties shall: '(iii) bear a unique or at least exceptional testimony to a cultural tradition or to a civilization which is living or which has disappeared [. . .] (v) be an outstanding example of a traditional human settlement, land-use, or sea-use which is representative of a culture (or cultures), or human interaction with the environment especially when it has become vulnerable under the impact of irreversible change; and (vi) be directly or tangibly

Additional conditions of integrity apply to each of these sub-paragraphs (vii)–(x).[41] This means that in following the Guidelines in relation to them, specific examples demonstrate that the absence of infrastructure (for the second wilderness quality), or size (for the third), are of considerable significance. Since this relates to both of these wilderness qualities, the Guidelines in these respects should also be emphasized for these wilderness qualities as a clear demonstration of the relevance of the Convention to wilderness protection.

In relation to (vii) therefore, an inscription based on a waterfall would need to include 'adjacent catchment and downstream areas';[42] for (viii) an ice age area, 'the snow field, the glacier itself and samples of cutting patterns, deposition and colonization', and for volcanoes, 'the magmatic series should be complete and all or most of the varieties of effusive rocks and types of eruptions be represented';[43] for (ix) an area of tropical rain forest 'a certain amount of variation in elevation above sea level, changes in topography and soil types, patch systems and naturally regenerating patches', a coral reef 'seagrass, mangrove or other adjacent ecosystems';[44] and for (x) a tropical savannah 'a complete assemblage of co-evolved herbivores and plants', an island ecosystem 'habitats for maintaining endemic biota', a property with wide ranging species 'should be large enough to include the most critical habitats essential to ensure the survival of viable populations', and an area containing migratory species, 'seasonal breeding and nesting sites, and migratory routes'.[45]

### *3.2 The absence of roads, buildings, bridges, tracks, cables or other proofs of the modern human society, as well as a minimum distance from such facilities and developments*

As seen from the overview section, the Convention is not intended to ensure the protection of all properties but only a selection of the most outstanding internationally. As seen from the extract from the Guidelines below, however, it is also recognized that properties in a pristine condition

associated with events or living traditions, with ideas, or with beliefs, with artistic and literary works of outstanding universal significance. (The Committee considers that this criterion should preferably be used in conjunction with other criteria).'

41 The Guidelines, para. 91.

42 *Ibid.*, para. 92.

43 *Ibid.*, para. 92.

44 *Ibid.*, para. 93.

45 *Ibid.*, para. 95.

will be rare. Furthermore, as emphasized below, a connection between human beings and the natural environment, particularly Indigenous peoples in their homelands that are the subject of several mixed inscriptions,[46] does not in itself necessarily compromise the condition of a property. The important consideration is that any such activities must be 'ecologically sustainable', which may negate the use of modern technology if the environment is harmed as a result.

The status of wilderness in Europe has much in common with such a finding, both as a result of Indigenous occupation of wilderness areas,[47] and because of the location of marginal wilderness areas proximate to 'modern human society', part of the second wilderness quality. Reference to 'modern human society' draws some distinction with Indigenous societies, although the key factor in the latter will be the extent to which subsistence lifestyles have been replaced by the capitalist economy. This is responsible for the infrastructure found in modern human society, which also reduces the traditional isolation of Indigenous societies. In relation to natural properties, the Guidelines therefore conclude that:

> For all properties nominated under criteria (vii)–(x), *bio-physical processes and landform features should be relatively intact. However, it is recognized that no area is totally pristine* and that all natural areas are in a dynamic state, and to some extent involve contact with people. *Human activities, including those of traditional societies and local communities, often occur in natural areas.* These activities may be consistent with the Outstanding Universal Value of the area where they are ecologically sustainable [all emphases by the author].[48]

### 3.3 *Relatively large in size*

The final wilderness criterion, the question of size, is also addressed by the Convention, specifically in connection with the concept of integrity as discussed previously. Any property listed under the Convention must be of 'adequate size' because integrity is a crucial determinant of OUV.[49]

[46] In the Australian context, the examples of Kakadu and Uluru / Kata Tjuta National Parks are prominent. See P. Figgis, A. Leverington, R. Mackay, A. Maclean and P. Valentine (eds.), *Keeping the Outstanding Exceptional: The Future of World Heritage in Australia*, (Sydney: Australian Committee for IUCN, 2012), https://portals.iucn.org/library/efiles/edocs/2013-026.pdf.

[47] The Swedish example of the Laponian Area is perhaps the best known, an extension to which may see it become a transboundary property with Norway in the future.

[48] The Guidelines, para. 90.

[49] For particular examples, see The Guidelines, paras 92–95.

Integrity also relates to the second wilderness criterion as seen above as the presence of infrastructure and its distance from wilderness is essential to 'wholeness and intactness'. To summarize, integrity is therefore defined as:

> [. . .] a measure of the *wholeness and intactness* of the natural and/or cultural heritage and its attributes. Examining the conditions of integrity, therefore requires assessing the extent to which the property:
>
> (a) includes all elements necessary to express its Outstanding Universal Value;
> (b) is of adequate size to ensure the complete representation of the features and processes which convey the property's significance;
> (c) suffers from adverse effects of development and/or neglect [emphasis by the author].[50]

## 4 Global examples of wilderness protection under the convention

To provide some context and comparison with wilderness protection in Europe, which is explained in the following two sections, this section provides two examples of Convention properties from the southern hemisphere.[51] Both are Australian properties: the first is Heard Island and the McDonald Islands (HIMI), an external territory of Australia to the far south-west of the Australian mainland in the sub-Antarctic; the second is the Tasmanian Wilderness on the Australian island state of Tasmania off the south-east of mainland Australia, which can be imagined by the late eighteenth Century quotation at the start of this chapter. Both are also defined as 'marine' properties by the IUCN;[52] HIMI is

[50] The Guidelines, para. 88.

[51] It is important to note that there are many omissions of natural properties from the List that could potentially satisfy the wilderness criteria, especially those located in the polar regions. One suggestion is Auyuittuk National Park (Canada), which is an Inuktitut word meaning the 'land that never melts'. This has the same symbolic significance as the already inscribed Ilulissat Icefjord, Heard Island and the McDonald Islands and the Pyrénées / Mount Perdu in a human-induced climate-changed world. Another is the Arctic National Wildlife Refuge in Alaska (USA), whose future free from drilling for oil may be secured by the resource security provided by shale gas fracking in the Lower 48. South Georgia (UK) in the sub-Antarctic also has potential for listing now that a comprehensive rat-eradication programme is complete, and Northeast Greenland National Park, the largest in the world, is another example.

[52] See A. Abdullar, D. Obura, B. Bertzky and Y. Shi, *Marine Natural Heritage and the World Heritage List: Interpretation of World Heritage Criteria in Marine Systems, Analysis of Biogeographic Representation of Sites, and a Roadmap for Addressing Gaps* (Gland: IUCN, 2013), at 3. For the purpose of this study, marine natural World Heritage is broadly defined and includes natural or mixed sites that have coastal components with no marine areas formally included, but with a clear marine/coastal aspect to their values. It therefore includes the islands identified as 'marine' in this chapter.

recognized for inscription in relation to marine values, and the Tasmanian Wilderness as including a marine component.[53]

### 4.1 *Heard Island and the McDonald Islands*

The telling comment in the Guidelines quoted above that 'no area is totally pristine',[54] unfortunately recognizes that direct human impact upon wilderness is no longer needed to result in environmental change.[55] UNESCO has increasingly recognized the effects of climate change,[56] and the indirect impact of human-induced climate change has affected Convention listed properties in the most isolated and least visited parts of the globe,[57] including in the Southern Ocean around Antarctica. While the Antarctic continent is itself not capable of listing under the Convention due to the contested nature of territory there, the sub-Antarctic property of HIMI, an external territory of Australia, is listed.[58]

Despite extremely limited visitation, evidence of indirect human impact has hence been suggested in relation to ice melt. This impact of human-induced climate change in one sense challenges the listing under the Convention, and relates potentially to the final component of integrity in the Guidelines, '(c) suffers from adverse effects of development and/or neglect'.[59] It also potentially relates to the obligation in the treaty text, 'not to take any deliberate measures which might damage directly or indirectly the cultural and natural heritage',[60] if the extraction, export or burning of fossil fuels falls within this. In another sense, however, it is an

[53] *Ibid.*

[54] The Guidelines, para. 90, see note 48.

[55] In relation to climate change and the Convention, see William C.G. Burns, 'Belt and Suspenders? The World Heritage Convention's Role in Confronting Climate Change', *Review of European Community and International Environmental Law*, 18(2) (2009), 148–163; Greg Terrill, 'Climate Change: How Should the World Heritage Convention Respond?', *International Journal of Heritage Studies*, 14(5) (2008), 388–404; and Anna Huggins, 'Protecting World Heritage Sites from the Adverse Impacts of Climate Change: Obligations for States Parties to the World Heritage Convention', *Australian International Law Journal*, 14 (2007), 121–136.

[56] See http://whc.unesco.org/en/news/319; and http://whc.unesco.org/en/climatechange/

[57] In relation to Arctic climate change, see www.npolar.no/en/the-arctic/environment-and-climate/

[58] For domestic implementation by Australia, see Simon Marsden, 'Protecting Sub-Antarctica via the World Heritage Convention: Recommendations for Improved Domestic and Transboundary Governance in Australasia', *Macquarie Journal of International and Comparative Environmental Law*, 9(1) (2013), 1–17.

[59] The Guidelines, para. 88, see note 50.

[60] The Convention, Art. 6(3).

excellent means of raising awareness of the issue.[61] A decade ago, before many scientists had fully accepted the reality of human-induced climate change, the following was said in relation to part of the HIMI inscription:

> If the climate changes responsible for glacier recession are of anthropogenic origin . . . then the wilderness values and natural process values upon which listing of this World Heritage property was partly based have in one sense been compromised. *Heard Island remains about as wild and untouched as any place can be. But the changes that are occurring raise the philosophical question of whether any place on an artificially warming planet can be regarded with any validity as an untouched wilderness* [emphasis by the author].[62]

## *4.2 The Tasmanian Wilderness*

Also in the southern hemisphere, a primarily successful example of the role of the Convention in the protection of wilderness and importantly in the application of the law in ensuring its protection, another Australian property, The Tasmanian Wilderness, is instructive. This covers an area of over 1 million hectares, and together with the cool, temperate regions of South America and New Zealand, constitutes one of the last expanses of temperate rainforest in the world. It was listed in 1982 and extended in 1989, on the basis of criteria (iii), (iv), (vi), (vii), (viii), (ix) and (x).[63] It consists of a large number of national parks and reserves that extend over much of South-West Tasmania, including several coastal islands.

The Tasmanian Wilderness highlights not only the potential use of the Convention by a State Party in the protection of wilderness, but also the attraction of the Convention by individuals and NGOs in ensuring that domestic obligations arising from membership are implemented and complied with.[64] It is furthermore an excellent example of how the law has been used to ensure wilderness protection. In a landmark case, *Commonwealth* v. *Tasmania*, the Australian High Court interpreted Articles 4 and 5 of the Convention and held that the provisions imposed

[61] See generally: http://whc.unesco.org/en/climatechange/ and note the situation concerning the Denmark/Greenland property, Ilulissat Icefjord, which has been shrinking since its inscription in 2004.

[62] Kevin Kiernan and Anne McConnell, 'Glacier Retreat and Melt-lake Expansion at Stephenson Glacier, Heard Island World Heritage Area', *Polar Record*, 38 (2002), 297, at 307.

[63] Criteria (iii), (iv) and (vi) are the cultural criteria. See The Guidelines, para. 77 for details.

[64] Note the practical measures based on partnership programmes used to support this; see Peter Mooney, 'Community Involvement in the Tasmanian Wilderness World Heritage Area', in Figgis et al., *Keeping the Outstanding Exceptional: The Future of World Heritage in Australia, supra* note 46, at 164–169.

an international obligation on Australia to take appropriate measures to preserve the World Heritage Area.[65] The outcome prevented the completion of a hydro-electric dam authorized by the state of Tasmania, which would have inundated a large part of the nominated area, which had been put forward by the Commonwealth of Australia (the national government) in November 1991.[66]

Recent moves by the Australian Government threaten this property.[67] The World Heritage Committee has been requested to consider a proposal to modify the boundaries to those in existence before the 2013 extension, which would remove an important buffer zone to the protection of the pre-2013 extension.[68] Furthermore, long-advocated further forest extensions to include the iconic area known as the Tarkine[69] are strongly resisted by the Australian Government and many in Tasmania. Recent changes to national legislation have also impacted the Tasmanian Wilderness, emphasizing the need for effective implementation and compliance.[70]

## 5 Relevance of the Convention for wilderness protection in Europe

European wilderness has decreased in size and quality as a result of many factors which are also relevant globally, such as climate change as noted. This section begins by summarizing the pressures upon European wilderness. By carefully reviewing inscribed properties, it next identifies those most likely to satisfy definitions of wilderness, and briefly explains why this is so for some but not others. It furthermore emphasizes the

[65] *Commonwealth of Australia and Another* v. *State of Tasmania and Others* (Judgment of 1 July 1983, 68 ILR 266. See T.C. Atherton and T. Atherton, 'The Power and the Glory: National Sovereignty and the World Heritage Convention', *Australian Law Journal*, 69 (1995), 631.

[66] Environmental NGOs have argued for decades that the Tarkine should also be included, but objections from industry groups and lack of support from the Tasmanian Government have prevented it proceeding. Ingloriously, the Tasmanian Government constructed a road across this area in the 1990s ('The Road to Nowhere'), the purpose of which may have had more to do with dissecting this huge area to reduce its wilderness qualities as to provide tourist infrastructure at a time of economic decline. See: www.abc.net.au/local/stories/2008/03/20/2196057.htm

[67] See Simon Marsden, 'Australian World Heritage in Danger', *Environmental and Planning Law Journal*, 31(2) (2014), 192–309.

[68] The Guidelines 103, see note 17.

[69] This is the largest area of Gondwanan cool-temperate rainforest in Australia, which also holds a high concentration of Aboriginal sites.

[70] Marsden, 'Australian World Heritage in Danger', *supra* note 67.

incompleteness of the List and the need for more natural inscriptions, particularly in under-represented areas.

### *5.1 Significant adverse impacts*

In addition to climate change, significant adverse impacts include settlement, land clearing and development, minerals extraction, and provision of infrastructure for transport and for energy generation and transmission. All of these have resulted in environmental harm in terrestrial, coastal and marine areas, and habitat loss or compromise. Other impacts, including species introduction and over-exploitation of natural resources, such as a fishery, may not be immediately apparent but can have detrimental effects upon ecosystems. Unless ecologically sustainable, all are wholly incompatible with wilderness protection and conservation.

As is the case on other continents, and as noted in the Introduction to this book (and in other contributions, notably Chapter 2), European wilderness is generally located far from the key population centres of continental Europe, most typically in the higher latitudes of the Nordic countries, or on isolated islands in the North Atlantic and the Arctic Ocean. It is here that direct human effects are more limited in their number or scale, although when they do occur they are more clearly observed in contrast to the surrounding land- or seascape. In a coastal and marine context, the World Heritage Marine Programme prepared a survey to discover perceived threats to OUV and management challenges affecting individual marine sites:

> Results of the survey show that habitat loss was the highest rated threat, closely followed by climate change, marine pollution, and overfishing [. . .]. Climate change and invasive species were identified as the biggest future threats. Overfishing was felt to be less of a problem in the future – sadly but likely because there will be less fish to catch.[71]

[71] See Charles Ehler and Fanny Douvere, *Navigating the Future of Marine World Heritage: Results from the First World Heritage Marine Site Managers Meeting Honolulu, Hawaii, 1–3 December 2010*, *World Heritage Series* No 28, 39 (Paris: UNESCO, 2011), http://whc.unesco.org/documents/publi_wh_papers_28_en.pdf.

Climate change is today likely to be the most significant, contributing to many of the other impacts. See further at 40–44, where tourism impacts are identified as the most important reason for habitat loss.

### 5.2 *Properties inscribed under the Convention*

The List identifies almost forty natural European properties, the majority domestic, but with a handful of transboundary properties. Those which potentially may satisfy the wilderness criteria are identified here. In the North the transboundary properties include the High Coast / Kvarken Archepelago (Sweden / Finland), and in the South and East the Primeval Beech Forests of the Carpathians and the Ancient Beech Forests of Germany (Germany / Slovakia), the Belovezhskaya Pushcha / Białowieża Forest (Poland and Belarus) and the Wadden Sea (Germany / The Netherlands).

Domestic properties include Surtsey (Iceland) and the West Norwegian Fjords – Geirangerfjord and Nærøyfjord (Norway) in the North-West, to the Virgin Komi forests in the extreme East (Russia). They also include Garajonay and Teide National Parks (Spain) in the far South-West to Pirin National Park (Bulgaria), the Danube Delta (Romania) and the Western Caucasus (Russia) in the South-East. However, given development pressures (tourism especially in relation to Garajonay, Pirin and the Western Caucasus[72]), definitions of wilderness may be compromised. Two other properties have direct experience of climate change, most tangibly Ilulissat Icefjord (Greenland / Denmark) – while not strictly geographically European – and also the Pyrénées / Mount Perdu (France / Spain).

Furthermore, none of the impacts to these properties appear significant enough to currently warrant consideration of inscription on the List in Danger, or worse, delisting. In relation to delisting, one of only two properties delisted under the Convention is in Europe. The integrity of the eighteenth- and nineteenth-century cultural landscape of Dresden Elbe Valley was destroyed when a bridge was constructed across the Valley. While this was not a natural or mixed property with any relevance for wilderness protection, the bridge is, however, an example of how the second (and perhaps third) wilderness qualities can easily be destroyed if such infrastructure is built across a natural property that satisfies the wilderness qualities.[73]

[72] Part of this area was impacted by the infrastructure constructed for the 2014 Winter Olympics in Sochi. See Ilara Bertini, 'Sochi 2014: How Russia's Winter Olympics Have Failed on Sustainability', 7 February 2014, http://blueandgreentomorrow.com/features/sochi-2014-how-russias-winter-olympics-has-failed-on-sustainability/

[73] *Supra* note 26.

The List also identifies many mixed properties, which, as the example of the Tasmanian Wilderness above illustrates, are potentially no less capable of meeting definitions of wilderness as properties solely listed in accordance with natural criteria. These include the transboundary property the Pyrénées / Mount Perdu (France / Spain), and the Laponian Area (Sweden). The second of these may satisfy most of the wilderness qualities, although questions have been raised regarding the use of modern technology for hunting and herding.[74]

It is also true that some European properties listed in accordance with cultural criteria alone, could in fact have sufficient wilderness qualities to justify a revised mixed listing. An example is Þingvellir National Park in Iceland, listed as a cultural property in 2004, but, as identified by the Committee when listing Iceland's other World Heritage property, Surtsey – noted further in the next section – this has potential to be also recognized for its geological and therefore natural / wilderness values.[75]

Significantly and finally, as noted,[76] there is a recognized need to ensure a representative scheme of listed properties. Not only are natural properties under-represented, but within this category marine and Arctic properties are currently also very limited and the potential exists to increase these.[77] This is particularly important given the threats to these properties which should be protected. This is the reason why the Guidelines give priority to these listings, which is potentially highly beneficial to the protection of European wilderness.[78]

## 6 European examples of wilderness protection under the Convention

The listing, protection and management of Surtsey (Iceland) and Svalbard (Norway) as marine and Arctic properties have all of the issues noted by the marine managers' survey. Both are classified by the IUCN as marine (Surtsey, Iceland), or potentially marine (on the Tentative List)

[74] See http://whc.unesco.org/en/list/774

[75] Decision 32COM 8B.11 – Examination of nomination of natural, mixed and cultural properties to the World Heritage List – Surtsey (Iceland).

[76] *Supra* note 13.

[77] For suggestions of potential general marine areas capable of inscription on the List, see Abdullar et al., *supra* note 52, pp. 29–38. For examples of polar properties capable of inscription, see *supra* note 51.

[78] *The Guidelines*, para. 61 (c).

(Svalbard, Norway), properties.[79] In addition to being examples of the unrepresented property types discussed, they have been chosen primarily because of their isolation. Each is found in or is part of the Nordic countries identified: the first is a very small island in the most southerly part of Iceland, which is itself located just south of the Arctic Circle; the second is extremely large even by continental European standards, and is located in the High Arctic. The geographical locations of both therefore suggest a much greater likelihood of satisfying definitions of wilderness, notwithstanding the vastly different size of each.

### 6.1 *Surtsey, Iceland*

Wilderness in Iceland is typified by the Central Highland, the largest remaining terrestrial wilderness in Western Europe (including Scandinavia but excluding Svalbard).[80] This does not prevent other claims to wilderness, however, particularly in the marine environment.[81] Surtsey is a fifty-year-old volcanic island, 32 km from the south coast of Iceland, formed by eruptions from 1963 to 1967. It is a pristine natural laboratory without human impact, and scientists have therefore been able to collect information on the colonization by flora, fauna and marine organisms.[82] Its values meet criterion (ix) of the Convention, ongoing biological and ecological processes. The whole island and marine area is listed to ensure the integrity of the entire property, and there is also an effective buffer zone of a similar size adjacent to it. Ironically part of the evolution of Surtsey is the coastal erosion which has halved its size and which is expected to reduce it further by two thirds, leaving only the hardest core.[83]

[79] Abdullar et al., *Marine Natural Heritage and the World Heritage List, supra* note 52.

[80] Thóra Ellen Thórhallsdóttir, 'Evaluating Nature and Wilderness in Iceland', in Alan E. Watson, Lilian Alessa and Janet Sproull (eds.), *Wilderness in the Circumpolar North: Searching for Compatibility in Ecological, Traditional, and Ecotourism Values*, proceedings of a workshop, 15–16 May 2001, (Ogden: USDA Forest Service Proceedings RMRS-P-26, 2002), pp. 96–104, at 98.

[81] For further information on the protection of wilderness in Iceland, see Chapter 16 of this book.

[82] See generally Ian Thornton and Tim New, *Island Colonization: The Origin and Development of Island Communities* (Cambridge: Cambridge University Press, 2007). See also AP, 'Volcano Raises New Japanese Island, 1000km from Tokyo', *The Australian*, 21 November 2013.

[83] Note that McDonald Island, part of the HIMI property, has undergone its own massive change, with volcanic activity in the 1990s resulted in it doubling in size. See Tony Fleming and Sandra Potter, 'Protecting Icy Islands – The Territory of Heard and

Surtsey has been legally protected since its birth by domestic legislation as noted below, although it was not listed under the Convention until 2008.[84] Human threats to Surtsey are reduced by prohibiting non-scientific visitation to avoid non-natural species introduction and minimize other human disruption, such as species removal and deposition of waste. Retaining this level of control is the most significant management issue because of the potential for human disturbance and pollution from a very wide area. Contingency planning for oil spills in particular is required, and a creative and positive approach is necessary to ensure that without physical visitation appreciation of its OUV is still possible.

At the time of listing, the Committee recommended that Iceland give consideration to a serial re-nomination and extension of Surtsey in relation to its geological values (criterion viii) to include a suite of sites that represents the great variety of unique geological features that are characteristic of tectonic plate margin separation. This could potentially be developed in the context of a serial nomination related to the Mid-Atlantic Ridge,[85] and/or as a serial nomination within Iceland which might include volcanic properties on Iceland's Tentative List, including the potential recognition of the significant geological values of Þingvellir National Park as noted.[86]

Although wilderness is defined in Icelandic legislation,[87] this does not in itself ensure its protection.[88] Special protection is, however, provided for certain natural features, including 'volcanic craters, rootless vents (pseudocraters) and lava fields'.[89] The effect of this is that any permit authorizations will be made subject to the opinion of the Nature Conservation Agency as to whether, if a project is permitted, disturbance to these features will be avoided. The only exception is where a master

McDonald Islands', in Figgis et al., *Keeping the Outstanding Exceptional: The Future of World Heritage in Australia, supra* note 46, pp. 72–75, at 74.

84 *Ibid.*

85 Note that the Islands of Jan Mayen and Bouvet as parts of a serial transnational nomination of the Mid-Atlantic Ridge system are on the Tentative List for Norway currently.

86 See note 75.

87 The Nature Conservation Act No 44/1999, Art. 3(4). This act will be replaced by the Nature Conservation Act No 60/2013, but because this new act had not entered into force when this chapter was finalized (1 February 2015), the 1999 Act is referred to. The new act will enter into force on 1 July 2015 (see Chapter 16, note 43).

88 As Aðalheiður Jóhannsdóttir explains in Chapter 16, the definition of wilderness in the new legislation is not as strict as in the old Act. The previous definition applied to any land, whereas the new applies to uninhabited land, which is a considerably smaller area. For full details of the new provisions, see Chapter 16 of this book.

89 The Nature Conservation Act No 44/1999, Art. 37.

plan has been previously approved, although an opinion on this, and environmental impact assessment,[90] will also have been required.[91] Surtsey is a nature reserve under Icelandic law,[92] protected by the Environment Agency of Iceland under the direction of the Minister for the Environment,[93] and public access is not permitted at all.[94]

### *6.2 Svalbard, Norway*

Svalbard is a large island group, and part of Norway, in the High Arctic. As noted above, despite its extreme northerly geographical location and separation from continental Europe as an island group – a situation shared with Iceland – it is technically the largest area of terrestrial wilderness in Western Europe.[95] It is also the largest and least disturbed wilderness area in Norway.[96] Biological diversity and ecological processes are largely intact, and major encroachments are largely concentrated in a few settlements.[97]

The stated objective of the Norwegian Government is that the large, continuous areas of wilderness must be protected from significant impacts.[98] The objective is for Svalbard to present itself as one of the best-managed wilderness areas in the world, with settlements organized in an environmentally sustainable manner to protect the environment and ensure well-being. Coastal waters must be preserved as some of the cleanest in the world, and resources utilized within limits to ensure the maintenance of biological diversity.

About sixty-five per cent of Svalbard is protected to preserve the unique natural environment, landscape and cultural heritage of Svalbard, with seven national parks, six nature reserves, fifteen bird sanctuaries and one protected geotope.[99] The Svalbard Treaty is the

[90] See the Act on Environmental Impact Studies 1993.
[91] The Nature Conservation Act No 44/1999, Art. 33.
[92] *Ibid.*, Art. 53.
[93] The Department of Nature of the Environment Agency of Iceland has assumed the responsibilities of the Nature Conservation Agency. See www.ust.is. It is understood that Art. 46 of the new legislation (see note 82) provides the Minister with the ability to protect the wilderness.
[94] See www.ust.is/default.aspx?PageID=6acceb5e-a96c-4ab3-96c8-d8bf88c18cae.
[95] Svalbard's claims to be part of Western Europe geographically are well founded and not comparable to the position of Greenland (see note 4), whose political status is also different since limited autonomy from Denmark.
[96] See Chapter 18 of this book.
[97] For further information see www.npolar.no/en/the-arctic/svalbard/index.html.
[98] Report No. 8 (1999–2000) to the Storting.
[99] For details, see www.npolar.no/en/the-arctic/svalbard/areas.html.

basis for protection and management and is a unique model in an international context.[100] Activities are strictly regulated by the Svalbard Environmental Act.[101] The purpose of this Act is 'to preserve a virtually untouched environment in Svalbard with respect to continuous areas of wilderness, landscape, flora, fauna and cultural heritage',[102] although wilderness is not specifically defined. It is a comprehensive statute with duty of care requirements and consideration of environmental principles underlying decision making.[103]

Protected areas are established under the Svalbard Environment Act,[104] one of the fundamental principles of which is to 'contribute to the maintenance of wilderness and untouched nature'.[105] 'Large untouched, or mainly untouched areas of natural habitat' may be designated national parks,[106] and 'untouched areas or largely untouched areas' may be designated as nature reserves,[107] as appropriate. International status for protected areas may be granted where an international convention applies.[108] In each of these cases activities may be prevented (national park), absolute protection given (nature reserve) or the obligations of the treaty be made binding under Norwegian law. Permits are required for activities carried out beyond settlement areas, with environmental impact assessment a requirement.[109] Koivurova concludes positively that '[...] so far, the environment is very well protected: a strict comprehensive environmental protection act is applied to the land areas and there is a fisheries conservation area covering the marine areas'.[110]

## 7 Conclusions

Wilderness protection has become more important over the history of the Convention given the decrease in the number, size and integrity of

100 While Norway acquired sovereignty over Svalbard in 1925, citizens from thirty-nine signatory nations were given equal rights to hunting, fishing, industrial activities, commerce and mining. For further information, see Timo Koivurova, *Introduction to International Environmental Law* (Abingdon: Routledge, 2014), at 95–96.

101 Act of 15 June 2001 No. 79 Relating to the Protection of the Environment in Svalbard.

102 *Ibid.*, Section 1.

103 *Ibid.*, Chapter II.

104 *Ibid.*, Chapter III.

105 *Ibid.*, Section 11 d.

106 *Ibid.*, Section 16.

107 *Ibid.*, Section 17.

108 *Ibid.*, Section 20.

109 *Ibid.*, Sections 57, 59–62.

110 Koivurova, *Introduction to International Environmental Law, supra* note 100, at 96.

wilderness areas globally, and its prioritized objective to represent the range of outstanding natural areas worldwide. While it is not directed towards wilderness protection explicitly, it is the most prominent global instrument in attempting to achieve this. The connection with wilderness protection is apparent from the provisions in the treaty text and supporting Guidelines, where definitions of OUV and integrity respond directly to the three wilderness qualities. As such, in theory it plays a significant role in the protection of wilderness in Europe as well as globally.

The polar and marine areas examined are notable examples of under-represented natural properties, and confirm the value of the Convention in wilderness protection, although this is enhanced by their relative isolation from human impacts.[111] In the case of Surtsey, isolation is important as geographical size, which suggests that this wilderness quality is not a prerequisite for the definition of wilderness. This may have broader implications for the other chapters in this book, and where remnant wilderness is all that remains. However, it is not suggested here that such remnant wilderness is capable for inscription under the Convention; while size may not be essential, the other two wilderness qualities are, for this author, closely linked with OUV and integrity, limiting listings to only the most exceptional properties.[112]

Much more can however be done, especially as natural properties constitute only around twenty per cent of the total inscriptions on the List. While achieving a numerical balance between natural and cultural properties may not be easily attainable, achieving a geographical balance may be more so, especially if attention is given to marine and Arctic listings as indicated. Despite comment that the natural list is 'an essentially closed one, whilst the product of human cultural endeavour continues to flourish in the more open category of cultural heritage'[113] this author respectfully disagrees for a number of reasons.

First, the example of Surtsey (and elsewhere),[114] indicates that the processes of the natural world are far from static and do not prevent

[111] Another example of this under the Convention is St Kilda in the Outer Hebrides of Scotland. This is a mixed property, a volcanic archipelago uninhabited since 1930 and with evidence of more than 2,000 years of human occupation in the extreme climatic conditions, http://whc.unesco.org/en/list/387.

[112] It is however acknowledged that if there were even less wilderness remaining, there would of course be a need to lower expectations of OUV if any natural inscriptions were to be made.

[113] Catherine Redgwell, 'Definition of Natural Heritage', in Francioni and Lenzerini (eds.), *The 1972 World Heritage Convention: A Commentary*, *supra* note 3, at 83.

[114] See note 82.

new properties being created. Second, there is little to prevent the discovery of existing natural properties, especially in the oceans as technology enables expeditioners and scientists to make new findings.[115] Third, a review of the Tentative List reveals many wilderness areas that can be added to the List (including Svalbard). Fourth, numerous other properties can potentially be added, especially in the two polar regions. For example, Finland and Sweden have just three natural properties between them on the List,[116] and just one on the Tentative List.[117] Fifth, transboundary and serial inscriptions should be added to increase geographical size and integrity. Finally, in Europe in particular, properties could also be inscribed if wilderness is restored, for example, in the UK.[118]

This chapter above all affirms the benefits of the Convention to the legal protection of wilderness, although it acknowledges that perceived compromises to national sovereignty may inhibit inscriptions.[119] The constant battle between promoters of economic development and advocates of environmental protection remains central to the reluctance of states to protect wilderness, by whatever legal means. A greater role for individuals and NGOs in the nomination and inscription process may be a way of providing a voice for the environment. Above all, if the difference between 'nature in all its vigour' and 'nature embellished by industry and by civilised man' – as observed by a European in the New World in the eighteenth Century – is to continue to exist and inspire future as well as current generations, the concepts of OUV and integrity must remain central to the process.

[115] The example of the Tasmanian Seamounts is instructive. See www.cmar.csiro.au/publications/facts/seamounts/. Furthermore, Papua New Guinea, which has just one cultural property listed under the Convention, is a treasure trove of potential wilderness listings in both the terrestrial and marine environments. See, for example www.conservation.org/newsroom/pressreleases/Pages/species_discoveries_papua_new_guinea.aspx.

[116] High Coast (Sweden) / Kvarken (Finland) and the Laponian Area (Sweden).

[117] Saimaa-Pielinen Lake System (Finland).

[118] The Cairngorms National Park is an example of this, while only a decade old, conservation efforts include restoration. See http://cairngorms.co.uk/look-after/conservation-projects.

[119] See further Natasha Affolder, 'Democratising or Demonising the World Heritage Convention', *Victoria University of Wellington Law Review*, 38 (2007), 341–362.

7

# Wilderness protection under the Bern Convention

## *The perspective of Europe's large carnivores*

ARIE TROUWBORST

### 1 Introduction

This chapter aims to assess the significance of the most comprehensive legal instrument for nature conservation in Europe, the pan-European 1979 Convention on the Conservation of European Wildlife and Natural Habitats (Bern Convention),[1] for European wilderness protection. The chapter consists of two main components. The first is a general analysis (in Section 2) of the Convention's relevance for wilderness protection. The second is an analysis (in Section 3) of the Convention's significance for a group of species that is of special interest from a wilderness protection perspective, namely the five European terrestrial large carnivores: brown bear (*Ursus arctos*), wolf (*Canis lupus*), wolverine (*Gulo gulo*), Eurasian lynx (*Lynx lynx*) and Iberian (or pardel) lynx (*Lynx pardinus*). The chapter ends with concluding remarks (in Section 4).

The methodology employed in this chapter chiefly comprises the identification and analysis of the main pertinent obligations of Bern Convention parties concerning the protection of species and habitats, relevant decisions and guidance adopted by the parties (particularly Standing Committee Recommendations and Action Plans), some national practice of interest, and biological data mainly concerning the five large carnivore species.[2]

[1] Convention on the Conservation of European Wildlife and Natural Habitats, 19 September 1979; entered into force 1 November 1983, *ETS* 104.

[2] The author gratefully acknowledges helpful comments by Eladio Fernández Galiano.

## 2 The Bern Convention and wilderness protection in Europe

### 2.1 *Aims of the Convention*

Of all regional legal instruments concerning European nature conservation, the Bern Convention has the broadest scope, both in terms of participation and objectives.[3] The Convention, which operates under the auspices of the Council of Europe, currently has fifty-one parties. These comprise virtually all European states (including the twenty-eight EU member states), the EU itself and four African states. The Convention's stated aims are 'to conserve wild flora and fauna and their natural habitats, especially those species and habitats whose conservation requires the co-operation of several States, and to promote such co-operation', giving particular emphasis to 'endangered and vulnerable species', including migratory ones.[4] The express emphasis on transboundary cooperation is the first of three characteristics of the Bern Convention that feature strongly when compared to other international conservation regimes. The second is the strictness of the obligations in the Convention. As Bowman and others put it, 'almost every one of its provisions is mandatory, as opposed to being couched in the hortatory language favoured by many conservation treaties'.[5] The third salient feature concerns the institutional mechanism provided for in the Convention to oversee its implementation.

These special features notwithstanding, wilderness protection as such is not included within the Convention's aims, which more narrowly focus on the protection of wild animals, plants and their habitats. Neither is wilderness protection addressed in so many words in any of the other

[3] Literature on the Bern Convention includes C. Lasén Díaz, 'The Bern Convention: 30 years of Nature Conservation in Europe', *Review of European Community and International Environmental Law* 19(2010), 185; M. Bowman, P. Davies and C. Redgwell, *Lyster's International Wildlife Law* (Cambridge University Press, 2010; 2nd edn.), at 297–345; F.M. Fleurke and A. Trouwborst, 'European Regional Approaches to the Transboundary Conservation of Biodiversity: The Bern Convention and the EU Birds and Habitats Directives', in L. Kotze and T. Marauhn (eds.), *Transboundary Governance of Biodiversity* (Leiden/Boston: Martinus Nijhoff Publishers, 2014), 128; S. Jen, 'The Convention on the Conservation of European Wildlife and Natural Habitats (Bern 1979): Procedures of Application in Practice', *Journal of International Wildlife Law and Policy* 2(1999), 224; and Y. Epstein, 'The Habitats Directive and Bern Convention: Synergy and Dysfunction in Public International and EU Law', *Georgetown International Environmental Law Review* 26(2014), 139.

[4] Art. 1.

[5] Bowman et al., *Lyster's International Wildlife Law, supra* note 3, at 298.

provisions of the Convention. This is not to say, of course, that the Convention is of no relevance from a European wilderness protection point of view, quite the contrary.

This becomes readily apparent when looking at the three 'wilderness qualities' distinguished in the introductory chapter to this book, which are reproduced here for convenience:

- Naturalness (native species and ecosystem and free functioning natural processes).
- Absence of roads, buildings, bridges, tracks, cables or other proofs of modern human society, as well as a minimum distance from such facilities and artefacts.
- Areas relatively large in size (often indicated by means of acres or hectares, the time needed to cross the area, or related to the effective ecological functioning).

As stated above, the overall aim of the Bern Convention is to conserve indigenous species in their natural surroundings. In this sense the treaty clearly promotes a measure of 'naturalness'. Likewise, the protection requirements under the Convention regarding species and their habitats, to be discussed in further detail, can have the effect of impeding the construction of human infrastructure (e.g., roads, wind turbines or cables) in areas with wilderness qualities. Similar considerations apply to the size aspect, as certain species require the protection of large areas in order to thrive, or even survive. Compliance with the Bern Convention thus appears to entail the advancement of all three wilderness qualities just cited. To what extent this is so will evidently vary according to the circumstances, such as the states parties, species, areas and threats involved. The other way around, it also appears that the protection of wilderness in Europe would, and to some extent already does, contribute to the achievement of the Convention's objectives, particularly by safeguarding the habitat of quite a few species protected under the Bern Convention. There is two-way traffic, so to speak.

It should be noted, however, that the overlap between the objectives of wilderness protection and the objectives of the Bern Convention is only partial. Many species, to take a straightforward example, can survive rather well in areas intersected by roads, as long as the latter are equipped with fences to avoid road-kill and a sufficient number of adequately constructed wildlife under- and/or overpasses to ensure connectivity. In such cases, road construction would *prima facie* be compatible with the Bern Convention, while ostensibly incompatible with the essence of wilderness protection. Similarly, there are instances where the conservation of populations of species listed under the Bern Convention would seem to require active human management, which is at odds with the notion of 'free functioning natural processes'. In such instances, the Convention may in fact hamper the *restoration* of areas to 'wilder' conditions. It is, however, more difficult to imagine situations where Convention obligations would require contracting parties to encroach upon *existing* wilderness qualities.

At any rate, in light of the above a considerable role appears to be reserved for the Bern Convention in the context of wilderness protection. To more accurately gauge this role, and in particular the (potential) contribution of the Convention to wilderness protection, a closer look is warranted at the Convention's legally binding provisions.

### 2.2 *Obligations under the Convention*

In order to achieve the broad aims cited previously, Article 2 of the Bern Convention stipulates with respect to *all* wildlife that parties:

> shall take requisite measures to maintain the population of wild flora and fauna at, or adapt it to, a level which corresponds in particular to ecological, scientific and cultural requirements, while taking account of economic and recreational requirements and the sub-species, varieties or forms at risk locally.

The Explanatory Report, written by the *ad hoc* committee that drafted the text of the Convention, describes this provision as 'a main obligation that follows from the aims stated in Article 1'.[6] What the 'level' referred to in Article 2 precisely amounts to is not defined in more detail in either the Convention or the Explanatory Report. Much will thus depend on the circumstances and the positions taken by contracting parties in each case, although it is probably safe to assume that species should at a minimum be conserved with the view to avoiding them being listed under the IUCN Red List.[7] The formulation of Article 2 also appears to suggest that conservation considerations will outweigh socio-economic ones in cases

[6] Explanatory Report Concerning the Convention on the Conservation of European Wildlife and Natural Habitats (Council of Europe, 1979), para 21. Para II states that the Report 'does not constitute an instrument providing an authoritative interpretation of the text of the Convention although it may facilitate the understanding of the Convention's provisions'.

[7] See also Bowman et al., *Lyster's International Wildlife Law*, *supra* note 3, at 300.

of irreconcilable conflict between the two.[8] It is evident, in any event, that the burden imposed on parties by this provision is a significant one. As Article 2 clearly focuses on the achievement of certain wildlife population levels, it is not plausible to read the much broader concept of wilderness protection into it. Nonetheless, achieving the conservation of certain populations at 'levels corresponding to ecological requirements' will entail the protection of large, undisturbed areas. In this indirect manner, Article 2 of the Convention may contribute to wildlife protection.

Similar considerations apply to Article 3, which calls for national conservation policies, 'with particular attention to endangered and vulnerable species, especially endemic ones, and endangered habitats'.[9] Furthermore, it commits parties to 'undertake' to 'have regard to the conservation of wild flora and fauna' in their 'planning and development policies' and when taking 'measures against pollution'.[10]

These general obligations are accompanied by specific duties concerning, as the Explanatory Report puts it, 'the two principal approaches to nature conservation',[11] namely, the conservation of habitats and the generic protection of species. These approaches are directed principally, albeit not exclusively, at plant and animal species listed in appendices to the Convention. These are: 'strictly protected flora species' (Appendix I), 'strictly protected fauna species' (Appendix II) and 'protected fauna species' (Appendix III). Over the years, these appendices have been amended following accession of new states parties and with a view to developments in scientific knowledge concerning the conservation status of species. It should be noted that the Convention does not set out any listing criteria.[12] Appendix I currently incorporates over 700 plant species, many of which are European endemics. Appendix II lists several hundred animal species, including birds, mammals, reptiles, amphibians and fish, as well as a number of insects and other invertebrates. Appendix III includes all reptile and amphibian species not included in Appendix II, virtually all bird species not included in Appendix II, and a significant number of mammal species, including various commonly occurring ones, and some invertebrates. The appendices include many species that appear to be associated with, or even dependent on, areas with wilderness qualities. To name a

[8] *Ibid.*, at 299.
[9] Art. 3(1).
[10] Art. 3(2).
[11] Explanatory Report, *supra* note 6, para 23.
[12] The adoption of amendments to the appendices requires a two-thirds majority in the Convention's Standing Committee, according to the procedure set out in Art. 17.

selection, Appendix II includes black stork (*Ciconia nigra*), white-tailed eagle (*Haliaeetus albicilla*), bearded vulture (*Gypaetus barbatus*), gyrfalcon (*Falco rusticolus*), capercaillie (*Tetrao urogallus*), European bison (*Bison bonasus*), Eurasian beaver (*Castor fiber*) and all large carnivore species mentioned in the introduction to this chapter except the Eurasian lynx, which is listed in Appendix III instead.[13]

As regards habitat protection, Article 4 of the Convention states that for *all* 'wild flora and fauna species' each party 'shall take appropriate and necessary legislative and administrative measures to ensure the conservation' of their habitats, with particular consideration for the habitats of species specified in Appendices I and II, and for 'endangered natural habitats'.[14] The parties 'in their planning and development policies shall have regard to the conservation requirements' of the areas thus protected, 'so as to avoid or minimize as far as possible any deterioration of such areas'.[15] Furthermore, parties 'undertake' to give 'special attention to the protection of areas that are of importance for the migratory species specified in Appendices II and III'.[16] With respect to transboundary habitat conservation, Article 4 calls on parties – using the word 'undertake' – to 'co-ordinate as appropriate' their efforts to conserve habitats 'when these are situated in frontier areas'.[17]

The obligations regarding habitat conservation laid down in Article 4 have been elaborated by the Standing Committee in a series of (non-legally binding) decisions.[18] The Standing Committee is the Convention's principal treaty body, in which all contracting parties are represented. Of particular significance are the decisions concerning the

[13] All of these species are mentioned in the indicative, albeit far from complete, list of species with 'wilderness values' in European Commission, *Guidelines on Wilderness in Natura 2000: Management of Terrestrial Wilderness and Wild Areas within the Natura 2000 Network*, Technical Report 2013–069 (Luxembourg: Publications Office of the European Union, 2013), at 88–91.

[14] Art. 4(1).

[15] Art. 4(2).

[16] Art. 4(3).

[17] Art. 4(4).

[18] See, inter alia, Resolution No. 1 (1989) on the Provisions Relating to the Conservation of Habitats; Resolution No. 3 (1996) Concerning the Setting Up of a Pan-European Ecological Network; Resolution No. 4 (1996) Listing Endangered Natural Habitats Requiring Specific Conservation Measures; Resolution No. 5 (1998) Concerning the Rules for the Network of Areas of Special Conservation Interest (Emerald Network); Recommendation No. 157 (2011) on the Status of Candidate Emerald Sites and Guidelines on the Criteria for their Nomination; Resolution No. 6 (1998) Listing the Species Requiring Specific Habitat Conservation Measures; Resolution No. 8 (2012) on the National Designation of Adopted Emerald Sites and the Implementation of Management, Monitoring and Reporting Measures.

Network of Areas of Special Conservation Interest, denominated 'Emerald Network'. Contracting parties are requested to designate areas of special conservation interest (ASCI) as part of this Emerald Network, and to ensure that the necessary and appropriate conservation measures are taken for each ASCI situated within their territory or under their jurisdiction. Both terrestrial and marine sites can be designated as ASCI. A site can become part of the Emerald Network if it meets one or several of the following conditions:

(a) it contributes substantially to the survival of threatened species, endemic species, or any species listed in Appendices I and II of the Convention;
(b) it supports significant numbers of species in an area of high species diversity or supports important populations of one or more species;
(c) it contains an important and/or representative sample of endangered habitat types;
(d) it contains an outstanding example of a particular habitat type or a mosaic of different habitat types;
(e) it represents an important area for one or more migratory species;
(f) it otherwise contributes substantially to the achievement of the objectives of the Convention.[19]

These criteria make clear that the Emerald Network can encompass areas with wilderness qualities. That the Network is indeed set to do so is borne out by the current list of sites that have been officially nominated by contracting parties as (candidate) ASCIs.[20] These include, to pick two examples, Berezinsky in Belarus and Borjomi-Kharagauli in Georgia, besides numerous other areas characterized by one or more wilderness qualities in the aforementioned countries and Albania, Armenia, Azerbaijan, Bosnia and Herzegovina, Croatia, Macedonia, Moldova, Montenegro, Norway, the Russian Federation, Serbia, Switzerland and Ukraine. In accordance with Article 4 of the Convention, however, the protection of the ASCIs is to be aimed primarily at the conservation of species and their habitats. Hence, the measures taken by parties in this regard need not directly target the protection of wilderness qualities as such, although, depending on the circumstances, they may evidently benefit those qualities. Incidentally, the EU and its member states implement their obligations under Article 4 of the Bern

[19] Recommendation No. 16 (1989) on Areas of Special Conservation Interest, para 1.

[20] See the *List of Candidate Emerald Sites*, Bern Convention Doc. T-PVS/PA (2013) 18; and the *List of Emerald Sites*, Bern Convention Doc. T-PVS/PA (2013) 15 (containing the Swiss sites, which are the only ones officially adopted at the time of writing).

Convention through the Natura 2000-protected area network, established pursuant to the Wild Birds and Habitats Directives.[21]

As regards generic species protection, each contracting party to the Bern Convention 'shall take appropriate and necessary legislative and administrative measures to ensure the *special* protection' of the wild flora species specified in Appendix I[22] and the wild fauna species specified in Appendix II.[23] Similar measures are required to 'ensure the protection' (without the adjective 'special') of animal species from Appendix III.[24] Specific prescriptions are added for each of these three groups of species including, inter alia, prohibiting the killing, capturing and the like of animals belonging to species from Appendix II. Before viewing these prescriptions in some more detail, it should be noted that it follows from the formulation of the provisions concerned that these so-called passive species protection requirements do not necessarily exhaust the obligation to take 'appropriate and necessary' measures, quoted above.

With respect to Appendix I flora, the '[d]eliberate picking, collecting, cutting or uprooting of such plants shall be prohibited'.[25] In regard of fauna from Appendix II, Article 6 of the Convention in similarly unequivocal terms requires parties to prohibit:

(a) all forms of deliberate capture and keeping and deliberate killing;
(b) the deliberate damage to or destruction of breeding or resting sites;
(c) the deliberate disturbance of wild fauna, particularly during the period of breeding, rearing and hibernation, insofar as disturbance would be significant in relation to the objectives of this Convention;
(d) the deliberate destruction or taking of eggs from the wild or keeping these eggs even if empty;
(e) the possession of and internal trade in these animals, alive or dead, including stuffed animals and any readily recognizable part of derivative thereof, where this would contribute to the effectiveness of the provisions of this article.[26]

[21] Directive 2009/147/EC of the European Parliament and of the Council of 30 November 2009 on the conservation of wild birds, [2010] OJ L20/7; and Council Directive 92/43/EEC of 21 May 1992 on the conservation of natural habitats and of wild fauna and flora, [1979] OJ L206/7. See Chapter 8.

[22] Art. 5 (emphasis added).

[23] Art. 6.

[24] Art. 7.

[25] Art. 5.

[26] Art. 6.

These prescriptions may, depending on the circumstances, have the effect of safeguarding or enhancing the wilderness qualities of particular areas. One instance is the application of the disturbance prohibition under (c) to brown bear or capercaillie populations. Regarding Appendix III, any exploitation of animals belonging to species listed therein 'shall be regulated in order to keep the populations out of danger', e.g., through closed seasons and regulation of trade.[27] In respect of animals from Appendices II and III, parties 'shall prohibit the use of all indiscriminate means of capture and killing and the use of all means capable of causing local disappearance of, or serious disturbance to, populations', and in particular 'the means specified in Appendix IV'.[28] Poisoned baits, snares and (semi) automatic weapons figure among the prohibited items included in this fourth Appendix. The Convention allows parties to grant exemptions from any of the above prohibitions only when all of the following three conditions are met: (i) the exception is made for one of the purposes stated in Article 9;[29] (ii) there is 'no other satisfactory solution'; and (iii) 'the exception will not be detrimental to the survival of the population concerned'.[30]

With regard to the reintroduction of native species of flora and fauna, the Convention specifies that when certain conditions are met, parties are to 'encourage' such reintroduction 'when this would contribute to the conservation of an endangered species'.[31] At the same time they are to 'strictly control the introduction of non-native species'.[32] The latter requirement is of evident significance with a view to the wilderness quality of 'naturalness'.

Article 10 of the Convention sets out an additional transboundary cooperation duty with respect to the migratory species listed in the Convention's appendices. Parties 'undertake', 'in addition to' the habitat and species protection measures required under Articles 4 and 6–8, to 'co-ordinate their efforts for the protection of the migratory species specified in Appendices II and III whose range extends into their territories'.[33] Article 11 supplements this with a general requirement for parties to 'co-operate whenever appropriate and in particular where

[27] Art. 7.

[28] Art. 8.

[29] These include, e.g., 'public health and safety', 'research and education', and the prevention of 'serious damage to crops, livestock, forests, fisheries, water and other forms of property'.

[30] Art. 9(1).

[31] Art. 11(2)(a).

[32] Art. 11(2)(b).

[33] Art. 10(1).

this would enhance the effectiveness of measures taken under other articles of this Convention'.[34]

The Bern Convention expressly allows states, when they become a party, to submit a reservation regarding specific species from Appendices I–III or means/methods from Appendix IV.[35] Over twenty contracting parties have availed themselves of this possibility. For some species this has resulted in something of a legal patchwork, with protected status varying from one country to the next. As detailed below, many reservations concern large carnivore species.

### *2.3 Standing Committee*

Since the Convention's adoption, many of the obligations set out therein have come to be informed by decisions adopted by the Standing Committee. The Committee has broad powers with regard to furthering the Convention's implementation, and has made specific recommendations concerning cases of non-compliance, produced guidance regarding legal aspects, issued action plans, set up the Emerald Network of protected areas and created several Groups of Experts charged with the development of guidance on specific topics like invasive alien species, large carnivores and climate change.[36] Although not legally binding by themselves, the decisions of the Standing Committee have considerable interpretive value, in accordance with the rules on treaty interpretation codified in the Vienna Convention on the Law of Treaties.[37] No such decisions have, however, hitherto been expressly devoted to wilderness protection proper, although it would clearly be within the Committee's mandate to do so. The Standing Committee has until now stuck closely to the vocabulary from the Convention text on species and habitat conservation and restoration, and has consistently refrained from any interpretations of the latter from the perspective of wilderness protection.

Specific mention should, finally, be made of the 'case file' procedure elaborated within the framework of the Convention to promote

[34] Art. 11(1)(a).

[35] Art. 22.

[36] See also S. Jen, 'The Convention on the Conservation of European Wildlife and Natural Habitats (Bern 1979): Procedures of application in practice', *supra* note 3.

[37] Convention on the Law of Treaties, 23 May 1969 (entered into force 27 January 1980), 1155 *UNTS* 331. See, in particular, Art. 31(3). For further discussion, see A. Trouwborst, *Conserving European Biodiversity in a Changing Climate: The Bern Convention, the EU Birds and Habitats Directive and the Adaptation of Nature to Climate Change*, Bern Convention Doc. T-PVS/Inf (2011) 21, at 13.

compliance.[38] Under this procedure, suspected concrete violations of the Convention by one or more contracting parties are investigated, and recommendations adopted by the Standing Committee as appropriate. Such potential violations are often brought to the attention of the Committee (or the Secretariat) by non-governmental organizations. It is then up to the Standing Committee to actually 'open' a file. Case file procedures may involve findings by the Standing Committee that a particular party has breached its obligations. One example is the 1992 declaration (later followed by others) that Greece had violated its treaty obligations concerning the conservation of the loggerhead turtle (*Caretta caretta*).[39] The case file system, with its 'naming and shaming' approach, has been more successful in some cases than in others, but is in any case more advanced than the non-compliance procedures under most other international wildlife treaties. The procedure has been used relatively often, and the list of closed and pending case files currently numbers over 130.[40] Many of these case files have hitherto concerned plans for wind farms, hydroelectric projects, roads and other human infrastructure in areas with wilderness qualities.[41]

## 3 Large carnivores, wilderness and the Bern Convention

In the field of international wildlife law the large carnivore species brown bear, wolf, wolverine, Eurasian lynx and (to a lesser degree) Iberian lynx stand out for their marked 'international' nature (most populations are shared between two or more countries) and for their elevated human–wildlife conflict potential (primarily in the sphere of livestock depredation and, for some species, human safety).[42] These species are, however, also eminently suited to the purpose of illustrating the subtle, mostly

[38] See Jen, 'The Convention on the Conservation of European Wildlife and Natural Habitats (Bern 1979): Procedures of application in practice', *supra* note 3; Bowman et al., *Lyster's International Wildlife Law, supra* note 3, at 338–342; and D.E. Pritchard, *Review of the Case File System*, Bern Convention Doc. T-PVS (2000) 16.

[39] Standing Committee Declaration concerning Laganas Bay, Zakynthos, of 4 December 1992. For discussion of this case, see Bowman et al., *Lyster's International Wildlife Law, supra* note 3, at 340–341.

[40] See the overview in the latest version of the *Register of Bern Convention Complaints*, Bern Convention Doc. T-PVS/Inf (2015) 4.

[41] *Ibid.*

[42] See A. Trouwborst, 'Managing the Carnivore Comeback: International and EU Species Protection Law and the Return of Lynx, Wolf and Bear to Western Europe', *Journal of Environmental Law* 22(2010), 347.

implicit, links between wilderness protection and international nature conservation instruments like the Bern Convention, identified above. (Other regional instruments of relevance to the conservation and management of large carnivores in Europe, with more restricted scopes, are the EU Habitats Directive and the mountain regimes of the Alpine[43] and Carpathian[44] Conventions, dealt with in other chapters.)

Large carnivores have traditionally been strongly associated with wilderness, and the notion that these species need wilderness in order to survive is still prevalent amongst the general public. In Europe, however, many populations of these species have adapted themselves to a variety of modified landscapes with different levels of human influences. Wolves, especially, have shown themselves capable of surviving in landscapes strongly dominated by human uses, as long as sufficient food is available and persecution levels are not too high. This is not to say that it is pointless to single out large carnivores in a wilderness context, quite the opposite.

As also noted in Chapter 3 of this book, all five species of large carnivore seem to prosper most in large, relatively undisturbed and non-fragmented areas.[45] This appears to be due to a combination of factors. Food, denning and other ecological conditions tend to be favourable in such areas. Brown bear den sites, for example, are associated with 'remote areas with low human disturbance'.[46] Wolverines also like to keep a safe distance between their den sites and human infrastructure such as roads.[47] Generally, fewer roads also mean less habitat

[43] Convention on the Protection of the Alps, 7 March 1991 (entered into force 6 March 1995); and the Protocol on the Implementation of the Alpine Convention of 1991 Relating to the Conservation of Nature and the Countryside, 20 December 1994 (entered into force 18 December 2002). See Chapter 9.

[44] Framework Convention on the Protection and Sustainable Development of the Carpathians, 22 May 2003 (entered into force 4 January 2006), and the Protocol on Conservation and Sustainable Use of Biological and Landscape Diversity, 19 June 2008 (entered into force 28 April 2010). See Chapter 10.

[45] For the most recent distribution data for bear, wolf, wolverine and Eurasian lynx, see P. Kaczensky et al., *Status, Management and Distribution of Large Carnivores – Bear, Lynx, Wolf & Wolverine – in Europe, Update 2012*, Large Carnivore Initiative for Europe report (Brussels: European Commission, 2013). See also M. Fisher et al., *Review of Status and Conservation of Wild Land in Europe* (Leeds: Wildland Research Institute, 2010); and European Commission, *Guidelines on Wilderness in Natura 2000: Management of Terrestrial Wilderness and Wild Areas within the Natura 2000 Network*, *supra* note 13, at 27.

[46] J.E. Swenson, N. Gerstl, B. Dahle and A. Zedrosser, *Action Plan for the Conservation of the Brown Bear (*Ursus arctos*) in Europe*, Nature and Environment No. 114 (Strasbourg: Council of Europe Publishing, 2000), para. 2.3.6.

[47] R. May et al., 'Habitat Characteristics Associated with Wolverine Den Sites in Norwegian Multiple-use Landscapes', *Journal of Zoology* 287(2012), 195.

fragmentation and less traffic mortality. Of particular importance for all large carnivores is the fact that in areas with little human activity, human-carnivore conflict levels – and by extension legal and illegal killing – tend to be low. At any rate, the occurrence of the most robust large carnivore populations in Europe appears to coincide to a significant degree with areas that have retained (or regained) relatively high wilderness qualities.[48] Fisher and others indeed confirmed a spatial correlation between Europe's 'wildest' areas – i.e., the higher end of the Wilderness Quality Index (WQI) – and Natura 2000 datasets for the natural range of bear, wolf, wolverine and the two lynx species.[49]

Moreover, as top predators these species represent key components of many native European ecosystems. Large carnivores provide a living for scavenging species[50] and affect the abundance and behaviour of prey species, thereby influencing plant communities and associated species. Their removal – and, conversely, their return – thus tends to have profound effects rippling through entire ecosystems, influencing biodiversity at large.[51] This has been especially well-documented with regard to recolonization by wolves in North America.[52] In brief, the occurrence

[48] Fisher et al., *Review of Status and Conservation of Wild Land in Europe, supra* note 45, and Kaczensky et al., *Status, Management and Distribution of Large Carnivores – Bear, Lynx, Wolf & Wolverine – in Europe, Update 2012, supra* note 45.

[49] Fisher et al., *ibid.*

[50] D.R. Stahler, B. Heinrich and D.W. Smith, 'Common ravens, *Corvus corax*, preferentially associate with gray wolves, *Canis lupus*, as a foraging strategy', *Animal Behavior* 64(2002), 283; C. Wilmers at al., 'Trophic facilitation by introduced top predators: gray wolf subsidies to scavengers in Yellowstone National Park', *Journal of Animal Ecology* 72 (2003), 909.

[51] B.E. McLaren and R.O. Peterson, 'Wolves, moose and tree rings on Isle Royale', *Science* 266(1994), 1555; J. Berger, 'Anthropogenic extinction of top carnivores and interspecific animal behaviour: implications of the rapid decoupling of a web involving wolves, bears, moose and ravens', *Proceedings of the Royal Society of London* 266(1999), 2261; J.A. Estes et al., 'Trophic downgrading of planet earth', *Science* 333(2011), 301; W.J. Ripple et al., 'Status and ecological effects of the world's largest carnivores', *Science* 343(2014), 151.

[52] W.J. Ripple et al., 'Trophic cascades among wolves, elk and aspen on Yellowstone National Park's Northern Range', *Biological Conservation* 102(2001), 227; D.W. Smith, R.O. Peterson and D.B. Houston, 'Yellowstone after wolves', *Bioscience* 53(2003), 330; W.J. Ripple and R.L. Beschta, 'Wolf reintroduction, predation risk, and cottonwood recovery in Yellowstone National Park', *Forest Ecology and Management* 184(2003), 299; C.A. White, M.C. Feller and S. Bayley, 'Predation risk and the functional response of elk-aspen herbivory', *Forest Ecology and Management* 181(2003), 77; W.J. Ripple and R.L. Beschta, 'Wolves and the ecology of fear: can predation risk structure ecosystems?', *Bioscience* 54(2004), 755; M. Hebblewhite et al., 'Human activity mediates a trophic cascade caused by wolves', *Ecology* 86(2005), 2135; W.J. Ripple, R.L. Beschta, J.K. Fortin and C.T. Robbins, 'Trophic cascades from wolves to grizzly bears in Yellowstone', *Journal of Animal Ecology* 82 (2013) (online first).

of large carnivores significantly contributes to a given areas' naturalness or ecological intactness, and thus plays a considerable role as regards the first of the three wilderness qualities mentioned above.

It is altogether not surprising that bear, wolf, wolverine and Eurasian lynx figure in the list of species with 'wilderness value' that was compiled in the context of the European Commission's wilderness guidance document.[53] This list was compiled by asking site managers of 'wilderness areas' to list the 'most important species representing wilderness value'.[54]

In view of the above, the targeted protection of wilderness, or wilderness qualities, would appear to be a good thing for bears, wolves, wolverines and lynx. Wilderness protection could thus clearly contribute to the achievement of the Bern Convention's objectives in respect of these species. It should be noted, nonetheless, that effective large carnivore conservation in Europe requires more than wilderness protection. A more comprehensive approach is called for, at the spatial scale of entire populations – including both wild and more cultivated landscapes, and both protected areas as well as generic species protection measures in the wider landscape outside protected areas.[55] Wilderness protection can, in any case, constitute an important element of this approach, by safeguarding core areas within large carnivore populations' ranges.

Besides, by requiring the conservation and restoration of large carnivore populations and their habitats, the Bern Convention must be deemed to contribute to some degree to the conservation and restoration of wilderness (qualities) in Europe. The Eurasian lynx is listed as a protected species in Appendix III, whereas bear, wolf, wolverine and Iberian lynx are listed as *strictly* protected species in Appendix II. A Swiss proposal in 2004 to downlist the wolf to Appendix III led the Standing Committee to commission ecological and legal studies on the issue, but did not succeed.[56] Several parties have, in any case, made reservations regarding the protected status

[53] European Commission, *Guidelines on Wilderness in Natura 2000: Management of Terrestrial Wilderness and Wild Areas within the Natura 2000 Network*, *supra* note 13, at 27 and 90.

[54] *Ibid.* at 27.

[55] See, e.g., J. Linnell, V. Salvatori and L. Boitani, *Guidelines for Population Level Management Plans for Large Carnivores*, Large Carnivore Initiative for Europe report (Brussels: European Commission, 2008).

[56] See V. Salvatori and J. Linnell, *Report on the Conservation Status and Threats for Wolf (*Canis lupus*) in Europe*, Bern Convention Doc T-PVS/Inf (2005) 16; and C Shine, *Legal Report on the Possible Need to Amend Appendix II of the Convention for the Wolf*, Bern Convention Doc. T-PVS/Inf (2005) 18.

of wolf and/or bear.[57] Aided by a Group of Experts on Large Carnivores, the Standing Committee has produced a significant body of Recommendations of relevance to the conservation of large carnivores and their habitat.[58] Species-specific Bern Convention Action Plans were launched for all five species in the year 2000.[59] These Recommendations and Action Plans offer important guidance for national policies and for the interpretation of nature conservation law in respect of large carnivores. As noted before, however, none of them explicitly address wilderness protection.

It is difficult to measure the effectiveness of the Bern Convention with any accuracy, whether in overall terms, for wilderness protection

[57] Bulgaria, Croatia, Finland, Latvia, Lithuania, Macedonia, Poland, Slovenia, Slovakia, Spain, Czech Republic, Turkey and Ukraine. Most reservations concern the exclusion of wolf and/or bear from Appendix II. Curiously, only few of these states have provided for protection through Appendix III instead.

[58] Recommendation No. 10 (1988) Concerning the Protection of the Brown Bear (*Ursus arctos*); Recommendation No. 17 (1989) on the Protection of the Wolf (*Canis lupus*) in Europe; Recommendation No. 19 (1991) on the Protection of the Pardel Lynx (*Lynx pardinus*) in the Iberian Peninsula; Recommendation No. 20 (1991) on the Protection of the European Lynx (*Lynx lynx*); Recommendation No. 37 (1992) on the Conservation of the Cantabrian Bear; Recommendation No. 43 (1995) on the Conservation of Threatened Mammals in Europe; Recommendation No. 59 (1997) on the Drafting and Implementation of Action Plans of Wild Fauna Species; Recommendation No. 74 (1999) on the Conservation of Large Carnivores; Recommendation No. 82 (2000) on Urgent Measures Concerning the Implementation of Action Plans for Large Carnivores in Europe; Recommendation No. 89 (2001) on the Conservation of the European Lynx in the Alps; Recommendation No. 94 (2002) on Urgent Measures for the Conservation of the Iberian Lynx (*Lynx pardinus*); Recommendation No. 100 (2003) on Conservation of Large Carnivores in the Carpathians; Recommendation No. 101 (2003) on the Implementation of the Pan-Alpine Conservation Strategy for the Lynx (PACS); Recommendation No. 115 (2005) on the Conservation and Management of Transboundary Populations of Large Carnivores; Recommendation No. 137 (2008) on Population Level Management of Large Carnivore Populations; Recommendation No. 162 (2012) on the Conservation of Large Carnivores Populations in Europe Requesting Special Conservation Action; Recommendation No. 163 (2012) on the Management of Expanding Populations of Large Carnivores in Europe; Recommendation No. 173 (2014) on Hybridisation between Wild Grey Wolves (*Canis lupus*) and Domestic Dogs (*Canis lupus familiaris*).

[59] M. Delibes, A. Rodríguez and P. Ferreras, *Action Plan for the Conservation of the Iberian Lynx* (Lynx pardinus) *in Europe*, Nature and Environment No. 111 (Strasbourg: Council of Europe Publishing, 2000); U. Breitenmoser et al., *Action Plan for the Conservation of the Eurasian Lynx* (Lynx lynx) *in Europe*, Nature and Environment No. 112 (Strasbourg: Council of Europe Publishing, 2000); L. Boitani, *Action Plan for the Conservation of the Wolves* (Canis lupus) *in Europe*, Nature and Environment No. 113 (Strasbourg: Council of Europe Publishing, 2000); J.E. Swenson et al., *Action Plan for the Conservation of the Brown Bear* (Ursus arctos) *in Europe*, *supra* note 46; A. Landa, M. Lindén and I. Kojola, *Action Plan for the Conservation of Wolverines* (Gulo gulo) *in Europe*, Nature and Environment No. 115 (Strasbourg: Council of Europe Publishing, 2000).

generally or for large carnivores. Across the board, however, its effectiveness appears to be less than that of the EU Wild Birds[60] and Habitats Directives (which benefit from the elaborate EU enforcement toolbox), but greater than that of most other international wildlife treaties.[61] There are, in any event, plenty of indications to suggest that the Bern Convention exercises a meaningful influence on relevant domestic policies. A pertinent instance of such an indication concerns wolves in Switzerland. In 2004, as mentioned above, the Swiss government (unsuccessfully) proposed the downlisting of wolves from Appendix II to III, and subsequently (again unsuccessfully) tried to amend Article 22 of the Convention in order to enable the filing of a Swiss reservation regarding the wolf.[62] Currently, there is discussion of the only remaining option, i.e., for Switzerland to resign from the Bern Convention as a contracting party and subsequently re-join the Convention *with* a wolf reservation. (Needless to say, this would be a rather embarrassing course of action – especially so in view of the fact that the Convention bears the name of the Swiss capital.) The above, at any rate, clearly points out that the Swiss authorities perceive their Bern Convention obligations concerning the conservation of wolves as a real constraint on their policy options.

## 4 Conclusion

Joint appraisal of this chapter's three main ingredients – wilderness, large carnivores and the Bern Convention – yields the following concluding observations. Wilderness protection as such is not required by the Bern Convention in so many words. Nonetheless, the protection of wilderness (qualities) can evidently serve the implementation by contracting parties to the Convention of their obligations under the treaty, although it will not do so in every instance. What is more, a faithful implementation of the Bern Convention by its contracting parties is likely to further the protection of wilderness (qualities), as a consequence of the close links between the latter and a number of species and habitats protected under the Convention. Large carnivores are a case in point. In certain instances,

60 Directive 2009/147/EC, *supra* note 21.

61 For a comparison between the Bern Convention and the Habitats Directive in this regard, both generally and with respect to wolf conservation, see Fleurke and Trouwborst, 'European regional approaches to the transboundary conservation of biodiversity', *supra* note 3.

62 Art. 22 conforms to the general rule from the law of treaties that reservations may only be entered at the moment when a state becomes a contracting party – not subsequently.

safeguarding and restoring particular wilderness qualities will actually be *required* by the Bern Convention. To illustrate, the implementation of the Convention's obligations concerning the protection of native species and their habitats can bar the construction of roads and other human infrastructure, and 'naturalness' is the direct beneficiary of the duty to control non-native species.

Clear potential thus exists for cross-fertilization between the Convention's objectives and obligations on the one hand, and the protection of wilderness on the other hand. The overlap between the two is not perfect, however. A further clarification of the relationship between the Bern Convention and wilderness protection is clearly desirable. The most authoritative and effective way to achieve this would be the development and adoption of a Standing Committee Recommendation, containing express guidance on the role of the conservation and restoration of 'naturalness' and other wilderness (qualities) in the implementation of the Convention by its contracting parties.

8

# Natura 2000 and the protection of wilderness in Europe

KEES BASTMEIJER

## 1 Introduction

The Natura 2000 network has been established under the European Union's Birds Directive (1979)[1] and Habitats Directive (1992).[2] Article 3(1) of the Habitats Directive describes it as a 'coherent European ecological network of special areas of conservation', which is 'composed of sites hosting the natural habitat types listed in Annex I and habitats of the species listed in Annex II' of the Habitats Directive. Likewise, the natural sites designated for the protection of bird species listed in Annex I to the Birds Directive and sites designated for 'regularly occurring migratory species not included in Annex I'[3] are part of the Natura 2000 network.[4] The central aim of Natura 2000 and other imperatives of the Habitats Directive is 'to maintain or restore, at favourable conservation status, natural habitats and species of wild fauna and flora of Community interest'.[5] This confirms that Natura 2000 represents – alongside species protection obligations in both directives – a core legal mechanism for implementing the 'EU Biodiversity Strategy to 2020',[6] 'constituting 'the centrepiece of EU nature & biodiversity policy'.[7]

[1] Directive 79/409/EEC on the conservation of wild birds, 1979, OJ L 103/1; consolidated version: Directive 2009/147/EC, OJ L 20, 26 January 2010, at 7 (hereinafter Birds Directive).

[2] Directive 92/43 on the Conservation of natural habitats and wild fauna and flora, 1992, OJ L 206/7, 22 July 1992 (hereinafter Habitats Directive).

[3] Art. 3(2) Habitats Directive.

[4] Art. 4(1) Birds Directive and Art. 3(1), last sentence, of the Habitats Directive: 'The Natura 2000 network shall include the special protection areas classified by the Member States pursuant to Directive 79/409/EEC.'

[5] Art. 2(2) of the Habitats Directive. See also the preamble and Art. 3(1).

[6] European Commission, *Our Life Insurance, Our Natural Capital: An EU Biodiversity Strategy to 2020*, COM(2011) 244 final (Brussels: European Commission, 2011).

[7] European Commission's website, http://ec.europa.eu/environment/nature/natura2000/index_en.htm.

In its resolution on 'Wilderness in Europe' of 3 February 2009,[8] the European Parliament '[c]alls on the Commission to ensure that the Natura 2000 network will be strengthened further to become a coherent and functioning ecological network in which wilderness areas have a central place'.[9] This is an interesting request as it presupposes the compatibility of wilderness protection with the Natura 2000 regime, an issue that has been regularly questioned in the European context. Accordingly, this chapter explores the extent to which wilderness areas within the European Union and their wilderness qualities[10] receive legal protection under the Natura 2000 system.

Section 2 briefly introduces the characteristics of Natura 2000 with special attention upon the strictness and focus of the regime. The following sections consider two central elements of the interrelationship between Natura 2000 and wilderness protection, namely the extent to which wilderness qualities are considered in selecting and designating protected sites (Section 3) and the extent to which wilderness qualities receive protection pursuant to Article 6 of the Habitats Directive (Section 4). Section 5 will identify pertinent legal issues in promoting wilderness protection under the Natura 2000 regime, with particular attention to ecological dynamics. The final section contains the main conclusions (Section 6).

The discussions are based on a desk-study (the directives, case law of the Court of Justice of the EU [CJEU/ECJ],[11] guidance documents of the European Commission and the literature). It should be noted that the discussions take a legal perspective; practical experiences with wilderness management in Natura 2000 areas are described elsewhere.[12]

[8] See Chapters 1 and 2.

[9] European Parliament Resolution of 3 February 2009 on Wilderness in Europe (Resolution 2008/2210(INI)), www.europarl.europa.eu/sides/getDoc.do?type=TA&reference=P6-TA-2009-0034&language=EN, para. 13.

[10] See the working definition in Chapter 1.

[11] For brief overview of ECJ Case Law on the Birds Directive, see European Commission, 'Summary of Important ECJ Case Law on Birds Directive, PowerPoint (Brussels: European Commission 2012), http://ec.europa.eu/environment/legal/law/pdf/nature_law/5%20Summary%20birds%20cases%20revised.pdf.

[12] See, e.g., European Commission, 'Guidelines on Wilderness in Natura 2000. Management of Terrestrial Wilderness and Wild Areas within the Natura 2000 Network', Technical Report – 2013 – 069, prepared with the assistance of Alterra, PAN Parks Foundation and Eurosite (Brussels: European Commission, 2013), http://ec.europa.eu/environment/nature/natura2000/wilderness/pdf/WildernessGuidelines.pdf.

## 2 Strictness of the Natura 2000 regime: cause of success and source of criticism

### *2.1 Strictness*

The Natura 2000 regime largely avoids the substantial weaknesses afflicting many other legal instruments concerned with nature protection.[13] For instance, the obligations concerning protected areas in many conventions are often vague or deliberately leave a broad margin of discretion to the Contracting Parties. As outlined in Section 3.1, this is different under the Natura 2000 system: the selection and designation of Special Protected Areas (SPAs) under the Birds Directive and Special Areas of Conservation (SACs) under the Habitats Directive are obligatory and must be based solely upon ecological criteria.

Similarly, where protected areas are designated under alternative regimes, they are often replete with opportunities for interpretation, the balancing of interests and political influences in the practical application of these mechanisms. While scope for the balancing of interests appears reasonable, this in practice is often weighted to the benefit of short-term socio-economic interests. The regime for Natura 2000 sites, as laid down in Article 6 of the Habitats Directive, is far stricter. Article 6(1) requires Member States to 'establish the necessary conservation measures' to achieve the conservation objectives that must be set for each site. Article 6(2) obliges Member States to avoid 'the deterioration of natural habitats and the habitats of species as well as disturbance of the species for which the areas have been designated, in so far as such disturbance could be significant in relation to the objectives of this Directive'. EU case law specifies that this means that obstacles for reaching the conservation objectives must be addressed, regardless of whether they are caused, for instance, by authorized human activities or natural causes.[14] This may not only require the prevention of adverse impacts, but also 'positive

[13] See also Kees Bastmeijer, 'Addressing Weak Legal Protection of Wilderness: Deliberate Choices and Drawing Lines on the Map', in Steffen Fritz and Steve Carver (eds.), *Mapping Wilderness: Concepts, Techniques and Applications of GIS* (Heidelberg/Dordrecht/New York: Springer, 2016, in press).

[14] ECJ, C-6/04 (*Com.* v. *United Kingdom*), para. 34: '[. . .] it is clear that, in implementing Article 6(2) of the Habitats Directive, it may be necessary to adopt both measures intended to avoid external man-caused impairment and disturbance and measures to prevent natural developments that may cause the conservation status of species and habitats in SACs to deteriorate'.

measures to preserve or improve the state of the area',[15] such as, for example, the removal of alien species that constitute a threat to a bird species to which the site pertains.[16]

For development programmes, Article 6(3) states that '[a]ny plan or project not directly connected with or necessary to the management of the site but likely to have a significant effect thereon, either individually or in combination with other plans or projects, shall be subject to appropriate assessment of its implications for the site in view of the site's conservation objectives'.[17] This paragraph further mandates that 'the competent national authorities shall agree to the plan or project only after having ascertained that it will not adversely affect the integrity of the site concerned [. . .].' Relevant case law clearly requires that in the case of 'reasonable scientific doubt' whether 'a plan or project is likely to undermine the conservation objectives of the site concerned',[18] the plan or project it may not be authorized, except where the exception of Article 6(4) is applied.

The difference in strictness between Natura 2000 and most international nature conservation conventions is starkly reflected in the ruling in case C-166/04. In this case the domestic protection regime for a Natura 2000 site was based, inter alia, upon international conventions; however, the ECJ ruled that the regime was 'too general and concerns neither the SPA in question specifically, nor the species living there'.[19]

The strictness of the Natura 2000 system is further enhanced through a relatively strong compliance system in the EU. The Commission regularly challenges the legislation, administrative decisions or practices of the Member States to enforce compliance with Natura 2000 before the CJEU, which substantially strengthens its 'watchdog-role'. The strict character of the regime and CJEU case law also increase the chance of

[15] ECJ, C-418/04 (*Com.* v. *Ireland*), 13 December 2007, para. 154.

[16] *Ibid.*, para. 87. This case related to Art. 4(4) Birds Directive, but Art. 6(2) Habitats Directive may also require positive measures. See C-535/07 (*Com.* v. *Austria*), 14 October 2010, paras 58–59.

[17] Art. 6(3) Habitats Directive.

[18] See, e.g., ECJ, C-127/02 (*Waddensea*), 29 January 2004, para. 48 and ECJ, C-404/09 (*Com.* v. *Spain*), 24 November 2011, para. 99, ECJ, C-182/10 (*Solvay and Others*), 16 February 2012, para 67, and CJEU case C-258/11 (*Sweetman*), 11 April 2013, para. 40.

[19] See ECJ, C-166/04 (*Commission* v. *Greece*), 27 October 2005 (only available in Greek and French; quote taken from European Commission, *Nature and Biodiversity Cases Ruling of the European Court of Justice* (Luxembourg: Office for Official Publications of the European Communities, 2006), at 14–15.

success of NGOs in domestic courts. Indeed, since the discretion of the competent authorities to allow activities that may have significant impacts on Natura 2000 sites is strictly regulated and limited, domestic courts also have less scope for a light marginal assessment.

### 2.2 *Criticism*

Given the comparative 'strictness' of Natura 2000, unsurprisingly the regime is subject to considerable criticism. While criticism from businesses and governments may be expected, managers of Natura 2000 sites sometimes also express the view that the regime is 'overly strict', too conservative and inflexible. This view is often based on the assumption that Natura 2000 sites must at all times be managed for the benefit of specific habitat types and species for which the site has been designated. This assumption underpins arguments that Natura 2000 is insufficiently flexible to respond to ecological changes, such as those related to climate change or non-intervention management. Against the backdrop of this sensitive debate on strict protection and flexibility, the European debate on wilderness protection and Natura 2000 has received increased attention.

## 3 Wilderness and the selection and designation of Natura 2000 sites

To what extent are wilderness qualities as distinguished in Chapter 1 taken into account in the process of selecting and designating Natura 2000 sites? As a preliminary point the designation process and the criteria used for the selection of sites requires explanation. It should be noted that the process of selection and designation of Natura 2000 sites in the EU has been almost completed; however, the network also requires continuous updating, hence Natura 2000 is not set in stone. For instance, ecological changes may justify amendments, although sites may not be de-listed when their ecological values have been degraded or lost as the result of non-compliance with the provisions of the directives.[20]

[20] See ECJ, C-418/04 (*Com.* v. *Ireland*), 7 December 2007, paras 83–89: Ireland had failed to comply with Art. 4 of the Birds Directive by not designating a site that had lost its relevant ornithological values (breeding sandwich terns) due to the lack of management measures.

### 3.1 *Selection and designation of Natura 2000 sites: criteria and ECJ case law*[21]

Special Protected Areas (SPAs) under the Birds Directive

Article 4(1) of the Birds Directive provides that 'species mentioned in Annex I shall be the subject of special conservation measures concerning their habitat in order to ensure their survival and reproduction in their area of distribution'.[22] To ensure this protection, 'Member States shall classify in particular the most suitable territories in number and size as special protection areas for the conservation of these species in the geographical sea and land area where this Directive applies.'[23] Protected sites must also be designated for 'regularly occurring migratory species not listed in Annex I', with 'particular attention to the protection of wetlands and particularly to wetlands of international importance'.[24] As explained elsewhere,[25] these fairly general criteria have been worked out in more detail by various Member States (e.g., the Netherlands and the United Kingdom). For instance, Schoukens and Woldendorp explain that in the Netherlands an SPA is designated if the area is one of the five most important sites for one or more Annex I bird species or 'if the areas is used regularly by one per cent or more of the biogeographical population of a bird species listed in Annex I [. . .] or a regularly occurring migratory species'.[26] An additional requirement set by the Dutch government is for the area to be larger than 100 hectares.[27] Some of these criteria are also endorsed by the European Commission, such as the 1%-criterion,[28] while others appear to be domestic policy choices and are thereby more questionable (e.g., the 100 ha.-criterion, which in the Netherlands has

[21] For a more comprehensive discussion on the selection and designation of Natura 2000 sites, see Hendrik Schoukens and Hans Erik Woldendorp, 'Site Selection and Designation under the Habitats and Birds Directives: A Sisyphean Task?', in Born et al., *The Habitats Directive in its EU Environmental Law Context: European Nature's Best Hope?* (Abingdon/New York: Routledge, 2015), pp. 31–55.

[22] Art. 4(1) Birds Directive.

[23] *Ibid.*

[24] Art. 4(2) Birds Directive.

[25] See Schoukens and Woldendorp, 'Site Selection and Designation under the Habitats and Birds Directives: A Sisyphean Task?', *supra* note 21, at 38. The authors also discuss the UK criteria.

[26] *Ibid.*, at 38. See also Ministry of Economic Affairs, Agriculture and Innovation, *Implementatie Natura 2000 in Nederland* (The Hague, 2011).

[27] *Ibid.*

[28] See the European Commission's webpage on Birds Directive Special Protected Areas, http://ec.europa.eu/environment/nature/natura2000/sites_birds/index_en.htm.

precluded the designation of agricultural areas of high ornithological importance).

Consequently, the selection of SPAs under the Birds Directive is primarily based on the distribution of certain listed bird species and migratory bird species and the importance of natural areas for such species. The European Commission accepts that 'Member States have a margin of discretion in determining the most appropriate criteria';[29] however, this margin of discretion is limited in various ways. For example, the ECJ has emphasized that only scientific criteria may play a role in the selection and designation of SPAs: 'It is the criteria laid down in paragraphs (1) and (2) of Article 4 which are to guide the Member States in designating and defining the boundaries of SPAs', and it is clear that 'the criteria in question are ornithological criteria'.[30] The ECJ has also clarified that this means that social and economic interests may not play a role in selecting Natura 2000 sites: 'a Member State is not authorized to take account of the economic requirements mentioned in Article 2 thereof when designating an SPA and defining its boundaries'.[31]

In a case against the Netherlands in May 1998, the ECJ stated that the margin of discretion is also limited as far as the number of SPAs are concerned. The obligation to designate SPAs cannot be avoided 'by adopting other special conservation methods',[32] and 'Member States are obliged to classify as SPAs all the sites which, applying ornithological criteria, appear to be the most suitable for conservation of the species in question.'[33] Based on the research report 'Inventory of Important Bird Areas in the European Community',[34] (IBA, July 1989), at that time seventy sites in the Netherlands qualified as SPAs, hence the actual designation by the Netherlands of only twenty-three SPAs constituted a violation of Article 4 of the Birds Directive. As discussed below, in the case relating to the natural area of *Basses Corbières* (France), the ECJ has also highlighted that the margin of discretion is limited as far as the size of

[29] *Ibid.*

[30] ECJ, Case C-44/95 (*Regina* v. *United Kingdom*), 11 July 1996, para. 26. See also ECJ, Case C-3/96 (*Com.* v. *The Netherlands*), 19 May 1998, para. 60, and ECJ, C-418/04 (*Com.* v. *Ireland*), 7 December 2007, para. 39.

[31] ECJ, Case C-44/95, *ibid.*, para. 27.

[32] ECJ, Case C-3/96 (*Com.* v. *The Netherlands*), 19 May 1998, para. 55. See also ECJ, C-418/04 (*Com.* v. *Ireland*), 7 December 2007, para. 38.

[33] ECJ, Case C-3/96, *ibid.*, para. 62.

[34] For a comprehensive explanation of the IBA reports, see Schoukens and Woldendorp, 'Site Selection and Designation under the Habitats and Birds Directives: A Sisyphean Task?', *supra* note 21.

individual SPAs are concerned: the full qualifying area must receive the status of a SPA, not merely a part of it.[35]

### Special Areas of Conservation (SACs) under the Habitats Directive

The selection and designation of SACs under the Habitats Directive must also be based solely on ecological criteria. Each Member State must have established (within three years of the notification of the directive) a 'list of sites indicating which natural habitat types in Annex I and which species in Annex II that are native to its territory the sites host'.[36] This is referred to as 'Stage 1' of the designation process.[37] The selection by the Member State must be based on the criteria in Annex III to the directive and relevant scientific information.[38] Annex III contains criteria to determine the 'relative importance of sites' for Annex I habitat types and Annex II species. For habitat types these criteria relate to the representivity, relative surface, degree of conservation and the restoration possibilities of the habitat type, as well as a global assessment of the importance of the site for the habitat type. For species they relate to the size and density of the population, the degree of conservation and isolation of the population and, again, a global assessment 'of the value of the site for conservation of the species'. These criteria also constitute an important basis for providing information on the listed sites through so-called Standard Data Forms (SDFs),[39] which must also be updated after the designation of the site.[40] Member States must specify the sites that host priority habitat types and priority species.

Based on the national lists and the criteria of Annex III of the Habitats Directive, the Commission will identify Sites of Community Importance (SCIs) – 'Stage 2' – within six years of the directive's notification.[41] The 'Union list' of SCIs consists of separate lists for the nine biogeographical

[35] ECJ, Case C-374/98 (*Com.* v. *France*), 7 December 2000. See Subsection 3.2.

[36] Art. 4(1) Habitats Directive.

[37] See Annex III to the Habitats Directive.

[38] Art. 4(1) Habitats Directive.

[39] *Ibid.*, and see the 'Commission Implementing Decision of 11 July 2011 concerning a site information format for Natura 2000 sites', notified under document C(2011) 4892, http://eur-lex.europa.eu/legal-content/EN/TXT/?uri=CELEX:32011D0484, para. 3 ('Ecological information').

[40] See Schoukens and Woldendorp, 'Site Selection and Designation under the Habitats and Birds Directives: A Sisyphean Task?', *supra* note 21, at 38. See also R.J. Bijlsma, K. Bastmeijer, M.E.A. Broekmeyer, R.J.F. Bugter, F.M. Fleurke, H.P.J. Huiskes, J.A.M. Janssen, 'Evaluatie samenvoeging Natura 2000-gebieden' (Wageningen/Tilburg: Alterra/Tilburg University, 2012), Chapter 2.

[41] Art. 1 (c) (iii), Art. 4(1) and Annex III Habitats Directive.

regions of the EU. After the adoption of these lists, for each SCI 'the Member State concerned shall designate that site as a special area of conservation as soon as possible and within six years at most'[42] ('Stage 3'). As explained above, most SACs have now been designated, but it is an ongoing process and the SCI-lists (and therefore the complex of SACs in the EU Member States) are regularly updated.[43]

Accordingly, the process of designating SACs is more complicated than the designation of SPAs and is based on the distribution of certain listed habitat types and species of wild plants and animals and the importance of natural areas for these specific ecological values. Additionally, ECJ case law makes clear that the margin of discretion of the Member States in SAC designation is also limited.[44] For example, the ECJ has specified that socio-economic interests are irrelevant to the process of selecting and designating SACs.[45] Member States should also list all areas that qualify under the Annex III criteria as it is the task of the Commission to select the various SCIs.[46]

### 3.2 *Relevance of the three main wilderness qualities to the Natura 2000 selection criteria*

A closer look at relevant provisions, policy documents of the European Commission and case law of the ECJ reveals that some wilderness qualities are reflected in the Natura 2000 selection criteria. For instance, of relevance to the wilderness quality of 'large size' is that the size of the surface of qualifying habitat type is one of the Annex III criteria for selecting sites under the Habitats Directive (Stage 1). The size of the area is also a central issue in the ECJ *Basses Corbières* case. France argued that the authorities were 'not required to classify the whole of the area listed in the national inventory of ZICOs as SPAs'.[47] This view was not accepted by the ECJ: 'It follows from the general scheme of Article 4 of the birds

[42] Art. 4(4) and Annex III Habitats Directive.

[43] See also the webpage of the European Commission: http://ec.europa.eu/environment/nature/natura2000/sites_hab/biogeog_regions/index_en.htm:

> 'Provided that Member States propose changes to the list of SCIs, and in order to ensure legal certainty about the status of any new sites that should be added to a Union List, the Commission proceeds with an annual updating of the Union Lists.'

[44] See Schoukens and Woldendorp, 'Site Selection and Designation under the Habitats and Birds Directives: A Sisyphean Task?', *supra* note 21.

[45] ECJ C-371/98 (*Com.* v. *United Kingdom*), 7 November 2000, paras 22–25.

[46] *Ibid.*, paras 22 and 23.

[47] ECJ, Case C-374/98 (*Com.* v. *France*), 7 December 2000, para. 12.

directive that, where a given area fulfils the criteria for classification as an SPA, it must be made the subject of special conservation measures capable of ensuring, in particular, the survival and reproduction of the bird species mentioned in Annex I to that directive.'[48] France had thereby 'failed to fulfil its obligations under Article 4(1) of the birds directive' [. . .] by 'not adopting special conservation measures for that site sufficient in their geographical extent.'[49]

The ECJ went one step further in its judgment concerning case C-418/04 (*Commission* v. *Ireland*) by stating 'that SPA classification cannot be the result of an isolated study of the ornithological value of each of the areas in question but must be carried out in the light of the natural boundaries of the wetland ecosystem [. . .].'[50] On this basis, the ECJ concluded that an area, which was used as a feeding ground by bird species for which a nearby located SPA was designated, should have been part of the SPA: 'it is an integral part of the entire wetland ecosystem and for that reason ought also to have been classified as an SPA'.[51] Here the ECJ explicitly acknowledged an ecosystem approach in setting the boundaries of SPAs, which is not only relevant for the size of the Natura 2000 sites but, to a certain extent, also for the quality of naturalness.

Other examples of relevant connections with the qualities of size and naturalness could be provided; however, none of these would justify the conclusion that wilderness protection is one of the aims of selecting and designating Natura 2000 sites. When wilderness qualities receive attention, it is because they are considered coincidentally relevant for the specific aims of the directives. The wilderness quality of 'undevelopedness' appears to be even less important. As McLeod et al. state in the context of SAC selection in the United Kingdom: '[a]rtificial areas need not be excluded from site selection if they have spontaneously given rise to Annex I habitat types or host Annex II species and if it is considered that they have exceptional value'.[52]

[48] *Ibid.*, para. 26.
[49] *Ibid.*, para. 59.
[50] ECJ C-418/04 (*Com. v. Ireland*), 13 December 2007, para. 142. Bijlsma et al., *Samenvoeging Natura 2000-gebieden, supra* note 40 and Schoukens and Woldendorp, 'Site Selection and Designation under the Habitats and Birds Directives: A Sisyphean Task?', *supra* note 21, at 36.
[51] ECJ C-418/04 (*Com.* v. *Ireland*), 13 December 2007, para. 145.
[52] C. McLeod, M. Yeo, A.E. Brown, A.J. Burn, J.J. Hopkins and S.F. Way (eds.), *The Habitats Directive: Selection of Special Areas of Conservation in the UK* (Peterborough: Joint Nature Conservation Committee, 2005), 2nd edn., http://jncc.defra.gov.uk/pdf/SAC-selection-background-T37.pdf, at 9.

Consequently, it is through the species and habitat types that wilderness may receive attention in the process of selection of Natura 2000 sites: a wilderness area receives Natura 2000 status if the area is important to ensure the favourable conservation status of the Habitat types of Annex I to the Habitats Directive or species of Annex I of the Birds Directive or Annex II of the Habitats Directive. This raises the question how 'wilderness dependent' these habitat types and species are.

### 3.3 *'Wilderness dependency' of species and habitat types for which Natura 2000 sites must be designated*

Fisher explains that certain species are characterized by a high 'wilderness dependency', for instance because their survival 'has a strong linkage to specific natural processes' or because they 'are only able to survive in areas with sufficient space and access to certain trophic functions of wild nature'.[53] In Natura 2000 terminology this means that for certain species wilderness is important for attaining a favourable conservation status. The European Commission's Guidelines on Wilderness and Natura 2000 (hereinafter Guidelines)[54] explicitly acknowledge this for both species and habitat types: 'Wilderness areas play a significant role in achieving favourable conservation status of many species and habitats of Community importance.'[55]

For several habitat types, the Guidelines stress the importance of 'natural processes', 'dynamics of ecosystems', 'allowance of natural disturbances' and other characteristics of wilderness.[56] According to the document, '[e]xamples of habitats that benefit from non-intervention management can be found under all habitat groups under Annex I to the Habitats Directive' and include 'aquatic as well as terrestrial, or closed woodlands as well as open grasslands, dunes, peatlands or rocky habitats'.[57] Examples include 'Pannonic salt steppes and salt marshes (habitat type 1530), Alpine and subalpine calcareous and siliceous grasslands (6150, 6170), Active raised bogs (7110), Western Taiga (9010), Bog

[53] Chapter 3. Fisher refers to Edit Borza and Vlado Vancura, 'Last of the Wild: Overview of Status and Monitoring of Some Wilderness Related Species in the Natura 2000 Network' (Budapest: PAN Parks Foundation/Kenguruprint, 2009; reprinted in 2011), www.europarc.org/uploaded/documents/1271.pdf.

[54] Guidelines on Wilderness in Natura 2000, *supra* note 12.

[55] *Ibid.*, at 23.

[56] *Ibid.*, at 25–26.

[57] *Ibid.*

woodland (91D0), and Riparian hardwood forests along rivers (91F0).'[58] Based on a survey of site managers of thirty-six Natura 2000 sites with high wilderness values, an annex to the Guidelines lists eighty habitat types 'representing wilderness values'.[59]

The Guidelines also provide examples of species that heavily depend on areas with relatively high wilderness qualities. The site managers' survey identified seventy-two Habitats Directive species and fifty-nine bird species 'for which wilderness management is important'.[60] This list included the large carnivores discussed in Chapters 3 and 7, alongside reptiles, amphibians and insects. For instance, in respect of forest species the Guidelines explain that 'many rare and threatened plant, fungi and animal species depend on the natural developmental stages of forests, rich in veteran trees and decaying wood' and that these species 'can develop only in forests subjected to a long-lasting regime of natural processes, including disturbances such as storms and wild fire'.[61]

The Guidelines pay special attention to wilderness-dependent birds species, distinguishing between those 'that are specialist of old-growth forest' in boreal and temperate areas (e.g., the Three-Toed Woodpecker and Red-Breasted Flycatcher), species that benefit from 'old, mature forest stands with dead or tall emergent trees' (e.g., Black Stork, Krüper's Nuthatch), species 'that need large areas' (e.g., Goshawk, Hazel Grouse, Black Woodpecker and Siberian Jay), species that need '[p]ristine riverine forests' (e.g., White-tailed Eagle, Little Egret, Night Heron) and 'species of taiga that benefit from the natural character of the forest' (e.g., Pygmy Owl, Nutcracker).[62]

In assessing the extent to which wilderness considerations are represented in the selection and designation process of Natura 2000 sites, it is of course important to assess whether these species and habitat types with relatively high wilderness dependency are listed in Annex I of the Birds Directive or Annex I or II of the Habitats Directive. Only if species and habitats are on one of these lists, must sites be designated to support their conservation status. The Guidelines are silent on this issue, but a comparison makes clear that almost all wilderness depending habitat types and species mentioned in the Guidelines are indeed to be found on one of the relevant Annexes, except for some species of birds (e.g., the common moorhen and the whimbrel).

[58] *Ibid.*
[59] *Ibid.*, at 26 and Annex A5.
[60] *Ibid.*, at 27–28 and Annex A6.
[61] *Ibid.*, at 26.
[62] *Ibid.*, at 29.

### 3.4 *Spatial overlap between wilderness and Natura 2000*

The available date reveals an interesting correlation between Natura 2000 and wilderness in Europe. On the one hand, the previously discussed importance of wilderness for Natura 2000 habitats and species seems to be reflected by the fact that almost all of the wildest places of the EU have a Natura 2000 status.[63] However, on the other hand it is also clear that only a very small proportion of the Natura 2000 network has high wilderness qualities: the European Wilderness Register, although not yet complete, indicates that '[m]ore than 500 protected areas were identified having wilderness qualities, of which 282 were qualified partly or total as wilderness category A, i.e. meeting the criteria set for wilderness, with an estimated total coverage of 4-5% of the Natura 2000 network.'[64] Possibly this may in part be explained by the limited role of wilderness qualities in selecting Natura 2000 sites; however, it may also underline that there is simply very little wilderness left within the EU's boundaries.

## 4 Article 6 and wilderness protection

### 4.1 *Importance of the conservation objectives for the scope of legal protection under Article 6*

Where an area with relatively high wilderness qualities has received the status of Natura 2000 site, the question arises as to what extent such a wilderness area and its wilderness qualities receive legal protection under the regime of Article 6 of the Habitats Directive.

In determining this issue, it is important to acknowledge that – as discussed above – the Article 6 regime is strict, but the scope of this regime is primarily determined by the conservation objectives of the site in question. For instance, the 'conservation measures' to be taken under Article 6(1) must be targeted towards realizing the conservation objectives of that site.[65] Furthermore, the terms 'significant' and 'significant effects' advanced, respectively, in Articles 6(2) and 6(3) must be

[63] A.T. Kuiters, M. van Eupen, S. Carver, M. Fisher, Z. Kun and V. Vancura, *Wilderness Register and Indicator for Europe*, Final report, October 2013, http://ec.europa.eu/environment/nature/natura2000/wilderness/pdf/Wilderness_register_indicator.pdf, at 39.

[64] *Ibid.*, at 73. See also the Guidelines on Wilderness in Natura 2000, at 17.

[65] See the Guidelines on Wilderness in Natura 2000, at 24. Reference is made to European Commission, 'Managing Natura 2000 Sites: The Provisions of Article 6 of the "Habitats" Directive 92/43/EEC', 2000, http://ec.europa.eu/environment/nature/natura2000/management/docs/art6/provision_of_art6_en.pdf.

interpreted in the light of the conservation objectives of the relevant Natura 2000 site.[66] For instance, as far as Article 6(3) is concerned, the ECJ has considered that 'where [. . .] a plan or project is likely to undermine the conservation objectives of the site concerned, it must necessarily be considered likely to have a significant effect on the site'.[67]

This strong connection between Article 6 and the conservation objectives of a site clearly limits the scope of legal protection of natural values under Article 6. As has been explained by the Advocate General of the ECJ in the Waddensea case, 'in principle any adverse effect on the conservation objectives must be regarded as a significant adverse effect on the integrity of the site concerned';[68] however, '[a]dverse effects, which are not obvious in view of the site's conservation objectives, may be disregarded'.[69]

### *4.2 The focus and scope of the conservation objectives*

In view of the strong focus of the objective of the directives and the Natura 2000 selection criteria upon specific (listed) habitat types and species, the conservation objectives of a Natura 2000 site will normally relate to the habitats and species for which the site has been designated. This is reinforced by Article 4(4) of the Habitats Directive that requires a Member State – when designating a SAC – to establish 'priorities in the light of the importance of the sites for the maintenance or restoration, at a favourable conservation status, of a natural habitat type in Annex I or a species in Annex II and for the coherence of Natura 2000 [. . .].'[70] The European Commission concurs by explaining that 'in its most general sense a conservation objective is the specification of the overall target for the species and/or habitat types for which a site is designated in order for it to contribute to maintaining or reaching favourable conservation status of the habitats and species concerned, at the national, the biogeographical or the European level'.[71] According to the Commission, a favourable conservation status must be defined 'at an appropriate level, such as for

[66] ECJ, C-127/02 (*Waddensea*), 29 January 2004, para. 46. See also the preamble to the Habitats Directive and the European Commission's note on setting conservation objectives for Natura 2000 sites, 23 November 2012, http://ec.europa.eu/environment/nature/legislation/habitatsdirective/docs/commission_note2.pdf.

[67] ECJ, C-127/02, *Ibid.*, para. 48.

[68] Opinion AG Kokott, C-127/02 (*Waddensea*), 29 January 2004, para. 85.

[69] *Ibid.*, para. 72.

[70] 'Commission Note on Setting Conservation Objectives for Natura 2000 Sites', *supra* note 66.

[71] *Ibid.* See also the Guidelines on Wilderness in Natura 2000 at 44.

example the national, the biogeographical or the European level',[72] and the conservation objectives at site level clarify the contribution of the site in achieving this status for the qualifying habitat types and species of that site.

This interpretation might give the impression that for each habitat and species, the conservation objectives must be specified or even quantified in domestic legislation or administrative decisions, but in relation to case C535/07, the ECJ makes clear that at least for SPAs this is not a general requirement: 'So far as concerns conservation objectives, it is apparent from paragraphs 20 and 21 of the judgment in Case C-374/98 *Commission* v *France* that the protective legal status which SPAs must obtain does not mean that those objectives have to be specified for each species considered separately.'[73] In Case C-374/98, France had adopted decrees that explicitly protected the Bonelli's eagle but not other bird species in these areas, an approach that was criticized by the Commission, but the Court considered the legislation was not 'insufficient in relation to the conservation requirements of any of the bird species present in the areas covered by those decrees'.[74] However, this does not justify the conclusion that the legal protection of a SPA may be 'disconnected' from the species for which the area qualifies as SPA. The Court makes clear that 'Article 4 of the Birds Directive lays down a regime which is specifically targeted and reinforced, both for the species listed in Annex I to the directive and for migratory species' and that this is 'the particular nature of the protection regime which SPAs must enjoy'.[75] It must therefore be clarified for which species the site is designated and the legal protection must meet the standards of the directive in relation to the protection of those species. One might therefore state that the conservation objectives of a site should be focused on the qualifying species, although there is no explicit requirement to specify such objectives in much detail.

### 4.3 *Wilderness protection under Article 6*

With conservation objectives being focused on specific habitat types and species, the degree of wilderness protection under Article 6 will depend heavily on the importance of wilderness to these habitats and species. It is clear that certain habitat types and species require active management

[72] 'Commission Note on Setting Conservation Objectives for Natura 2000 Sites', *supra* note 66.

[73] ECJ, C-535/07 (*Com.* v. *Austria*), 14 October 2010, para. 65. See also para. 111.

[74] See ECJ, C-374/98 (*Commission* v. *France*), 7 December 2000, paras 18–21.

[75] ECJ, C-535/07 (*Com.* v. *Austria*), 14 October 2010, para. 66.

and may even be threatened by non-intervention management.[76] In such cases, Article 6(1) will require conservation measures that will probably limit wilderness qualities (e.g., naturalness) or prevent the area from becoming 'wilder'. However, as discussed in Subsection 3.3, other habitats and species depend on wilderness – or certain qualities of it – to maintain or achieve a favourable conservation status. When conservation objectives are focused on these species, the same Article 6 regime may actively require wilderness conservation under Article 6(1) and prohibit adverse wilderness impacts under Articles 6(2) and 6(3). Generally, one could state that the more wilderness-dependent habitats and species are, the stronger the 'wilderness protection' under the Article 6 regime will be.

An example of an ECJ case whereby Article 6(2) resulted in protection of the wilderness qualities of large size and undevelopedness to prevent significant effects for a Natura 2000 species relates to the unauthorized operation of a mine in Spain:

> Since the Kingdom of Spain does not produce evidence refuting the conclusions of that report [. . .] it must be held that the [. . .] operations are capable of producing a barrier effect likely to contribute to the fragmentation of the habitat of the capercaillie and the isolation of certain sub-populations of that species.[77]

However, similarly to the position in relation to the selection of Natura 2000 sites, and indeed the operation of the Bern Convention,[78] Article 6 offers 'indirect' wilderness protection, as the application of this provision in this context depends upon whether the habitats and species in question are wilderness-dependent. This weakens wilderness protection under this legal system substantially, not only because certain species will not benefit from wilderness management, but also because those that do may under certain circumstances not require the full protection of all three wilderness qualities. For instance, establishing permanent infrastructure in an old-growth forest will certainly limit the wilderness quality of 'undevelopedness' of the site, but may not cause negative impacts on Natura 2000 species that highly depend on the 'naturalness' and large size of the old-growth forest. In such a situation, Article 6(3) may prevent intensive forestry but not the construction of a road or building, since preventing permanent facilities is not an independent objective of the Natura 2000 regime. As explained by Advocate General Mazak in a case relating to wind turbines:

[76] See the Guidelines on Wilderness in Natura 2000 at 45.
[77] See, e.g., ECJ, C-404/09 (*Com.* v. *Spain*), 24 November 2011, para. 148.
[78] Chapter 7.

> the referring court, the applicant companies and the Commission correctly state that the classification of a zone as a site of Community importance or special protection area forming part of the ecological network Natura 2000 does not result in all construction therein being banned in accordance with the Birds and Habitats Directives.[79]

Even in Natura 2000 sites that have been selected and designated for large carnivores, Article 6 may not ensure full wilderness protection. This is illustrated by the ECJ case C-308-08, relating to the upgrade of a road in the Doñana Natura site in Spain, which site has been designated for (among others) the Iberian Lynx.[80] The project had 'led to an increase in traffic, particularly private cars, travelling at higher speeds'[81] and the European Commission stated that the upgrade resulted in 'natural habitat of that species to be fragmented and exposed the animals to the risk of fatal accidents'.[82] However, the Court disagreed, considering that significant impacts upon lynx populations had been averted because the road was fenced over a distance of 9,300 metres on both sides of the road and safe road-crossing options had been established.[83] In this case these developments clearly limited the wilderness qualities of the site, but did not cause significant effects under Article 6(3).[84]

## 5 Options for strengthening wilderness protection under the Natura 2000 regime

The above discussions show that, despite the strictness of Natura 2000, the regime as such does not guarantee comprehensive wilderness protection in the European Union in either the phase of site selection or in the application of the Natura 2000 regime. But what *if* wilderness protection is an explicit policy aim? Could wilderness protection then be established through Natura 2000 or should we conclude that the latter system fails to accommodate wilderness approaches?

[79] Opinion AG Mazak, C- 2/10, 14 April 2011, para. 30.
[80] ECJ, C-308–08 (*Com.* v. *Spain*), 20 May 2010, para. 47.
[81] *Ibid.*, para. 24.
[82] *Ibid.*, para. 12.
[83] *Ibid.*, in particular paras 31–47.
[84] In other situations, building a road or other physical developments may result in significant effects for the qualifying values of the site. See, e.g., ECJ, C-404/09 (*Com.* v. *Spain*), 24 November 2011, para. 117 and 148. See also the discussion in Chapter 18 by Sergiusz Urban of the Rospuda River valley case in Poland.

The Guidelines on Wilderness in Natura 2000 adopt a cautiously optimistic tone,[85] which is significant as the document 'reflects the view of the Commission services'.[86] The document has a strong practical value as it demonstrates through case studies 'that a good degree of conservation of habitats and species of Community interest can be achieved in the Natura 2000 sites through management which pursues the preservation of wilderness qualities'.[87] Notwithstanding its wider significance, however, legal aspects receive little attention in the Guidelines; the document makes no reference either to ECJ/CJEU case law or the legal literature.[88]

Based on the previous discussions in this chapter and the Guidelines, a number of issues of particular legal relevance for the 'wilderness protection potential' of Natura 2000 are identified below.

### (a) Greater scope for ecological changes by ensuring favourable conservation status at the national level and incorporating foreseeable ecological changes into the conservation objectives

It follows from Section 4 and Subsection 5.1 that reflecting wilderness qualities in the conservation objectives of a Natura 2000 site can strengthen the integration of wilderness protection and Natura 2000 implementation. However, an important question is whether the regime leaves space for ecological dynamics that are so characteristic of wilderness. What if – due to natural processes and succession stages shifts – certain habitat types or species for which the site has been designated decrease in quality or size?

Under these circumstances it is envisaged that natural processes will profit certain Natura 2000 values, while other values will decrease. The Commission appears to contemplate such developments as the Guidelines state that, '[n]atural fluctuations at the individual site level following natural processes fit well within the Natura 2000 requirements, even if the area of some habitat types may locally and temporarily decrease and while other habitats may develop or improve as a result of the same natural

[85] See also the summary of the views expressed by Ladislav Miko (in 2007 Director General Environment of the European Commission) at the conference 'Nature – Bridging Borders', 26–30 September 2007, Cesky Krumlov, Czech Republic (Grafenau: Europarc Federation, 2007), www.europarc.cz/download/conf2007/conference_report.pdf, at 24.

[86] *Ibid.*, at 2.

[87] Guidelines on Wilderness in Natura 2000 at 43.

[88] The only reference in the Guidelines to the Court may be found in the general statement that '[i]t rests with the EU Court of Justice to provide definitive interpretation of a Directive' (p. 8).

processes'.[89] In this case, one approach to avoiding difficult discussions on compliance with Article 6(2) in relation to the decreasing values may be to incorporate such prospective developments into the conservation objectives of the site. In the Netherlands, this approach has already been applied and explicitly accepted by the highest administrative court.[90]

However, the consequences of natural processes for qualifying habitats and species are often uncertain and it is not always possible to build anticipatory measures into the individual conservation objectives. The Guidelines appear to leave space for '[l]ocal fluctuations [of habitats or species] as a result of natural processes at the site level [. . .], provided the FCS [favourable conservation] status at the national and biogeographical level is ensured'.[91] Consequently, it must in principle be certain that the habitats and species for which the area has been designated will be maintained or restored at a favourable conservation status at, e.g., national level, despite possible unexpected negative effects for these values in the relevant site. It is uncertain whether the ECJ would agree with this position as wilderness approaches have not yet been the subject of a preliminary ruling or infringement procedure. However, this standard appears to be an essential condition: if this cannot be guaranteed on the basis of solid ecological knowledge, it appears difficult to argue that the decrease of a qualifying habitat or species is not a violation of Article 6(2) of the Habitats Directive.

This invites a Member State to integrate wilderness approaches in Natura 2000 sites into a more comprehensive national policy directed at meeting the objectives of both EU directives. It also suggests that wilderness approaches in Natura 2000 sites are likely to be less problematic in countries where many habitats and species are already in a favourable conservation status.

### (b) Prevention of the extinction of habitats and species, particularly those with priority status

One might question whether it would also be acceptable if a habitat type or species for which a site has been designated could completely disappear as a result of 'wilderness management'. It appears that the Guidelines seek to avoid discussion of this situation. One might argue

[89] Guidelines on Wilderness in Natura 2000, at 44–45.

[90] See, e.g., Afdeling Bestuursrechtspraak Raad van State, 23 July 2014 (in Dutch), para. 14.1, https://www.raadvanstate.nl/uitspraken/zoeken-in-uitspraken/tekst-uitspraak.html?id=80198.

[91] Guidelines on Wilderness in Natura 2000, at 44.

that such a consequence would still be acceptable as long as the favourable conservation status at national level is guaranteed; however, this interpretation is questionable, particularly in respect of habitat types or species that have priority status. In respect of Article 6(3), the ECJ has concluded that '[t]he competent national authorities cannot [. . .] authorise interventions where there is a risk of lasting harm to the ecological characteristics of sites which host priority natural habitat types'.[92] The Court states that this 'would particularly be so where there is a risk that an intervention of a particular kind will bring about the disappearance or the partial and irreparable destruction of a priority natural habitat type present on the site concerned'.[93] This judgment relates to an 'intervention' to which Article 6(3) applied; however, because the Court has also stated in various other judgments that 'Article 6(2) and Article 6(3) are designed to ensure the same level of protection',[94] this standard may also apply to *non*-intervention (wilderness management) subject to Article 6(2).

### (c) Limiting legal risks by zoning

Chapters in Part III of this volume illustrate that in various countries large National Parks have wilderness zones. The Guidelines further note that '[a] non-intervention core zone with wilderness values can be distinguished from zones with active management where other ecological values or socio-economic factors are essential'.[95] Such approaches may also avoid difficult legal discussions and related uncertainties. For instance, if the conservation objectives of the site for a particular species are met in the more intensively managed areas, the decreased presence of this species in the wilderness zone as a result of natural processes will probably not breach Article 6(2).

### (d) Adopting stricter domestic standards to ensure protection of all three wilderness qualities

Case 404/09 above illustrates that even in respect of species that strongly prefer wilderness areas, the Natura 2000 regime may not result in a comprehensive protection of all three wilderness qualities. However, it should be noted that both EU directives permit the Member States to adopt stricter nature conservation rules. This is illustrated by ECJ case C- 2/10, in

[92] ECJ case C-258/11 (*Sweetman*), 11 April 2013, para. 43.
[93] *Ibid.*
[94] *Ibid.*, para. 32.
[95] Guidelines on Wilderness in Natura 2000 at 45.

which the general prohibition of wind turbines in Natura 2000 sites, established by the Italian government, was challenged. While such turbines may under certain circumstances be in compliance with Article 6, the Court concluded that the Italian legislation complied with the Natura 2000 regime:

> the Birds and Habitats Directives, in particular Article 6(3) of the Habitats Directive, do not preclude a more stringent national protective measure which imposes an absolute prohibition on the construction of wind turbines [. . .] within areas forming part of the Natura 2000 network [. . .].[96]

## 6 Conclusion

To what extent do wilderness areas within the European Union and their wilderness qualities receive legal protection under the Natura 2000 system? Despite the unique characteristics of the regime, Natura 2000 does not as such guarantee comprehensive wilderness protection, at least not without an explicit policy for integrating wilderness protection and the implementation of EU commitments. The criteria for the selection and designation of Natura 2000 sites do not refer explicitly to wilderness. Although the wilderness qualities of 'large size' and 'naturalness' are to a certain extent reflected in the criteria, their relevance is 'indirect': the wilderness qualities of such areas is only relevant to the selection process if they are considered important for achieving the objective of maintaining or restoring the favourable conservation status of habitat types and species of Community interest. Furthermore, *if* areas with relatively high wilderness qualities receive Natura 2000 status, wilderness protection under Article 6 is also 'indirect': the protection accorded by this provision focuses on the conservation objectives of a Natura 2000 site and relates solely to the conservation status of habitat types and species for which the site was designated. Consequently, the greater the importance of wilderness to the conservation and restoration of habitat types and species for which the site was designated, the stronger the wilderness protection under Article 6 will be. However, it was also illustrated that even in Natura 2000 sites that host typical wilderness species, the three main wilderness qualities may not necessarily all receive protection.

[96] ECJ, case C- 2/10, 14 April 2011, para. 58.

However, this may not be the final answer to the central question. As wilderness may be dynamic, so too is the wilderness debate and the wider role of law in protecting such areas. The good news for wilderness in the EU is that the European Commission has been shown to be receptive to wilderness approaches in Natura 2000 sites. This is clear from the Guidelines, but is also illustrated by the explicit option provided to applicants for LIFE projects to consider a wilderness approach, not merely as 'a substitute to best practices currently used', but as an approach that 'could be tested as a complementary way of biodiversity conservation for species and habitats identified in the Habitats and Birds Directives'.[97]

From a legal perspective, and particularly in the light of ECJ/CJEU case law, there are some uncertainties in respect of the scope for wilderness management under Article 6; however, as discussed in Section 5, certain approaches may limit these uncertainties. Furthermore, through various active NGOs, wilderness workshops, LIFE projects and research initiatives, there is a wider appreciation of wilderness approaches to Natura 2000 sites and the importance of wilderness to Natura 2000 habitats and species. This may also further reduce legal ambiguities, given that they are often driven by wider gaps in ecological knowledge. It would be prudent to heed these lessons, since they may well lead to a greater role for wilderness considerations in achieving the Natura 2000 objectives, and correspondingly to a greater role for the Natura 2000 regime in protecting wilderness in Europe.

[97] European Commission, Guidelines for applicants 2014, *LIFE Nature and Biodiversity*, 2014, http://ec.europa.eu/environment/life/toolkit/pmtools/life2014_2020/documents/2014nat_application_guide.pdf, at 19.

9

# The Alpine Convention and wilderness protection

VOLKER MAUERHOFER, EWALD GALLE AND MARCO ONIDA*

## 1 Introduction

The international treaty on the protection of the Alps ('Alpine Convention', hereafter 'AC'[1]) was signed during the Second International Alpine Conference on 7 November 1991 in Salzburg (Austria) by the representatives of the Alpine countries (Austria, Germany, France, Italy, Liechtenstein and Switzerland) and the European Community. The Republic of Slovenia signed the AC in March 1993 and the Principality of Monaco followed in 1994. The AC came into force on 6 March 1995.[2]

It constitutes a Multilateral Environmental Agreement (MEA) taking a specific regional geographical approach. The AC is an international legal instrument for sustainable development and is based on the awareness that environment and development have close interlinkages.[3] It is an

* The authors write in a purely personal capacity and this chapter does not reflect the official opinion of the European Commission or Austrian government.

1 Alpine Convention, Salzburg, 7 November 1991, www.alpconv.org

2 See www.alpconv.org/en/convention/history/default.html; W.E. Burhenne, 'The Alpine Convention – An Update', *Environmental Policy and Law*, 27(5) (1997), 407; W.E. Burhenne, 'A Big Day for the Alpine Convention', *Environmental Policy and Law*, 30(6) (2000), 278.

3 For further information see E. Galle, *Das Übereinkommen zum Schutz der Alpen (Alpenkonvention) und seine Protokolle*, Beiträge zur Umweltgestaltung: A 148, (Berlin: Erich Schmidt Verlag, 2002); also published in Ergänzungsband A 148, Alpine Umweltprobleme Teil 39, (Berlin: Erich Schmidt Verlag, 2007); A. Dallinger, 'An Alpine Convention – Solution for an Avalanche of Problems', *Environmental Conservation*, 21 (1994), 279–280; M. Onida, 'A Common Approach to Mountain Specific Challenges: The Alpine Convention', in P. Quillacq and M. Onida (Eds.), *Environmental Protection and Mountains. Is Environmental Law Adapted to the Challenges Faced by Mountain Areas?* (Innsbruck: Permanent Secretariat of the Alpine Convention, 2011), 94–112; and M.F. Price, 'Towards Co-operation across Mountain Frontiers: The Alpine Convention', *European Environment*, 9(3) (1999), 83–89.

instrument that, with its all-encompassing and cross-border approach, has attained a special status among regional environmental agreements. Unlike other MEAs, the AC does not exclusively address certain ecosystems, habitat types and species, but instead has a very broad thematic scope relating to a whole mountain region. It can be therefore considered one of the general MEAs related to, among other aspects, biodiversity protection.[4] Furthermore, in view of its geographic scope, the AC can be considered as being based on an ecosystem approach: it is the occurrence of certain geomorphological and biological characteristics that determines the geographical scope of application of the AC, rather than national or regional borders.

The AC applies to an area of approximately 190,000 km$^2$ across eight States, with a population of 14 million people.[5] Austria and Italy account for about two-thirds of the area and population.[6] Some twenty-five per cent of the territory of the AC is addressed through different protection regimes.[7] Population density in the Alps is high if only the area suitable for human settlement is taken into account. For obvious reasons, the concentration of wilderness is greater at higher altitudes. The Western Alps account for eighty-one of the eighty-two peaks that exceed 4,000 metres in altitude (these are mostly concentrated around the Regions of Haute Savoie, Valle d'Aosta and Valais).[8] Clearly, these least accessible regions, as well as some scarcely inhabited valleys in the Maritime, Cottian and Julian Alps, host the largest unspoiled natural areas. At the same time, in these regions, which are 'naturally' protected, wilderness protection tends to receive less attention compared to regions in which human settlements occupy almost the entirety of the mountain areas (e.g., Tirol, South Tirol), and where new developments always raise strong opposition among nature protection associations and concerned citizens.

This chapter first provides a short overview of the objectives, the structure and the organization of the AC (Section 2). Next, the wilderness-related content of the AC and its protocols is presented in greater detail

4 See V. Mauerhofer and F. Nyacuru, 'Biodiversity, Migratory Species and Natural Heritage', in P.G. Harris (ed.), *Handbook of Global Environmental Politics* (Abingdon: Routledge, 2013), 481–493, at 486. M. Onida, 'Plaidoyer pour une politique communautaire des Montagnes: l'exemple à prendre de la Convention alpine', *Revue du Droit de l'Union Européenne*, 4/2008, Paris.

5 See www.alpconv.org/en/convention/default.aspx.

6 See www.alpconv.org/en/convention/default.aspx.

7 *Ibid.*

8 See www.club4000.it/en/the-4000-of-the-alps/information-about-the-4000s/official-listofl-the-4000-in-the-alps.

(Section 3). The following section provides a short overview of the interplay of the AC with other international legal instruments, particularly to show that the overlap of different regimes may result in the protection of Alpine wilderness (Section 4). To illustrate the relevance of the AC framework for wilderness protection in the Alps at a domestic level, the implementation of the AC in Austria is discussed (Section 5). This section pays special attention to the only official 'Wilderness Area' in Austria (in the sense of the IUCN classification): 'Wilderness Dürrenstein'. Next, a number of specific projects, based on funding programmes, with relevance for the protection of Alpine wilderness receives attention (Section 6). Finally, conclusions and an outlook on wilderness protection and the AC are provided (Section 7).

## 2 Objectives, structure and organization of the Alpine Convention

Wilderness protection features highly within the AC, both directly through specific provisions in relevant protocols, and indirectly through the promotion of a model of development whereby nature also plays an active role for economic purposes (e.g., regarding tourism).

Art. 2 ('General obligations') is the core provision of the AC for protecting the Alps and defines the general obligations of the parties in order to implement an environmentally friendly use of the area in all sectors and to preserve the Alpine range as a living and economic space for its populations. Art. 2(2) of the AC states that, in order to preserve and to safeguard the Alps, the parties shall adopt suitable measures in specific fields and identifies twelve different thematic objectives. The parties have agreed on the creation of additional Protocols, where the general obligations of the AC have been elaborated in greater detail (Art 2(3)). Between 1994 and 2000, eight thematic Protocols have been signed on spatial planning, soil conservation, conservation of nature and the countryside, mountain farming, mountain forests, tourism, transport and energy. A further protocol was adopted on the settlement of disputes.[9]

[9] Four Protocols regarding the following sectors are still open: population and culture, protection of air quality, water management and waste management; however, only the 'population and culture' sector, as requested by the Ministers, has been further examined through a Declaration, which was adopted in autumn 2006, during the IXth Meeting of the Alpine Conference in Alpbach. The other subject areas have not yet been addressed and it is not clear if work on new Protocols will commence in the near future; see Onida, 'A Common Approach to Mountain Specific Challenges: The Alpine Convention', *supra* note 3, at 95.

The Protocols are legally binding agreements, which further specify the more general obligations outlined by the AC. The Protocols are currently in force in Austria, France, Germany, Italy, Liechtenstein and Slovenia. Monaco ratified four of these protocols, the EU five, whereas Switzerland remains the only State not to have ratified any of the Protocols of the AC (as by January 2016)[10], a rather paradoxical situation given its location in the centre of the Alps.[11]

As regards organizational aspects, the AC sets up the Alpine Conference,[12] the highest decision-making body formed by the Ministers of the Parties, and the Permanent Committee, which is the executive organ at administrative level. A decision based on Article 9 of the AC to establish a Secretariat was taken in 2002 and since 2003 the Permanent Secretariat has been based in Innsbruck, with an external office in Bolzano. The 2002 Alpine Conference also set up a Compliance Committee to monitor the implementation of the Convention and its Protocols by the parties. The AC provides for the establishment of Working Groups (WGs) in order to prepare decisions on specific issues.[13]

## 3 The wilderness-related content of the Alpine Convention

Due to its framework approach, the AC has a broad objective, including the preservation of biodiversity. In the AC and its Protocols, the term 'wilderness' is not explicitly used; however, various components of the AC framework are relevant for the protection of one or more of the three main qualities of wilderness as described in Chapter 1 (naturalness, absence of proof of modern human society and relatively large size).

### *3.1 Naturalness*

Article 2(2)(f) of the AC obliges Contracting Parties to 'take appropriate measures' to protect, conserve and, where necessary, rehabilitate the natural environment and the countryside,

[10] Apart from the Monaco Protocol.

[11] The Report 'Switzerland's International Environmental Policy 2012, State and Outlook', published by the Federal Office for the Environment, and which, inter alia, contains a chapter on MEAs in which Switzerland participates, does not even mention the Alpine Convention.

[12] This Ministerial meeting later established itself as 'Alpine Conference', and was finally included in the AC as its decision-making body.

[13] The full list of the existing WGs is available at www.alpconv.org/en/organization/groups/default.html.

> so that ecosystems are able to function, animal and plants species, including their habitats, are preserved, nature's capacity for regeneration and sustained productivity is maintained, and the variety, uniqueness and beauty of nature and the countryside as a whole are preserved on a permanent basis.

This formulation explicitly refers to 'naturalness' as one of the three main qualities of wilderness. For this quality, also the Protocols are of central importance, particularly the Protocol 'Conservation of the Nature and the Countryside' (short hereinafter 'Nature Conservation Protocol'). Article 2 of this Protocol ('fundamental commitments') states that

> each Contracting Party undertakes to adopt the measures necessary to ensure the protection, care and, to the extent necessary, the restoring of nature and the landscape of the Alpine territory, together with the wild animal and plant species, their diversity and their habitat, while also considering the possibility of their ecologically tolerable usage.

This general obligation has been worked out in several more concrete obligations. For instance, under Article 9 of the Nature Conservation Protocol the Contracting Parties are asked to create appropriate conditions for all types of activities which are able to affect nature. The second sentence of the first paragraph of this article goes even further: the Parties are committed to considering the interests of nature and landscape by conducting an examination of possible impacts of and alternatives for the proposed activity.[14]

Numerous other provisions also have the potential to address issues related to wilderness. For example, Article 11 of the Nature Conservation Protocol contains an obligation to preserve protected areas. The term 'protected areas' covers a variety of sites, such as National Parks or Biosphere Reserves. The core obligation of this provision is the duty to preserve, manage and to eventually extend such areas in order to attain their specific conservation objectives. The content of this objective is different for each protected area, but often the naturalness constitutes an essential motivation for its designation and protection. Of particular interest for the wilderness quality of naturalness is the third paragraph of this provision, obliging the Parties to 'set aside areas of respect and tranquillity that ensures giving priority to the wild animal and plant species over other interests', in which areas the Parties must ensure that:

[14] For a comprehensive discussion of these issues see M. Hautzenberg, 'Das Naturschutzprotokoll und seine unmittelbare Anwendbarkeit im österreichischen Naturschutzrecht', *Recht der Umwelt* (2013), at 237.

> there is the peace necessary for the ecological process typical of the species to take place undisturbed, and shall reduce or prohibit any form of use incompatible with the ecological processes of these areas.[15]

Art. 13 obliges the parties more generally and also outside of protected areas to implement the necessary measures to ensure the preservation of natural and near-natural biotope types in sufficient quantities and to guarantee their effective spatial distribution. Until now the implementation of this provision has been unsatisfactory, although as regards the obligation laid down in paragraph 2 implementation is in progress. This obligation relates to the preparation of reports on national measures. A questionnaire has been prepared to this end and the five Alpine countries of the EU referred to European sources of law, like the Wild Birds Directive[16] and the Habitats Directive.[17]

Furthermore, the Protocol also contains some very specific obligations and prohibitions that directly promote 'naturalness': Parties have to implement a fishing and hunting ban for specific animal species (Art. 15), ensure the recovery of endemic species (Art. 16) and prevent the settlement of animal and plant species which do not belong to the natural habitat (Art. 17). Also other Protocols under the convention contain prohibitions of activities or effects that promote 'naturalness', such as the prohibition in the Soil Protocol on impacts on labile areas, briefly discussed in the next subsection.

### 3.2 *Absence of proof of modern human society*

Article 11 of the Nature Conservation Protocol on the duty to preserve areas obliges the Parties to also avoid all activities which would conflict with the conservation purpose. Although there is no prohibition *per se* to build infrastructure facilities in protected areas, in practice the preservation of a natural area generally implies that the impact on the territory by means of man-made structures is strongly regulated and limited.

Likewise, the Protocol on Spatial Planning and Sustainable Development, which primarily concerns procedural aspects, contains the commitment to delimit areas for the protection of nature and the

[15] Article 11(3) of the Nature Conservation Protocol.

[16] Council Directive 79/409/EEC of 2 April 1979 on the conservation of wild birds (Bird Directive), *Official Journal* L, 103(25/04), 1–18, replaced by Directive 2009/147/EC of 30 November 2009, *Official Journal* 2010 L 20, 7–25.

[17] Council Directive 92/43/EEC of 21 May 1992 on the conservation of natural habitats and of wild fauna and flora (Habitats Directive), *Official Journal* 1992 L 206, 7–50.

landscape and areas which should be partially or totally free from buildings and disturbing activities (Art. 9(4)). The implementation of these restrictions or even prohibitions positively contributes to the enhancement of wilderness qualities, such as the naturalness and the absence of proof of modern human society.

Similarly, Article 10 of the Tourism Protocol obliges the Parties to 'undertake, in accordance with their laws and ecological criteria, to establish designated quiet areas where no tourist facilities will be developed'. This obligation is also codified in the AC under Art. 2 (2)(i), albeit less explicitly. Such areas, which are free from technical and touristic infrastructures, such as lifts, ramps or public transport facilities, are special areas for recovery; however, in view of the definition of wilderness, such areas could only be effectively protected as or restored to wilderness if the application of Article 10 would be combined with norms prescribing the naturalness of these areas. To comply with Article 10, only the absence of touristic activities (including infrastructure) is required and not, for instance, forest clearances or agricultural measures.

The Protocol on Mountain Forests includes several further obligations. Art. 6(1), for instance, states that in respect of mountain forests that have highly protective functions for human settlements, transport infrastructure and agricultural farmlands, 'Contracting Parties undertake to give priority to that protective function, focusing the forest's management to that purpose.' It is also established that these mountain forests shall be preserved where they are located. Even more significant for the concept of wilderness is that this Protocol also requires the representative selection and demarcation of natural forest reserves, where any form of exploitation is suspended or adapted to the purposes of the reserve (Art. 10(1)).

The Protocol on Soil Conservation also contains provisions of great relevance to wilderness. For instance, Article 7(3) obliges the Parties to take into account 'soil conservation and the scarcity of space in the Alpine region' in their national procedures regarding 'large-scale projects in the fields of trade and industry, construction and infrastructure, especially in the transport, energy and tourism sectors'. Article 8(2) of this Protocol obliges parties to prevent mineral resource activities that may affect designated drinking water and those areas which are particularly significant for safeguarding soil functions. Furthermore, in the context of the protection of wetlands and moors, dewatering measures may only be authorized in exceptional cases. In principle, moor soils shall not be used; they may only be farmed for agricultural purposes in a manner that preserves their characteristics (Art. 9(2)(3)).[18]

For mountain forests with a high protective function (see Art. 6(1) of the Protocol on Mountain Forests), the Protocol on Soil Conservation requires in Article 13(1) that this protective effect should be considered a priority. Thus it repeats the rather vague obligation advanced by the Protocol on Mountain Forests.

Also relevant is Article 14(1) of the Protocol on Soil Conservation, which obliges the Parties to prevent the detrimental impact of tourist activities[19] on the Alpine soils. In particular, authorizations for the building and planning of ski slopes in forests with a protective function shall only be granted in 'exceptional cases' and together with compensatory measures (Art. 14(3)).

Finally, for the quality of the absence of permanent human infrastructure, Article 11 of the Transport Protocol is also noteworthy as this provision aims to limit the construction of new large-capacity roads in the Alps. New trans-alpine large-capacity roads are prohibited (Art. 11(1)), whereas intra-alpine large-capacity roads need to undergo a number of prior assessments on their environmental impacts and economic viability (Art. 11(2)). The underlying principle is that traffic should be shifted from road to rail.

### 3.3 *Relatively large in size*

Although, neither the AC nor its protocols determine any minimum size for wilderness areas, this need not necessarily constitute an operational disadvantage. Articles 11 and 13 of the Nature Conservation Protocol discussed previously could be construed in the spirit of wilderness conservation by interpreting the size requirement as needing to be sufficiently large in order to maintain or restore effective ecological functioning. This interpretation provides for greater flexibility but of course does not guarantee that sites of a minimum size will ultimately be protected. It should also be emphasized that the size of the wilderness area might not be so decisive, in the sense that several relatively small but connected areas forming an ecological continuum might provide greater shelter for wilderness than a large but isolated area.

[18] For a comprehensive discussion see S. Schmid, 'Alpenkonvention und Moorschutz', *Recht der Umwelt* (2007), 158.

[19] For a more general discussion on tourism impacts, see D. Cigale, 'Environmental Impacts of Tourism and Recreation in the Slovenian Alps' [Okoljski učinki turizma in rekreacije], *Geografski Obzornik*, 51(4) (2004), 4–10.

### 3.4 Interim conclusion

The above discussion shows that several Protocols to the AC contain an array of provisions that may play a role in protecting wilderness qualities. In particular, articles that result in the protection of the second quality of wilderness may also have positive effects for the two other qualities of wilderness. It is also clear that there are substantial differences in the way in which obligations and prohibitions have been formulated. Some provisions contain fairly strict and clear wording, while the majority leave considerable space for interpretation.[20]

Initially, the AC was conceived by many as a nature protection instrument, as the name 'Convention for the Protection of the Alps' implies. However, the convention has developed over time and today the broad framework (the AC and its Protocols) may be characterized as a system to promote sustainable development in which social and economic dimensions also play an important role. This has certainly resulted in a situation in which the wilderness dimension cannot always be considered a leading element in politics and decision making. It should not be forgotten that one of the main goals of the AC is to fight the depopulation of rural areas and high-altitude settlements. A clear mission of the Protocols is therefore to provide opportunities to the Alpine population, including future generations, so that they are not forced to migrate to the cities and the plains. This does not imply that social and economic developments will always result in a loss of wilderness. Certain types of outdoor recreation even require the active preservation of wilderness. Nonetheless, a certain tension between these interests is inevitable.

It should also be kept in mind that biodiversity in the Alps is often the result of hundreds of years of human occupation of land. The depopulation that is currently being experienced in high altitude villages is not necessarily beneficial for biodiversity: the uncontrolled growth of forestry may in some cases lead to the disappearance of some wild species of plants and animals. Consequently, a balance has to be found between wilderness protection and the preservation of culture and human-related biodiversity as we know it today.

Tensions generated by different perceptions of these priorities are visible within the AC decision-making bodies: it is often the case that States like Germany or Liechtenstein and even some heavily inhabited and

[20] See Onida, 'A Common Approach to Mountain Specific Challenges: The Alpine Convention', *supra* note 3, at 103.

intensively-visited regions of Austria such as Tirol or Salzburg, which have a relatively small share of wilderness within their territory, promote a more 'conservationist' agenda than States in which wilderness still occupies a large portion of their alpine territory, such as Italy and France.

Furthermore, the situation is dynamic: in recent times, climate change has helped to place biodiversity and wilderness more centrally upon the political agenda. The Alps experience a higher rise in temperature than the average rate within the Northern hemisphere (2 degrees Celsius instead of 1 on average). Global warming pushes plants and species to higher altitudes, which makes connectivity between ecosystems and populations of wild species more difficult. For this reason the issue of green corridors, ecological networks and connectivity in general has gained momentum.

Recently, the Ecological Network Platform has been established under the aegis of the Alpine Convention with the objective of supporting the creation of a cross-border alpine network of protected areas and connecting elements,[21] which can also contribute substantively to wilderness conservation within the Alps. The AC secretariat also participated in the recent Green Infrastructure Initiative of the EU Commission,[22] which, inter alia, emphasizes the Alps as transboundary aspect of the EU's shared natural and cultural heritage.

## 4 The interplay between the Alpine Convention and other legal instruments at international, regional, national and subnational level

Once the AC and its Protocols entered into force, they became part of the legal framework at the international as well as at respective regional, national and subnational level and related to 'international grades' based thereon.[23] Categories that are not derived from a formal convention also exist, such as the protected area categories of the International Union for Conservation of Nature (IUCN),[24] which also includes the category Ib of 'Wilderness Areas'. Although not legally binding, this category was

21 See www.alpconv.org/en/organization/groups/WGEcologicalNetwork/default.html.

22 See, for example, Communication of the European Commission, 'Green Infrastructure (GI) – Enhancing Europe's Natural Capital' (COM(2013)0249), at 9.

23 For example, the grade 'World Natural Heritage' based on the World Heritage Convention of the UNESCO, see V. Mauerhofer and F. Nyacuru, 'Biodiversity, Migratory Species and Natural Heritage', in P.G. Harris (ed.), *Handbook of Global Environmental Politics*, Chapter 37 (Abingdon: Routledge, 2014).

24 N. Dudley, J.D. Parrish, K.H. Redford and S. Stolton, 'The Revised IUCN Protected Area Management Categories: The Debate and Ways Forward', *Oryx*, 44 (2010), 485–490. See also Chapter 1.

particularly influential for the designation of wilderness areas in the territories of AC signatories.[25] Wilderness areas can also be geographically covered by other categories such as certain zones of 'National Parks' designated in accordance with IUCN category II or of 'Biosphere Reserves' declared under the Man and Biosphere (MaB) programme of UNESCO.[26]

At the regional level there is also a full geographical overlap between the areas of application of the AC and, for example, the Bonn Convention on Migratory Species, which all AC parties have ratified.[27] Sometimes there is a partial overlap, for instance with the EU Wild Birds Directive[28] and the Habitats Directive,[29] which do not apply to the territory of Switzerland and Liechtenstein. Nevertheless, if areas with high wilderness qualities have been designated under these Directives as Natura 2000 sites, they nevertheless provide a very strong implementation mechanism that, depending on certain factors, may also strengthen wilderness protection within the geographical range of the AC, especially due to the 'watchdog' function of the European Commission and the jurisdiction of the Court of Justice of the European Union (CJEU).[30]

One example is the Austrian Republic being censured for the incorrect designation and inadequate legal protection of Special Protection Areas under the Natura 2000 regime,[31] in which case part of the incorrect

[25] See, e.g., V. Mauerhofer, 'Nationalparkrecht – Im Spannungsfeld von bundesstaatlicher Kompetenzverteilung, Europarecht und Naturschutzpolitik' [National Park Law – In the area of conflict between competence distribution in a Federal State, EU-law and Nature Conservation Politics], Umweltbundesamt Bericht [Federal Environmental Agency Report] *Bericht*, 129 (1998), at 375, www.umweltbundesamt.at/fileadmin/site/publikationen/BE129.pdf.

[26] See on these reserves, e.g., M. Elbakidze, T. Hahn, V. Mauerhofer, P. Angelstam and R. Axelsson, 'Legal Framework for Biosphere Reserves as Learning Sites for Sustainable Development: A Comparative Analysis of Ukraine and Sweden', *Ambio*, 42 (2013), 174–187.

[27] S. Lyster, 'Convention on the Conservation of Migratory Species of Wild Animals (The Bonn Convention)', *The Natural Resources Journal*, 29 (1989), at 979.

[28] Bird Directive, *supra* note 16. See Chapter 8.

[29] Habitats Directive, *supra* note 17. See Chapter 8.

[30] S. Grohs, 'Commission Infringement procedure in environmental cases', in M. Onida (ed.) *Europe and the Environment* (Groningen: Europa Law Publishing, 2004); L. Cashman, 'Commission Compliance Promotion and Enforcement in the Field of Environment', *Journal for European Environmental and Planning Law*, 5 (2006), 385–394; V. Mauerhofer, '3-D Sustainability: An Approach for Priority Setting in Situation of Conflicting Interests towards a Sustainable Development', *Ecological Economics*, 64(3) (2008), 496–506. See also Chapter 1.

[31] See Case C-535/07 of 14 October 2010, *European Court Reports* 2010 I-09483.

designation related to areas with wilderness qualities,[32] falling within the scope of application of the AC. Recently, the EU Commission initiated a new complaint procedure (no. 2013/4077) against Austria addressing a lack of designations of areas for Natura 2000, including one relatively large alpine riverine area at the river Isel with wilderness qualities for the highly dynamic and natural habitat type 3230, Alpine rivers and their ligneous vegetation with *Myricaria germanica*.[33] Another example, relevant for the theme of this book, would be Case C-304/05, in which Italy was sanctioned for infringing the Habitats Directive in the case of a World Championships skiing event in 2003 in the *Parco Nazionale dello Stelvio*.[34] The area concerned was described as having 'great natural qualities' and according to the CJEU the development constituted measures with a potential significant effect.[35]

Neither the AC nor its Protocols were mentioned in these legal proceedings. Nevertheless, their implementation at the EU level is mandatory and these two EU Directives clearly contribute to achieving the objectives of the AC, although they entered into force before the AC and its Protocols. In this connection, it is important to note that non-compliance with one or more provisions of a Protocol to the AC may trigger a case before the CJEU, since the EU has ratified the AC and five of its protocols. A precedent exists whereby the CJEU sanctioned an EU Member State for the breach of an international convention.[36]

Connections between the AC and other legal frameworks[37] have been advanced through collaboration, for example, through the 2006 Memorandum of Cooperation (MoC) with the Carpathian Convention and the 2008 MoC with both the Carpathian Convention and the CBD.[38] In the framework of this cooperation a map has been produced that shows the distribution of protected areas (including wilderness sites)

[32] This concerned areas above the tree line within the site 'Niedere Tauern' appropriate for the Euroasian Dotterel and not appropriately delimitated (para. 28ff) as well as the lack of designation of the whole alpine site of the Verwall (para. 97f), Case C-535/07 of 14 October 2010 ECR 2010 I-9483; see also the opinion of the Advocate General Sharpston, 25 February 2010, para. 38ff.

[33] www.umweltdachverband.at/fileadmin/user_upload/pdfs/Natura_2000/130530_Mahnschreiben_EU_KOM_Natura2000_-_ohne_Anhang_B.pdf.

[34] See Case C-304/05 of 20 September 2007, ECR 2007 I-7495.

[35] *Ibid.*, paras. 24, 35 and 73.

[36] Court of Justice of the EU, Case C-239/03, *Etang de Berre*, ECR 2004 I-09325.

[37] For a general discussion on mountain-related norms, see A. Villeneuve, P. Talla and M.A. Mekouar, 'The Legal Framework for Sustainable Mountain Management: An Overview of Mountain-specific Instruments', *Unasylva*, 53(208) (2002), 56–65.

[38] See www.erneuerbare-energien.de/inhalt/41686/36296/#memo.

within the separate geographic ranges of both regional conventions. An important motivation for this initiative was the promotion of wildlife corridors for migratory species, in accordance with Article 7(a) and Annex 1.1 of the CBD.[39]

Another partial overlap exists between the AC and the European Landscape Convention,[40] signed by the Parties of the AC except for Austria, Liechtenstein, Monaco and Germany. Art. 1(a) of this Convention defines 'landscape' as 'an area, as perceived by people, whose character is the result of the action and interaction of natural and/or human factors'. This definition – due to the use of the word 'or' – also covers naturally shaped areas, such as wilderness areas.

Furthermore, important overlaps exist between the AC and other conventions in respect of more procedural aspects that also have relevance for wilderness conservation. Of particular interest are the 'Aarhus Convention'[41] and the 'ESPOO Convention',[42] that have been concluded under the aegis of the United Nations Economic Commission for Europe. These regional conventions deal with the participation of citizens and Non-Governmental Organizations (NGOs) in decision-making processes relating to environmental matters and Environmental Impact Assessment (EIA), respectively. The scope of these instruments also covers, for example, the assessment and authorization of large projects in reserves,[43] including those areas that have relatively high wilderness qualities.

The Permanent Secretariat of the AC is not a member of the United Nations but it was granted Observer Status as an Intergovernmental Organization by the UN General Assembly to participate in the work of the Preparatory Committee for the UNCSD[44] held in Rio de Janeiro in 2012. There, it actively cooperated with the organs of that Committee in the drafting of the 'Rio+20' outcome-document *The Future We Want.* The Secretariats of the AC and the Carpathian Convention cooperated closely with the EU Commission and the States interested in sustainable

[39] *Ibid.*

[40] Concluded under the aegis of the Council of Europe in Florence, 20 October 2000 and entered into force in March 2004, conventions.coe.int/Treaty/en/Treaties/Html/176.htm.

[41] See ec.europa.eu/environment/aarhus/index.htm.

[42] See www.unece.org/env/eia/about/eia_text.html.

[43] V. Mauerhofer, 'Missing Links: How Individuals Can Contribute to Reserve Policy Enforcement on the Example of the European Union', *Biodiversity and Conservation*, 19 (2010), 601–618.

[44] For an overview of inter-governmental organizations that were involved in this conference, see http://www.uncsd2012.org/igos.html.

mountain development (SMD) to include the needs of mountainous regions in this final document. As a result, the document approved by the Conference contains three paragraphs on mountains.[45] The conservation of mountain ecosystems and biodiversity stands out in this text.

In summary, with regard to wilderness conservation the AC also provides an innovative legal framework that is applicable throughout the territories of its parties. Moreover, it interacts with several other legal frameworks within this geographical area and exerts influence at both the EU and international levels within a multitude of institutions and organizations.

## 5 The implementation of the Alpine Convention: Austria

### (a) Overview of the Austrian legal system

A land-locked state in central Europe, the Austrian Republic is about 83,000 km$^2$ in size with a population of about 8 million and is geographically divided into nine provinces (*Bundesländer*). Article 15 of the Federal Austrian Constitution (*Bundesverfassungs-Gesetz* or 'B-VG') defers competence over legislation regarding nature conservation and its implementation to the nine provinces and thus no specific nature conservation law exists at the Federal level.[46] However, the Federal government has the authority to sign and ratify international treaties, such as the AC.

### (b) The implementation of the AC and its Protocols in Austria

The AC and its Protocols have been approved as individual agreements following the same national procedure.[47] However, during the parliamentary procedure all Protocols – in contrast to the framework Convention itself – have been given direct applicability in national legislation since the moment of their entry into force in order to make the adoption of new laws unnecessary. As provided by the Austrian Constitution, the direct applicability of a provision by administrative and judicial officials depends on whether the provision is sufficiently precise. If the suitability of a provision for direct application is ('merely') doubtful, the non-existence of a legal discretion on the part of the

[45] See www.alpconv.org/en/convention/agreements/OtherConventions/rio20mountains/default.html.

[46] For further details, see Chapter 11 of this volume.

[47] E. Galle and M. Reiterer, 'Implementation of the Alpine Convention in Austria', in T. Treves, L. Pineschi and A. Fodella (eds.), *International Law and Protection of Mountain Areas* (Milan: Giuffré, 2002), 89–99.

implementing (administrative and/or judicial) authorities can be a reason to assume the provision's direct applicability.[48]

### (c) The consequences of implementation

Although the bodies responsible for the application of a provision of the Protocols initially decide whether such provision is directly applicable, the ultimate decision is provided for in the judgments of the Administrative Court of Austria ('Verwaltungsgerichtshof' – VwGH) and the Constitutional Court of Austria ('Verfassungsgerichtshof' – VfGH), the two highest judicial offices at the national level in public law affairs, as well as the CJEU. As a consequence of the system and case law of these courts, the following rough classification of AC Protocol provisions into three categories is useful:

(1) Provisions which are *directly applicable* (self-executing) are those that can be applied by executive authorities without any further transposition or change;
(2) Clauses that aim to bring about *legal adjustments or additions* to laws and regulations;
(3) Provisions with a *declarative character*, but which should still be taken into account by the authorities as argumentative, explanatory and motivating instruments.

The majority of the provisions of the AC Protocols have a declarative character, but shall still be referred to for interpretational purposes, for setting political goals and for benchmarking when weighing any possible interest.

### (d) Specific implementation steps

When the Protocols of the AC became effective in December 2002, the implementation of the AC entered into a new era in Austria. Since then, various decisions have been taken by administrations and courts in which an explicit reference has been made to the AC Protocols. For instance, the independent Environmental Senate (*Umweltsenat*)[49] based

[48] For a detailed discussion of this topic, see S. Cuypers, 'Die Alpenkonvention und ihre Durchführungsprotokolle: Einen alpinen Werkzeugkoffer für die Naturschutzarbeit öffnen in Fachbeiträge des Österreichischen Alpenvereins', *Alpine Raumordnung* Nr. 24 14, (2004); P. Bußjäger, 'Die unmittelbare Anwendung der Protokolle der Alpenkonvention in Österreich, *Natur und Recht*, 32(11) (2010), 759–766.

[49] This is a special institution, set up as court of appeal for procedures to examine decisions in matters of Environmental Impact Assessments (EIA).

its refusal to authorize the expansion of a skiing area[50] on Article 14(1) of the Protocol on Soil Conservation (see above), a provision that was considered directly applicable. It stated that this project could significantly affect highly dynamic, natural alpine slopes. This opinion of the Environmental Senate was subsequently confirmed by the Administrative Court of Austria.[51]

In the field of national cooperation, the 'Austrian National Committee for the AC' was established in 1990 to launch policies and agreements. This domestic coordination platform comprises representatives from the various provinces, the Ministries concerned, national NGOs and the trade unions and business sector. This institution, which is quite similar to a consultation committee, makes it possible not only to lead international negotiations on the basis of a large national consensus, but also to launch a whole series of actions at the national level.

One essential cornerstone of the efforts to support the national implementation of the AC and its protocols is a *manual* for the application of the AC of 2007, a document that has the objective of providing uniform Austrian legal definitions. This work of reference, published by the Ministry of Agriculture, Forestry, Environment and Water Management, includes framework conditions, guidelines and practical proposals for the legal application of the AC and its Protocols.

The last highlight to mention here was the establishment of a *service centre of law* at the branch office of CIPRA-Austria. This centre has the challenging task of finding answers to questions relating to the interpretation of the AC and its Protocols. This service provides any person the opportunity to receive general, non-binding and free legal advice, without needing to substitute expert opinions or to give specific project evaluations. This service may well be of relevance to wilderness-related issues in the Austrian part of the Alpine Region. Complementing this initiative, a database[52] has been made publicly available that includes additional literature as well as the various decisions taken by administrations and courts that refer to the AC and its Protocols.

[50] Decision of the independent Environmental Senate of 22 March 2004, US 6B/2003/8–57 (*Case Mutterer Alm*).

[51] VwGH 8 June 2005, 2004/03/0116 (after refusal of the VfGH with decision dated 2004, B581/04).

[52] See www.umweltbundesamt.at/alpenkonvention.

### (e) 'Wilderness Area Dürrenstein'

Although the criteria of the IUCN have played a considerable role in Austria's nature conservation,[53] only one area has as yet been officially declared a 'Wilderness Area' in accordance with the criteria of the IUCN.[54] The alpine site 'Wilderness Dürrenstein' covers an area of nearly 6177 acres,[55] is located in the Alpine bio-geographical region of the province Lower Austria and is characterized by the largest natural forests of Austria, which have not been cultivated or managed since the last ice age.[56] Through provincial regulation based on a provincial nature conservation law, parts of this area were already designated as a nature conservation reserve in 1942.[57] Until 2001 the Federal forestry law contained certain duties for the forest owner that contradicted the conservation aims.[58] These problems were overcome by applying for a certain status under the forestry law, which may be given to forests that protect human settlements and other constructions (the so-called status of a *Bannwald*). In 2001, the Federal forest law was amended, also under the pressure of binding EU law, and since then the law left scope for failing to execute the relevant duties for the benefit of nature conservation.[59]

In 2002, the area was designated the 'Wilderness Dürrenstein' Natura 2000 site by an administrative regulation of the province Lower Austria and a special management unit for this area was established. It is a private

[53] For a discussion on National Parks, see Mauerhofer, 'Nationalparkrecht', *supra* note 25.

[54] See also Chapter 1. The IUCN criteria constituted an important foundation for the European Commission's working definition of wilderness in a European context, which has also been adopted as the working definition of wilderness for this book.

[55] See www.wildnisgebiet.at/en.html.

[56] See B.E. Splechtna, G. Gratzer and B.A. Black, 'Disturbance History of a European Old-growth Mixed-species Forest – A Spatial Dendro-Ecological Analysis', *Journal of Vegetation Science*, 16 (2005), 511–522; B.E. Splechtna and G. Gratzer, 'Natural Disturbances in Central European Forests: Approaches and Preliminary Results from Rothwald, Austria', *Forest Snow and Landscape Research*, 79 (1/2) (2005), 57–67; S.A. Pietsch and H. Hasenauer, 'Evaluating the Self-initialisation Procedure for Large Scale Ecosystem Models', *Global Change Biology*, 12 (2006), 1658–1669.

[57] 'Verordnung vom 9. November 1942 über das 'Naturschutzgebiet Rothwald' in, der Katastralgemeinde Neuhaus, Landkreis Scheibbs, Niederdonau (VABl Niederdonau 463/1942)'. This regulation was replaced by the 'Verordnung über die Naturschutzgebiete 5500/13–0, Stammverordnung 40/78', 3 March 1978.

[58] For these duties, see Mauerhofer, 'Nationalparkrecht', *supra* note 25, at 375, and Volker Mauerhofer, 'Forstrechtlicher Handlungsbedarf durch EU-Richtlinien' [Action need in forestry law through EU-Directives], *RdU, Law of the Environment*, 4 (2001), 130–137.

[59] Article 32a of the Federal Forestry Act, *Federal Law Gazette* No. 440/1975, 3 July 1975, latest version published in *Federal law gazette* No. I 189/2013.

association that works on a contractual basis with the province of Lower Austria and this province also provides the basic funding.[60] This management unit closely cooperates with the management unit of the nearby 'Gesäuse' National Park, which is characterized by similar natural features.[61] The international recognition as a 'Wilderness Area' under IUCN- category I followed in 2003 with the inclusion of the site into the list of the IUCN.[62]

Currently, the area is divided into four zones,[63] a natural zone of about eighty-five per cent of the area (subject only to game regulation and spatially limited tours), a natural zone with silvicultural management of less than five per cent (for a limited period, secondary spruce forests are transformed into mixed forests with a high amount of deciduous trees), a management zone of alpine pastures of about ten per cent (with cattle grazing for nature management purposes) and a wildlife management zone comprising twenty-five per cent of the area (with regulation of the management of ungulates, such as red deer, roe deer and chamois due to the only occasional appearance of large predators). This wildlife area overlaps partly with other zones.

A funding contract under the LIFE programme[64] of the European Union with co-financing by the former Austrian Federal Ministry for Youth, Family and Environment[65] paved the way for the legal establishment of this wilderness area in 2003 through administrative regulation.[66] The Dürrenstein Wilderness Area is also closely connected to the ECONNECT project,[67] which indicates the close relationship of the site with the AC. Although the area is not explicitly presented as a direct implementation measure of the AC or one of its Protocols, it certainly

[60] See www.wildnisgebiet.at/en/portrait/aims-a-tasks.html.

[61] See www.wildnisgebiet.at/en.html.

[62] Consisting of the areas Rothwald I-III Nature Reserves in the World Database on Protected Areas, which are the only three Areas listed in the category 1b 'Wilderness' (see www.protectedplanet.net/search?iucn_category_id=1&q=Austria).

[63] See www.wildnisgebiet.at/en/portrait/zoning.html.

[64] See Regulation (EC) No 1404/96 and Regulation (EC) No 1682/2004; repealed by Regulation (EC) No. 614/2007 of the European Parliament and of the Council of 23 May 2007 concerning the Financial Instrument for the Environment (LIFE+) OJ L 149, 9.6.2007, 1–17; see also http://ec.europa.eu/environment/life/about/index.htm#history.

[65] Now Federal Ministry for Agriculture and Forestry, Environment and Water Management.

[66] www.wildnisgebiet.at/en.html.

[67] See in detail on this connection www.wildnisgebiet.at/de/projekte/netzwerk-naturwald/econnect.html.

contributes to an improved implementation of the AC and, in particular its Protocol on Conservation of Nature and the Countryside.

## 6 Conservation of alpine wilderness through funding programme projects

Apart from the EU LIFE programme noted above, there are several other temporary projects, including those financed under the EU structural funds instruments, that may have relevance for wilderness protection in the Alpine Region.[68] Many of these projects have a basis in public law, but some are based solely on private contracts.

One of the projects based on public law was ECONNECT, implemented from September 2008 to August 2011, with total financing of €3,198,240.[69] Co-funded by the EU within the legal framework of the European Territorial Cooperation Alpine Space Programme, ECONNECT strived towards an ecological continuum across the Alps with a focus on linking protected areas, including wilderness areas (such as Dürrenstein), as core zones of ecological networks in order to also achieve legal connectivity between alpine ecosystems.[70] The project was implemented in seven pilot regions, most of which host core areas with wilderness qualities conserved through protected area status.[71] Public authorities responsible for wilderness areas, such as the government of Lower Austria, actively promote in their information material the AC and projects such as ECONNECT.[72]

A recent type of follow-up project is the 'GreenAlps' project, funded under the same scheme from September 2013 until the end of 2014 (total eligible costs of €644,506 including an ERDF grant of €398,713).[73] The aim

[68] See in general J. Brun, 'Alpine Research Today: Planning, International Coordination and Anchor Projects [La recherche alpine aujourd'hui: Programmation, coordinations internationales, projets structurants]', *Revue De Geographie Alpine*, 96(1) (2008), 77–99.

[69] See www.econnectproject.eu/about_the_project.php?lang=en.

[70] Y. Kohler, G. Plassmann, A. Ullrich, A., Götz, T. Scheurer, S. Hölscher and S. Savoia, 'The Continuum Project: Establishing Ecological Networks throughout the European Alps', *Mountain Research and Development*, 28(2) (2008), 168–172, www.econnectproject.eu/about_the_project.php?lang=en; see also ECONNECT, *Webs of Life – Alpine Biodiversity Needs Ecological Connectivity Final Project Booklet* (2011) (www.econnectproject.eu/cms/sites/default/files/EN_3.pdf).

[71] See in detail the descriptions at www.econnectproject.eu/pilot_regions.php?lang=en#pilotregion2.

[72] See http://alpenkonvention-noe.at/uploads/docs/InfoFolder_Alpenkonvention_Niederoesterreich_Web.pdf.

[73] See www.greenalps-project.eu/project/.

of the project is to develop the basis for a European-wide environmental policy for the protection of biodiversity in the Alps, drawing on previous experiences. The project had a strong focus on the required multilevel legal framework and it also intended to promote connectivity and sustainable use of resources for successful ecosystem management policies in the Alps. One of the official Observers of this project was the French-German Presidency of the Platform Ecological Network of the AC for 2013 and 2014, which ensured a direct link to the AC and allowed a direct involvement of decision makers at the political level, as well as a direct connection with European policies.[74] Both projects, ECONNECT and GreenAlps, have been run by a larger consortium of public and private stakeholders, including Alpine protected area management organizations and NGOs.

Another example of a wilderness-related project is 'RowAlps' (Recovery of Wildlife in the Alps), which is privately funded by the MAVA foundation.[75] The project started in 2012, and has been preliminarily planned for three years,[76] while its objective is strongly connected to the AC and to wilderness as it focuses on wilderness-related species.[77] It aims to present practical conservation and management options to implement the so-called WISO Guidelines, especially for wolf and lynx in the Alps. WISO (Wildlife & Society) is an expert-platform created by the Alpine countries within the framework of the AC to address pan-Alpine challenges in wildlife conservation.[78]

This project is challenging as its implementation takes place in a time period in which Alpine governments, NGOs and other stakeholders have adopted different positions in respect of carnivores. For instance, while in 2012 in Switzerland the first new generation of wild-born wolves for 150 years was celebrated by NGOs, the Administrative Council of a national park in the Southern Alps of France decided that wolves should be shot even in the Park's core zone to protect animal husbandry practised in the Park.[79] The Swiss government also took a different view to the NGOs: in 2012 it proposed (albeit unsuccessfully)[80] to change the status of the wolf

[74] See www.greenalps-project.eu/partners-observers/.

[75] See www.kora.ch/index.php?id=283&L=0.

[76] See http://en.mava-foundation.org/what-we-fund/list-of-projects/alpine-arc-switzerland/.

[77] These species include particularly species with relatively large home ranges, such as wolf, lynx and bear.

[78] See www.wup.wi.tum.de/index.php?id=126.

[79] See www.cipra.org/en/alpmedia/news-en/4738/?set_language=en.

[80] See www.swissinfo.ch/eng/swiss_news/Convention_rejects_Swiss_wolf_protection_change.html?cid=34051932.

under the Convention on the Conservation of European Wildlife and Natural Habitats ('Bern Convention')[81] in order to make it easier to kill wolves for reasons of livestock protection, and afterwards even examined the option to withdraw from this convention as a Contracting Party.[82]

## 7 Conclusions and outlook

Within the geographic range covered by the AC, among the large portion of protected territory (up to twenty-five per cent of the Alpine territory) there are several areas with relatively high wilderness qualities. Most of these areas are located at high altitude (more than 2,500 metres above sea level), with the exception of some low altitude wilderness areas especially in the Maritime, Cottian and Julian Alps. To what extent does wilderness receive protection under the AC?

This is not a question that can receive a straightforward reply. Rather it requires a careful analysis of the legal texts of the AC and its Protocols, as well as their implementation, for instance, through the designation of protected areas, application of the relevant provisions in the decision-making processes regarding large projects, as well as the conduct of wilderness-related projects.

As far as the legal texts are concerned, neither the AC nor its Protocols explicitly use or define the term 'wilderness'; however, a closer analysis reveals that there are many provisions that are relevant for the protection of the main wilderness qualities as distinguished in Chapter 1. For instance, numerous provisions of the AC and its Protocols oblige or enable the Parties to maintain or restore the naturalness of Alpine areas within and outside of protected sites. The AC and its Protocols also contain obligations for the parties regarding impact assessments for planned constructions or other activities or even to keep areas totally free of infrastructure. This contributes to the implementation of the second main component of the wilderness definition. These provisions may relate to large areas and also to smaller areas that may still have important ecological functions.

The effectiveness of these legal provisions remains difficult to evaluate. Their effectiveness will depend heavily on the political will to embrace the concept of wilderness in the Alpine Region and to actually apply the relevant provisions for protecting and restoring wild nature. In this

[81] See www.coe.int/t/dg4/cultureheritage/nature/bern/default_en.asp.

[82] See on this convention Chapter 7.

context, it should however also be noted that many parts of the Alpine region have been influenced by humans for hundreds of years. If wilderness values, as well as cultural landscapes and related biodiversity shall be fostered, a balance has to be found between wilderness protection and the preservation of culture and human-related biodiversity.

Currently, the issue of wilderness is often obscured by general discussions on how to deal with the so-called periphery areas. Despite the fact that biodiversity protection remains a challenge, since nature is gradually on the retreat due to the cumulative effects of direct anthropocentric interventions, not to mention the effects of climate change, new challenges also arise.[83] There is, for instance, a growing issue of alpine depopulation. Many alpine valleys struggle with existential problems, with ever-increasing exploitation, compounded by unemployment levels that are amplified by the phenomenon of 'brain drain', with structural changes within the alpine mountain agriculture[84] or with forms of public transport that are unable to fulfil the basic needs of the working population.

The interplay of each of these influences leads to opportunities to promote new wilderness in the Alpine Region. People are leaving these peripheral alpine regions, farmers are giving up their homesteads and cultivated lands morph into abandoned lands. Currently, this 'new (*or second*) alpine wilderness' has little to do with the wilderness as defined for the purpose of this book, but in the longer-term these areas may yet qualify as wilderness again. However, this is dependent upon public support and the need to counteract undesirable developments and to use existing instruments and tools, such as those available in the AC framework. One thing is clear: when discussing wilderness-related issues, one should be aware of the fact that the transformation of previously

[83] For an overview, see V. Briquel, 'Development Issues for the Alps: Survey of Convergences and Divergences in Their Meaning' [Les enjeux de développement des Alpes: Enquête sur les convergences et divergences dans leur signification], *Revue De Geographie Alpine*, 94(2) (2006), 57–84. See also M. Boesch, 'Is "culture" Still Relevant to Regional Policy? Conclusions from DIAMONT, a European Union Research Project', *Mountain Research and Development*, 27(1) (2007), 4–10. P. Haßlacher, 'The Alpine Convention – Instrument of a Lasting Regional Development?' [Die Alpenkonvention: Instrument einer nachhaltigen Raumentwicklung?], *Berichte Zur Deutschen Landeskunde*, 77(2–3) (2003), 133–149.

[84] See more in detail, e.g., T. Streifeneder, U. Tappeiner, F.V. Ruffini, G. Tappeiner and C. Hoffmann, 'Selected Aspects of Agro-structural Change within the Alps: A Comparison of Harmonised Agro-structural Indicators on a Municipal Level' [Éclairage sur les transformations des structures agricoles dans les Alpes: Comparaison des indicateurs agro-structurels harmonisés à l'échelle locale], *Revue De Geographie Alpine*, 95(3) (2007), 27–52.

cultivated or managed land into wilderness is likely to raise doubts and fears among local communities. This issue has a huge social dimension. The successful establishment of wilderness areas often strongly depends on how the local stakeholders have been involved in the process and whether an open and honest discussion has been facilitated from the very beginning.

With the entry into force of all the Protocols to the AC, new opportunities and possibilities for wilderness protection have emerged, alongside new questions and challenges related to social developments, conservation objectives that focus on biodiversity, climate change and landscape developments. The legal implementation and enforcement of the AC is still in an early phase and it will take some time before well-established traditions or practices are reconsidered. It took years to identify, recognize and gradually make use of the potential of the AC and more specifically of the Protocols. It is therefore fair to expect that it will also take more time to embrace the wide range of possibilities of this regional legal framework and to use them for the relevant objectives, ideally across the whole Alpine space. Whether the various options for wilderness protection will actually be used will heavily depend on the political will of the Contracting Parties. However, one thing is clear: the political attention and related debate on wilderness protection is definitely higher today than it was in the past. This is also one of the merits of (or the reasons behind) the AC. The various bodies of the AC are active in this field and – at least – specific decisions at the local level which impact on wilderness are undergoing debate (and in many cases, legal challenges). All this shows that the general attention for wilderness in the Alps is on the rise.

In this way the AC is an enduring political programme, that offers a credible perspective to the Alpine area as a living, economic and cultural space with all its diversity and its problems, as well as to the humans, non-humans, ecosystems and its remaining remnants of wilderness.

# 10

# Wilderness protection under the Carpathian Convention

HARALD EGERER, CAI LIN GWEE, ELEONORA MUSCO AND MATHILDE KOECK

## How the Carpathians were born

Many years ago, there was a plain with agricultural fields owned by giant Sylun. Many people worked for him and had no rights to leave. A young guy Carp Dniprovsky worked for the giant and decided to return back home. The giant didn't allow him, they fought, Carp took power from the land and won, got Sylun under the land. Sylun tried to get out but couldn't, the land became as waves – mountains were created. People decided to stay in this place, some of them in the mountain, some in the lowland. Sylun is still under ground, sometimes storming, but he is very old and not able to get out.[1]

## 1 Introduction

The Carpathians are one of the largest mountain ranges in Europe, covering an area of more than 200,000 km$^2$ shared by seven Central and Eastern European countries:[2] the Czech Republic, Hungary, Poland, Romania, Serbia, the Slovak Republic and Ukraine. The Carpathians are the most extensive mountain system in Europe after the Alps. The Carpathian region includes a mountain core area. The total length of the Carpathians is over 1,500 km and their width varies between twelve and 500 km. Their highest range is the Tatra Mountains with the Gerlachovský peak at 2,655 m, located in the Slovak Republic close to the Polish border.[3] The wider Carpathian region, including forelands and surrounding

[1] Adel Grygoruk and Yulia Lyamzina, *Carpathian Legends and Fairy Tales* (Martin: Vydavateľstvo Matice slovenskej, 2011), at 47.

[2] See www.carpathianparks.org/index.php?option=com_content&view=frontpage&Itemid=1.

[3] *Strategic Action Plan for the Carpathian Area*, (Vienna: United Nations Environment Programme-Interim Secretariat of the Carpathian Convention, 2011), at 03.

foothills and lowlands, is home to a human population of nearly 53 million inhabitants, which represents approximately seven point six per cent of the European population, and covering less than five per cent of European territory.[4] Five of the seven Carpathian countries are members of the EU (the two non-EU countries are Ukraine and Serbia).

Known as the 'Kingdom of Carnivores', the region supports viable populations of large carnivores, an estimated 8,000 brown bears, 4,000 wolves and 3,000 lynx.[5] The region also contains the last virgin forests in Europe except for the Russian forests, and harbours more than one-third of all European plant species.[6] Besides this ecological value, the Carpathian forests also have significant socio-economic value through the timber and tourism industries, as well as through preserving the region's natural and cultural heritage.

The Carpathian Convention was set up as a transnational framework for the sustainable management of the Carpathian forests, the protection of its remaining virgin forests and the preservation of the region's unique heritage. The key strength of the Carpathian Convention is its transnational nature, facilitating cross-borders and inter-institutional collaboration, which is particularly important for wilderness protection and would otherwise be difficult to achieve. Based on a brief introduction to the convention and its main bodies (Section 2), this chapter gives an insight into the functioning of the Carpathian Convention and its contribution to the protection of the Carpathian wilderness through its provisions, its protocols and the work of the various working groups (Section 3). This will be further highlighted using an example of a project that is of particular importance for the implementation of the Convention (Section 4). The final section includes the main conclusions (Section 5).

## 2 The Carpathian Convention: a brief overview

### *2.1 History, geographical scope and institutional arrangements*

People living in the Carpathians have had to deal with harsh socio-economic conditions, such as the lack of infrastructure, geographical

[4] *Ibid.*

[5] There are also estimates which are considerably lower pointing at declining populations in some countries. Further research and transnational data collection and harmonization would be required.

[6] E. Samec, *The Carpathians 'Existing Instruments and Programmes and a Carpathian Sector Analysis'* (Vienna: United Nations Environment Programme, 2002), 3–27.

isolation, high unemployment rates and poverty, political and economic marginality. The region is still facing challenges due to the transition from communism to a free market economy. The ongoing European enlargement process has also major implications for the development of the region. Joining the EU offers both challenges and opportunities for most of the Carpathian countries. Despite many efforts during the past, the loss of biodiversity has continued due to habitat fragmentation and destruction, over-harvesting, pollution and inappropriate management methods.

In order to preserve the extraordinary and unique natural and cultural heritage of the Carpathians, and at the same time support the development of the region, a legal framework and a platform for cooperation between different stakeholders acting in the Carpathian region was needed. The 'Carpathian Convention process' started in 2001, when the Government of Ukraine requested the United Nations Environment Programme (UNEP) to facilitate an intergovernmental consultation process among the Carpathian countries with the aim of drafting an international convention for the Carpathian Mountains. The Framework Convention on the Protection and Sustainable Development of the Carpathians (Carpathian Convention) was adopted and signed by the seven Parties (the Czech Republic, Hungary, Poland, Romania, Serbia, Slovak Republic and Ukraine) sharing the Carpathians in May 2003 in Kyiv, Ukraine, and entered into force in January 2006.

The Convention is a Framework Convention that includes general principles and objectives that are further specified by its Protocols, adopted at the meetings of the Conference of the Parties (COP), the Conference of the competent ministers of the Parties that is the decision-making body of the Convention. These Protocols are the main instruments to fulfil and facilitate the implementation of the Convention's main provisions.

The executive body of the Convention, established by the COP under Article 14(2)(e) of the Convention,[7] is the Carpathian Convention Implementation Committee (CCIC), which is constituted by the Carpathian Convention National Focal Points (NFPs) and other country representatives. The CCIC is responsible for the preparation of the decisions of the COP, including the development and recommendation for the adoption of new Protocols and other relevant documents significant for reaching the objectives of the Convention. The Carpathian

[7] See Art. 14(2)(e) and Art. 16 of the Convention.

Convention Working Groups (WGs), also established by the COP under Article 14(2)(e) of the Convention,[8] contribute to the elaboration of the Protocols, their Strategic Action Plans and other relevant documents. The eight WGs relate to:

- Conservation and Sustainable Use of Biological and Landscape Diversity
- Spatial Development
- Agriculture and Rural Development
- Sustainable Forest Management
- Sustainable Industry, Energy, Transport and Infrastructure
- Sustainable Tourism
- Cultural Heritage and Traditional Knowledge
- Adaptation to Climate Change

The Secretariat of the Carpathian Convention (SCC), established on 1 May 2004 and hosted by the UNEP Vienna Office with the support of EURAC Research through the EURAC Representing Office in Vienna, services the Parties in implementing the Convention.[9] The Secretariat supports the work of the Convention bodies, coordinates the implementation of the Convention Programme of Work and promotes Carpathian Convention-related projects. It organizes the CCIC and COP meetings and prepares the draft documents that are submitted for discussion and final adoption of the Parties. It also enables and facilitates research, communication and information exchange between relevant stakeholders and represents the Convention in external relations.

### *2.2 Implementation of the Carpathian Convention*

The Carpathian Convention is the only multi-level governance mechanism for the entire Carpathian region and, besides the Alpine Convention, the only regional treaty-based regime related to the sustainable development and protection of a mountain region in the world. The Carpathian Convention has established linkages and partnerships with networks and organizations at regional and international levels, in particular with the

[8] *Ibid.* For an overview of the WGs and the WG-meetings, see http://www.carpathianconvention.org/working-groups.html.

[9] After the fourth Conference of the Parties (COP), the Parties asked UNEP to continue to administer the Secretariat in Vienna and to review this decision at COP5. The term 'interim' was dropped from the designation, now being called 'Secretariat of the Carpathian Convention'.

Alpine Convention but also with the Ramsar Convention (Convention on Wetlands of International Importance), the Convention on Biological Diversity (CBD) and the 'Science for the Carpathians Initiative' (S4C), a network of scientific institutions in the Carpathian Region. The Carpathian Convention also cooperates with the EU, in particular for the implementation of the EU Strategy for the Danube Region (EUSDR) through the BIOREGIO Carpathians project and as the body responsible for the implementation of EUSDR Priority Area 6 (biodiversity, landscapes, quality of air and soil). Other partners include NGOs, like the World Wide Fund for Nature – Danube Carpathian Programme (WWF DCP), which has been a long-term supporter of the Convention since the early days of its negotiation and development.

An institutional framework at different administrative levels is in place for the implementation of the Carpathian Convention in each country.[10] The governmental bodies that represent the Parties to the Convention are the main driving forces for the implementation of the Carpathian Convention, but other stakeholders acting in the Carpathian region at different levels play important roles in the implementation process too. The relevant ministries of the Carpathian countries work together with regional and local authorities, scientific institutions and NGOs to coordinate activities. In order to strengthen this framework, coordination committees have been established to coordinate implementation efforts at local and regional levels. The Carpathian countries have also drawn up national/strategic actions plans for certain themes and they recognize the importance of cooperation at international level across institutions, especially for interdisciplinary issues. NGOs are also involved in promoting the Carpathian Convention at national and local levels.

The implementation of the Carpathian Convention at a national level has resulted in the introduction of around sixty regulatory documents by the Carpathian countries since 2007: ten governmental laws, sixteen decrees, three ministerial orders/decisions, nine national strategies and plans, eleven national programs, seven protocols and three rulebooks.[11] The commitment of the Carpathian countries towards fulfilment of the objectives under the Carpathian Convention is also evident from the large number of activities initiated within the policy, legislative and institutional framework, particularly in the areas of forestry and

[10] M.L. Weiss, H. Egerer and G. Luciani, *National Achievements and Challenges Related to the Implementation of the Carpathian Convention* (Bolzano/Vienna: EURAC research, 2011), at 11.

[11] *Ibid.*, at 11.

biodiversity (detailed below). The general three-pronged approach taken for the implementation of the Carpathian Convention by the Carpathian countries is as follows: (a) identification of thematic priorities for each focus area, (b) policy and legal assessment and (c) development of projects, initiatives and other activities.[12]

## 3 The Carpathian Convention and wilderness protection

### *3.1 Carpathian wilderness: fact finding*

As discussed in Chapter 1, the debate on the definition of 'wilderness' is ongoing and unsettled. When applied strictly, it is concluded that there is no wilderness left in Europe, not even in the Carpathians. It is therefore critical to ensure the protection of areas with high wilderness qualities as described in Chapter 1, such as naturalness, the absence of roads, buildings, bridges, tracks, cables or other proof of modern human society and large size.

Forest cover in the Carpathians extends to about 10 million hectares, about half of the area of the Carpathians, with approximately fifty per cent of the forest area located in Romania.[13] However, due to natural and anthropogenic reasons, the current state of the Carpathian forests is less than desirable. A 'State of the Carpathian Forest' report[14] has been prepared, providing an overview of the state of nature protection and forest health in the Carpathians, the disturbances and damages to forest resources, and the challenges and priorities for the future sustainable management of Carpathian forests. Forest management practices in the past have rendered the Carpathian forests very vulnerable to external factors. Natural threats include winds, air pollution, floods and droughts, as well as attacks by insect and fungal species. Anthropogenic factors are the harvesting of timber from as early as Roman times, and the practice of monocultures during the more recent communist times. These practices led to sharp declines in the condition of the forests. Illegal logging and tourism have also caused long-term environmental damages.

The many damaging human activities in the Carpathian forest that have been conducted for a long time led to the disturbed condition of part of the forests.[15] Nevertheless, at higher elevations with less significant

[12] *Ibid.*, at 18.

[13] University of Padova, Dept TeSAF, *Report on Current State of Forest Resources in the Carpathians*, Carpathian Project Activity 2.7: Forestry and Timber Industry (Legnaro: University of Padova, 2008), at 13.

[14] *Ibid.*, at 13.

[15] *Ibid.*, at 14.

human pressure vast areas of untouched forests – the last remnants of 'wilderness' in Europe outside Russia – remain. These virgin forests are a unique part of the Carpathian heritage. Currently, about 225 virgin forests with areas larger than 10 ha have been identified in the Carpathians.[16] In 2008, the University of Padova provided an overview of how the total virgin forest area of more than 300,000 ha is spread within the Carpathian countries: Czech Republic: 463 ha, Poland: 55,645 ha, Romania: 207,500 ha (about sixty-five per cent), Serbia: 3,248 ha, Slovakia 15,428, Ukraine 40,300 ha.[17]

In view of these large areas of virgin forest that are unique for Europe, the case for the preservation of the existing wilderness areas in the Carpathians is real and pressing. For protecting these remaining virgin forests, protected area regimes in the Carpathian countries are of crucial importance. The website of the 'Carpathian Network of Protected Areas' (CNPA) includes '36 national parks, 51 nature parks and protected landscape areas, 19 biosphere reserves and around 200 other protected areas'.[18] Nearly all the remaining natural and semi-natural forests in the Western Carpathian (Czech Republic, Hungary, Poland and Slovakia) are now protected as nature reserves or national parks. However, as also illustrated by discussions in other chapters of this book, legal protection does not always guarantee the adequate protection of the wilderness qualities of these areas.[19] For instance, in relation to Romania's old growth forests, Jan Knorn et al. concluded in 2013 that 'seventy-two per cent of the old-growth forest disturbances are found within protected areas.'[20] Furthermore, large areas of primeval and natural forests in Romania and Ukraine are not yet protected by law. The University of Padova concluded in 2008:

[16] Samec, *The Carpathians 'Existing Instruments and Programmes and a Carpathian Sector Analysis'*, *supra* note 6, at 36.

[17] University of Padova, *Report on Current State of Forest Resources in the Carpathians*, *supra* note 13, at 18.

[18] See http://www.carpathianparks.org/description.html. For a map distinguishing the various types of protected area categories in the Carpathian region, see http://www.carpathianparks.org/map.html.

[19] See Chapters 12, 15 and 18.

[20] Jan Knorn, Tobias Kuemmerle, Volker C. Radeloff, William S. Keeton, Vladimir Gancz, Iovu-Adrian Biri, S. Miroslav Svoboda, Patrick Griffiths, Adrian Hagatis and Patrick Hostert, 'Continued Loss of Temperate Old-growth Forests in the Romanian Carpathians Despite an Increasing Protected Area Network', *Environmental Conservation*, 40(2) (2013), 182–193, at 182.

> At present about sixteen per cent of the total area of the Carpathian Mountains is protected, with land under protection varying between nine and thirty-two per cent of the territories in the respective countries, spanning from small-scale nature reserves to large-acreage landscape protected areas, national parks and UNESCO biosphere reserves.[21]

Many of the virgin forest areas suffer from problems because of the limitations in legal protection and additional factors like poor management, pollution, tourism, over-hunting, grazing and illegal felling.[22] Hence, not only the conservation of remaining wilderness is important, but also the restoration of areas, which could potentially be developed into 'new wilderness areas', should be considered.

Below, the provisions of the Convention and relevant Protocols, which are of special relevance for the protection of wilderness in the Carpathians, are discussed in detail. The efforts to implement these provisions are also discussed. But first the values of wilderness in the Carpathians will be discussed in some more detail.

### 3.2 *Value of Carpathian wilderness*

Forests and their wilderness qualities support the diverse ecological, economic and social functions of forests.[23]

#### Ecological

Forests have an impact on the global and local climate, atmospheric composition and the water cycle in nature. The productive function of the Carpathian ecosystems is demonstrated by its ability to generate more biomass, resulting in an increase in growing stock, which in its turn act as carbon sinks. 'Old-growth forests in the Carpathian Mountain region of Europe store very high levels of carbon in comparison to younger and managed forests.'[24] Data indicate that the average wood removal is about seventy per cent of the growing increment. Hence, considering only the above-ground biomass the Carpathian forests provide a total carbon sink of about 10 M Mg per year.[25] As mountains are early indicators of climate

[21] University of Padova, *Report on Current State of Forest Resources in the Carpathians*, *supra* note 13, at 18.

[22] Robin Webster, Suzie Holt and Charlie Avis, *The Status of the Carpathians. A Report Developed as a Part of the Carpathian Ecoregion Initiative* (Vienna: WWF, 2001), at 18.

[23] See also Chapters 3, 4 and 5.

[24] Knorn et al., 'Continued Loss of Temperate Old-growth Forests in the Romanian Carpathians Despite an Increasing Protected Area Network', *supra* note 20, at 182.

[25] Webster et al., *The Status of the Carpathians*, *supra* note 22, at 15.

change, the Carpathians also serve as important grounds for research on the impact of climate change.[26]

Forests also have a protective function, as they counteract floods, avalanches and landslides and protect soil against erosion. Moreover, they play important roles as reservoirs for biodiversity, helping to protect and preserve a large number of species and ecosystems.[27] Different kinds of protected areas have been established in large areas of the Carpathians.

### Economic

Healthy forest ecosystems produce timber for the timber industry and also non-timber forest resources, e.g., for agriculture and hunting purposes. Tourism is also an emerging industry and sustainable or eco-tourism is a priority for Romania and Ukraine.[28] Adequate transport infrastructure is essential to facilitate tourism. These infrastructure would also give a boost to the industry and the labour market. The Protocol on Sustainable Tourism and the European Transnational Cooperation South East Europe 'ACCESS2MOUNTAIN project',[29] under which a Protocol on Sustainable Transport was under elaboration, respond to these needs. The Transport Protocol implementing Article 8 of the Carpathian Convention requires transport policies to promote an efficient transport system, aiming at guaranteeing accessibility in the Carpathian region and to manage freight and passenger traffic flows, meeting the economic and social needs of the region. On the other hand, transport policies should also consider environmental needs and the harmful effects of freight and passenger traffic on the Carpathian environment should be minimized.[30]

26 For an overview and current status of 'global change research in the Carpathians' (climate, water, land use, forestry, biodiversity and conservation, tourism and ecosystem services), see Astrid Björnsen Gurung, Anita Bokwa, Wojciech Chełmicki, Marine Elbakidze, Manuela Hirschmugl, Patrick Hostert, Pierre Ibisch, Jacek Kozak, Tobias Kuemmerle, Elena Matei, Katarzyna Ostapowicz, Joanna Pociask-Karteczka, Lars Schmidt, Sebastian van der Linden and Marc Zebisch, 'Global Change Research in the Carpathian Mountain Region', *Mountain Research and Development*, 29(3) (2009), 282–288, http://boris.unibe.ch/36463/1/mrd%252E1105.pdf.

27 *Ibid.*, at 282: 'The region is important for biodiversity, hosting the largest unmanaged old-growth ("virgin") forests of Western and Central Europe, many endemic species, and Europe's largest wolf and brown bear populations.'

28 For a discussion on tourism developments in the Carpathian Mountain Region, see (authors unknown) *Strategy for the Sustainable Tourism Development of the Carpathians* (Vienna: Carpathian Convention Working Group on Sustainable Tourism, 2014).

29 See www.access2mountain.eu/en/project/default.html.

30 Massimo Santori and Andrea Barisiello, *Overview on Transport System in the Carpathian Space* (Bolzano: EURAC, 2008), at 5.

In order to implement the provision of the Protocol and to guarantee a follow up of the European Transnational Cooperation South East Europe ACCESS2MOUNTAIN and BIOREGIO Carpathians Projects, the Secretariat is now working towards the development of a project proposal with the general aim to contribute to defining and applying the EU concept of Green Infrastructure by fostering integrated, participatory planning processes. More concretely, the project aims at protecting ecological connectivity and improving awareness about the benefits of Green Infrastructure in protected areas and Natura 2000 sites, which are under infrastructure development pressure.

#### Social

Forests also have a social function, providing green spaces and recreational landscapes for the society and communities living in the mountains. Preserving forests also serves to preserve the specific cultural heritage of the region which would otherwise be lost. Lastly, forests provide excellent learning grounds for younger generations to increase their awareness of the importance of protecting forest ecosystems.

### *3.3 Working group on sustainable forest management*

Article 7 of the Carpathian Convention contains the following provisions for sustainable forest management (SFM, *italic* added by the authors):

3. The Parties shall pursue policies aiming at promoting and supporting the use of instruments and programs, compatible with *internationally agreed principles of sustainable forest management.*
4. The Parties shall apply *sustainable mountain forest management practices* in the Carpathians, taking into account the multiple functions of forests, the high ecological importance of the Carpathian mountain ecosystems, as well as the less favourable conditions in mountain forests.
5. The Parties shall pursue policies aiming at designating *protected areas in natural, especially virgin forests* in sufficient size and number, with the purpose to restrict or adapt their use according to the objectives of conservation to be achieved.[31]

The Working Group aims at supporting the implementation of the relevant provisions under Article 7 of the Convention and of the

[31] Framework Convention on the Protection and Sustainable Development of the Carpathians (The Carpathian Convention), Art. 7, paras 3–5.

Protocol on Sustainable Forest Management (Forest Protocol). This Protocol was adopted at COP3 on 27 May 2011 and entered into force in November 2013. From a wilderness perspective, it is particularly relevant that Article 7(5) of the Convention has been worked out in more detail in the Protocol. According to Article 10 of the Protocol on Sustainable Forest Management:

1. Each Party shall take measures in its national territory aimed at identifying and protecting natural, especially virgin forests of the Carpathians, by establishing Protected Areas in sufficient size and number and implementing other specific measures of protection.
2. Each Party shall take measures for the inclusion of sufficient areas of all types of identified natural forests from its Carpathian region in Protected Areas.
3. In particular, each Party should take specific measures for the preservation of genetic resources of natural, especially virgin forests.
4. Each Party shall take specific measures for compensation of costs or economic losses resulting from measures taken in accordance with paragraph 1, 2 and 3 of this Article.[32]

Virgin forests are defined in the Protocol as 'natural forests which have not been influenced directly by human activities in their development'.[33]

The tasks of the Working Group include the implementation of the previous provisions and the elaboration of a strategic action plan (SAP) for the implementation of the Forest Protocol, the analysis of the available information and the identification of gaps requiring further research in the forest field. The Working Group also provides guidance and recommendations for the development of follow-up projects related to the implementation of the Forest Protocol. Of particular relevance for the theme of this book is the establishment of a 'Carpathian Inventory on Virgin Forests', in cooperation with the European Environment Agency (see Subsection 3.4) and other relevant institutions.

In order to establish the inventory, common criteria for the definition of virgin forests and a methodology for their identification were elaborated under the leadership of WWF DCP. The Working Group members and experts from all the Carpathian countries contributed to this activity. A first draft of the common criteria has been developed at the Forest WG

[32] Protocol on Sustainable Forest Management to the Framework Convention on the Protection and Sustainable Development of the Carpathians, Art. 10, paras. 1–4.

[33] *Ibid.*, Art. 7(k).

meeting held in Baia Mare, Romania, in June 2013 and was further discussed during the Forest Working Group meeting which took place in Rzeszow, Poland, in September 2013. The final version of the 'Criteria and Indicators for selection of virgin forests in the Carpathians'[34] was submitted and adopted by the Parties to the Carpathian Convention during COP4, held in Mikulov on 23–26 September 2014. During the meeting the Parties finally adopted also the 'Strategic Action Plan for Implementation of the Forest Protocol to the Carpathian Convention',[35] this Protocol being currently the only international instrument on sustainable forest management in force in Europe.

Sustainable forest management is a main thematic priority, particularly for Romania and Ukraine, which countries are working with WWF DCP on the development of criteria of High Conservation Value Forests (HCVF). Romania is also working with WWF DCP on Responsible Forest Management, Pristine Forest Conservation and Protected Areas Development. The use of the criteria of HCVF allows the elaboration of sustainable resource management strategies for local people and forest authorities and companies. Policy and legal instruments, such as national strategic action plans and new laws and programmes, are also common tools for implementing the Carpathian Convention. Examples include Hungary's and Serbia's new national laws on forests to promote nature conservation and Slovakia's National Forest Programme and National List of Special Protection Areas for sustainable forest management.

Several more concrete forestry initiatives and projects relevant for the theme of wilderness protection have been initiated. For instance, Ukraine has launched activities to protect mountain forests, such as the 'Moratorium on the main cutting and use of the crawler transport in high-mountains in force', the 'Improvement of forest system use FORZA' (Forestry development in Zakarpattya), and the 'Certification of forests'. The WWF and IKEA jointly developed a programme for responsible forest management and protection, under which workshops and trainings were held for hundreds of Romanian and Ukrainian foresters.[36] The WWF is also working with Romania to save and protect Romania's virgin

[34] See www.carpathianconvention.org/tl_files/carpathiancon/Downloads/03%20Meetings%20and%20Events/COP/2014_COP4_Mikulov/Follow%20Up/DOC13_Criteria_Indicators_virginforests_FINAL_26SEP.pdf.

[35] *Ibid.*

[36] Weiss, Egerer and Luciani, *National Achievements and Challenges Related to the Implementation of the Carpathian Convention*, *supra* note 10, at 25.

forests, which represent an estimated sixty-five per cent of the virgin forests still remaining in Europe.

### 3.4 *Cooperation between the Carpathian Convention and the European Environment Agency on forest activities*

The Secretariat of the Carpathian Convention (SCC), with the support of EURAC Research through the EURAC Representing Office in Vienna, finalized a Partnership Agreement (PA) and a related Work Plan 2013–2015 with the European Environment Agency (EEA). The PA aims to provide a durable basis for the collaboration between the EEA and the Carpathian Convention regarding the observation, collection of data, monitoring and information analysis with relevance to the protection and sustainable development of the Carpathians. The goals of collaboration include the management of data flow between the EEA and the Carpathian Convention and the harmonization of the use of Carpathian indicators with EEA Indicators and their application.

Follow-up of the PA in accordance with the Joint Work Plan 2013–2015, will be the cooperation with the European Topic Centre on Spatial Information and Analysis (ETC – SIA) on forest issues. This cooperation relates to various types of activities, including the monitoring of land use and land cover of the Carpathian region and the identification of available data sets and indicators on sustainable forest management, including forest classification and forest type indicators. Particularly relevant for wilderness protection is the collaboration on the:

- application of the common criteria for the definition of virgin forests on the basis of the document on 'Criteria & indicators for selection of virgin forests in transboundary region', prepared in the context of the CC WG Forest;
- realization of a 'Carpathian Inventory on Virgin Forests'.

These activities also contribute to the interpretation of data for the Carpathian area, the collection of additional data and information at regional and local levels, and the development of qualitative analysis useful for further implementation of the Carpathian Convention. More specifically, these activities may also support the implementation of Article 7(5) of the Convention and Article 10(1) of the Protocol on Forestry concerning the designation and protection of the remaining virgin forests in the Carpathian region.

### 3.5 *Working Group on Conservation and Sustainable Use of Biological and Landscape Diversity*

Article 4 of the Carpathian Convention[37] contains the following provisions for Conservation and Sustainable Use of Biological and Landscape Diversity (*italic* added by the authors):

> 1. The Parties shall pursue policies aiming at conservation, sustainable use and restoration of biological and landscape diversity throughout the Carpathians. The Parties shall take appropriate measures to ensure a high level of protection and sustainable use of *natural and semi-natural habitats*, their continuity and connectivity, and *species of flora and fauna* being characteristic to the Carpathians, in particular the protection of endangered species, endemic species and large carnivores.
> 2. The Parties shall promote adequate maintenance of semi-natural habitats, the *restoration of degraded habitats*, and support the development and implementation of relevant management plans.
> 3. The Parties shall pursue policies aiming at the prevention of introduction of alien invasive species and release of genetically modified organisms threatening ecosystems, habitats or species, their control or eradication.
> 4. The Parties shall develop and/or promote compatible *monitoring systems*, coordinated regional *inventories of species and habitats*, coordinated scientific research, and their networking.
> 5. The Parties shall cooperate in developing an ecological network in the Carpathians, as a constituent part of the Pan-European Ecological Network, in establishing and supporting a *Carpathian Network of Protected Areas*, as well as enhance conservation and sustainable management in the areas outside of protected areas.
> 6. The Parties shall take appropriate measures to integrate the objective of conservation and sustainable use of biological and landscape diversity into *sectoral policies*, such as mountain agriculture, mountain forestry, river basin management, tourism, transport and energy, industry and mining activities.

The Working Group aims at supporting the implementation of these provisions as well as the provisions of the Protocol on Conservation and Sustainable Use of Biological and Landscape Diversity (Biodiversity Protocol, entered into force in 2010) and its Strategic Action Plan (SAP) through the elaboration of official documents and strategic projects, such as the European Transnational Cooperation South East

[37] *Framework Convention on the Protection and Sustainable Development of the Carpathians (The Carpathian Convention)*, Art. 4, para. 1–6.

Europe BioREGIO Carpathians project. It facilitates the cooperation with other relevant Conventions and Organizations, such as the Convention on Biological Diversity (CBD), and ensures the coordination of its activities with the Carpathian Network of Protected Areas Steering Committee (CNPA SC) and the Carpathian Wetlands Initiative (CWI).

The Carpathian Network of Protected Areas facilitates the implementation of the Biodiversity Protocol and its Strategic Action Plan. The Network was established in 2006 and promotes cooperation among protected areas in the Carpathians, facilitates information exchange and develops projects to strengthen the ecological coherence of the Carpathian Ecoregion.[38] The CNPA comprises thirty-six national parks, fifty-one nature parks and protected landscape areas, nineteen biosphere reserves and around 200 other protected areas.[39] The level of protection within each category varies considerably and heavily depends on the status of the relevant areas under domestic legal systems. The protection ranges from strictly protected areas which are protected from most human development and pollutions (e.g., those designated as National Parks) to areas that focus mainly on rural development. Consequently, wilderness protection is not an explicit aim of the network, but as the approach ensures that a spectrum of different types of natural areas is protected, the efforts may also be beneficial for the relatively undisturbed areas that form part of the network. The network is coordinated by the CNPA Steering Committee, which is constituted of a representative for each Carpathian Country.

At the national level examples of policies and programmes implementing the Biodiversity Protocol include the National Environment Programmes (NEP) by Hungary (NEP III, 2009–2014) and Serbia (2010–2019), Poland's strategy of nature protection of the Silesian province (2011–2030) and presidential decrees on endangered species and regional programmes on econet development by Ukraine.

At the transboundary and transnational level key transnational projects implementing the Biodiversity Protocol are the BioREGIO Carpathians project[40] (2011–2014), which is considered a flagship

[38] See www.carpates.org/.

[39] See www.carpathianparks.org/index.php?option=com_content&view=frontpage&Itemid=1.

[40] See www.bioregio-carpathians.eu.

project within the EU Strategy of the Danube Region (EUSDR), and the Alpine Carpathian Corridor (AKK) project.[41] This AKK project aims at improving ecological connectivity between the Alps and the Carpathians.

### 3.6 *Cooperation and the role of non-governmental organizations and non-profit organizations*

The Carpathian countries work very closely together towards wilderness protection. Examples of joint initiatives include the BioREGIO Carpathians project and the Forest WG activities on the Carpathian virgin forests (see Section 4). Besides the relevant governments of Carpathian countries, Non-Governmental Organizations (NGOs) and Non-Profit Organizations (NPOs) play a significant role in promoting the Carpathian Convention in the Carpathian countries. According to research by Weiss, Egerer and Luciani, institutions involved in promoting the convention in the Carpathian countries include Ministries (seventeen per cent), other public (state) bodies (twenty-three per cent) and institutions for research and higher education (fourteen per cent. However, the largest category is formed by NGOs and NPOs (forty-six per cent).[42] For instance, WWF–DCP embodies WWF's efforts to preserve, restore and sustainably manage the natural values of the Danube-Carpathian Ecoregion. In 2011, WWF DCP launched a campaign to save Romania's virgin forests and prevent further human intervention. This was followed by a Memorandum of Understanding (MoU), signed by WWF Romania and the Ministry of Environment and Forests of Romania, with the objective to identify, map and protect virgin forests. More than 100,000 people had signed a petition in support of this initiative to secure the protection of Romania's virgin forests.[43]

## 4 Implementing the Convention: The BioREGIO Carpathians project

The Carpathian Convention is a common platform for the Parties and the stakeholders acting in the region to collaborate and achieve overall

[41] See www.alpenkarpatenkorridor.at.

[42] Weiss, Egerer, Luciani, *National Achievements and Challenges Related to the Implementation of the Carpathian Convention, supra* note 10, at 12.

[43] See wwf.panda.org/?202898/WWF-campaign-gains-protection-of-Romanias-virgin-forests.

protection of the Carpathians through cross-border and transnational projects. The Convention achieves its objectives also in cooperation with other relevant Conventions such as the Alpine Convention. Such projects are crucial for nature and biodiversity issues across boundaries.

The Carpathian Project (2005–2008) was developed within a trans-Carpathian partnership platform, involving eighteen project partners from ten countries. These countries analysed and made recommendations on the Carpathians and implemented pilot activities for selected topics. Several publications have been developed from the project, such as the Carpathian Environment Outlook[44] (environment assessment of the mountain region), the Carpathian Spatial Development Vision (VASICA)[45] and the Atlas of the Carpathian Macroregion[46] (databases including spatial and environment indicators). The project outcomes, together with the Strategic Action Plan of the Carpathian Area and the various reports mentioned in earlier sections, served as a good basis for further activities. Most of these outcomes were relevant for wilderness protection in the Carpathian Area.

Of particular importance for the central theme of this chapter and book are the activities of the Carpathian Convention Working Group on Sustainable Forest Management (Forest WG) on the Carpathian virgin forests. The relevance of the Convention and implementation process for wilderness protection is also reflected in the BioREGIO Carpathians project.

### BioREGIO Carpathians project[47]

The BioREGIO Carpathians project (2011–2014) is a transnational cooperation project, co-financed under the second call of the European SEE Transnational Cooperation Programme, priority area 'Protection and Improvement of the Environment'. It is a flagship project included in the EU Strategy for the Danube Region. The main aim of the Project is to implement the main provisions of the Carpathian Convention

[44] United Nation Environment Programme, *Carpathians Environment Outlook* (Vienna: Carpathian Project, 2007).

[45] M. Borsa, C. Chifelea. H. Egerer, Z. Gal, W. Glowacki, M. Halas, V. Hopfgartner, I. Illes, Z. Niewiadomski, P. Ptacek and D. Wiederwald, *VASICA – Vision and Strategies in the Carpathian Area*, (Vienna: Carpathian Project, 2009)

[46] F.V. Ruffini and P. Ptacek (eds.), *Atlas of the Carpathian Macroregion* (Olomiuc: Palacky University, 2009)

[47] The text in this subsection builds on the information available on the website of the BioREGIO Carpathians' website, www.bioregio-carpathians.eu/.

Biodiversity Protocol[48] through the development, harmonization and implementation of integrated management plans for natural areas to promote regional development in the region and to improve the ecological connectivity in the Carpathians. This focus corresponds mainly to the following Articles of the Biodiversity Protocol under the Convention:

| | |
|---|---|
| Article 4 | Policies aiming at conservation, restoration and sustainable use of biological and landscape diversity of the Carpathians; |
| Article 5 | Integration of the objectives of conservation and sustainable use of biological and landscape diversity of the Carpathians into sectoral policies; |
| Article 6 | Participation of regional and local authorities, and other stakeholders; |
| Article 9 | Continuity and connectivity of natural and semi-natural habitats, ecological network in the Carpathians; |
| Article 15 | Enhancing conservation and sustainable management in the areas outside of protected areas; |
| Article 16 | Consultation, harmonisation and coordination of measures undertaken in border areas; |
| Article 17 | Development and implementation of management plans. |

The BioREGIO project involves sixteen partners from the seven Carpathian Countries (with the lead partner being the Piatra Craiului National Park in Romania) and the Alps (Austria and Italy). The Ministries of Environment of the seven Carpathian countries are also observers of the project.

The main objectives/outputs of the project include:

- Development and promotion of compatible biodiversity indicators and monitoring systems and regional inventories of species and habitats;
- Harmonization of management plans aimed at achieving common standards for the protection and sustainable use of habitats and species;
- Encouraging and supporting cooperative agreements for the management of protected areas in border regions;
- Fostering ecological connectivity in line with the requirements of NATURA 2000 and the pan-European Ecological Network;

[48] Protocol on Conservation and Sustainable Use of Biological and Landscape Diversity to the Framework Convention on the Protection and Sustainable Development of the Carpathians, Art. 4, 5, 6, 9, 15, 16 and 17.

- Promoting sustainable regional development initiatives based on the economic value of areas with high biodiversity;
- Promoting an intensive knowledge transfer to stakeholders at all levels and with other mountain regions (Alps, SEE);
- Increasing awareness on the importance of an integrated management of the Carpathians' natural assets as a development factor;
- Building on existing cooperation tools in the Carpathians (such as Carpathian Convention, Biodiversity Protocol).

Wilderness protection is not an explicit purpose of the project. For instance, the term 'wilderness' does not appear in the seventy-six-page 'Final Publication' of the project of June 2014.[49] A closer look at this project makes clear that the project and recommendations resulting from it may be of value for the protection of wilderness or wilderness qualities in the Carpathian region. For instance, in respect of forests (one of the four natural assets that receive attention in the project), the first three recommended measures are:

> F1. Identify and protect all near-natural, old growth and virgin forests
> F2. Establish non-intervention zones in all large forest protected areas.
> F3. Maintain different structural elements in forests: deadwood, hollow trees, microhabitats, rare tree species.[50]

Also with regard to other types of ecosystems (natural assets of 'high nature value grasslands' and 'wetlands'), similar measures were recommended. For instance, in respect of grasslands the document recommends to '[a]dopt non-intervention management for alpine and remote subalpine grasslands',[51] and for wetlands it recommends to '[a]dopt passive (minimal intervention) management for suitable sites (e.g. wetland forests, raised bogs, swamps)'.[52]

Furthermore, Carpathian wilderness may also profit from the efforts regarding the strengthening of the connectivity of natural areas. For instance, in respect to forest areas, the final publication recommends to '[p]revent forest fragmentation and maintain the integrity of forest

[49] ISCC, *BioREGION Carpathians. Integrated Management of Biological and Landscape Diversity for Sustainable Regional Development and Ecological Connectivity in the Carpathians*, Final Publication (Vienna: UNEP Vienna – Interim Secretariat of the Carpathian Convention (ISCC), 2014), www.bioregio-carpathians.eu/tl_files/bioregio/donwnloads_resources/Key%20Outputs%20and%20Publication/BioREGIOCarpathians_FINAL Publication.compressed.pdf.

[50] *Ibid.*, at 31.

[51] *Ibid.*, at 32, recommendation G1.

[52] *Ibid.*, at 33, recommendation W1.

ecological corridors'.[53] For wetlands, it is recommended to '[e]stablish ecological networks and restoration of river and wetland connectivity'. [54] This connectivity may be of crucial importance for the free functioning of natural ecosystems and is therefore relevant for the wilderness quality of 'naturalness'. In order to protect naturalness, the recommended active control of invasive species in respect of forests and wetlands is important.[55] As far as research is concerned, it is recommended to '[e]stablish regional methods for the assessment of forest naturalness'.[56]

Finally, the 'Final Publication' includes recommendations with regard to the fourth natural asset of the project, 'large carnivores and herbivores'. While most recommendations directly relate to species protection (prevention of poaching, establishing of a 'special regional project for lynx conservation', monitoring), some recommendations are also relevant from a wilderness perspective. For instance, the establishment of an 'ecological corridor system based on habitat use and species occurrence data'[57] is recommended. For the wilderness quality of 'naturalness', it is also interesting to note that the Final Publication recommends to '[p]lan a coordinated extension of the bison breeding and reintroduction programme'.[58]

Other deliverables of the project include a geo web-referenced interactive Carpathian Joint Biodiversity Information System (CJBIS) and Common Integrated Management Measures (CIMM) for natural assets and protected areas and for strengthening transboundary cooperation in protected areas. Three different transboundary pilot areas have been identified for intensified cooperation for protection. These areas also provide opportunities for regional development:

- Duna Ipoly National Park (Hungary)/Poiple (Slovakia)
- Iron Gates Nature Park (Romania)/Djerdap National Park (Serbia)
- Maramures Nature Park (Romania)/Carpathian Biosphere Reserve (Ukraine)

The project builds on existing frameworks of cooperation in the Carpathians such as the CNPA as well as the CWI, which provide multi-level governance and cross-sector integration of the project

[53] *Ibid.*, at 31, recommendation F14.
[54] *Ibid.*, at 33, recommendation W18.
[55] *Ibid.*, at 31, recommendation F13 and at 33, recommendation W14.
[56] *Ibid.*, at 31, recommendation F29.
[57] *Ibid.*, at 34, recommendation LM7.
[58] *Ibid.*, at 34, recommendation LM4.

outcomes and recommendations. Experience gained from the project will be shared with the Alps and project results are transferred to the Dinaric Arc and the Balkans.

## 5 Conclusion

The Carpathian Convention provides a transnational cooperation platform, which is important for the protection of nature including the remaining wilderness and wilderness qualities in the Carpathian region. Through the Convention, an institutional framework for different administrative levels in the various Carpathian countries has been developed, together with the introduction of about sixty regulatory documents for the implementation of the Convention, such as governmental laws, decrees, national strategies and plans and programs as well as protocols and rulebooks. The Carpathian countries have identified thematic priorities for each focus area, drew up policy and legal instruments and embarked on projects, initiatives and other activities to implement the provisions set out under the Convention. Transnational cooperation networks have also been established, such as the CNPA, and strategic projects have been developed and implemented, such as the BioREGIO Carpathians project.

In most of these legal instruments, plans, programmes and projects, there appears to be little explicit attention for the wilderness concept, as described in Chapter 1. This may in part be explained by the fact that, until recently, wilderness has not been a broadly discussed concept in environmental law and policy making in Europe. The Carpathian Convention framework complements existing legal instruments (e.g., the CBD and Natura 2000) by fostering regional cooperation to sustain further activities in the region aimed at promoting its sustainable development. This explains its fairly strong focus on sustainability and biodiversity. However, the Convention and its protocols also provide certain legal tools that are quite unique and more directly relevant for the protection of remaining wilderness areas in Europe, even if the term 'wilderness' is not used explicitly. Relevant are the efforts under the Convention to protect European virgin forests. Of particular interest is the legal obligation of each Party under Article 10 of the Forest Protocol to 'take measures in its national territory aimed at identifying and protecting natural, especially virgin forests of the Carpathians, by establishing Protected Areas in sufficient size and number and implementing other specific measures of protection'. Also, other provisions and initiatives, such as those relating to the promotion of non-intervention management, the strengthening of connectivity between protected areas and the control of invasive species, have relevance for wilderness protection, particularly the quality of 'naturalness'. The recommendations resulting from the BioREGIO Carpathians project illustrate the importance of these issues in the Carpathian Convention's framework.

It should also be noted that sustainable development is still a vague or even unknown concept for many inhabitants of the Carpathian area. One of the key mechanisms to establish awareness and to ensure sustainable development of the mountain communities in the long term is to work closely with NGOs and reach out to the local communities and by incorporating these efforts into school educational programmes. A particular challenge will be to balance social and economic development of the region with the protection of the remaining wilderness qualities. As the region develops, new infrastructure development and growing tourism bring about many economic benefits, yet at the same time result in greater ecological deterioration of the fragile ecosystems. Hence, it is critical that the Carpathian countries and relevant partners work together to ensure synergies especially for transnational and particularly interdisciplinary or intersectoral activities, minimizing the negative impact on ecosystems as much as possible. In this respect, eco-tourism has great potential. One example in the Carpathians is the successful development of the Piatra Craiului National Park in Romania under the WWF-supported Carpathian Large Carnivore Project. This initiative demonstrates the importance and possibility of developing the region whilst keeping the forest habitats intact through controlling pollution, recycling waste products and careful spatial planning.

In the future, wilderness protection in the Carpathians will also become more important due to the impact of climate change. As mountains are usually the first indicators of climate change, many aspects from the water cycle to carbon sequestration and impacts on biodiversity in the Carpathians need to be considered, for instance through the existing collaborations with various research institutions and NGOs.

In summary, the Carpathian Convention provides a good basis for wilderness protection in the Carpathians. It will continue to be a platform for future development of the region, while ensuring that the Carpathian Mountains region retains its name as the 'green jewel of Europe'.

# PART III

## The role of national law in protecting wilderness in Europe

# 11

# Wilderness protection in Austria

VOLKER MAUERHOFER

## 1 Introduction

'Nature needs protection and refuge areas where it can unfold without influence from the human hand'.[1] This statement was made in 2012 – not by a classical deep ecologist – but by the CEO of the publicly owned company Österreichische Bundesforste (OeBf). This company is responsible for managing ten per cent of the national territory of Austria, including fifteen per cent of its woodlands and over one hundred lakes.[2] This statement was not unexpected. It was made in connection with the presentation of a study entitled 'Wilderness in Austria? Challenges for society, nature conservation and the management of areas of unspoiled nature in times of climate change', co-launched with the World Wide Fund for Nature Austria (WWF Austria) in September 2012.[3] This initiative is illustrative of a new type of collaboration in relation to wilderness protection in Austria, mainly addressing one specific wider type of ecosystem, namely forests, but also alpine moorlands which are managed by the OeBf.[4] These moorlands and the only officially declared wilderness area of Austria, all of which are located in the Alpine Region, in conjunction with the specific legal aspects of forestry have already been covered in Chapter 9 of this book.[5] This

[1] Translation from www.wwf.at/de/menu447/subartikel2292/: 'Die Natur braucht Schutz und Rückzugsgebiete', sagt Georg Erlacher, Vorstandssprecher der Österreichischen Bundesforste, 'wo sie sich unbeeinflusst von Menschenhand entfalten kann.' All translations in this chapter are the author's.

[2] See www.bundesforste.at/index.php?id=554

[3] WWF/ ÖBf AG, Wildnis in Österreich? Herausforderungen für Gesellschaft, Naturschutz und Naturraummanagement in Zeiten des Klimawandels, (Purkersdorf: Österreichische Bundesforste AG (ÖBf AG)/Kompetenzfeld Naturschutz, 2012), www.wwf.at/de/view/files/download/showDownload/?tool=12&feld=download&sprach_connect=2203.

[4] See www.bundesforste.at/index.php?id=990.

[5] See Chapter 9.

chapter instead focuses on the role of law in protecting wilderness in Austria in areas beyond alpine habitats. The analysis is grounded in an in-depth review of literature, relevant legal sources and legal databanks.[6] Based on these sources, more detailed information has been collected with respect to a number of specific areas.

After discussing the relevance of the wilderness concept in Austrian society (Section 2), attention is given to the definition of wilderness in an Austrian legal context (Section 3). The main body of this chapter addresses the relevance of Austrian law in protecting wilderness (Section 4). The extent to which this protection is also ensured in practice is discussed subsequently (Section 5). The final section includes some main conclusions and the author's personal reflection on the future of wilderness protection in Austria (Section 6).

## 2 Relevance of 'wilderness' to Austrian society

In 1985, successful public resistance to the destruction of the largest Austrian lowland wetlands alongside the Danube River near the town of Hainburg (east of Vienna), marked the birth of the green political movement in Austria. This area was widely recognized as an area of wilderness (despite the former physical river adjustment) and was intended as the construction site of a river dam for hydropower production. The peaceful occupation of this site by various social actors in winter 1984 and its forceful dissolution by the police generated a huge public discussion on the value of the area. This discussion resulted in a preliminary political 'Christmas peace-decision' by the Austrian Chancellor to stop the ongoing forest clearances that were being conducted in preparation for the construction activities. At the time of this discussion, all legal preconditions were fulfilled to proceed with the construction work; however, on 1 July 1986, the highest Administrative Court of Austria ('Verwaltungsgerichtshof' – VwGH) declared the permission, which was granted pursuant to the Austrian Water Law Act, unlawful.[7] After that decision, the construction plans were cancelled, the creation of a National Park announced and this lowland river wetland area now constitutes a main part of the core zone of the 'National Park

[6] For the databases see www.ris.bka.gv.at/default.aspx.

[7] See VwSlg 12188 A/1986, but see also the preliminary measures granted at 2 January 1985 – after the commencement of the forest clearance activities – by the same court in VwSlg 11632 A/1985.

Donau Auen' ('Danube Wetlands National Park').[8] Meanwhile, the specific site near Hainburg was subsequently partly exempted from physical river management measures through a river restoration project, co-funded by the European Union's Life funding scheme,[9] which restored the river dynamics (e.g., flooding) in adjacent areas.

This success story of public action to protect relatively untouched nature also served to strengthen the legal protection for other pre-existing wild areas and the designation of new areas (particularly national parks, areas recognized under the 'Man and Biosphere programme' of the UNESCO and Natura 2000 sites[10]) and more generally broadened public appreciation of the intrinsic values of nature.

This development has resulted in a mutually cooperative relationship between these areas and society, with increasing numbers of visitors and a broad recognition of these sites as an important economic factor in their respective surroundings. The administrative units responsible for these areas ('National Park authorities') regularly organize events whereby tourism opportunities and local products from their surroundings are showcased, even in the centres of the largest cities of Austria.

Finally, in the societal context it should be observed that the German word for wilderness (*Wildnis*) is widely used within Austrian society, but often with a negative connotation. For instance, the term is still regularly used in relation to small scale areas that have not been 'cultivated' through gardening, agriculture, forestry or other types of human uses.[11] Consequently, the term 'wilderness' may also be found in certain decisions of the highest Courts of Austria in which the parties have used this term for particular purposes.[12] For instance, in one particular

[8] See www.donauauen.at/?language=english.

[9] Project Donauufer – Restoration of Danube river banks LIFE02 NAT/A/008518, selected as one of the twenty-six 'Best' LIFE Nature projects in 2007–2008, see http://ec.europa.eu/environment/life/project/Projects/index.cfm?fuseaction=home.search.

[10] V. Mauerhofer, 'Conservation of Wildlife in the European Union with a Focus on Austria', in R. Panjwani (ed.), *Wildlife Law–A Global Perspective* (Cleveland: American Bar Association (ABA)-Publishing, 2008), 1–55, and V. Mauerhofer, 'Missing Links: How Individuals Can Contribute to Reserve Policy Enforcement on the Example of the European Union', *Biodiversity and Conservation*, 19 (2010), 601–618.

[11] See the discussion in Chapter 1 on the meaning of wilderness prior to the Romantic Period.

[12] Supreme Court ('Oberster Gerichtshof – OGH') 7Ob209/98f of 28 April 1999, which dealt with the issue of an easement and whether or not one party would have been able to recognize the use of a certain parcel of land. For a similar case, see OGH of 07 December 1995, 2Ob521/94. See also the judgment of the OGH of 11 November 2011, 10 Ob 52/11m,

Supreme Court judgment,[13] the defendant named an area with bushes and shrubs 'wilderness' in order to avoid censure for illegal forest cutting. The administrative authority successfully argued that parts of the area consisted of natural wetland forests. Conversely, in another judgment of the VwGH[14] the defendant administrative authority claimed that a particular area was a 'forest' while the (successful) private appellant emphasized its non-wilderness character due to its careful use. Strikingly, in both cases, the party using the term 'wilderness' applied it with a negative connotation in order to disqualify the claim of the opponent.

## 3 What is 'wilderness' in the Austrian legal context?

### *3.1 The issues of a definition: potential wilderness areas in Austria*

Article 15 of the federal Austrian Constitution ('Bundesverfassungs-Gesetz' – short 'B-VG') leaves the competence for the development and implementation of nature conservation legislation to the nine Austrian provinces ('Bundesländer'[15]), thus no specific nature conservation law exists at the federal level.[16] The respective laws of the provinces dealing with Nature Conservation and Nature Protection do not advance any explicit definition of wilderness. However, as observed in Chapter 9, the province of Lower Austria explicitly established a 'wilderness area' and even successfully applied for its recognition by the IUCN through the IUCN list of Protected Areas under category I. Thus, this province implicitly recognizes the IUCN definition and it can be argued that this definition is also valid for wilderness areas in this province that are located outside the Alpine Region.

Similarly, the law establishing the latest (alpine) Austrian National Park 'Gesäuse' in the province of Styria lists in its annex I all the current six IUCN protected areas categories (including 'Wilderness Area'), while also reproducing the general IUCN criteria for zoning of protected areas

wherein the dispute concerned the question whether hens had to be prevented from entering a parcel of neighboring land that had fallen into temporary disuse and was called 'Wildnis' by the hen-owning defendant.

13 See OGH, 7 December 1995, 2Ob521/94.

14 Judgment of 20 June 1994, 90/10/0064.

15 Burgenland – Castle Land, Kärnten – Carinthia, Niederösterreich – Lower Austria, Oberösterreich – Upper Austria, Salzburg – Salzburg, Steiermark – Styria, Tirol – Tyrol, Vorarlberg – Vorarlberg, Wien – Vienna.

16 For more details, see, inter alia, Mauerhofer, 'Conservation of Wildlife in the European Union with a Focus on Austria', *supra* note 10.

as well as their specific requirements for National Parks.[17] Again, there is a strong assumption that the IUCN criteria would also be applicable if specific wilderness areas were to be created within this province, either within its Alpine part or the lowlands outside the Alpine Region.

Potential wilderness areas in the Austrian lowlands comprise in particular larger areas dedicated to military use (under federal legislation), wetlands alongside rivers, reed belts, forest areas outside the Alpine Region and moorlands. These are all habitat types that, in their growth and breakdown cycles, do not depend on human management or use. Applying the criteria for wilderness, as described in Chapter 1, to these areas provides an ambiguous picture. Among the larger areas dedicated to military use (under federal legislation) one area is particularly noteworthy: the area of 'Allentsteig' in Lower Austria that is some 152.49 $km^2$ in size.[18] This whole area was requisitioned without compensation during the National Socialism regime in the 1940s. At that time the area consisted of mixed farmland and woodland with numerous villages and has since developed naturally, as well as under the influence of the military (including fires), to a type of 'secondary wilderness'. Nevertheless, while the existing ruins of these villages will deteriorate further, they will still represent manifestations of modern civil society for a number of decades to come. Meanwhile, this naturalization widely occurs within existing ecosystems, in conjunction with military uses which also include certain forestry activities. In all other provinces, military areas were developed away from human-dominated landscapes, and in various types of natural habitats (e.g., forests, wetlands, grasslands discussed later). In most cases, these other military areas cannot be considered 'relatively large in size'. One exception, however, is the area of 'Bruckneudorf' in Lower Austria spanning 33.2 $km^2$, which, with its open meadow landscape, constitutes part of a Natura 2000 site.[19]

Relatively natural riverine wetlands can be mainly found alongside the Danube River, in particular within the Danube Wetlands National Park of about 9,300 hectares stretching from Vienna approximately 100 km east towards the Slovakian border.[20] But the naturalness of these wetlands has also been heavily affected by man-made changes of the riverbed

[17] Gesetz vom 12. März 2002 über den Nationalpark Gesäuse (Nationalparkgesetz Gesäuse, Stmk. NPG) Provincial Law Gazette – Landesgesetzblatt (short LGBl.) No. 61/2002.

[18] See federal law gazette II No. 441/2005, latest version II No. 477/2008.

[19] Information was forthcoming in late 2014 at www.burgenland.at/natur-umwelt/geschuetzte-gebiete/natura-gebiete/leithagebirge (no longer available).

[20] See www.donauauen.at/?area=nationalpark&subarea=numbers&language=english.

and measures to facilitate international shipping in the past. However, the maintenance of the Danube in particular as an international waterway is stipulated in the legal basis of that National Park,[21] while in recent years a programme to destroy side dams over several kilometres was commenced to restore the ecological functioning of the river system, including the flooding of the wetlands behind these dams.[22] Furthermore, the graduated reduction of artificial plantations of non-native tree species has been mandated as part of the management plan of the National Park.[23]

In addition to these areas with comparatively high wilderness qualities, relatively large reed belts exist within the Region of the Neusiedler See – Seewinkel. These belts may span up to 5 km in breadth and the area has received international recognition as a Ramsar Site, World Heritage Site and Austria's first internationally designated National Park under the IUCN's category II.[24] It is the westernmost steppe lake in Europe, with a surface of 178 km$^2$ (providing a combined lake coverage of approximate 320 km$^2$), of which eighty per cent is located in Austria, and twenty per cent in Hungarian territory.[25] Large parts of the reed belt even fall within the Nature Reserve Zone of the National Park accounting for fifty per cent (about 4,500 ha) of the entire National Park, wherein human access is very strictly regulated.[26]

Woodlands beyond the Alpine Region are usually used for forestry; for those laying beyond the protected areas the duty to implement phytosanitary and similar measures regularly fall upon forest owners. Usually these obligations apply even if the area is protected under the provincial nature conservation legal framework. One exemption, apart from miscellaneous forested areas falling under the Natura 2000 network, is the forested area of the Thaya Valley National Park, comprising 1,330 hectares located in the Bohemian highland alongside the border with the Czech Republic.[27] Whether this can be considered as 'relatively large' (as indicated in Chapter 1 as one of the main wilderness qualities), may be questioned; however, the Austrian woodland is connected to an area on

[21] Art. 3(2) of the Nature Park Law of Lower Austria 5505–2 and – based on this provision – the Regulation on the National Park Danube Wetlands, Provincial Law Gazette 5501/1–0 of 19 December 1996.

[22] See www.donauauen.at/?area=nature&subarea=riverregulation.

[23] See www.donauauen.at/?area=nationalpark&subarea=numbers&language=english.

[24] See www.eulakes.eu/upload/eulakes/gestionedocumentale/output_2.2.4–2.%20join%20bulletin_784_2451.pdf.

[25] See www.nationalpark-neusiedlersee-seewinkel.at/lake-neusiedl-and-its-reed-belt.html.

[26] See www.nationalpark-neusiedlersee-seewinkel.at/key-facts.html.

[27] For a description see e.g. www.np-thayatal.at/en/pages/key-data-132.aspx.

the other side of the river within the Czech Republic that is much larger and has also been designated as a National Park under category II of the IUCN criteria.[28] Certain management measures apply to 70 hectares within the nature zone for the protection of ecosystems, for example on behalf of traditionally used meadows alongside the Thaya River.[29]

Moorlands have almost disappeared in Austria beyond the Alpine Region. Some examples of remaining moorland complexes can be found in areas protected within the Natura 2000 network, such as a Special Protection Area within the Ibmer moorlands in the province of Upper Austria,[30] spanning about 152 hectares[31] and the Special Protection Area in the North-Western part of the province of Lower Austria[32] which comprises 13.9 ha.[33] These areas are on the one hand subject to specific restorative management measures that aim to improve their naturalness, while on the other hand their size may be considered insufficient in order to fulfil the 'relatively large' criterion. Furthermore, several species formerly typical to these areas, such as the Black Grouse and the Great Shrike, are extirpated and have not yet returned.

### 3.2 *Different levels of 'wilderness areas'*

Based on the above inventory of Austrian natural areas that may qualify as wilderness, it must be concluded that – outside of the Alpine Regions – few of the 'last remnants of true wilderness'[34] can be found. The aforementioned reed belts appear to most closely represent the three criteria of the definition outlined in Chapter 1, although many of them outside of the Neusiedler See – Seewinkel National Park are regularly cut during winter.

[28] See, e.g., Mauerhofer, 'A bottom-up "Convention-Check" to Improve Top-down Global Protected Area Governance', *supra* note 10.

[29] See www.np-thayatal.at/en/pages/key-data-132.aspx.

[30] See Provincial Law Gazette number 2011/22 of Upper Austria, which is based on the EU Birds Directive, www.ris.bka.gv.at/Dokumente/Lgbl/LGBL_OB_20110331_22/LGBL_OB_20110331_22.pdf.

[31] See http://portal.wko.at/wk/format_detail.wk?angid=1&stid=607823&dstid=7067.

[32] SPA 'Waldviertler Teich-, Heide- und Moorlandschaft' ('Waldviertler Pond, Heather and Moor Landscape') Regulation 5500/6-4 of the Provincial Law Gazette of Lower Austria, which is based on the Habitats Directive.

[33] Size and code AT1201A00 according to the EU Standard Data Form www.noel.gv.at/bilder/d37/4_01_Gebietsbeschreibung.pdf?15098.

[34] See Chapter 1.

The forests of the Thaya Valley National Park should not be considered 'natural' due to forestry activities conducted prior to its inauguration as a National Park on 1 January 2000, although the area still exhibits relatively high wilderness qualities. Similarly, the management of the meadows near the river to support the conservation of traditionally used meadow ecosystems demonstrates clear and direct human influences.

The wetlands along the River Danube described above currently exhibit relatively low wilderness qualities but do have strong potential for restoration towards an area with relatively high wilderness qualities ('new wilderness').[35] Restoration measures in these wetlands have already been implemented, but measures to ensure international waterway navigation continue to play a primary role therein.

A similar conclusion may be drawn in respect of the moorland Natura 2000 sites insofar as their restoration measures have been successfully implemented. But certain influences such as hunting in the surrounding areas and diffusion of other human-based activities into the relatively small sites still serve to reduce their specific wilderness qualities.

Other areas within the wetlands of the Danube River Wetland National Park and the moorland mentioned previously also show relatively low wilderness qualities but have high potential to be restored to 'new wilderness'.[36]

## 4 Legal protection of wilderness areas

### *4.1 General: wilderness protection as a policy objective?*

Wilderness protection is a policy objective at the federal Austrian level insofar as the federal government has influenced – by means of financial incentives – several provinces to establish National Parks that fulfil the criteria of IUCN Category II, which has been particularly relevant for the exclusion of certain human uses of these relatively wild areas.[37] As outlined in Chapter 9, the federal government also contributed financially

[35] *Ibid.*

[36] *Ibid.*

[37] See, for instance, V. Mauerhofer, 'Nationalparkrecht – Im Spannungsfeld von bundesstaatlicher Kompetenzverteilung, Europarecht und Naturschutzpolitik' ['National Park Law – In the Area of Conflict of Competence Distribution in a Federal State, EU-law and Nature Conservation Politics'], Umweltbundesamt [Federal Environmental Agency], *Bericht* Nr. 129 (1998), www.umweltbundesamt.at/fileadmin/site/publikationen/BE129.pdf.

from the outset to the establishment of the only Austrian Wilderness Area listed under IUCN category I.

Despite intensive discussions, no quantitative goal was included in the Austrian National Biodiversity strategy released at the end of 2014.[38] But goal 10 (entitled 'Species and Habitat types have to be maintained')[39] of that strategy lists as one of the sixteen measures the 'elaboration of options for the designation of natural sites (areas without intervention with wilderness character) within the frame of existing conservation site concepts by means of conservation contracts'.[40] This measure is also explicitly considered as a tool to serve goals 3 ('Agronomy and forestry contribute to the maintenance and betterment of biodiversity)[41] and 4 ('Wildlife stock and fish stock are adapted to the natural conditions')[42] of this strategy.[43]

While in the realm of environmentalists the term 'wilderness' is also romantically associated with and expressed by landscape paintings from the 'Biedermeier' period by famous artists, such as Ferdinand Georg Waldmüller (1793–1865[44]) and Friedrich Gauermann (1807–1862[45]), the term still has a relatively negative connotation in Austria, associated with danger and untidiness. Consequently, politicians are still rather reluctant to use the term. In recent decades, other categories of protected sites – which also may include areas with wilderness qualities but are christened with a different and more popular designation, such as 'National Parks' and 'Biosphere Parks' – have increased in numbers and have been subject to considerable outreach activities and awareness

38 Biodiverstäts-Strategie Österreich 2020+ (Vienna: Umweltbundesamt, 2014); and personal communication with the Bundesministerium für Land- und Forstwirtschaft, Umwelt und Wasserwirtschaft (Hrsg.).

39 *Ibid.*, at 23: 'Arten und Lebensräume sind erhalten'.

40 Biodiverstäts Strategie Österreich 2020+, *ibid.*, at 23: 'Erarbeitung von Optionen zur Ausweisung von Naturgebieten (eingriffsfreie Flächen mit Wildnischarakter) im Rahmen bestehender Schutzgebietskonzepte mittels Vertragsnaturschutz.' For a discussion of specific forests reserves based solely on contractual arrangements, see G. Frank and F. Müller, 'Voluntary approaches in protection of forests in Austria', *Environmental Science and Policy*, 6 (2003), 261–269.

41 *Ibid.*, at 12: 'Land- und Forstwirtschaft tragen zur Erhaltung und Verbesserung der Biodiversität bei.'

42 *Ibid.*, at 14: 'Wildtierbestand und Fischbestand sind an die naturräumlichen Verhältnisse angepasst.'

43 *Ibid.*, at 46.

44 See http://geschichte.landesmuseum.net/index.asp?contenturl=http://geschichte.landesmuseum.net/personen/personendetail.asp___id=948544823.

45 *Ibid.*

raising.[46] Educational programmes and specific events of certain parks focus explicitly on wilderness[47] and therefore raise awareness and understanding of wilderness issues among the Austrian population. Large carnivores that have re-established regular breeding in areas with wilderness qualities, such as lynx and, from about 1990 to 2000, the brown bear, often form some of the 'spearhead species' of such campaigns in order to promote a more positive perception among locals and visitors. The wolf receives a rather lower degree of support among local people, whether based upon perceptions that are rooted still in fairy tales or due to its carnivore diet, alongside the presence of larger packs (although this is not the case in Austria).

The re-establishment of wilderness may also sometimes be politically attractive in addressing emerging environmental threats. For example, the destruction of the dams in the Danube Wetlands National Park, described as restoration measures previously, enhanced the wilderness qualities of the wetlands and led to an increased number of flooding events on the northern riverside. In conjunction with their ecological motivations, these measures also aim to reduce the likelihood of flooding, especially for the town Hainburg on the south bank of the Danube. From a political perspective, such measures are easier to justify, in particular in the context of unpredictable flooding events due to climate change.

Another interesting initiative is that of 'city wilderness' ('*Stadtwildnis*'), which is promoted by several Viennese public authorities. Also, areas within the city (public areas or those under public management) are being developed with a more natural status in mind.[48] One example is the extension of a small park in the fifth Viennese district from 1,500 $m^2$ to 3,100 $m^2$ and its reopening as a park and city wilderness.[49]

[46] See, e.g., www.nationalparksaustria.at/ and www.unesco.org/new/en/natural-sciences/environment/ecological-sciences/biosphere-reserves/europe-north-america/austria/.

[47] See, for example, the 3rd International Wilderness Days, which took place in the (Alpine) National Park 'Kalkalpen', 13–15 September 2012. www.kalkalpen.at/system/web/sonderseite.aspx?menuonr=221633442&detailonr=221633442&sprache=2; furthermore, the umbrella organization National Parks Austria convened its public annual conference 2012 from 11–12 December under the slogan 'Call of the Wilderness' ('Ruf der Wildnis') and attracted about 150 visitors; see www.nationalparksaustria.at/nationalparks-360-grad/die-nationalparks/aktuelles/#sthash.bdc8HgjF.dpuf.

[48] See www.wien.gv.at/umwelt/parks/anlagen/stadtwildnis.html and www.wua-wien.at/natur-wien/stadtwildnis.

[49] 'Scheupark und Margaretner Stadtwildnis', www.wien.gv.at/umwelt/parks/anlagen/scheupark.html.

These developments show a gradual process of increasing societal and political acceptance of wilderness in certain regions of Austria at least.

### *4.2 The use of the term 'Wildnis' in Austrian legislation to implement international law*

The Austrian federal legal framework is not the primary means of providing legal protection to wilderness areas, due to the distribution of competences by the Constitution as described above. However, the federal legislative body can – and in case of binding international and regional agreements, must – implement obligations pertaining to wilderness protection by modifying legislation and enforcing these commitments. This has been explained already in the context of duties stated in the federal forestry law that contradicted EU-related conservation obligations regarding areas with wilderness qualities. (see Chapter 9, Section 5, under e).

Additionally, some of the multilateral environmental agreements concluded by the federal government and published in the Federal Law Gazette for further implementation by the competent provincial authorities, expressly contain the term 'wilderness'. A particular example relates to the implementation of Art. 7(a)[50] of the Convention on Biological Diversity (CBD),[51] since Annex I to this convention lists 'wilderness' among the criteria[52] for the identification of components of biological diversity important for its conservation and sustainable use, especially in connection with in-situ conservation, ex-situ conservation and sustainable use.

It must however be noted that in some instances the German translation of a treaty refers to '*Wildnis*', the German translation of 'wilderness', while the treaty itself in fact only uses the term 'wild'. For instance, the Annex to the Convention on International Trade on Endangered Species

[50] See Article 7 on 'Identification and monitoring': 'Each Contracting Party shall, as far as possible and as appropriate, in particular for the purposes of Articles 8 to 10: (a) identify components of biological diversity important for its conservation and sustainable use having regard to the indicative list of categories set down in Annex I.'

[51] Published in the federal law gazette ('Bundesgesetzblatt-BGBl') No. 213/1995 of 24 March1995.

[52] The relevant first point of Annex I reads as follows: 'IDENTIFICATION AND MONITORING 1. Ecosystems and habitats: containing high diversity, large numbers of endemic or threatened species, or **wilderness**; required by migratory species; of social, economic, cultural or scientific importance; or, which are representative, unique or associated with key evolutionary or other biological processes' (emphasis added).

(CITES),[53] wherein the endangered species are listed[54] for two families of species (the family of the *Manidae* – Pangolins and the family of the *Testudinidae* – Tortoises) for which a zero annual export quota has been established for certain specimens of these families removed from the 'wild' and traded for primarily commercial purposes. The word 'wild' is translated in the German language version as '*Wildnis*',[55] a translation that is not consistent since in the context of certain other species[56] the German version uses the phrase 'taken from nature' ('*der Natur entnommene*').

The examples above provide interesting insights into the ambiguous use of 'wilderness' in the German language and legal documents.

### *4.3 Domestic legislation providing legal protection to wilderness areas*

Apart from these examples from international conventions, the term 'wilderness' can also be found in other sectors of federal law, such as military law. The so-called *Flexibilisierungsverordnung Heeresforstverwaltung Allentsteig*[57] (Flexibility regulation military forestry administration Allentsteig) defines the obligations of the authority that is specifically responsible for the military exercises areas of Allentsteig and Bruckneudorf outlined previously in this chapter. Point 4 of the Annex to that regulation defines among its key obligations the implementation of management measures for specific land that is allocated to the military exercises areas of Allentsteig according to a special military spatial use plan. This land covers, for example, fire protection strips, shooting strips and '*Wildnisflächen*' (Wilderness areas), but only applies up to a maximum size of 95 hectares. This number appears rather small given the total area of both military exercise areas of more than 185 km$^2$; moreover, the regulation neither defines the term 'wilderness area' nor does it prescribe its aims.

Within its wide range of protected area categories, the Austrian provincial legal framework does not provide for a separate category of

[53] Published in the federal law gazette ('Bundesgesetzblatt-BGBl') No. 188/1982; latest version in federal law gazette III No. 55/2014. On its implementation generally, and the directly binding regulations in an Austrian context at the EU level, see http://ec.europa.eu/environment/cites/legislation_en.htm.

[54] See http://cites.org/eng/app/2013/E-Appendices-2013-06-12.pdf.

[55] Federal law gazette III Nr. 69/2012.

[56] For example, in respect of the family of the *Crocodylidae* – Crocodiles, *Geoemydidae* – Box turtles, freshwater turtles.

[57] See federal law gazette II No. 441/2005, latest version II Nr. 477/2008.

'wilderness areas'. The province that established the only Austrian wilderness area listed under IUCN's category I so far ('Wilderness Area Dürrestein', October 2014[58]), simply referred an area protected as a 'Nature Conservation Area' ('*Naturschutzgebiet*') to the IUCN for recognition.[59] Additionally, the area is also protected as a '*Europaschutzgebiet*' ('Europe Protection Area'), a separate category of protected area within the Nature Protection Act of Lower Austria[60] to implement the Natura 2000 regime, which has received further attention in regulations under the Act.[61]

Many of the areas previously described have the status of National Parks as well as of EU Natura 2000 sites. In fact, all Austrian National Parks are also covered either by the Habitats Directive and/or the Birds Directive. The protection under these Directives is mainly oriented towards certain species and habitat types, while National Parks aim in particular for the establishment and maintenance of natural processes.[62] These differing directions can lead to conflicts within conservation aims. This is the case when the Habitats Directive aims for the maintenance of a favourable conservation status of a certain habitat type or species, while the more wilderness-oriented National Park concept of IUCN Category II supports natural developments (e.g., the growth of forests or the natural breakdown of rocks), developments that may in fact be detrimental for this habitat type or species. This is, for example, the case for the Thaya Valley National Park on the border with the Czech Republic. There the question arises as to whether to protect certain natural meadow

[58] The current Protected Area database indicates three areas named 'Rothwald I, II and III', respectively, as these are the names of the officially designated Nature Conservation Areas based on which the IUCN status Ia was granted (www.protectedplanet.net/search?q=rothwald+III).

[59] For more information, see Chapter 9.

[60] Law 5500/9 of the Provincial Law Gazette of Lower Austria.

[61] Para. 9 of Regulation 5500/6–6 of the Provincial Law Gazette of Lower Austria.

[62] As for the criteria for the establishment of National Parks, the National Park Act of Lower Austria (para. 2 in the Law 5505–3 of the Provincial Law Gazette of Lower Austria) refers to the criteria of the IUCN (para. 2 para 1, number 1), the vast nativeness of the area and the possibility of a widely uninfluenced dynamic of the ecosystems of the area. Similar formulations can be found in Art. 44(1)(b) and 45(3) of the National Park Act of Burgenland (Provincial Law Gazette number 27/1991, latest version 79/2013). The latter two paragraphs were even adopted – uniquely for National Park definitions in Austria – as constitutional norms of the Province by 2/3-majority voting (requiring the presence of a minimum of half of the parliamentarians), in order to make it politically impossible to modify them by simple majority (requiring only a 1/3 presence) based on para. 33 of the Provincial Constitution of Burgenland (para. 31 provincial law gazette no. 42/1981, latest version 64/2014).

habitat types on rocks or to leave the park to its natural processes, leading to a more forested habitat type.

Although all Austrian National Parks received their Natura 2000 status at a later point than their National Park status, it is hard to identify a shift from 'wilderness oriented protection' towards the protection of specific species and habitat. To start with, the majority of the species or habitat types protected through Natura 2000 have already previously been subjected to management measures under the National Park regime. This is valid for many species or habitat types such as old-growth forests and dynamic wetland areas. Furthermore, National Parks in Austria instead aim to extend their core zones, and therefore their wilderness qualities. The reasons for this differ: either a National Park has had an explicit wilderness strategy and could quite easily reach or even exceed the IUCN seventy-five per cent goal (e.g., Kalkalpen National Park) or a National Park has too little wilderness (below seventy-five per cent) and therefore strives for an increase in wilderness in order not to lose its position on the IUCN list (e.g., Neusiedler See – Seewinkel National Park).

For some areas with this double status (National Park and Natura 2000) existing provincial National Park laws contain more stringent assessment requirements for activities that are potentially harmful for Natura 2000 habitats and species. Certain provinces provide in these cases legal norms that explicitly uphold those more stringent requirements.[63]

### 4.4 *Wilderness protection through protected area legislation*

The above discussion indicates that the Austrian legislation contains three protected area categories that are particularly well-equipped to protect wilderness qualities: Nature Conservation Areas, National Parks and Biosphere Reserves. Nature Conservation Areas exist in all nine provinces,[64] National Parks in eight,[65] while seven provinces[66] have

[63] For example, para. 24 of the Landesgesetz über die Erhaltung und Pflege der Natur (Oö. Natur- und Landschaftsschutzgesetz 2001 - Oö. NSchG 2001) Provincial Law Gazette No. 129/2001, version No. 35/2014.

[64] For example, para. 24 of the Gesetz vom November 1990 über den Schutz und die Pflege der Natur und Landschaft im Burgenland (Burgenländisches Naturschutz- und Landschaftspflegegesetz – NG 1990) Provincial Law Gazette No. 27/1991, version No. 79/2013.

[65] Gesetz vom 12. März 2002 über den Nationalpark Gesäuse (Nationalparkgesetz Gesäuse, Stmk. NPG) Provincial Law Gazette – Landesgesetzblatt ( short LGBl.) No. 61/2002.

[66] All except Styria and Upper Austria.

legally established 'Biosphere Parks', recognized as Biosphere Reserves by UNESCO under its Man and Biosphere Programme.[67] Generally, the National Parks follow the IUCN criteria in terms of protection of natural processes and zoning. They are spread over several square kilometres and have their own management units, although the provincial administration is designated as the formal competent authority. Some Nature Conservation Areas may be significantly larger than the smallest National Parks and they theoretically cover a broader spectrum of aims, ranging from the conservation of natural processes to the sustainable use of certain man-made habitat types. With regard to natural processes, smaller Nature Conservation Areas can impose even more stringent prohibitions than some National Parks. For example, hunting in some Nature Conservation Areas is prohibited in order not to disturb waterbirds,[68] while in several National Parks certain wildlife management measures are implemented. With regard to the sustainable use of certain man-made habitat types, Nature Conservation Areas usually lack their own management unit in comparison to National Parks, and therefore depend heavily on the work of volunteers and are accordingly often 'candidates for secondary wilderness'.

Some of the seven Biosphere Reserves in Austria[69] include – as their 'core zone' in the sense of the UNESCO zoning concept[70] – pre-existing Nature Conservation Areas with quite stringent legal protection schemes. For instance, the 'Viennese Forests' Biosphere Park, located at the easternmost Alpine foothills, contains the 'Lainzer Tiergarten' Nature Conservation Area[71] that surrounds a site of 70 hectares, called the 'Johannser Kogel' Natural Forest Reserve,[72] which is even considered

[67] E.g. NÖ Biosphärenpark Wienerwald Gesetz Provincial Law Gazette No. 5760–0.

[68] See, for example, the administrative regulation on the area of 'Gralla' in Styria, which was subject to a judgment of the Constitutional Court of Austria of 18 June 1983, V30/80, number 9724 of the official collection of judgments.

[69] See www.unesco.org/new/en/natural-sciences/environment/ecological-sciences/biosphere-reserves/europe-north-america/austria/.

[70] See M. Elbakidze, T. Hahn, V. Mauerhofer, P. Angelstam and R. Axelsson, 'Legal Framework for Biosphere Reserves as Learning Sites for Sustainable Development: A Comparative Analysis of Ukraine and Sweden', *Ambio*, 42 (2), 174–187.

[71] See the related regulation in the Provincial Law Gazette number 46/2008 of 28 November 2008.

[72] The 'Johannser Kogel' is also an officially designated Natural Heritage Site, established under para. 28 of the Viennese Nature Conservation Law, Provincial Law Gazette number 45/1998, latest version number 31/2013; see also the regulation related to the 'Lainzer Tiergarten' in the Provincial Law Gazette number 46/2008 of 28 November 2008.

to be a virgin forest and of which 45 hectares are fenced and only accessible through guided tours.

The 'Viennese Forests' Biosphere Park is one of the two parks in Austria with its own formally institutionalized management organization, while the former logging operators are responsible for the operational activities regarding its practical forest management.[73]

In addition to these three categories, wilderness may also receive legal protection as a 'Natural Heritage Area', an instrument that can be found in the conservation laws of all nine Austrian provinces and which is usually applied in a quite stringent way to individual features of a relatively small size (e.g., old trees, gorges and short river stretches).

### 4.5 *Wilderness and 'ex lege protection'*

Wilderness in Austria may also be the subject of '*ex lege* protection'.[74] Several conservation laws contain this instrument that already defines protected zones by broad typologies of ecosystems within the legislative act without an administrative regulation stipulating in detail the borders as well as specific prohibitions and duties. One example is the *ex lege* protection of glaciers in the Nature Protection Law of Carinthia, declaring that in the area of glaciers and their catchment areas every sustainable deterioration is prohibited.[75] Similar general prohibitions can be found in varying formulations regarding, for example, the *ex lege* protection of wetlands.[76]

### 4.6 *Wilderness protection through spatial planning law*

Austrian spatial planning legislation does not play any role in constituting conservation areas. Rather, it has a declarative function in terms of making conservation areas visible during spatial planning processes for purposes other than nature conservation. Nonetheless, spatial planning law has a more indirect relevance for wilderness conservation as

[73] www.bundesforste.at/index.php?id=315. The other example is the Biosphere Park Nockberge.

[74] See more in detail Mauerhofer, 'Conservation of Wildlife in the European Union with a Focus on Austria', *supra* note 10.

[75] Para. 7 of the Nature Conservation Law of Carinthia, Provincial Law Gazette number 79/2002, latest version 85/2013.

[76] Para. 8 of the Nature Conservation Law of Carinthia Provincial Law Gazette; paras 8 and 9 of the Tyrolean Nature Conservation Act Provincial Law Gazette Provincial Law Gazette number 26/2005, latest version 87/2015.

provincial conservation laws use zoning terms such as '*Bauland*' ('construction land') defined by spatial planning legislation, and therefore bind themselves to categories of spatial planning law. This is especially important in connection to the *ex-lege* protection typologies explained above. For example, the Carinthian Nature Conservation law prohibits activities that may threaten a wide range of enumerated wetland types; however, these prohibitions are no longer valid once the wetland has been designated for over ten years as 'construction land' and is located within a 'closed construction area', with both zones defined in spatial planning law and implemented by legally binding decisions by provincial and local spatial planning authorities. Here, nature conservation law is clearly subordinate, rendering the *ex-lege* protection of areas with wilderness qualities quite ineffective in practice.

### *4.7 Consequences of 'wilderness protection' for recreational activities*

Several groups of people usually have access to officially protected areas with a wilderness character, although in a restricted manner. One such group is researchers, who implement the scientific assessments foreseen in management plans or independently of the plan permitted by the competent authorities.[77] The second group are visitors that regularly have to join guided tours to enter.[78] Exceptions to this general visitor rule exist at both ends of the spectrum. Visitors may not be allowed to enter certain areas at all (even as part of a guided tour), for instance in specific core zones, or they must stay on certain pathways. Both examples can be found in the zoning policy of the Lake Neusiedl National Park.[79] At the other end of the spectrum, visitors can enter every part of an area with wilderness qualities, even without guided tours. An example is the Thaya Valley National Park.[80] Biosphere Reserves also partly follow this

[77] Art. 6(2) and 6(3) of the Nationalparkgesetz Neusiedler See – Seewinkel, Provincial Law Gazette No. 28/1993, latest version 79/2013.

[78] 'Verordnung vom 9. November 1942 über das 'Naturschutzgebiet Rothwald', in der Katastralgemeinde Neuhaus, Landkreis Scheibbs, Niederdonau (VABl Niederdonau 463/1942)'; this regulation was replaced by the 'Verordnung über die Naturschutzgebiete 5500/13–0, Stammverordnung 40/78' of 3 March 1978.

[79] Art. 6(2) and 7(2) Nationalparkgesetz Neusiedler See – Seewinkel, Provincial Law Gazette No. 28/1993, latest version 79/2013.

[80] See Art. 5(2)(3) of the Niederösterreichisches Nationalparkgesetz, Provincial Law Gazette No. 5505–3 in connection with para. 7 NÖ Verordnung über den Nationalpark Thayatal Provincial Law Gazette No. 5505/3–0; see also V. Mauerhofer, 1998. Nationalparkrecht – Im Spannungsfeld von bundesstaatlicher Kompetenzverteilung, Europarecht und

open access approach in respect of their core zones,[81] although sometimes certain areas therein are fenced and only accessible through a guided tour.[82]

### 4.8 *Protecting wilderness as 'property'*

The case of the planned river dam in the Danube wetlands was detailed at the outset of this chapter. Some years after the escalation of the conflict an NGO started a national campaign, which culminated in a fundraising evening that was even supported by the national broadcasting cooperation.[83] The campaign was successful and provided the NGO with the financial means to buy over 400 hectares of forests offered by a landowner on the southern bank of the Danube River. This land area was later included as part of the core zones of the Danube Wetlands National Park, established in 1996.

In a similar way, environmental NGOs occasionally gain certain property rights related to strategically located parcels of land to at least gain legal standing in legal procedures to determine whether certain modifications of the site may be permitted. This acquisition of any property rights does not of course restrict the general right of the competent public authorities, laid down in all Austrian conservation laws, to fully or partially restrict these property rights or to expropriate them under certain circumstances.

## 5 Practical implementation and supervision and enforcement

The term 'wilderness' also plays an occasional role in the implementation and enforcement of procedures of environmental law. Examples can be

Naturschutzpolitik [National Park Law – In the area of conflict between competence distribution in a Federal State, EU-law and Nature Conservation Politics], Umweltbundesamt [Federal Environmental Agency], *Bericht* [Report] Nr. 129, pp. 375 (81f). www.umweltbundesamt.at/fileadmin/site/publikationen/BE129.pdf.

[81] Paras 3 and 6 of the Gesetz über den Wiener Teil des Biosphärenparks – Wienerwald (Wiener Biosphärenparkgesetz), Provincial Law Gazette No. 47/2006.

[82] For example, the Hermannskogel as part of the Viennese Corezone of the Biosphärenpark – Wienerwald (see Art. 3(2)(7) of the Gesetz über den Wiener Teil des Biosphärenparks – Wienerwald [Wiener Biosphärenparkgesetz]), Provincial Law Gazette No. 47/2006 in connection with para. 2 Erklärung von Teilen des 19. Wiener Gemeindebezirkes zum Landschaftsschutzgebiet (Landschaftsschutzgebiet Döbling), Provincial Law Gazette No. 21/1990.

[83] See www.donauauen.at/?area=nationalpark&subarea=history&language=english.

found within EIA procedures which are applicable to envisaged activities in or near all categories of protected areas, including those discussed above (Nature Conservation Areas, National Parks, and Biosphere Reserves). For example, in 2007 the Constitutional Court was petitioned by a Civil Society Organization (CSO), challenging a regulation defining the route of a road through the aforementioned Danube River Wetlands National Park by claiming that this 'wilderness' should be preserved.[84] The Court did unfortunately not enter into the substance of the dispute and summarily dismissed the appeal on the basis that the CSO was not correctly represented at the time at which the appeal was submitted.

'Wilderness' can also play a role in discussions as to whether an EIA must be made for a certain project. This was, for instance, the central topic in an appeal case before the independent Environmental Senate ('Umweltsenat') regarding an alpine ropeway construction near a glacier. This case was based on a report of an official expert ('*Amtssachverständiger*'), wherein the potential effects on 'wilderness' qualities of the site were emphasized.[85] As the ropeway allegedly did not use the space of the glacier, the central question concerned whether the planned ropeway would influence the landscape. In this context, the official expert had to appraise the legal term of a '*Naturlandschaft*' ('natural landscape'). He emphasized that this glacier area is a part of a landscape unmodified by humans, and that those wilderness areas have particular importance because of their inherent uniqueness in comparison to the nearby long history of settlement, the most elevated settlement density and cultural heritage in central Europe and in the Alps.[86] The VwGH subsequently confirmed[87] the importance of this decision by the Environmental Senate and approved the decision that an EIA was necessary.[88]

Another interesting case decided by the VwGH[89] concerned the decision of an administrative authority to declare an area of dry meadows as a Natural Heritage Site and to authorize a NGO to take management measures to keep its meadowland character. The landowner appealed unsuccessfully against the decision. A private expert engaged by the

[84] Judgment of 2 March 2007, V66/06, number 18075 in the official collection of the judgments.
[85] Decision of 30 April 2008, US 6B/2008/5-8.
[86] *Ibid.*
[87] VwGH, Judgement 2008/03/0086 of 26 April 2011.
[88] An EIA has not yet been conducted, according to the database. www.umweltbundesamt.at/umweltsituation/uvpsup/uvpoesterreich1/uvpdatenbank/uvpgenehmigung/.
[89] Judgment 2002/10/0017 of 19 December 2005.

authority highlighted, inter alia, the value of such meadows for small animals, the 'island' character of these areas in the agricultural landscape and the high importance of 'even small areas and even the smallest areas of such "wilderness"' as a living and surviving space and as a 'stepping stone' for such species.[90] This shows that the term 'wilderness' has to be closely connected with related species and their habitats, and such correlations might be possible regarding a habitat of hundreds of square metres (or less) – or, alternatively may be ruled out as such due to the presence of national borders (notably a species such as the wolf with potentially wide migration routes). This idea is also supported by the fact that the judgment did not precisely indicate the size of the area in dispute. Nevertheless, it was mentioned that the area fulfilled the legal requirement of the Nature Conservation Law of Lower Austria, according to which Natural Heritage Areas cover 'small-scale' issues, whether of natural or semi-natural character. The wider area, of which the above meadow area formed part, was the subject of a EU-LIFE Project[91] between 2006 and 2010, with total costs of €726,000 (sixty per cent of which was EU co-financed),[92] and in 2011 a Natura 2000 site based on the Habitat Directive was designated by the Province of Lower Austria.

Apart from these particular wilderness-related judgments, other more general notions apply to all areas with relatively high wilderness qualities. For instance, it is quite clear that the establishment and maintenance of these areas is better secured if financial resources are continuously provided and adapted to increasing prices and salaries.

Furthermore, effective protection is particularly closely related to the question of whether a special body for the management of the site should be established and what competences it should have. The more this body has an ownership-like position, the more effective management measures can be implemented and the stronger the position of the body in administrative procedures against projects that threaten nature will be. In the Austrian National Parks and Biosphere Reserve the management bodies do not usually have full ownership rights. These rights largely remain

[90] *Ibid.*

[91] See the formerly valid Regulation (EC) No 1404/96 and Regulation (EC) No 1682/2004; repealed by Regulation (EC) No. 614/2007 of the European Parliament and of the Council of 23 May 2007 concerning the Financial Instrument for the Environment (LIFE+) OJ L 149 (9 June 2007), 1–17; see also http://ec.europa.eu/environment/life/about/index.htm#history.

[92] See www.life-natur-noe.at/pages/Projekte_Beschreibung.htm#Bisamberg and www.life-bisamberg.at.

with private owners or public authorities represented by certain public departments[93] or privatized entities such as the OeBf mentioned above. These private owners or entities then conclude contracts with the public body that is officially in charge for the protected area and implement particular management practices. Problems usually occur in cases in which other public authorities (in particular federal bodies responsible for forest or water issues) make prescription to the *owner* of the site with regard to, for instance, phytosanitary measures and/or precautionary measures. The public body officially in charge of the protected area often lacks full standing in these procedures and is widely dependent upon how the private owners or public authorities represented by certain public departments or privatized entities react to this authoritative prescription. This reaction can be to challenge it (including applying for injunctive relief), running the risk of civil liability for damages,[94] or to follow and respect it immediately. Alongside, the nature conservation authority of the respective province can designate the activity as one that requires an Appropriate Assessment in accordance with Article 6(3) of the Habitats Directive.

A practical situation in this regard arose in which a provincial nature conservation authority threatened with such an Appropriate Assessment related to Kalkalpen National Park. After the storms of 2009, the federal forest authority prescribed to the OeBf (as a privatized entity representing the Republic of Austria as the *owner*) comprehensive logging measures (based on federal-forestry law) in areas with relatively high wilderness qualities in order to reduce the spread of bark beetles. The 'National Park Kalkalpen Ltd' as the public body officially in charge of this National Park (together with the OeBf as the implementing unit based on a private contract) disagreed, but did not have legal standing in this administrative procedure. The situation was partly eased by the existence of paragraph 32a of the Forestry Act, established in 2002, which allows bodies to apply in advance for exemptions from these federal prescriptions (but only with prior permission from the *owner*), as well as by the collaborative long-term working relationship between National Park Kalkalpen Ltd. and the local management unit of the OeBf.

93 Such as the forestry department of the province of Vienna regarding large areas of the Viennese part of the Biosphere Park Viennese Forest.

94 For instance, if bark beetles from the forested area with wilderness qualities spread into forests outside the area, or if old trees adjacent to hiking routes fall and injure hikers. Similar questions of liability can arise if damage sustained by neighbouring landowners is caused because prescribed flood protection measures have not been implemented.

## 6 The future of wilderness protection

The future of some areas with wilderness qualities in the Austrian lowlands appears to be quite secure. This is particularly valid for the areas related to protected area categories, such as National Parks, Biosphere reserves and Natura 2000 sites. Their management is strongly guaranteed by the majority of administrative units and their popularity among the Austrian population is continuously fostered by specific awareness-raising campaigns and eco-education activities.

This rather positive outlook should not hide the fact that a number of these areas are rather small and that, outside these existing sites, few areas with similar wilderness qualities exist. This is in particular due to the high economic value of the land concerned in terms of agriculture and forestry, the long history of colonization and prevalence of private property. These factors make it difficult to establish new areas with high wilderness qualities (if there are indeed any left in the lowlands) or to restore wilderness qualities in existing sites.

12

# Wilderness protection in the Czech Republic[1]

ZDEŇKA KŘENOVÁ AND JIŘÍ ZICHA

## 1 Introduction

As in many European countries there has been considerable debate in the Czech Republic throughout the past decade over wilderness *sensu lato* and non-intervention management in protected areas. Critics may describe this as following a fashion, but they cannot fully dispel the fact that there are several strong motivating factors behind the pursuit of such a policy. From an ecological point of view it is obvious that severe natural disturbances have occurred in Europe (e.g., cyclones and windstorms, such as Lothar, Vivian and Kyrill, insect outbreaks, large fires and floods) resulting in discussions about appropriate ways of managing ecosystems, including whether it is acceptable to use non-intervention management in protected areas. In addition, there are also sociological and cultural aspects to the wilderness discussion. After the collapse of the Iron Curtain and the re-opening of previously closed frontiers, people were able to travel more readily and visit new places, during which they were exposed to new ideas. This has helped to inspire new regulatory approaches, including calls for the implementation of new concepts of nature conservation and ecosystem management. In addition, the development of information technologies has offered new channels for sharing ideas, including the promotion of a greater degree of global responsibility and care for our common natural heritage.

The idea of wilderness attracts a broad audience and is widely debated. Some people have personally experienced the wilderness, while others have just a romantic notion of something they have never experienced, whereas others strongly reject the notion that wild nature or wilderness should be protected. In the Czech Republic, the ecological and social changes that have occurred over the last decade have stimulated an

[1] This research was supported by the grants No. 14–36098G of the GA CR and No. LO1415 of the MSMT.

increasing interest in wilderness, although the prevailing regulatory conservativism has meant that new ideas have not been adopted easily. Wilderness is still more about emotions than serious arguments, legal definitions and protective legislation.

This chapter accordingly provides a concise overview of the nature conservation policy and legislation in the Czech Republic and outlines milestones in the Czech implementation of the European wilderness concept (Section 3). As a case study, the Europe's Wild Heart project is examined, alongside the importance of a powerful legislative framework for wilderness protection (Section 4). Finally, the future of wilderness protection in the Czech Republic is evaluated (Section 5). Prior to this, it is first important to appraise the relevance of wilderness to society, to which this chapter now turns (Section 2).

## 2 Relevance of wilderness to society

The landscape of continents, including Europe, has been shaped by humans for centuries. Consequently, the wilderness has not only been physically diminished on many continents, but has also receded somewhat from human minds and experiences. The Czech economist Tomáš Sedláček reminds us that probably the oldest known work of literature, the Epic of Gilgamesh, which was written more than four thousand years ago in Mesopotamia, has served as an inspiration for many subsequent stories and continues to dominate current mythology, to varying degrees.[2] One aspect addressed in this epic work is the change in our external environment from nature to city, which closely reflects the internal change from a savage to a civilized person. When we talk about city and nature, our thoughts are directed towards viewing nature as a symbol of a natural state into which we are born, while the city represents a symbol of the exact opposite: development, civilization and progress. There are wild creatures similar to the savage Enkidu living in nature and it is where one goes to hunt, collect crops or gather the harvest. Nature is perceived solely as the provider of our needs. One returns to the city to sleep and be 'human'.

In addition, evil resides in nature, which is typified by Humbaba, who lives in a cedar forest and therefore needs to be eradicated. It is necessary to separate the city, the symbol of people, civilization, *non*-nature, from its surroundings with a strong wall. The wall around the city of Uruk is,

[2] T. Sedlacek, *Economics of Good and Evil: The Quest for Economic Meaning from Gilgamesh to Wall Street* (Oxford: Oxford University Press, 2011), p. 19.

among other things, a symbol of an internal distancing from nature, a metaphor for the refusal to submit to laws that are not determined and controlled by man and from which he benefits. Enkidu becomes human by moving into a city. The natural state of things, such as at birth, is imperfect according to this epic; it is evil and nature has to be transformed, civilized, cultured and resisted. The unspoken message of the entire epic is that civilization and progress are confined to cities, which are the true 'natural' dwelling-place of the people, and in the end cities prove not only to be the home of people but also of the gods.[3]

In accordance with the basic idea of the Epic of Gilgamesh, the word 'wilderness' has been translated into Czech – and, with some minor variations into most Slavic languages – as 'divočina' or 'pustina', which means a desolate, wild and unpopulated part of the world. It is understood as a dangerous and unfriendly place where large predators and many strange creatures are considered to live and is accordingly located well away from our homes. Our ancestors fought against the wilderness in order to define their cultural space, their community. People were afraid of the wilderness, but for many of them it was the only available refuge in times of war or when they were desperate for food or needed to hide from the authorities. They also used to search for food in wilderness areas when starving. For centuries, various fairy tales, myths and legends have saved many old religions from becoming extinct and have nurtured feelings and respect for wild nature. While many of them have been lost, there are still a number of well-known stories, for example, those about nymphs called '*divoženky*' in Czech, which are wild ('*divo*') women ('*ženky*').[4] Old storytellers used to say that these nymphs or wild-women are called ugly and raw fairies. They live in forests or caves and like to dance in misty woods or marshlands. They often steal human babies and exchange them for theirs. There are also various local depictions of wilderness, such as the Swiza,[5] a woman allegedly dressed in a wolf's skin and antlers who dwelt in the area around Kašperk Castle in the Bohemian Forest, the western part of the Šumava National Park. She has been told of since pagan times and is said to be able to turn those who damage nature into stone. Some legends, myths and superstitions prohibited various human activities in 'forbidden places or certain periods of

[3] *Ibid.*, at 31–32.

[4] I. Šindlářová and J. Růžička, *Mýty a báje starých Slovanů: božstva, svatyně, bájesloví, tradice* (Olomouc: Fontána, 2003).

[5] M. Stejskal, *Labyrintem tajemna, aneb Průvodce po magických místech Československa*, (Prague: Paseka, 1991).

the year' and served to protect wild nature for centuries. People are complex creatures. They are afraid of the wilderness but may depend on it during difficult times. On a scientific, cultural and legal level the current generation may appreciate the value of wilderness better than our ancestors, but previous generations protected the wilderness by complying with ancient rules that resulted in a harmonious coexistence with nature.[6]

In recent history, humanism in particular has served to stimulate interest in acquiring knowledge about nature. The historical perception of wilderness was thus transformed and the first modern appreciation of wild nature or wilderness is likely to have developed during the second half of the nineteenth century, when romantic painters, composers and writers extolled the beauty and mystery of nature. Beautiful pictures of the wilderness hang in the Czech National Gallery. Yet even in the 1930s the Czech writer, mystic and wood engraver Josef Váchal, who produced only eleven hand-made copies of his iconic work 'Šumava Dying and Romantic', lamented that wild nature is disappearing year by year, depriving people of part of their identity.[7]

From a legal perspective it is important that artists were also the first to call for the protection of nature. The exploitation of natural forests varied in the nineteenth century and only a few fragments of primeval forest survived in the most remote areas or in the domains of enlightened owners, who issued private decrees that they should be protected. This was the case for the Žofín and Hojná Voda primeval forests in 1838 and the Boubín primeval forest in 1858.[8] The system of state nature conservation came about much later with the establishment of the first protected areas in 1933.

Young people turned to hiking and discovered the charm of wilderness soon after the establishment of Czechoslovakia in 1918. This rambling, called 'tramping' in Czech, was – and remains – a Czech and Slovak folk civic movement inspired by woodcraft, scouting and romantic dreams about the American Wild West inspired by Jack London's novels and western films. The first ramblers belonged to the poorer social classes and were often unemployed. Later the movement was popularized and attracted ramblers from a broader spread of society. During communism, rambling became a way of escaping from the grey everyday life and

[6] P. Taylor (ed.), *Rewilding* (Oxford: BANC & Ethos, 2011).

[7] J. Váchal, *Šumava umírající a romantická* (Prague: Josef Váchal, 1931).

[8] M. Šíp, *Boubínský prales: Národní přírodní rezervace a její dějiny* (Oldenburg: Ed. Sagitta, 2006), translated in German: M. Šíp, *Boubínský prales: Das Nationalreservat und seine Geschichte* (Oldenburg: Ed. Sagitta, 2006).

mandatory social activities. Hundreds of people camped in the open at weekends, which was again inspired by the first settlements in the American West, and walked through a wild landscape. These ramblers did not respect the official state authorities, nature conservation legislation and the regulation of tourist clubs, but they did nonetheless appreciate and protect wildlife, the landscape and the wilderness.[9]

Rambling as a social phenomenon has almost disappeared due to the profound social changes that occurred after the Velvet Revolution. Currently, there are only a few small groups of ramblers in the Czech Republic who still find wild nature attractive, especially the young. Nowadays, several NGOs (e.g., Hnutí Duha – Friends of the Earth Czech Republic), intellectuals and public activities aim to promote the wilderness concept.

More recently, a new and interesting concept of the new wilderness[10] has been proposed. The adjective 'new' emphasizes that it differs from the original, 'old' wilderness, which consists of small remnants of old growth forests. The new wilderness is much younger and has become established on land that was previously cultivated by man over various periods of time. It is characterized by relatively early successional stages of vegetation. The old wilderness is rare and sometimes protected, whereas the new wilderness is generally perceived as unwanted and unprotected, yet its potential scope for further development as a wilderness area is increasing. The current trend in the development of the Czech cultural landscape, as in other parts of Europe, is characterized by two contradictory processes – intensification and extensification. Both processes are complementary and lead to significant polarization in land use. In the vicinity of intensively cultivated fields there can be abandoned areas that have successively returned to a natural or near-natural state. This, step by step, has affected the common perception of the Czech landscape.[11]

## 3 Legal protection of wilderness

### *3.1 Definition of wilderness*

The cultural and historical records mentioned above indicate that the wilderness was never legally protected *per se* in the Czech Republic. Its survival previously depended on generally shared rules, traditional restrictions or

[9] B. Hurikán, *Dějiny trampingu* (Prague: Novinář, 1990).

[10] C. Cílek, D. Dreslerová, P. Hájek, P. Pokorný and J. Sádlo, *Krajina a revoluce. Významné přelomy ve vývoji kulturní krajiny Českých zemí* (Prague: Malá Skála, 2006).

[11] Z. Lipský, 'Nová divočina v české kulturní krajině I', *Geografické rozhledy*, 4 (2009), 12–13.

even the fear of something mysterious and dangerous. Efforts to protect wilderness areas usually begin with debates about a proper definition for such areas. Currently, there is still no official definition of the term 'wilderness' in the Czech Republic, despite many discussions on this topic in recent years.

One such forum is the wilderness working group operating under the auspices of the Europarc Federation,[12] outlined in Chapter 1. The European concept of wilderness was adopted and promoted at the EU Conference that took place in Prague in May 2009, during the Czech Presidency. The Conference participants agreed that nature in Western Europe had been altered by human intervention to such an extent that a long and gradual rehabilitation will be required. Conversely, however, as discussed in other chapters of this book, in some Northern and Eastern European countries there are large areas that are completely or virtually untouched by humankind. The general view is that these areas of European importance must be protected in this relatively pristine condition.[13] In the context of Central Europe, the quality of and attitudes to wilderness areas are somewhat mixed. For some areas conservationists have preferred non-intervention, while in others nature should recover spontaneously, and there are also advocates for supporting natural processes through restoration projects.[14]

Thus, wilderness in Central Europe should not be seen only as encompassing primeval forests or pristine areas that have not been affected by man throughout their history. There are many areas with a high potential for redeveloping wild nature or wilderness. Primeval forests or wilderness areas cannot be cultivated; it is, however, possible to allow their spontaneous and natural development.[15]

### 3.2 *Wilderness in policy making*

There are currently several policy and legal documents relating to nature conservation in the Czech Republic. The most general document is the State Environmental Policy,[16] which defines a consensual framework for

[12] See www.europarc.org.

[13] European Parliament Resolution of 3 February 2009 on Wilderness in Europe (2008/2210 (INI); see also Chapters 1 and 2.

[14] 'Poselství from Prague. Summary of the Conference on Wilderness and Large Natural Habitat Areas', Prague, Czech Republic, 27–28 May 2009, www.wildeurope.org/inde.php/about-us/prague-conference.

[15] I. Míchal, 'Divočina jako kulturní objekt. Chráněná území a spontánní vývoj', *Vesmír*, 81 (1981), 187–188.

[16] Ministry of the Environment, 'The State Environmental Policy of the Czech Republic 2012–2020', www.mzp.cz/en/state_environmental_policy.

long- and medium-term sustainable development of the environment. It includes measures related to nature conservation, although it does not explicitly mention wilderness as such.

Nature conservation is more specifically covered by two other strategic documents. The Nature Conservation and Landscape Protection Programme of the Czech Republic was adopted in June 1998 and updated in 2009. This document analyses the former situation and financial resources and defines more than forty medium- and long-term priorities based on a cross-sectoral approach, which integrates nature management issues across various sectors. In 2005, shortly after the accession of the Czech Republic to the European Union, the government adopted a National Biodiversity Strategy. It is based on the activities and tools of the Convention on Biological Diversity, especially its thematic programmes of work, and was prepared in accordance with the Biodiversity Strategy of the European Community. The Programme further elaborates the aims and targets of the Strategy, while reflecting also the requirements set by the Ramsar Convention and the European Landscape Convention. But unlike other national biodiversity strategies, such as in Germany, none of the Czech strategic documents deal directly with the term 'wilderness' or 'wild nature', or its conservation or restoration. After the successful European wilderness symposium in Prague in 2009, one might have expected more attention to wilderness in policy-making in the Czech Republic, but so far it has not yet attracted any greater degree of importance. And the same is true in respect of the legal framework.

### 3.3 *Legislation of the Czech Republic: protected areas relevant for wilderness protection*

#### National nature reserves and national parks

The principal source of law for nature conservation in the Czech Republic is the Act on Nature and Landscape Protection (hereinafter also 'the Act').[17] It establishes regulations for the general and special protection of landscape, areas and species, and rules pertaining to the national contribution to the EU's Natura 2000 network form an integral part of the Czech system of nature conservation.

Specially protected areas are divided into six categories: national parks, protected landscape areas, national nature reserves, nature reserves,

[17] Act No 114/1992 Coll., on Nature and Landscape Protection, as amended.

national natural monuments and natural monuments.[18] None of these categories correspond precisely to the categories of protected areas advanced by the IUCN; accordingly, it is necessary to consider each protected area, or part or zone on an individual basis in order to fully appreciate and understand their respective management objectives.[19] The precise mission of a nature conservation area, alongside detailed conditions for its protection are proclaimed by a regulatory act or decree. This measure establishes each individual protected area, whereas the basic conditions of protection for such categories of site are set directly by the Act. The most valuable natural areas are covered by the 109 national nature reserves and four national parks.[20]

National nature reserves are smaller areas of exceptional natural value, with important and unique ecosystems from a national or international point of view. The Act sets out the basic conditions for the protection of national nature reserves in Articles 28–32. It establishes a prohibition on altering or damaging these areas, and that their utilization is contingent upon preserving or improving the existing state of the natural environment. In national nature reserves farming of the land is prohibited if it involves intensive infrastructure or technologies, such as breeding of game, new buildings or extraction of minerals. Forests in national nature reserves cannot be categorized as timber forests. Furthermore, restrictions are placed on driving motor vehicles, with some exceptions, for instance, state administration authorities, forestry and agriculture, state defence and protection of state borders, fire protection, and medical and veterinary services. Restrictions also apply to deviating from marked paths without the approval of a nature protection authority, collecting plants or catching animals, camping and outdoor activities such as climbing. Detailed conditions are specified in the decree of proclamation for each reserve.

National parks are defined under Article 15 of the Act as extensive areas that are unique nationally or internationally, a considerable part of which is covered by natural ecosystems or ecosystems that are little affected by human activities, where plants, animals and abiotic nature are of exceptional scientific and educational importance. This provision further states that the utilization of national parks must defer to the preservation and improvement of their natural conditions and must

[18] Section 14 of the Act.

[19] L. Miko, *Zákon o ochraně přírody a krajiny: komentář* (Prague: C.H. Beck, 2007), at 134.

[20] The Central Register of Nature Conservation is available online: http://drusop.nature.cz/ (in Czech).

conform to the scientific and educational objectives of national parks. In general terms, this characterization of national parks already indicates that the instrument may be of high importance for protection of wilderness areas as defined in Chapter 1. The methods for protecting national parks are based on dividing national parks into usually three zones in which nature protection is delimited by natural values. The strictest regime is applied in the first zone, whereas protection in the second and third zones is less stringent. The delimitation and changes in individual zones are set out by the Ministry of the Environment after consultations with the municipalities concerned, and detailed regimes for the zones in question are specified in generally binding legal regulation, which proclaims individual national parks.[21]

Consequently, the protection of national parks is 'tailor-made'; however, the general protection regime, as laid down in the Act on Nature and Landscape Protection, is also of particular relevance to the topic of wilderness protection. According to Article 16 of the Act, intensive farming, breeding of game, extraction of minerals, disposal of waste originating from outside national parks, changing the existing water regime and building new highways, roads, railways, industrial buildings, settlements, navigation canals, high voltage transmission lines and long-distance product pipelines are prohibited within these parks. As in national nature reserves, further restrictions focus on the use of motor vehicles, with some exceptions such as for the vehicles of state authorities, vehicles necessary for forestry and agriculture, state defence and protection of the state borders, fire protection, and medical and veterinary services. Restrictions also relate to deviation from marked pathways without the approval of a nature protection authority, collecting plants or catching animals, camping, climbing or organizing mass sporting, tourist and other public events.

In the first zone of a national park it is further prohibited to construct new buildings or leave marked pathways without the approval of a nature protection authority, although exceptions apply to owners and tenants of the land. It is also prohibited to alter the existing composition and area of plant cultures, unless this alteration is in accordance with the management plan for the national park, or to fertilize the land with farm sewage or liquid from silage and other wastes. So we can say that the first zones, which are delimited in all four Czech national parks, are the most relevant parts of national parks for wilderness protection. The qualities of large size and

[21] Section 17 of the Act.

naturalness receive attention for the whole area of national parks, but the absence of permanent infrastructure is a special and important requirement established by the law for especially these first zones.

For historical reasons, some smaller protected areas, usually strictly protected nature reserves, can occur inside the confines of national parks. These nature reserves pre-date the national park and their protected status should have been incorporated into the conservation status of the national park conservation. Nevertheless, in some cases these areas have been subject to pre-existing regulations that are more rigorous than those for national parks and are still valid in respect of these individual sites. Wilderness protection is therefore more robust where the decree of proclamation explicitly addresses the protection of wild nature *sensu lato*, various wilderness attributes or non-intervention management. For example, the nature reserve Trojmezná, with a strict non-intervention regime, was established already before the Šumava NP in 1991. After designation of the National Park the whole nature reserve was the 'first zone' but several years later the first zone in ŠNP was fragmented and opened for cutting the bark beetle-infected trees.[22] The original status of the nature reserve (supported by a civil blockade organized by NGOs) helped to protect the most valuable parts of this area against logging and the degradation of ecosystems.

## Management plans and visitors' rules

In addition to the legal framework laid down in the Act, or in the specific instruments establishing individual national nature reserves or national parks, a series of additional mechanisms are presumed to apply pursuant to the Act to further regulate activities in these protected areas. First, the management plan serves as a conceptual document for the protection of nature. This instrument will be prepared and adopted by the nature protection authority on the basis of data on the previous development and present status of a specially protected area. The Ministry of the Environment has set out the requirements in a legal decree on the content of the management plans and the procedure for preparing and implementing such instruments.[23] Prior to the approval of a management plan, a nature protection authority is obliged to notify the public and consult

[22] Z. Křenová and J. Hruška, 'Proper Zonation – An Essential Tool for the Future Conservation of the Šumava National Park', *European Journal of Environmental Sciences*, 2(1) (2012), 62–72.

[23] Decree No. 64/2011 Coll., on management plans, documentation of designation, registration and marking of protected areas.

the municipalities and regions concerned. The plan will include proposals for preserving or improving the status of the protected values within such as site, and for safeguarding the protected area against adverse influences from adjacent land. The management plan, which usually runs for periods of ten to fifteen years, serves as a basis for other types of planning documents and for further decision-making by the nature protection authorities. The management plan, however, is binding only upon the nature conservation authority, and does not apply to other natural or legal bodies.

Another instrument issued by the nature protection authority is a generally binding decree for each national park or part of its territory, which establishes the rules concerning visitation. Following the basic rules for protection, which are stated in the Act on Nature and Landscape Protection, these rules may further limit access of vehicles, free movement of people outside the currently built-up areas of municipalities and recreational and tourist activities of visitors. The procedures for approving and applying the visitors' rules sometimes result in judicial disputes. And perhaps surprisingly, these are generally challenges not because they are too strict but rather that they have been too liberal, or for a failure to follow the specific procedures prior to their adoption. This has been the case in respect of the Šumava National Park. There have been several situations in which an NGO or individual has challenged the insufficient protection of nature provided by visitors' rules in the Highest Administrative Court, which has resulted in rulings against the National Park Authority.[24]

## Wilderness protection through a mix of instruments

Currently there is no specific wilderness legislation in the Czech Republic. Although neither the Act nor its implementing decrees use the term wilderness, it is nonetheless apparent that the legal framework relating to national nature reserves and national parks can facilitate a relatively strong level of protection for wilderness. The general definition and legal regimes for both categories of protected areas connect well with the three main wilderness qualities described in Chapter 1. More specifically, the combination of the general conservation obligations laid down in the general legislation, the special regulations for particular zones of

[24] Case 6 Ao 5/2010 – 43 Okrašlovací spolek Zdíkovska v. Správa Národního parku a chráněné krajinné oblasti Šumava, or case 7 Ao 6/2010 – 44 V. Ř., v. Správa Národního parku a chráněné krajinné oblasti Šumava, available in Czech through www.nssoud.cz.

National Parks, and the requirements formulated in the complementary management plans and visitors' rules may in principle constitute a robust regime for the protection of wilderness areas in the Czech Republic. However, while wilderness protection *may well be* established, the *actual* value of this framework for wilderness protection depends heavily upon how and whether these instruments are applied and implemented in practice, as illustrated by the following case study.

## 4 Practice: the Wild Heart project

The great forester and ecologist Igor Míchal wrote:

> The protection of wilderness (the area in which man purposefully and voluntarily waives any intervention) in Central Europe is a challenging project, probably more difficult in socio-psychological than in ecological terms.[25]

Based on his long experience of nature conservation and seeking appropriate ways of managing ecosystems, Míchal knew that although the time may be right for natural development or rewilding, such a process is contingent upon human respect for and understanding of nature and natural processes. Social aspect can be more changeable. In order to determine the relevance of the above statement for the Czech Republic, this chapter will proceed to focus on a case study of the 'Wild Heart project'.

### *4.1 A transboundary wilderness area*

Few places within the central European landscape remain essentially unmodified or at least exhibit potential for becoming wilderness areas. Two such areas are the Šumava National Park (ŠNP) and neighbouring Bavarian Forest National Park (BFNP), which together constitute a unique forest zone in the middle of Europe. In this large area natural forest dynamics and ecosystem processes occur. From a biodiversity perspective they also constitute very important Natura 2000 sites. Transboundary cooperation between both national parks has improved since 1990, when the former Iron Curtain Corridor was opened, culminating in the inauguration of Europe's Wild Heart project[26] in 2008. The

[25] I. Míchal, 'Divočina jako kulturní objekt. Chráněná území a spontální vývoj', *supra* note 15. Translation into English by the authors.

[26] Z. Křenová and H. Kiener, 'Europe's Wild Heart – Still Beating? Experiences from a New Transboundary Wilderness Area in the Middle of the Old Continent', *European Journal of Environmental Sciences*, 2(2) (2012), 115–124.

main goal of this project, which was initiated by ŠNP and BFNP headquarters and supported by several NGOs, is to develop a transboundary wilderness area incorporating the core zones of these two national parks.

This project includes an area of 13,060 ha, comprising 5,797 ha within the BFNP and 7,263 ha within the ŠNP. The BFNP is listed as a protected area carrying an IUCN Protected Area Category II[27] status, and the Bavarian part of Europe's Wild Heart is located in the core zone of BFNP ('*naturzone*'), where a non-intervention management policy has been operational since the 1980s. Hunting is prohibited and public access is restricted in the breeding seasons of the most important species (e.g., capercaillie, hazel grouse, woodpeckers and lynx) as well as within the most sensitive habitats (e.g., peat bogs, marshlands and screes).

The ŠNP too is listed as a protected area, also carrying the status of an IUCN Protected Area Category II, but the current zonation of this NP is very fragmented. The Czech part of Europe's Wild Heart area is located in the non-intervention part of the ŠNP, where no trees have been harvested since 1997. Non-intervention management in this segment of the ŠNP is prescribed in the Management Plan and confirmed by several administrative rulings from the Ministry of Environment. Moreover, in 2012 the Municipal Court in Prague formally confirmed that non-intervention management ought to be the optimal method of managing this part of the ŠNP.[28] Water regime restoration projects, i.e., re-establishment of peat bogs,[29] have been undertaken throughout the last decade, while hunting has been prohibited in this area since 2008. These new management regulations were agreed by the director of the ŠNP and subsequently incorporated into the new Management Plan of the ŠNP.

### *4.2 Combining the status of National Park and Natural Reserve*

Over half of this wilderness area overlaps with the strictly protected Nature Reserve of Modravské slatě mires (NRMS; 3,615 ha, established in December 1989), which is listed as a protected area carrying the status of an IUCN Protected Area Category Ia. From a legislative perspective,

[27] See the World Database on Protected Areas, www.wdpa.org.

[28] Case 6 Ca 231/2008-172 Město Kašperské Hory a další v. Ministerstvo životního prostředí a další.

[29] I. Bufková, F. Stibal and E. Mikulášková, 'Restoration of Drained Mires in the Šumava National Park, Czech Republic', in G. Likens and M. Eiseltová (eds.), *Restoration of Lakes, Streams, Floodplains, and Bogs in Europe: Principles and Case Studies* (Dordrecht: Springer, 2010), 331–354.

the NRMS is a strictly protected and integral part of the ŠNP. From a practical perspective, the level of management required by the NRMS Decree is included in the Management Plan of the ŠNP. Although the overlap between two protected area regimes (Nature Reserve and National Park) is a consequence of the area's conservation history, the strictly protected Nature Reserve serves as a strong legislative tool for protecting this wilderness area. This can be of particular importance if nature conservation principles and rules in the ŠNP are weakened by pressure from politicians, lobbyists and developers.[30]

For the purpose of Europe's Wild Heart project, the wilderness area is understood to be a large intact area of high biological value, which is mostly undisturbed by man, roadless and without other industrial infrastructure or permanent habitation, and in which the extraction of resources is not permitted. This description is very close to the working definition of wilderness as explained in Chapter 1, and the regulations applicable to this site clearly aim to protect its wilderness qualities. Visitor access is only permitted along certain hiking trails, with a preference for guided tours rather than individual and unmonitored access. Scientific research is permitted, although subject to prohibitions on intrusive and potentially damaging activities. Guidelines for the uniform management[31] of the united core zone were incorporated in the management plans of both NPs. With regard to public and scientific outreach, information concerning this project[32] has been presented at several international conferences, including the World Wilderness Congress (WILD9) in Merida, Mexico.[33]

The directors of both the ŠNP and BWNP signed a joint initiative entitled 'Vision 2020' in 2007, under the auspices of the Europarc Transboundary Certification. Under this programme, both parks have

[30] Z. Křenová and J. Vrba, 'Just How Many obstacles Are There to Creating a National Park? A Case Study from the Šumava National Park', *European Journal of Environmental Sciences*, 4(1) (2014), 30–36.

[31] Z. Křenová and H. Kiener, *Společné jádrové území Národních parků Šumava a Bavorský les – Divoké srdce Evropy / Gemeinsamer Kernbereich der Nationalparke Šumava und Bayerischer Wald – Europas wildes Herz.* (bilingual common management guidelines), (Grafenau: Vimperk, 2009).

[32] T. Meyer, H. Kiener and Z. Křenová, 'Wild Heart of Europe', *International Journal of Wilderness*, 15(3) (2009), 33–40.

[33] H. Kiener and Z. Křenová, 'Europe's Wild Heart – New transboundary wilderness in the middle of the Old Continent', in A. Watson, J. Murrieta-Saldivar and B. McBride (eds.), *The Symposium on Science and Stewardship*, WILD9 Congress Proceedings, 2009, pp. 65–71.

committed, inter alia, to 'achieve a joint core area of about 15,000 ha with harmonized management principles, information services and monitoring networks to officially become the first and largest transboundary wilderness area in Central Europe'.[34] This document followed an international agreement between the Ministers of the Environment on transboundary cooperation between both national parks and other specified topics of cooperation. Vision 2020 was understood as a transboundary declaration of a common responsibility to protect wild nature in the region in which these national parks are sited.

### *4.3 Political uncertainties and the long-term future of wilderness protection*

Unfortunately, the bark beetle outbreak that followed hurricane Kyrill in 2008 and 2009 exacerbated the debate concerning the appropriate management of the forest areas of the ŠNP. Opponents of the core principles of the national park of non-intervention and the wilderness concept became increasingly vocal. The situation escalated after the election in 2010 when the representatives of the Green Party in the Czech Ministry of Environment were replaced by conservatives from the Civic Democratic Party. Clear cutting started in some of the former non-intervention parts of the ŠNP and hunting was reinstated in the core zone, where both activities had been previously banned by the administration in accordance with valid Czech legislation. A former ŠNP director listened to the politicians' wishes and made these changes without reference to the administrative process.

Consequently, management strategies and practical measures in ŠNP and BFNP, respectively, have become increasingly divergent since 2010. Opponents of the wilderness concept in both countries took advantage of the situation and, currently, Europe's Wild Heart project is on hold in both countries. The latest public discussion on this project and on the societal importance of wilderness generally was convened by Havel's cabinet on 17 November 2010. At that meeting the cultural commentator Petr Mikšíček argued that:

> Today comes a time when you need to protect nature and wildlife from the position of culture and civilization. Culture is no longer in thrall to

[34] A. Ahokumpu and M. Solar, *Verification Report for the Bavarian Forest National Park / Germany & Šumava National Park / Czech Republic*, Application for the EUROPARC certificate: Transboundary Parks – Following Nature's Design (Grafenau: BWNP Administration, 2009) www.infodatasys.cz/sumava/Europarc_NPBW_NPS2009.pdf, Annex II, p. 23.

nature, but nature is at the mercy of culture. We have extricated ourselves from nature. At the same time due to the level of our civilization our nature suffers.[35]

## 5 The future of wilderness protection in the Czech Republic

*Ex definitione* wilderness cannot be created, it can only be admitted.[36] The state of an ecosystem is not defined in terms of its ultimate climax state, but rather as a series of permanent adjustments, including randomness and unexpected changes.[37] The re-naturalization of areas, even when planned in extensive detail and including consideration of unexpected contingencies, cannot necessarily create a real wilderness. The decision to endorse the protection of the national wilderness entails a long-standing commitment and one that is best pursued without a preconceived idea of a specific type of wilderness or pre-assigned functions for the site in question. In other words, for particular areas of our natural environment we should be willing to accept the unpredictable outcomes of allowing nature to take its course. The ecological and anthropogenic benefits of this approach are well documented.[38]

Wilderness is a specific state of affairs that encompasses both natural and social aspects. The ecological arguments for the protection of wilderness are doomed to failure if society fails to understand and appreciate the social and cultural aspects engaged by the conservation of wilderness. Our experience in the Czech Republic is that the wilderness cannot solely be created and preserved by passing laws, although well-developed legislation can be an effective tool to protect wilderness if accompanied by social acceptance and the requisite political will to promote this as a clear objective. It is always difficult to prepare and enact strong and effective legislations that will subsequently be respected and adhered to. Moreover, it is clear that this process will involve a race against time to find effective tools for wilderness conservation before the last remnants

[35] M.M. Ondřej, 'Kabinet Havel: Je dobré mít a chtít divočinu?'s, *Ekolist.cz* – 25 November 2010, http://ekolist.cz/cz/zpravodajstvi/zpravy/kabinet-havel-je-dobre-mit-a-ctit-divocinu.

[36] I. Míchal, 'Divočina jako kulturní objekt. Chráněná území a spontánní vývoj', *supra* note 15.

[37] J.H. Connell and R.O. Slatyer, 'Mechanisms of Succession in Natural Communities and Their Role in Community Stability and Organization', *The American Naturalist*, 111 (1977), 1119–1144.

[38] See Chapters 3, 4 and 5. See also H.K. Cordell, J.C. Bergstrom and J.M. Bowke, *The Multiple Values of Wilderness* (State College, PA: Venture Publishing, Inc., 2005).

of wilderness disappear from our homeland. Experts estimate that the current state of wilderness coverage throughout the Czech Republic is less than one per cent,[39] and there is strong scientific support for the view that the protection of these remaining areas is a pressing necessity.

We can conclude that there is no Wilderness Act or any other regulation that explicitly aims to protect wilderness in the Czech Republic; however, the protected area regimes established by the Act on Nature and Landscape Protection, in combination with the detailed conservation regulations in the designation decrees and management plans, can function as an alternative 'legal toolkit' for protecting the main wilderness qualities (i.e., large area, absence or regulation of building new infrastructure, relatively natural intactness) addressed in this volume. This is particularly true in relation to national nature reserves and national parks, where this mixture of legal instruments can provide a relatively strong degree of legal protection for wilderness areas in the Czech Republic. This overall framework works well in cases in which wilderness qualities are protected simultaneously with other conservation values, for example in relation to rare species, sensitive habitats, old growth forests or important migration corridors. Nonetheless, a particular challenge that remains to be addressed is how wilderness conservation can be accommodated within other legal frameworks for the protection of natural areas, particularly the Natura 2000 regime. The European Commission[40] has developed guidance on this issue, but its implementation in the Czech Republic will not be straightforward because of the lack of political will as well as the limited number of inhabitants interested in this.

Overall, the need for more explicit legislation to protect wilderness increases as pre-existing regimes, common agreements and habits are diminished. This is relevant not only for the 'old wilderness', but also for 'new wilderness' Wilderness deserves to be protected both for its importance as a biodiversity hot spot in the desert of an industrial landscape, as well as an important cultural milestone in our largely uncultured landscape. However, with the current political situation in the Czech Republic, which is characterized by limited respect for strict nature

[39] T. Vrška, P. Šamonil, P. Unar, L. Hort, D. Adam, K. Král and D. Janík, *Developmental Dynamics of Virgin Forests in the Czech Republic. III – Šumava Mts. and Český les Mts.*, (Prague: Academia, 2012).

[40] European Commission, EU Guidelines on Wilderness in Natura 2000. *Management of Terrestrial Wilderness and Wild Areas within the Natura 2000 Network*, Technical Report - 2013 - 069 (Brussels: European Commission, 2013).

conservation regulations, there is little chance that a national Wilderness Act or similarly strong legal instruments will be adopted in the near future. Support from the international community (including that of governments as well as NGOs) and inspiration from other EU countries appear to be important elements in improving the prospects for wilderness protection in the Czech Republic.

# 13

# Wilderness protection in Estonia

RICHARD CADDELL*

## 1 Introduction

Concerns have long been raised that the remaining areas of wilderness in Europe are fragmented, threatened by multiple anthropogenic pressures and in collective retreat. However, as a striking national exception, it has been consistently observed that Estonia has not only retained significant tracts of wilderness-quality land, but concurrently imposes some of the most stringent legal controls over such areas within the EU.[1] Since its inception Estonia has proved to be a nature conservation actor of understated significance, with an extensive history of environmental innovation, both as an independent state and as a constituent Republic of the Soviet Union.[2] Within modern-day Estonian territory, the designation of areas subject to minimal human intrusion can be traced back to the thirteenth century. More recently, the coordinated legal protection of natural features by Estonians dates back to 1910, with the designation of the first formalized *zapovednik* in the Russian Empire,[3] thereby

* The author is indebted to Uudo Timm and Piret Kiristaja of the Estonian Ministry of the Environment, Kaidi Aher of the Office of the President of the Republic of Estonia, Eleri Lopp-Valdma of Estonian Wildlife Tours (www.estonianwildlifetours.com) and Aivar Ruukel of Sooma.com for additional information on wilderness management and policy in Estonia; the usual caveats apply. This chapter seeks to outline the legal position as of 30 May 2015.

[1] See M. Fisher et al., *Review of Status and Conservation of Wild Land in Europe* (Edinburgh: Scottish Government, 2010), 45–69 and European Commission, *Guidelines for the Management of Wilderness and Wild Areas in Natura 2000* (Brussels: European Union, 2012), at 15.

[2] On the historical development of Estonian environmental law see R. Caddell, 'Nature Conservation in Estonia: From Soviet Union to European Union', *Journal of Baltic Studies* 40 (2009), 307–332.

[3] F. Shtilmark, Историография Российских Эаповсдников (1895–1995) (Edinburgh: Russian Nature Press, 2003), at 16. The *zapovednik* system would ultimately govern wilderness areas across the USSR and has remained a highly influential mechanism in many independent post-Soviet states. See also Chapter 19.

inaugurating what would eventually become an extensive collection of purportedly pristine and undisturbed areas across Eurasia. Numerically, Estonia has established significantly more sites corresponding to the IUCN's specific wilderness Category Ib than any other European jurisdiction and is second only to Sweden in the size of areas so designated.[4] Indeed, as the national authorities have rather pointedly observed, the '[p]reservation of nature free from human interference is a principle that has been utilized quite often since the earliest days of Estonia's nature conservation system; many countries are now making their first encounter with this idea'.[5]

Estonia accordingly represents an intriguing case study of the protection of wilderness characteristics in a European context. Although the reasons underpinning the success or otherwise of national wilderness policies are essentially peculiar to each jurisdiction, the Estonian experience nonetheless provides insightful lessons for other states, not least in its innovative system of zoning and in regulating the coexistence between protected sites and the burgeoning ecotourism industry. To this end, this chapter first outlines the importance of wilderness in Estonia, detailing the combination of historical factors and the unique physical, social and political geography of the country that has facilitated the retention of considerable areas of wilderness-quality land. There then follows an appraisal of the legal protection of wilderness areas, predominantly through forestry and nature conservation legislation and the management of protected sites. Finally, reflecting the recent views of the European Parliament that wilderness areas are not intended to be hermetically sealed to human interaction,[6] this chapter examines the regulation of Sooma National Park, which encompasses arguably Estonia's most significant area of wilderness, before drawing some concise conclusions as to the future challenges facing wilderness conservation and management in Estonia.

[4] Fisher et al., *Review of Status and Conservation of Wild Land in Europe, supra* note 1, at 53–55. Nevertheless, wilderness-quality areas may also be protected under IUCN Category Ia, with a number of states establishing considerably more and larger areas under this designation.

[5] L. Klein and I. Hermet, *Estonian Nature Conservation in 2011* (Tallinn: Estonian Environmental Information Center, 2012), at 24.

[6] As the European Parliament has observed, '[w]e have to protect the [*sic*] nature, but through human use. The territory of Europe is too small to have forbidden areas for its citizens . . . Sustainable tourism development is used as a means to give economic value to wilderness and to create support for conservation': European Parliament, *Report on Wilderness in Europe*; Document (2008/2210(INI)), at 7.

## 2 Wilderness in Estonian geography, culture and society

The modern Republic of Estonia is a relatively diminutive jurisdiction, comprising a landmass of 45,227 $km^2$. Estonia is a lowland coastal state fringed by over 1,500 separate islands, many of which are sparsely habited or otherwise devoid of human activity. Historically, Estonia has been a primarily agrarian society and remains home to an exceptional variety of biodiversity, given its northern latitude, hosting a vast array of flora and fauna. Most significantly from a wilderness standpoint, however, approximately half the Estonian mainland is composed of woodland, while peat bogs occupy a further twenty per cent of national territory,[7] creating significant tracts of little-populated and rarely-accessed terrain and presenting clear natural barriers to urban spread and accretion.

Specific data on wilderness coverage throughout Estonia are not readily available, nor has a national inventory of wilderness-quality land yet been instituted. Within the context of the Wilderness Quality Index for Europe, however, Estonia is considered to have high areas of wilderness across its eastern frontier with Russia and throughout its western parameters and coastal fringe.[8] A high number of sites within the Estonian network of protected areas correspond to the IUCN's Categories Ia and Ib, denoting areas that are under strict protection from human influence and those containing a significant volume of wilderness, respectively. The national wilderness may therefore be mapped with some degree of clarity with reference to the legal protection accorded to particular locations. Additional areas of wilderness-quality land may also exist beyond this specific legal network. Indeed, numerous areas of the Estonian mainland exhibit at least two of the three wilderness qualities considered within the present project, namely naturalness and an absence of other manifestations of human interaction. Unlike neighbouring territories in Russia and Scandinavia, however, Estonian wilderness areas are comparatively smaller in net length, yet are nonetheless substantial in relative proportion to the national landmass.

Estonia was founded as a sovereign nation in 1918, incorporating the provinces of Estland and northern Livonia, which had been historically controlled by a succession of conquering powers. During World War II, Estonia was annexed by the USSR and, to a considerable degree, the

[7] T. Leito, K. Kimmel and A. Ader, *Estonian Conservation Areas* (Tallinn: Ministry of the Environment, 2008), at 7.

[8] Fisher et al., *Review of Status and Conservation of Wild Land in Europe, supra* note 1, at 45.

current wilderness footprint is attributable – in both a positive and negative sense – to Soviet development policies. As with many former entities of the USSR, the Soviet system bequeathed Estonia a contradictory ecological legacy of ruin and bounty. Indeed, it is an ironic paradox that, although Soviet economic policies were often synonymous with environmental calamity, they simultaneously secured large swathes of pristine wilderness across the various territories of Eurasia. While the fall of communism duly revealed a disturbing litany of environmental degradation throughout the region, the totalitarian shroud of the Iron Curtain also obscured a substantial network of protected sites, alongside numerous additional areas largely untouched by anthropogenic influences.[9]

Three key historical factors may be considered to be especially important in retaining extensive wilderness coverage in Estonia. First, and while hardly a laudable mechanism for the protection of European wilderness, strict controls were established over population movement throughout the Estonian SSR, which ultimately facilitated the maintenance and (re-)establishment of pristine areas. Rural localities in Estonia – which had previously hosted small villages and homesteads – were swiftly cleared, thereby perpetuating large tracts of *de facto* wilderness. Mass deportations were instituted throughout the 1940s to quell the guerrilla resistance of the *Metsavennad* ('Forest Brothers') to Soviet control, as well as prospective opposition to the impending policy of agricultural collectivization. In 1945, some 136,000 individual farmsteads were operational in Estonia;[10] by May 1949 sixty-nine per cent of these had been subsumed into the *kolkhoz* system,[11] while living conditions within the countryside steadily deteriorated, which further incentivized urban migration.[12] Meanwhile, from 1946 onwards, large segments of the north and north-western coastline of Estonia were precluded from settlement or were subject to sweeping legal constraints upon access and transit due to their military sensitivity. Consequently, many settlements were virtually abandoned and these areas were subject to minimal

[9] Approximately thirty per cent of Central and Eastern European landmass lay under some form of legal protection upon the dissolution of the USSR: P. Pavlínek and J. Pickles, *Environmental Transitions: Transformation and Ecological Defence in Central and Eastern Europe* (London: Routledge, 2000), at 42.

[10] A. Plakans, *A Concise History of the Baltic States* (Cambridge: Cambridge University Press, 2011), at 367.

[11] A. Statiev, *The Soviet Counterinsurgency in the Western Borderlands* (Cambridge: Cambridge University Press, 2010), at 178.

[12] R. Misiunas and R. Taagepera, *The Baltic States: Years of Dependence, 1940–1990* (London: Hurst, 1993), at 232.

development. Accordingly, even some twenty years after the resumption of independence, the majority of Estonia's numerous islands and coastal regions 'are still well preserved and in a relatively untouched state'.[13]

Second, the pristine nature found across the former USSR is often attributable as much – if not more so – to the wholesale inefficiencies in and arbitrary application of centralized economic policies as to deliberate attempts to preserve significant tracts of land. These initiatives often prioritized grandiose industrial projects and failed to exploit natural resources in a rational manner, ensuring that some areas were subject to devastating over-exploitation and inappropriate development, while others remained essentially neglected and underdeveloped, yet also fundamentally unsullied. While Estonia endured the heavy exploitation of its famed reserves of phosphates and oil shale,[14] such activities were generally concentrated within specific and predictable locations, thereby ensuring that other areas remained essentially untouched. Moreover, the Baltic region was largely spared the more outlandish manifestations of the Soviet determination to 'master' the forces of nature, ensuring that many elements of the natural ecosystem remained fundamentally intact.

Third, these trends were complemented by a strong history of environmental regulation in Estonia that even pre-dates independence.[15] During the Soviet era, the Estonian authorities adopted the first Republican law on nature protection, thereby placing the procedures for the designation of protected areas on a regularized footing and, as noted below, pioneered a series of conservationist mechanisms with clear benefits for wilderness areas. Indeed, and rather counter-intuitively, Soviet annexation led to little discernible change in proactive environmental management in Estonia,[16] which suggests that the Estonian authorities exercised a dramatically disproportionate influence over the trajectory of nature conservation policies on both a central and local level.

[13] H. Järve et al., 'Comprehensive Study of Estonia's Coastal Zone Protection and Conservation', *Coastline Reports*, 20 (2012), 63–76, at 64.

[14] P.R. Pryde, *Environmental Management in the Soviet Union* (Cambridge: Cambridge University Press, 1991), at 263.

[15] See Caddell, 'Nature Conservation in Estonia: From Soviet Union to European Union', *supra* note 2, at 310 and R.W. Smurr, *Perceptions of Nature, Expressions of Nation: An Environmental History of Estonia* (Köln: Lambert Academic Publishing, 2009), especially 27–129.

[16] E-L. Tuvi et al., 'Establishment of Protected Areas in Different Ecoregions, Ecosystems, and Diversity Hotspots under Successive Political Systems', *Biological Conservation* 144 (2011), 1726–1732, at 1728.

The continued wilderness presence within Estonia is not the mere product of historical accident; demographic trends in the post-Soviet era have generally militated against population shifts that might adversely affect impact upon the volume of national wilderness coverage. The population of Estonia is small and contracting. The latest census data establishes a national population of 1,294,455 permanent residents, a reduction of five point five per cent from 2000, which is largely attributable to a low birth-rate and significant emigration following EU accession in 2004.[17] The population is also primarily urbanized and remains located within predictable areas of habitation. Some sixty-seven point nine per cent of the population live in cities, predominantly in the capital Tallinn, which accommodates almost 400,000 residents or approximately one-third of the entire population. Meanwhile, the rural population is generally falling. Of the 4,438 officially registered villages in rural areas, within which wilderness and protected sites are most prevalent, only twelve have a population above 1,000 residents (predominantly those located in the Harju region, on the fringes of Tallinn), while 3,781 have less than 100.[18] Road and rail networks follow well-established routes connecting the major population centres; hence the primary areas of habitation are clearly and predictably contained. Allied to this, as noted in Section 3, Estonia has retained a strong regulatory emphasis upon nature conservation and the wilderness areas protected during the Soviet era were reinforced by a series of legal initiatives following the return to independence to ensure the ecological integrity of these sites. Moreover, within these protected areas in Estonia, the general population trend is one of 'rapid decline', especially among the younger generation, notwithstanding a small degree of inverse migration from wealthier citizens seeking to escape the rigours of urban life.[19]

Despite the seemingly favourable conditions for the promotion of wilderness values in Estonia, considerable challenges are nonetheless also apparent. In the first instance, the concept of 'wilderness' as expressed in English has little direct equivalent in many other

[17] The most recent census was undertaken in 2011 and concluded in March 2012; the results are published at www.stat.ee (last visited 30 May 2015).

[18] *Ibid.*

[19] J. Kliimask et al., 'Nature Conservation in Remote Rural Areas: A Win-Win Situation?' in F. Dünkel, M. Herbst and T. Schlengel (eds.), *Think Rural! Dynamiken des Wendels in peripheren ländlichen Räumen und ihre Implikatationen für die Daesinsvorsorge* (Dordrecht: Springer, 2014), 193–208, at 198.

languages,[20] and there is no truly comparable term in Estonian, which may hinder national policies to protect such areas. While Estonian most closely resembles modern Finnish, there is no equivalent to the unique Finnish notion of *erämaa* outlined in Chapter 14.[21] Instead, the most common contemporary articulation of the term is *metsik loodus*, literally translated as 'forest-like nature'. Nevertheless, numerous areas in Estonia that exhibit the three core wilderness qualities lie outside the woodland and include the country's many bogs, mires, bays, floodplains, islands and *klint*, the extensive limestone escarpments unique to the Baltic region. An alternative – if lesser used – term is *kõnnumaa*, with *kõnd* describing land (*maa*) that is of modest value in supporting agrarian activities. This, however, raises the false assumption that wilderness protection is accordingly based on default, in the sense that the pristine integrity of an area has endured due to a lack of economic prospects rather than its inherent value as an untouched ecosystem meriting a state of perpetual preservation. As observed below, Estonian nature conservation law provides for the establishment of Wilderness Conservation Zones within protected national areas. This term, however, is used solely in English; the more generic phrase *looduslik sihtkaitsevöönd* is used in Estonian, literally translated as a conservation zone for nature. Ultimately, many modern conservation terms have little historical resonance in the Estonian language, with concepts such as 'landscape' (*maastik*) having only entered popular usage in the 1990s and bearing a closer linguistic resemblance to the German *landschaft*, as opposed to the more internationally prevalent English terminology.[22] Ironically, concepts such as 'wilderness' may be subject to a proactive legal framework in Estonia that is perhaps more capably articulated in other languages than the native tongue.

[20] This is starkly exemplified by the Celtic languages of the UK, which struggle to articulate an equivalent concept of wilderness, which is often used interchangeably with a 'desert' or 'uncultivated land' in Scots (*fàsach*), Irish (*fásach*), Manx (*aaisagh*), Cornish (*defyth*) and Welsh (*anialwch*). The closest equivalent is arguably the antiquated Welsh word *diffeithwch*, used predominantly in classical and religious texts, which conveys the sense of an open or 'unmade' place.

[21] The popular understanding of *luonto* in Finnish as denoting 'nature' or 'the natural world' is, however, largely mirrored by the Estonian term *loodus*.

[22] H. Palang et al., 'Social Landscape: Ten Years of Planning "valuable landscapes" in Estonia', *Land Use Policy* 19 (2011), 19–25, at 23. This is perhaps unsurprising given that the Baltic German community exercised a considerable cultural and linguistic influence over the regime of natural features in the pre-1918 provinces that would ultimately form the territories of Estonia, Latvia and Lithuania.

Just as the linguistic understanding of the wilderness paradigm in Estonia is markedly distinct to its Anglo-American foundations, so too are national attitudes towards the natural environment in general and uncultivated land subject to minimal human interaction in particular. The Baltic peoples have long identified themselves as having a strong attachment to the natural world, historically worshipping natural features in the Pagan tradition.[23] This has been particularly pronounced in Estonia, which has retained a strong attachment to particular groves, woodlands and individual natural features, while the traditional nature-orientated festivals to mark the summer solstice, or *jaanipäev* in Estonian, continue to be celebrated with great fervour across the Baltic States. As with many other civilizations, the natural world has inspired significant works of literature, art and music in Estonia. From the ancient legends of the *Kalevipoeg*, depicting the playful use of natural features by mythical giants, to the celebrated modern composition *Tuul Kõnnumaa Kohal*,[24] the untouched landscape has traditionally provided a notable creative undertone to Estonian culture. Likewise, Estonian literature has long evoked wistful reflection on the preservation of the natural environment and the restoration of virgin land, albeit with additional layers of context and complexity: throughout much of the twentieth century this was primarily asserted as a subversive metaphor for the restoration of Estonian statehood and the dispersal of invasive occupants, rather than a simple paean to the rugged beauty of the Baltic landscape.[25]

Indeed, this complexity is reflected in attempts to ascertain popular attitudes to wilderness protection in Estonia. The available data suggests that unlike the more preservationist stance of Western Europe, a seemingly prevalent view within Estonia is that protected areas 'should not be seen as a system of orders and prohibitions, but the rational and flexible way to maintain the inherited relationships between nature and local people',[26]

[23] Plakans, *A Concise History of the Baltic States, supra* note 10, at 20–25; see also Smurr, *Perceptions of Nature, Expressions of Nation: An Environmental History of Estonia, supra* note 15, at 2–26. As Smurr observes, even today most ethnic Estonian surnames are directly derived from nature: *ibid.*, xviii.

[24] This noted choral work by the Estonian Veljo Tormis, a world-renowned classical composer, is most usually translated as *Wind over the Barrens*, again reflecting the notion of *kõnnumaa* as a landscape that is less conducive to cultivation and human utility.

[25] See further K. Tüür and T. Maran, 'On Estonian Nature Writing', *Estonian Literary Magazine* 13 (2001), 4–10.

[26] C. Bosangit, J. Raadik and L. Shi, *Perception of Wilderness in Finland and Estonia* (Wagenigen: WWF, 2004), at 25. While this study should be treated with a degree of caution – canvassing a small pool of national experts and the managers of protected areas, rather than the general public, and eliciting a relatively low response rate – the results are nonetheless illuminating.

while the national relationship with the 'wilderness' appears to favour human interaction over voluntary avoidance.[27] More recent investigations of popular interest in the protection of wild animals that thrive in wilderness habitats reveal a notable ambivalence towards wild nature, with at least fifty per cent of those surveyed of the view that it is 'not important'.[28] Such surveys have, however, been primarily conducted in the context of large carnivores, where there remains a considerable degree of regional antipathy towards wolves in particular,[29] hence the population may be favourably disposed to certain elements of a resurgent wilderness yet antagonistic towards others. Attitudes towards abandoned and re-wilded land in the Baltic region are, however, generally negative among the local population,[30] and attempts to celebrate and promote uncultivated land for its own intrinsic merit have been received with hostility and suspicion in rural areas.[31] Accordingly, as with other jurisdictions, the legal framework of wilderness conservation in Estonia has sought to reconcile the traditional entitlement of human access to the natural environment with the possibility of securing anthropogenic absence and the maintenance of pristine nature sites, to which this chapter now turns.

## 3 The legal protection of wilderness

### *3.1 Introduction*

Although Estonia can be generally considered a jurisdiction within which wilderness values have received a strong measure of protection, the notion of 'wilderness' itself is paradoxically absent from national legislation. There is no specific wilderness statute in Estonia, nor indeed is the

[27] *Ibid.*, at 67.

[28] L. Balčiauskas, M. Kazlausakas and T. Randveer, 'Lynx Acceptance in Poland, Lithuania and Estonia', *Estonian Journal of Ecology* 59 (2010), 52–61, at 58. The most negative attitudes were recorded in South Estonia, where the potential impact of resurgent carnivores would be keenest felt; approximately forty per cent of those polled in Tallinn, however, considered wild nature to be 'very important'.

[29] T. Randveer, 'The Attitudes of Estonians to Large Carnivores', *Acta Zoologica Lituanica* 16 (2006), 119–123.

[30] See A. Ruskule et al., 'The Perception of Abandoned Farmland by Local People and Experts: Landscape Value and Perspectives on Future Land Use', *Landscape and Urban Planning* 115 (2013), 49–61. The authors note, however, that a higher value is generally placed on the revival of wild land by city-dwellers and those with an advanced educational background.

[31] K.Z.S. Schwartz, 'Wild Horses in a "European wilderness": Imagining Sustainable Development in the Post-communist Countryside', *Cultural Geographies* 12 (2005), 292–320 (examining the clash between Western preservationism and Baltic utilitarianism in the context of reintroducing wildlife to abandoned Latvian farmland).

term either defined or even explicitly referenced within current legal provisions. Nevertheless, a broad mosaic of legal instruments provides a discernible foundation for the protection of wilderness in Estonia. Of these, the most pertinent in safeguarding the three core wilderness qualities considered herein is the Nature Conservation Act 2004, which envisages the maintenance of certain categories of land in an unaltered state and subject to minimal human interaction. In addition, given the dense woodland coverage across many areas of the Estonian mainland, forestry law will also play a significant role in reinforcing national wilderness protection. Other relevant provisions supplementing this broad framework include legislation governing hunting and fishing, agriculture, land regulation, tourism and rights of way, natural heritage and general principles of environmental protection and stewardship.

### *3.2 The history of wilderness protection in Estonia*

Despite its truncated history as a sovereign nation, the creation of protected areas subject to minimal human interference has a long heritage in Estonia. The earliest recorded measures for strict nature protection within Estonian territory date back to 1297, where the Danish King Menved prohibited logging on a series of islands fringing the northern coastline so as to assist maritime navigation. Later, under Swedish rule, further restrictions were placed upon the felling of valuable trees and the destruction of forestry resources in 1647 and 1664, culminating in the establishment in 1764 of an extensive protected forest zone, spanning some fifty fathoms in width, across the Baltic coast.[32] The first formalized nature reserve was inaugurated in Estonia in 1910, with the acquisition of a sizeable tract of land by the Riga Naturalists' Society on the large western island of Saaremaa, inspired by the private lease in 1909 of the Vaika Islands to secure nesting and hatching sites from human intrusion. The Vaika Islands Bird Sanctuary, which remains protected today, was soon joined by a series of nature reserves designated in 1924 by the government of the newly founded Estonia and, although difficulties were encountered in developing a specific national law on nature conservation, which was belatedly concluded in 1935,[33] regular conservation designations continued throughout this era. By 1940, at which point Estonia succumbed to a

[32] K. Sepp et al., 'Prospects for Nature and Landscape Protection in Estonia', *Landscape and Urban Planning* 46 (1999), 161–167, at 163.

[33] Caddell, 'Nature Conservation in Estonia: From Soviet Union to European Union', *supra* note 2, at 310.

series of wartime annexations, some forty-seven separate nature reserves had been established across the country, a considerable number of which encompassed significant areas of pristine wilderness.

The Vaika Islands reserve is widely credited as being the first *zapovednik* within the then Russian Empire, a system of nature conservation that was retained by the USSR and subsequently reapplied in Estonia. In principle, *zapovednost* – the conceptual foundation of the *zapovednik* system – remains arguably the most explicit legal mechanism for the protection of wilderness values to have been applied in Europe. The term *zapovednik*, which has little direct equivalent in English, was initially conceived as the complete withdrawal of an area from any form of economic usage, within which the sole permissible anthropogenic activity would be the study of pristine nature.[34] Soviet-era *zapovedniki* nonetheless endured a schizophrenic and precarious existence. While the abolition of the private ownership of land in the USSR and the legislative designation of *zapovedniki* as 'forever withdrawn from economic utilization for scientific-research and cultural-education purposes'[35] provided conditions that were highly conducive to proactive wilderness protection, preservationist intent was frequently subordinated to industrial reality. By 1933 the 'fetish of inviolability' incumbent in *zapovednost* had been stridently rejected by influential Soviet scientists,[36] mindful of Stalin's ruthless pursuit of economic progress and the Socialist 'transformation of nature' as a central component of this objective; hence *zapovedniki* became increasingly zoned to facilitate development projects. *Zapovedniki* were also viewed with suspicion by the KGB as havens for dissidents, further inhibiting proponents of

[34] Shtilmark, Историография Российских Эаповедников (1895–1995), *supra* note 3, at 1.

[35] P.R. Pryde, *Conservation in the Soviet Union* (Cambridge: Cambridge University Press, 1972), at 212.

[36] D.R. Weiner, *Models of Nature: Ecology, Conservation and Cultural Revolution in Soviet Russia* (Pittsburgh: University of Pittsburgh Press, 1988), at 195. This infamous pronouncement was made at the 1933 annual meeting of the All-Union Conference on Nature Conservation, at a point at which the trend of 'self-criticism' was prevalent and a concerted purge of perceived opponents of Socialist economic progress was firmly underway. While there were many genuine antagonists to the notion of unqualified *zapovednost*, Shtilmark considers that for others tactical opposition to 'bourgeois' wilderness sites perversely represented the only realistic opportunity to secure their protection – by embracing (and accordingly controlling) the seemingly inevitable process of zoning, important areas of *zapovedniki* could nonetheless be potentially maintained in a pristine state: Shtilmark, Историография Российских Эаповедников (1895–1995), *supra* note 3, at 58–83.

wilderness values.[37] In the Estonian context, given that the *Metsavennad* were primarily active in what is now Karula National Park, this is perhaps one instance of Soviet paranoia that was not entirely misplaced. Most significantly, however, responsibility for *zapovednik* affairs was frequently reassigned between ministries, notably those with a marked pliancy towards industrial production and limited empathy for plaintive supplication as to the innate value of pristine nature. In 1952 Stalin presided over the 'liquidation' of the *zapovedniki*, from which 128 areas spanning 12.5 million hectares (over zero point five per cent of the entire territory of the USSR) were culled to forty sites with a net volume of approximately 1.5 million hectares.[38] From 1957 onwards, prompted by Estonian developments, the individual Republics introduced nature conservation laws that would eventually restore *zapovednost* as a central objective of Soviet protected areas, although in many instances this was 'blatantly disregarded'[39] and the *zapovedniki* never collectively realized their full wilderness potential.

*Zapovedniki* nonetheless enjoyed a distinctly more favourable existence in the Estonian SSR, in which five were established during the Soviet era. The first four designations were made in 1957, in the wake of the Republic's pioneering Nature Conservation Act, in Matsalu (to protect waterfowl), Nigula (to promote research into bog ecology, also becoming a bird area of international importance in 1979), Viidumäe (to conserve the Saaremaa ecosystem, and which was subsequently expanded in 1979) and Vilsandi (incorporating the original Vaika Islands Bird Sanctuary), while the Endla *zapovednik* was instituted in 1985 as a wetland reserve. That the Estonian *zapovedniki* fared considerably better than their eastern counterparts appears attributable both to a proactive system of environmental management and influential conservation personnel, alongside the otherwise poor industrial prospects for this land.[40]

Other legislative possibilities were also deployed to protect the pristine integrity of particular sites, including designation as a *zakhaznik*. While *zakhazniki* were not centrally envisaged as wilderness reserves, '[t]he Russian republic and some others use[d] this category primarily for game management purposes, whereas the Baltic republics have

[37] Weiner, *ibid.*, at 227.
[38] *Ibid.*, at 237.
[39] Shtilmark, Историография Российских Эаповедников (1895–1995), *supra* note 3, at 134.
[40] Tuvi, 'Establishment of Protected Areas in Different Ecoregions, Ecosystems, and Diversity Hotspots under Successive Political Systems', *supra* note 16, at 1728–1730.

established them mainly to preserve specific features of the landscape'.[41] In Estonia, *zakhazniki* supplemented the main *zapovedniki* by establishing new nature reserves in 1979 at Karula and Otepää and in 1981 at Haanja, Peipsiveere and Piusa. A further *zazhaznik* established in 1981 for mire protection at Endla was swiftly reconstituted as the Republic's fifth *zapovednik*, while the Vorsmi *zakhaznik* (1987) operated in reality as a wilderness reserve, since the island had been abandoned after World War II and visitor access was subsequently precluded for security purposes. By the time at which Soviet power disintegrated in 1991, some seven point three four per cent of the Estonian landmass was under formal legal protection, which thereby included a considerable proportion of areas exhibiting distinct wilderness qualities.[42]

The immediate post-Soviet period presented particular challenges to the integrity of the wilderness in the newly re-independent Estonia. The withdrawal of Soviet forces duly facilitated the sudden release of significant areas of *de facto* wilderness, for which public access had previously been heavily restricted. The ecological effects of the convulsions of regime change have only recently begun to be quantified, for which in Estonia there appears to have been a discernible adverse impact upon species most attenuated to wilderness habitats.[43] Moreover, the chronic understaffing of the national nature conservation authorities and their limited capacity to enforce protective ordinances facilitated some distinctly rapacious behaviour within these locations.[44] Ecological considerations would also have to compete for the legislative attention of the nascent government with a host of other pressing matters, while nature conservation itself was a less immediate environmental priority than addressing significant pollution concerns and land remediation requirements. In 1994 a Law on Protected Natural Objects was enacted and, while this facilitated the establishment of four significant nature reserves at Alam-Pedjar (1994), Naissare (1995), Osmussaare (1996) and Silma (1998), this provision is considered to have

[41] P.R. Pryde, 'The Environmental Basis for Ethnic Unrest in the Baltic Republics', in J.M. Stewart (ed.), *The Soviet Environment: Problems, Policies and Politics* (Cambridge, Cambridge University Press: 1992), 11–23, at 12.

[42] S. Sööt, 'Estonia', in P.R. Pryde (ed.), *Environmental Resources and Constraints in the Former Soviet Republics* (Boulder: Westview Press, 1995), 95–108, at 105.

[43] E.V. Bragina et al., 'Rapid Declines of Large Mammal Populations after the Collapse of the Soviet Union', *Conservation Biology* 29 (2015), 844–853.

[44] M.R. Auer, 'Estonian Environmental Reforms: A Small Nation's Outsized Accomplishments', in M.R. Auer (ed.), *Restoring Cursed Earth: Appraising Environmental Policy Reforms in Eastern Europe and Russia* (Lanham: Rowman & Littlefield, 2005), 117–143, at 133–34 (noting wholesale logging and illegal construction in previously secured sites).

been overly dependent upon a framework approach and the corresponding need to elaborate regular delegated legislation and was thus less able to facilitate proactive nature conservation.[45] Meanwhile, further complications were raised by the protracted process of land restitution following the confiscation of private property by the Soviet authorities, which could prospectively serve to fracture the connectivity of existing or future protected sites or pockmark particular elements of the remaining Estonian wilderness with development projects.

### 3.3 *The Nature Conservation Act 2004*

Upon accession to the EU, the 1994 statute was repealed and replaced with the Nature Conservation Act 2004 (NCA),[46] which seeks to promote a closer legislative alignment with the Habitats Directive.[47] While the wilderness credentials of the Habitats Directive are somewhat qualified,[48] the NCA has nonetheless served to facilitate a concerted degree of protection for wilderness sites in Estonia, notably through clear provisions on the zoning of conservation areas to facilitate minimal interference with pristine land. The basic tenet of the NCA is for nature conservation to be realized 'by means of restricting the use of areas important from the aspect of preservation of the natural environment, by regulating steps involving specimens of wild fauna, flora and fungi and specimens of fossils, and by promoting nature education and scientific research'.[49]

The primary mechanism for wilderness conservation within the NCA is Section 4, under which six distinct categories of 'protected natural objects' (*kaitstavad loodusobjektid*) are recognized,[50] of which 'protected

45 H. Veinla, 'Environmental Considerations in Estonian Land-use Legislation', *Juridica International* 1 (1996), 48–56, at 50. Similar concerns were raised by the European Commission during Estonia's EU accession process: Caddell, 'Nature Conservation in Estonia: From Soviet Union to European Union', *supra* note 2, at 315–317.

46 On the NCA generally see H. Veinla and K. Relve, *Environmental Law in Estonia* (Aalpen aan den Rijn: Kluwer, 2012), at 153–167.

47 Council Directive 92/43/EEC of 21 May 1992 on the conservation of natural habitats of wild flora and fauna [1992] OJ L206/7.

48 See further Chapter 8.

49 Section 2(1). The protection of 'animals living freely in the wild' is vested exclusively in the NCA: see the Animal Protection Act 2000, Sections 1(2) and 6(1). Hunting and fishing is generally prohibited within designated conservation zones and is regulated respectively under the specific legislation governing these activities.

50 Namely, protected areas, limited conservation areas, protected species and fossils, species protection sites, individual protected natural objects and natural objects protected at the local government level: Section 4(1).

areas' (*kaitsealad*) present the clearest possibilities for the untrammelled protection of pristine nature. Indeed, protected areas are to be 'maintained in a state *unaltered by human activity* or used subject to special requirements where the natural environment is preserved, protected, restored, researched or introduced'.[51] Responsibility for the designation of protected natural objects – including protected areas exhibiting wilderness qualities – is vested in the Ministry of the Environment,[52] although '[e]veryone' may propose additional sites for incorporation into the national network.[53] Once designated, protected areas are subject to individual protection rules,[54] through which the distinct ecological character of each site – including any specific wilderness requirements – will be managed. In this regard, the protection rules are to establish 'one or several protected zones with equivalent or different degree of strictness of restrictions',[55] while a specific management plan is also to be established for the site,[56] providing further scope to address particular wilderness considerations.

Three specific categories of 'protected area' are envisaged under the Estonian system, namely national parks (*rahvuspargid*), nature reserves (*looduskaitsealad*) and landscape protection areas (*maastikukaitsealad*).[57]

## Protected areas

National parks are defined in Section 26(1) as 'a protected area prescribed for the preservation, protection, restoration, research and introduction of the natural environment, landscapes, cultural heritage and balanced use of the environment of the protected area'. Five such areas have been established to date: Laahemaa, initially created in 1971 during the Soviet period, to protect the coastal landscapes of Northern Estonia; Karula, established in 1993 from an earlier *zakhaznik*, to protect the hilly moraine landscapes of Southern Estonia; Soomaa, established in 1993, to

[51] Section 4(2) (emphasis added).
[52] Section 9.
[53] Section 8(1).
[54] Section 12(1).
[55] Section 12(2).
[56] Section 25.
[57] There is some inconsistency in the official English translation of the NCA, with *looduskaitsealad* described in Section 4(2)(2) as 'nature conservation areas' but as 'nature reserves' in Section 27. The latter construction has been used in this chapter, since Section 27 establishes the definition and functions of *looduskaitsealad* on a more extensive basis and the term 'nature reserve' is predominantly used in the English translation of official documents pertaining to this category; the original Estonian language version is clear that the areas addressed by Sections 4(2)(2) and 27 are one and the same.

protect the mire and floodplain landscape of *Estonia intermedia*; Vilsandi, designated in 1993 to protect the Western Estonian archipelago and Matsalu (2004) in the Väinameri Sea region, both of which had been previously established as *zapovedniki* in 1957. National parks are therefore intended under the NCA to operate as multi-use sites, wherein wilderness objectives are to be reconciled with recreational uses and cultural heritage considerations.

This approach reflects the historical practices of such sites in Estonia, which, alongside other national parks in the Baltic region, have a multifaceted provenance. Lahemaa is notable as the first national park to have been created within the USSR, then representing a novel designation of protected area beyond the *zapovednik* system. While it was (and remains) unquestionably significant from an environmental perspective, nature protection was nevertheless far from the sole objective underpinning its creation, for Lahemaa was conceived as a means of preserving indigenous Estonian culture just as much as its native ecosystem.[58] Mixed motives notwithstanding, as one of Estonia's most pristine and sparsely populated areas, Lahemaa swiftly assumed a significant role in wilderness preservation and a core part of its original mandate was 'to preserve special regions within the park in conditions of pristine natural condition for the observance and research of natural processes'.[59] Indeed, some six to eight per cent of the park was ultimately withdrawn specifically to preserve its wilderness character, while a further two-thirds of the park was available only to the most passive forms of recreation.[60]

This broad practice has endured within the current legislative framework. Three distinct types of zones are envisaged within national parks, namely 'strict nature reserves' (*loodusreservaat*), 'conservation zones' (*sihtkaitsevöönd*) and 'limited management zones' (*piiranguvöönd*).[61] Of these, strict nature reserves and conservation zones present the clearest mechanisms for the protection of wilderness values within nationally protected areas. From a specific wilderness standpoint, limited management zones are generally unsuited to wilderness conservation since an array of intrusive economic activities may be permitted within these sites,

[58] R.W. Smurr, 'Lahemaa: The Paradox of the USSR's First National Park', *Nationalities Papers* 36 (2008), 399–423, at 411. Similar parks – with broadly similar objectives – were soon established in Latvia (Gauja, 1972) and Lithuania (Augštaitija, 1974).

[59] *Lahemaa Rahvuspargi Põhimäärus*; reproduced *ibid.*, at 404.

[60] Pryde, *Environmental Management in the Soviet Union*, *supra* note 14, at 162.

[61] Section 26(3).

including mineral extraction, landscape modification and extensive access by visitors and most forms of vehicles.[62]

Strict nature reserves are defined in Section 29(1) as 'a land or water area of a protected area whose natural status is unaffected by direct human activity and where the preservation and development of natural biotic communities is ensured only through natural processes'. More significantly from a wilderness perspective, '[a]ll types of human activity' are prohibited within such areas,[63] with exceptions granted solely for supervision, rescue work and to organize the protection of the area itself,[64] or for the monitoring and assessment of the site,[65] a position largely reflective of the original intentions of *zapovednost*.

Conservation zones are defined as 'a land or water area of a protected area prescribed for the preservation of natural and semi-biotic communities established or to be developed therein. Mineral resources present within a conservation zone are not deemed to be resources intended for exploitation.'[66] Within designated conservation zones, general prohibitions are imposed upon economic activities, the use of natural resources, construction work, interference with protected habitats, driving motor vehicles, off-road vehicles or vessels, as well as camping, building fires or organizing public events.[67] Likewise, the protection rules established for a conservation zone may, with the approval of the responsible authorities, permit a wider degree of human interaction with the site than is contemplated for strict nature reserves. This will include, to a greater or lesser extent and on the proviso that the preservation of the area is not compromised, maintenance work, development of biotic communities, gathering berries, fungi and other forest products, hunting and fishing, the establishment of roads, conservation activities and the gathering of reed and seaweed.[68] In practice, and although no explicit distinction is made concerning *sihtkaitsevöönd* within the MCA, two broad categories of conservation zone have been established, namely Wilderness Conservation Zones (WCZs) and Managed Conservation Zones (MCZs). The distinction is drawn depending on whether the area in question is to be maintained in either a natural or

[62] Section 31.
[63] Section 29(2).
[64] Section 29(3).
[65] Section 29(4).
[66] Section 30(1). This latter position is reinforced in Section 20(1)(1) of the Earth's Crust Act 2004, which precludes the granting of permits where the proposed activities would damage a protected natural object.
[67] Section 30(2).
[68] Section 30(4).

semi-natural state: MCZs are generally applied where some form of human intervention is necessary to preserve the natural values of the land, in particular maintaining the wooded meadows (*puisniidud*) that remain a unique feature of the Estonian countryside, while WCZs are considered to be essentially free from anthropogenic activities.

A broadly similar position applies in the other two categories of protected area recognized under the NCA. As with national parks, a nature reserve – which is 'prescribed for the preservation, protection, restoration, research and introduction of the natural environment'[69] – may also comprise a series of strict nature reserves, conservation zones and limited management zones.[70] Landscape protection areas, in contrast, are specifically established to preserve the integrity of the landscape, rather than the natural environment,[71] with wilderness conservation a lesser priority. Strict nature reserves are not contemplated for these areas, although they may incorporate *sihtkaitsevöönd*,[72] which will in practice include a smaller number of designations as WCZs.

## Current status of 'wilderness designations'

Inventories of protected areas are conducted periodically in Estonia, most recently in 2011, which provides an official record of the current status of wilderness designations under the NCA. To date, twenty-nine strict nature reserves have been established, comprising a combined total of 7,958 hectares or some 0.002 per cent of Estonian territory,[73] with such designations having remained static in number and area since the previous inventory in 2007. As of 2011, 316 WCZs had been created, comprising a total area of 189,246 hectares, which represents a numerical increase by two sites but a net reduction of 516 hectares.[74] Protected wilderness sites are most prevalent within nature reserves: three per cent of the net territory of these zones has been designated as strict nature reserves and forty-three per cent as WCZs.[75] Across the five national parks, one per cent of the land cumulatively constitutes a strict nature reserve and thirty-three per cent has been established as a network of

[69] Section 27(1).
[70] Section 27(2).
[71] Section 28(1). Unlike the other two categories of 'protected area', the protection of the natural environment is absent from the definitional objectives of a landscape protection area.
[72] Section 28(2).
[73] Klein and Hermet, *Estonian Nature Conservation in 2011*, *supra* note 5, at 54.
[74] *Ibid.*, at 55.
[75] *Ibid.*, at 41.

WCZs.[76] Additionally, some six per cent of the combined total of land designated as landscape protected areas has been established as a WCZ.[77]

### Public access to wilderness sites

Public access to wilderness sites is not precluded, although it is subject to extensive regulation. Reflecting its early heritage as an outpost of a succession of Scandinavian empires, Estonia has retained the Nordic tradition of the 'everyman's right' (*igameheõigus*), prescribing a customary privilege to freely roam the land between sunrise and sunset. Although there is no general public right of access to strict nature reserves,[78] the *igameheõigus* expressly applies, inter alia, to conservation zones,[79] which would accordingly extend to sites designated as WCZs. The specific parameters of the *igameheõigus*, which had previously lay scattered across a disparate array of statutes, have recently been collated in the Environmental Code Act 2011 (General Part), for which the relevant provisions formally entered into force on 1 August 2014. The exercise of the *igameheõigus* is a residual freedom, contingent upon the permission of the owner of the land – whether public or private – which is deemed to have been granted 'if the owner has not fenced the plot or marked it in a manner that demonstrates the intent to restrict strangers' stay on the plot.'[80] On 3 March 2015, the Act was amended to withdraw this general presumption in the specific case of power-driven or off-road vehicles;[81] the Estonian legislation therefore provides a clear regulatory position on activities that have raised significant concerns in the wilderness environments of other jurisdictions.

Where applicable, the *igameheõigus* prescribes a general entitlement to pick berries, mushrooms and nuts and to take any other natural products, unless this is clearly prohibited by the owner.[82] Permission to camp on land is presumed only for one day,[83] while fires may be lit solely in areas for which specific authorization has been granted.[84] Visitor access to

[76] *Ibid.*, at 40.
[77] *Ibid.*, at 42.
[78] Section 29(2).
[79] Section 15(1).
[80] Section 32(2). Access to shores and banks is guaranteed under Section 36 of the NCA.
[81] Section 32(2); the amendments entered into force on 14 March 2015. Provision for further restrictions on vehicular access to remote areas is established under Section 5(1) of the Roads Act 1999.
[82] Section 34. This general position is reinforced by Section 35 of the Forest Act 2006 in relation to woodland areas.
[83] Section 35(3).
[84] Section 36.

protected areas across Estonia has accordingly been clearly demarcated through suitable fencing and signposting. The State Forestry Management Centre has also established an authoritative list of sites suitable for public amenity, while specifying locations that are not to be disturbed and within which the *igameheõigus* will explicitly not apply.[85] Responsibility for the enforcement of these provisions is vested in the Environment Board, which has established a 24-hour hotline for the anonymous reporting of environmental infractions. There has generally proved to be a high level of compliance with the relevant wilderness restrictions,[86] a position that appears largely attributable to the clear information concerning limitations upon access to particular areas and the concerted provision of amenities and recreational sites for visitors.

## Wilderness and forestry protection

Given that significant areas of pristine nature remain located within the extensive Estonian woodland, the regime of forestry protection is also highly pertinent in promoting wilderness conservation. Land-use changes and the collectivization of agriculture led to a dramatic increase in forest coverage during the Soviet era,[87] which now accounts for approximately fifty per cent of the national landmass. Forestry resources are regulated under the Forest Act 2006, which prescribes a legal requirement that state-owned forestry shall encompass at least twenty per cent of the total area of the Estonian mainland.[88]

The Forest Act presents particular scope to assist in wilderness conservation through the establishment of a network of Woodland Key Habitats (WKHs), each of which span at least seven hectares.[89] Economic activities may be restricted or even prohibited entirely within WKHs;[90] approximately thirty-one per cent of Estonian forestland is currently subject to management restrictions.[91] Privately owned forestry may also be co-opted into this network, whereby a mandatory twenty-

85 For full details see www.looduseakoos.ee (last visited 30 May 2015).

86 Personal communication with Mr Uudo Timm of the Estonian Ministry of the Environment (on file with the author).

87 Forest coverage increased from 929,000 hectares in 1940 to 2,022,000 hectares in 1993: E. Urbel-Piirsalu and A-K. Bäcklund, 'Exploring the Sustainability of Estonian Forestry: the Socio-economic Drivers', *Ambio* 38 (2009), 101–108, at 101.

88 Section 5(1).

89 Article 23(1).

90 Article 26(6).

91 R. Sirgmets, P. Kaimre and A. Padari, 'Economic Impact of Enlarging the Area of Protected Forests in Estonia', *Forest Policy and Economics* 13 (2011) 155–158, at 155.

year lease is concluded for the land in question.[92] Private owners have nevertheless proved reluctant to participate in voluntary initiatives to withdraw their forestry from economic usage, unsurprisingly so where individual sites may have been regained through protracted land restitution proceedings; hence compulsory leases have been an important tool in maintaining the integrity of the WKH network.[93]

Significantly, from a wilderness standpoint, forest resources are also subject to an overarching development plan to be concluded on a ten-yearly basis.[94] This includes provision for the withdrawal of a certain volume of forestry from economic use and its preservation as a *de facto* wilderness area. The latest Forest Development Programme, concluded in 2010, mandates the strict protection of at least ten per cent of the total area of Estonian forestry, thereby supplementing current wilderness designations under the NCA for an extended period of time.

### Wilderness and heritage law

Finally, the network of protected wilderness areas established under the NCA may be complemented to some degree by designations for heritage purposes. Given Estonia's pagan heritage, and a post-Soviet revival of the indigenous nature-based religions of *Maausk* and *Taarusk*, the natural environment has retained a strong cultural resonance. Numerous sites protected under the NCA also host natural features that are significant examples of cultural heritage. This includes an extensive volume of *hiied* (sacred groves), within which ancient lore has traditionally mandated an absence of cultivation.[95] A definitive inventory of sacred natural sites is currently being compiled in Estonia,[96] for which the Heritage Conservation Act 2002 facilitates the designation of heritage conservation areas to preserve monuments of national significance.[97]

Unlike other jurisdictions, however, cultural heritage legislation is of comparatively modest utility in protecting wilderness values in Estonia: a

[92] Section 26(4).

[93] P. Põllumäe, H. Korjus and T. Paluots, 'Management motivations of Estonian forest owners', *Forest Policy and Economics* 42 (2014), 8–14, at 11.

[94] Section 7(2). Approximately one quarter of all WKHs are located on privately-owned land: Klein and Hermet, *Estonian Nature Conservation in 2011, supra* note 5, at 51.

[95] On the pristine nature of *hiied* see T. Jonuks, 'Holy groves in Estonian religion', *Estonian Journal of Archaeology* 11 (2007), 3–35, p.17.

[96] *State Conservation Plan for Sacred Natural Sites 2008–12* (Tallinn: Estonian Ministry of Culture, 2008), Objective 1. Placing such items under formal legal protection remains an on going process (Objective 2).

[97] Section 15.

protected zone is presumed to extend for only 50 metres around the monument,[98] public access is to be guaranteed[99] and the designation criteria applies to sites that 'have developed under the joint influence of natural phenomena and human activities'.[100] Moreover, *hiied* aside (which often vary substantially in size), natural items of cultural significance in Estonia have generally comprised individual features, such as glacial erratic boulders, cross-trees, cup-stones and traditional boundary markers, rather than large sites valued for their wilderness characteristics. Most significantly, perhaps, the relationship between wilderness values and cultural heritage in Estonia remains complex and divisive. Attempts to reintroduce primordial nature within protected rural areas that are also representative of longstanding agrarian traditions have been staunchly resisted by supporters of heritage values. Indeed, this dichotomy has been most starkly illustrated in the context of Lahemaa National Park, where proponents of wilderness restoration have faced concerted opposition from those seeking to preserve its distinct traditions of cultivation.[101]

## Future challenges

The current legislation provides an effective template for the preservation of significant areas of land in Estonia exhibiting a high state of naturalness and a general absence of anthropogenic infrastructure. Indeed, it can be seen that this framework has facilitated the withdrawal of a significant volume of territory across Estonia as pristine wilderness, for which a high degree of public cooperation has been forthcoming. However, the perceived conflict with cultural values and the Baltic heritage of shaping the landscape is not the only challenge to coordinated wilderness conservation in Estonia. It would appear that the current range of wilderness designations is approaching its full capacity within a relatively small

98 Section 25(3).

99 Section 27.

100 Section 4(1). Likewise, Estonia has also nominated a series of *puisniidud* for inclusion upon the Tentative List of the World Heritage Convention, although this specifically celebrates the fact that human cultivation prevents these distinct natural areas from becoming overgrown and subsumed into a wilderness environment.

101 M. Kõivupuu, A. Printsmann and H. Palang, 'From Inventory to Identity? Constructing the Lahemaa National Park's (Estonia) Regional Cultural Heritage', in T. Bloemers, H. Kars, A. van der Valk and M. Wijnen (eds.), *The Cultural Landscape and Heritage Paradox* (Amsterdam: Amsterdam University Press, 2010), 115–131, at 124–125. Similar conflicts have occurred in Latvia: K.Z.S. Schwartz, '"Masters in Our Native Place": The Politics of Latvian National Parks on the Road from Communism to "Europe"', *Political Geography* 25 (2006), 42–71, at 55.

territory and the scope to withdraw further expanses of land as pristine sites may be decidedly limited. Indeed, the more recent trend is for conservation designations to be established as managed zones, which remain under protection but with a clear toleration for socio-economic activities. Moreover, there appears to be discernible pressure to renew the protection rules for existing conservation areas in favour of a softer management regime within particular sites.[102] Ultimately, support for the economic transformation of land previously precluded from use under the Soviet regime has proved to be rather more vociferous across the Baltic States than advocacy for its continued enclosure.[103]

Likewise, land ownership also presents further complications. While a considerable number of land restitution claims have been settled and the overwhelming majority of wilderness designations concern state-owned land,[104] questions over title to parcels of territory in remote areas remain outstanding. Moreover, although the European Commission has considered that clear lines of communication with those affected by the withdrawal of land – whether as landowners or traditional land-users – remains an essential component of effective national wilderness policies,[105] there has been a decidedly chequered record of consultation within the Baltic States concerning conservation designations.[106] Tensions also remain concerning the balancing of nature protection considerations with economic development, especially in remote areas: in this respect, industrial activities in the Selisoo bog region, a candidate site for the Natura 2000 network, will constitute a significant test case for Estonia's application of the Habitats

[102] Personal communication with Uudo Timm, *supra* note 86.

[103] Ü. Mander and R. Kuuba, 'Changing Landscapes in Northern Europe Based on Examples from Baltic Countries', in R.H.G. Jongman (ed.), *The New Dimensions of the European Landscape* (Dordrecht: Springer, 2004) 123–134, at 124.

[104] Currently, ninety-nine point eight per cent of all strict nature reserves are located on state-owned land, while ninety-two per cent of WCZs are state-owned, six per cent lie on unregistered land and two per cent occur upon private property: Klein and Hermet, *Estonian Nature Conservation in 2011, supra* note 5, at 62.

[105] European Commission, *Guidelines for the Management of Wilderness and Wild Areas in Natura 2000, supra* note 1, at 65–66.

[106] This has been particularly acute in Estonia: see M. Suškevičs and M. Külvik, 'The Role of Information, Knowledge, and Acceptance During Landowner Participation in the Natura 2000 Designations: The Cases of Otepää and Kõnumaa, Estonia', in M. Jones and M. Stenseke (eds.), *The European Landscape Convention: Challenges of Participation* (Dordrecht: Springer, 2011), 275–294. Similar problems have been experienced in Latvia: see I. Pavasars, 'Environmentalism in Latvia: Two Realities', *Journal of Baltic Studies* 45 (2014), 39–54, at 42–51.

Directive.[107] Ultimately, it appears that for wilderness conservation to further thrive in Estonia, clear accommodations must be made between ecological, developmental and cultural values. To this end, ecotourism constitutes an intriguing prospect for reconciling these competing interests, which this chapter now moves to consider.

## 4 Wilderness management and the regulation of ecotourism

An issue of emerging significance for the protection of wilderness areas is the prospect of increasing ecotourism within the Estonian hinterland. The exploration of the natural environment has long been a favoured recreational pursuit in Estonia and an organized nature tourism industry can be traced back to the 1930s,[108] although this largely fell into abeyance during the Soviet period, due to transit restrictions throughout the Estonian SSR and the promotion of tourism to sites of supposed Socialist importance.[109] Following the resumption of independence, the national authorities and individual entrepreneurs were swift to appreciate the significant tourism potential of Estonia's pristine landscape,[110] even if the facilities and infrastructure necessary for viable rural tourism were distinctly lacking in the immediate post-Soviet period.[111] Although still relatively small, the ecotourism sector has expanded considerably over the past decade, with a consistent market for wilderness experiences having emerged in recent years. Of particular significance in this context is the regulatory regime established in respect of Soomaa National Park, although a degree of well-managed wilderness tourism also occurs in a considerable number of sites throughout Estonia.

The Soomaa region, located in the south-eastern corner of the country, constitutes the most significant area of wilderness in Estonia. Soomaa

107 On these developments see A. Marandi, H. Veinla and E. Karro, 'Legal Aspects Related to the Effect of Underground Mining Close to the Site Entered into the List of Potential Natura 2000 Network Areas', *Environmental Science and Policy* 38 (2014), 217–224.

108 H. Tooman and A. Ruukel, 'Sustainable Development of a Remote tourist Destination: The Case of Soomaa National Park, Estonia', in P. Sloane, C. Simons-Kaufman and W. Legrand (eds.), *Sustainable Hospitality and Tourism as Motors of Development: Case Studies from Developing Regions in the World* (Abingdon: Routledge, 2012), 276–295, at 278.

109 See A.E. Gorusch, *'All This Is Your World': Soviet Tourism at Home and Abroad after Stalin* (Oxford: Oxford University Press, 2011), 49–78.

110 R. Jaakson, 'Tourism in Transition in Post-Soviet Estonia', *Annals of Tourism Research* 23 (1996), 617–634, at 628.

111 T. Unwin, 'Tourist Development in Estonia: Images, Sustainability and Integrated Rural Development', *Tourism Management* (1996), 265–276, at 269–272.

('land of swamps') comprises a sparsely populated network of large bogs, woodland and floodplain and is notable for its pristine mire ecosystem and the so-called fifth season, during which the area is subject to extensive flooding. Elements of Soomaa have been protected since 1981, with conservation designations made for its four main bogs of Kuresoo, Valgeaba, Kikipera and Öördi; the area was subsequently reconstituted in 1993 as Estonia's youngest and second-largest national park. Soomaa has been designated a Ramsar Wetland of International Importance since 1997 and, most significantly from the perspective of wilderness ecotourism, received PAN Park status in 2009, the only such designation in Estonia and one of two within the Baltic states.[112]

Soomaa is subject to multiple conservation designations under the NCA. A small area of Kikipera has been established as a strict nature reserve, with extensive WCZs instituted across its main bog areas, alongside a small proportion of MCZs and limited management zones to facilitate visitor access and human habitation.[113] Ecotourism activities are therefore largely regulated under the NCA in relation to these protected sites. In practice, however, tourism management has been facilitated through the further zoning of the area of the national park under the Management Plan developed for the site, establishing four clear zones of activity. Minimal visitation is to occur within the zones subject to strict protection rules and those under WCZ status, while tourism is instead largely confined to the 'immediate surroundings' of the national park and the 'further surroundings' provide scope for more intrusive activities, such as off-road driving.[114] Following the practices generally adopted for protected areas, the authorities have clearly designated locations within which tourist access is prohibited, while maintaining a network of paths and walkways to ensure that visitors remain within the minimal infrastructure established within the confines of the site. This has helped to avoid some of the initial difficulties posed to wildlife habitats by poorly planned tourism facilities that had been previously encountered in other protected areas.[115]

[112] Cepkeliai-Dzukija National Park, located on the Lithuania–Belarus frontier, was incorporated into the PAN network in 2011. Soomaa National Park also received the EU's EDEN award in 2009 for promoting sustainable ecotourism.

[113] A clear map of the regulatory area is reproduced in Fisher et al., *Review of Status and Conservation of Wild Land in Europe, supra* note 1, at 105.

[114] *Sustainable Tourism Strategy of the Soomaa NP Region 2009–2013* (Soomaa: Soomaa National Park, 2009), at 20–24.

[115] Some of the walkways placed for visitor access within Nigula National Park were subsequently considered to have affected the distribution pattern and population of

In essence, the relatively small number of ecotourism operators has served to ensure that the anthropogenic footprint implanted by the industry in the Estonian wilderness has been as innocuous as possible. Such operators are generally well apprised of their responsibilities towards the wilderness environment[116] and, ultimately, a sense of economic Darwinism prevails. Ecotourism entrepreneurs have swiftly appreciated that a high level of compliance with environmental provisions imbues their operations with a high degree of reputability that is a significant marketing benefit for the lucrative foreign market.[117] Nor has the cultural significance of wilderness tourism been lost on domestic constituents, with the protective environment of Soomaa having facilitated a re-engagement with regional traditions, notably a revival of the crafting of *haabja* (traditional canoes), which had lapsed almost to extinction during the Soviet period.[118] Moreover, many such operators are also trained ecologists – a number of whom are noted experts in their fields – and have generally taken a long-term view of the wilderness environment and their role in its preservation.[119] A significant unifying ethos between nature tourism operators is accordingly to foster a strong understanding of, and concern for, wilderness values among visitors, which is intended in turn to promote the ongoing cause of wilderness protection in Estonia.[120]

## 5 Concluding remarks

As one of the few remaining territories of Europe within which extensive wilderness coverage has endured, Estonia represents an illuminating case study of the legal protection of wilderness values. A unique combination of

birds: K. Kimmel et al., 'The Status, Conservation and Sustainable Use of Estonian Wetlands', *Wetlands Ecology and Management* 18 (2010), 375–395, at 389.

116 Tooman and Ruukel, 'Sustainable Development of a Remote Tourist Destination: The Case of Soomaa National Park, Estonia', *supra* note 108, at 292.

117 See M. Reimann, M-L. Lamp and H. Palang, 'Tourism Impacts and Local Communities in Estonian National Parks', *Scandinavian Journal of Hospitality and Tourism* 11 (2011), 87–99.

118 Tooman and Ruukel, 'Sustainable Development of a Remote Tourist Destination: The Case of Soomaa National Park, Estonia', *supra* note 108, at 291.

119 As one leading operator notes in the context of the popular flying squirrel, tours should not be given in relation to species that are not currently able to support such activities and prospective clients are instead referred to reputable operators in Finland, with a view towards establishing a more ecologically viable experience in Estonia within 5–10 years: personal communication with Mr Eleri Lopp-Valdma of Estonian Wildlife Tours (on file with the author).

120 Personal communication with Mr Aivar Ruukel of Soomaa.com (on file with the author); similar sentiments were expressed by Mr Lopp-Valdma, *ibid.*

circumstances has facilitated the retention of significant tracts of wilderness-quality land in Estonia. The primary drivers of this have been a small demographic with predictable areas of population density, the limited industrial utility of a number of remote locations and the involuntary withdrawal and rewilding of substantial volumes of land, imposed at a time at which many European countries were heavily exploiting their remaining wilderness resources. Since re-independence, Estonia has continued its longstanding traditions of protecting large tracts of territory subject to minimal human intrusion. While the notion of wilderness is not formally articulated within current Estonian legislation, a clear legal platform has nonetheless been established for the preservation of pristine nature. This has been facilitated primarily through nature conservation law, which prescribes a clear basis for the withdrawal of extensive areas from anthropogenic use. These provisions have been instituted effectively in Estonia and a discernible network of protected wilderness areas has emerged across the course of the past twenty years. This regime has been buttressed by forestry regulations, which have secured the further withdrawal of land from economic use and established a legal guarantee that a substantial volume of the national mainland is to remain carpeted by pristine endemic woodland for the long-term future. Moreover, the proactive management of visitor access to natural sites has ensured a high level of compliance with these restrictions, in tandem with the development of a nascent but responsibly operated ecotourism industry.

Notwithstanding the significant wilderness designations made to date in Estonia, pressures upon the current volume of wilderness coverage are nonetheless apparent. Given the large amount of land already withdrawn from economic use across a diminutive territory, it appears unlikely that extensive further designations will be forthcoming in the immediate future. Indeed, there is some movement to downgrade elements of existing WCZs to facilitate a greater degree of economic activity across the fringes of the national wilderness, alongside the application of a lighter regulatory touch concerning the management regime for such areas. Wilderness ideals also cohabit uneasily with cultural heritage considerations within particular sites, where the abandonment and rewilding of land is largely antithetical to longstanding agrarian traditions. The long-term future of wilderness management in Estonia accordingly depends upon the ability of the national authorities to balance these various interests. In the meantime, however, Estonia remains a jurisdiction in which wilderness enthusiasts can not only observe significant expanses of pristine nature, but also the clear and pragmatic application of legal principles to facilitate its ongoing protection.

# 14

# Wilderness protection in Finland

KAI KOKKO AND MARKKU OKSANEN

## 1 Introduction[1]

Originally, *erämaa*, the modern Finnish word for 'wilderness', referred to a hunting area located outside farming villages.[2] Yet, historically, farming was not the only basis of land ownership within and between villages in Northern Finland (Lapland). A varied and vague ownership terminology was used to define the access of local and other people to resources in hunting, fishing and reindeer husbandry.[3] In its traditional and etymological sense, 'wilderness' denotes an area that sustains and provides natural resources for human use and consumption. The specific type of North European subsistence economy associated with such areas has been called *erätalous* in Finnish historiography. Accordingly, in the traditional Finnish understanding of nature – as well as that of the Sámi – there is no clear distinction divide between natural and cultural landscapes; an area that others call 'wilderness' may be a cultural landscape for the Sámi.[4]

1 The chapter for this book has been written as background material for the projects 'Development of the Natural Resource Research Cluster system' (LUODE) and 'Constraints and Opportunities of Assisted Dispersal of Plants in Climate Change Adaptation – Biological, Legal and Ethical Analyses' (CO-ADAPT). The first project was funded by the ERDF and the second by the Academy of Finland. In addition, Markku Oksanen was supported by the Academy of Finland (grant no. 218139). The chapter has been proofread by Richard Foley and Richard Caddell.

2 M. Rapola, 'Suomen kielen sanat erä ja erämaa', *Virittäjä*, 40 (1936), 106–121, at 117; J.-P. Taavitsainen, 'Wide-range Hunting and Swidden Cultivation as Prerequisites of Iron Age Colonization in Finland', *Suomen antropologi*, 12 (1987), 213–233.

3 See K. Korpijaakko, *Saamelaisten oikeusasemasta Ruotsi-Suomessa*, (Mänttä: Lakimiesliiton kustannus, 1989), at 589. On ownership, see V. Hyvönen, *Kiinteistönmuodostamisoikeus I. Yleiset opit* (Jyväskylä: KY Veikko O. Hyvönen & CO, 1998), 82–104; and J. Sillanpää, 'Ylä-Lapin isojaot ja saamelaisten maaoikeudet', *Maanmittaus*, 81(2006), 49–79, at 76.

4 P. Magga, *Rakennuksia, kotasijoja, muistoja*, Suomen ympäristö 34/2007 (Rovaniemi: Lapin ympäristökeskus, 2007).

The recent discussion in Finland about wilderness led to harmonization of the classification of Finnish nature protection areas with the IUCN Protected Areas Categories System, which emphasizes wilderness as a place free from human influence. This is a new idea of wilderness in the Finnish context which, alongside concerns over the environmental vulnerability of such areas, clearly clashes with the much older concept of *erämaa* (and its equivalents in Sámi culture). In this chapter, we examine how these different conceptions of and approaches to wilderness areas and their protection have been reconciled in the Finnish legislation.

In the section that follows, we shed light on the historical meaning of wilderness in Finnish culture and society (Section 2). In Section 3 we focus on the meaning of the term 'wilderness' in the Finnish legal context and in current national legislation, drawing on relevant case law. Next, we analyse policy instruments and provisions that aim to protect wilderness (Section 4). Based on this analysis, we assess the practical implementation, supervision and enforcement of the current instruments for wilderness protection (Section 5). Subsequently, we reflect on potential future developments in the legal protection of Finnish wilderness areas (Section 6) and elaborate insights into directions for future research and policy (Section 7).

## 2 Wilderness in Finnish culture and society

The modern English notion of wilderness has no straightforward translation in Finnish.[5] The conventional translation is *erämaa*, although in current legal terminology, as well as in everyday parlance, *luonto* (*nature* or *the natural world* in English) is widely used. Like *wilderness, erämaa* intertwines many historical elements and layers, some of which are still very much alive.[6]

Etymologically, *wilderness* (Middle English *wildern, wild*, from Old English *wilddeoren* 'of wild beasts') and *erämaa* are different, although they both connote the presence of untamed animals. *Erämaa* is a compound expression consisting of two words, *erä* 'share' and *maa* 'land, earth'. In this context, *erä* denotes one's share of the total catch to be had and *maa* denotes the land or earth. *Erämaa* refers to an uninhabited area for hunting, fishing, berry-picking and, in some regions, burn-beating for cultivation. In short, *erämaa* is a place in which to acquire one's share of

[5] The same applies in the case of the Sámi languages.

[6] Y. Haila, '"Wilderness" and the Multiple Layers of Environmental Thought', *Environment and History*, 3 (1997), 129–147.

nature's bounty.[7] The landscape in wilderness areas includes forests, lakes, swamps, fells and valleys.

In the oral mythology and vernacular (non-Christian or syncretistic) religion of the Baltic-Finnic peoples, the natural world was seen as crowded with spirits. Game animals were not just resources but beings with souls and guardian gods, examples of the latter being *Ahti* for fish and *Tapio* for forest animals.[8] Indeed, respect for guardian gods is still expressed in the saying 'go and ask one's prey' (*eränkäynti, pyynti*), a euphemism for hunting or making a catch. These folkloric, religious and economic threads are embodied in the poem of the *Kalevala* (1837), the Finnish national epic:[9]

| | |
|---|---|
| Be kind, forest, soften, wilds | miesty, metsä, kostu, korpi |
| and bend, precious tapio; | taivu, ainoinen tapio! |
| bring a man to the islet | saata miestä saarekselle, |
| lead him to that mound | sille kummulle kuleta, |
| where a catch is to be made | jost' on saalis saatavana, |
| and a prey-task carried out! | erän toimi tuotavana! |

Hunting not only involved ceremonies and rituals but also the inter-community regulation of the resource base. *Erämaa* is not an unmanaged open-access resource base; resource use was governed by customary law within and between historical villages.[10] Customary law not only governed entitlements to resources but also when, where and how such resources could be used and the responsibilities attendant thereto. Also important was the concept of sacredness (*pyhä*), which had not only a religious but also an economic meaning: the use of resources in particular places defined as 'sacred' was restricted for neighbouring communities.[11]

Originally, wilderness areas were not owned in a formal sense;[12] the specific rules of ownership, such as rules governing access, usufruct and exclusion, were parts of customary, and often unwritten, law. Customary law has since evolved to some extent as a result of the expansion of monarchic and, later, state power; partly it has survived and is still exemplified in the form of everyman's rights (*jokamiehenoikeudet*). The

[7] Rapola, 'Suomen kielen sanat erä ja erämaa', *supra* note 2.

[8] A.-L. Siikala, *Itämerensuomalaisten mytologia* (Helsinki: SKS, 2012), at 368 ff.

[9] Keith Bosley (trans.), 'Be Kind, Forest, Soften, Wilds...', in Elias Lönnrot (ed.), *The Kalevala* (Oxford: Oxford University Press, 1989) (no page numbering).

[10] Cf. E. Ostrom, *Governing the Commons* (Cambridge: Cambridge University Press, 1990).

[11] V. Anttonen, *Uskontotieteen maastot ja kartat* (Helsinki: SKS, 2010), at 160–165; see also Siikala, *Itämerensuomalaisten mytologia, supra* note 8.

[12] See Ostrom, *Governing the Commons, supra* note 10, at 51.

continued validity of the system of everyman's rights still precludes imposing entry fees for access to wilderness areas. The Swedish King Gustav I Vasa declared in 1542 that uninhabited regions, including forests, belong to God, the King and the Swedish Crown (*silva regalis*). The claims of the Crown regarding forests did not, however, extend to Finnish Lapland.[13] At that time Lapland was very sparsely populated and the main means of subsistence for the Sámi and the Finns were reindeer husbandry, fishing, hunting and gathering.

Lapland represented both a frontier to and the aggregation of the Swedish (-Finnish) and Sámi economies. The Sámi community did not constitute a state and the geopolitical situation of Sámi lands remained unresolved until the mid-eighteenth century, as Sweden, Denmark-Norway and Russia each had territorial claims in the region. For the Sámi people of 'the cap of the North', the borderless region above the Arctic Circle provided freedom to move but also the potential risk of having to pay levies to three rival governments.[14]

The border regions between Norway and Sweden in Lapland were settled for the first time in 1751. In 1809 the borders between Sweden and Russia were redrawn when Sweden lost its eastern province to Russia and the Russian autonomous Grand Duchy of Finland was created. Even today, King Vasa's *silva regalis* forms the basis for state ownership of the uninhabited wilderness areas throughout Finland. However, in Lapland, and especially in the Sámi Homeland, state ownership is a matter of continuing national debate.[15] Legal historical studies by Korpijaakko-Labba emphasize that Sámi land rights were never transferred to the Finnish state by statutory enactment or court decisions.[16] With the passage of the Act on Wilderness Reserves (hereinafter AWR)[17] in 1991, all the wilderness areas mentioned in the Act became established as state property.

Finland became independent in 1917. As elsewhere in Europe, the elite in Finland were fervently nationalistic during the nineteenth and

[13] Hyvönen, *Kiinteistönmuodostamisoikeus I*, *supra* note 3, at 85.

[14] H. Hyvärinen, *Saamelainen kiinteistö oikeudessamme*. Saamelaisvaltuuskunnan julkaisuja No 1 (Helsinki: Komiteanmietintö 30, 1979), at 9; A. Aikio, 'Suomen saamelaisten historiallinen erilliskehys', in K. Kokko (ed.), *Kysymyksiä saamelaisten oikeusasemasta*, (Rovaniemi: Lapin yliopiston oikeustieteellisiä julkaisuja B 30, 2010), 186–198, at 189.

[15] See, e.g., the Statement of the Constitutional Law Committee of the Finnish Parliament (PeVL 29/2004).

[16] K. Korpijaakko-Labba, 'Valtionmaat Suomen kiinteistöjärjestelmässä – erityisesti silmällä pitäen saamelaisten maaoikeusasiaa', *Oikeustiede-Jurisprudentia*, XXXVI (2003), 299–350, at 349.

[17] AWR 62/1991.

the early twentieth centuries. This ideology, known as romantic nationalism, was strongly embodied in the arts, in literature (Topelius, Kivi, Aho, Leino), landscape painting (Gallen-Kallela, Halonen, Edefelt), symphonic music (Sibelius, Järnefelt), architecture (Saarinen, Geselius, Lindgren, Sonck) and even in photography (Inha) and popular printed landscape imagery.[18] A common theme was to create a Finnish national identity through artistic narratives of Finnish nature and its inhabitants.[19] Consequently, certain places – both cultivated and uncultivated landscapes – were held in high esteem as national landscapes. According to the art historian Reitala, certain artists criticized commercial logging and sought to save old-growth forests through their paintings. Moreover, artists were well aware of the mythological and spiritualist dimensions of nature as expressed in the *Kalevala*.[20]

Romantic nationalism played an important role in the creation of nature protection legislation and, in some cases, its results; works of art created in the period have provided a central basis for later protection policies in some areas (e.g., Koli National Park, the Huopanankoski rapids). In 1923, the first Nature Conservation Act[21] was passed, the preparatory works for which highlighted the need to preserve the monuments representing nature for the benefit of science and the education of future generations.[22] According to parliamentary documents, strict nature reserves have a primarily scientific purpose and national parks 'are to be fun and a source of enjoyment for all the friends of free nature, sightseers and artists and all who admire land, air, water and animals'.[23]

The present Nature Conservation Act (hereinafter NCA)[24] reflects the same ideology: strict nature reserves are mainly protected for scientific purposes and national parks are fairly open outdoor areas. National parks are established only in state-owned areas, while smaller strict nature reserves may also be set up on privately owned land. However, the Natura 2000 protection provided for by the Act, implementing the

[18] M. Häyrynen, 'The Kaleidoscopic View: The Finnish National Landscape Imagery', *National Identities*, 2 (2000), 5–19, at 8.

[19] Haila, '"Wilderness" and the Multiple Layers of Environmental Thought', *supra* note 6.

[20] A. Reitala, 'Metsä suomalaisessa kuvataiteessa', *Silva Fennica*, 21(1987), 436–444, at 441–442.

[21] The old Nature Conservation Act (luonnonsuojelulaki) 71/1923.

[22] Government Proposal 24/1922.

[23] Report of the Legal Affairs and Commerce Committee of Parliament No 4/1922.

[24] NCA 1096/1996.

Habitats Directive,[25] brings in an ecological approach focused on species and habitats, as explained later in this chapter. The new aims of the Act are to (1) maintain biological diversity and to (2) promote the sustainable use of natural resources and the natural environment. Both objectives are based on the Convention on Biological Diversity 1992. The other aims enumerated in the Act – (3) to conserve the beauty and scenic values of nature, (4) to promote awareness and general interest in nature and (5) to promote scientific research – are grounded in the cultural and legal history of nature protection in Finland.

## 3 Wilderness in Finnish legislation

### *3.1 Wilderness as a legal concept*

In Finnish legislation, wilderness is not simply a category of protected area but also encompasses people and nature-based use. The twelve wilderness reserves listed in Section 3 of the AWR fall under this conventional idea. According to Section 1(1) of the Act, the reserves have been established to preserve the wilderness character (*erämaaluonne*) of the areas, to safeguard Sámi culture and natural sources of livelihood and to improve multiple use of nature and the prerequisites for such use.[26] This characterization also differentiates the Act from many other 'wilderness acts' in the world. In the English translation of the Act, provided by the Ministry of the Environment, the wording 'to preserve wild areas' is inaccurate. We propose the following translation: the wilderness areas are established in order 'to preserve the wilderness character of the areas'.

The meaning of 'wilderness character' is ambiguous. It is not defined in the legislation and neither do the preparatory documents for the Act provide full clarity on its projected meaning. What is being preserved? The Government Bill on which the Act was based states that one aim of the Act was, as far as possible, to maintain in an unaltered state the most original and typical wilderness nature to be found in Lapland.[27] In the absence of a clear definition, this description may be understood as encompassing the three main wilderness qualities of naturalness, absence of infrastructure and size described in Chapter 1, especially in light of the

[25] Council Directive 92/43/EEC of 21 May 1992 on the conservation of natural habitats and of wild fauna and flora, *OJ* 1992 No. L 206, 22 July 1992. See also Directive 2009/147/EC of the European Parliament and of the Council of 30 November 2009 on the conservation of wild birds (codified version), *OJ* 2009 No. L 20, 26 January 2009.

[26] Unofficial translation by the authors.

[27] Government Proposal 42/1990, detailed explanation of Section 1.

present discussion over the IUCN classification. Yet, 'wilderness character' may equally well refer to natural features or only the protected species of wild flora and fauna and their habitats within these wilderness areas. At a minimum, the latter, narrow, interpretation can be easily defended, because most of each of the wilderness reserves has been designated as Natura 2000 sites under the EU Habitats Directive. Moreover, Finland has ratified the Convention on Biological Diversity and the Bern Convention 1979. The Natura 2000 network and the Bern Convention in particular adopt a strong species-oriented approach.[28] However, biodiversity protection is not mentioned in the AWR, which makes it questionable whether biodiversity-based protection should give meaning to the term 'wilderness character' in the AWR.

The objectives of the AWR include the safeguarding of Sámi culture. The basis of Sámi culture lies in its livelihoods – reindeer herding, fishing and hunting – which are also protected under Section 17.3 of the Finnish Constitution. Yet, the term 'natural source of livelihood' also refers to the means by which other local people earn their living; for example, they may also herd reindeer. Thus, safeguarding natural sources of livelihood in a wilderness area can protect not only Sámi interests, but also other local nature-based economic activities.

In view of these objectives of the AWR, it is particularly interesting to observe that reindeer herding that requires more lichen than the pastures produce has been seen as a major threat to wilderness characteristics.[29] This argument entails two presumptions: first, that wilderness character is indeed associated with ecological factors (possibly even naturalness) and, second, that effective wilderness protection may depend on finding the right balance between ecological considerations and the use of natural sources of livelihood. From a biodiversity perspective, it has been observed that the AWR has not been successful in balancing intensive reindeer herding and biodiversity protection in wilderness areas. Indeed, it has been proposed that activities that significantly decrease the ecological value of a Natura 2000 site should be prohibited.[30] This policy has

[28] See Chapters 7 and 8. In the specific context of Finland, see also the Decree on the conservation of European wildlife and natural habitats, *Convention in Finnish Treaty Series*, SopS 29/1986.

[29] T. Helle, 'Luonnollista vai ihmistoimintaa: poron laidunnusvaikutukset luonnonsuojelu- ja erämaa-alueilla', in J. Saarinen (ed.), *Erämaapolitiikka* (Rovaniemi: Metla, 2002), 57–65, at 58–63.

[30] J. Similä, A. Raunio, M. Hildén and S. Anttila, *Luonnonsuojelulainsäädännön arviointi*. Suomen ympäristö 27/2010 (Helsinki: Edita, 2010), at 95–96.

been implemented, and applies to the Natura 2000 sites (including wilderness reserves with Natura 2000 status).[31]

Wilderness reserves have also been established to enhance the relationship between nature and recreation,[32] for example, by allowing public access to wilderness areas to pick berries. Moreover, the state enterprise the *Metsähallitus* (the former National Board of Forestry) issues permits for fishing or hunting in reserves.

To conclude, it can be stated that the four original objectives for the establishment of the Finnish wilderness reserves aim to balance the protection of wilderness characteristics with human use of nature as a source of livelihood or based on Sámi culture. In practice, this means that a compromise must be brokered between land uses by local and other people. Any such balancing rests on the Finnish concept of wilderness: nature-based use[33] is an integral part of wilderness as long as it does not harm the wilderness characteristics of the reserves.[34] Consequently, the AWR does not relate exclusively to the protection of the three main wilderness *qualities* as defined in Chapter 1 of this book.

Another important consideration here is that there are areas in Finland that may be considered wilderness as defined in Chapter 1 of this book, but have not been designated as wilderness reserves under the AWR, for instance because safeguarding subsistence lifestyles was not among the primary aims of protecting these areas. Therefore, to fully understand the protection of wilderness as defined in this book, we must also examine other legal instruments addressing nature protection in Finland. However, before discussing these in more detail, we will first briefly consider the question of the influence that IUCN classification may have on the traditional Finnish conception of wilderness reserves.

[31] Government Proposal to amend the Nature Conservation Act, 77/2014.

[32] Government Proposal 42/1990, detailed explanation of Section 1, *supra* note 27 and Ministry of the Environment and Metsähallitus, *IUCN: n suojelualueluokituksen soveltaminen Suomessa* (Application of the IUCN classification of the protection areas in Finland), 11 October 2013, YM6/5711/2013 at 39.

[33] A relevant distinction is also the difference between nature-based uses by local people and recreational uses by others, although in public discussions they are often indistinguishable. J. Valkonen, 'Erämaa, paikallisuus, hallinta', in Saarinen (ed.), *Erämaapolitiikka, supra* note 29, pp. 43–55, at 51–53. In fact, local people have some special rights to get permits for fishing and hunting. See the Fishing Act (FiA) 286/1982, Section 12, the new Fishing Act 379/2015, Section 10 and the Hunting Act (HA) 615/1993, Section 8.

[34] P. Veijola, 'Metsähallituksen kokemuksia erämaa-alueiden hoidosta ja suunnittelusta', in Saarinen (ed.), *Erämaapolitiikka, supra* note 29, pp. 13–20, at 16.

### 3.2 *Categories of protected areas and their wilderness qualities*

In April 2013, the Ministry of the Environment invited various stakeholders to express their views on the proposal to harmonize the classification of Finnish nature protection areas with that of the IUCN Protected Areas Categories System. In October 2013, the final guide on the application of the IUCN classification in Finland was accepted. In the guide wilderness reserves established under the AWR form the backbone of the IUCN's 'wilderness' category in Finland. Lemmenjoki National Park also falls into this category. In addition, areas over 1,000 hectares subject to formal protection other than national parks and strict nature reserves are mainly considered to be IUCN wilderness areas. Furthermore, areas over 1,000 hectares that currently belong to the governmental nature conservation programme, but which have not yet been established as nature protection areas, are also considered to belong to this category.[35] For example, according to the proposal even the network of Old-growth Forest Reserves, established under the old Nature Conservation Act and Mire Conservation Reserves, would belong within the IUCN's category of 'wilderness', although both reserves are based only on a Government decision in principle and will not achieve their final legal status until they are implemented as nature protection areas under the NCA.

#### Wilderness reserves

There are twelve officially designated wilderness areas in Finland:

(1) Northwest Lapland, 221,000 hectares in the municipality of Enontekiö;
(2) Tartovaara wilderness area, 67,000 hectares in the municipality of Enontekiö;
(3) Pöyrisjärvi wilderness area, 128,000 hectares in the municipality of Enontekiö;
(4) Muotkatunturi wilderness area, 157,000 hectares in the municipalities of Utsjoki and Inari;
(5) Paistunturi wilderness area, 157,000 hectares in the municipalities of Utsjoki and Inari;
(6) Kaldoaivi wilderness area, 294,000 hectares in the municipalities of Utsjoki and Inari;

[35] Ministry of the Environment and Metsähallitus, *supra* note 32, at 34, 38 and 39. For the IUCN definition of 'wilderness', see Chapter 1.

(7) Vätskäri wilderness area, 155,000 hectares in the municipality of Inari;
(8) Tsarmituntuturi wilderness area, 15,000 hectares in the municipality of Inari;
(9) Hammastunturi wilderness area, 182,000 hectares in the municipalities of Inari, Sodankylä and Kittilä;
(10) Pulju wilderness area, 61,000 hectares in the municipalities of Enontekiö and Kittilä;
(11) Kemihaara wilderness area, 31,000 hectares in the municipality of Savukoski; and
(12) Tuntsa wilderness area, 21,000 hectares in the municipalities of Salla and Savukoski.

These reserves are clearly wilderness areas within the meaning of the IUCN system and Chapter 1 of this book as they are all relatively large areas, which have a high degree of naturalness and have no roads or permanent structures.[36]

### National parks and strict nature reserves

The establishment of a national park and its management objectives require an Act of Parliament.[37] A national park can only be established on state-owned land that is 1,000 hectares in size or larger and the area should hold general interest as a natural attraction or raise general awareness of, or interest in, nature. Establishing a strict nature reserve also requires an Act if the site is at least 1,000 hectares in size; otherwise it is established by a Decree. A strict nature reserve can only be established on state-owned land and it should have significance as a location for safeguarding undisturbed natural development or as a place for scientific research or education.[38]

These criteria make it possible that national parks and natural reserves include wilderness areas; however, the criterion of a 'large size' is not a strict requirement for these areas. Consequently, the smallest national parks and strict nature reserves do not satisfy the size criterion for wilderness. These smaller areas may also fail to dovetail with the Finnish concept of wilderness outlined above, as the prospects for using such areas for hunting or other nature-based livelihoods is very limited because of their size.

[36] See the area descriptions in Government Proposal 42/1990, *supra* note 27 and the explanation of Section 3.
[37] NCA, Section 11.
[38] NCA, Section 12.

In further examining specific areas, Lemmenjoki National Park is an important example. This national park was established in 1956 and enlarged in 1971 and 1982 by Acts of Parliament. The total area now covers 285,790 hectares in the municipalities of Inari and Kittilä. According to the regulations on the national park, the area is a public attraction in which the wilderness of Lapland is protected.[39] Although some fairly small areas of the Lemmenjoki National Park are still in use for small-scale gold mining, most parts of the park meet the wilderness area criteria. However, after accepting one national park in the category of wilderness area, as the Ministry of the Environment proposes, one could ask what should be decided in respect of the country's other national parks and nature reserves, for instance the largest national park, Urho Kekkonen (254,000 hectares). For wilderness protection, one of the most important strict nature reserves is Kevo (71,000 hectares).[40] These parks and reserves include areas with almost no influence from modern human society and have relatively high wilderness qualities. Furthermore, wilderness protection is sometimes explicitly acknowledged as a management objective. For example, one of the specific purposes of Urho Kekkonen National Park, a large area located in several municipalities (Savukoski, Sodankylä and Inari) is wilderness protection.

### Other nature reserves

In the NCA, the term 'other nature reserves' refers to areas other than national parks or strict nature reserves.[41] The above-mentioned guide of the Ministry of the Environment and the Metsähallitus also places other nature reserves over 1,000 hectares in the IUCN category of wilderness area. Moreover, the guide leaves some space for a case-by-case interpretation. It would be problematic if too strict hectare limits were set for such areas. Quite often, these state-owned protected areas are too small to qualify as wilderness areas without due consideration of local conditions. The establishment of other nature reserves and the objectives of doing so on state-owned land must be set out in a government decree or, if the area is 100 hectares or smaller, a decree of the Ministry of the Environment.[42] Other nature reserves may also be established on privately owned land. However, they are seldom large enough to constitute wilderness reserves. They may nevertheless fulfil the above-mentioned requirements

[39] Decision 1021/623/2009 of Metsähallitus, 18 March 2009, at 2.
[40] Government Proposal 42/1990, *supra* note 27.
[41] NCA, Sections 11 and 12.
[42] NCA, Section 17.1.

concerning native species, ecosystem, free-functioning natural processes and absence of roads.

### Nature conservation programme sites

The state uses nature conservation programmes to protect significant nature values. Such programmes were the main basis on which new nature conservation reserves were selected from the mid-1970s to the mid-1990s. Primarily, the areas are established as part of state nature reserves or national parks by an Act or decree and managed by the *Metsähallitus*. Many of the 'other nature reserves' (see above) have also been established on private land. The Finnish Government has issued decisions in principle on the programmes.[43] Finland has six national nature conservation programmes that cover the following types of ecosystems:

- Mires, set up in 1978 and 1981 and covering 650,000 hectares;
- Waterfowl habitats, set up in 1982 and covering 74,750 hectares;
- Eskers, set up in 1984 and covering 97,000 hectares;
- Herb-rich forests, set up in 1989 and covering 5,300 hectares;
- Shore areas, set up in 1989 and 1990 and covering 134,000 hectares; and
- Old-growth forests, set up in 1993, 2005 and 2006 and covering 320,000 hectares.[44]

The Mire Conservation Programme and the Programme for the Protection of Old-Growth Forests are central to wilderness protection. The mire area Sammuttijänkä-Vaijoenjänkä (52,000 hectares) and the old-growth forest area of Korouoma (26,000 hectares) are among the best examples of wilderness protection. These reserves include areas which show almost no influences of modern human society and have relatively high wilderness qualities. The areas may also be protected under the Ramsar Convention on Wetlands[45] and/or as part of the Natura 2000 network.

A supplementary programme has also been established to improve the state of mires and their protection, especially in Southern Finland. It

[43] Ministry of the Environment, *Nature conservation programmes*, 30 July 2013, and L. Suvantola and J. Similä, *Luonnonsuojeluoikeus* (Helsinki: Edita, 2011), at 52.

[44] *Ibid.*, Ministry of the Environment, *Nature Conservation Programmes*; Suvantola and Similä *Luonnonsuojeluoikeus*, at 52–55.

[45] Convention on Wetlands of International Importance especially as Waterfowl Habitat (Ramsar Convention), Ramsar (Iran), 2 February 1971, UN Treaty Series No. 14583, as amended by the Paris Protocol, 3 December 1982, and Regina Amendments, 28 May 1987. See the Introductory Decree and the *Convention in Finnish Treaty Series*, SopS 3/1976.

complements the basic programme for mire conservation from 1979 and 1981. Most of the programme areas (ninety-nine per cent) were already established nature conservation areas or state-owned in 2010.[46]

As a consequence of commercial forestry and other historical forms of use, old forests are rare and pristine forests non-existent. Most of the programme areas lie in Northern and Eastern Finland and, again, ninety-nine per cent of these areas were established nature conservation areas or state-owned in 2010.[47]

In addition to the comprehensive nature conservation programmes based on the NCA, the Government has initiated a variety of action plans to secure the diversity of nature. The most important of these in the light of wilderness protection is the Forest Biodiversity Programme for Southern Finland (METSO).[48]

#### Commercial forests

Commercial forests are not wilderness areas according to the IUCN categorization; however, they are not irrelevant for protection of wild nature. Private owners may protect their forests in a voluntary and unofficial capacity. In addition, commercial forests are subject to some habitat protection requirements,[49] and may function as corridors to connect wilderness areas for certain species. Furthermore, certain areas may exhibit strong potential to be restored to a state with relatively high wilderness qualities ('new wilderness').

## 4 Legal protection of wilderness in Finland

### *4.1 The regime applicable to wilderness reserves*

The AWR pertains to areas controlled by the Metsähallitus and owned by the state. The Metsähallitus manages the areas in accordance with a plan, which it creates and submits to the Ministry of the Environment for approval. During the preparation of the plan, the Sámi Parliament should be heard on matters relating to the Sámi Homeland and some of the decisions in the plan may be challenged by the Parliament in court.[50] The plan provides guidelines on how to manage each reserve for the different

46 Suvantola and Similä, *Luonnonsuojeluoikeus, supra* note 43, at 52.
47 *Ibid.*, at 55.
48 www.metsonpolku.fi/en/METSO_programme/index.php.
49 Forest Act 1093/1996, Section 10.
50 The Supreme Administrative Court, KHO 11 March 2003/516; Veijola, 'Metsähallituksen kokemuksia erämaa-alueiden hoidosta ja suunnittelusta', *supra* note 34, at 18.

nature-based livelihoods in the area and in accordance with the objectives of the Act. Stricter regulation on the pursuit of livelihoods is set out in special legislation.[51] The plan also provides clear principles for cross-country and snowmobile traffic, which are regulated by the Cross-country Traffic Act.[52] Building projects in shore areas of wilderness reserves are not allowed, unless a contrary decision is obtained and the management and use plan is confirmed by the Ministry.[53] Thus, in a legal sense, the plan is more than a mere guide.

Forestry is allowed only in limited parts of the reserves and only in accordance with special natural resource planning by the Metsähallitus.[54] Critics, however, have observed that the existing wilderness reserves include only two extensive forest areas, Kessi and Hammastunturi, and that plans called for harvesting 58,000 hectares in these areas according to the natural resource planning.[55] In 2006, negotiations between WWF and the Metsähallitus resulted in an agreement to complement the protection of old-growth forests in Northern Finland. In 2006, the Metsähallitus amended its plans and in practice protected an additional 20,000 hectares of state forests in the wilderness reserves of Vätskäri and Hammastunturi.[56]

Permits from the Government are required for mining, road construction, selling or leasing use-rights or renting land in these areas. According to a decision of the Supreme Administrative Court,[57] the Ministry of the Environment is the competent authority in granting permission for mining in wilderness reserves but it must take into account various aspects and conditions in its decision-making process, since the activity

[51] See, e.g., The FiA, the HA, *supra* note 33, and the Reindeer Husbandry Act (RHA) (poronhoitolaki) 848/1990.

[52] CCTA (maastoliikennelaki) 1710/1995.

[53] Land Use and Building Act (LBA) (maankäyttö ja rakennuslaki) 132/1999, Section 172 and the Supreme Administrative Court, KHO:2004:18.

[54] See Veijola, 'Metsähallituksen kokemuksia erämaa-alueiden hoidosta ja suunnittelusta', *supra* note 34, at 18; and www.metsa.fi/sivustot/metsa/en/naturalresources/planning methods/Naturalresourceplanning/Sivut/NaturalResourcePlanning.aspx.

[55] A. Lehtinen, 'Kenen maa?', in Saarinen (ed.), *Erämaapolitiikka, supra* note 29, pp. 21–41, at 29.

[56] Metsähallitus, 'WWF and Metsähallitus: Old-growth Forest Dispute Settled through Extended Protection in Northern Finland', press release of 22 February 2006, and Metsähallitus, 'Metsähallitus tarkisti Ylä-Lapin luonnonvarasuunnitelmaa', Bulletin of 1 November 2006. For another conflict on forest felling in 2007, which resulted in an agreement to protect the forest at least for the next twenty years, see Metsähallitus, *Metsähallitus ja Inarin paliskunnat sopivat porolaitumista*, Bulletin of 10 December 2010.

[57] The Supreme Administrative Court KHO:2004:23.

for which a permit is applied always alters the wilderness character of the reserve.[58] Permanent roads are usually not allowed,[59] but the Government may grant a permit for the construction of a permanent road that clearly serves the public good or provides a natural source of income in the area.[60] Some of the land areas inside a wilderness reserve may be under private ownership. If a private owner had a right to build a road before the AWR was enacted (e.g., in the form of an easement or a usufruct or as part of a full private property right on the land), this right is usually respected. In other situations, the Government can give permission for the state to expropriate the right to a permanent road, and sometimes, upon a special request by the private land owner, the private ownership over the area if the road damages the wilderness character of the area.[61]

### *4.2 The regimes applicable to national parks, strict nature reserves and Natura 2000 sites*

Any activity altering the natural surroundings within a national park or strict nature reserve, for instance the building of roads, extraction of sand and stone materials and minerals and the construction of buildings, is prohibited.[62] This prohibition also applies to nature conservation areas, which are listed as wilderness reserves according to the IUCN categorization. There are exceptions, however: for example, in national parks the building of roads is allowed when it is necessary for park maintenance and the road does not jeopardize the purpose for which the park has been established. It is also possible to obtain permits for geological surveys and prospecting provided that the conservation objectives of the site are not endangered.[63]

In addition, the Natura 2000 regime may provide a certain level of wilderness protection and, as explained above, natural areas may fall under two or even more protected area regimes. For instance, all Finnish wilderness reserves belong to the Natura 2000 network. As explained further in Chapter 8, the core element of the Natura 2000 regime in respect of plans and project is laid down in Article 6(3) of the Habitats Directive: if a project has a significant adverse effect on the

[58] Government Proposal 42/1990, *supra* note 27, especially detailed explanation of Section 6.
[59] AWR, Section 5.1.
[60] AWR, Section 5.2.
[61] See the AWR, Sections 5.3 and 8.1, Government Proposal 42/1990, *supra* note 27, and the Supreme Court, KKO:2004:125.
[62] NCA, Section 13.
[63] NCA, Sections 14 and 15.

Natura 2000 values of the site, the developer should conduct an appropriate assessment.[64] This assessment of impacts on a Natura 2000 area can also be carried out as part of the wider Environmental Impact Assessment (EIA) procedure.[65]

The Natura 2000 assessment may include public participation, if appropriate, as provided in Article 6(3) of the Habitats Directive. Section 65 of the NCA aims to implement the Article 6(3) requirements, but it is silent on the public participation. However, in practice permit procedures under other legislation usually require public participation, albeit originally considered for other purposes. If an EIA is prepared, two phases of public participation must always be conducted in accordance with the Finnish EIA Act: the first phase relates to an assessment programme (EIA programme) for environmental impacts at the beginning of the process; the second relates to an assessment report (EIA report, or statement) at the end of the assessment procedure. The assessment is to be carried out before any decisions are made.[66]

No authority may grant a permit for the implementation of a project if the assessment procedure or the requested opinion indicates that the project may or will have a significant adverse impact on ecological values within the Natura 2000 site.[67] If significant adverse impacts can be demonstrated, the public authority cannot grant a permit for the project without an exception granted by the Government and possible compensation measures. The requirements for such an exception are strict and must respect Article 6(4) of the Habitats Directive.[68] Consequently, any project in a wilderness reserve may require two different exceptions: one engaging specific wilderness protection provisions and a second derived from the Natura 2000 protection provisions.

Although acquiring Natura 2000 status and the protection under Article 6(3) of the Habitats Directive and Section 66.1 of the NCA significantly[69]

[64] On interpretation in practice, see for example the Supreme Administrative Court, KHO: 2013:102.

[65] NCA, Section 65.1.

[66] Act on Environmental Impact Assessment Procedure (EIA Act) 468/1994, Chapter 2 and especially Sections 7 and 13.

[67] See the NCA, Section 66.1. On the interpretation in practice, see, for example, K. Kokko. 'Weighing Environmental Information and Its Sources in Legal Decision Making', in L. Gippert and C. Zettenberg (eds.), *Miljörättsliga perspektiv och tankevändor* (Uppsala: Iustus Förlag, 2013), 285–317, at 311–315.

[68] NCA, Sections 66.2 and 66.3 and 69 and the Habitat Directive (92/43/EEC), *supra* note 25, Art. 6.

[69] NCA, Sections 64a, 65a, 65b and 65c.

strengthen the level of protection of a wilderness reserve, the particular Natura 2000 site does not necessarily cover the whole reserve. For example, about 14,400 hectares (eight per cent) of the Hammastunturi wilderness reserve is still a logging area, managed through natural resource planning. The area is not part of the Natura 2000 site in the reserve.[70]

In sum, national parks and other strict nature reserves, listed as IUCN wilderness areas, are quite strictly protected by law. Thus, any action altering the natural surroundings is prohibited in these areas, albeit subject to certain exceptions. The NCA explicitly prohibits the building of roads, the extraction of sand and stone materials and minerals or any other action that endangers the conservation purposes. In addition, passage, camping, mooring and landing, and the use of vehicles can be prohibited or restricted. However, passage that is necessary for reindeer farming is usually relatively unrestricted, even in protected areas.[71] The original idea of the AWR was that the wilderness reserves would not be used for commercial purposes, but would also not be as strictly protected as nature conservation areas.[72] After the main parts of the wilderness reserves were included in the Natura 2000 network, the legal protection of ecological values in the reserves and, indirectly also the wilderness character, has become stronger.[73]

### 4.3 Other environmental legislation and wilderness protection

The consequence of the applicability of various laws to projects in natural areas may ensure that the legal protection also 'accumulates' in respect of specific wilderness sites. For instance, mining activities in natural areas are subject not only to the provisions of the Mining Act,[74] but also those of the NCA and the AWR. Decisions made according to the old Mining Act[75] also have to respect the provisions of the NCA.[76] Thus, the special decisions mentioned above granting exceptions to wilderness or Natura 2000 protection are always required for mining projects before developers can establish mines within wilderness or Natura 2000 areas. Furthermore, lifting the legal protection accorded to national parks for

[70] Metsähallitus. *Hammastunturin erämaa-alueen hoito- ja käyttösuunnitelma* (Metsähallituksen luonnonsuojelujulkaisuja, Sarja C XX, 17.12.2012), at 11.

[71] NCA, Sections 13, 14, 15 and 18.3.

[72] See Government Proposal 42/1990, *supra* note 27.

[73] See Chapter 8.

[74] MA (kaivoslaki) 621/2011.

[75] The old MA (kaivoslaki) 503/1965.

[76] See the new MA Section 3 and the old MA Section 71.2 and the Supreme Administrative Court, KHO 26 January 2009/175.

mining purposes always requires the Parliament to pass an amendment to the Act under which the park was originally established.

Spatial planning legislation is also relevant to the legal protection of wilderness. Wilderness reserves are incorporated into regional plans, which set out the principles of land use and community structure. Areas are designated as reserved only to the extent and level of detail required by national or regional land use goals or by harmonizing the use of land in more than one municipality. Strategic environmental assessment (SEA) is carried out during the planning process.[77] In planning, special attention must also be paid to the ecological sustainability of land use and the protection of landscape and natural values. Moreover, the plans are accompanied by particular building restrictions in the form of special orders. These orders are in force in areas designated by the regional plan as recreation or protection areas, among other uses.[78] For example, the Regional Plan of Fell Lapland[79] includes both types of designated areas and wilderness reserves with the appropriate building restrictions. However, the building restrictions in regional plans are quite weak.[80]

The regional plan is quite general (1:250,000); it is used as a guideline in drawing up and amending local master plans and local detailed plans, as well as where any other measures are taken to organize land use. When developing planning measures concerning land use and deciding on their implementation, the authorities must take the regional plan into account and seek to promote its implementation. Generally speaking, the regional plan is not valid in areas with a legally binding local master plan or local detailed plan.[81] If needed in wilderness areas, local plans are drawn up providing stricter protection. The strongest aggregation of policy instruments in the context of wilderness (nature) protection is the establishment of a strict nature reserve, complemented by the appropriate map symbols and regulations in a land use plan.

Wilderness reserves and their status as Natura 2000 areas may even hinder private building projects on the shores of lakes and rivers in the vicinity of the reserves, if such developments are not based on a local master plan or a detailed plan. Having a plan for shore areas is a basic rule in Finland. Although a right to deviate from the basic rule may usually be granted in particular circumstances, the requirement that a building

77 LBA132/1999, Sections 9 and 25.4.

78 *Ibid.*, Sections 28.3, 29, 30 and 33.1.

79 Tunturi-Lapin maakuntakaava, 25 November 2009.

80 LBA, Section 33.2.

81 LBA, Section 32.

project must be guided by such a plan is stronger in closer proximity to wilderness reserves.[82]

Thus, depending on particular circumstances, the land use planning legislation, and even forestry legislation, can complement the above-mentioned wilderness protection under the AWR and NCA, although this additional protection is more or less indirect.

## 5 Practical implementation, supervision and enforcement

Wilderness reserves are under the management and control of the Metsähallitus,[83] which exercises official authority by granting permits for hunting and fishing and by acting as an enforcement body for wilderness (*erävalvoja*) with special inspectors (*erätarkastajat*). The decisions of an official authority can be appealed by the party concerned (*asianosainen*). In hunting cases, for example, 'party concerned' has sometimes been interpreted in the light of the fundamental right to the environment established under the Finnish Constitution, to include a non-governmental nature conservation organization.[84]

The Act on the Metsähallitus (hereinafter AM) makes clear that the management, use and protection of natural resources governed by the Metsähallitus in the Sámi Homeland are modified to maintain the necessary conditions for the Sámi to practice their culture.[85] To this end, the Metsähallitus uses for instance the *Akwé: Kon guidelines*. In the reindeer herding area, governance must also fulfil the obligations laid down in the Reindeer Husbandry Act.[86]

[82] LBA, Sections 72, 172 and the Supreme Administrative Court, KHO:2013:110.

[83] AWR, Section 10.

[84] See the Constitution of Finland (731/1999), Section 20, the Act on Metsähallitus (AM) (laki Metsähallituksesta) 1378/2004, Sections 6–9, 11, the Act on Wilderness Supervision of the Metsähallitus (AWM) (laki Metsähallituksen erävalvonnasta) 1157/2005, Sections 2 and 3, the Administrative Judicial Procedure Act (AJPA) (hallintolainkäyttölaki) 586/1996, Sections 4–6, for example the Supreme Administrative Court, KHO:2007:74 and K. Kokko,'Ympäristöperusoikeuden evoluutio kirjallisuuden ja erityisesti korkeimman hallinto-oikeuden vuosikirjaratkaisujen valossa', in M. Aarto and M. Vartiainen (eds.), *Oikeus kansainvälisessä maailmassa* (Helsinki: Edita, 2008), 309–341, at 339–340.

[85] AM, Section 4(2). The government has developed proposal (132/2015) on the new Act on the Metsähallitus.

[86] *Ibid.* See also Secretariat of the Convention on Biological Diversity, *Akwé: Kon Guidelines*, 2004 and Ministry of the Environment, *Akwé: Kon -ohjeet*, ympäristöhallinnon ohjeita 1/2011 (Helsinki: Edita, 2011) and Metsähallitus, *Application of Guidelines in the Management and Land Use Plan for the Hammastunturi Wilderness Area* (Natural Heritage Services, 2013).

The regional ELY centres (Centres of Economic Development, Transport and the Environment) promote and supervise nature and landscape protection and make decisions concerning protection. In national parks and strict nature reserves located in the Sámi Homeland, the conditions for the maintenance and development of Sámi culture must also be secured through the work of the centres.[87]

A decision taken by the Metsähallitus or an ELY centre can be appealed in an administrative court. A ruling made by an administrative court in respect of the provisions of the NCA can be appealed in the Supreme Administrative Court with or without permission to appeal. The Ministry of the Environment is responsible for the overall guidance and supervision of nature and landscape conservation. A decision taken by the Government or the Ministry can be appealed directly in the Supreme Administrative Court.[88]

The right of appeal usually belongs to those whose rights or interests are directly affected. In nature conservation matters other than compensation, a local authority also has the right of appeal. In particular matters, appeals may also be filed by any registered local or regional association that has the purpose of promoting nature conservation or environmental protection. A decision taken by the Government concerning the adoption of a nature conservation programme can also be appealed by landowners' and conservationists' organizations.[89]

## 6 Future challenges for wilderness protection in Finland

Because wilderness reserves and other nature protection areas are mainly located in the northerly areas of the country and sometimes at high altitudes, the flora and the fauna there are very susceptible to the effects of global climate change. Some of the species populations are the southernmost to be found and the sea constitutes an obstacle to their moving northwards. Even where an area may remain otherwise unmodified by virtue of a wilderness protection policy, the habitats are subject to change. Given the increasing effects of global warming, it is an issue for debate whether we should attempt to maintain current species populations or let ecosystems adapt to the new conditions. One specific issue is

[87] NCA Sections 6.2, 16.1 and 24.1 and Section 4 of the Act on the Sámi Parliament (laki saamelaiskäräjistä 974/1995).

[88] AWR Sections 13 and 13a (into force 1 September 2014) and NCA Sections 6.1, 61, 62.

[89] AJPA Section 6 and the NCA Section 61.3.

the acceptability of assisted migration, that is, the intentional relocation of species that are considered endangered because of global warming.

A more politically sensitive topic is whether Finland should ratify ILO Convention No. 169,[90] the legally binding international instrument to protect the rights of indigenous and tribal peoples. The Sámi are the only European people who are clearly recognized as indigenous. Thus far, political reasons relating to land rights have stalled ratification of the Convention. For the theme of this book, the key issue is what it would mean if the governance of large areas of public land currently undertaken by the Metsähallitus were to be reassigned somehow or other to the Sámi people.

The question of poaching of predators has been and will remain a subject of continuous debate due to reindeer management. The same is true of the classic overstocking problem: how many reindeer can the common pastures sustain and does reindeer herding damage wilderness areas?

Other considerations can also be significant for the future of wilderness in Finland. These are more universal in nature, relating to the reconciliation of economic activities with wilderness preservation. Examples are the above-mentioned conflicts between reindeer husbandry and timber production by the Metsähallitus.[91] The expansion of tourism, with the cross-country and snowmobile traffic it involves, windmill parks and the role of the extractive industries (mining) are quite new, emerging issues.

The Constitutional Law Committee of Parliament stated in 2004 that modern ways of practising traditional livelihoods are a part of Sámi culture.[92] Modern ways of practising nature-based livelihoods can also be divisive among different users, particularly in Northern Finland. In other parts of Finland, the situation is perhaps less sensitive where nature-based livelihoods is concerned, with the exception of coastal areas and archipelagos, where people are more dependent on primary production than those located inland near urban areas.

Finally, it should also be noted that the expansion of land use for second homes might reduce wilderness coverage. Issues relating to building second homes have been largely local and there has been much less public discussion about their environmental impacts as a whole.

90 ILO Convention No. 169, Convention concerning Indigenous and Tribal Peoples in Independent Countries (ILO No. 169), 72 *ILO Official Bull.* 59.

91 See K. Raitio, 'New Institutional Approach to Collaborative Forest Planning on Public Land: Methods for Analysis and Lessons for Policy', *Land Use Policy*, 29, (2012), 309–316.

92 See the Statement of the Constitutional Law Committee (PeVL 38/2004).

## 7 Conclusions

In recent years, Finnish governments have had a common policy objective for nature protection: to promote the conservation of biodiversity and its sustainable utilization.[93] Thus, the emphasis has been less specifically on wilderness conservation (*erämaasuojelu*). There are several reasons behind the prioritization of biodiversity and sustainable utilization. First, as it stands, the use of the Finnish term *erämaa* has proved to be confusing: commercial forests are also used as hunting grounds (as wilderness areas in the original meaning of the term), but they are not really areas for protecting wild nature. Second, there has probably also been a certain shift in policy objectives in response to the Convention on Biological Diversity 1992 and EU legislative *aquis* that became applicable to Finland upon accession to the EU in 1995. Third, the network of protected and wilderness areas is already quite large in Northern Finland and the limited financial resources available have been re-targeted to establish new protected areas mainly in Southern Finland and the Baltic Sea and its coastal archipelagos. At these locations, the human presence is very clear and the landscapes are essentially cultural landscapes, which also render a focus on biodiversity more logical than one that prioritizes wilderness.

The aim set out in Section 1 of the AWR is exceptional in Finnish nature protection legislation and differentiates the Act also from many other 'wilderness acts' throughout the world. In the English translation of the Act, provided by the Ministry of the Environment, the wording 'to preserve wild areas' is inaccurate and should be replaced with the expression 'to preserve the wilderness character of the areas'. In Finnish culture, this 'wilderness character' is not a synonym for the three main wilderness qualities as described in Chapter 1 of this book. In fact, wilderness reserves are not strict nature protection areas, not even when the majority of a reserve is protected as a Natura 2000 site. Instead, preserving a reserve's wild nature is balanced against the cultural and economic objectives for which the reserve has been established, particularly the interest of Sámi and other local people in using natural sources of livelihood.

This may also explain the international criticism of the Finnish AWR as a faux or misleading wilderness act because it does not categorically outlaw large-scale exploitation of resources (e.g., logging). This criticism

[93] See the website of the Ministry of the Environment, www.ym.fi/en-US/Nature.

may rest on a linguistic misunderstanding stemming from the inaccurate translation cited above, but may also possibly result from an unduly limited acknowledgement of the fact that the people of different countries may have different perceptions of what 'wilderness' entails. Furthermore, since a significant amount of each wilderness reserve has become protected under Natura 2000, the status of the reserves as nature protection areas has also changed. At present, the ecological values of a particular Natura 2000 site receive special protection under Sections 64a, 65 and 66 of the NCA and can thus – depending on the conservation objectives of the sites – also promote the wilderness character of reserves. In addition, as explained above, wilderness as understood internationally may well receive protection under other Finnish legal instruments for nature protection. Indeed, many old national parks and strict nature reserves qualify as wilderness areas.

Despite these clear legal options for protection of wilderness (as defined for this book) in Finland, the previous section also explains that there are considerable challenges that may limit the effectiveness of these instruments. For instance, climate change may radically influence the wilderness character of land areas and active management of wilderness areas may therefore be needed. The main threats to the wilderness character of land in Finland come from activities that form part of the global economy, such as forestry, building projects, mining and mass tourism projects, as well as wind and water energy projects. Addressing these threats requires a continuous balancing act between modern economic uses and traditional nature-based uses of wilderness areas. In this context, Sámi cultural rights in wilderness areas still need further clarification. Consequently, the Finnish Act on Wilderness Reserves clearly merits improvement to clarify the meaning of the term 'wilderness character' and to address locally the new challenges of the global world.

# 15

# Wilderness protection in Hungary

SANDOR FULOP

## 1 Introduction

As identified and discussed below, numerous legal tools in Hungary target the protection of wilderness in either a direct or indirect manner.[1] This chapter examines a number of pertinent questions, including whether the available legal tools are sufficiently interconnected to ensure effective protection of the most important wilderness areas in Hungary.[2] Attention will also be paid to the question of whether the necessary budgetary, institutional and procedural guarantees are in place to ensure their effective implementation. A decisive factor in wilderness protection is the value that social and political decision-makers attach to it. There is a lack of reliable opinion polls on this issue, but based on hundreds of practical cases and intensive interactions with the concerned professional and NGO communities, the 2008–2009 Annual Report of the Hungarian Ombudsman for Future Generations (FGO) highlights the core social attitudes:[3]

1 While system sciences are widely used in environmental and sustainable development studies, the system approach is seldom present in legal matters. In this chapter we try at least to name the major elements of the law concerning wilderness protection, together with some initial thoughts about their interrelationship and joint effect.

2 According to the most recent data (Nature Protection Bulletin, 2012), there are ten national parks in Hungary (483,078 ha), thirty-nine landscape protection districts (336,875 ha), 168 national level nature protection territories (30,701 ha) and 939 local level nature protection territories (46,138 ha), while the Natura 2,000 territories (1.44 m ha) occupy twenty-three per cent of the total territory of the country (6.195 m ha). Other forms of protection relevant from a wilderness viewpoint cover a less significant portion of the territory of the country. See earlier data for comparison in Attila Pánovics, 'Recuperation of the Protected Lands in Hungary', in Pál Bobvos (ed.), *Reformator Iuris Cooperandi, Studies for the Honour of Professor József Veres* (Szeged: Pólay Elemér Foundation, 2009), 419–431, and note 13.

3 2008–2009 Report of the Future Generations Ombudsman Office (hereafter FGO), at 136–137.

> a quite lenient practice of the environmental authorities and the social conviction that small pieces of green spots can be taken away with no harm, 'just now and just for us', lead to the gradual eradication of the remainders of wilderness in the country. This is not going to change unless our moral convictions, low level responsibility towards the protection of nature and lack of honour for the interests of our future generations change dramatically and, as concludes, the available legal tools together with necessary new, creative approaches, are used in a systemic way.

Section 2 provides an introduction to the place and relevance of the concept of wilderness in Hungarian society. Section 3 includes a general inventory of potentially relevant legal instruments for wilderness protection in Hungary, distinguishing instruments concerning nature protection law from other relevant legal tools. Based on this general inventory, Section 4 examines whether wilderness protection is a policy objective of the Hungarian government and studies in greater detail the extent of wilderness protection advanced through the current legislation. Next, Section 5 discusses issues in relation to implementation, supervision and enforcement to clarify the extent of wilderness protection in practice. Finally, Section 6 contains the most important conclusions and discusses possible ways forward to strengthen wilderness protection in Hungary, paying special attention to the potential value of the concept of intergenerational justice and environmental principles.

## 2 Relevance of wilderness in society

Nature[4] protection seldom breaks through the perception threshold of Hungarian society. The River Danube however, is amongst the rare exceptions. The Danube is a largely unconscious, yet archetypical social factor in the life of the people.[5] Almost all of the Hungarian shore of the river carries pristine nature protection and it has multiple social uses and

[4] Wilderness protection is even less prevalent in the social awareness of the Hungarian public. Hungary is a predominantly agricultural nation with no high mountains or any other places in which agricultural activities were not feasible during the previous centuries. If one conducts a Google search for wilderness, pristine nature or similar terminology, only references to foreign places, such as the Alps, several sea-shores and islands will be found.

[5] This appears to be a general feature. For instance, the key relevance of the Chattanooga River in the revitalization of the city of Chattanooga, Tennessee, is reinforced in David Eichenthal and Tracy Windeknecht, *A Restoring Prosperity Case Study: Chattanooga, Tennessee* (Washington, DC: Brookings Institution, 2008), 1–27, at 11–12 or at http://planphilly.com/design-matters/case-studies/chattanooga. See also Nancy Cook, 'Chattanooga's Makeover Secret: A River Flows through It', *National Journal*, 19 August, 2013.

meanings. Nature forms the basis for the life of our society but we do not really appreciate that. The ecological services of the Danube,[6] for instance, are widespread: regulating services (flood regulation, agricultural water regulation, underground water regulation and river bank regulation), supply services (forestry, grazing lands, game and fishery, drinking water, renewable energy, sewage sinking, industrial cooling water, transport and pebble production), sustaining functions (nature protection, including wilderness) and cultural functions (recreation, sport, tourism). Many of these functions are not widely known, yet arbitrary plans to dramatically change or exhaust the river usually raise enormous public attention and lead to political turbulence. Such was the case of the Gabcikovo-Nagymaros Dam, where the uprising of Danube protection groups played an important role in the change of the Hungarian political system in 1989.

Other issues of nature protection and wilderness trigger off smaller and shorter social reaction that nonetheless could remain for a couple of weeks in the headlines of newspapers. In the recent past, such issues included peat bog harvesting by major mining companies, larger urban sprawl and real estate speculation cases when precious green spots were endangered around major cities.[7]

As concerns the time dimension of the social recognition and commitment towards wilderness protection a sad declining curve can be observed in Hungary. Shortly after the enthusiastic years of the first part of the 1990s, the social attention and resources allocated to nature protection diminished gradually. As an outstanding feature of this loss of social and political position of nature protection we had to witness a gradual degradation of the formerly independent nature protection administrative bodies and thereafter their total merger into the environmental administration system.[8]

[6] Representatives of seventeen professions, representing these ecological services, took part in the ground breaking conference in October 2010 in the Future Generations Ombudsman Office, 2010 Annual Report of FGO, at 255–262.

[7] See their descriptions in the 2011 Annual Report of FGO, at 145 and 167–185.

[8] In 1998 a major military radio locator plan could not receive its nature protection permit because of a steady objection from the National Nature Protection Directorate, the second level administrative body in the case. As a consequence, the system of the Hungarian nature protection administration was reorganized in a way that the second instance nature protection cases were hitherto handled by the National Environmental Protection Chief Inspectorate. The radio locator received its permit within months. In the following decade the independent first instance nature protection administrative body has been eradicated too. See László Fodor, *Environmental Legal Traits of the Permitting Procedure of the Zengő*

## 3 'Wilderness' and relevant legal instruments

The term 'wilderness' is not explicitly used or defined in the domestic law of Hungary, however, there are several terms in the nature protection law that are related to it. These terms can be arranged in a line according to their severity. In reality, the notion of true wilderness and the respective forms of its handling are missing too. As a nature protection expert states: 'In our country – since not having untouched natural territories – the methodology of passive protection cannot be applied in wider circles.'[9] However, the *core zones* of *national parks* and the parts of the national parks that were designated as *biosphere reserves*[10] are very close to the wilderness as defined in Chapter 1. The national parks themselves are defined as large territories, having valuable natural traits that are not yet changed significantly.[11] While this definition reflects two of the main qualities of wilderness (large size and relatively untouched nature), the third major quality, lack of human infrastructural or other permanent facilities, does not appear in these definitions. However, as will be discussed later, this third quality receives attention in practice through the active, normative rules concerning the protection and management of national parks.

The Hungarian legislature, however, also acknowledged that the majority of the valuable natural lands are less pristine and therefore created other, less stringent protection grades. The *landscape protection district* is also rich in natural values, but mostly as a result of combined natural and man-made processes, and as such it can be more mosaic (patchwork) like. The next grade, the unqualified[12] *natural protection areas* (both on local and national scale) represent smaller territories, albeit still rich in natural values. Peat bogs and the territories of natural springs are qualified (highly protected) nature protection areas. The Hungarian natural protection law also contains detailed regulations on

*Mountain Locator Station, Sectio Juridica et Politica, Miskolc Tomus XXII* (Miskolc: Miskolc University Press 2004), at 234, and Sándor Fülöp, 'Reduction of the Environmental Administration to a Lower Rank', *Green Law*, 11/12 (1998), at 11.

9 Zoltán Rakonczay, *Nature Protection* (Budapest: Szaktudás Publishing House, 2002), at 67.

10 Decree of the Minister of Environment and Water Management No. 7/2007. (III. 27.) KvVM

11 Act LXIII of 1996 on Nature Protection, Article 28, para. 2.

12 National parks, biosphere reserves and landscape protection districts belong to the qualified, i.e., the so-called highly protected nature protection areas, while the rest of the protected territories under nature protection belong to nature protection lands with no adjective in the term.

*Natura 2000 territories* that represent a compromise between nature protection and competing social and economic interests. As such they fall outside the scope of this study.[13]

It should be emphasized that environmental and nature protection laws are not the only provisions to protect territories for their natural values. Cultural heritage laws also arrange for the protection of natural world heritage sites, while land use and construction regulations provide detailed rules on *ecological networks* and *ecological corridors* as well. As a third relevant non-environmental administrative law, the land protection branch of agricultural law should also be noted, as it advances the important notion of *valuable lands*. Other branches of agricultural law (forestry, plant protection laws, etc.) might be relevant as well.

Due to historical reasons (notably the relative abundance of natural territories[14]), the size of these territories is not yet typically emphasized in Hungarian nature protection law. Hungarian law is largely silent about the presence of human constructions as well, while this feature presents less a substantive, rather a methodological problem: the general focus of the nature protection law concerns the activities, rather than the objects and also addresses the species, not the territories.

Consequently, wilderness areas or areas with high wilderness qualities do not constitute a single category of natural areas that receive special legal protection, but are instead protected by a sophisticated web of different legal tools in Hungarian law. The coherence between nature protection law and other relevant branches of law, however, is quite questionable. To provide a better understanding and enable an evaluation of this system, a comparison of the intensity of wilderness protection within the various categories of protected areas and related nature protection laws is provided in Table 1.

Table 1 shows that there is a clear differentiation between land areas protected by nature protection laws and areas protected by other

[13] While Natura 2000 territories partly overlap with territories with higher levels of protection and the specific legal tools of Natura 2000 can also be used for the protection of these territories, the connection is only indirect. In Hungary the substantial protection of territories close to wilderness qualities ensue from these other legal titles, not from the Natura 2000 label.

[14] At the end of 2008 almost ten per cent of the territory of Hungary was under some form of protection, although the majority of this fell under national level protection (873,000 ha as compared to 39,000 ha local level protection); see Pánovics, 'Recuperation of the Protected Lands in Hungary', *supra* note 2, at 420. Other titles of protection add to this coverage, especially large Natura 2000 areas (more than twenty per cent of the territory of the country), which justifies the estimation that about a quarter of the territory of Hungary is protected because of its natural value.

Table 1 *Comparison of various forms of protection of natural lands in Hungary and their relevance for wilderness protection. Empty boxes indicate the absence of characteristic information*

| Category protected site | Naturalness | Absence of permanent infrastructure | Size | Special traits | National legal source of protection | International source of protection |
|---|---|---|---|---|---|---|
| **National parks (NP)** | Natural traits are not changed significantly | Natural systems of biodiversity shall be maintained undisturbed | Relatively large | Special important for protection of wild plants, animals, soil and water, landscape and cultural values | Act LIII of 1996 on the protection of nature | |
| **Biosphere reserves** | Highly valuable part of NPs, protected zones or landscape protection districts | Same as NPs | Same as NPs | Representing high level international scientific values | Act LIII. of 1996 Governmental Decree. No. 7/ 2007. (III. 22.) Korm. on assigning 7 biosphere reserves | UNESCO 'Man and Biosphere Program' |

| | | | | | | |
|---|---|---|---|---|---|---|
| **Core zone of NPs and other biosphere reserves** | No national level rules | Same as NPs | Same as NPs | | Same as the reserves | Guidelines UNESCO 'Man and Biosphere Program' |
| **Landscape protection districts** | Aesthetic, cultural or nature protection values of the interaction of man and nature | | Relatively large, but not always in one block | Landscape, typical to the country | Act LIII. of 1996 and also several other laws on wild species protection and hunting | |
| **Protected zones** | Close to natural status; self-regulation is typical and can be sustained without human interference | Man played no role or hardly any role or a little role in forming (except in restoring) | | | Act LIII of 1996 and many other laws (e.g., water management, forestry, fishery, mining, spatial planning, GMOs) | |

*cont.*

Table 1 (*cont.*)

| Category protected site | Naturalness | Absence of permanent infrastructure | Size | Special traits | National legal source of protection | International source of protection |
|---|---|---|---|---|---|---|
| **National ecological network** | Close to natural status | No endangerment of habitats and their connections or only with compensative measures | | National level significance | Act XXVI of 2003 on the National Spatial Plan | |
| **Ecological corridors** | Close to natural status | No endangerment of habitats and their connections or only with compensative measures | Mostly linear or discursive, mosaics or fragments, chains of habitats | | Act XXVI of 2003 on the National Spatial Plan | |
| **Sensitive natural territories** | | Nature saving agricultural activity takes place, mostly historical activity | Min. 3,000 ha | | Different legislation, e.g., Decree No. 2/2002. (III. 23.) KöM-KVM | |
| **World heritage scenes** | | | | Exceptional value; its maintenance is the interest of the whole world and the future generations | Act LXXVII of 2011 on World Heritage Act | 1972 UNESCO Convention on World Heritage |

branches of laws, such as cultural heritage, agriculture or spatial planning laws. In the former category of nature protection laws, all the three main wilderness qualities are somehow addressed. In the second category the nature protection elements are mixed with other social interests and the result is a protection of the valuable territories that is strongly based on a series of compromises. These compromises make wilderness protection under these instruments more difficult.

## 4 Legal protection of wilderness areas in Hungary

### *4.1 Wilderness protection as a policy objective*

While the several legal branches serving the aims of wilderness protection could form a horizontal system, we need to examine the vertical system, too. This involves consideration of the interplay of several levels of State decision-making, starting from the expression of the major values of the State relevant to the wilderness topic in constitutional principles and major planning documents, through acts, governmental and ministerial decrees down to the individual decisions and implementation measures performed by the competent administrative bodies. At the top level of this vertical system, wilderness protection is a policy objective of the Government of Hungary, but a careful analysis is needed to establish how far the ambitious goals set in the Parliamentary and Governmental documents have been realized in actual institutional and budgetary allocation, procedures and sanctions introduced – in essence, whether such objectives have led to discernible changes in the actual legal practice of our nature protection and related laws.

In Hungary at the central level the most important relevant plan is the National Environmental Protection Plan,[15] which has a separate Nature Protection Part with three chapters with relevance for wilderness protection. In the main text of the plan a large chapter deals with biodiversity, nature and landscape protection, including the maintenance of the protected zones, protection of biodiversity outside these zones, ex situ protection (genebanks), and integration of biodiversity protection into plans and policies of agriculture, forestry, fishery, spatial planning, energy, transport, industry, tourism, mining and commercial activities. The first attachment

[15] Parliamentary Decision No. 96/2009. (XII. 9.) Ogy., on the National Environmental Program for 2009–2014. See, e.g., point 1.2: 'Hungary still has an ecological *network* of natural or close to natural territories under different levels of protection that represent a significant biodiversity value as a specific bioregional unit.'

of the Plan covers the Hungarian Biodiversity Strategy, with detailed plans in connection with the mentioned topics, while the third attachment covers the National Nature Protection plan, with further details on the management of the protected zones. We can see in every subchapter for each plan item the concretization of the goals, the measures to be taken and the indicators to evaluate the effectiveness of the measures. However, no mechanisms are determined for implementing and monitoring them.

In Hungary there are numerous planning documents on regional, county and especially on local level, because State functions were vastly decentralized after the change of regime in the early nineties. At the local level there is an optional planning instrument; the municipality environmental plan and municipality spatial planning documents also contain several environmental and nature protection chapters.[16]

### 4.2 *Domestic legislation providing legal protection to wilderness areas*

There are three levels of legal protection in the Hungarian nature protection system. The first is the *general protection* of organisms, systems and habitats of wild species, especially native ones, without having any specific legal title of protection.[17] Any economic activity using or burdening such species or habitats (including hunting and fishery) shall be performed without harming these natural values and biological diversity.[18] It is prohibited to collect, cull or capture such species in a way that is not selective or results in the mass destruction or harm to them. Also, any change of their genetic pattern, dissemination of modified species or purposeful transfer of them is strongly prohibited.[19] This general protection is provided for the natural territories, i.e., all forests, grasslands and reeds and even any lands that are not designed, or are unsuitable, for agricultural, industrial or extractive activities. Even in such cases, the protected status shall be noted on the land register sheets of these lands.[20] Detailed rules on handling such natural territories are also

[16] While there are several cities and villages in Hungary where the municipality councils have created their environmental plans, in the practice of spatial planning and city development programmes the spirit and the letter of these environmental plans are seldom followed. See the 2011 FGO Report, at159.

[17] This general level of protection encompasses all the types of protection of more valuable natural territories described in Table 1.

[18] Article 9(1) and Article 11 of Ttv.

[19] Article 9(2) and (3) of Ttv.

[20] Article 15(1)-(3) of Ttv.

provided in the Nature Protection Act[21] and these rules shall be obeyed by those who deal with such lands. These rules therefore are self-executing, bolstered only with sporadic monitoring by the environmental authorities.

The second level of legal protection ensues from special administrative and legislative procedures resulting in unqualified (basic level) *protected zones*[22] that are determined by their scientific, cultural, aesthetic, educational and other public interests and by their role in maintaining biological diversity.[23] Such protection may be established at the national or local level. In the former case protection is established by a decree of the minister responsible for environmental protection, while in the second case the concerned municipality council issues a local ordinance. In the second procedure, as well as for the reverse decision on the cessation of protection, public participation is to be ensured. Two further layers are advanced at the national level: a normal and an enhanced degree of protection. The latter forms the basis for specific and stronger nature protection regimes described in Table 1, which are therefore most relevant for wilderness protection. In each of these cases, close control of the handling of the protected zones is facilitated by a set of environmental administrative permits and the enhanced protection means there are severe conditions attached to such permits.[24]

Finally, the most valuable objects of nature protection, such as peat bogs, springs and caves, are *protected by the force of law*, without any specific procedure. In principle such objects enjoy the highest level of protection (enhanced protection) without any administrative procedure. This so-called '*ex lege*' protection, however, was controversial from the viewpoint of constitutional law, as the Hungarian Constitutional Court has pointed out.[25] While the high level protection seriously constrains or, in some cases excludes, the exercise of property rights, concerned land owners had no legal remedies and might not even be sure whether their lands belong to these areas or not. Therefore, the Constitutional Court obliged the environmental authorities to take decisions on the concrete extension of the territories of *ex lege* protection. The critics of this decision say, however,

[21] Articles 16–18.

[22] Three categories from Table 1, natural parks, biosphere reserves and landscape protection districts, belong to this second level of protection under Ttv. All general rules described hereinafter are also relevant to these three categories. There are, however, lower level regulations and especially bylaws issued by the minister responsible for nature protection that contain specific rules that apply to them.

[23] Article 22 of Ttv.

[24] Articles 31–41 of Ttv.

[25] Decision 964/B/1998 AB (ABH 2002, 873, 878)

that this additional *contra legem* requirement of the Court strongly reduces the strength of the *ex lege* protection. The Office of the Ombudsman for Future Generations (FGO) dealt with that problem too, and interpreted the decision of the Constitutional Court in the only way that would not make the *ex lege* protection futile.[26] According to the FGO, the *ex lege* protection has created a presumption of protection of the widest possible territorial scope, while, if the land owner requests so, the expert-based decision of the environmental authority might remove the ambiguity by precisely delineating the parameters of the *ex lege* protection.

Now, in the context of the horizontal system, let us turn our attention to the other branches of law that perform certain nature protection tasks. The major tool for wilderness protection in spatial planning under construction law is the National Physical Plan,[27] which has the objective of harmonizing the conditions of use of territory and development of technical infrastructure network with landscape, nature, ecology and cultural heritage protection in the spirit of sustainable development.[28] The *national ecological network* within the National Physical Plan consists of core regions, ecological corridors and buffer zones. No zones for social and economic purposes can be assigned to these territories if they endanger the habitats and their connections in the ecological network. Mining and linear transport or energy installations can take place on such territories only under strict conditions and, if appropriate, with compensation measures. No construction zones can be assigned in the core territories.[29] Regional size waste management facilities (landfills) cannot be sited in any parts of the ecological network.[30] While at the national level the spatial planning policy of the country is seemingly quite supportive of nature protection, the major stresses on wilderness area are exerted by the local spatial plans, where the social and economic pressure for development is at its strongest. After the change of regime in the early 1990s, the local municipality councils became the major players in spatial planning and they rarely hesitate to sacrifice green lands for local taxes and employment and for other possible public and private advantages.

Outstanding values of nature may also be the subject of *world heritage protection*, not only for aesthetic and cultural reasons, especially if we return to the core meaning of the heritage that we pass to future

26 JNO-702/2010
27 Act XXVI of 2003
28 Article 1 of SP Act
29 Articles 9, 13 and 17–19 of SP Act
30 Article 22 of SP Act

generations. The protection and restoration of world heritage values are the tasks of the cultural administration, but they have to take into account the rules of nature protection.[31] In this way cultural heritage can secure additional resources for the protection of wilderness and strengthen the understanding and appreciation of our responsibilities to maintain it.

Ideally, agricultural regulation could also provide a significant contribution to wilderness protection. According to the joint decree of the Ministries of Agriculture and the Environment,[32] the aim of assigning sensitive natural territories is to sustain or introduce nature-friendly agricultural practices for the protection of *lands that are ecologically sensitive*, in order to avoid their degradation and sustain biological diversity and connectivity.[33] Old, sustainable agricultural practices might secure not only the past, but also the future of these lands, especially grazing lands, grasslands, reeds and fishery ponds, as well as old arable lands and fruit gardens. The assignment is decided by the national park directorate, with the support of the agricultural and land protection authorities,[34] and the owners of the assigned lands can in turn apply for special state subsidies.[35]

In the context of agricultural law, the 2009 Forestry Act[36] might be especially relevant for the central theme of this book. In this Act forests are grouped according to their ecological values and there are legal tools to prevent forests from degrading from a better to a worse category and to encourage forest owners and managers to 'upgrade' their forests. In general, some solutions of the centuries-old forestry law, a branch of administrative law with a high prestige and social embeddedness, could be quite useful for nature protection. The declared aim of the Forestry Act is sustainable forestry and especially to contribute to climate resilience, biodiversity, protection of surface and underground waters and top soils, as components of the fulfilment of the constitutional right to a healthy environment.[37] Forests are classified in the Act according to their status of naturalness:

[31] Article 3(3) of Act LXXVII of 2011 on World heritage.
[32] Joint Decree No. 2/2002. (I. 23.) KöM-FVM.
[33] Articles 1 and 3(1) Joint Decree.
[34] Articles 4 and 5 Joint Decree.
[35] Article 8 Joint Decree.
[36] Act XXXVII of 2009 on the forests, on the protection of them and on forestry.
[37] Article 1 Forestry Act.

- natural forests (undisturbed, their content, structure and dynamics are natural, with no alien or invasive species[38]);
- natural-like forests (similar to natural forests, but alien species can be found up to twenty per cent, with no invasive species);
- originated forests (transformed by human interference, with non-native species between twenty and fifty per cent and invasive species not more than twenty per cent);
- transitional forests (strongly transformed, with non-native species between fifty and seventy-five per cent and invasive species between twenty and fifty per cent);
- culture forests (the same as transitional ones with more than seventy per cent non-native and more than fifty per cent invasive species);
- tree plantations (typically non-native species and their artificial hybrids planted in a regular grid arrangement, intensively managed with clear-cutting in at least every fifteen years).[39]

In preparation of the district forestry plans, natural or natural-like forests shall be preferred and maintained to the maximum extent possible.[40] The establishment of forests with non-native species shall be banned by the forestry authorities within the vicinity of 200 metres to natural and natural-like forests to ensure that the naturalness of these forests is not endangered.[41] The same applies to the renewal of existing forests with non-native species.[42] Where forests are transformed into other uses, the forest protection fee will be increased fourfold in the case of natural and natural-like forests compared to other types.[43] The owner or manager of the forest would escape payment of this considerable fee if he re-establishes a similar or larger forest at another location with at least the same level of naturalness.[44] The re-establishment of the forest is mandatory in the cases of natural or natural-like forests.[45]

[38] Measures against invasive species are apparent in several legal branches of Hungarian law: nature protection legislation, public health laws, food safety laws and also laws relating to the protection of city parks and streets.
[39] Article 7(1)(a-f) Forestry Act.
[40] Article 34(2)(a) Forestry Act.
[41] Article 45(1) and 47(2) Forestry Act.
[42] Article 51(6) Forestry Act.
[43] Article 81(2) (ba) and (bb) Forestry Act.
[44] Article 82(2) Forestry Act.
[45] Article 82(4) Forestry Act.

### *4.3 Consequences of 'wilderness protection' for human activities*

The above discussion shows that nature protection is supported by several other branches of the law that are not primarily concerned with environmental conservation. Our nature protection law also contains many concrete rules on these related branches of social and economic activities.[46] However, difficulties are raised in reconciling the multidisciplinary, harmonized use of several laws with different legal culture, independent, separate administrative bodies and procedures towards the wider objective of nature protection.

As far as forest management is concerned, in forests under nature protection the agricultural methods of soil preparation and burning are 'avoidable',[47] while renewal and management of the forests shall take place in harmony with the protection goals through natural methods, taking into consideration the native compound of species and structure of forests. On protected lands new forests shall be established exclusively with native species, in accordance with their natural, historical rate on a given territory.[48] Any tree cutting shall be performed in non-vegetation seasons, while clear-cutting shall not exceed three ha of territory and only when the trees are full grown.[49] In addition, on enhanced protected lands any forest management measures can be designed and implemented according to the natural protection management plans.[50]

With regard to hunting, nature protection lands shall be designated as *special hunting zones* in harmony with the relevant hunting rules.[51] Specific conditions for hunting shall be determined by individual decisions of the hunting authorities.[52] Furthermore, the manager of a hunting area shall keep the game population within the limits determined by the nature protection authorities.[53]

Apart from these cross-cutting rules, the nature protection act – in harmony with the integration principle – contains a series of constraints

[46] As noted above, the nature protection rules on several human activities refer to all categories of nature protection territories, including nature parks, biospheres reserves and landscape protection districts as defined in Table 1.
[47] Article 33(2) NP Act.
[48] Article 33(3) NP Act.
[49] Articles 33 (4), (5) and (8) NP Act.
[50] Articles 33(1) and 33(6) NP Act.
[51] Article 34(1) NP Act.
[52] Article 21(1) Act LV of 1996 on the protection of game, game management and hunting.
[53] Article 34(3) NP Act.

in connection with other fields of law, such as those relating to construction, soil protection, water management and transport.[54] Activities under these branches of social and economic life shall not endanger the status of the protected lands, nor may they disturb the unity of the landscape or lead to disturbance of protected species through noise or light.[55] A permit from the nature protection authority is needed for any research on protected lands as well as for certain other activities, such as collection or experimentation, watering, grazing, burning or otherwise eliminating plants, spreading pesticides or bioregulators and even the use of artificial fertilizers. A permit is also needed for organizing community sport events and for conducting any technical sports individually and using any vehicles on roads not specially designated for this purpose on the protected lands.[56] In addition, on enhanced protection lands any access is subject to a specific permit from the environmental authorities, with the exception of tourist routes and education paths.[57]

### 4.4 *Protecting wilderness as 'property'*

The civil law aspects of wilderness protection can generally be considered at least from three perspectives: first, damage payments to the owners and the users of protected lands for expenses incurred in performing specific duties in connection with nature protection; second, a similar position arises for the victims of damage caused by protected species and third, damage payments may be due to the State (as well as several fines) when economic activities harm nature protection interests.[58] The first situation will be addressed here in detail. This entails a very sophisticated set of legal and theoretical problems concerning the issue of how much of a

[54] These rules again underline the inherent multidisciplinary features of the law on nature protection. According to the Tvt: 'On protected natural territories any construction of buildings, linear objects, facilities that endangers or damages these territories or alters the landscape shall be prohibited.'

[55] Article 35 NP Act.

[56] Article 38(1)(a-j) NP Act.

[57] Article 40(1) NP Act.

[58] There is a fourth civil law aspect, not connected to damages: that is the ownership and (re-) acquisition of the most valuable protected lands by the state. As Pánovics points out, following a Constitutional court decision, all privatized protected lands should have been re-purchased, while the proper legislation has been brought, the state budget could only cover half of the acquisition, and since 2005 no budget has been allocated to this task. Pánovics considers it a shame that the State failed to amend its obviously irresponsible privatization acts. See Pánovics, 'Recuperation of the Protected Lands in Hungary', *supra* note 2, at 431.

burden private owners should carry in order to protect wilderness, nature and, ultimately, the interests of future generations.

The starting point of the Hungarian nature protection law is clear: on one hand the owner, manager, user of the land is obliged to tolerate all the necessary measures pursued by the nature protection authorities and managing organizations, such as those necessary for the protection, maintenance, control or even exhibition of natural values; scientific research and administrative measures such as the installation of signs, plates or information tables. These measures are acknowledged by the law as constraining property rights.[59] On the other hand, effective compensation for these constraints (*damnum emergens*) shall be covered by the State.[60] This issue has been further elaborated by the practice of the environmental authorities and the courts. Based on a Constitutional Court decision[61] the Jász-Nagykun-Szolnok County Court declared[62] that no payment is due to the owners of protected lands when the constraints of their property rights ensue from such decisions of the environmental authorities that prevent an unlawful situation, i.e., any harm to or endangerment of the protected lands or species. This position arises most obviously in a situation where the environmental authorities are not in a position to prevent such harm or endangerment, and therefore the responsible owners, managers and so on of the land shall face sanctions and other measures. Therefore, the State will have no obligation to compensate the owners for the financial consequences of failing to adhere to their environmental obligations. Likewise, according to the court's decision, no compensation obligation arises where measures are imposed by the environmental authorities to prevent such situations from arising.

We note here that with regard to administrative laws in particular cases of higher social importance, such as national defence, public health, water management (e.g., flood protection), the question of compensation does not apply in similar situations when social interests would require some constraints of personal property. Even under the construction law, compensation is quite limited in cases where the value of private property is decreased due to a public project or the spatial plan for the community concerned. There are time constraints and further limitations on the

[59] Articles 41(1) and (2) NP Act.
[60] Article 41(3) NP Act.
[61] Decision of the Constitutional Court No. AB 597/B/2007.
[62] Jász-Nagykun-Szolnok County Court Decision No. 12.K.27.248/2008/3, 13 November 2008.

financial responsibility of the municipalities towards land owners, such as measures taken to address natural dangers.[63]

## 5 Practical implementation, supervision and enforcement

Central and Eastern European countries are often considered to have ambitious environmental and nature protection rules that are nonetheless undermined by far poorer levels of implementation. This is a false dichotomy: if the implementation of the law is not effective, there must be serious shortcomings in the relevant legal regimes too. In such situations laws tend to be only wishful thinking or political slogans rather than serious considerations of legislators. This can be clearly exemplified by inadequate or absent institutional and procedural parts of the relevant laws.

The above discussion shows that some activities are prohibited or constrained by the force of law itself, while others are subject to a permit from the environmental authority, which is to be assessed and issued on the basis of the specific facts and circumstances of the given situation. However, the Hungarian concept of wilderness protection can be criticized as being overly subjective. Practical cases indicate that there is no legal sanction where the Hungarian environmental authorities are too lenient in addressing the use and abuse of protected lands arising out of competing social and economic interests.

In the Hungarian Dakar Rally case,[64] a large international car race was permitted to proceed through a highly protected area in the Bakony Mountains in central Hungary. It was obvious that the cars would use different routes during the race, thereby damaging a wide range of unpaved roads in the enhanced nature protection area. Furthermore, the large audience of the event would cause further damage. Nonetheless, the regional environmental authority issued the permit for this activity using an expedited procedure.

In a similar case in the Ócsa marshland area[65] that is under *ex lege* protection, the relevant regional environmental authority granted a permit for a movie set to be established. Several façades of castles and houses were built on pristine nature land and even although the staff tried to remove everything carefully afterwards, the unavoidable access through this highly sensitive area caused irreversible damage.

[63] Articles 30(3) and (5) of Act LXXVIII of 1987 on the protection and shaping of built environment.

[64] Case No. JNO-544/2010, at 148–149 of the 2012 FGO Report.

[65] Case No. JNO-116/2011, at 151 of the 2012 FGO Report.

Probably the worst example of the practice of the Hungarian FGO was the Nagyberek wetland wildlife resort case,[66] where the long-term lease holder of the territory used the land for commercial hunting purposes and – to facilitate this use – attempted to dry out the wetlands. This caused irreversible damage to a Ramsar site and disturbed thousands of protected birds and other water-bound animals. In this latter case a contract between the Hungarian state and the lease holder had been in place for almost twenty years, and the water management and environmental authorities issued several consenting decisions during this period.

A common feature of all of these cases was that the environmental authorities considered certain major social and economic interests as overriding the theoretically strict nature protection rules of the country. In striking contrast to this, it should be briefly noted that, according to experiences in national park management research, the most stringent protection rules are quite strictly applied against poor rural minority groups that used to collect several forest commodities on a relatively small scale.[67]

Nevertheless, it should be added that the whole territory of the ten national parks represents one-third of the total surface of protected territory under almost a dozen other legal titles. The substantial size of the natural parks in itself ensures a convenient distance from human settlements and human activities in general, which results in the *de facto* protection of the other features of the wilderness definition (undisturbed and natural) in many of these territories. Therefore, the management of national parks can use a large part of their resources for professional activities other than monitoring, supervision and enforcement activities. Yet the fringes of large nature parks and the smaller protected territories are much more exposed to activities that are incompatible with the objectives of long-term nature protection.

## 6 The future of wilderness protection

Hungary is losing 130 ha of green surface each day.[68] Unless the attitudes of our decision-makers (not only politicians, chief administrators and the

[66] Case No. JNO-400/2011, at 154 of the 2012 FGO Report.

[67] P. 15, TAI Forestry, Hungary.

[68] Personal communication with the head of Pestterv Ltd, a major spatial planning firm, at the occasion of the Conference of the Hungarian Nature Protection Alliance on public participation in spatial planning, Vecsés city, April 2008.

managers of large companies, but also voters and consumers) change dramatically, the future of wilderness in Hungary is dim. While in principle decision-makers profess to love nature and appreciate the values of the wilderness, they also consider that pieces of it can be sacrificed for social and economic interests from time to time. This 'slicing' of our precious green spots will lead to their eradication unless the impacts of climate change – to which Hungary is especially exposed – does the job more quickly.

A widespread acknowledgement and promotion of intergenerational justice might be a possible way out of these monumental 'prisoners' games'.[69] This would need a dramatic change in morals and attitudes as well as a creative use of our existing legal concepts. We are responsible for the well-being of our offspring, regardless of the exact composition of the coming generations.[70] The continuity between the past, present and future generations, as part of the identity of the communities and their members, was accepted as natural at a time when people fought with nature for their everyday sustenance. In the current era we have conquered nature, filled in almost all the available space on Earth and over-consumed many of its resources. However, biologists warn that in such a situation the world of competition might eventually end. During the so-called succession phases of the development of ecosystems the species on the same trophic level keep fighting to occupy the largest possible part of the given space and resources. In the climax phase, though, when they have reached the spatial and other physical limits of the given place, the compromise between sharing resources becomes prevalent. According to Professor Vida[71] this phenomenon might occur at the present moment in the history of humankind: we have just reached our limits, frequently denoted as planetary boundaries, and therefore the only way ahead for our civilization is a significantly better cooperation within and between generations.

[69] Garret Hardin's classic essay 'The Tragedy of the Commons' is put into an environmental legal context by Bosselmann. See Klaus Bosselmann, 'Losing the Forest for the Trees: Environmental Reductionism in the Law', *Sustainability*, 2(8) (2010), 2424–2448, at 2426–2427.

[70] I refer here to the *non-identity problem*, the philosophical dilemma that whatever illegitimacy the present generation leaves to the following ones, they cannot claim to have suffered harm because of this since these very acts created the conditions upon which that given set of future generations could come into existence. An important summary of the ways of handling the non-identity problem can be found in SEP, at 9–11.

[71] Gábor Vida, 'A fenntarthatóság és a tudósok felelőssége' (Sustainability and Responsibility of the Scientists), *Magyar Tudomány* (*Hungarian Science*), 12 (2007), at 1600.

There needs to be considerable changes to the development of our constitutional, environmental and other laws. It should become natural for every lawyer that a certain set of human rights belongs to the members of the future generations, in a similar way as are claimed by past and present generations, although, naturally with different content. Also, once a certain set of rights has been established, future generations should have recognition of their standing in certain relevant cases with proper representation. Why do elderly professors raise their eyebrows on hearing this idea? The abstraction for giving legal personality to those other than an individual or to a group of individuals is not at all alien to our legal systems, for instance a sum of money (in the case of a foundation) can enjoy all the advantages of having legal personality. It would be a pity to deny the rights of our grandchildren and great-grandchildren on a merely formal basis.

We cannot contest, however, that our environmental laws already contain several creative solutions. Public participation and environmental impact assessment (EIA) procedures[72] are just two outstanding examples of new legal institutions that have been created for more effective environmental protection. Further cultivation and systemic application of these instruments may promise a better future for nature and wilderness protection too.

From the existing set of legal tools, principles of environmental law might also play a key role in facilitating a more effective degree of environmental protection and promoting intergenerational justice. A possible implementation of one of the leading environmental principles, the integration principle, has been already referred to in this chapter in relation to the interplay between environmental law and several other associated fields of law. At the same time, we have sufficient reason to consider the integration principle a double-edged sword. While it is important that all the relevant branches of administration monitor the process of sustainable development, it is difficult to commission them to perform major environmental tasks on their own because of their inherent professional biases and competing interests. In fact, the competition between nature protection, forestry and gaming interests for the remaining most pristine protected lands indicates the limitations of the integration principle.[73]

[72] Actually, we can speak about a 'family' of EIA legal institutions, starting from an impact assessment for strategic decisions (SEA), through international assessments (Espoo procedures) to the local procedures for SME facilities.

[73] On 21 June 2011, FGO has organized a ground-breaking workshop for the professionals, authorities and NGO representing hunters, foresters and nature protection professionals to discuss the definition and measuring problems relating to game populations.

Other principles, such as the precautionary principle, might play a decisive role in, for instance, determining the boundary between wilderness protection areas *vis a vis* Natura 2000 territories with less stringent protection regimes. Furthermore, international networks for saving the last wilderness areas of the world cannot be imagined without the principle of common but differentiated responsibility (CBDR). An old principle of general international law, the non-regression principle would also be worth further consideration in the field of environmental protection as the Hungarian Constitutional Court has indeed advanced in its famous 'basic' environmental decision.[74] Several other principles, such as the polluter pays principle, might also play a decisive role in ensuring a viable future for the wilderness areas, although none of these can do so in isolation. Only a coherent system of environmental legal principles[75] might be able to determine the proper legal responses to the system of ecological catastrophes that threatens the last remainders of the green surfaces of European countries, including those in Hungary.

This chapter raised the question as to whether the use of all these principles and instruments could really assist in the protection of wilderness in Hungary. The limit of each of these instruments is that they leave space for balancing interests. This position lies at the heart of the notion of sustainable development, but the balancing act often proves most beneficial to short-term economic interests. If we really want to be fair to future generations, there will have to be situations in which we protect wildernesses in an absolute way, without any exceptions at all. This leads us back to a central perspective of this chapter: without a better knowledge and higher appreciation of the values of nature and wilderness, our major 'decision makers' (consumers and voters) will consequently deliver decisions that are deleterious for our societies and for future generations.

## 7 Conclusions

The above discussion shows that, although the term 'wilderness' is not explicitly used or defined in Hungarian law, areas that exhibit the wilderness qualities as defined in Chapter 1 may well receive legal protection through several branches of law in Hungary. In theory, the bulk of this protection is established by environmental and nature protection laws, particularly the

[74] Decision No. 28/1994. (V. 20.) AB.

[75] See Klaus Bosselmann, 'Losing the Forest for the Trees: Environmental Reductionism in the Law', *note* 68, at 2431–2432.

legislation on protected areas. Other branches of administrative law, such as laws on spatial planning and agricultural laws, also contain relevant provisions. However, these only play a supplementary role, and are always subject to compromises with other social and economic interests. As discussed in Sections 5 and 6, even wilderness protection as advanced through the designation of protected areas presents considerable practical challenges.

These problems notwithstanding, progressive elements of Hungarian law offer some hope for more effective nature protection, notably its holistic approach and problem-oriented handling. Hungarian law as such also creates conditions for concerted efforts to protect nature through ancillary fields, such as agricultural regulation and spatial planning. However, we do not yet see mechanisms prescribed in the legal regime governing these additional fields to ensure effective information flow between these administrative bodies or harmonized planning and implementation efforts. However, the participation of the concerned communities might substitute such provisions solely by the fact that local communities and their nature protection organizations are not interested in the division of competences between several administrative offices; they rather deal with the problem itself and demand the contribution of all the State bodies that could possibly help.

Certainly, in the local social-economic-ecological conflicts the concerned communities and NGOs also regularly apply the tools of the general environmental law (e.g., EIA) and principles (some of which are reinforced by the Constitution); however, effective public participation is nowadays quite different from the green movement projects that were prevalent some decades ago. To have a fair chance in the administrative and legal procedures, the actors need proper information about the professional and legal background of given cases and a wide range of support from the authorities or from larger, professional mainstream NGOs, a complex of measures that is often referred to as 'capacity building'. Without active, well informed and well trained public participation we cannot envisage a successful use of the available set of legal tools of nature protection, yet public participation without well designed, systematic capacity building cannot be effective either. In the specific context of wilderness protection, capacity building programmes should encompass not only the technical-legal issues of public participation but also general questions, such as the concept of ecological services and the basic moral elements of intergenerational justice.

# 16

# Wilderness protection in Iceland

AÐALHEIÐUR JÓHANNSDÓTTIR

## 1 Introduction[1]

With a population of 330,000, a land area of 103,000 km$^2$ (~3 habitants per km$^2$),[2] and with its inhabited regions (which constitute a mere twenty-five per cent of the total territory) primarily confined to coastal areas and lowlands below 200 m above sea level,[3] Iceland is usually pictured as a place within which one can not only enjoy unspoiled nature but also experience the uniqueness of the Icelandic highlands,[4] including their wilderness.[5] More than half of Icelandic territory lies higher than 400 m above sea level, which predominantly comprises an uninhabited interior highland plateau (400–700 m above sea level), and about sixteen per cent of the land is covered by glaciers, lava flows, lakes and rivers.[6]

[1] Icelandic laws and decrees included in the references of this chapter are available through www.althingi.is.

[2] 'Statistics Iceland', www.statice.is/Statistics/Population, and also www.statice.is/Statistics/Geography-and-environment/Geographical-data.

[3] See further T.E. Thórhallsdóttir, 'Environment and Energy in Iceland: A Comparative Analysis of Values and Impacts', *Environmental Impact Assessment Review*, 27 (2007), 522–544, at 523.

[4] A reference to the 'highlands', which is not an accurately defined area, is usually considered to be land higher than 200, 300 or 400 m above sea level, or land above the so-called highland edge. See the Icelandic science web: www.visindavefur.is/svar.php?id=59622. The term 'mid-highlands' that has, inter alia, been defined as a planning term, will be detailed further in Subsection 4.5.

[5] See, inter alia, the mapping available by the *Wilderness Quality Index* of the European Environment Agency, www.eea.europa.eu/data-and-maps/figures/wilderness-quality-index, indicating a high degree of wilderness quality in Iceland. On Icelandic wilderness see also, T.E. Thórhallsdóttir, 'Evaluating Nature and Wilderness in Iceland', in Alan E. Watson, Lilian Alessa and Janet Sproull (eds.), *Wilderness in the Circumpolar North: Searching for Compatibility in Ecological, Traditional, and Ecotourism Values* (Ogden: Forest Service, Rocky Mountain Research Station, 2002), 96–104, www.fs.fed.us/rm/pubs/rmrs_p026.html.

[6] Thórhallsdóttir, 'Environment and Energy in Iceland: A Comparative analysis of Values and Impacts', *supra* note 3, at 523–525.

Around 17,000 km$^2$ of the land mass has already been formally protected[7] (~ seventeen per cent of Iceland).[8] From the outset these characteristics should endow Icelandic wilderness with a degree of natural protection. However, a recent wilderness study reflects a troubling trend.[9] In the period from 1936 to 2010, the development of road and power infrastructure (including dams and reservoirs),[10] located in or dependant on the natural resources of the highlands,[11] has led to a reduction of nearly seventy per cent of wilderness areas.[12] Furthermore, tourism has grown considerably[13] and, as Taylor points out, tourism and wilderness 'have both a beneficial and conflicting relationship'.[14] However, the fragile ecosystem of remote wilderness, such as that of Iceland, necessitates carefully managed tourism to prevent the destruction of the resource.[15]

As will be further elaborated in this chapter, the term 'virgin wilderness' was specifically defined as a legal concept in Act No 44/1999 on Nature Conservation (NC-1999) that entered into force on 1 July 1999.[16] This act has recently been replaced by the Act No 60/2013 on Nature Conservation (NC-2013), that came into force on 15 November 2015. In this new act, the term 'virgin wilderness' has been replaced by the term 'uninhabited wilderness'. Furthermore, also two other Acts currently in force, Act No 106/2000 on Environmental Impact Assessment

[7] Including national parks, nature reserves, natural monuments, community parks and particular nature conservation areas. See www.ust.is/default.aspx?PageID=6acceb5e-a96c-4ab3-96c8-d8bf88c18cae.

[8] See 'Statistics Iceland', *supra* note 2, and www.statice.is/Statistics/Geography-and-environment/Geographical-data.

[9] V.F. Taylor, *GIS Assessment of Icelandic Wilderness from 1936 to 2010* (Reykjavík: University of Iceland/Faculty of Life and Environmental Sciences, 2011), 1–43.

[10] *Ibid.*, at 9–12 and 23–30.

[11] *Ibid.*, at 4. Taylor relied upon the wilderness definition in Article 3 of the NC-1999; see further below.

[12] *Ibid.*, at iv and 34 *et passim*. Interestingly glaciers cover eighty-eight per cent of the remaining areas of wilderness.

[13] *Ibid.*, at 32–33, and *supra* note 1, www.statice.is/Statistics/Tourism,-transport-and-informati.

[14] Taylor, *GIS Assessment of Icelandic Wilderness from 1936 to 2010*, *supra* note 9, at 32.

[15] *Ibid.*, at 32–33. See also a recent study on the influence of tourism on the mid-highlands regarding the wilderness qualities of the highlands that make the area a very valuable but also vulnerable resource, which should be carefully utilized for tourism: A.D. Sæþórsdóttir, *Ferðamennska á miðhálendi Íslands: Staða og spá um framtíðarhorfur* (Reykjavík: Land- og ferðamálafræðistofa, Líf- og umhverfisvísindadeild Háskóla Íslands, 2012), www.skipulagsstofnun.is/media/landsskipulagsstefna/Ferdamennska_a_midhalendi_Islands_loka_ths_ad%5B1%5D.pdf. Sæþórsdóttir also points out (see at 20–21) that different approaches have been used in evaluating Icelandic wilderness; some, but by no means all, rely upon the NC-1999 concept.

[16] In Icelandic, lög nr. 44/1999 um náttúruvernd.

(EIA-2000)[17] and Act No 123/2010 on Spatial Planning (SP-2010),[18] make direct reference to the concept of wilderness, as will be further outlined in Section 4.

The operational function of the wilderness concept in NC-1999 has seemingly been rather limited and legal research in this field is accordingly scarce. This makes it difficult to evaluate whether the relevant legislation has actually contributed to wilderness protection. Furthermore, although it is possible to trace some examples from legal practice, explicit references to the wilderness concept or wilderness qualities are seldom found in environmental decision-making, including in court judgments.

Against this backdrop, the overall objective of this chapter is to examine the effectiveness of the current legal framework in protecting Icelandic wilderness. Placing this discussion in context, this chapter will not only scrutinize the above mentioned laws that explicitly refer to (virgin or uninhabited) wilderness, since other important terms (including landscape,[19] uninhabited areas[20] highlands[21] and mid-highlands[22]) are also of importance. By way of background, Section 2 briefly discusses the competing interests that shaped the scope of the first legislative concept of wilderness that emerged in the late 1990s. In Section 3, the current legal definition for wilderness will be examined, inter alia, in relation to the IUCN definition and the three main wilderness qualities (derived from this IUCN definition[23]) as explained in Chapter 1. Thereafter, in Section 4, the relevant legal framework relating to the protection of wilderness areas and qualities will be outlined and discussed. Finally, Section 5 advances the chapter's main conclusions.

## 2 Wilderness protection and Icelandic society: competing interests

### *2.1 The purpose of wilderness protection*

The primary objective of wilderness protection is the preservation of particular natural qualities, including the long-term ecological integrity

[17] In Icelandic, lög nr. 106/2000 um mat á umhverfisáhrifum.
[18] In Icelandic, skipulagslög nr. 123/2010.
[19] *Ibid.*
[20] In Icelandic: *óbyggðir*, which literally means 'uninhabitable area'. See also Thórhallsdóttir, 'Evaluating Nature and Wilderness in Iceland', *supra* note 5, at 97.
[21] See note 4.
[22] See Subsection 4.5.
[23] N. Dudley, *IUCN Guidelines for Applying Protected Area Management Categories* (Gland: IUCN, 2008), at 14–16.

of natural areas that have not been significantly disturbed by human activity and are free from modern infrastructures, in the interests of present and future generations.[24] Hence, the safeguarding of particular qualities and functions of nature and natural surroundings, which cannot be enjoyed elsewhere, is central to wilderness protection. Based on the IUCN definition of wilderness[25] and other sources, Chapter 1 of this book distinguished three main wilderness qualities: (1) naturalness (relatively ecological intactness); (2) the absence of permanent facilities (e.g., roads, buildings, bridges, tracks) or other evidence of modern human society, and (3) relatively large size of the area. As will be further elaborated in Section 3, the Icelandic definitions of wilderness correspond to and reflect these three basic wilderness qualities.

### *2.2 Competing interests*

Wilderness protection in Iceland is a complex and, if not always overtly, a rather politicized issue. As a rule, wilderness discussions have tended to reflect the broad philosophies of the traditional political blocs. Left-wing advocates have generally sought to promote environmental conservation, including wilderness protection, while those to the right have usually argued in favour of economic development and the utilization of the nation's natural resources.[26] The debate has also been inextricably linked to two fundamental economic considerations: the richness of energy resources, hydropower and geothermal, many of which are either located within the highlands or adjacent to them, and the growing business of tourism.[27] Moreover, some aspects of national energy policy – particularly electricity production for energy-intensive industries, including aluminium smelters – have from the outset been sensitive, not the least due to the fact that large scale hydropower electricity production requires water collection in the highlands as well as a considerable area for water storage. Against this backdrop, it would not be unfair to describe the wilderness issue as a clash between two competing interests: environmental interests

[24] *Ibid.*

[25] *Ibid.*, particularly at 14–15.

[26] See further, 'Tillaga til þingsályktunar um varðveislu ósnortinna víðerna' ('Proposal for Althingi´s Resolution, on the Preservation of Virgin Wilderness'), þskj. 27–27. mál, 1996–1997.

[27] See further 'þingsályktun um áætlun um vernd og orkunýtingu landsvæða', ('Althingi's resolution on Strategic Planning for Conservation and Energy Utilisation of Land Areas'), þskj. 892–89. mál, 2012–2013. See also Sæþórsdóttir, *Ferðamennska á miðhálendi Íslands: Staða og spá um framtíðarhorfur, supra* note 15, at 15–36.

(public), emphasizing nature conservation, including wilderness protection, in the interests of present and future generations, and economic interests (public and private), which prioritize economic development, including the furtherance of electricity generation for industrial uses and also tourism.

### *2.3 Wilderness concept*

The national recognition that the Icelandic highlands represent natural qualities that are rapidly disappearing elsewhere, alongside a growing degree of environmental pressure and underlying concerns that the ecological integrity of the highlands could be compromised by specific activities[28] led to the establishment of an official working group in 1997. The working group was given the task of defining the concept of wilderness.[29] The following year, the group introduced the concept of *virgin wilderness*,[30] which was eventually enshrined in law through the NC-1999.[31] As the definition reflects (see further Section 3), particular infrastructure – i.e., power lines, power stations, reservoirs, as well as other wilderness threats and main roads – became integral components of the NC-1999 concept. This was not coincidental, as the same infrastructure projects are usually thought to constitute the main challenges to the integrity of the Icelandic wilderness.[32] Moreover, the primary emphasis of this concept was clearly to respond to the core elements of the energy policy.

### *2.4 Reluctance to commit to the concept*

Although the wilderness concept became law in 1999, and has been referred to in environmental decision-making (see Section 4), it has nonetheless had a limited function and has generally failed to provide effective protection for wilderness. The reason for this is partially related to the fact that the Althingi, at that time, was not prepared to take the necessary additional steps to equip the NC-1999 with the requisite legal

[28] See further note 26.

[29] *Ibid.*

[30] See, 'Tillaga til þingsályktunar um kortlagningu ósnortinna víðerna á Ísland, fylgiskjal' ('Annex to proposal for Althingi's resolution, on the Mapping of Virgin Wilderness in Iceland'), þskj. 404–327. mál, 1998–1999.

[31] In its work, the working group was seemingly inspired by the wilderness definitions advanced under Norwegian and US law. See also note 26.

[32] Taylor, *GIS assessment of Icelandic wilderness from 1936 to 2010*, *supra* note 9, pp. 1–43.

and administrative tools to protect a defined wilderness area in a meaningful way. In the view of Althingi's Environmental Committee (Althingi's Standing Committee for Environmental issues), the concept had not acquired the necessary legitimacy in relation to spatial planning and land use issues. Therefore, the Committee held that the Nature Conservation Strategy (NCS)[33] – whose purpose was, inter alia, to list and describe the nature conservation areas that should be formally designated and protected – was to take wilderness qualities into account, but was not required to directly include defined wilderness areas within this document.[34] Ultimately, the most likely reason for the Committee's reluctance to fully commit to the concept is related to an underlying political disagreement on the national energy policy and the plans for future hydropower plants that were dependant on water resources located in the Icelandic highlands.[35]

### *2.5 A social status beyond the traditional political disagreement?*

In spite of the practical implications of the developments outlined above, it is nonetheless clear that by defining wilderness in the NC-1999, the inherent qualities were given a particular status that went beyond the traditional political disagreement on land-use policy. In this respect, the unique circumstances of *Supreme Court Case 19 March 2009 No 425/2008* are particularly revealing.

> The plaintiffs, land owners of Brekka land, argued for the annulment of the development consent for a road construction on their land and claimed that the consent had been incorrectly prepared. They furthermore argued for the annulment of the Road Administration's decision to expropriate a part of the Brekka land. Of interest in this case is that the experts that evaluated the monetary value of the Brekka land that needed to be expropriated were specifically asked to evaluate the loss of wilderness

[33] See further Art. 66, *cf.* Art. 65, of the NC-1999. Now referred to as the Nature Conservation Action Plan, see Art. 33(2) of the NC-2013.

[34] See further the view of Althingi's Environmental Committee, 'nefndarálit um frv. til l. um náttúruvernd' ('Committee's view on the proposal for Act on Nature Conservation'), þskj. 1111–1528. mál, 1998–1999, and 'þingsályktun um náttúruverndaráætlun 2009–2013', ('Nature Conservation Strategy 2009–2013'), þskj. 654–200. mál, accepted by Althingi, 2 February 2010.

[35] The preparation of these plans began as early as 1995. For further information see 'þingsályktun um áætlun um vernd og orkunýtingu landsvæða' ('Strategic Plan for Conservation and Energy Utilisation of Land Areas'), þskj. 892–889. mál, 2012–2013, No. 13/141.

> as the Brekka land would lose its value as a virgin land with the road construction.[36]

The above dispute indicates that the loss of wilderness qualities could have an impact upon the value of real-estate and could be considered a matter of private law. Had the concept of wilderness not been defined by the NC-1999 it is unlikely that this kind of argumentation would have been advanced before the court. Furthermore, this also indicates that, interestingly, the wilderness concept would appear to have a particular social status beyond that commonly espoused in traditional politics.

## 3 Defining wilderness under Icelandic law

### 3.1 *From virgin wilderness to uninhabited wilderness*

The term *virgin wilderness*[37] formally attained legal recognition with the entry into force of the NC-1999 on 1 July 1999. However, this initial legislation may be considered somewhat flawed, since it lacked the necessary tools to legally designate and protect a defined wilderness area and was, moreover, influenced by, inter alia, the possible negative impact from the growing demand for electricity production and tourism.[38] Nevertheless, Article 3(6) NC-1999 accorded wilderness the following definition:

> an area of land at least 25 $km^2$ in size, or in which it is possible to enjoy solitude and nature without disturbance from man-made structures or the traffic of motorized vehicles on the ground, which is at least 5 km away from man-made structures or other evidence of technology, such as power lines, power stations, reservoirs and main roads, where no direct indications of human activity are visible and nature can develop without anthropogenic pressures.[39]

While it is for each individual jurisdiction to further elaborate the IUCN wilderness criteria in domestic law, the definition of wilderness advanced in the NC-1999 was considered unnecessarily strict. In particular, the highly specific wording of the size requirements precluded some valuable wilderness areas in Iceland[40] – essentially uninhabited

[36] See further http://haestirettur.is/.

[37] In Icelandic: *ósnortið víðerni.*

[38] See Subsection 2.3.

[39] Unofficial English translation of NC-1999 available at http://eng.umhverfisraduneyti.is/legislation/nr/389. Note that the definition was originally advanced in Article 3(4).

[40] See further explanations to Article 46 in frumvarp til laga um náttúruvernd (proposal for Act on Nature Conservation), 2012–2013, þskj. 537–429. mál, which became NC-2013, and also nefndarálit um frumvarp til laga um náttúruvernd (the view of Althingi's Environmental Committee on the proposal), 2012–2013, þskj. 1113–1429. mál.

areas that are not located in the traditional highlands – from otherwise meeting these conditions.[41] In addition, the NC-1999 definition was also considered to be incompatible with the wilderness definitions of other states,[42] and is indeed only partially compatible with the IUCN wilderness guidelines.

These inherent weaknesses in the NC-1999 definition led to the reformulation of the wilderness concept in Icelandic law. Accordingly, Article 5(19) of the new Act No 60/2013 on Nature Conservation (NC-2013)[43] introduces a revised and more flexible wilderness concept under the heading *uninhabited wilderness*.[44] The new definition reads as follows:

> an area of uninhabited land that is usually at least 25 km$^2$ in size or so that one can enjoy solitude and nature without disturbance from man-made structures or the traffic of motorized vehicles and at least 5 km away from man-made structures and other evidence of technology, such as power lines, power stations, reservoirs and main roads.[45]

There are accordingly two main differences between the definitions advanced in NC-1999 and NC-2013:

(1) The unnecessary strictness of the NC-1999 has been softened by changing the fundamental concept from *virgin wilderness* to *uninhabited wilderness*, and
(2) the addition of the word *usually* to the qualifying criterion makes it possible to formally protect a *defined wilderness area even if it* does not fully satisfy the size requirement.

As a result of these developments, the new wilderness definition prescribed under NC-2013 now facilitates the recognition of particular areas as 'wilderness', even though they do not strictly fulfil the size criterion, which is definitely a step forward. Furthermore, it is no longer a condition that the area in question represents virgin land, as the definitional emphasis has shifted to the term 'uninhabited'. Both of these changes, in conjunction with the wording of Article 46, are thus likely to strengthen wilderness protection in Iceland.

41 *Ibid.*
42 *Ibid.*
43 See also recent changes that were made on NC-2013 in 2015 http://www.althingi.is/altext/145/s/0432.html.
44 In Icelandic: *óbyggt víðerni*, see further NC-2013, Art. 5.
45 Author's translation. A similar definition of wilderness was initially advanced in Art. 46 of the original proposal that would ultimately become NC-2013. See note 40.

### *3.2 The three main wilderness qualities – comparison*

Comparing the wilderness definition of the NC-2013 to the three main wilderness qualities distinguished in Chapter 1 (derived from IUCN's basic criteria[46]), and taking into account Article 46 of the NC-2013, it seems evident that the new definition will broaden the scope of the legal protection of wilderness in Iceland, while the definition is still very much in line with the IUCN criteria. The wilderness quality of naturalness (ecological intactness) as reflected in the NC-1999 definition is currently part of the definition in Article 5 and Article 46 NC-2013. Furthermore, the size requirement of the area has become a less absolute criterion, a development noted in the context of other regimes discussed in this book (see, e.g., Chapter 6).

However, a mere legal definition is, in itself, insufficient to adequately protect the national wilderness. Therefore, the next section will address the relevant legal framework relating to wilderness areas and wilderness quality protection in Iceland.

## 4 Legal instruments for wilderness protection

### *4.1 Introduction*

This section discusses the main instruments of Icelandic law that are relevant to wilderness protection.[47] To limit the coverage to laws explicitly referring to the term wilderness would be an oversimplification of the legal situation. Other important terms, including landscape, uninhabited land, the highlands and mid-highlands, are also of importance as most surviving areas of wilderness would be located in either uninhabited or highland areas. Thus, the following Section first outlines the relevant wilderness principles of the NC-1999 and NC-2013 before discussing salient features of other acts with relevance to wilderness. This includes Act No 60/2007 on Vatnajökull National Park

[46] Dudley, *IUCN Guidelines for Applying Protected Area Management Categories*, *supra* note 23, at 14–15.

[47] Due to spatial constraints, several additional pieces of legislation – all of which have a limited geographical scope of application – could also have some relevance to wilderness protection but are not specifically discussed in this chapter. These acts include: lög nr. 54/1995 um vernd Breiðafjarðar (Act No 54/1995 on the Conservation of Breiðafjörður); lög nr. 47/2004 um þjóðgarðinn á Þingvöllum (Act No 47/2004 on the National Park at Þingvellir), and lög nr. 97/2004 um verndun Mývatns og Laxár í Suður-Þingeyjarsýslu (Act No 97/2004 on the Conservation of Mývatn and Laxá in South-Þingeyjarsýsla); see www.althingi.is.

(VNP-2007),[48] Act No 123/2010 on Spatial Planning (SP-2010) and Act No 106/2000 on Environmental Impact Assessment (EIA-2010). Although performing different roles, each of these acts has the potential to contribute to the legal protection of wilderness qualities. To place this broad framework in context, it is first appropriate to briefly discuss the relationship between Icelandic nature conservation legislation and that of the European Union.

### *4.2 Relationship to the European Union's nature conservation policy*

The European Union (EU) has placed a considerable emphasis on the conservation of European biodiversity; however, more recently the European Parliament and European Commission have each paid substantial attention to wilderness protection.[49] Iceland, which is not an EU Member State, is nevertheless a party to the Agreement on the European Economic Area (EEA).[50] According to Article 7 of the EEA Agreement, Iceland is under an obligation to implement particular EU provisions into its legal order. The material scope of the EEA Agreement is defined by several annexes listing the relevant EU legislation to be incorporated into national law. Even though one of them, Annex XX, *Environment*, contains the most important EU provisions in the environmental field,[51] EU acts that are directly focused on nature conservation, such as the Habitats Directive[52] and the Birds

[48] Lög nr. 60/2007 um Vatnajökulsþjóðgarð.

[49] See European Parliament Resolution of 3 February 2009 on Wilderness in Europe (2008/2210(INI)), discussed in Chapters 1 and 2. See also European Environmental Agency, *Wilderness Quality Index* (Copenhagen: EEA, 2011), www.eea.europa.eu/data-and-maps/figures/wilderness-quality-index, and European Commission, *Guidelines for the Management of Wilderness and Wild Areas in Natura 2000* (Brussels: European Commission, 2012), http://ec.europa.eu/environment/nature/natura2000/wilderness/pdf/WildernessGuidelines.pdf. See also Chapter 8.

[50] Agreement on the European Economic Area, 2 May 1992, OJ 1994 L 1, p. 3 (EEA Agreement); see www.efta.int/eea/eea-agreement.aspx.

[51] Including the Directive 2011/92/EU of 13 December 2011 on the assessment of the effects of certain public and private projects on the environment (EIA directive; consolidated version), OJ L 26, 28 January 2012, p. 1; Directive 2000/60/EC of 23 October 2000 establishing a framework for Community action in the field of water policy (Water Framework Directive), OJ L 327, 22 December 2000, p. 1, and the Directive 2004/35/EC of 21 April 2004 on environmental liability with regard to the prevention and remedying of environmental damage (Environmental Liability Directive), OJ L 143, 30 April 2004, p. 56.

[52] Directive 92/43/EEC of 21 May 1992 on the conservation of natural habitats and of wild fauna and flora (Habitats Directive), OJ L 206, 22 July 1992, p. 7. See also Chapter 8.

Directive,[53] are excluded from the material scope of the Agreement. Iceland is therefore not required to designate Special Areas of Conservation or to participate in the *Natura 2000* network pursuant to the Habitats Directive. Due to this legal situation, the EU's nature conservation policy, including its recent increasing emphasis on the potential inter-relationship between biodiversity and wilderness, has no formal relevance for nature conservation policy or the legislative process in Iceland.

### 4.3 *Nature conservation legislation*

#### Wilderness provision

As noted above, the wilderness concept that was established under the NC-1999 has been revised, and a new legal regime the NC-2013, came into force 15 November 2015. The definition of wilderness has been changed and one of the core weaknesses of the NC-1999 – the lack of legal tools to designate and protect wilderness areas – is now rectified through Article 46 of NC-2013. This provision, entitled *uninhabited wilderness*, prescribes unprecedented powers to formally designate and protect a defined wilderness area:

> Large land areas wherein human influences are minimal and where nature can evolve without the pressure from human activities can be formally protected as uninhabited wilderness.
>
> The protection should aim to safeguard the characteristics of the areas, *e.g.* to maintain diverse and unusual landscapes, panoramas and/or conserve complete large ecosystems, and ensure that present and future generations can enjoy therein solitude and nature without disturbance from man-made infrastructures or traffic from motor vehicles.[54]

Article 46 of the NC-2013 has two important elements from the standpoint of wilderness protection. First, Article 46(1) grants a general power of authorization to the Minister for the Environment and Natural Resources, pursuant to Article 38(1) of the NC-2013, to formally designate and protect an uninhabited wilderness. In the event that the Minister takes such a decision, the criteria in Article 46(1), as well as those comprising the wilderness definition of Article 5(19), have to be fulfilled. Second, Article 46(2) stipulates the general aims and objectives

[53] Directive 2009/147/EC of 30 November 2009 on the conservation of wild birds (Birds Directive; consolidated version), OJ L 20, 26 January 2010, p. 7. See also Chapter 8.

[54] Author's translation from the original Icelandic.

of wilderness protection. These objectives shall be elaborated further in a subsequent officially published regulation, which will have a general legal effect and be applicable to the designated wilderness area in question. No stand is taken on the ownership of the land area that would be protected as a wilderness according to Article 46, accordingly both public and privately owned areas could be designated.[55] Article 46(1) is a passive provision, unless the Minister decides to designate and protect a defined wilderness area accordingly. Nevertheless, although Article 46(2) refers to particular wilderness aims, they do not as such create rights or duties unless a wilderness area has been formally designated and protected in line with Article 46.

## Conservation objectives

With the entering into force of the NC-2013, specific conservation objectives established under Articles 2 and 3 NC-2013 will have to be taken into account in environmental decision-making. Article 2 concerns biotopes, ecosystems and species and emphasizes, inter alia, the protection of biological diversity and the favourable conservation status of species. Article 3 applies to geological formations, water basins, landscape and wilderness and addresses, inter alia, the conservation of geological and landscape diversity, protection of unique or rare landscapes, and the safeguarding of uninhabited wilderness. These conservation objectives are a new feature of Icelandic nature conservation legislation and have the ability to enhance the quality of environmental decision-making, including the ones that affect wilderness and wilderness qualities.

## Environmental principles

Another novel feature of the NC-2013 is the incorporation of several important environmental principles, cf. Articles 8–11. These principles are to be taken into account in environmental decision-making, including general decisions, such as general regulations, and individual decisions,

[55] Although not without possible exceptions, wilderness areas and other uninhabited areas in Iceland would generally fall under the concept of *public land* (in Icelandic: *þjóðlenda*), even though private individuals or legal persons may enjoy limited rights of ownership there; see Art. 1 of lög nr. 58/1998 um þjóðlendur og ákvörðun marka eignarlanda, þjóðlendna og afrétta (Act No 58/1998 on public lands and the determination of the boundaries of private land, public land and upland ranges). The Icelandic State is the owner of such land and of all entitlements and natural harvests from it that are not governed by proprietary law, in line with Art. 2 of the Act.

which usually concern licensing of some kind. The first principle stipulates that decisions should be based upon scientific information and knowledge of the favourable conservation status of species population size, distribution and conservation status of biotopes and ecosystems and geology. The second mandates the application of the precautionary principle in decision-making and the taking of preventive measures. The third principle establishes that environmental impact should be evaluated by assessing the total ecological impact or total critical load of the activity in question. Finally, the fourth tenet incorporates a general polluter-pays principle, obliging the developer to pay reasonable costs of preventing impacts or damage connected with development projects. Although these environmental principles are rather general, they should nonetheless enhance environmental decision-making and, as such, could contribute to the conservation of wilderness qualities. Some of them, inter alia, the precautionary principle is further elaborated in the NC-2013 and the SP-2010 notably in its Article 13 on developing consent.

### General duty of care

As the NC-2013 has only recently entered into force, no wilderness area has as yet been formally designated and protected under the legislation. Wilderness qualities may nevertheless enjoy some legal protection by virtue of the general nature conservation provisions advanced therein, which provisions have been strengthened compared to the NC-1999. In line with Article 12(2) of the NC-1999, everyone was obliged to treat the natural environment with respect and take the utmost care to avoid damaging it.[56] A similar, yet more advanced, provision is now found in Article 6 of the NC-2013, which not only stipulates a general duty of precaution and care for nature, but also emphasizes that every reasonable preventive measure should be taken in order to diminish impacts on nature from development projects and other operations with a potential environmental impact.

### Special protection

As outlined above, the NC-1999 did not advance a particular provision for the designation of a defined wilderness area. Even so, Article 37 of this

[56] Art. 12(2) NC-1999 did not turn out to be effective as the Icelandic courts deemed its wording to be too general and imprecise. Accordingly, if the environment was treated in a disrespectful manner that resulted in environmental damage, no criminal liability would follow. See, e.g., Judgment of the Supreme Court of Iceland, *ákæruvaldið gegn Jóni Guðmundssyni*, Case No 458/2006, available through http://haestirettur.is/.

act, which addressed special protection, should have contribute to the protection of wilderness qualities. According to Article 37(1) several types of ecosystems and geological formations enjoyed special protection and their disturbance should be avoided, if at all possible. The ecosystems and geological formations that fell under Article 37(1) were: (a) volcanic craters, rootless vents (pseudo craters) and lava fields; (b) freshwater lakes and pools, 1,000 $m^2$ or more in size; (c) bogs and fens, 3 hectares or more in size; (d) waterfalls, hot springs and other thermal sources, as well as surfacial geothermal deposits (sinter and travertine), 100 $m^2$ or more in size and (e) salt marshes and mudflats. In line with Article 37(2), particular procedural requirements were established to facilitate the special protection of these features. If the proposed project involved the disturbance of an ecosystem or landscape type covered under Article 37 (1), the relevant licensing authority was obliged to obtain an opinion from the Environment Agency of Iceland (EA) and the local environmental committee before issuing development consent and a building permit. Although the EA and the local committee do not ultimately have the power to prevent the licensing of an activity, these opinions usually have some effect and could prompt modifications to the original plans so as to minimize their environmental impacts. In reality, however, the special protection has not transpired to be very effective and has provided only modest protection against the disturbance of the respective ecosystems or geological formations.[57]

A similar but more advanced provision on the special protection of particular ecosystems and geological formations is however found in Article 61 NC-2013. Two additional categories of ecosystems have been added to those protected under NC-1999, namely several types of wetlands that are 20,000 $m^2$ or larger in size and natural birch forests, and one type of geological formations, i.e., lava caves that formed in the early post-glacial period. The wording of the disturbance criterion has also been strengthened as disturbances should be avoided unless they are absolutely necessary. Furthermore, these disturbances are subject to a developing consent, issued according to Article 13 of SP-2010 that is based on the precautionary principle. This is very important as it necessitates an objective assessment of the likelihood of environmental disturbance that may result in a decision of not allowing any disturbance at all. Finally, the conservation objectives and environmental principles of

[57] See further comments advanced in frumvarp til laga um náttúruvernd (proposal for an Act on Nature Conservation), þskj. 537–429. mál, 2012–2013.

the NC-2013 have to be taken into account in the decision-making process.

The changes that have been made concerning the special protection provision should contribute to the protection of wilderness qualities.

### Off-road driving

In spite of the prohibition against off-road driving the negative impact of off-road driving has been environmentally problematic in Iceland for years.[58] Off-road driving has been a particular problem in the fragile highlands, largely due to a lack of paved roads, which has led to the development of a system of country roads and unofficial rural roads and tracks, with the latter usually emerging without any formal preparation or consent. Until now the main practical problem has been tied to the definition of a road, since – in line with established human rights principles – the benefit of the doubt in relation to whether a vehicle has been actually driven off-road has been applied in favour of the accused, rather than the wider interests of nature.[59] Moreover, several entities produce and sell maps, including road-maps, which depict these unofficial rural roads and tracks. Similar to Article 17(1) NC-1999, Article 31 NC-2013 also prohibits and criminalizes all off-road driving. Since there has been no improvement in the current situation of unofficial rural roads and tracks, the Icelandic Road and Coastal Administration (IRCA) has been charged with developing an official database to collate information on the roads and tracks that can be legally driven by vehicles, see further Article 32 of the NC-2013. To ensure the administrative legality of the measures, the Minister will formally approve the road database, which, when available, shall be officially published. Those entities producing and selling road-maps, including digital GPS-maps, will then be under an obligation to reflect, as far as possible, the information in the official database. When operational, the new system should contribute to nature conservation in general and should also improve the official surveillance of off-road driving, particularly in the highlands, which has not been sufficiently effective.[60]

[58] See, inter alia, *Skýrsla umhverfisráðherra Þórunnar Sveinbjarnardóttur um Alþingis um umhverfismál* 2007–2008 (Report of the Minister for the Environment to Althingi on Environmental Issues, 2007–2008), particularly p. 12.

[59] See, e.g., Judgment of the Supreme Court of Iceland, *ákæruvaldið gegn X*, Case No 331/ 2006, available through http://www.haestirettur.is/.

[60] *Ibid.*

### Summing up

In principle, the new approach to off-road driving (Articles 31–32 NC-2013), the provision of more focused rules relating to the special protection of particular ecosystems and geological formations (Article 61 NC-2013), and the inclusion of conservation objectives and environmental principles should, in theory, contribute to the protection of wilderness qualities. As outlined above, the NC-1999 did not contain a specific provision for the formal designation and protection of a defined wilderness area, even if some of its wider provisions could have been considered to contribute to the general protection of wilderness qualities, notably Article 37. This legal obstacle has now been removed with the entering into force of the NC-2013, as the inclusion of the new wilderness provision in Article 46 allows the Minister for the Environment and Natural Resources to formally designate and protect a defined wilderness area. Whether these tools will be used in the future, however, remains to be seen.

## *4.4 Vatnajökull National Park*

Act No 60/2007 on Vatnajökull National Park (VNP-2007) protects a spacious, uninhabited and, to a large extent, a wilderness area, comprising thirteen per cent of Icelandic territory,[61] – including Europe's largest glacier, Vatnajökull, which spans 8,000 $km^2$ – endowing it with a unique governance system and a legal framework of protective measures.[62] Vatnajökull National Park was formally established in 2008; see regulation No 608/2008 on Vatnajökull National Park. In line with VNP-2007 Articles 6 and 7, the National Park is governed by its own management board and is divided into four administrative units, namely the Northern region, Eastern region, Southern region and Western region. The rationale behind the establishment of the National Park was primarily to protect the area's landscape, biosphere, geological formations and

[61] See further www.vatnajokulsthjodgardur.is/english/education/.

[62] See further Act No 60/2007 on Vatnajökull National Park and Regulation No 608/2008 on Vatnajökull National Park with amendments. See particularly regulation amendment No 3 (No 463/2013), which includes maps, www.reglugerd.is/interpro/dkm/WebGuard.nsf/key2/463-2013. Vatnajökull National Park includes two national parks, Skaftafell and Jökulsárgljúfur, and several other smaller protected conservation areas that had been formally protected according to law before the entering into force of VNP-2007 but are now enjoying protection by the NVP-2007. See the map at www.vatnajokulsthjodgardur.is/media/skjol/Heildarkort_ISL-12okt2011.jpg. See also http://whc.unesco.org/en/tentativelists/5590/.

cultural heritage and to facilitate opportunities for the general public to visit the Park without damaging its natural features, see further VNP-2007 Article 2. Aside from a general obligation to take due care (see further VNP-2007 Article 14), and the prohibition of off-road driving in line with Article 15, the National Park's main management tool consists of a strategic management plan.[63] The plan is prepared in line with a formal procedure and must eventually be approved by the Minister for the Environment and Natural Resources according to VNP-2007 Article 12. Under Article 13(2) the fundamental principle of the VNP-2007 is that construction projects and the taking of material within the National Park should only be allowed if they have been integrated into the plan; if necessary, individual construction projects can be undertaken subject to particular conditions in order to protect the integrity of the National Park. The strategic management plan is legally binding upon the local governments in the vicinity of the park, in line with Article 13(1), who must follow them in their spatial planning, see further Subsection 4.5. Compared to other unprotected areas of Iceland, both the VNP-2007 and the management plan provide the National Park with a relatively good level of wilderness protection, although negative impacts upon wilderness qualities may still be possible. Nevertheless, taking into account the size and the wilderness quality of Vatnajökull National Park in general, it would be fair to say that the legal approach that was chosen for this area does contribute to the protection of its inherent wilderness qualities.

## *4.5 Spatial planning legislation*

### Spatial plans

As established under Article 78(1) of the Icelandic Constitution,[64] the municipalities (local governments) manage their administrative affairs independently. Competence over spatial planning – which is regulated by Act No 123/2010 on Spatial Planning (SP-2010) – and decision-making powers over land-use is exercised by the seventy-four municipalities.[65] Moreover, each such body holds independent planning jurisdiction

[63] See the documentation at www.vatnajokulsthjodgardur.is/verndun-og-stjornun/stjornunar–og-verndaraaetlun/.

[64] See further lög nr. 33/1944 stjórnarskrá lýðveldisins Íslands (Act No 33/1944 on the Constitution of the Republic of Iceland); English translation available at www.government.is/constitution/.

[65] For further information see www.samband.is/sveitarfelogin/sameining-sveitarfelaga/.

within a defined area that constitutes a municipality.[66] Effective and sympathetic spatial planning could therefore offer a degree of protection to wilderness qualities. One of the principal objectives of SP-2010 is landscape and nature protection and the prevention of environmental damage and overuse in the light of sustainable development.[67] The term 'landscape' carries a specific definition in Article 2(13) of the SP-2010:

> Landscape means an area that has an appearance and characteristics due to natural and/or man-made factors and their interaction. Landscape thus covers the everyday environment, environment having conservation value and environment that has been disturbed. Landscape includes, inter alia, urban areas, rural areas, virgin wilderness, rivers, lakes and marine areas.[68]

Also of importance is Article 3(3), *cf.* Article 12 SP-2010, stipulating the general duty of the local governments to prepare spatial plans, whose content must correspond to the principal objectives of the SP-2010, and the centralized Strategic Planning Policy (SPP; see further below). Three types of municipal spatial plans are envisaged under the SP-2010:

(1) regional plans for two or more municipalities containing a common land-use policy and land-use policy that municipalities deem necessary to synchronize due to common interests. This is an optional planning level except for the greater capital area: see further Article 22 SP-2010;
(2) master plans for each municipality as a whole, which are mandatory, and wherein all present and future land-uses policy must be reflected: see further Article 28 SP-2010, and
(3) zoning of particular areas or zones, e.g. building and development sites, within a municipality under Article 37 SP-2010.

These plans operate on a hierarchical basis. If a regional plan has been formulated, it will rank higher than a master plan, to which a zoning plan will also be subordinated. Moreover, each planning level or type of plan must be compatible with one above it; see further Article 12(7) of the SP-2010. The plans are essentially differentiated by their purpose and level of detail. These objectives also permeate localized decision-making processes since, as a general rule, all licensing decisions, including for

[66] See further Art. 3 and 12 of SP-2010 and Art. 1 and 4 of sveitarstjórnarlög nr. 38/2011 (Act No 38/2011 on Local Government).
[67] Art. 1(b), SP-2010.
[68] Author's translation from Icelandic.

those concerning development and building permits, would be based on either the master or the zoning plans.

Spatial planning has a clear role to play in establishing the developmental conditions necessary for the protection of wilderness. Locations that have been planned as uninhabited areas by the municipalities as well as formal nature conservation areas (namely those areas that have been formally designated and protected in line with the NC-2013 or NC-1999 or any of the other nature conservation acts outlined above and formally designated wilderness areas that could be established in the future according to Article 46 NC-2013) must be reflected in the spatial plans in order to ensure that they remain protected and to prevent the erroneous approval of developing and building permits that could operate contrary to these planning objectives.[69] Furthermore, in line with Article 6(3) of the Spatial Planning Regulation No 90/2013, the ecosystems and geological formations that enjoy the special protection in line with Article 61 of the NC-2013 (previously Article 37 NC-1999) must also be reflected in the master plans. However, as noted in Subsection 4.3, this protection is not absolute and will be subject to the balancing of the competing interests. Conversely, however, individual municipalities can of course demonstrate a clearer commitment to wilderness protection in their land-use planning by limiting the issue of developmental and building permits accordingly.

### The pre-1998 position and the mid-highlands plan

Prior to the entry into force on 1 January 1998 of Act No 73/1997 on Spatial Planning and Building Issues, the predecessor of SP-2010, national planning law was unclear on spatial planning responsibilities and whether all areas of Iceland – particularly the mid-highlands – were officially located within a defined municipality.[70] The term 'mid-highlands', which is primarily a planning term,[71] refers to the highland area of

[69] Landscape protection is further elaborated in the Spatial Planning Regulation No 90/2013, Art. 6.2 and 6.3.

[70] Art. 4 of skipulagslög nr. 19/1964 (Act No 19/1964 on Spatial Planning) stipulated that all municipalities were subject to physical planning. However, Art. 9(1) of skipulags- og byggingarlög nr. 73/1997 (Act No 73/1997 on Spatial Planning and Building Issues) subjected all land in Iceland to physical planning and required that all buildings and other man-made structures should be addressed in accordance with such plans; see also A. Jóhannsdóttir, Breytingar á fyrirkomulagi skipulagsmála á miðhálendi Íslands, *Afmælisrit Páll Sigurðsson sjötugur 16. ágúst 2014*, E.G. Gunnarsson, et al. (eds.) (2014), pp. 1–31, at p. 5.

[71] The definition was inserted into Act No 19/1964 in 1993 with amendments according to lög nr. 73/19973 um breytingu á skipulagslögum, nr. 19/1964, ásamt síðari breytingum (Act No 73/1993 on the Amendment to Act No 19/1964 on Spatial Planning, with amendments).

mid-Iceland, including traditional grazing lands, uninhabited areas and principal glaciers. The uncertain legal status of this area, alongside other developments affecting the mid-highlands, including enhanced accessibility for motor vehicles, increasing levels of tourism, unregulated building activities and the expanding needs of the energy sector,[72] led to the establishment in the early 1990s of a cooperative committee, tasked with preparing a spatial plan for the area. The municipalities closest to the mid-highlands participated in the work of the committee, which was chaired by a representative of the Ministry for the Environment.[73] The committee's main task was to prepare a planning proposal for the mid-highlands, which was eventually approved as a regional plan for the mid-highland area and entered into force in 1999.[74] The performance of the mid-highlands plan is due to be formally evaluated but it is likely that this development has had a broadly positive effect. Indeed, given the principles of hierarchy and compatibility exercised in national spatial planning as outlined above (see also Article 9(7) of Act No 73/1997), the mid-highlands regional plan did ultimately bind the relevant local governments in their planning efforts.[75] The current mid-highland plan will remain in force until it will be replaced by the SSP which is currently under preparation.[76]

### Strategic planning policy

As indicated above, the spatial planning system underwent considerable adjustment with the entry into force of the SP-2010. The new centralized SPP could be of considerable importance in the context of wilderness protection. Under Article 10 SP-2010 the Minister for the Environment and Natural Resources is responsible for the SPP, which is to be submitted to the Althingi in the form of a proposal for a parliamentary resolution.[77] The SPP will eventually establish a long-term centralized

[72] See further frumvarp til laga um breytingu á skipulagslögum, nr 19/1964, ásamt síðari breytingum (proposal on an Act on the Amendment to Act No 19/1964 on Spatial Planning, with amendments), þskj. 1259–1455. mál, 1992–1993.

[73] *Ibid.*

[74] For further documents and maps, see http://halendi.is/Svaedisskipulag2015/.

[75] See further, note 71, at 12–13.

[76] See further provisional Art. 4, SP-2010, and www.skipulagsstofnun.is/skipulagsmal/svaedisskipulag/svaedisskipulag-midhalendisins/.

[77] The first proposal for a SPP was submitted to the Althingi on 28 February 2013 but was not accepted. See further tillaga til þinsályktunar um landsskipulagsstefnu 2013–2024 (Proposal for an Althingi's Resolution on the Strategic Planning Policy 2013–2024), þskj. 1087–623. mál. At the time of writing a new proposal is being developed by Althingi, see further tillaga til þingsályktunar um landsskipulagsstefnu 2015–2026 (Proposal for an Althingi's Resolution on the Strategic Planning Policy 2015–2026), þskj. 101 - 101. mál.

planning policy, valid for twelve years and subject to regular revision, that integrates several official strategies relating to transportation, population patterns, nature conservation, energy utilization, and other issues concerning land-use.[78] At the time of writing the SPP has been prepared by the National Planning Agency (NPA) and was submitted to the Althingi in the spring of 2015. The SPP emphasizes four main issues: (1) planning policy for the mid-highlands; (2) policy relating to settlement patterns and distribution of settlement; (3) planning policy for marine and coastal areas, and (4) planning of land-use in rural areas.[79] Once the SPP has been approved by the Althingi, it will replace the current mid-highlands plan.[80]

The first of these policies in particular could play an important role in wilderness protection. In the light of the experience of the current mid-highlands plan of 1999 the new policy should, inter alia, reflect a synchronized land-use policy based upon several official plans and policies, including the NCS (now Nature Conservation Action Plan, see Art. 33(2) of NC-2013), tourism, transportation and the conservation and energy utilization of land areas. Furthermore, issues concerning landscape protection, wilderness protection and soil protection should also be reflected in the policy, as well as issues relating to transportation and the road system in the area.[81] Eventually, when the SPP has been accepted by the Althingi, the further elaboration of the policy will be the responsibility of the local governments that exercise planning jurisdiction in the mid-highlands, which will be primarily facilitated through the spatial plans established under SP-2010.[82] Depending on the final content of the planning policy for the mid-highlands, the SPP, when accepted, could provide some protection for wilderness qualities as the municipalities have to take content of the SPP into account in further elaborating their spatial planning, as stipulated by the first sentence of Article 10(4). Conversely, however, the effectiveness of the SPP may be undermined by the second sentence of Article 10(4), which stipulates that:

> [if] a local government is of the opinion that an accepted strategic planning policy should not be taken into account in the spatial planning then it

[78] See further Art. 10 of the SP-2010.

[79] See further the letter to the NPA from the Minister for the Environment and Natural Resources, dated 25 October 2013, www.landsskipulag.is/um-landsskipulagsstefnu/frettir/nr/858.

[80] This is in line with para. 4 of the provisional Article of the SP-2010.

[81] See note 79,

[82] See further Art. 12, and 21–44 of SP-2010.

can present a reasoned opinion that should be attached to the proposal for a spatial plan when it is sent to the National Planning Agency.[83]

Moreover, the SPP is essentially expressed in a less-binding legal format. Indeed, while explicitly based on the foundation of Article 10 of the SP-2010, it is nonetheless a resolution that has limited legal effect and primarily reflects the intentions of the Althingi. This provides scope for a local government body to present reasons to thereby disregard one or several parts of the SPP in its spatial planning. The text of SP-2010 is silent as to the consequences of such a move. However, in the light of Article 78 of the Constitution, which stipulates that local governments manage their affairs independently as laid down by law, it appears likely that the will of a local government body that argues against the SPP would ultimately prevail.[84]

This position is in marked contrast to the current mid-highland regional plan that formally binds the local governments.

### Limitations on planning powers

The planning powers exercised by the municipalities are not absolute and the content of the spatial plans may be clearly limited by allied legislation. In relation to wilderness qualities the most important limitations relate to: (1) formally protected conservation areas according to the NC-2013 (NC-1999), such as the nature reserves and a defined wilderness area protected in line with Article 46; (2) the protection of defined nature conservation areas in line with special Acts;[85] and (3) VNP-2007. What these limitations have in common is that the protected areas must be shown in the spatial plans and the respective local government is not competent to dispose of the areas for other uses.[86] Apart from these and other clear legal limitations, each local government can legally decide the land-use policy for the respective municipality; however, the general principles and objectives of the SP-2010 and the SPP should be respected.

[83] Author's translation from Icelandic.

[84] See also the underlying principle reflected in Judgment of the Supreme Court of Iceland: *Íslenska ríkið gegn Flóahreppi*, Case No 579/2010, where the refusal of the Minister for the Environment to validate a particular part of Flóahreppur's (municipality) master plan was annulled. The contested part concerned the location of a hydropower project, *Urriðafossvirkjun*, and the National Power Company's involvement during the plan's preparation. See www.haestirettur.is/.

[85] See note 47.

[86] See, inter alia, Art. 12 SP-2010 and the Spatial Planning Regulation No 90/2013, Art. 6.2 and Art. 6.3.

### 4.6 Environmental Impact Assessment

The Environmental Impact Assessment process under Act No 106/2000 on Environmental Impact Assessment[87] (EIA-2000) has exercised some influence over the protection of wilderness qualities, particularly in circumstances whereby it has been questionable whether an EIA should ultimately be conducted. Although the EIA-2000 does not explicitly mention wilderness in its operational text, it nonetheless incorporates a reference to 'landscape' in its definition of the term 'environment', which is usually considered to include wilderness.[88] The question as to whether wilderness is likely to be affected by an individual project should thus be taken into account in the EIA process. Current practice indicates that direct references to wilderness values in EIA reports or in the NPA EIA decisions are rather scarce, although some examples can be found. In any event, two kinds of projects, if situated in the highlands, but both subject to a mandatory EIA,[89] are likely to affect wilderness values. These are: (1) large scale energy resources utilization and related installations, such as dams, reservoirs, power lines located in or adjacent to the mid-highlands, and (2) the construction of new roads in the same areas. As yet, it appears that no such projects have been cancelled due to their effects on wilderness qualities.

In this context the Kárahnjúkar Hydropower Plant Project is worthy of closer examination. In an EIA decision from 1 August 2001 the NPA decided that the Project, located in the mid-highlands, could not proceed due to its significant environmental impact and a lack of information on the environmental effects.[90] The NPA decision was appealed to the Minister for the Environment who, on 20 December 2001, overturned the decision and approved the project, albeit subject to several conditions.[91] In the court proceedings that followed, three individuals and one NGO challenged the EIA decision.[92] They argued for an annulment, inter alia, on the basis that the project would have a significant and irreversible environmental impact on vegetation, animal life, panorama and natural beauty, and due to the insufficient evaluation

[87] EIA-2000 implements the EU EIA directive, *supra* note 51, which is a part of the EEA Agreement; however, the annexes of the EIA directive have been slightly adjusted to reflect circumstances in Iceland.

[88] See Art. 3 EIA-2000 and Art. 1(13), SP-2010.

[89] Art. 5, EIA-2000, Annex 1.

[90] See www.skipulagsstofnun.is/umhverfismat/urskurdir/2000–2006/nr/577.

[91] See www.urskurdir.is/Umhverfis/UrskurdirRaduneytisins/nr/836.

[92] See www.haestirettur.is/.

of the effects on wilderness that would be permanently affected by the execution of the project.[93] The outcome was, however, unfavourable to the plaintiffs as the Supreme Court of Iceland, Case No 280/2003,[94] arrived at the conclusion that the EIA, although not perfect and containing some methodological flaws, should nonetheless not be annulled.

Had the critical highland area in question in Kárahnjúkar been formally designated a wilderness area and thus fallen under official protection, the legal situation would have been different. Indeed, it is likely that such protection would have precluded the execution of the project, inter alia, due to the location of the main reservoir, Hálslón. That, however, was not the case and the project was ultimately approved. Nevertheless, it is interesting to note that the location of the Hálslón reservoir prompted changes to be made to the boundaries of the Kringilsárrani natural reserve, which *had* been formally designated a nature reserve and was protected according to advertisement No 524/1974, resulting in a substantive reduction in the size of the protected area, see further advertisement No 181/2003.[95]

In contrast to development proposals caught under Article 5 of the EIA-2000, the need to conduct an EIA for other projects, such as smaller scale energy resources utilization, power lines, dams and reservoirs on protected areas, new roads within protected areas and tourist service installations in the highlands, is to be evaluated on a case-by-case basis.[96] Such a decision must be based on the criteria established in Annex 2 to the EIA-2000, which includes the location criterion that specifically mentions virgin wilderness.[97] Accordingly, a number of EIA decisions are particularly revealing in this context, given that some explicitly refer to the wilderness concept advanced in Article 5(19) NC-1999:

- In an EIA decision from 6 June 2001 the NPA decided not to subject a small scale enlargement of a tourist service facility in the heart of the mid-highlands (Drekagil) to an impact assessment and the decision did not directly mention wilderness considerations.[98]

[93] See also A. Jóhannsdóttir, 'Breytingar á mörkum friðlýstra svæða með áherslu á Ramsarsvæði', *Náttúrufræðingurinn*, 79(1–4)(2010), 68–74, at 73–74, commenting on the changes that were made on the delimitation of the Kringilsárrana nature reserve in 2003 due to the Kárahnúkar Project.

[94] See www.haestirettur.is/.

[95] See note 93.

[96] In line with Art. 6, EIA-2000.

[97] Regulation on Environmental Impact Assessment No 1123/2005 provides more information on the environmental report, particularly Art. 18.

[98] See www.skipulagsstofnun.is/media/attachments/Umhverfismat/495/2001010101.PDF.

- Also relevant is an EIA decision from 27 December 2000 concerning the environmental effects of drilling a borehole for geothermal research, road construction and related activities, where the NPA arrived at the conclusion that the operations, planned in a valley (Grænidalur), that had not been formally protected but listed in the Nature Conservation Registry (Hengilsvæði), and thus considered to have high conservation value, were deemed unacceptable due to their significant environmental impact on virgin land.[99] The EIA decision was appealed to the Ministry for the Environment, which did not consider the valley to be a wilderness within the meaning of the NC-1999 concept. The decision was annulled and the operations approved subject to particular conditions.[100]
- Finally, attention should be paid to an EIA decision from 27 May 2007, concerning a small scale hydropower station (Hverfisfljót) and road construction that did not subject the project to an EIA. However, the Ministry for the Environment annulled the EIA decision and subjected the project to an EIA, inter alia, by referring to the possible effects on wilderness and the uniqueness of the area's lava fields, which were protected by Article 37 of the NC-1999 (equal to Article 61 of the NC-2013).[101]

Although an EIA may be of importance for the protection of wilderness qualities, the assessment alone will not ensure that wilderness values will actually enjoy legal protection. The formal protection of a defined wilderness area could, however, change this position.

## 5 Conclusion

The main objective of this chapter was to evaluate the role and effectiveness of the law in protecting Icelandic wilderness. The coverage was placed within the particular context of the decline of Icelandic wilderness, which is seemingly attributable to the development of particular infrastructures and growing tourism activities. As has been demonstrated, there is relatively little indication from current legal practice that the wilderness concept as reflected in the NC-1999 has secured a substantial improvement in the protection of this type of land. The reason for this is most likely the fact that the NC-1999 lacked a provision

[99] See www.skipulagsstofnun.is/umhverfismat/urskurdir/2000–2006/nr/536.
[100] See www.urskurdir.is/Umhverfis/UrskurdirRaduneytisins/2001/11.
[101] See www.umhverfisraduneyti.is/media/PDF_skrar/hverfisfljoturskurdur.pdf.

for the designation and formal protection of a defined wilderness area. Yet the changes that have now been accepted in the new nature conservation legislation (NC-2013), particularly the redefinition of the wilderness concept, have widened the regulatory scope of this provision by allowing for particular sites to be qualify as wilderness areas even if they do not strictly meet the relevant size criterion. Furthermore, the new approach to off-road driving, in conjunction with a revised and more effective approach to the protection of ecosystems and geological formations according to the special protection provisions, as well as a new material provision for the designation and formal protection of a defined wilderness (Article 46), should contribute to more effective wilderness conservation in the future. It cannot, however, be overlooked that the application of Article 46 is not mandatory and will be subject to the exercise of political discretion. Indeed, Article 46 will only function effectively in this context if it is actually used to designate and formally protect a defined wilderness areas. Other legislative provisions, which do not necessarily mention wilderness as directly in their operative texts, are also of relevance to the protection of wilderness quality land. These include the VNP-2007; the new approach adopted in the SP-2010 – not least the new SPP, which will eventually replace the special mid-highlands plans – and the EIA-2000. On the other hand the ability of the local government bodies to avoid the full implementation of SPP policies renders the promotion of wilderness qualities in the mid-highlands a matter of some uncertainty. It remains to be seen whether such policies will ultimately be followed by the local governments. The Icelandic wilderness and wilderness qualities will however not protect themselves. From the preceding discussion it is clear that, while this disparate legal framework is important in the protection of the wilderness, it cannot provide any absolute wilderness guarantees for future generations.

# 17

## Wilderness protection in Norway

OLE KRISTIAN FAUCHALD

### 1 Introduction

Norway has always been a sparsely populated country. As of January 2015 there were sixteen persons per km$^2$ on the Norwegian mainland. Mainly because of low soil productivity and reliance on natural resources, the population has traditionally been spread throughout the country, except at high elevations (forty-seven per cent of the Norwegian mainland is mountainous).[1] Hence, even if population density has been low, most areas in Norway have been subject to significant human interference throughout the past 800 years.[2] The emerging valuation of wilderness in the Norwegian context coincided with efforts to gain independence from Sweden and burgeoning nationalist sentiments during the nineteenth century. It also coincided with significant population growth and greater use of nature for hunting, fishing, farming and forestry. There was thus tension between the valuation of wilderness among intellectuals and the wealthy, and the increasing dependence of the rural poor on scarce natural resources.[3] Also today we find tensions along similar lines: farmers – especially those engaged in forestry – generally oppose initiatives to protect wilderness and emphasize voluntary approaches to the establishment protected areas; by contrast, national authorities and NGOs have tended to promote a top-down approach to nature protection – inter alia, through the wilderness concept.[4]

[1] See www.ssb.no/en/natur-og-miljo/statistikker/arealstat. This includes the three categories 'open firm ground', 'bare rock, gravel and rock fields' and 'perpetual snow and glaciers'.

[2] See B. Berntsen, *Grønne linjer: Natur- og miljøvernets historie i Norge* (Oslo: Unipub, 2011), 15–23.

[3] *Ibid.*, 25–35.

[4] For a relevant case study, see M. Reitan and F.E. Holm, 'Staten, kommunene og Trillemarka: lokal mobilisering forankret nasjonale politiske konflikter', in M. Reitan, J. Saglie and E. Smith (eds.), *Det norske flernivådemokratiet* (Oslo: Abstrakt forlag, 2012), 167–195.

Currently, Norway ranks among the European countries with highest population growth, and the medium estimate is that the population will grow from today's 5 million to close to 8 million by 2100.[5] Despite the long-term general policy of maintaining a geographically spread population, including very high support to agriculture,[6] there has been significant increase in the urban population and decrease in the rural population in many areas.[7]

Against this background, we should expect pressures on wilderness areas in Norway to be modest.[8] However, there are many factors that point to increased pressure on wilderness areas – not least the construction of cabins and holiday homes, expansion of energy production and infrastructure, construction of roads and railways, the need for increased extraction of natural resources due to expected lower revenues from fossil energy resources, as well as the general increase in economic activity.[9]

Wilderness protection has been on the agenda of the Norwegian administrative authorities for several decades. One early definition of 'wilderness' was developed in the 1970s by Statistics Norway for a committee established to propose reforms to the country's nature protection policy.[10] By this definition, the term 'wilderness' applied to areas

[5] See www.ssb.no/en/befolkning/statistikker/folkfram.

[6] See OECD, *Agricultural Policy Monitoring and Evaluation 2013: OECD Countries and Emerging Economies* (Paris: OECD, 2013) at 42–43, where support in Norway is highest among the countries examined, and is estimated at more than sixty per cent of gross farm receipts.

[7] See www.ssb.no/en/befolkning/statistikker/beftett.

[8] A. Skonhoft and H. Solem, 'Economic Growth and Land-use Changes: The Declining Amount of Wilderness Land in Norway', *Ecological Economics*, 37 (2001), 289–301, at 296, finds, on the basis of data from 1988 and 1994, 'that the consumption of wilderness land is greatly influenced by crowding in a broad sense, interpreted as county-specific demographic and geographic factors in this cross-section analysis. The population density effect is particularly strong for wilderness land of the least restrictive character [i.e. more than one km from major infrastructure.]'

[9] *Ibid.*, at 298: 'the level of economic activity, correcting for variations in population density, explains between forty-six per cent and sixty-five per cent of the variations in the amount of wilderness land among the counties for the two broadest categories of wilderness land. Hence, in these cases, the higher level of GDP per capita in a region, the less wilderness land. [. . .] Secondly, the fixed effects models reveal a negative, and linear, connection between GDP per capita growth and conversion of wilderness land; the higher the economic growth, the higher the consumption of wilderness land.'

[10] See *Norges offentlige utredninger* (Norwegian Official Reports; hereinafter NOU) 1980:23, *Naturvern i Norge*, 33–35. The maps show areas located more than 5 km from roads, railroads, human settlements and regulated waterways, and were originally prepared for southern Norway only. The maps were extended to the rest of the Norwegian mainland in

located more than 5 km from significant infrastructure. The definition has subsequently been further refined; in its early form, it listed the following types of technical infrastructure that would prevent an area from qualifying as 'wilderness':[11]

- public roads and railways, except tunnels
- forest roads, farm tracks, access roads and roads to summer farms exceeding 50 m in length
- tracks improved to enable use by tractors and off-road vehicles
- tracks approved for motor vehicles when the ground is not snow-covered (in Finnmark, the northernmost county of Norway)
- power lines carrying 33 kV or more
- reservoirs (entire extent of water at highest regulated water level), regulated rivers and streams
- above-ground pipelines
- power plants, penstocks, canals, levees, embankments and flood protection works.

The definition of wilderness was initially developed to assist committees established to work on further developing Norwegian nature conservation policy, in particular in the context of national parks.[12] As further discussed below, the definition has since been revised and has become a decision-making tool for other policy and administrative decisions. It is currently administered by the Norwegian Environment Agency.

A new approach to wilderness issues can be derived from the Norwegian Nature Index, which was first published in 2010.[13] The Index provides a general overview of the status and trends of ecosystems based on expert opinions of natural scientists. Among its purposes is to serve as a tool for decision-making authorities. Most of the reference

NOU 1986:13 *Ny landsplan for nasjonalparker*, 31–32. On the historical background, see also T. Skjeggedal, T. Arnesen, J. Kveli, G. Markhus, P.G. Thingstad, G. Wollan and J. Aasetre, *Inngrepsfrie naturområder som verktøy for arealforvaltning* (Steinkjer: Nord-Trøndelagsforskning, 2005) (NTF-notat 2005, 6), 20–21. The authors trace the concept back to the 1960s and 1970s as being inspired by the 1964 US Wilderness Act. The concept of wilderness as used in Norway has close links to the 'purism construct' as elaborated in the United States; see O.I. Vistad and M. Vorkinn, 'The Wilderness Purism Construct: Experiences from Norway with a Simplified Version of the Purism Scale', *Forest Policy and Economics*, 19 (2012), 39–47, at 40.

[11] See Statistics Norway, *Natural Resources and the Environment 2007: Norway* (Oslo, 2008), at 131.

[12] See NOU 1974B:30 *Hardangervidda*, NOU 1980:23 *Naturvern i Norge*, and NOU 1986:13 *Ny landsplan for nasjonalparker*.

[13] See www.environment.no/Topics/Biological-diversity/The-Norwegian-Nature-Index-/

values for the indicators are set as the status of ecosystems without human interference ('undisturbed environment'). However, as has been pointed out, it would be a misconception to interpret this as if the general objective were to achieve an undisturbed environment.[14] Even though the Nature Index is related to wilderness and might significantly influence how the concept is used in future nature management, this will not be explored in detail here, due to its recent development and current lack of formal linkage to decision-making processes. That said, this recent development may contribute to developing the wilderness concept in Norway along lines that fit in well with the general description of the concept in the first chapter of this book, by promoting greater emphasis on the undisturbed and natural character of wilderness.

In the following, we explore the definition of wilderness in the Norwegian legal context, analysing the legal protection of wilderness in Norway, and discussing the implementation and enforcement of the legal framework for wilderness areas. The chapter concludes with some reflections on the future of wilderness protection in Norway.

The discussion focuses on the Norwegian mainland. However, it should be noted that Norway also exercises jurisdiction over several remote islands: Svalbard, Jan Mayen, Bouvet and Peter I Island, and has claims to Queen Maud Land in Antarctica. Norway has adopted the Svalbard Environmental Protection Act[15] and established extensive protected areas on Svalbard and Jan Mayen. These islands and areas are characterized by very limited human interference, and therefore vast tracts of wilderness.

## 2 What is 'wilderness' in the Norwegian legal context?

Norway adopted a comprehensive and updated act on nature protection, the Nature Diversity Act, in 2009.[16] The Act does not single out 'wilderness' as a concept deserving particular attention; and in the preparatory works, there was limited focus on wilderness.[17] The concept was

[14] S. Nybø, G. Certain and O. Skarpaas, *The Norwegian Nature Index 2010* (Trondheim: DN-report 1–2011), 18.

[15] See www.regjeringen.no/en/doc/Laws/Acts/Svalbard-Environmental-Protection-Act.html (English translation).

[16] See www.regjeringen.no/en/doc/Laws/Acts/nature-diversity-act.html (English translation).

[17] NOU 2004:28, *Lov om bevaring av natur, landskap og biologisk mangfold (Naturmangfoldloven)*, report of an expert committee, Chapter 17, see in particular pp. 320–321. The concept is barely mentioned in the government's proposal: see Ot.prp. no. 52 (2008–2009), *Om lov om forvaltning av naturens mangfold (naturmangfoldloven)*.

discussed mainly in the context of protected areas, in particular in relation to national parks, which may be established only 'where there is no major infrastructure development'.[18]

One of the most controversial topics discussed during the preparation of the Act was whether areas should be subject to automatic protection due to their current status of vulnerability. The result was Chapter VI on 'selected habitat types', according to which the government may adopt regulations designating specific habitat types as 'selected' throughout or in parts of Norway. Such decisions are to be based on (1) trends for or the status of the habitat type, (2) whether the habitat type is important for 'priority species' (see Sections 23 and 24 of the Act), (3) whether a significant proportion of the natural range of the habitat type is found in Norway and (4) whether international obligations apply to the habitat type. While the degree of wilderness as defined by the Norwegian Environment Agency may be relevant under these criteria or as a separate criterion (the above-mentioned criteria are not exhaustive), it does not appear to be particularly important and it was not mentioned in relevant parts of the preparatory work. However, virgin or old forests are among the nature types mentioned as particularly significant.[19]

Wilderness has been of some importance under planning and agricultural legislation. There are two main instruments under the Planning and Building Act (2008)[20] that are of relevance to wilderness areas. Wilderness areas may be identified in municipal plans and may thus be afforded protection against specific projects.[21] Further, wilderness issues are relevant to environmental impact assessments.[22] The regulations under the Forestry Act (2005)[23] mention wilderness as an essential factor when applications for financial support to forest roads are to be considered.

18 Section 35 of the Nature Diversity Act.

19 The proposal was based on an extensive mapping and assessment of nature types in Norway, which identified sixty-three nature types as particularly important from a biodiversity perspective. Many of the vulnerable or threatened nature types are situated in cultural landscapes: see NOU 2004:28, *supra* note 17, pp. 434 and 626 and Ot. prp. no. 52 (2008–2009), *supra* note 17, 271–288. See also A. Lindgaard and S. Henriksen (eds.), *Norwegian Red List for Ecosystems and Habitat Types 2011* (Trondheim: Norwegian Biodiversity Information Centre, 2011).

20 See www.regjeringen.no/en/doc/laws/Acts/planning-building-act.html (English translation).

21 See Chapters 11 and 12 of the Planning and Building Act, in particular Sections 11–8, 11–9, 12–5 and 12–7.

22 See Chapters 4 and 14 of the Planning and Building Act and the associated government regulation (Forskrift om konsekvensutredninger, FOR-2014–12–19–1726 and 1758.

23 See www.ub.uio.no/ujur/ulovdata/lov-20050527-031-eng.pdf (English translation). For more details, see the discussion below.

It is against this background that the 'wilderness' concept as administered by the Norwegian Environment Agency has been further developed. One reason appears to be the loss of relevance of the original concept for management purposes, as there seemed to be no significant changes in the extent of wilderness in recent years. Another, perhaps more important, reason seems to be the trend towards using the wilderness classification for administrative processes – in particular in connection with establishing new protected areas, drafting land-use plans, designing agricultural support schemes, and deciding on specific development projects.

The revised definition introduces a new concept: 'interference-free areas' *(inngrepsfrie områder)*,[24] by which is meant areas that are between 3 and 5 km ('zone 1') and between 1 and 3 km ('zone 2') from significant technical infrastructure. Moreover, the revised definition adds new categories of infrastructure that would prevent areas from qualifying as wilderness, or interference-free:

- massive towers and wind power turbines
- stone quarries
- infrastructure for winter sports (downhill installations and ski jumps)
- minor hydropower stations that do not involve the construction of reservoirs.

The use of the revised definition as a basis for land-use planning has been controversial.[25] One argument has been that the definition means that minor projects may lead to highly significant loss of wilderness and interference-free areas. Another argument has been that the informal introduction of the concepts into public administrative practices lacks political legitimacy. It has also been held that there is a weak connection between the concepts and officially endorsed environmental objectives such as biodiversity and recreation.

Against this background, the concepts as developed in Norway can be subjected to critical examination based on the purposes that they serve. First, we may ask whether the concepts take sufficient account of user

[24] See www.miljødirektoratet.no/no/Tema/Miljoovervakning/Inngrepsfrie-naturomrader-i-Norge-/Hva-er-INON/ (available in Norwegian only).

[25] The government that took office in October 2013 promised to discontinue the use of 'interference-free areas' as a tool in land-use planning, see Politisk plattform for en regjering utgått av Høyre og Fremskrittspartiet, Sarbuvollen, 7 October 2013, at 60. See also the Proposal from several members of the Storting (Parliament) regarding interference-free areas, Parliamentary Document 8:37 S (2009–2010).

interests, ecosystem services, biodiversity and restoration capacity.[26] It can be argued that infrastructure that is highly relevant for such purposes has been omitted – not least, private cabins and infrastructure for farming, reindeer herding, hunting and tourism. Moreover, the focus on infrastructure means that activities that can be conducted independent of infrastructure are not taken into account, such as tourism, sports, hunting and fishing, and gathering of berries, mushrooms and so on. Finally, the Norwegian definition does not include any definition of the status of the area in terms of previous human interference. This is significant, since many areas in Norway are still recovering from extensive logging that took place more than 100 years ago. Against this background, we may question whether the wilderness according to the Norwegian definition is sufficiently 'wild' or 'interference-free' in the sense of being unaffected by human activities.[27]

Second, the definition is based on distance from significant infrastructure. This means that certain important areas that have wilderness characteristics – in particular, virgin and old forests in southern Norway – fall outside the scope of the concept since they do not fulfil the distance criterion. If we assume that infrastructure has been constructed mainly in areas with valuable natural resources, it can be argued that the Norwegian definition is not sufficiently representative of the diversity of nature types, and that there is an inherent overrepresentation of unproductive land and underrepresentation of productive land.

Third, the wilderness concept encounters particular challenges when applied to areas used by nomadic indigenous populations, such as Sami reindeer herders, or other areas where local traditional use of natural resources takes place. Traditional use may serve to protect particular habitats or species and thus have lasting impact on biodiversity in an area. The biodiversity thus developed may be viewed as worthy of conservation. However, new lifestyles and technical innovations may change traditional use of the land and extend the use to new areas. It has been argued that application of the wilderness concept to areas subject to

[26] Concerning human user interests, see Vistad and Vorkinn, *supra* note 10. The categories of infrastructure in the revised definition do not reflect the eight items used in the simplified purism scale in several wilderness studies in Norway. See also W.E. Hammitt, B.P. Kaltenborn, O.I. Vistad, L. Emmelin and J. Teigland, 'Common Access Tradition and Wilderness Management in Norway: A Paradox for Managers', *Environmental Management*, 16:2 (1992), 149–156.

[27] In these respects, the Norwegian definition deviates from the IUCN definition of wilderness areas (category Ib): see N. Dudley (ed.), *Guidelines for Applying Protected Area Management Categories* (Gland, Switzerland: IUCN, 2008), 14–16.

indigenous and local use may be alien to the views of indigenous or local populations.[28] Against this background, it is often challenging to apply the wilderness concept to the Sami areas and areas that have been subject to extensive use by local populations.[29]

## 3 Legal protection of wilderness areas

This section first examines how Norway has provided legal protection to wilderness areas through legislation on protected areas, focusing on national parks and nature reserves.[30] Thereafter follows a discussion of how wilderness issues are addressed in legislation regarding land planning, forestry, energy production and management of water resources.

### *3.1 National parks and nature reserves*

Norway has assigned protected area status to approximately seventeen per cent of the Norwegian mainland, of which thirty-six national parks amount to nine point seven per cent and 2,051 nature reserves amount to one point seven per cent.[31] According to Section 35 of the Nature Diversity Act, *national parks* may be established only on '[l]arge areas of natural habitat ... where there is no major infrastructure'.[32] Hence, national parks were generally established in mountainous areas otherwise used mainly for grazing, hunting, gathering of mushrooms and berries, sports, and tourism. In recent years, however, some national parks have been established in areas that are closer to significant human settlements and are subject to more extensive human activities.[33] Section 35 of the Nature Diversity Act does not provide for any possibility of restoring wilderness for the purpose of establishing a national park.

[28] Chapter 21 of NOU 2004:28, *supra* note 17.

[29] In this context, the Nature Diversity Act includes specific procedural provisions aimed at ensuring that proper account is taken of the interests of Sami and local populations, see Sections 8, 14, 41 and 43 of the Act.

[30] Protected landscapes fall outside the scope of this chapter as they are essentially established in areas where human interference is significant: see Section 36 of the Nature Diversity Act.

[31] www.miljostatus.no/Tema/Naturmangfold/Vernet-natur/Vernet-areal-Norge/.

[32] The preparatory works indicate that Section 35 should be read as referring only to the original list of infrastructure: see Ot.prp. no. 52 (2008–2009), *supra* note 17, p. 410. Norwegian national parks have generally been categorized as IUCN category II (national parks) and not as IUCN category Ib (wilderness areas).

[33] Ytre Hvaler National Park, established in the coastal region just south of Oslo in 2009, is the most clear cut example to date: see www.ytre-hvaler.no/hovedEnkel.aspx?m=66538.

This means that the authorities have few options when considering whether to establish national parks on productive land. Moreover, the establishment of national parks in such areas would entail significant challenges in terms of striking a balance between a low degree of human interference and the interests of local populations in harvesting natural resources, such as hunting and fishing, and in promoting recreational and commercial use. Many national parks have been established on private land and include private cabins.

Traditionally, Norwegian *nature reserves* have been established in areas that have been subjected to negligible human interference and are of great importance to biodiversity. Section 37 of the Nature Diversity Act has extended nature reserves so that they may be established also in areas with significant human interference, and where the purpose of the protected area is dependent on continued human interference. Moreover, Section 37 promotes restoration of areas, for example in order to re-establish wilderness characteristics. We may safely assume that the vast majority of Norwegian nature reserves contain biodiversity that has not been subjected to significant human interference. Nature reserves tend to be small (average size: 2.75 $km^2$), and many are located close to significant infrastructure. While such reserves do not qualify as wilderness or interference-free areas according to the above definitions, they may qualify as wilderness areas according to IUCN category Ib. Some nature reserves are located within national parks or protected landscapes. Especially where they are located within national parks,[34] nature reserves can be assumed to cover areas with a high degree of wilderness.

In sum, while Norway's national parks do protect significant wilderness areas, they do not ensure representativeness of nature types. Moreover, they may fail to ensure effective protection of wilderness if the concept is extended beyond the infrastructure covered by the Norwegian concepts – for example, to private cabins, recreational use, hunting, fishing and grazing. Nature reserves, on the other hand, are more useful for protection of a broader range of nature types, and they normally afford a stricter level of protection. Many nature reserves are located close to human infrastructure and activities, and may therefore not qualify as wilderness. Other nature reserves are located within national parks and thereby constitute core areas of wilderness.

[34] For example, Dovre National Park contains three nature reserves: Kattuglehøi, Mesætermyre and Veslehjerkinntjønnin.

### 3.2 *Spatial planning and environmental impact assessment legislation*

Two major elements of the Planning and Building Act are relevant to the legal protection of wilderness areas: the adoption of municipal plans ('municipal master plans' and 'zoning plans'), by which municipalities regulate construction and activities outside of national parks and nature reserves; and the duty to conduct environmental impact assessments. There is no explicit reference to wilderness areas or interference-free areas in the Act. Such areas are mentioned only in the Regulation on Environmental Impact Assessments.[35]

Most of the Norwegian mainland consists of zones for agriculture, nature, outdoor recreation and reindeer husbandry according to *municipal master plans* under Section 11–7 of the Planning and Building Act. Such zoning protects the areas against major infrastructure projects, but not against agricultural activities, including forestry. We find wilderness and interference-free areas within these zones. In addition, wilderness and interference-free areas may be protected as 'zones requiring special consideration' under Section 11–8(c) of the Act. Such zones can be established as buffer zones to national parks or protected landscapes (but not as buffer zones to nature reserves). Municipalities may also adopt binding decisions that protect wilderness and interference-free areas against certain projects and activities (e.g., construction of cabins and agricultural infrastructure, and recreational activities) within zones for agriculture, nature, outdoor recreation and reindeer husbandry according to Section 11–11 of the Act.

*Zoning plans* are more specific than municipal master plans. Zoning plans may be used to safeguard wilderness and interference-free areas on the basis of Sections 12–5 no. 5, 12–6 and 12–7 of the Act. Due to the option of prohibiting for example cabins and agricultural infrastructure, zoning plans may establish protection that goes beyond the Norwegian concepts of wilderness and interference-free areas.

In 2011 the government adopted 'National Expectations regarding Regional and Municipal Planning', according to which counties and municipalities are expected to take into account the need to protect interference-free areas in their planning procedures.[36] Decisions

[35] See Annex III (f) of the Regulation on Environmental Impact Assessment, FOR 2014–12–19 nos. 1726 and 1758.

[36] See Section 6–1 of the Planning and Building Act and Ministry of Climate and Environment, *Nasjonale forventninger til regional og kommunal planlegging*, adopted 24 June 2011, document T-1497 (www.regjeringen.no/pages/16723462/T-1497.pdf).

regarding municipal master plans and zoning plans may be subject to objections by national or regional authorities.[37] Based on the National Expectations, the existence of wilderness or interference-free areas may justify such objections. The Ministry of Climate and Environment has not integrated wilderness or interference-free areas in general guidelines regarding regional and municipal planning, but the Norwegian Environment Agency has issued specific guidelines on how interference-free areas should be taken into account.[38] At the time of writing (December 2014) the government has not yet decided how it will proceed with its plans to discontinue the use of interference-free areas as a tool in land-use planning. Protection of wilderness and interference-free areas through planning decisions remains essentially within the discretionary power of the municipal authorities.

Section 4(b) of the former Regulation on Environmental Impact Assessment requires that environmental impact assessments be conducted where planning or project decisions concern activities that 'are located in or are in conflict with important interference-free areas'.[39] The duty to assess implications for interference-free areas has not been further specified in the Regulation or in associated guidelines. Nevertheless, we may assume that such environmental impact assessments must evaluate the consequences on interference-free areas, and that failure to do so might provide legal grounds for invalidating subsequent planning and project decisions. That said, however, given the reluctance of the Norwegian Supreme Court in a case to invalidate a decision regarding the location of the US Embassy due to lack of an environmental impact assessment,[40] Norwegian courts may be unlikely to contribute to strict enforcement of such environmental impact assessment requirements.

Decisions other than those that are subject to environmental impact assessment under the Planning and Building Act are subject to the Instructions for Official Studies and Reports (*utredningsinstruksen*).[41] The Instructions establish the duty of public authorities to take account of environmental considerations when taking decisions regarding regulations

[37] See Sections 4–2 and 5–4 of the Planning and Building Act.

[38] www.miljokommune.no/Temaoversikt/Naturmangfold/Inngrepsfri-natur-i-planleggingen/ (in Norwegian).

[39] Forskrift om konsekvensutredninger, FOR 2009–06–26 no. 855 (translation by the author). The rules are slightly revised, see note 35 supra.

[40] *Norsk Retstidende* 2009, 661.

[41] See www.regjeringen.no/upload/FAD/Vedlegg/Statsforvaltning/Utredningsinstruksen_eng.pdf (English translation).

and implementation guidelines. Subsection 2.3.2 of the Instructions defines environmental considerations as 'other significant consequences' that shall be considered where relevant. According to Section 2.3 of the Guidelines issued by the Ministry of Climate and Environment, the public authorities are expected to consider whether proposals will have significant consequences for interference-free areas.[42] However, failure to take such considerations does not affect the legal validity of decisions.

### 3.3 *Other legislation*

In the following, we briefly discuss obligations concerning wilderness and interference-free areas under the Forest Act (2005), the Energy Act (1990) and the Water Resources Act (2000).[43]

#### The Forest Act (2005)

The Forest Act contains several provisions aimed at ensuring the ecological sustainability of forestry.[44] However, wilderness and interference-free areas are not explicitly mentioned in these provisions, or in the Regulation on Sustainable Forestry or the associated Living Forest Standard.[45] While significant resources have been expended on mapping environmentally valuable forests, in particular virgin and old forest, the forest legislation contains no legal requirements and few incentives against forestry in wilderness or interference-free areas, including virgin and old forests.[46] Nevertheless, the effects of forestry on such areas are relevant and may in certain cases be mandatory considerations. The only

[42] Ministry of Climate and Environment, *Miljøutredninger etter utredningsinstruksen*, document T-1349, adopted December 2000.

[43] See www.ub.uio.no/ujur/ulovdata/lov-20050527-031-eng.pdf and www.ub.uio.no/ujur/ulovdata/lov-19900629-050-eng.pdf (English translations).

[44] See in particular Sections 4, 5, 7 and 13.

[45] See Sections 4 and 5 of Forskrift om berekraftig skogbruk, FOR 2006-06-07 no. 593 (in Norwegian), and www.levendeskog.no/levendeskog/vedlegg/51Levende_Skog_standard_Engelsk.pdf (in English). The Living Forest Standard contains the following standard (Section 20): 'In larger continuous forest areas with particular environmental and recreational value due to the limited scope of technical encroachments, new forest road construction should be avoided.'

[46] The authorities may require notification when forest owners plan to conduct logging in virgin or old forests: see Section 11 of the Forestry Act. As yet, no regulation has been adopted to implement Section 13 of the Act, which provides for protection of forest areas of particular environmental value. According to Section 4 of the Living Forest Standard: 'At least five per cent of productive forest areas shall be managed as areas of ecological importance.'

regulation adopted under the Forest Act that contains explicit reference to wilderness areas concerns subsidies.[47] It stated that subsidies cannot be provided for the construction of permanent roads that reduce wilderness areas, but that such subsidies may still be provided if the roads only reduce interference-free areas. Moreover, the regulation states that subsidies may be provided to cover losses from not being able to construct roads in wilderness areas. Such support could be used to facilitate logging in interference-free and wilderness areas.[48] In addition, applications to construct roads for agricultural purposes must provide information on whether they will affect wilderness or interference-free areas.[49] Hence, the impacts on wilderness and interference-free areas shall be taken into account when permits are granted for the construction of agricultural roads, and until May 2015 subsidies could not be provided to such roads if they interfered with wilderness areas.

### The Energy Act (1990)

The Energy Act and its associated regulations set the general framework for the establishment of infrastructure for wind power and hydropower, as well as power lines. While the Act and associated regulations do not mention wilderness or interference-free areas, there is significant focus on such issues in the guidelines published in 2007 by the Ministry of Climate and Environment and the Ministry of Petroleum and Energy. The guidelines on wind power state that the degree of conflict with interference-free areas shall be considered, and identify the following interference-free areas as having high conflict potential: interference-free areas that contain wilderness, that cover areas that are uninterrupted from the sea to the mountains and that are located in regions with few interference-free areas. The guidelines state that it is a general objective to preserve interference-free areas, but they do not set norms for when small hydropower plants may be established in conflict with existing interference-free areas: they merely advise applicants to contact the county

[47] Forskrift om tilskudd til nærings- og miljøtiltak i skogbruket, FOR 2004-02-04 no. 447, Sections 5 and 6. The government amended Section 5 of the Regulation in May 2015, and removed the prohibition on providing subsidies to roads that interfere with wilderness areas, see FOR 2015-05-28 no. 551.

[48] An assessment from 2010 indicates that there had been little use of such support: see Statens landbruksforvaltning and Direktoratet for naturforvaltning, Skogsveibygging og hensynet til inngrepsfrie naturområder i Norge (INON), April 2010, 30–31.

[49] See the application form referred to in Section 2-1 of Forskrift om planlegging og godkjenning av veier for landbruksformål, FOR 1996-12-20 no. 1200.

governor's office where conflicts may arise. There are no relevant rules or guidelines on the construction of power lines.

### The Water Resources Act (2000)

Hydropower is relevant under both the Energy Act and the Water Resources Act. As is the case with the Energy Act, the Water Resources Act and its associated regulations do not mention wilderness or interference-free areas. Since 1973, the Norwegian Parliament has adopted plans for protecting rivers against the establishment of hydropower plants. Currently, 394 rivers are subject to such restrictions.[50] However, in 2005 the Parliament decided that hydropower plants of up to 1 MW may be established in protected rivers.[51] Guidelines on small hydropower plants (up to 10,000 kW) were issued in 2007, establishing a detailed framework for considerations of impact on wilderness and interference-free areas. Interference-free areas that contain wilderness, that cover areas that are uninterrupted from the sea to the mountains and that are located in regions with few interference-free areas are identified as being of high value; other interference-free areas are identified as being of medium value. The guidelines state that projects which entail significant interference in wilderness areas or a significant reduction of high-value interference-free areas should be avoided. Moreover, the degree of conflict with interference-free areas may justify requirements that the project be adjusted.

## *3.4 Concluding remarks*

The definition of wilderness and interference-free areas is not set out in any legally binding document, and may be amended through administrative decisions. It is unclear whether such decisions must be taken by the Norwegian Environment Agency, the Ministry of Climate and Environment or the government. Since government regulations refer to the concept, it can be argued that any amendments to the definitions should be decided by the government.

Wilderness protection in Norway has been conducted mainly through the establishment of national parks and nature reserves. Norway has fulfilled its political commitment under the CBD to protect seventeen per cent of the mainland area, and current policy focuses more on

[50] See St.prp. no. 53 (2008–2009), 1 and Decision 414 of the Parliament 2008–2009.
[51] Decision 240 of the Parliament 2004–2005.

management issues than on protection of new areas. One remaining main challenge, however, is to increase the representativeness of nature protection in Norway. This challenge is closely associated with the protection of remaining wilderness in ecologically productive and densely populated areas. The concept of interference-free areas is of particular relevance in this context, due to the lower requirement concerning distance to major infrastructure.

Outside of national parks and nature reserves, there is only weak legal protection of wilderness and interference-free areas. Such areas may be subject to development based on political decisions by municipalities, but with the possibility of transferring such decision to the Ministry of Local Government and Modernisation if objections are raised by the relevant public authorities. There are no legal restrictions regarding forestry, wind power plants, hydropower plants or power lines in wilderness or interference-free areas. The existing guidelines may be revised by the relevant ministries. Private parties cannot invoke violation of the guidelines as a basis for invalidation of administrative decisions by the courts.

## 4 Implementation and enforcement

### *4.1 Loss of wilderness in Norway*

The area of wilderness has been estimated at forty-eight per cent of the total land area of mainland Norway in 1900, thirty-four per cent in 1940, twelve point two per cent in 1988, eleven point seven per cent in 2008 and eleven point six per cent in 2013.[52] The loss of wilderness has thus been significantly reduced,[53] but may be increasing in recent years.[54] One major reason for the reduction appears to have been the establishment of national parks, which prohibits the construction of major infrastructure.[55] Another

[52] www.miljodirektoratet.no/no/Tema/Miljoovervakning/Inngrepsfrie-naturomrader-i-Norge-/Statistikk-inngrepsfrie-naturomrader/. The figures for 1900 and 1940 are only rough estimates. The Norwegian Environment Agency has published maps and statistics for 1988, 1994, 1998, 2003, 2008 and 2013.

[53] This is despite predictions to the contrary: see Skonhoft and Solem, *supra* note 8, p. 299.

[54] The Norwegian Environment Agency has reported that the loss of wilderness increased from 130 km$^2$ in the period 2003–2007 to 183 km$^2$ during 2008–12, see www.miljødirektoratet.no/no/Nyheter/Nyheter/2014/Mars-2014/Fortsatt-press-pa-inngrepsfri-natur/.

[55] Twenty-four of a total of thirty-seven national parks have been established since 1986, including most of the national parks of more than 1,000 km$^2$ in area (four before 1986, and nine subsequently).

important reason may be the limited interest in human use of the remaining wilderness areas – but this seems to be changing due to increasing interest in, inter alia, mining, hydropower, tourism and construction of cabins.[56]

The situation regarding interference-free areas is likely to be more nuanced, as many such areas are located outside of national parks. Approximately forty-five per cent of Norway's mainland area is interference-free. The reduction of interference-free areas is higher than for wilderness, and has been increasing significantly in recent years, from 726 $km^2$ during 1998–2002 to 860 $km^2$ during 2003–2007 and 888 $km^2$ during 2008–2012.[57] The percentage lost is almost identical to that for wilderness. The main reasons for loss of interference-free areas between 1988 and 2013 was roads for forestry (4,373 $km^2$) and generation and transport of electric power (1,626 $km^2$).[58] Even if there has been a decrease in the construction of forest roads, such infrastructure is likely to remain a significant cause of loss of interference-free areas, especially in regions with few of these areas remaining. The main reason is the call for increased subsidies in order to facilitate the availability of forest resources in remote areas.[59] The focus on the production of renewable energy as a means to mitigate climate change can be expected to lead to further loss of interference-free areas due to power generation and transport.[60]

[56] See Norwegian Ministry of Trade and Industry, *Strategy for the Mineral Industry* (Oslo, 2013, www.regjeringen.no/pages/38262123/strategyforthemineralindustry_2013.pdf), the so-called 'fjellteksten' (the mountain text) in St.prp. no. 65 (2002–2003), 140–153, and Riksrevisjonen, Riksrevisjonens undersøkelse av bærekraftig arealplanlegging og arealdisponering i Norge, Dokument 3:11 (2006–2007), 52–53, 56.

[57] See www.environment.no/topics/biodiversity/areas-without-major-infrastructure-development/

[58] See www.miljodirektoratet.no/no/Tema/Miljoovervakning/Inngrepsfrie-naturomrader-i-Norge-/ and www.miljostatus.no/miljomal/Mal-og-nokkeltall/Fjell/Ta-vare-pa-natur mangfaldet/Utvikling-i-areal-av-inngrepsfrie-naturomrade-INON/Areal-av-inngreps frie-naturomrade-INON/ (in Norwegian).

[59] See Riksrevisjonen, Riksrevisjonens undersøkelse av bærekraftig forvaltning av norske skogressurser, Dokument 3:17 (2011–2012), 13, 73–75, 103–104, where the Offiice for the Auditor General and the Ministry of Agriculture and Food emphasized the need to focus on infrastructure to facilitate forestry, and where unclear policy regarding interference-free areas is singled out by regional authorities as a major concern. See also Statens landbruksforvaltning and Direktoratet for naturforvaltning, Skogsveibygging og hensynet til inngrepsfrie naturområder i Norge (INON). Vurderinger og anbefalinger til Landbruks- og matdepartementet og Miljøverndepartementet, April 2010, pp. 15–16.

[60] The number of hydropower plants has increased from about 900 in 2004 to 1443 by the end of 2012: see Torodd Jensen (ed.), Beregning av potensial for små kraftverk i Norge. Forutsetninger, metodebeskrivelse og resultater, Norges vassdrags- og energidirektorat report 19/2004, p. 10, and www.nve.no/no/Energi1/Fornybar-energi/Vannkraft/ (in Norwegian). As of June 2013, there were 696 applications for small hydropower plants

### 4.2 *The practice of wilderness protection*

From the above statistics, it may seem that the rules and procedures regarding construction of forest roads have not been effective in containing their impact on wilderness and interference-free areas in Norway. This is confirmed by a geographically limited assessment of the cases at one county governor's office, which indicates that construction of such roads is accepted in almost all instances.[61] But the figures may also indicate that the number of applications has gone down, and that applications are limited to those cases where construction of such roads is expected to yield significant economic returns.

Infrastructure for electricity transportation is exempted from the rules concerning zoning under the Planning and Building Act (Section 1–3), and the construction of power plants can be made subject to a fast-track procedure (Section 6–4). Hence, the extent to which such projects are allowed to reduce wilderness and interference-free areas essentially depends on decisions at the national level. Effective implementation of the guidelines regarding small hydropower plants may possibly reduce the loss of interference-free areas. There are no corresponding guidelines applicable to the construction of power lines, so such infrastructure is subject to relevant procedures only in cases where environmental impact assessments are required.

It has not been possible to carry out an exhaustive assessment of how wilderness and interference-free areas have been taken into account in planning decisions and environmental impact assessments. One assessment of cases in 2010 concerning planned activities that would affect interference-free areas revealed that few such cases were brought to the offices of county governors (fifty-four) and that the governors advised against the plans in forty per cent of the cases. Information concerning final decisions was available for eight plans only: six were accepted, one was accepted with amendments, and only one plan was rejected.[62]

and 106 applications for wind power plants pending before the Directorate, and the Directorate has been criticized for taking too much time to finalize such cases: see Riksrevisjonen, Riksrevisjonens undersøkelse av effektivitet i konsesjonsbehandlingen av fornybar energy, Dokument 3:5 (2013–2014), and Chapter 7 of NOU 2012:9 Energiutredningen – verdiskaping, forsyningssikkerhet og miljø.

[61] Statens landbruksforvaltning and Direktoratet for naturforvaltning, *supra* note 48, pp. 28–29.

[62] Direktoratet for naturforvaltning, Notat. Oversikt over saker som berører inngrepsfrie naturområde (INON) – 2010, dated 1 November 2011. See also cases and statistics provided by Skjeggedal et al. *supra* note 10, pp. 123–126.

Against this background, it may seem that wilderness or interference-free status rarely prevents plans from being adopted. However, as in the case of forest roads, wilderness or interference-free status may prevent such plans from being elaborated in the first place, ensuring that only the most economically significant plans are brought forward. The latter point could be supported if wilderness and interference-free areas are addressed effectively in environmental impact assessments. A significant number of assessments deal with wilderness and interference-free areas. Moreover, the electronic maps of wilderness and interference-free areas are user-friendly and should facilitate appropriate consideration of such areas.[63] As pointed out above, municipalities may also protect wilderness or interference-free areas more proactively through planning decisions. Municipalities have been encouraged to adopt such decisions through the 'National Expectations regarding Regional and Municipal Planning' and guidelines, but information on the extent to which municipalities have used planning decisions to protect wilderness or interference-free areas does not seem to be available. Nevertheless, at least some counties have elaborated plans that address wilderness and interference-free areas.[64] So far, evidence regarding implementation through planning and environmental impact assessments may indicate a relatively high degree of effectiveness in the use of the instruments – but significant uncertainty remains as to the effects for wilderness protection.

### 4.3 *Implementing wilderness protection under the Nature Diversity Act (2009)*

The core protection of wilderness and interference-free areas takes place through the establishment of national parks and nature reserves. In 2003, the government and the Parliament adopted a policy of more extensive recreational and commercial use of national parks.[65] Moreover, in 2009 a local management reform was introduced, to extend to all national parks: decision-making power will be moved from regional government agencies (county governors) to local management boards composed of municipal,

[63] www.miljodirektoratet.no/no/Tjenester-og-verktoy/Database/INON/ (in Norwegian).

[64] The only regional plan for wilderness and interference-free areas was adopted by Møre and Romsdal County in 2000. In addition, wilderness and interference-free areas have been taken into account in some other area-specific and sector-specific plans.

[65] This was done in the context of the revised budget, St.prp. no. 65 (2002–2003), 140–153.

county and, where relevant, Sami politicians.[66] Against this background, it can be questioned whether national parks will preserve their character of wilderness or interference-free areas. According to Section 35 of the Nature Diversity Act, '[n]o activity that has a lasting impact on the natural environment [...] is permitted [...] unless such impact is essential to achieving the purpose of protection.' Section 48 of the Act permits local management boards to 'grant exemption' from the protected area regulation and from Section 35 of the Act[67] if 'important public interests make it necessary'. The decision shall weigh the 'important public interests against the interests promoted by the protected area', and 'particular emphasis shall be placed on the importance of the protected area for the overall network of protected areas and on whether a corresponding protected area can be established or developed elsewhere'. The decisions of local management boards can be appealed to the Norwegian Environment Agency. While certain categories of infrastructure that are considered to be essential from the perspective of the public interest, such as power lines and water reservoirs, may be allowed in protected areas, the preparatory works indicate that this option is to be available only in exceptional cases.[68]

According to Section 37 of the Nature Diversity Act, within a nature reserve no activity is allowed that 'reduces the conservation value of the area as described in the purpose of protection'. Nature reserves are generally subject to stricter regulations than are national parks. Section 37 states that nature reserves 'may be given absolute protection from all activity, projects and access or passage'. Section 48 of the Act, as discussed above, also applies to nature reserves. Moreover, even if the vast majority of nature reserves are not subject to the local management reform of 2009,[69] almost all nature reserves located within national parks and many nature reserves located within protected landscapes are subject to the reform. Hence, the reserves that are most likely to qualify as wilderness areas are managed by local management boards, and these reserves would also be subject to the policy decision of 2003 on more extensive use. However, this decision aims at striking a balance between

[66] This decision was made as part of the budget: see Det kongelige miljøverndepartement, Prop. 1 S (2009–2010). *Proposisjon til Stortinget*, 218–226. See also O.K. Fauchald and L.H. Gulbrandsen, 'The Norwegian Reform of Protected Area Management: A Grand Experiment with Delegation of Authority?' *Local Environment: The International Journal of Justice and Sustainability*, 17:2 (2012), 203–222.

[67] Ot.prp. no. 52 (2008–2009), *supra* note 17, at 425.

[68] *Ibid.* 237–240, 425.

[69] In addition, 171 nature reserves had been subject to a previous local management reform initiated in 1998, see Fauchald and Gulbrandsen, *supra* note 66, pp. 208–209.

conservation and user interests, and in nature reserves the former are likely to prevail.

A number of interference-free areas and some wilderness areas are located within protected landscapes. Such protected area status affords some protection, since projects that 'substantially alter the nature or character of the landscape' are prohibited (Section 36 of the Nature Diversity Act). However, many of the important landscape protection areas are subject to the local management reform, and they are subject to less strict protection against new infrastructure than are national parks and nature reserves.

Against this background, the local management reform, taken together with policy decisions to promote more extensive use of protected areas, may possibly undermine the legal protection provided to national parks, nature reserves and protected landscapes. Protected landscapes and national parks seem vulnerable to such developments, whereas nature reserves are much more likely to preserve their wilderness characteristics. Nature reserves are likely to afford protection against recreational use, hunting and fishing. However, the Ministry of Climate and Environment has recently accepted significant interferences with nature reserves by reference to Section 48 of the Nature Diversity Act and by redefining the borders of protected areas.[70] Moreover, cancellation of protected area status and redefinition of the borders of protected areas are political decisions that cannot be overturned by courts. It remains to be seen whether the courts will accept extensive use of Section 48 in cases involving wilderness or interference-free areas.[71] Current efforts at adopting and updating management plans for protected areas may assist in preventing loss of wilderness and interference-free areas.

### *4.4 The role of the public in challenging decisions that impact on wilderness*

There are few possibilities for environmental NGOs or other interested parties to initiate court cases regarding projects that are planned in wilderness or interference-free areas, due in part to the lack of legal bases for claims, and in part to the high costs of bringing cases to

[70] One famous case involves Åkersvika Nature Reserve, a Ramsar Site.

[71] One case before a court in the first instance concerning Sørdalen Nature Reserve provides decision-makers with extensive margins of discretion under Section 48 (decision Oslo Tingrett 23 December 2013). The decision was overturned on appeal (decision Borgarting lagmannsrett 12 March 2015).

Norwegian courts.[72] A search of the Norwegian database on court decisions revealed only two appeal court cases in which wilderness or interference-free areas had been mentioned.[73] One case concerned reconstruction of accommodation in connection with summer pasture, where interference-free area was mentioned as one factor of importance when determining the rights of location of the building.[74] The second case concerned compensation for lost opportunity to construct a hydropower plant as a consequence of the establishment of a nature reserve. The court referred to the fact that the plant would have been located in an interference-free area as one reason for deeming it unlikely that a concession would have been granted for constructing the plant, and thus as a reason for not awarding compensation.[75]

### *4.5 Concluding remarks*

Against this background, we can observe that, except for those that have protected area status, enforcement of the protection of wilderness and interference-free areas in Norway is problematic from a legal perspective, as this protection is established primarily by non-binding instruments. Moreover, with the exception of electricity production and transportation, decision-making power is largely delegated to political bodies at the local level. The procedures for securing implementation of the non-binding instruments are to some extent transparent and allow for involvement of the public. Beyond the statistics on the loss of wilderness and interference-free areas and a few limited studies, however, little aggregate information is available on how the non-binding instruments are followed up. Moreover, the non-binding status of the instruments means that stakeholders are unable to prevent incursions into wilderness and interference-free areas where there is lack of political will to protect such areas. Restoration of wilderness or interference-free areas is mentioned in some documents, but there is currently no policy decision promoting this approach.

[72] See O.K. Fauchald, 'Environmental Justice in Courts – A Case Study from Norway', *Nordic Environmental Law Journal*, 1/2010, 49–67 and H.T. Anker, O.K. Fauchald, A. Nilsson and L. Suvantola, 'The Role of Courts in Environmental Law – A Nordic Comparative Study', *Nordic Environmental Law Journal*, 1/2009, 9–34.

[73] See www.lovdata.no. The database contains all Supreme Court and appeal court decisions, but only a small selection, approximately one per cent, of decisions from courts of first instance. Hence, there may exist other cases than those mentioned here.

[74] *Rettens gang* 2007, 5.

[75] *Rettens gang* 2012, 1421.

## 5 The future of wilderness protection in Norway

In Norway, the extension of the 'wilderness' concept to interference-free areas and the use of the concepts as a basis for land-use planning have been controversial – in particular in relation to the forest industry, but also as related to the production and transport of electric power.[76] The government that took office in October 2013 promised to discontinue the use of 'interference-free areas' as a tool in land-use planning,[77] and the Ministry of Climate and Environment has followed up by ceasing to mention wilderness and interference-free areas in relation to the Norwegian mainland in its budget and announcing that formal references to interference-free areas have been deleted in rules concerning forestry.[78] This chapter has shown that the legal protection of wilderness and interference-free areas is weak when such areas are located outside protected areas, and that protection seems to be weakening also for areas located within protected areas. Due to the lack of legal instruments that mention wilderness and interference-free areas, the government can decide to abandon these concepts as nature management tools without having to propose legislation to the Norwegian Parliament.

In the Norwegian context, the wilderness concept is also vulnerable from a natural science perspective. Studies have shown that there is no particularly strong link between biodiversity and wilderness areas in Norway.[79] One main reason is that the remaining wilderness areas are located in mountainous areas with low levels of biological productivity and biodiversity (diversity of nature types in particular). A further important reason is that the Norwegian criteria for defining wilderness seem disconnected from concerns regarding loss of biodiversity. However, the inclusion of interference-free areas may change this situation significantly. It seems clear that interference-free areas are regarded as biologically important in many municipalities and regions, especially in regions with few such areas remaining.

The 'wilderness' and 'interference-free areas' concepts as defined in Norway are more closely related to landscape effects and the interests of

[76] See Proposal from several members of the Storting (Parliament) regarding interference-free areas, Parliamentary Document 8:37 S (2009–2010).

[77] Politisk plattform for en regjering utgått av Høyre og Fremskrittspartiet, Sarbuvollen, 7 October 2013, p. 60.

[78] See Klima- og miljødepartementet, Prop. 1 S (2014–2015). The Ministry refers extensively to wilderness in the context of Svalbard and Jan Mayen.

[79] See, e.g., Skjeggedal et al. *supra* note 10, pp. 43–89.

recreational users than to biodiversity. Consequently, even if the concepts lack clear links to biodiversity, they may still be justified on the basis of aesthetical and ethical arguments. However, even if we take this point into account, the Norwegian concepts will need to be redefined in light of recent developments and international trends in wilderness protection, if they are to continue to serve as administrative tools for land planning and project decisions.[80] The three basic characteristics of wilderness as set out in this volume – size, absence of permanent human interference and degree of natural intactness – could constitute useful points of reference for such a revision.

Due to the current legal status of the country's remaining wilderness areas – they are essentially protected as parts of national parks – abandoning the use of the Norwegian 'wilderness' concept as an administrative tool may not be significant for future protection of wilderness in Norway. Essentially, the future protection of these areas will depend on the enforcement of protected area legislation. By contrast, abandoning the concept of 'interference-free areas' as an administrative tool can be expected to have important negative implications for future protection of wilderness in Norway.

[80] See Riksrevisjonen, *supra* note 56, at 51–52 and 57–60.

# 18

## Wilderness protection in Poland

SERGIUSZ URBAN

### 1 Introduction

The term 'wilderness' is not used in the Polish legislation and is even not easy to translate into Polish with a single word. Probably closest to the term wilderness is the phrase 'wild nature': *dzika przyroda*. In common understanding this phrase means natural ecosystems, not affected, or only slightly affected, by human civilization (e.g., buildings and roads) – although not necessarily very large in size. Despite the absence of the term 'wilderness' in Polish legislation and language, Poland hosts quite many areas with relatively high wilderness qualities,[1] particularly in comparison to West- and North-West Europe. Statistics regarding the surface area of 'wilderness' in Poland are not available, as the term is not defined nor formally used in, for instance, Polish policy making. Based on the working definition of this book, the most important wild areas – mainly forests – are located in the Eastern and North-eastern part of Poland, although certain old grown forest complexes are to be found also in Central and Western Poland. Part of these areas are mountains (Southern frontier of the country), which due to their geomorphology are less accessible for human activity.

The available data show that Natura 2000 sites cover twenty per cent of the land territory of Poland[2] (the entire territory of Poland is 311,904 km$^2$); however, not all of these areas may be regarded as wilderness with the qualities as described in Chapter 1. The national parks and nature reserves, the two most strict forms of nature protection provided by national law, cover as little as one point five per cent of the country only, but also these areas do not all necessarily qualify as wilderness. *Vice versa*, not all areas that have the quality of being 'wild' are

[1] For the working definition of wilderness, see Chapter 1.

[2] Environment 2014, Central Statistical Office, 2014, Section. 40, http://stat.gov.pl/obszary-tematyczne/srodowisko-energia/srodowisko/ochrona-srodowiska-2014,1,15.html.

protected as Natura 2000 sites, national parks or nature reserves. Those wilderness areas that have a protected status under a protection regime often have an overlapping status of National Park and/or Nature Reserve (see beneath for further explanations) and Natura 2000.

One of the most important areas in Poland is the Bialowieska Forest (Puszcza Białowieska), located on the territories of Poland and Belarus,[3] which area is one of the last primeval forests in Europe. The Polish part of the Forest is about 630 km$^2$, which is forty-two per cent of the entire area. The Bialowieski National Park (Białowieski Park Narodowy) covers only eight point five per cent of the Polish part of Bialowieska Forest (53.48 km$^2$). Unfortunately, due to the interests of local people and a forest administration, an important portion of the most valuable areas is protected only partially under less strict regimes.

Among other important relatively wild areas in Poland are the Biebrzański National Park (Biebrzański Park Narodowy, 592 km$^2$) and Puszcza Romincka (Landscape Park of Romnicka Primaval Forest, 146 km$^2$ on the Polish side of the border), both located in the North-eastern part of Poland; Knyszyńska Forest (Puszcza Knyszyńska, 1,396 km$^2$, 745 protected as the landscape park) in the Eastern part of Poland; Notecka Forest (Puszcza Notecka, 1,362 km$^2$) in the Western part of Poland, and Bieszczady Mountains in the South-eastern part of Poland (the Natura 2000 site in Bieszczady is about 1,115 km$^2$).[4] Due to the geography, climate and history, these areas are mainly forest ecosystems (about sixty-two per cent).

Unfortunately, the aforementioned areas are under constant pressure of human activities, mainly by logging, housing developments, building infrastructure intersecting habitats such as roads, as well as by the expansion of urbanization. Another source of pressure is the growing number of tourists visiting these areas. A good example of an area that is experiencing this threat is the Tatra Mountains National Park (surface area of 211 km$^2$), which is visited every year by more than a million people during the summer season only.[5]

This chapter discusses the relevance of Polish law and policy in protecting wilderness in Poland. The chapter presents first the relevance of the

[3] For a discussion of the transboundary management aspects, see Arun Agrawal, 'Adaptive Management in Transboundary Protected Areas: The Bialowieza National Park and Biosphere Reserve as a Case Study', *Environmental Conservation* 27(4) (2000), 326–333.

[4] More data available at Environment 2014, Central Statistical Office, *supra* note 2, at 285–310.

[5] *Ibid.*, at 287: A total of 2,764,000 visitors in 2013. See also *Tatra National Park newsletter* 2(13) (2010), at 16 http://tpn.pl/filebrowser/files/Biuletyn_TPN/biuletyn_tpn_02_2010.pdf.

term 'wilderness' in Polish society (Section 2), particularly based on available information on results of surveys carried out by other institutions. Next, the legal protection of wilderness in Poland is discussed, including the topic of protection of wilderness through property rights (Section 3). This more theoretical part is followed by a discussion on the practical aspects of implementation and enforcement of the relevant legal provisions (Section 4). Finally, conclusions are drawn and some recommendations for the future of the wilderness protection in Poland formulated (Section 5). Information provided in this chapter is based on a desk-study and the experience of the author. Information on the number and surface area of protected areas are derived from the materials published by the Central Statistical Office and other central administration bodies in Poland (mainly the Ministry for the Environment), unless indicated otherwise.

## 2 Relevance of 'wilderness' in Polish society

### *2.1 A brief historic overview*

Historically, the first attempts to protect 'wild nature' in Poland (as noted above, the term 'wilderness' is not used in Poland) took place in the Middle Ages, although originally they had utilitarian goals as they were aimed at preserving certain elements of nature, especially certain species of animals (such as beaver, deer and bison) in their habitats for the sovereigns, who were exclusively entitled to hunt them. Through the centuries various aspects of nature protection were regulated in a number of statutes issued by Polish kings;[6] for example, the 1423 Statute of Warta (*Statut Warcki*) enacted protection of yews (as a particularly valuable tree) and the 1519 First Lithuanian Statute (*I Statut Litewski*) enacted protection of beaver lodges, which may be regarded as an early example of 'habitats protection'.[7] In a few cases the motivations for the protection were even similar to current convictions, for instance that biodiversity is worth preserving independent from

[6] See also Artur Pawlowski, 'The Historical Aspect to the Shaping of the Sustainable Development Concept', in Lucjan Pawlowski, Marzenna R. Dudzinska and Artur Pawlowski (eds.), *Environmental Engineering* (London: Taylor & Francis Group, 2007), 21–30, at 22.

[7] See also Jerzy Jendrośka and Magdalena Bar, *Prawo ochrony środowiska. Podręcznik*, (Wrocław: Centrum Prawa Ekologicznego, 2005), at 495, J. Boć, K. Nowacki, E. Samborska-Boć, *Ochrona środowiska*, (Wrocław: Kolonia Limited 2002), at 31, and Wojciech Radecki, 'Zarys dziejów prawnej ochrony przyrody i środowiska w Polsce', (Kraków: Oddział Akademicki PTTK RPK, 1990).

direct human use. This was, for instance, the case of the attempt to save the aurochs from extinction, although the efforts were not successful.

In the nineteenth century, Poland did not exist as a sovereign country since its territory was at that time divided between its three neighbours: Germany, Russia and Austria. Due to that fact, the protection of Polish nature was considered as part of protecting general national heritage and therefore regarded as part of aspirations to independence. Activities in this regard were undertaken in particular on the Polish territories under Austrian rule (in so-called Galicja), which enjoyed certain autonomy. In 1868 the Parliament of Galicja (*Sejm Galicyjski*) adopted the Act on the protection of chamois and marmots (animals living in the Tatras) as well as the Act on the protection of birds.[8]

The Tatra mountains, due to their alpine nature combined with cultural heritage, continued to be the focal point for growing interest in nature protection. Also, the idea to create the first national park in Poland related to this mountain range. Of course, other grounds justifying the protection of nature, such as aesthetic and philosophic beliefs, were also present to a certain degree, steadily gaining in importance. Due to the political circumstances, the initiative of individuals and bottom-up approaches were of significant importance for nature protection in this time period.[9] At the beginning of the twentieth century, several patriotic landowners transformed parts of their properties into nature reserves, giving the origin and inspiration for further protection of these areas.

After regaining its independence in 1918, Poland took up the duty of protecting its nature based on a modernized approach to this issue, inspired mainly by scientific motivations. In 1919 the Temporary State Commission for the Nature Conservation was created. In 1926 it was further transformed into the National Council for Nature Conservation. The council was composed of scientists and academics with several universities and associations, such as the Nature Protection League (created in 1928), collaborating.

The initiative of the National Council for Nature Conservation[10] led to the adoption of the Nature Protection Act in 1934[11] and allowed for creation of several nature reserves (180 reserves and a further 200

[8] See also Jendrośka and Bar, *Prawo ochrony środowiska. Podręcznik*, *supra* note 7, at 496.

[9] See also Chapter 1, Subsection 3.1.

[10] For a comprehensive discussion on the institutional and organizational aspects of nature protection in Poland, see Kamila Sobieraj, 'Organization of Environmental Services in Poland', *Polish Yearbook of Environmental Law* 31 (2011), 153–173.

[11] Nature Protection Law of 1934 (*Ustawa o ochronie przyrody z dnia*), 10 March 1934, *DZIENNIK Ustaw* No. 31(274).

planned) and national parks[12] (Białowieski NP, Pieniński NP, Czarnohora NP).[13] Worth mentioning is that the Pieniński National Park encompassed not only Polish territory but also land in the Czech Republic. During those challenging times of rebuilding the public administration and unifying law over three parts of the country that were separated for over 120 years, the role of social organizations was crucial. These organizations not only identified the natural areas worth protecting, but were also building public support for this goal and collecting the financial means necessary to buy valuable areas from private owners. This was, for instance, the case for the Tatra National Park.[14]

### *2.2 Increasing public awareness of the importance of nature under the communist regime*

Despite the existence of legislation and a public administration responsible for nature protection, little attention to this policy field was paid in reality under the communist regime. The goals of industrialization and urbanization of the country prevailed over care for the environment,[15] leading to its serious deterioration over the years. However, during the second half of the twentieth century, public awareness with regard to environmental concerns increased and the conservationist movement also provided opportunities to express opposition towards the oppressive authorities. This anti-system character of nature protection survived the fall of the communists and was also present at the beginning of the 1990s, when the modernization of the country significantly accelerated with numerous infrastructural projects being developed.

A good example of such a clash between the members of civil society willing to stop nature degradation and the administration blindly pursuing its goals of infrastructural development, was the well-known protest at Mount St. Anna in the Opolskie region in 1998. The A-4 highway, to be built in such a way that it would fragment highly valuable natural habitats, initiated open protest and substantial media attention.

[12] Daniel H. Cole, 'An outline history of environmental law and administration in Poland', *Hastings International Law and Comparitive Law Review* 18 (1995), 297–358, www.repository.law.indiana.edu/facpub/691, at 303–304.

[13] Institute of Environmental Protection, 'Dzieje ochrony przyrody w Polsce', www.ios.edu.pl/biodiversity/4/r4_511.htm.

[14] *Ibid.* See also Władysław Szafer, *Tatrzański Park Narodowy*, Zakład Ochrony Przyrody PAN, 1962.

[15] See also Cole, 'An Outline History of Environmental Law and Administration in Poland', *supra* note 12, at 305–306. See also Chapter 20.

However, the protestors lost their cause due to the persistence of the government and relative lack of support of the wider general public.[16] Another example of public protest is the quite famous Rospuda case. As will be discussed in more detail in Section 4, in this case environmental NGOs were effective in protecting an important wilderness area through open protest, media activities and legal procedures based on the European Natura 2000 regime.

### *2.3 Recent decrease of public support for nature protection*

More recently, Polish society appears to consider nature protection less important. Nature is not commonly perceived by the general public as the stand-alone value, important and precious for its own sake, but more as a resource that can be traded-off for other values. For example, there appears to be a general agreement that habitat fragmentation is inevitable and that projects, such as road constructions, should in most cases be considered acceptable as these projects represent prevailing public interest. The same attitude towards the protection of nature is often shared and openly expressed by officials of the public administration.

This attitude towards nature appears also to apply to the 'wilder part' of nature. This may be illustrated by the fact that since the beginning of this century no new National Park has been created in Poland, although there are several areas of the highest natural value that could qualify as a National Park. Examples include the Mazurian Lakes, Jura Krakowsko-Częstochowska Region (potential Jurajski National Park) or Pogórze Przemyskie Region (potential Turnicki National Park). Białowieski National Park has not been extended either despite the fact that currently a large proportion of the natural habitats are located outside the boundaries of the Park. An important hurdle for establishing or extending National Parks is that, according to the Nature Protection Act 2004,

[16] Adam Grzeszczak, 'Ekolog schodzi z drzewa', *Polityka*, nr 2151 (25 July 1998), 25–26. See also the article from the local press: www.nto.pl/apps/pbcs.dll/article?AID=/20141110/HISTORIALOKALNA/141109521, and Mateusz Fałkowski, Mikołaj Lewicki and Alek Arkowski, 'The 1998 Environmental Protests at Mount St. Anna', in Fredrik Bynander, Piotr Chmielewski and Greg Simons (eds.), *The Politics of Crisis Management in Transitional Poland from 1990–1999, Crisis Management Europe Research Program Volume 19* (Vällingby: Elanders, 2008), 303–349, www.fhs.se/Documents/Externwebben/forskning/centrumbildningar/Crismart/Publikationer/Publikationsserier/VOLUME_19.pdf.

local authorities have a veto in respect of such proposals.[17] In practice these authorities often oppose such initiatives, as in their perspective the stricter protection of nature is only an additional burden or even an obstacle for the development of the local economy. This has also been concluded in a study on the implementation of Natura 2000 in Poland:

> In the case of Natura 2000, opposition was expressed mainly by the local governments of those municipalities where new protected areas were designated. Analysis of their comments shows negative opinions with regard to both the very idea of the programme and the need to introduce it in Poland.[18]

According to the National Biodiversity Strategy 2007–2013, similar opposition exists among members of the general public in Poland: according to the Strategy, one of the weaknesses of biodiversity conservation in Poland is '[t]he difficulties in winning the public approval of the creation of new protected areas or the expansion of the existing ones, also including the Natura 2000 sites'.[19]

This connects well with public perception research in Poland. According to a public awareness study of 2010, financed by the National Fund for Environmental Protection and Water Management, Polish people support nature protection and landscape conservation in general;[20] however, their opinion significantly changes when this would result in a situation where personal interests are sacrificed. For example, there is a common consent on cutting the trees, draining the wetlands and destroying the habitats of rare species when these natural values create an obstacle for the existing traffic or planned roads. As many as eighteen per cent of those participating in this study stated that humans can freely transform the environment according to their will and needs.

[17] Art. 10.2 of the Nature Protection Act 2004 (*Ustawa o ochronie przyrody*), 16 April 2004 (in force 1 May 2005), *Official Journal of Laws (OJ)* 2013, Pos. 627, consolidated version of 14 May 2013, available in Polish: http://faolex.fao.org/docs/pdf/pol129607.pdf.

[18] Malgorzata Grodzinska-Jurczak and Joanna Cent, 'Expansion of Nature Conservation Areas: Problems with Natura 2000 Implementation in Poland?', *Environmental Management* 47(1) (2011), 11–27, www.ncbi.nlm.nih.gov/pmc/articles/PMC3016195/, at 14. See also the 'non-binding inquiry No. 8762 to the President of the Council of Ministers on the practices applied in designating Natura 2000 sites', 20 March 2009, http://orka2.sejm.gov.pl/IZ6.nsf/main/2D37B0B7.

[19] Poland Council of Ministers, 'The National Strategy for the Conservation and Sustainable Use of Biodiversity, 2007–2014', available through www.cbd.int/countries/?country=pl, at 11.

[20] 'Survey on the knowledge and attitudes of Polish people towards nature and the idea of its conservation', funded by the National Fund for Environmental Protection and Water Management, March-May 2010, www.jestemnaptak.pl/public/media/org/11/polska-i-polacy-z-lotu-ptakaraportlist2010.pdf.

This attitude is also reflected by the position towards the environmental non-governmental organizations, which are critically perceived by approximately fifty per cent of the respondents. This also explains why the number of members of these NGOs has been decreasing.

An even more recent insight into the perception of the public on nature protection is provided by a survey conducted by the Ministry for the Environment in 2014.[21] While this study, which is conducted every year, focuses on general environmental awareness of the public, it includes also a component referring to the perception of the public on nature protection. In the opinion of most respondents of the 2014 survey, nature protection is not the crucial policy challenge for the country. According to the authors of the study, it is due to the economic problems of Polish society that people focus on everyday needs: 'For most Polish citizens, the economic considerations prevail over the care for the environment.'[22] The survey also shows that many Polish people take an instrumental perspective towards nature. When asked for the reasons to protect the environment, the answer that nature has value for its own sake was given by only thirty-three per cent of the respondents. Reasons such as 'care for the generations to come' (forty-nine per cent) and 'beneficial effects on human health' (forty-eight per cent) clearly were more popular. Another reason mentioned quite often by the respondents was the economic benefit (including the negative financial effect of using fewer resources) (eighteen per cent). The issue of keeping large areas free from human influence, especially as far as infrastructure is concerned, was not explicitly discussed in this survey.

## 3 Legal protection of wilderness in Poland

### *3.1 The absence of a definition*

The notion of 'wilderness' is not used and, consequently, not defined in Polish legislation. As mentioned above, the term 'wilderness' as such does even not exist in the Polish language. The introduction of such a definition was never debated during any legislative process. For this reason, any reference to it in the following discussion is based on the working definition included in Chapter 1: An area characterized by a relatively

[21] Ministry for the Environment, *Badanie Świadomości Ekologicznej* (Study on Environmental Awareness), latest survey conducted in October–November 2014, www.mos.gov.pl/g2/big/2014_12/3cd08e737106bd35c7a6e3128e9abbbd.pdf.

[22] *Ibid.*, at 16.

high degree of naturalness (native species and ecosystem and free functioning natural processes), undevelopedness (absence of roads, buildings, bridges, tracks, cables or other proof evidence of the modern human society, as well as a minimum distance from such facilities and development), and a relatively large size (scale).[23]

Polish nature protection legislation uses the term 'nature' ('przyroda') and 'nature protection' ('ochrona przyrody'). According to Article 2(1) of the 2004 Nature Protection Act,[24] nature protection consists of preserving, sustainable use and restoration of the resources and elements of nature: wild plants, animals and fungus, plants, animals and fungus subject to species protection, migratory animals, natural habitats, habitats of endangered, rare and protected species of plants, animals and fungus, elements of living and inanimate nature as well as fossil plants and animals, landscape, urban greenery, and trees. The scope of the notion of 'nature protection' is therefore quite broad, encompassing all components of nature. Although the various legal instruments in Polish law concentrate on certain specific components of nature and not on wilderness, these components do frequently form areas that fulfil the criteria of 'wilderness' as defined in Chapter 1. Furthermore, some definitions of categories of protected areas refer to the wilderness qualities of 'large size' or 'naturalness' (see Subsection 3.3).

Therefore, to assess the extent to which wilderness receives legal protection in Poland, it is necessary to take a closer look at these various nature protection laws and instruments; however, first the relevance of the wilderness concept in policy making receives attention.

### 3.2 *Wilderness and policy making*

The main policy document regarding nature protection in Poland is the National Biodiversity Strategy and Action Plan, as required under Article 6 of the 1992 Convention on Biological Diversity (CBD) and foreseen by Article 111 of the Nature Protection Act. A first strategy was adopted for the period of 2003–2006 and the second strategy related to the period 2007–2013.[25] A draft of the third revised strategy for the period 2014–2020, dated 24 September 2014, was prepared by the Ministry for Environment and is still awaiting adoption by the Council

23 See Chapter 1, Subsection 1.5.2.

24 Nature Protection Act of 16 April 2004, *supra* note 17.

25 See a presentation by Ewa Pisarczyk, 'Polish National Biodiversity Strategy and Action Plan 2007–2013', www.cbd.int/doc/nbsap/nbsapcbw-eur-02/nbsapcbw-eur-02-pl-01-en.pdf.

of Ministers.[26] In general, the strategic goals of the strategies, as well as the operational objectives and related text of the documents, focus strongly on biodiversity conservation and the sustainable or rational use of biodiversity.[27] This is fully in conformity with the CBD and appears to be the effect of the strong influence of international and European nature conservation law on Polish domestic policy and law making.[28] This focus on threatened species and habitat types and the sustainable use of natural resources may also at least partly explain why the concept of wilderness receives little attention in Polish policy making. Only some of the 'Operational objectives' of the 2007–2013 strategy related to issues that relate more closely with wilderness: '(11) The improvement of the state of the most valuable, damaged ecosystems, including river valleys, wetlands and forestland', and '(13) *In-situ* protection of valuable natural and semi-natural landscapes.'[29] However, these objectives have not been worked out in more detail in relation to wilderness areas in Poland.

Another policy document that should be noted in this context is the strategy on Energy Safety and the Environment, adopted by the Council of Ministers in 2014.[30] Currently it is the main policy document on environmental protection in Poland. It aims to merge energy production and environmental protection and has a tendency to focus on environmental protection in the context of climate change policy. This discussion is closely connected with coal-based energy production, which is one of the major sources of environmental problems in Poland.[31] The document is relatively general and does not refer to the protection of 'wilderness' or the areas having wilderness qualities, and neither are tensions between the energy projects and wilderness discussed. While it provides for some general concepts related to the 'synergies' between the energy

[26] *Program ochrony i zrównoważonego użytkowania różnorodności biologicznej*, 24 September 2014, www.mos.gov.pl/g2/big/2014_10/8c378a334f0822e09b2fa3d5c8293b33.pdf.

[27] Poland Council of Ministers, 'The National Strategy for The Conservation and Sustainable Use of Biodiversity', *supra* note 19. See also the 'Fifth National Report on the Implementation of the Convention on Biological Diversity', Poland, March 2014, www.cbd.int/doc/world/pl/pl-nr-05-en.pdf.

[28] See also Chapter 1.

[29] Poland Council of Ministers, 'The National Strategy for The Conservation and Sustainable Use of Biodiversity', *supra* note 19, at 24–25.

[30] Council of Ministers, 'Resolution No. 58 on the Adoption of a Strategy on Energy, Food Safety and the Environment. A Perspective for 2020', 15 April 2014.

[31] See Jerzy Jendrośka and Magdelena Bar, 'Nowe podejście do polityki ekologicznej' ('A New Approach to Environmental Policy'), *Prawo i Środowisko* 79(3) (2014), 74–80.

sector and the environment, these concepts do not receive more concrete meaning and both issues tend to be discussed separately.[32]

Chapter 1.3 of this Strategy, entitled 'Maintaining the biodiversity, including multifunctional forest management', stresses the importance of protecting biodiversity due to, e.g., the development of housing and infrastructure.[33] Again, the wording of the Strategy is, however, quite vague and general.

While there are some discussions on connectivity and robustness of areas having a relatively high degree of naturalness,[34] they haven't influenced the country's policies in such a way that concrete action is proposed to implement such approaches. Generally speaking, these topics are mainly raised by NGOs and scientists, but not by politicians, and the general public also seems quite indifferent about it.

### *3.3 Legal protection of wilderness*

The three qualities of wilderness, discussed in Chapter 1, are not recognized by domestic law and therefore do not receive explicit legal protection as such; however, there are some general legal instruments that set a general standard for environmental protection, as well as several more specific legal instruments that aim to protect one or more wilderness qualities without any reference to the wilderness concept.

#### The Constitution

The Constitution of the Polish Republic of 2 April 1997[35] is the legal cornerstone for the protection of the environment in Poland. It is the basis for the more specific nature protection legislation discussed below. The Constitution refers to the term 'environment' and not to nature or nature protection; however, it may be assumed that nature is covered by

[32] Resolution No. 58, *supra* note 30, at 5.

[33] *Ibid.*, at 34–37.

[34] Mariusz Kistkowski and Michał Pchałek, *Natura 2000 w planowaniu przestrzennym – rola korytarzy ekologicznych (Natura 2000 in land-use planning – The role of ecological corridors)* (Warsaw: Ministry for the Environment, 2009), and Michał Pchałek, Paulina Kupczyk, Piotr Matyjasiak and Adam Juchnik, *Efektywność ochrony korytarzy ekologicznych, Koncepcja zmian legislacyjnych (The effectiveness of the protection of the ecological corridors, the concept of legislative changes)* (Warsaw: WWF Poland, 2011), http://pracownia.org.pl/korytarze-konferencje.

[35] Constitution of the Polish Republic of 2 April 1997, *OJ* 1997 No 78, item 483, with further amendments.

the broader concept of 'environment'.[36] The Constitution establishes the duty for the public authorities to protect the environment (Art. 74(2)) and to prevent the degradation of the environment (Art. 68(4)). Furthermore, the public authorities shall pursue policies ensuring the ecological security of current and future generations (Art. 74(1)). Further still, care for the quality of the environment is not only the duty of the government, but is the duty of 'everyone', and 'everyone' shall be held responsible for causing environmental degradation (Art. 86).

### Nature Protection Act 2004 – national parks and natural reserves

The key act implementing these general constitutional provisions is the Act of 16 April 2004 on Nature Protection.[37] The act enables the designation of various categories of protected areas[38] and some of these categories are relevant for wilderness qualities. For instance, the definitions of 'national parks' and 'natural reserves' clearly reflect the quality of 'relatively large size' and 'naturalness':

- national park (*park narodowy*) is described as 'an area of outstanding natural, scientific, social, cultural and educational values, with the surface area of not less than 1000 ha, in which the entire nature as well as the landscape is subject to protection' (Art. 8.1).
- natural reserve (*rezerwat przyrody*) 'encompasses areas preserved in their natural state, as well as habitats of plants, animals and fungus, elements of inanimate nature of outstanding natural, scientific or landscape values' (Art. 13.1). For nature reserves, there is no minimum size threshold and in practice these areas are often relatively small (the smallest occupies as little as 0.1 ha).[39]

In Poland, twenty-three national parks have been established. Their total area covers 314,600 ha, which is a little more than one per cent of the area of Poland.[40] Some twenty-one per cent of the area of these national parks is protected under the severe regime of 'strict protection' (*ochrona*

[36] Please see the definition of the term 'environment' in Art. 3 point 39 of the Environmental Protection Law Act of 27 April 2001, *OJ* 2013, item 1232, text consolidated.
[37] Nature Protection Act 2004, *supra* note 17.
[38] *Ibid.*, Art. 6(1).
[39] See the website of the Institute for Sustainable Development, http://obszary.natura2000.org.pl/index.php?s=obszar&id=329.
[40] Environment 2014, Central Statistical Office, *supra* note 2, at 283.

*ścisła*).[41] For the theme of this book, this level of protection is particularly interesting: strict protection implies a total and permanent abandonment of human interference with ecosystems and their natural components.[42] In the remaining areas of the national parks, the protection of nature may be less strict and may involve also 'landscape protection', focused mainly on landscape characteristics but not necessarily on excluding human interference.

Furthermore, 1,479 nature reserves have been established in Poland, covering approximately 165,500 ha.[43] As described in the above quoted Article 13(1), they serve to protect natural or insignificantly changed ecosystems and habitats and formations and elements of inanimate nature, having outstanding natural, scientific or landscape values.

In order to assure protection of national parks and nature reserves against adverse human influences, Article 15 of the Act on Nature Protection contains a large list of activities that are forbidden in these areas. Several of these prohibitions relate directly to biodiversity protection (e.g., prohibitions to harm protected wild flora and fauna); however, a closer look at this list of twenty-six categories of prohibited activities makes clear that quite a number are very relevant for protecting wilderness qualities. For instance, for the wilderness quality of absence of human permanent facilities and infrastructure, such as roads, buildings and power lines, it is relevant that Article 15 prohibits:[44]

- the construction or reconstruction of buildings and technical equipment, with the exception of facilities and equipment serving the purposes of national park or nature reserve (Art. 15(1));
- the destruction or change of the land designation and use (Art. 15(9));
- manufacturing business, trade and agricultural activity, with the exception of locations designated in the plan of protection (Art. 15(11));
- the use of vehicles off the public roads and roads situated on the real estate owned by the national parks or which are in perpetual usufruct of national parks, indicated by the director of the national park or the regional director for environmental protection in the case of the nature reserve (Art. 15(18));
- placing tables, inscriptions, advertisements and other landmarks not related to nature conservation or making the national park or a nature

[41] *Ibid.*, at 285.

[42] See Article 5(9) of the Nature Protection Act 2004. See also www.mos.gov.pl/artykul/2236_parki_narodowe/311_parki_narodowe.html.

[43] See the website of the Directorate General for Environmental Protection, www.gdos.gov.pl/formy-ochrony-przyrody.

[44] Translation by the author.

reserve accessible or environmental education, with the exception of road signs and other signs relating to the protection of public order and safety (Art. 15(19));

- the execution of earth works permanently changing the shape of land (Art. 15(22));
- the organization of recreational and sports events in the national park without the consent of the director of the national park or the regional director for environmental protection in the case of the nature reserve (Art. 15(27)).

For the wilderness quality of naturalness, it is relevant that Article 15 prohibits:

- hunting (Art. 15(4)), harvesting of wild plants and fungi (Art. 15(13)) and catching fish and other aquatic organisms (Art. 15(14)), except in areas designated in the plan of protection or plan of conservation;
- use, destruction, damage, pollution and alteration of natural objects, sites and resources, and wildlife components (Art. 15(6));
- changes in the water resources, regulation of rivers and streams, as long as these changes do not serve to protect nature (Art. 15(7));
- acquisition of rocks, including peat, and fossils, including the fossil remains of plants and animals, minerals and amber (Art. 15(8));
- using open fire and smoking tobacco as well as use of light sources with an open flame, except for the places designated by the director of the national park or the regional director for environmental protection in the case of the nature reserve (Art. 15(10));
- use of chemical and biological plant protection products and fertilizers (Art. 15(12));
- walking dogs in areas under strict protection and active protection, with the exception of locations designated in the plan of protection, herding dogs in the areas under active protection where the plan of protection or plan of conservation tasks set for the nature reserve allow grazing, as well as assistance dogs (Art. 15(16));
- climbing, exploration of caves or bodies of water, with the exception of places designated by the director of the national park or the regional director for environmental protection in the case of the nature reserve (Art. 15(17));
- disturbing the silence (Art. 15(20));
- use of motor boats and other motorized equipment, water sports and motor sports, swimming and sailing, with the exception of water bodies and trails designated by the director of the national park or the regional

director for environmental protection in the case of the nature reserve (Art. 15(21));

- camping, except in places designated by the director of the national park or the regional director for environmental protection in the case of the nature reserve (Art. 15(23));
- conducting scientific research without the consent of the director of the national park or the regional director for environmental protection in the case of the nature reserve (Art. 15(24));
- introduction of species of plants, animals and fungi without the consent of the Minister for the Environment (Art. 15(25));
- introduction of genetically modified organisms (Art. 15(26)).

The prohibitions described above do not apply to activities that are required to execute the plan of protection or plan of conservation, to rescue missions and public safety measures, national defence measures in case of a threat to state security, to economic activities in landscape conservation areas, and to the exercise of the right to property in accordance with the provisions of the Civil Code.[45]

Furthermore, it is possible to obtain a derogation from the prohibitions on the basis of a request addressed to the Minister for the Environment (for national parks) or the General/Regional Director for the Environmental Protection (for nature reserves). Such a consent is issued in the form of an administrative decision and is valid for no more than five years. A derogation in respect of national parks and nature reserves may be granted if this is justified by reasons listed in Article 15 (3), (4) and (5) of the Act on Nature Protection. These reasons refer to:

- nature protection, the conduct of scientific research, and educational, cultural, tourist, recreational or sport or religious objectives, as long as the planned activity will not have an adverse impact on the nature of the national park;
- the need for linear investments for public purposes (e.g., roads, power lines, pipelines), in the absence of alternatives and after ensuring environmental compensation.

In theory, this set of concrete prohibitions and relatively limited grounds for exceptions may well constitute a regime for comprehensive protection of areas with high wilderness qualities. In fact, there are not many domestic nature conservation acts that include such a comprehensive set

[45] Art. 15(2) of the Nature Protection Act 2004.

of clear and concrete prohibitions. However, there is a constant pressure from developers, local governments and society in general to convert these lands for more 'useful' purposes. Actually, nature protection has often been criticized as being a hurdle for economic growth and local development. This conviction appears to be commonly shared among public authorities, business people and the general public, and results in high expectations regarding an extensive use of the competences to grant derogations, as well as in expectations that the law will be changed to provide more space for human uses. This is also the case in relation to protected areas, such as National Parks or Nature Reserves, especially in the mountains. A strong example is the Tatra National Park, an area with relatively high wilderness values, where the legal protection regime is seen as obstacle for the ski industry and economic development.[46]

### Nature Protection Act 2004 – Natura 2000

In addition to the above discussed instruments of national parks and natural reserves, the Nature Protection Act 2004 also provides the legal basis for designating Natura 2000 sites to implement the European Union's Bird Directive and Habitat Directive. Article 5(2b) and Article 25(1) of the Act make clear that Natura 2000 areas include areas designated under both directives. The number of Natura 2000 areas in Poland in 2013 was equal to 845 'habitat areas' and 145 'bird areas',[47] covering 68,296 km$^2$ (of which 61,059 km$^2$ are terrestrial areas) or nineteen point five per cent of the country's land area.[48]

Article 25(2) states that protected area categories in Poland may overlap: a Natura 2000 area may also have a status as, for instance, national park or natural reserve. Actually, all of the National Parks and most other protected areas, including landscape parks, contribute also to the Natura 2000 protection regime, benefiting from double protection status.[49] Competences and procedures relating to the designation of Natura 2000 areas, the development and adoption of various categories of plans for Natura 2000 areas and competences regarding supervision of compliance have been regulated in Articles 26 to 32 of the Act. The substantial protection regime of Article 6 of the Habitat Directive has been implemented through Articles 33 and 34 of the Act. The theoretical meaning of this regime for wilderness protection is not discussed here, as

[46] See Section 4.
[47] Environment 2014, Central Statistical Office, *supra* note 2, at 40.
[48] *Ibid.*, Tabl. 28(397), Natura 2000 areas, at 526. See also Tabl. 23(197) at 299.
[49] *Ibid.*, at 40.

this is the main topic of Chapter 8; however, an important example of wilderness protection in Poland through public pressure and compliance measures within the Natura 2000 regime (relating to the Rospuda Valley) is discussed in Section 4.

### Spatial planning legislation

As far as the spatial planning legislation is concerned, protection of landscape could in theory – if properly tailored – provide a certain degree of legal protection of wilderness qualities in Poland. Also the quality of 'large size' could benefit from this. Unfortunately, the protection of this quality is a very delicate matter in Poland. For many years, the existing instruments that would serve this purpose proved to be quite ineffective. In 2013 a draft Act was prepared by the President of Poland.[50] The aim of the proposal is to implement the provisions of the Council of Europe's European Landscape Convention and to provide for instruments allowing for enhanced protection of Polish landscape, especially through planning tools. Unfortunately, the legislative process has been extremely slow due to lack of political will to adopt it. Among those opposing the regulation are the local communities that are afraid of losing control over spatial development (to be more precise – over the designation of land for new investments), and the developers who fear that the public would be vested with more power to hinder their projects. Due to this unfavourable political atmosphere, the legislative draft has got stuck in the Parliamentary sub-commission.[51]

### Protection of wilderness through property rights

Protection of wilderness through property rights is not frequent in Poland. The only modern example that is commonly known in Poland occurred during the Rosupda case, discussed in the next section. In order to be considered a party to the administrative proceedings related to the construction of the Augustów bypass, several environmental organizations and a few individuals bought a small parcel of 0.7 ha, located in the area where the road had been planned. In this way, they were able to appeal the construction permit for the Augustów bypass once this decision was issued. However, it is far more common that property rights

[50] See the President's website, 'The Draft Law on the Strengthening of Landscape Protection', www.prezydent.pl/prawo/ustawy/zgloszone/art,15,projekt-ustawy-o-wzmocnieniu-narzedzi-ochrony-krajobrazu.html.

[51] See the media article, 'What to Do with the Landscape?', www.propertydesign.pl/prawo/131/co_z_ustawa_krajobrazowa,2955.html.

create an obstacle for the protection of sites of high natural value since the owners tend to consider the related requirements as impeding regular use of the land and causing financial losses. These complaints are especially frequent in relation to Natura 2000 sites, where certain activities are not allowed.[52] Generally, farmers seem to be particularly prejudiced against nature protection.[53]

## 4 Wilderness protection in practice

The discussion in the previous section shows that Polish law pays little explicit attention to wilderness or 'wild nature' protection, although there are several legal instruments that could provide wilderness protection. The actual use of these instruments depends heavily on political will to do so and practice has shown that this political will has often been absent. Even when there was intensive protest by action groups against the road construction project in the Mount St. Anna region in 1998,[54] it was decided to proceed with the project. This was not only the result of domestic politics, but also Poland's ambitions towards the EU played an important role. Fałkowski et al. explain that the road construction was financed by the EU and that 'the crisis could weaken Poland's international credibility'.[55] The authors state: 'In the rhetoric of both Polish and EU politicians, the construction of motorways in Poland is both a real and symbolic unification of Poland with the EU. It is also treated as a necessary condition for the Polish access to the EU structures.'[56]

This attitude of the Polish government has also been reflected during societal discussions on developments in other relatively wild natural areas in Poland. A more recent example relates to plans to expand the ski lift capacity or to develop infrastructure for artificial snow at Kasprowy Wierch Mountain in the Tatra Mountain National Park. The efforts of the parliamentary commission for sport and tourism have been concentrated on introducing changes to the current legislation in order to facilitate these plans, while this area belongs to the most natural and

[52] See, for example, the letter of the Ombudsman to the Minister of the Environment, 12 September 2011, www.sprawy-generalne.brpo.gov.pl/pdf/1998/08/286012/1591525.pdf.

[53] See, e.g., www.tygodnik-rolniczy.pl/articles/interwencja/chroniac-przyrode-niszcza-rolnikow/.

[54] See Subsection 2.2.

[55] Fałkowski, Lewicki and Arkowski, 'The 1998 Environmental Protests at Mount St. Anna', *supra* note 16, at 329.

[56] *Ibid.*, at 345.

relatively large areas in Poland. The commission representatives admit frankly that it perceives the environmental regulations as the greatest obstacle for the development of new projects and for the economy in general and that therefore its purpose is to significantly reduce the requirements related to nature protection.[57] The draft act is expected to be published in January 2015.[58]

However, environmental pressure groups and the EU – through its nature protection legislation – may also be successful in protecting wilderness, as is shown by the case concerning the Rospuda Valley. In this case the Polish government had planned the construction of a section of the Via Baltica Trans-European Network, a road crossing the valley of the Rospuda River serving as the bypass of the town of Augustów in North-eastern Poland. The plan dates back to the mid-1990s. At that time, little attention was paid[59] to the fact that the wetland was characterized by a peat bog of a quality that takes approximately 10,000 years to form. In fact, no similar habitat exists in Central or Western Europe any more. The area should be considered a unique wilderness area in Europe: '[t]he valley contains a rare mosaic of unspoilt habitats within one of the largest and best maintained primeval forests in central Europe. The expressway would cross a unique wetland system considered to be of exceptional European value by scientists.'[60] The area is also home to numerous rare bird species.

After Poland's accession to the EU in 2004, Poland was obliged to designate its most important wildlife sites as protected areas under the European Natura 2000 Network.[61] The Rospuda Valley was listed as a Bird Directive area and qualified as a Habitat Directive site and therefore required protection under Article 6 of the Habitat Directive. Causing significant effects on the qualifying values of the area should be prevented, especially if there are reasonable alternatives for the project.

[57] See the online news at Wyborcza.pl, 16 December 2014, http://wyborcza.pl/1,75478,17136615,Narciarski_biznes_chce_armatek_w_parku.html.

[58] It is worth mentioning that the development of ski resorts and ski lifts is the arena for constant struggle between developers and members of the local communities on one side and the environmental non-governmental organizations on the other side, sometimes supported by the public authorities responsible for environmental protection. See, for example, the website of the Polish NGO that is very active in this field: http://pracownia.org.pl/inwazyjna-turystyka-gorska.

[59] Julia Szulecka and Kacper Szulecki, 'Analysing the Rospuda River Controversy in Poland: Rhetoric, Environmental Activism, and the Influence of the European Union', *East European Politics* 29(4) (2013), 397–419, at 405.

[60] European Commission, Brussels, 'Commission Asks the European Court of Justice to Order Poland Not to Start Road Construction in Rospuda Valley', IP/07/1191, 30 July 2007.

[61] See also Chapter 8.

However, the authorities refused to acknowledge this and just wanted to proceed with the project. 'At this stage, the government's practices of denial in the face of environmental protest were not followed by any concrete arguments, apart from the calling-up of the value of development and the idea of modernisation.'[62] In 2006, the coalition of Polish ecological NGOs submitted a complaint to the European Commission[63] and petitioned the European Parliament on the grounds that the project would violate EU law.[64] The authorities ignored all actions and formally approved the launch of the construction works in 2007.[65] 'As a result the Commission accelerated an existing infringement procedure against Poland over these two roads, known respectively as the Augustow and Wasilkow bypasses.'[66] The Commission took the view 'that Poland has a duty to protect this site and that the assessments and examination of alternatives are weak and unconvincing'.[67]

Efforts to resolve the conflict informally failed, and the European Commission initiated a legal infringement procedure against Poland before the European Court of Justice. The Commission requested 'an order asking Poland not to go ahead with the construction of the bypass through Rospuda Valley while the case is pending'.[68]

Parallel to the more formal procedures, the non-governmental organizations launched a public-awareness campaign, highlighting the threats to the Rospuda Valley and explaining that more eco-friendly and even less expensive alternatives existed.[69] Despite the strong

[62] Szulecka and Szulecki, 'Analysing the Rospuda River Controversy in Poland: Rhetoric, Environmental Activism, and the Influence of the European Union', *supra* note 61, at 405.

[63] Environmental NGOs had already informed the Standing Committee of the Bern Convention some years earlier and the Standing Committee adopted a Recommendation on this case on 4 December 2003. See Standing Committee of the Convention on the Conservation of European Wildlife and Natural Habitats (Bern Convention), 'Recommendation No. 108 (2003) on the proposed construction of the *Via Baltica* (Poland)', 4 December 2003, www.rspb.org.uk/Images/Rec108_2003_ en_tcm9-228496.pdf.

[64] See Birdlife International, 'BirdLife's Polish Partner (OTOP) Campaigned to Save the Rospuda Valley from Road Development', http://www.birdlife.org/datazone/sowb/case study/25 and http://bankwatch.org/documents/via_baltica_issue_paper_0606.pdf.

[65] European Commission, Brussels, 'Commission Asks the European Court of Justice to Order Poland not to Start Road Construction in Rospuda Valley', IP/07/1191, 30 July 2007.

[66] *Ibid.*

[67] *Ibid.*

[68] *Ibid.*

[69] See Birdlife International, 'BirdLife's Polish Partner (OTOP) Campaigned to Save the Rospuda Valley from Road Development', http://www.birdlife.org/datazone/sowb/case study/25.

opposition of environmentalists and numerous scientists, both domestic and foreign, the construction was carried out.[70] This has caused even more fierce protests, including a camp set in the area of the future road in order to block the progress of construction works in February 2007:[71] 'ENGOs, including Greenpeace Poland, organised a protest camp in the Rospuda Valley, proclaiming the "Republic of Rospuda", which granted citizenship and issued its own passports.'[72] As a result of these actions and nationwide media coverage, the social opposition to the project grew to almost 150,000 citizens, who have signed a petition to halt the project and to fulfil the legal requirements. It was only in 2009 that the Polish authorities decided to refrain from the plan to build the road through the very heart of the Rospuda valley and to study the alternative routes. On the basis of a Strategic Environmental Assessment, an alternative route was selected, saving the wild nature of this area for future generations. The building permit for an alternative route was issued in 2012 and today the road is open for the public. The case has been considered as an important example of the key role that environmental NGOs may play in ensuring compliance with EU environmental law:

> Altogether, the case can be regarded as a success for Polish ENGOs that were empowered both by European laws and transnational policy networks in their attempts to pull the Polish government towards compliance with EU environmental law.[73]

Despite this example that has received much attention in the field of nature conservation policy and research in Europe, wilderness protection in Poland through the enforcement of the law should generally be considered problematic. One of the relevant factors is, as already mentioned and illustrated by the previous cases, the strong emphasis on economic growth in Poland. Directors of the national parks and the regional directors for environmental protection in the case of the nature

[70] One of the leaders of the protests Małgorzata Górska was awarded the 2010 Goldman Environmental Prize in 2010 as a way to honor her efforts in this respect, see http://www.goldmanprize.org/2010/europe.

[71] See the online news articles at http://www.greenpeace.org/poland/pl/wydarzenia/polska/ob-z-w-dolinie-rospudy-ju-dzi/ and http://wwf.panda.org/?94820/Via-Baltica-expressway-construction-to-destroy-Polands-Rospuda-Valley.

[72] Tanja Börzel and Aron Buzogány, 'Environmental Organisations and the Europeanisation of Public Policy in Central and Eastern Europe: The Case of Biodiversity Governance', *Environmental Politics* 19(5) (2010), 708–735, http://dx.doi.org/10.1080/09644016.2010.508302, at 723.

[73] *Ibid.*, at 724.

reserves experience direct involvement of actors at the national level (e.g., the Minister for the Environment and the General Director for the Environmental Protection) and an emphasis on the importance of economic development. This relates to the continuous increase of infrastructural projects (such as housing, roads and power lines), as well as the increasing number of tourists willing to visit the nature protection sites. Furthermore, protected area managements are increasingly forced to undertake activities to make money themselves. A strong example is the recently adopted law forcing the authorities responsible for the State Forests in Poland (fully self-financed) to transfer 1.6 billion PLN (375.6 million Euro) in 2014 and 2015 to the State budget and a further two per cent of their income from timber sold in the coming years.[74] It must be admitted that in this period of economic troubles the protection of nature is not the focal point of state policy.

Another factor is that the general public is less 'environmentally aware' compared to some decades ago. Non-governmental organizations may still play an important role in challenging plans and projects that may affect wilderness in Poland; however, their role is weakened if they are not backed up by the general public. Furthermore, they often lack necessary financial means to conduct research and start public or legal action. While formal instruments, such as environmental impact assessments (EIAs) and the Natura 2000 procedures, provide opportunities for NGO involvement, the actual influence of NGOs is generally inadequate in order to stop the loss of wilderness qualities. Furthermore, there are regular attempts of the government to limit the right of NGOs to participate in the proceedings related to nature protection matters.[75]

## 5 Conclusions and the future of wilderness protection in Poland

Despite the falling birth-rate in Poland[76] and population decrease in peripheral regions of the country, the demand for land will most probably not decrease. The scarcity of 'geographical space' will probably continue to grow and the pressure on relatively untouched places is not

[74] See the online news article on the State Forest website, 24 January 2014, www.lasy.gov.pl/informacje/aktualnosci/zmiany-w-ustawie-o-lasach-przyjete-przez-sejm.

[75] See, e.g., the legislative proposal of the General Director for Environmental Protection of 29 June 2011, www.mos.gov.pl/g2/big/2011_07/dc2efa299136db8a9209c3ac965c702a.pdf.

[76] See the press release of the Central Statistics Office of the Department of Demographic and Labour Market Research, 30 January 2014, http://stat.gov.pl/cps/rde/xbcr/gus/L_podst_inf_o_rozwoju_dem_pl_do_2013.pdf.

likely to decrease. Wilderness does not receive explicit attention in Polish law or language; however, Polish legislation provides some instruments that, in theory, may constitute strict protection of some of the qualities that characterize wilderness areas. For instance, the set of concrete prohibitions of human activities and influences for national parks and natural reserves is quite unique and connects well with protecting naturalness and preventing buildings, roads and other permanent proof of modern human society. The case of the Rospuda Valley also shows the potential of the Natura 2000 regime and public protest for wilderness protection. However, as discussed in the previous section, numerous factors weaken wilderness protection in practice. These factors, in combination with the lack of attention for the concept of wilderness as such, may result in the situation that not only space becomes more scarce, but wilderness does as well, even in a country like Poland.

To make wilderness protection in Poland more effective, an important first step would be to increase the awareness of the general public and the government with regard to the values (and therefore importance) of wilderness. This may also constitute the basis for addressing the various other factors. Some of these changes may be quite fundamental and therefore sensitive. For instance, in Poland the competent authorities involved in the execution of the nature protection legislation should become more independent of day-to-day politics, and gain better understanding of their role. Political parties are too influential and many politicians are not real supporters of high environmental standards, particularly not when they conflict with the short-term economic benefits.

Most likely, if wilderness is to be better protected and enforced in Poland, there is a need for external inspiration, coming from international and regional (for example, the European Union or the Council of Europe) legislation. As the Rospuda Valley case illustrates, this is particularly important for environmental NGOs, which are subjected to continuous criticism at the domestic level as organizations that hinder investments and tame the economic development of the country. However, it is also clear that law making in itself will not provide the full answer. Probably, a combination of increased awareness on wilderness conservation, more effective command-and-control tools, more independent administrative supervision and financial incentives need to be implemented. Such tools may require a more intensive collaboration between the policy makers, economists and NGOs in Poland. It is hoped that this cooperation is established soon enough so that the remaining wilderness areas in Poland could be saved before they disappear.

# 19

# Wilderness protection in Russia

NATALIA DANILINA, ANTJE NEUMANN AND KEES BASTMEIJER

## 1 Introduction

Russia covers a vast territory with significant areas of nature, which are relatively untouched by human activity. Considerable spaces in the North, Siberia and the Far East are sparsely populated, while in the European part of Russia many areas are also still relatively large, ecologically intact and free from permanent human infrastructure. In part this is due to the low population density (by European standards), which in the Central European part of Russia is a mere 59.5 persons per $km^2$.[1] Nevertheless, Russian economic policies are strongly focused on the active exploitation of natural resources. The intensive use of nature has increasingly focused on the Russian Arctic regions, where areas have relatively high wilderness qualities. This makes the central theme of this book, the role of law in protecting wilderness, also very relevant for the European part of Russia.

This overarching theme is not only relevant from a nature conservation perspective but also in the social context. It has been increasingly acknowledged that the general notion that Russia has inexhaustible supplies of wild nature is misleading. The general public is increasingly disturbed about the threat to Russia's wilderness since wild nature has always been of great importance to the country's inhabitants.

This chapter first discusses the societal relevance of the concept of wilderness in Russia (Section 2). Next (Section 3), the relevance of Russian environmental protection and nature conservation law for wilderness protection will be examined, with a particular focus on the Federal Law 'On protection of the environment' (2002), the Federal Law 'On specially protected natural areas' (1995), the 'Forest Code' of the Russian

* The authors would like to thank Peter Schütz (Alterra, The Netherlands) for his support for developing this chapter.

1 Russian State Register, 1 January 2012.

Federation (1997) and the Federal Law 'On Ecological Expertise' (1995).[2] Attention will then be focused on the category of protected areas that is most relevant for protecting the three main wilderness qualities identified in the introductory chapter of this book: namely '*zapovedniki*' (traditional Russian strict nature reserves) (Section 4). The original purposes of establishing *zapovedniki* and the influences of different political time periods upon the designation and managements of *zapovedniki* also receive attention. The final section provides a brief conclusion and future perspectives on wilderness protection in Russia (Section 5).

## 2 Wilderness in Russian society

Until the mid-twentieth century, the majority of the Russian population lived in villages surrounded by nature. Large natural areas with rich natural resources and significant space for wildlife have traditionally been commonplace in Russia. Throughout the duration of the Soviet Union governmental efforts for the protection of wilderness were minimal. For a number of decades there was little public dissent to this lack of protection. For instance, the closure of most of the *zapovedniki* between 1951 and 1961 generated little public response beyond the protests of a small number of active scientists (see Section 4).

One of the first examples of vociferous popular action to protect nature was the protest against the construction of a hydroelectric power station in the Katun River (Altai) in the 1980s. These proposals threatened many valuable wildlife areas as well as sacred places for indigenous people. Scientists played a leading role in this protest and public support for environmental causes in this context led to the establishment of the first truly non-governmental organization (NGO) 'Socio-Ecological Union'. Due to the protest, the power station was never built and in the 1990s it was subsequently determined that the development of Altai would focus on tourism.

While this may not have been a mass public protest, it nonetheless foreshadowed a sea-change in attitude among the general public towards wild nature. The increase in the urban population has fostered a greater public awareness for the importance of nature, notably in the context of

[2] It should be noted that regional and local legislation may also have relevance for wilderness protection in Russia. Furthermore, other federal laws not addressed in this chapter due to spatial constraints may also be pertinent: see, for instance, the Federal law 'On the Animal World' of 24 April 1995, No. 17, as amended on 21 November 2011, which focuses on wildlife protection and the human use of wild animals, and the Federal Law 'On Hunting and the Preservation of Game Resources', adopted on 24 July 2009 (# 209-FL).

human health. The distance between people and nature has increased and the absence of nature has become keenly felt. These benefits, as reflected in Chapter 5, have also had economic consequences, such as the increase in value of houses near national parks and *zapovedniki*, which is a new phenomenon for Russia. At the same time, public protest has become more prevalent, against both exploitation and development plans and projects in forests and other natural areas. As a member of the Public Chamber of Russia from 2011 to 2014, Natalia Danilina received numerous complaints of citizens and requests to prevent the destruction of wildlife areas.

The most active individuals have also established new NGOs and have used social networks to fight for the preservation of parks, *zapovedniki* and forests. For instance, action has also been initiated by Moscow residents for the protection of nature in the city, such as the 'Bitsevskiy Forest' Park.[3] Such actions have also been directed at wilderness areas. For example, for about ten years, the association 'Save Utrish'[4] has been campaigning for the establishment of the 'Zapovednik Utrish' in the Krasnodar region near the Black Sea coast. This action has been successful, as the *zapovednik* was established in 2010. Another better-known example is the Russian NGO 'Save Hoper'.[5] Through the establishment of this NGO, citizens sought to block copper-nickel mining in the Voronezh region, since this project threatened the whole Chernozem (Black Earth) Region. People were concerned by adverse impacts on agricultural interests as well as the wilderness qualities of the nearby (about 15 km) Khoper Zapovednik. This *zapovednik* was established in 1935, covers about 16,178 ha of wilderness and hosts various rare species, such as the white-tailed eagle, the peregrine falcon, the golden eagle and the Russian Desman (a threatened semiaquatic mammal).[6]

## 3 Russian nature conservation legislation and wilderness protection

In the 1990s, increased awareness of the gravity of environmental problems[7] made the development of effective environmental legislation an important issue: indeed, '[e]stablishing a modern environmental management system that would match new economic and social realities was one of the challenges that Russia faced during the transition

[3] See http://vk.com/club13780936.
[4] See http://vk.com/club1183453.
[5] See http://savekhoper.ru/.
[6] *Ibid.*
[7] See, e.g., Boris Porfiriev, 'Environmental Policy in Russia: Economic, Legal, and Organizational Issues', *Environmental Management* 21(2) (1997), 147–157.

period'.[8] As Ostergren notes, during the 1990s Russia has been 'rewriting the entire body of conservation and environmental laws enacted during the Soviet era'.[9] Certain fundamental provisions on environmental protection were included in the 1993 Constitution of The Russian Federation (*Konstitutsiia Rossiiskoi Federatsii*). Notably, Article 9(1) states: 'Land and other natural resources shall be utilised and protected in the Russian Federation as the basis of life and activity of the people living in the corresponding territories.'[10] As with many federal laws that have been developed over the last two decades, this provision was primarily based on laws and policies adopted at the international level, as previously noted in Chapter 1 of this book. As the OECD observed in 2006:

> In the mid and late 1990s, regulatory and institutional frameworks rapidly expanded. At that stage, environmental policies were largely guided by the international environmental agenda, most importantly by the outcomes of the Rio Summit and the emergence of sustainable development.[11]

Russia is a Contracting Party to a number of international nature conservation conventions, some of which have received attention in Chapter 1 and Part II of this volume: notably the Convention on Biological Diversity, the World Heritage Convention, the UN Convention to Combat Desertification, the Convention on International Trade in Endangered Species of Wild Fauna and Flora (CITES) and the Convention on Wetlands of International Importance Especially as Wildlife Habitat (Ramsar Convention). In the Russian legal system, provisions of such international agreements have priority over national laws.

As discussed in Part II of this book, wilderness protection receives little explicit attention in the nature conservation conventions. This is also true in Russia, where there is no specific law that defines and aims to protect wilderness. Therefore, to assess the extent to which wilderness and its constituent qualities as described in Chapter 1 may be subject to legal protection in Russia, several federal laws require closer investigation.

[8] OECD, *Environmental Policy and Regulation in Russia. The Implementation Challenge*, (Paris: OECD, 2006), www.oecd.org/env/outreach/38118149.pdf, at 5.

[9] David Ostergren, 'An organic act after a century of protection: The context, content, and implications of the 1995 Russian Federation Law on Specially Protected Natural Areas', *Natural Resources Journal* 41 (2001), 125–152, at 126. See also Chapter 1.

[10] Constitution of The Russian Federation (Konstitutsiia Rossiiskoi Federatsii), www.wipo.int/edocs/lexdocs/laws/en/ru/ru003en.pdf, Art. 9(1). See also Article 58: 'Everyone shall be obliged to preserve nature and the environment, treat and carefully the riches of nature.'

[11] OECD, *Environmental Policy and Regulation in Russia, supra* note 8, p. 8.

### 3.1 *The Federal Law 'On protection of the environment'*

Many of the important terms and concepts of the aforementioned environmental treaties can be recognized in the Federal Law 'On protection of the environment'.[12] The preamble to this act stresses the importance of nature as the foundation of life:

> The present Federal Law governs relations in the field of interaction of the society and the nature occurring in economic and other activities affecting the natural environment as a most important component of the environment as a whole being the foundation of life on the Earth [. . .].[13]

This statement has been operationalized in various more specific legal instruments. A concept that is closely related to wilderness is the 'natural landscape', defined in Article 1 of the Act as a territory that has not undergone modification as a result of economic and other activity and which is characterized by a combination of specific types of terrain, soil and vegetation that have shaped up in uniform climatic conditions. Article 3 on 'the Basic Principles of Environmental Protection', states:

> The economic and other activities of the governmental bodies of the Russian Federation, the governmental bodies of Russian regions, local government bodies, legal entities and natural persons that exert effects on the environment shall be pursued on the basis of the below principles: [. . .]

- the priority of preservation of natural ecological systems, natural landscapes and natural complexes; [. . .]

This prioritization has been laid down explicitly in Article 4(2) of the Act: 'The following shall be subject to priority protection: the natural ecological systems, natural landscapes and natural complexes which have not been exposed to man-made effects.' The scope of these general obligations has been further elaborated by requiring protection of natural landscapes in various other provisions of the act (e.g., those relating to chemical substances); however, the way in which this set of ancillary protective provisions is being implemented in practice has not been assessed for the purpose of this chapter.

[12] Federal Law on Environmental Protection, No. 7-FZ of January 10, 2002, www.asser.nl/upload/eel-webroot/www/documents/Federal%20Law%20on%20Environmental%20Protection%20Russia_ENG.pdf. The act builds on the Federal Law No. 2060-1 of 19 December 1991).

[13] *Ibid.*, preamble.

The protection of natural landscapes as relatively untouched natural areas depends heavily on the designation and protection of these areas as specially protected natural areas. According to Article 1 of the act, 'natural landscapes' form part of a broader concept of 'natural facility',[14] which is the main subject of regulation under Article 58 of the act. This article describes the 'protective measures' for natural facilities and states in paragraph 1:

> The natural facilities of special nature preservation, scientific, historical and cultural, aesthetic, recreational, health rehabilitation and another valuable significance are under special protection. For the purpose of protecting such natural facilities a special legal regime shall be established, in particular, specially protected natural areas shall be created.

Paragraph 2 specifies that '[t]he procedure for the creation and operation of specially protected natural areas shall be regulated by the legislation on specially protected natural areas', which is discussed next.

### *3.2 Federal Law 'On specially protected natural areas'*

The designation and protection of natural areas in Russia has a rich history and, as with many other countries discussed in previous chapters, 'Russian protected natural areas evolved from seventeenth century hunting and forest preserves set aside by nobility.'[15] The first state natural reserve was Barguzinski Zapovednik, established by the Regnant Senate of the Russian Empire in December 1916.[16] Since then, 'Russian conservation interests have experienced the rise and fall of political favour and a shifting, fluctuating strategy towards protecting natural resources.'[17] However, as a discrete area of environmental policy, protected areas enjoyed considerable government in the early 1990s. Presidential Decree 1155 of 2 October 1992 considered the conservation of specially protected natural areas as one of the main priorities of State Environmental Policy of the Russian Federation,[18] and in 1994 the

[14] Federal Law on Environmental Protection, *supra* note 12, Article 1: '"natural facility" is a natural ecological system, natural landscape and the components thereof that retain their natural properties'.

[15] David Ostergren, 'An organic act after a century of protection: The context, content, and implications of the 1995 Russian Federation Law on Specially Protected Natural Areas', *supra* note 9, at 126. See also Chapter 1.

[16] See Felix Shtilmark, The historiography of Russian Zapovedniks, (Moscow, LLP "Logata", 1996), at 38.

[17] *Ibid.*, at 151.

[18] Decree No. 1155 'On Specially Protected Nature Areas of the Russian Federation', Decree of the President of the Russian Federation, October 2, 1992.

'Federal Programme of State Targeted Support for State Zapovedniks and National Parks' was adopted by the Government of the Russian Federation. The Programme guaranteed financial support for protected areas over the next ten years, a period that was also characterized by difficult political and economic changes.

In 1995 the Federal Law 'On specially protected natural areas' was adopted,[19] which still constitutes one of the main legal fundaments for the designation and protection of different categories of 'Specially Protected Natural Areas'. In the act, the overarching concept of a specially protected natural area has been defined as:

> areas of land, water and the air space above them, where the natural complexes and objects have special environmental, scientific, cultural, aesthetic, recreational and health value, and which are by a public authority decision in whole or partly withdrawn from economic use for special protection.[20]

Although wilderness qualities or values are not explicitly mentioned, certain categories of protected areas have been and remain of great relevance for wilderness protection in Russia. Before focusing our discussions on the most relevant category in the next section, it should be noted that the system of protected areas in Russia is complex, not only because of the many different names that are used, but also because the network of protected areas has evolved over almost 100 years. Protected areas have been created in different time periods, where approaches to and objectives for the establishment and management of these areas have varied significantly. Furthermore, the competence to designate and manage protected areas has been divided between various government levels for a considerable number of years. Based on the 1995 act and the

[19] Federal Law of the Russian Federation 'On specially protected natural areas', No. 33-F3 of 14 March 1995 (revised on 25 June 2012). See Vsevolod Stepanitsky, *Commentaries to the Federal Law 'On Specially Protected Natural Areas'*, Series: *Handbook for managers of Protected Areas* (Moscow: BCC, 1997).

See also Ostergren, 'An organic act after a century of protection: The context, content, and implications of the 1995 Russian Federation Law on Specially Protected Natural Areas', *supra* note 9, at 131. Ostergren explains that 'the stated purpose of the 1995 Law [. . .] is to define the legislative mechanism for natural area protection and the categories of areas for protection, to delineate the level of protection for those areas, and to designate the agencies and political entities responsible for the management and funding of said areas' (p. 131).

[20] Federal Law of the Russian Federation 'On specially protected natural areas', *supra* note 19 (translation by WWF-Russia). According to the act, specially protected areas can relate to federally, regionally or locally owned natural areas.

database of the Ministry of Natural Resources and Environment of Russia and literature,[21] Table 1 summarizes the main objectives and features of some of the most important categories of protected areas in the Russian Federation and indicates to which IUCN category[22] these areas most closely connect.

By January 2015 over 13,000 protected areas with federal, regional and local status had been established in the Russian Federation. Their total area covers over 200 million hectares – eleven point eight per cent of the landmass of Russia. Regional protected areas make up eighty-four per cent of the total number and occupy fifty-four per cent of their total area, while for local protected areas these percentages are thirteen and fourteen per cent respectively. The total area of the 215 federal PAs – 103 State *Zapovedniki*, 47 National Parks and 70 State Nature Sanctuaries – is 53.6 million hectares or three point one four per cent of the total area of Russia.[23]

For the near future, the key policy document determining the development of SPNAs in Russia is *The Development Concept for Specially Protected Natural Areas of Federal Significance for the Period till the Year 2020*, which was adopted by Presidential Decree in 2011.[24] This document announces the creation of new *zapovedniki* and national parks and determines the basic principles, priorities and directions of protected area development. Among other issues, it emphasizes the priorities that should be considered for the conservation of natural complexes and sites

[21] Vladimir Krever, Mikhail Stishov, Irina Onufrenya, Protected Areas of the Russian Federation: Gap Analysis and Perspective Framework (Moskow: WWF, 2009), at 8, and Ostergren, 'An organic act after a century of protection: The context, content, and implications of the 1995 Russian Federation Law on Specially Protected Natural Areas', *supra* note 9, at 133.

[22] See Chapter 1 and Nigel Dudley (ed.), *Guidelines for Applying Protected Area Management Categories* (Gland: World Conservation Union/IUCN, 2008), http://cmsdata.iucn.org/downloads/iucn_assignment_1.pdf.

[23] State report on the state and protection of the environment of the Russian Federation in 2013.

Also see Decree No. 153 of the Government of the Russian Federation on the establishment of the National Park Onezhskoye Pomorye, 26 February 2013; Order No. 947r on the establishment of the National Park Beringia, 10 June 2013; and Decree No. 1035 on the establishment of Zapovednik Shaitan Tau, 9 October 2014.

[24] Decree No. 2322-r, 'The Development Concept for Specially Protected Natural Areas of Federal Significance for the Period till the Year 2020', Decree of the President of the Russian Federation, 22 December 2011.

Table 1 *Categories of protected areas in Russia and their primary objectives and distinguishing features*[25]

| Category of Russian PA/ Category IUCN | Primary objective(s) | Distinguishing features |
|---|---|---|
| State *Zapovednik*/mainly, IUCN cat. I.<br>Some PAs named *Zapovednik* perform the functions of IUCN cat. II or V | • Protection of biodiversity, ecosystems and wilderness;<br>• scientific studies, environmental monitoring;<br>• environmental education; and limited visitation. | • as a rule a rather large natural area,<br>• has been formed mostly or entirely by non-human forces;<br>• human use and impacts are strictly controlled;<br>• any economic activities are prohibited by law. |
| National Parks/ IUCN cat. II. Some PAs named NP perform the functions of cat. V | • protection of ecosystem, natural and cultural heritage;<br>• environmental education, tourism and recreation;<br>• scientific studies. | • quite a large natural area with nationwide significance, which may include human settlements;<br>• uses functional zoning, including allocated strictly protected zones (*zapovednik* zones), in which all activities are prohibited. |

[25] Natalia Danilina, 'The role of Zapovedniks in the system of specially protected natural areas: history and current situation' in *Russia in the World: 2010. Sustainable Development: Ecology Politics, Economy. Analytical Annual.* (Moscow: MNEPU, 2010), pp. 121–146.

| | | |
|---|---|---|
| Regional Natural Parks/ IUCN cat. II or V. Unlike NPs, these areas have a regional dimension and are administered by the regional government | • protection of biodiversity, natural and cultural heritage;<br>• environmental education, tourism and recreation;<br>• scientific studies. | • a natural area, which may include human settlements;<br>• uses functional zoning, including allocated strictly protected zones (*zapovednik* zones), in which all activities are prohibited. |
| Natural Monuments/ IUCN cat. III | • protection of unique or specific natural features. | • predominantly small areas beyond human activities. |
| State Nature Sanctuaries (*Zakazniki*) / IUCN cat. IV | • To maintain, conserve and restore species and habitat. | • Status is determined individually for each reserve, taking into account its goals. As a rule, certain activities are prohibited (e.g., removing eggs, logging, hunting and mowing);<br>• management is carried out in order to preserve or restore some species or habitats. |

in state protected areas, priorities that also have relevance for areas with relatively high wilderness qualities:

- The importance of preserving a comprehensive natural biological and landscape diversity;
- Maintaining specially protected natural complexes and avoiding fragmentation of the landscape;
- Ensuring visitors' awareness of the biological and landscape diversity of specially protected natural areas.
- The need to reach a reasonable compromise between protection of the environment and the interests of socio-economic development in the regions;
- Encouraging models of land use, which do not destroy the environment or exhaust biological resources.

Section 4 focuses on federal *zapovedniki* and their relevance for the protection of the three main qualities of wilderness as identified in Chapter 1. As explained by Shestakov and Kats, *zapovedniki* 'are clearly not the only mechanism for wilderness protection in Russia', but 'are clearly the closest analogous entity to designated wilderness areas'.[26]

### *3.3 The Forestry Code and wilderness*

Russia is the largest forested country in the world, accounting for a quarter of global forest land cover. Forests cover almost half of the area of Russia and feature great natural diversity as well as wilderness qualities, while 'more than 25 percent of the world's old-growth forests are found in Russia'.[27] The Forestry Code of the Russian Federation was adopted in 2006.[28] Experts believe that this piece of legislation roundly fails to protect forests, and has not ensured effective protection

[26] Alexander Shestakov and Dmitry Kats, 'The Russian Federation', in Cyril F. Kormos (ed.), *A Handbook on International Wilderness Law and Policy* (Golden: Fulcrum Publishing 2008), 215–239, at 221.

[27] *Ibid.*, at 216. See also Ellen Hitchcock, 'The 2006 Forest Code of the Russian Federation: An Evaluation of Environmental Legislation in Russia', *Australian Slavonic and East European Studies* 24(1–2) (2011), http://miskinhill.com.au/journals/asees/24:1-2/2006-forest-code. Hitchcock refers to J. Howard, 'Saving Russia's Forests: The Finnish–Russian Development Program on Sustainable Forest Management and Conservation of Biological Diversity in Northwest Russia', *Colorado Journal of International Environmental Law and Policy* 14(2) (2003), at 274.

[28] Forest Code of the Russian Federation, 4 December 2006, No. 166-FZ, www.fire.uni-freiburg.de/GlobalNetworks/BalticRegion/ForestCode-3rdReading-061108-eng.pdf.

for old-growth forests. Non-governmental organizations have criticized the code for various reasons, particularly the decentralization of competences which makes the designation of transboundary natural areas more difficult, the limitation of environmental assessment requirements in relation to forestry activities and the problematic character of public participation.[29] According to other experts, the implementation of the new Code has been blamed as the main cause of major forest fires in recent years, especially in 2010.[30] As Hitchcock concludes:

> A key failing of the Forest Code is its lack of provisions for ensuring the protection of forests, a focus of concern for Russian environmental groups in particular. This absence of protection has occurred in a number of ways, particularly through the expansion of permissible types of forest use, changes to the classification of forest types, and the transfer of formerly protected areas to new forest categories that allows for their exploitation. Aspects of the Code are focused on the direct stimulation of the forest industry and the attraction of investment into the sector [. . .]. In comparison with both the 1997 and 1993 forestry laws, the 2006 Forest Code does shift the focus away from the protection of forests quite noticeably towards a more utilitarian approach.[31]

In September 2013, after a strong campaign by the professional forestry community and the general public, the Government of Russia developed and approved its policy through the adoption of the document *Principles of State Policy in the use, protection and regeneration of forests in the Russian Federation for the period up to 2030.*[32] It defines the principles, objectives and tasks of the state in relation to the use, conservation and regeneration of forests. The policy includes measures to prevent the fragmentation of forests (mainly forests of a high ecological value), the formation of a national forest heritage in the Russian Federation (a forest fund that should not be dependent on economic development) and measures to adapt to climate change. While laudable, the new policy is, however, only the first step in improving forestry from the perspective of nature protection.

[29] Anonymous, 'New forest legislation for Russia', *Russian Conservation News* 42 (2006/07), 29, www.wild-russia.org/pubs/pdfs/42.pdf.

[30] Eugene Schwartz and Dmitry Aksenov, 'Forest fires: Looking from the ground', *Vedomosti* 11 August 2010, 148 (2666)

[31] Hitchcock, 'The 2006 Forest Code of the Russian Federation: An Evaluation of Environmental Legislation in Russia', *supra* note 27.

[32] 'Principles of State Policy in the use, protection and regeneration of forests in the Russian Federation for the period up to 2030', Order of the Government of the Russian Federation of 26 September 2013, No. 1721-p, Moscow, 1 October 2013, www.rg.ru/2013/10/01/lesa-site-dok.html.

### 3.4 *Environmental Impact Assessment and wilderness*

Although Russia has not yet ratified the UNECE Convention on Environmental Impact Assessment in a Transboundary Context (Espoo Convention) 1991,[33] regulatory approaches are in place to cover assessments of environmental impacts. In this regard, the main legal instruments are the 'Ecological Expertise', regulated by the Federal Law 'On Ecological Expertise' of 1995,[34] and the Environmental Impact Statement of Project Planning (Russian: OVOS – assessment of environmental impacts), guided by the Regulation 'On the Assessment of Environmental Impacts of Economic and Other Activities in the Russian Federation' of 2000.[35] From a procedural point of view, the OVOS has to be prepared prior to the 'Ecological Expertise', and is generally conducted by the project developer.[36]

In respect of the 'Ecological Expertise', two forms can be distinguished: the 'State Ecological Expertise', regulated by Chapter III of the Federal Law 'On Ecological Expertise', and the so-called 'Public Environmental Expertise', contained in Chapter IV of this law. The general aim of both forms is, according to Article 1 of the law, to assess the compliance of the project documentation with environmental requirements, technical standards and the applicable environmental legislation in order to avoid negative impacts on the environment caused by the project. Articles 11 and 12 of the Law 'On Ecological Expertise' state which documents and initiatives are subject to the 'State Ecological Expertise'. These include, for instance, drafts of technical specifications and methodological instructions on environmental protection, federal target programmes, documents for obtaining authorization for projects with potential environmental impacts and documents for the examination of areas of federal or regional importance with respect to their certification as protected areas, or as ecological emergency areas.

[33] The Russian Federation signed the Espoo Convention on 6 June 1991, but has not yet ratified it. For the status of ratifications of the convention see https://treaties.un.org/Pages/ViewDetails.aspx?src=TREATY&mtdsg_no=XXVII-4&chapter=27&lang=en.

[34] Federal Law 'On Ecological Expertise' of 23 November 1995, No. 174-F3, available in Russian at: www.consultant.ru/document/cons_doc_LAW_166215/.

[35] Regulation 'On the Assessment of Environmental Impacts of Economic and Other Activities in the Russian Federation' of 16 May 2000, No. 372, available in Russian at: www.ohranatruda.ru/ot_biblio/normativ/data_normativ/10/10349/index.php.

[36] For an outline of the general procedure of the assessment of environmental impacts, including public participation during this process, see N. Kovalev and J. Koeppel, 'Introduction to the Environmental Impact Assessment System and Public Participation in the Russian Federation', *Journal of Environmental Assessment Policy and Management* 5(3), 2003, 325.

Although the wilderness qualities addressed in Chapter 1 are not explicitly referred to in this legislation, it is still of relevance to wilderness protection, since Articles 11(6) and 12(4), require consideration of any negative impacts on protected areas, including *zapovedniki* in the context of conducting an 'Ecological Expertise'. In practice, however, empirical data is difficult to obtain and examples are rather sporadic.[37] Additionally, it must be noted that the Federal Law 'On Ecological Expertise', together with other relevant legislation, like the Federal Law on Environmental Protection of 2002[38] and the Federal Urban Planning Code of 2004, have been amended several times in the course of different administrative and procedural reforms. The main aim behind these reforms was to reduce the administrative and procedural efforts required for the approval of construction projects, e.g., the number of assessment authorities, and the time required for granting permission.[39] Especially in respect of the latter law (the Federal Urban Planning Code), the Federal Law No. 232 of 2006[40] introduced significant changes to the EIA regulations. One notable development was that all official ecological assessments of project documentation on the construction, reconstruction and repair of buildings were abolished. Instead of these previously separate ecological assessments, a uniform state expertise is required, which streamlines various technical, epidemiological and safety requirements, as well as requirements for the protection of cultural heritage.[41]

With regard to the second form of ecological expertise, the 'Public Environmental Expertise', Articles 11 and 12 of the Law 'On Ecological Expertise' are also applicable,[42] with the consequence that wilderness

[37] See, e.g., K. von Ritter and S. Zirkunow, 'How Effective Is the System of Environmental Assessment in Russia?' (in Russian language), 2003, www.alexpublishers.ru/envassess.pdf; N. Kovalev and J. Koeppel, 'Democracy and the Environment in Russia', *Journal of Environmental Assessment Policy and Management* 11(2), 2009, 161–173.

[38] Federal Law on Environmental Protection of 2002, *supra* note 12.

[39] Anja May, Wolfgang Wende, Adrian Hoppenstedt, Valery Kravchenko, Anatoly Ignatov and Victoria Venchikova, *Assessment of Environmental Impacts and Ecological Expertise: Professional Experience of EIA Issues in Russia and Germany*, (Irkutsk/Dresden: Publishing House of the Sochava Institute of Geography of the SB RAS, 2012), www.umweltbundesamt.de/sites/default/files/a7_publikation1_umweltfolgenbewertungs-kompendium_en_0.pdf, at 5.

[40] Federal Law on Amendments of the Urban Planning Code, No. 232-FZ of 18 December 2006, available in Russian at: www.consultant.ru/document/cons_doc_LAW_169786/.

[41] May et al., 'Assessment of Environmental Impacts and Ecological Expertise - Professional experience of EIA issues in Russia and Germany', *supra* note 39, at 10.

[42] With the exception of projects which contain classified or commercially sensitive information, or other secret information protected by law. Art. 21 of the Law 'On Ecological Expertise', translation by the authors.

qualities of protected areas can be theoretically subject to an environmental impact assessment. It should, however, be noted that the right of citizens to initiate a 'Public Environmental Expertise'[43] is rarely available in practice as this right is usually reserved for public organizations and associations that have – accordingly to their statutes – the organization and conduct of environmental impact assessments as their main activity.[44] Further constraints result from amendments to the Federal Law 'On Non-Profit Organisations' of 2012,[45] which led to comprehensive administrative obstacles (e.g., new obligations for registration and reporting) for Non-Governmental Organizations (NGOs) that are financially supported by foreign funds.[46] As regards the practical relevance of the 'Public Environmental Expertise' towards wilderness qualities, verified statements are not available to the authors. Nevertheless, it should be mentioned that the relevance of this instrument, in general, has risen constantly since 2000,[47] and examples of the 'Public Environmental Expertise' in respect of *zapovedniki* are evident as well.[48]

## 4 Russian zapovedniki[49]

### 4.1 *The original idea of zapovedniks: strict protection for scientific research*

In the early phase of designation, the term '*zapovednik*' was understood almost as a synonym for 'national park'. In a popular article, A.P.

43 *Ibid.*, Art. 20.

44 See M. Brintschuk, Commentary to the Federal Law 'On Ecological Expertise' (2009), Comments on Art. 11.

45 Federal Law 'On Non-Profit Organizations', No.7-FZ of 12 January 1996; in connection with Federal Law on Amendments of individual legislations of the Russian Federation in the regulatory area of Non-Commercial Organizations with the function of a 'Foreign Agent', No. 121-FZ of 20 July 2012.

46 Numerous Russian NGOs, acting in the environmental protection context, are still dependent on foreign financial support; see Laura A. Henry and Vladimir Douhovnikoff, Environmental issues in Russia, *The Annual Review of Environment and Resources* 33 (2008), 437–460, at 450.

47 Kovalev and Koeppel, 'Introduction to the Environmental Impact Assessment System and Public Participation in the Russian Federation', *supra* note 36, at 332.

48 See, for example, the 'Public Environmental Expertise' regarding the *zapovednik* of 'Utrish' (North Caucasus), News of 23 March 2010, www.ewnc.org/node/5407; or the 'Public Environmental Expertise' regarding the Federal Target Program 'Development of Sochi as a mountain resort – 2006–2014'', www.greenpeace.org/russia/Global/russia/report/2007/4/1010413.doc.

49 Parts of this discussion build on Natalia Danilina and Vladimir Boreyko, 'Strictly Protected Areas: The Russian System of Zapovedniks', in David Harmon and Alan D. Putney (eds.),

Semenov-Tyanshanski (1911) wrote: 'Significant areas of wild forests must in good time be turned to conservation areas, to national parks, where taiga could be preserved in its untouched condition as it is done in many areas of North America.'[50] Thus, the exemplary role of the 'national park' concept from the US for other parts of the world, as discussed in Chapter 1, also applied to the designation of protected areas during the early decades of the twentieth century in Russia.

However, unlike the US, where recreational use was an important purpose of designating the first national parks, the early *zapovedniki* in Russia were characterized by a strict protection regime that was strongly focused on limiting human access to protect the value of these areas for ecological research.[51] The Russian *zapovednik* network was based on a scientific biogeographic approach that provided for the maximum representation of the natural diversity of the whole country. Natalia Danilina and Vladimir Boreyko explain that:

> as early as 1910, at a congress of Russian naturalists and physician, a professor, Ivan Borodin, and a famous Russian forestry specialist, Grigory Morozov, suggested that 'allotment of the protected sites should be done according to a plan, if possible, based on botanic-geographical divisions.... Protected areas should be situated in each botanic-geographical region representing in their totality a range of characteristic and most valuable types of plants...' (Congress of Russian Naturalists 1911).[52]

The authors explain that 'Borodin and Morozov's principles are to a great extent realized in the modern network of zapovedniks of Russia.'[53] Professor Grigory Kozhevnikov, who also played a crucial role in this

*The Full Value of Parks: From Economics to the Intangible* (Oxford: Rowman & Littlefield, 2003), 227–238. For a comprehensive debate on the history of zapovedniki and the influences of politics, see Feliks Shtilmark, *History of the Russian Zapovedniks 1895–1995*, translated from Russian by G.H. Harper (Edinburgh: Russian Nature Press, 2003).

50 Benjamin Semenov-Tyanshansky, 'The Types of Terrain, Which Should Establish Reserves Such as the American National Parks', Paper presented at the joint meeting of the Main Department of the Land Committee, the Scientific Committee of the Ministry of Agriculture of Russia and the Permanent Environmental Commission of Russian Geographical Society, 17–20 October 1917, cited in Feliks Shtilmark, *The Historiography of Russian Zapovedniks, supra* note 49, at 22.

51 David Ostergren and Steve Hollenhorst, 'Converging Protected Area Policy: A Case Study of the Russian Zapovednik (Strict Nature Reserve) and American Wilderness Systems', *USDA Forest Service Proceedings RMRS-P-14*, 2000, at 3.

52 Danilina and Boreyko, 'Strictly Protected Areas: The Russian System of Zapovedniks', *supra* note 49, at 227–228.

53 *Ibid.*, at 228.

early phase of creating nature reserves in Russia, considered such a strict 'regime of untouchability' the most important feature of such reserves:[54]

> In relation to flora, it is necessary to cancel the cutting of clearings, the pruning of wood growth, even grass cutting – and certainly all sorts of sowing and planting. Nothing should be eliminated, added, or improved. One should leave nature to itself and observe the results.[55]

According to Kozhevnikov, leaving nature to itself was necessary for scientific research: 'To be able to study nature, we must try to preserve it in its primordial intactness, in the form of its most typical formations.'[56] This approach to *zapovedniki* as 'nature laboratories' or 'science laboratories in nature' was approved by many outstanding scientists of that time, including the member of the Academy of Sciences V. Sukatchev, who proposed one of the first programmes of scientific research under *zapovednik* conditions.[57] As commentators have observed, this 'focus on scientific research clearly distinguishes the Soviet system from those around the world'.[58]

As explained by Danilina and Boreyko, 'the specific political conditions of the former Soviet Union' made it possible to designate exclusive state-owned land as strictly protected areas:

> From the creation of the very first zapovedniks, an important principle of complete nonintervention in natural processes was laid down, as called for by the Russian scientific community. The management regime of a zapovednik completely forbids any kind of economic activity on its territory. No use of protected natural resources is allowed, whether it be mining, hunting, or haymaking. The only activities allowed are those required of managers to protect the zapovednik, scientific research, and [. . .] educational programs and tourist excursions on specially selected routes or at designated sites.[59]

[54] Grigory Kozhevnikov, 'On the Necessity for Setting up Preserved Areas for the Protection of Russian Nature', in Proceedings of the All-Russian Acclimatization Anniversary Congress in 1908 in Moscow. B.1, MA, 1909, http://ecoethics.ru/on-the-necessity-for-setting-up-preserved-areas-for-the-protection-of-russian-nature/.

[55] *Ibid.*

[56] *Ibid.*

[57] Vladimir Sukachev *On Environmental Protection in the Zhiguli*, (Simbirsk: Simbirsk Western Science Museum, 1914).

[58] See also David Ostergren and Evgeny Shvarts, 'Protected Areas in Russia: Management Goals, Current Status, and Future Prospects of Russian Zapovedniki', in Alan E. Watson, Greg H. Aplet and John C. Hendee, *Personal, Societal, and Ecological Values of Wilderness: Sixth World Wilderness* (Ogden: Forest Service, Rocky Mountain Research Station, 1998), 11–16, www.fs.fed.us/rm/pubs/rmrs_p004/rmrs_p004_011_016.pdf, at 11.

[59] Danilina and Boreyko, 'Strictly Protected Areas: The Russian System of Zapovedniks', *supra* note 49, at 228.

For the central theme of the book, this history makes the *zapovedniki* especially valuable and '[t]here is no doubt that the strict nature protection regime of the zapovedniks, along with the great amount of area they cover, contributed to the effective conservation of nature on the protected sites'.[60] However, it is important to stress that since the establishment of the first State *Zapovednik* (Barguzinski) in 1916 in Russia, this protected area category has been the subject of significant regulatory fluctuations in respect of their main objectives and institutional arrangements (e.g., division of administrative competences), caused by the shifting political landscape.

### *4.2 The influence of politics: 'good times' and 'bad times' for zapovedniki*

The governmental approach to zapovedniki has been strongly dependent upon the political and economic situation in Russia.[61] For instance, in 1929 '[a] change in policy from protection to utilization of nature was outlined by the Nature Protection Congress'.[62] In the 1930s numerous experiments for 'nature improvement' were carried out in the zapovedniki, for instance, acclimatization of non-indigenous plants and animals of particular economic value, such as the raccoon dog. Simultaneously, species that had adverse impacts for human interests were eliminated. Those species mainly included predators, such as wolves and even tigers, along with many carnivorous birds. Hunting such animals created a 'favourable environment' for species that were considered valuable from the perspective of human interests. Furthermore, the protection of certain commercially interesting species played an important role in the designation and protection of certain *zapovedniki*. For instance, Voronezhski Zapovednik was established in 1927 for the preservation and breeding of beaver, and Khoperski (1935) was designated for the protection of desman. Generally, the *zapovedniki* were successful in fulfilling these tasks. In 1933 the State Committee of Zapovedniks, affiliated with the Presidium of the All-Russian Central Executive Committee, was created. In this period of political repression (especially in the years 1937–1941), many scientists moved to work within remote

[60] *Ibid.*
[61] For a comprehensive discussion, see Shtilmark, *History of the Russian Zapovedniks 1895–1995*, *supra* note 49.
[62] Douglas R. Weiner, *A Little Corner of Freedom. Russian Nature Protection from Stalin to Gorbachëv*, (Berkeley/Los Angeles/Oxford: University of California Press, 1999), at 37–57.

*zapovedniki*,[63] and the science in the nature reserves was probably at its peak during this time period.

Since World War II, there have been several periods in which *zapovedniki* received little or no political support. For instance, in the beginning of the 1950s Stalin endorsed the ideas of Professor Lysenko, who denied genetics and claimed that ancestral features could be changed by altering environmental conditions. The realization of Lysenko's principle of 'changing nature for satisfying human demands' led to the decision to dissolve the state institution responsible for managing *zapovedniks* and to the liquidation of many such areas: of the 128 *zapovedniki*, only forty survived, while the territory of some of these forty areas was also reduced significantly. The total area of *zapovedniks* was reduced from 12.5 million hectares to less than 1.5 million hectares. By the end of the 1950s, after Stalin's death, scientists managed to restore some of the reserved territories and to increase their total area up to five million hectares; however, in 1962 'Khrushchev launched another attack on the system in order to bring more land into economic production'[64] and half of this territory was again handed over to the 'needs of the national economy'.[65] However, after the Khrushchev era, a gradual restoration of the destroyed *zapovednik* network began, a process that was influenced by the international conservation movement briefly discussed in Chapter 1.

In 1988, the State Committee on Nature Conservation was established. Social changes stimulated people to become more aware and involved in environmental issues and '[t]he "Perestroyka period" [. . .] was a time of reconstruction and opened a new phase in zapovednik history'.[66] In the early 1990s, the protected area network in Russia started to grow more rapidly. Political reforms made it possible to withdraw valuable nature complexes from land development. Up to six new *zapovedniki* were established each year. These represented urgent measures for the rescue

[63] Shtilmark, *History of the Russian Zapovedniks 1895–1995, supra* note 49.

[64] *Ibid.* See also Ostergren and Shvarts, 'Protected Areas in Russia: Management Goals, Current Status, and Future Prospects of Russian Zapovedniki', *supra* note 58, at 11–12.

[65] Alexei Blagovidov, Vsevolod Stepanitsky, Natalie Troitsky and Alexey Troitsky, *Protected Areas of Russia after the Collapse of the Soviet Union 1992–2003* (Gland/Moscow: IUCN and the Ministry of Natural Resources of the Russian Federation, 2003), at 5. See also Ostergren and Shvarts, 'Protected Areas in Russia: Management Goals, Current Status, and Future Prospects of Russian Zapovedniki', *supra* note 58, at 11–12.

[66] M.A. Spetich, A.E. Kvashnina, Y.D. Nukhimovskya and O.E. Rhodes, 'History, Goals, Administration, Value and Long-term Data of Russia's Strictly Protected Scientific Nature Reserves', *Natural Areas Journal* 29(1) (2009), 71–78, www.srs.fs.usda.gov/pubs/ja/ja_spetich010.pdf, at 73.

of rare (and frequently endangered) plant and animal species, unique wetland and tundra complexes and steppe areas that had remained intact. A stimulating factor for the designation of *zapovedniki* was that this procedure was easier and faster than that in respect of a national park. Furthermore, the legislation relating to *zapovedniki* was more effective from the perspective of nature protection due to the direct involvement of federal environmental bodies: *zapovedniki* were established and administered by nature protection authorities, while national parks were established by authorities responsible for forestry.

### *4.3 Existing zapovedniki and their importance for wilderness protection in European Russia*

The long and complex history of Russian *zapovedniki* discussed above has resulted in a continuously changing number of *zapovedniki* in Russia.[67] Today, there are 103 State *zapovedniks*, while almost half of these sites are situated in European Russia, which also features the highest population density in Russia. These areas therefore often appear like 'islands', surrounded by farmland, industrial zones, cities and villages, road and rail networks. These *zapovedniki* are relatively small in size, although this is a relative concept and 'small' by Russian standards nevertheless covers substantial areas of territory: seven of them cover less than 10,000 hectares each, while most other *zapovedniki* span between 10,000 and 100,000 hectares. Only the largest of all European *zapovedniki* – Pechoro-Ilych – covers over 721,000 hectares of virgin forest in the Northern foothills of the Ural Mountains. Below are a few examples of *zapovedniki* located in the European part of Russia.[68]

Significant onshore and offshore territories have been designated in the Arctic Region and in little-developed areas in Siberia and the Far East. The largest *zapovednik* of Russia is the Great Arctic Zapovednik on the Taymyr Peninsula, covering an area over 4 million hectares of tundra. Komandorski Zapovednik in the Far East is just a little smaller – 3.6 million hectares together with an offshore part.[69]

[67] See Christel Elvestad, Frode Nilssen and Ludmila Ivanova, 'The New Paradigm for Nature Protection: A Model for Russia's High North?', *Arctic Review on Law and Politics* 3(2) (2011), 199–221, at 206, Table 2.

[68] Natalia Zabelina, Ludmila Isaeva-Petrova and Ludmila Kuleshova, *Zapovedniks and National Parks of Russia* (Moscow: Logata, 1998).

[69] Natalia Danilina, 'Protected Areas in Condition of Democratic Changes in Russian Society', *Parks* 6(3) (1996), 8–13.

Not all areas that have received *zapovednik* status have management objectives that are characteristic of wilderness areas, because the different political time periods discussed above have resulted in significant differences between zapovedniki established in the modern era and those of more historic vintage. For instance, in some *zapovedniki* extensive management measures are taken to sustain biological diversity. One such example is the Centralnochernozemny Zapovednik, where a mowing regime is carried out in respect of thirty per cent of the area in order to implement scientific recommendations of several generations of botanists. Today, such management measures are the only way to preserve the floral biodiversity of the steppe, because the huge herds of wild ungulates no longer graze on the territory. Some other *zapovedniki* aim to protect certain types of landscape or human social values, such as historical and cultural values. Examples include Zapovednik Shulgan Tash (Ural), which protects lime forests and the traditional Bashkir craft of beekeeping; Khakasky (Southern Siberia) steppes, where historical monuments of the ancient Khakassians are to be found and Uvs Nuur Basin (Republic of Tuva), where nature surrounds many archaeological sites.[70] Furthermore, Ostergren and Hollenhorst state that designation policy of *zapovedniki* was broadened from the original designations for ecological research to include ecotourism and environmental education in more recent years.[71]

Nonetheless, in most *zapovedniki* the original purpose to protect large natural systems as natural science laboratories has continued to play an important role and the vast majority of the *zapovedniki* in Siberia, Northern European Russia and the Far East remain wilderness areas. These include also very large areas of untouched wild nature, such as the Central Siberian (1,019,899 hectares), Sayano-Shushensky (390,368) and Putoransky Zapovedniki (1,887,251) and many others.

## 5 Conclusion and future challenges

The above discussions show that, although Russia does not have legislation explicitly referring to the term 'wilderness', a considerable amount of

[70] Natalia Danilina, 'The Role of Zapovedniks in the System of Specially Protected Natural Areas: History and Current Situation', in *Russia in the World: 2010. Sustainable Development: Ecology Politics, Economy. Analytical Annual* (Moscow: MNEPU, 2010), 121–146.

[71] Ostergren and Hollenhorst, 'Converging Protected Area Policy: A Case Study of the Russian Zapovednik (Strict Nature Reserve) and American Wilderness Systems', *supra* note 51, at 4.

domestic legislation has relevance for the central theme of this book. Most important is the protected area regime of the *zapovedniki*. Depending on political conditions, this regime has experienced 'good times' and 'bad times'; however, over the past century many areas with high wilderness qualities in Russia have received relatively strict legal protection under this regime.

As for the future it is also clear that wilderness in Russia faces particular challenges. Institutional concerns continue to exist. The effective management of 150 *zapovedniki* and national parks would be a challenge for any organization, but the abolition of the State Committee for Environmental Protection in 2000 and reduction of the budgets of relevant actors have increased this challenge dramatically.[72] The establishment in 2008 of a relatively small ministerial unit responsible for the management of federal protected areas[73] did not really address this concern. When the Russian Government approved *The Development Concept for Specially Protected Natural Areas of Federal Significance for the Period until the Year 2020* in 2011, the funding for *zapovedniki* was improved; however, the available budgets are still inadequate for effective management of the large areas. Furthermore, the wages for PA staff members are too low to attract highly qualified personnel.

Challenges are further increased by the development of tourism in *zapovedniki*. Discussions on the desirability of tourism in *zapovedniki* have taken place throughout the history of these protected areas,[74] and, motivated primarily by educational opportunities, some of *zapovedniki* have been accessible for recreational purposes. Examples include Teberdinski Zapovednik in the Caucasus (established in 1936), and the Stolby (Krasnoyarsk Krai), close to Yenisei River (established in 1925) and Kivatch Zapovedniki (Karelia, established in 1931). Small-scale recreational visitation may be highly important in making people aware of the importance of protecting wilderness, but there is a real risk that pressure for allowing greater tourist activities in *zapovedniki* will become too high.

In March 2015, the Ministry of Natural Resources of Russia acknowledged the importance of this issue by approving a Strategy on the

[72] See, inter alia, Laura A. Henry and Vladimir Douhovnikoff, 'Environmental Issues in Russia', *supra* note 46, at 440.

[73] The Resolution of the Government of Russian Federation, 'On the Ministry of Natural Resources and Environment', 29 May 2008, No. 404.

[74] Quoted in: Vladimir Boreyko, *'Don Quixotes': History, People and Zapovedniks* (Moscow: Logata, 1998), at 158.

development of educational tourism (visitation) in protected areas. This document constitutes the basis for rather strict regulations on the visitation of protected areas, particularly *zapovedniki*. The document states categorically that no more than five per cent of the total area of each *zapovednik* may be opened for visitation.

This recent development may give hope that the various challenges discussed above will be addressed in time in order to prevent irreparable damage to Russia's wildernesses. This would be of great value not only for Russia, but for Europe as well. The scarcity of relatively untouched nature in Europe underlines the special value of the large wilderness areas that still exist in Russia, and the discussions in this book show that the category of *zapovedniki* is of special importance for the long term protection of remaining wilderness.

20

# Wilderness protection in Spain

AGUSTÍN GARCÍA-URETA

## 1 Introduction

Spain is the fourth largest European country (504,645 km$^2$) with a population of forty seven million (ninety-three inhabitants per km$^2$).[1] The length of Spanish coasts spans some 7880 km; the fourteen most important rivers stretch over 6,479 km. With an average altitude of 650 metres Spain is one of the most mountainous countries in continental Europe, with thirteen mountain chains. Its geographical and climatic conditions shelter a large variety of species and habitats. Spain includes four of the nine biogeographical regions under the EU Natura 2000 network (Atlantic, Mediterranean, Alpine and Macaronesian, the latter being exceptional in Europe)[2] and hosts 118 of 235 EU habitats of Community interest. It gives refuge to approximately 90,000 species of fauna and flora (approximately fifty-four per cent of the total number of European species, and about fifty per cent of which are endemic to Spain) including about 8,000 vascular plants, 23,000 fungi and lichens, 57,000 invertebrates and 635 species of vertebrates. Due to its geographical location, the Spanish landmass is also one of the main migration routes for wild birds to Northern Europe (spring migration) and to Africa (autumn migration). Spain has the second largest collection globally of biosphere reserves classified under UNESCO rules (forty-five in 2013). By late 2013 Spain had designated more than 1,449 sites of Community importance under the EU Natura 2000 network (11,731,366,44 terrestrial ha; 101,150,029 marine ha.), and 598 special protection areas for birds (1,012,128,753 terrestrial ha; 26,637,512 marine ha).[3] While this corresponds to roughly twenty-seven per cent of Spanish territory, this does not mean that those sites contain similar features or, for

[1] 2013 census.
[2] This biogeographical region is shared with Portugal.
[3] Spanish Ministry for the Environment (Magrama).

the purposes of this contribution, could be regarded as highly valuable areas free from human intervention. The surface covered by protected natural areas in Spain encompasses 6.9 million ha (6.5 million terrestrial and 490,000 marine). Sierra Nevada (85,883 ha) and Tablas de Daimiel (1928 ha.) are the largest and smallest respectively of Spain's fifteen national parks. The Canary Islands and the Autonomous Communities of Andalusia and Castilla-León are the regions with the largest proportion of protected areas.

Notwithstanding the foregoing, defining 'wilderness' in Spanish law is not a simple task. This term could either encompass untouched habitats or wild fauna and flora species not subject to the dominion of man,[4] but also other situations subject to a certain degree of anthropic traits, a situation that is far from infrequent. Wilderness is a notion normally equated to 'nature' as opposed to areas or zones subject to (intense) human presence (or influence), such as housing and the corresponding services, and other man-made infrastructures. As considered below, from a strict legal viewpoint the basic piece of Spanish legislation (Law 42/2007, on the Natural Patrimony and Biodiversity) does not provide a definition of 'wilderness' but instead articulates the notions of 'natural patrimony' and 'biodiversity'. The former term is defined as a set of goods and natural resources representing the basis of biological and geological diversity having relevant environmental, landscaping, scientific or cultural values.

It should also be noted that Spain has not yet discharged the mandate contained in Law 42/2007 requiring the competent authorities to adapt the existing Spanish designations of protected areas to the categories adopted by the IUCN. This represents an apparent hurdle to providing clear-cut conclusions regarding the current status of wilderness quality areas in Spain. To date only forty-three per cent of all areas have been classified under the respective IUCN categories, the most common being category V (Protected Landscape/Seascape), whilst categories Ia (Strict Nature Reserve) and Ib (Wilderness Area) are scarce due to the absence of sufficiently extensive natural spaces and entirely natural ecosystems. By late September 2014, category Ia areas were mainly found in the Canary Islands (eleven sites) and Catalonia (six sites), whereas category Ib areas were located in the Canary Islands (fifteen sites), the Autonomous Community of Aragón (three sites) and Madrid (one site).[5] The general percentage of the surface protected (data for forty-three per cent of natural

[4] This latter definition was included in the Hunting Act of 1902.

[5] Europarc España, www.redeuroparc.org/consultaespaciosprotegidos.jsp.

spaces) would be as follows: Ia (less than one per cent); Ib (one per cent); II (fifteen per cent); III (two per cent); IV (one per cent); V (seventy-six per cent) and VI (five per cent).[6]

This chapter deals with a series of significant matters regarding wilderness areas in Spain, such as the historical evolution of wilderness protection, its position in the existing political and legal framework; as well as the current hindrances those areas face owing to diverse reasons, notably relentless infrastructure development, the weaknesses of protective instruments, lack of management plans, or the ancillary position of nature protection *vis-à-vis* other public policies. It is important to note that unlike many other European States, Spain is a highly decentralized country, both generally as well as in the specific context of environmental law and management. The State is empowered to adopt basic laws that must be complied with throughout Spain. The seventeen regions (Autonomous Communities) are entitled to develop those rules, theoretically for the setting out of *their own* policies, and also to approve more protective measures.[7] This represents an additional difficulty to provide definite conclusions regarding the topic addressed by this contribution.

The chapter employs standard legal research methodology based on the analysis of Spanish law, as well as case studies, legal and biological literature and interviews with academics, officials and experts dealing with the abovementioned matters.[8]

## 2 Wilderness in Spain: historical account

The current legal framework and the intervention of the public authorities in the protection of wilderness cannot be understood without recourse to an historical account of nature conservation in Spain. Broadly speaking, nature protection had little relevance for the Spanish public authorities until the beginning of the twentieth century. Spain was essentially a rural country until the second half of that century, the main influx of population to cities taking place in the late 1950s. Wild animals were (and still are, at least formally) defined as *res nullius* in the Spanish Civil Code of 1889. Therefore, they could be freely hunted or possessed

[6] Europarc España, *2011 Yearbook*, www.redeuroparc.org/anuario_europarc_espana.jsp.

[7] Article 149.1.23; I. Lasagabaster, A. García-Ureta and I. Lazcano, *Derecho Ambiental. Parte General* (Bilbao: Lete, 2007), at 105–120.

[8] The author wishes to thank Europarc-España, in particular Marta Múgica, for their invaluable data, and also Iñigo Lazkano, José Manuel Marraco, Eduardo Salazar, Jaime Doreste and Mario García Paris for their comments and information.

subject to hunting regulations or those concerning fauna.[9] Active protection of nature was not needed in so far as it was not under threat or experiencing an acute unfavourable status. What is nowadays considered as 'nature' was conceived as an economic resource for humankind. Wild animals and plants and other resources, like watercourses, were a source of food and financial revenue for local communities and society at large. The exploitation of forests was sustainably managed by municipalities (a practice that remains) through the concept of communal forests. The land sheltering wild species was not subject to intense exploitation in comparison with current trends and technologies.

While nature was considered important for subsistence, areas that are nowadays specially protected, such as wetlands,[10] were conceived at the beginning of the twentieth century as little more than an indication of poverty, a source of infection (malaria)[11] and an obstacle for the development of extensive agricultural exploitations. Areas free from the impact of humankind were not inherently valued but were rather considered as wastelands that required cultivation to become fruitful. Therefore, under a 1918 Law (not formally repealed until Water Law 29/1985) many wetlands (continental and coastal) were intensively drained, providing new areas for extensive agriculture. Needless to say, there was also an undeclared interest in gaining property titles through wetland drainage.

In 1916 Spain adopted a Law on National Parks, albeit predicated mainly on protecting certain landscapes for their aesthetic features. They were conceived as nature sanctuaries similar to other historic or cultural monuments.[12] The 1916 Law was formally in force until 1957 when the 'Mountains Law' was adopted. Its title notwithstanding, this Law did not relate to the common notion of mountains (natural elevations of the earth surface rising more or less abruptly from the surrounding level),[13] but to any surface covered with vegetation, either trees or bushes, and carrying out environmental, landscape, productive, amenity or protective functions.[14] Consequently, this Act also had the main

[9] Articles 610 and 611, respectively.

[10] According to the Spanish inventory of wetlands, there are currently 267 sites.

[11] This was the case of Doñana.

[12] F. López Ramón, *Política ecológica y pluralismo territorial* (Madrid: Marcial Pons, 2009), at 35–36.

[13] *Oxford English Dictionary*.

[14] Article 5. The definition excludes fields devoted to agriculture, urban areas and any other territories so excepted by the laws of the Autonomous Communities.

purpose of protecting human interests that were provided by nature. In fact, the overriding position of forestry exploitation was explicit within the law. Accordingly, rules on national parks shared the same chapter on forestry regulations. In spite of certain provisions aimed at protecting forests and watercourses, the effects of the 1957 law were detrimental in environmental terms. Deforestation steadily (but stubbornly) continued to invade large portions of Spain, thereby heavily affecting the naturalness of areas and limiting the total amount of relatively wild areas. Local species of trees were replaced by fast-growing ones, like eucalyptus,[15] providing swift economic benefits at the expense of diversity and soil quality.

This state of affairs altered little with the creation of an authority in charge of nature conservation in 1971,[16] and the adoption of a new Law on nature conservation areas in 1975. Needless to say, these policies were very much centralized during the dictatorship. Nature protection was not perceived as a matter requiring a coherent policy. Accordingly, it was subordinated to other prevailing interests, e.g., the execution of public works. Indeed, the second half of the twentieth century saw the establishment of a large number of infrastructure projects, such as the building of roads, airports, urban developments, and dams designed to modernize Spain and move on from the stagnation that characterized the decades following the civil war. Among the different projects undertaken, those regarding water projects could be regarded as the most damaging in terms of environmental aggression. However, intense urbanization, water drainage and demanding agriculture also gravely affected areas subject to minor human intervention, notably Doñana, the Guadarrama mountain range near Madrid and Tablas de Daimiel National Park. Successive land laws have purportedly sought to protect rural lands (as opposed to urbanized ones) with different approaches. Law 6/1998 (which has since been repealed) set out one of its main aims as being to facilitate the offer of land, permitting land that had not at that time been incorporated into the urban process and was not subject to special preservation features, to be urbanized. The strict provisions of successive land laws have neither avoided continuous declassifications of rural lands nor halted a steady invasion of unspoilt natural areas. According to the Spanish Observatory for Sustainability, in the period from 1987 to 2005 more than double the land necessary for the corresponding increases in

[15] This species roughly covers 760,000 ha in Spain.
[16] Institute for the Conservation of Nature (ICONA).

population was classified as land of an urban nature. The average growth of the provincial capitals in this period was thirty-eight point one three per cent, six times their population growth in the same period.[17]

In spite of the laws of 1916 and 1975 previously mentioned, Spain's accession to the EU in 1986 could be regarded as the boundary dividing nineteenth century and present-day approaches, albeit with a differing impetus. First, a new law on nature conservation was not adopted until 1989,[18] three years after EU Membership. Even though it was believed that it implemented basic EU requirements, in fact it had partially incorporated certain matters that accordingly required subsequent amendments in successive years. An example was the absence of the notion and criteria for the designation of Special Protection Areas (SPAs) for wild birds under Directive 79/409 (as it was then),[19] a deficiency that was not completely remedied until 2003 in order to stave off the threat of infringement procedures by the EU institutions. However, the lack of consistency was apparent, since nature protection, i.e., the basic elements enshrined in the Wild Birds Directive, were again inserted within forestry matters in an additional clause to Mountains Law 43/2003. In broad terms, the period ranging from 1989 to 2003 was characterized by a lack of clear policy strategies – even though it also led to the progressive abandonment of town planning matters as a guiding instrument for the protection of nature – and the increasing importance of legislation directly addressing these concerns as required by the Habitats Directive.[20]

The Autonomous Communities conducted the designation of a significant number of sites, although the adoption of their management plans continued at a slow pace. In addition, the legal framework was incongruous. The Habitats Directive was essentially implemented by government regulations contradicting Law 4/1989 and allowing for the application of exceptions contrary to general prohibitions protecting wild species.[21] This latter trend may also be explained by the tendency of Spanish authorities to transpose EU law in literal terms without assessing the impact of European rules. The State legal framework was a leaking boat requiring continuous repairs in order to comply with EU law. This was not achieved until the adoption of Law 42/2007, on the natural patrimony and biodiversity, which provides a modern

[17] *Local Sustainability: An Urban and Rural Approach* (2008).

[18] Law 4/1989.

[19] Directive 147/2009.

[20] López Ramón, *Política ecológica y pluralismo territorial*, *supra* note 12, at 107–113.

[21] Royal Decree 1997/1995; this provision is still in force.

perspective on the protection of nature, requiring the adaptation to IUCN categories and creating a wide range of national lists to inventory the existing nature patrimony. However, it remains to be seen whether this law and its practical implementation may counter the relentless degradation of wilderness areas.

## 3 Political (Ir)relevance among the public authorities and the position of wilderness in general society

### *3.1 Wilderness in public policy*

Nature protection cannot be considered in isolation since it is part of a broader environmental policy.[22] Before accession to the EU in 1986 it could not realistically be asserted that Spain had framed a coherent policy (or even, more to the point, a policy as such). Nature conservation and enhancement has been mainly influenced by the EU. Long-term strategies and plans have been adopted in recent years to specifically address nature protection.[23] However, they are usually policy documents lacking binding effect and, on many occasions, illustrate the gap between well-oriented purposes and their practical implementation. In addition, it should be observed that nature protection concerns are diluted within administrative institutions that are already multi-faceted. Environmental departments, let alone those specifically dealing with wilderness protection, do not enjoy a strong or privileged position within the hierarchy of the public authorities, whether at the level of the central government or the Autonomous Communities (the two basic tiers of government dealing with this matter). A ministry for the environment was created in 1996 but it was latterly merged with agriculture, paving the way for the adoption of a similar approach in several Autonomous Communities. Therefore, as illustrated in the ensuing paragraphs, wilderness interests do not usually take priority over other matters in the political agenda, such as industry, housing, transport or energy, a trend that is not only restricted to periods of economic downturn.

[22] See A. García-Ureta and I. Lasagabaster Herrarte, 'Environmental Governance in Spain', in F. Palermo and M. Alberton, *Environmental Protection in Multi-Layered Systems. Comparative Lessons from the Water Sector* (Leiden: Martinus Nijhoff, 2012), 113–133.

[23] Spanish strategy for the conservation and sustainable use of biodiversity (1998) and Royal Decree 1274/2011, adopting the Strategic Plan for the natural patrimony and biodiversity 2011–2017. The Autonomous Communities have also adopted similar strategies.

Arguably, wilderness protection is one of those fields in which the gap between political slogans and results is wider. Whilst it is easier to publicise the designation of new protected areas, such as national parks or, in particular, biosphere reserves, with the accompanying national and international media impact, it is far more difficult to curtail the progressive fragmentation of areas of species distribution as well as preserving largely untouched portions of territory from human intervention, e.g., tourism. It is doubtful whether political institutions, which are theoretically designed to supersede the limited lifespan of humans, guarantee the long-term protection of wilderness. The most damaging activities to unspoilt areas have taken place during the last fifteen years of economic expansion. According to estimates by the EU Corine programme, the increase in artificial areas in Spain accelerated from 13,112 ha/year in the period 1987–2000 to 29,500 ha/year between 2000 and 2006.[24] Some eighteen per cent of the new artificial areas created between 1987 and 2000, and fourteen point nine per cent of those created between 2000 and 2006 were established at the expense of agricultural mosaics and natural vegetation.[25] Between 1987 and 2006, the surface covered by artificial areas increased by thirty-three point nine per cent within protected areas, by sixty-seven per cent within the Natura 2000 network, and by fifty-two point one per cent in unprotected areas. By contrast, the economic downturn initiated in 2008 has led to the progressive abandonment of projects, notably harbours,[26] and the rearrangement of others which initially envisaged the transformation of large parcels of land. The increase of artificial infrastructures, such as dams, windmills and roads, some of which have been supported by EU funds, has represented a burden on wilderness areas, although the Natura 2000 regime may – depending on the specific situation – constitute a barrier for such projects, for instance the extraction and storage of natural gas in Doñana national park, an extensive development comprising fourteen wells and 20 km of pipelines (see also Chapter 8).

[24] Spanish Observatory for Sustainability, *Biodiversity in Spain. The Basis for Sustainability in the Face of Global Change* (Madrid: Universidad de Alcalá, 2012), at 25. The term 'artificial uses' is not defined in the document, but relates to 'urban spaces and other artificial uses' (p. 27). The Observatory was closed in 2013 due to a lack of public funding to sustain its activities.

[25] *Ibid.*, at 25.

[26] For instance, the extension of Pasaia harbour in the Basque Country, a 765 million euro project that had already been challenged by the French authorities due to its likely impact on a Natura 2000 site.

### 3.2 *Wilderness in Spanish society*

The relevance of wilderness to Spanish society presents different facets. To begin with, a significant part of the population lives in urban areas (roughly forty per cent reside in coastal municipalities). The natural environment comprises ninety per cent of Spain's territory and contains eighty per cent of its municipalities, but contains only about thirty-five per cent of the population.[27] A constant migratory flux from small villages to cities in recent decades has not only depopulated the countryside, but has also served to detach citizens from the natural world. A majority of the population believes that wilderness is a value deserving of greater protection. Visitor numbers to national parks and other designated sites have increased in recent years, a trend that is encouraged by the Spanish government.[28] However, according to a survey carried out by the Spanish Society for the Protection of Birds (SEO) in 2011 eighty-five per cent of the population was unaware of the meaning of Natura 2000 and fifty-one per cent failed even to link it to the environment. Generally, as was also noted in the chapter on wilderness protection in Poland, the environment is not perceived as a cause for concern. Indeed, on the contrary, it occupies one of the lowest positions in opinion polls.[29] Arguably, only NGOs can be regarded as the bulwark pressing for better and improved nature protection. However, they lack a large number of affiliates to sustain their activities.[30] Unlike other EU Member States, green political parties obtained less than 0.5 per cent of the votes in the general elections held in 2011.

Overall, this appears to reflect a more generalized contradiction between (a) what the population would defend as citizens, i.e., a high regard for wilderness areas or for wild species, and (b) what they desire as individuals or consumers, for instance, the use of transportation infrastructures (airports or roads) that may serve to fragment or conflict with habitats and migratory routes of species (e.g., bears in Northern Spain or the *Iberian lynx* in Doñana national park); fresh water supplies, which

[27] Spanish Observatory for Sustainability, *Biodiversity in Spain. The basis for sustainability in the face of global change, supra* note 24, at 30.

[28] According to the Ministry for Agriculture, Food and the Environment, 14,307,591 people visited fourteen National Parks in 2014; approximately 11,500,000 million visited 149 parks during 2012. In 2014 the Spanish government adopted a Plan on nature and biodiversity tourism 2014–2020.

[29] See the July 2014 barometer of the Centre for Sociological Surveys (CIS); http://www.cis.es/cis/export/sites/default/-Archivos/Marginales/3100_3119/3104/es3104mar.pdf.

[30] Greenpeace Spain has approximately 100,000 affiliates; Ecologistas en Acción has a similar number; the Spanish Society for the Protection of Birds (SEO) 12,000 affiliates.

would require the construction of dams that would flood the habitats of highly protected species (*Iberian lynx* or eagles) and areas already protected under Natura 2000;[31] or the right to enjoy a private dwelling occupying further portions of valuable territory.[32]

## 4 Wilderness in a legal context

### *4.1 A constitutional notion*

From a strict legal viewpoint, a legal notion of 'wilderness' has only recently been elaborated in Spanish law. The Spanish Constitution of 1978 neither refers to biodiversity nor to wilderness. It employs the term 'environment' and indicates, inter alia, that the public authorities shall safeguard the rational use of all natural resources with a view to protecting and improving the quality of life and preserving and restoring the environment, by relying on essential collective solidarity.[33] Natural resources is a very broad notion encompassing, inter alia, continental and maritime waters, coasts, air, soil, fauna and flora, forestry, as well as other, less tangible, matters, such as the landscape.

The laws setting out the powers of the Autonomous Communities (*Estatutos*) contain references to the environment, protected areas, hunting, fishing and ecology in general. A more specific regulation was enshrined in Law 4/1989, on the conservation of natural spaces and wild fauna and flora.[34] The preamble to the Law indicated that nature is the context in which the essential ecological processes and the basic vital systems take place, but also constitutes the set of resources that is indispensable for nature itself. Assessing the compatibility of the Law 4/1989 with the allocation of powers between the State and the Autonomous Communities, the Constitutional Court held in its ruling 102/1995 that the environment cannot be conceived as a mere sum or juxtaposition of natural resources and its physical base. Rather, it is a complex framework of relations between each of these elements that, by themselves, have an independent and previous existence, yet their interconnection gives them a significant meaning. In other words, the environment is a structural concept whose governing

31 See the case of La Brena dam in Southern Spain; ec.europa.eu/environment/nature/natura2000/management/docs/art6/labrena_en.pdf.

32 See M. Sagoff, *The Economy of the Earth* (Cambridge: Cambridge University Press, 2008), at 59–62.

33 Article 45(2).

34 This Law was repealed by the aforementioned Law 42/2007.

idea is the balance of all its factors, static and dynamic, in space and time.[35] In a similar sense, the Criminal Code punishes a series of activities affecting 'the balance of the natural systems',[36] thus reflecting the importance of at least one wilderness quality, i.e., that of relatively intact natural processes.

### 4.2 *The role of current Spanish biodiversity legislation*

Spanish Law 42/2007 on the natural patrimony and biodiversity reflects the rationale underlying international and EU legal instruments regarding nature protection. First, it defines the natural patrimony as a set of goods and natural resources establishing the basis of biological and geologic diversity and encompassing relevant environmental, landscaping, scientific or cultural values. According to the Law, the natural patrimony and biodiversity carry out a relevant social function owing to their close relationship with development, health and well-being of people, as well as their contribution to social and economic development. In its ruling 69/2013 concerning the reach of Law 42/2007 and of the aforementioned notions, the Constitutional Court has acknowledged that it reflects the evolution regarding the public interest of the natural patrimony and biodiversity and regardless of legal titles (public or private) and even of their definition as *res nullius*. Hence, species, habitats and areas with high wilderness qualities cannot be conceived as freely available resources.[37] In this sense, the Supreme Court has held in a case concerning bear hunting that the animal was a legal good relevant for society as a whole due to its ecological value.[38]

Even though wilderness is a public interest, there is not an overriding presumption placing it over other competing interests. Therefore, when conflicts arise it is for the public authorities to balance the different interests that may be at stake, e.g., energy supply *versus* species and habitat protection. The scales usually tilt in favour of nature conservation areas provided that they have already been designated.[39] It is considerably more difficult to guarantee the preservation of areas that have not achieved such a status.[40] Whilst highly valuable areas are sheltered from

[35] Constitutional Court Judgment (CCJ) 102/1995, at para. 6.
[36] Article 325.
[37] The two references to an open-ended notion of 'development' in Law 42/2007 cannot contradict the aforementioned conclusion.
[38] Supreme Court Judgment (SCJ) (Criminal Law chamber) of 1 April 1993, appeal 594/1990.
[39] SCJ (Administrative Law Chamber) of 14 July 2014, appeal 3636/2011.
[40] SCJ (Administrative Law Chamber) of 13 October 2003, appeal 8065/2000.

direct intervention, it is rather more problematic to assess whether external interferences may really leave them untouched, notwithstanding the application of Article 6(2) of the Habitats Directive. Consequently, the areas are usually surrounded by a variety of activities likely to cause harm to their integrity, e.g., coastal tourism, agriculture, mining operations and energy infrastructures.

This situation is well illustrated by the collapse of a retaining wall of a tailings lagoon in Aznalcóllar mine near Doñana national park in 1998. The wall was used to store pyrite tailings from the mine works. As a result, the rivers were flooded with more than two billion litres of tailings with a high metal content that affected the border areas of the park. A series of walls constructed by the Spanish authorities were finally able to keep almost all of the spilled materials from entering the park. However, there may be *prima facie* less apparent activities that also affect the dynamics of protected areas, e.g., illegal agricultural activities and water abstractions or the construction of residential areas with accompanying services. On many occasions nature conservation interests have to be balanced against nebulous criteria (notably sustainable development) alongside legal support for economic intervention, e.g., energy supply.[41] In addition, Law 42/2007 does not segregate wilderness areas or species from human intervention. Arguably, the Achilles heel of the system remains, since it is for nature management plans, which are to be adopted on a case-by-case basis,[42] to specify zones that should remain intact within a protected area owing to their characteristics.[43]

### *4.3 Criteria for the classification of protected areas in Spanish law: nature protection areas, Natura 2000 sites and international law sites*

According to the Constitutional Court, the establishment of a protected area requires three factors: (a) the presence of certain geological, zoological, botanic, environmental and human features; (b) an official designation; and (c) a teleological factor, i.e., the protection of its characteristics.[44] Under Spanish law there are essentially three categories of areas:

[41] SCJ (Administrative Law Chamber) of 30 April 2008, appeal 3516/2005.

[42] Sixty-six per cent of national parks and eighty-four per cent of parks, respectively, have a management plan.

[43] The significance of natural resource management plans was highlighted by the ECJ in a 1993 landmark case against Spain (*Santoña Marshes*); Case C-355/90, *Commission* v. *Spain*.

[44] CCJ 234/2012; CCJ 102/1995.

(1) protected areas (parks, nature reserves, monuments, protected landscapes and marine areas);
(2) areas of EU origin (Special Protection Areas for birds (SPA) and Special Areas of Conservation (SAC)); and
(3) areas established pursuant to international commitments (Ramsar wetlands, sites under the Convention Concerning the Protection of the World Cultural and Natural Heritage; the Convention for the Protection of the Marine Environment of the North-East Atlantic; and the Convention for the Protection of the Marine Environment and the Coastal Region of the Mediterranean; UNESCO geoparks; biosphere reserves; and Council of Europe's biogenetic reserves).

The reasons behind this distinction are not elaborated in the Law. In the case of protected areas and areas of EU origin, the Constitutional Court has highlighted the different rules and designation procedures to which they are subject.[45] In addition, an area may embrace different categories (e.g., Doñana is a national park, a biosphere reserve, SPA, SAC, Ramsar wetland and a World Natural Heritage site). National Parks have their own legal regime laid out in Law 30/2014 on National Parks.

The first group (protected areas) does not substantially depart from the categories previously included in the former Law 4/1989, that is to say, parks, nature reserves, monuments and protected landscapes. The novelty is the category of 'marine areas' absent in the 1989 Law. These sites are to be respected by the Autonomous Communities, although these communities may create other additional categories of protected areas. As a result, there is a surfeit of protective labels (over forty) raising the question of whether they really highlight outstanding natural values or whether they have been employed so as to differentiate a particular Autonomous Community from its neighbours. In other cases certain categories have arguably blurred those of EU origin by including SPAs and SACs within a general (regional) category.[46] This approach is disputable in strict legal terms because Spain lacks the power to alter the title and meaning of SPAs and SACs, this competence having been attributed to the EU. Be that as it may, the criteria for the classification of protected

[45] CCJ 234/2012.

[46] This is the case of Law 9/2001, on the conservation of nature of the Autonomous Community of Galicia. This Law creates a so-called Special Protection Zone of Natural Values (*Zona de especial protección de los valores naturales*) that includes, inter alia, SPAs and SACs.

Table 1 *Categories of protected areas (not based on EU or international law)*

| Type | Criteria for classification | Values to protect |
|---|---|---|
| Parks | Landscape, representativeness of ecosystems, fauna, flora and geomorphology | Ecological, aesthetic, educational scientific |
| Nature reserves | Ecosystems, biology | Rarity, frailty, importance |
| Monuments | Geomorphological features | Singularity, rarity, beauty |
| Protected landscapes | Particular location of landscapes | Aesthetic, cultural |

areas and the values that such a classification is to represent remain unaltered since 1989. The values are set out in Table 1.

Some of the above-mentioned criteria address the need to protect areas with high wilderness qualities. It is for this reason that a majority of IUCN category Ia sites in Spain are classified under Spanish law as 'nature reserves' or 'integral nature reserves'. This category is defined by the legislation of some Autonomous Communities as a space of moderate dimension that, owing to its fragility and scientific importance, must be preserved in an integral way with all its biotic and abiotic elements and natural ecological processes, while human occupation is considered incompatible with that objective.[47]

This description connects well with the wilderness concept, although the quality of relatively large size is not explicitly addressed. Neither Law 42/2007 nor the laws of the Autonomous Communities include express references to minimum territorial dimensions in the case of candidate sites. In contrast, Law 30/2014 on National Parks explicitly establishes such requirements for terrestrial or maritime-terrestrial national parks situated in mainland Spain or in Spanish maritime waters (≥ 20,000 ha), and for terrestrial or maritime-terrestrial national parks situated on islands (≥ 5,000 ha). National parks must span a continuous and non-fragmented area that is sufficiently large to permit their natural evolution, without or

[47] Article 14(2)(a) of Law 5/2005, on the conservation of areas of environmental relevance, of the Autonomous Community of the Balearic Islands. In similar terms, Article 24 of Law 12/1985 on nature protected areas of the Autonomous Community of Catalonia.

with minimal human intervention, to maintain their physical and biological characteristics, and to ensure the functioning of natural processes. National parks must therefore be characterized by territorial continuity, understood as the absence of fragmentation of their areas, save in properly justified exceptions. Agriculture, forestry, hydraulic or mining exploitations, or construction projects that may significantly alter the aesthetics of the scenery or the functioning of the ecosystems are in principle not envisaged in respect of these areas.[48] Likewise, a national park is not to encompass land capable of town-planning transformation or urbanized land. Whilst this latter criterion follows the rationale of the above-mentioned standards, it may reduce the size of candidate sites as illustrated by Guadarrama national park (designated in 2013), where intense urban sprawl had taken place in the last decades, thus limiting the available territory meeting the foregoing criteria.[49]

Even though Law 42/2007 requires the public authorities to adapt the existing Spanish categories of protected areas to the classifications adopted by IUCN,[50] it has not replaced the criteria for these categories by those of this international organization. This has resulted in an inconsistent approach: on the one hand any Spanish category must be accompanied by the corresponding IUCN classification but, on the other hand, the IUCN criteria are not expressly enshrined as binding standards for future classifications. Therefore, the position of IUCN criteria *vis-à-vis* Spanish law is feeble. In fact, as indicated above, in 2014 only forty-three per cent of sites designated according to Spanish law had been adapted to the IUCN labels. Labels for categories Ia and Ib are not frequently used and sites deserving this classification often form part of larger Spanish categories, e.g., a national park or a nature reserve, although the area complying with IUCN criteria may only cover a relatively small proportion of their whole area. Cartographical data is not usually available, thus adding further difficulties in determining the extent of those particular areas with relatively high wilderness qualities. These assertions may be exemplified in the case of national parks.[51]

[48] Law 30/2014, Article 6(1).

[49] E. Saez Pombo and G. Madrazo García de Lomana, 'La Sierra de Guadarrama. Una Montaña transformada por el ser humano', *Revista Ambienta* 103 (2013) 68–89.

[50] Article 51(2) reads as follows: 'the natural spaces inscribed in the Spanish Inventory of Protected Natural Spaces will be assigned, together with its original denomination, to the categories established internationally, especially by the International Union for the Conservation of Nature (IUCN)' (translation by the author).

[51] Source: Europarc-España.

Table 2 *Size of National Parks and of strictly protected areas within National Parks*

| National park | Surface (ha) | Strictly protected area (ha) | % |
|---|---|---|---|
| Archipiélago de la Cabrera | 10,021.00 | 820.57 | 8.19 |
| Aigüestortes i Estany de Sant Maurici | 14,119.00 | 317.63 | 2.25 |
| Cabañeros | 40,828.60 | | |
| Caldera De Taburiente | 4,397.89 | 21.61 | 0.49 |
| Tablas De Daimiel | 1,928.00 | | |
| Doñana | 54,252.00 | 11,029.43 | 20.33 |
| Garajonay | 3,984.00 | 2,035.00 | 51.08 |
| Islas Atlánticas de Galicia | 8,480.00 | 545.85 | 6.44 |
| Monfragüe | 18,396.00 | 10,171.48 | 55.29 |
| Ordesa y Monte Perdido | 15,608.00 | 770.00 | 4.93 |
| Picos de Europa | 64,660.00 | | |
| Sierra Nevada | 85,883.00 | 303.00 | 0.35 |
| Teide | 18,990.00 | 1,265.00 | 6.66 |
| Timanfaya | 5,107.00 | 4,938.92 | 96.71 |
| Guadarrama | 33,960.00 | 7.011 | 20.64 |

Table 2 summarizes their surface and the proportion of strictly protected areas.

Second, even though Law 42/2007 employs terms such as singularity or frailty, it does not set out a classification depending on the degree of preservation required, whereas the exploitation of resources 'shall be limited' in nature reserves it 'may be limited' in parks. As indicated above, it is essentially left to nature management plans to define zones within a protected area, e.g., strict protection or zones subject to certain types of exploitation. The reference to IUCN categories (and designation criteria) should guide the competent authorities in this particular respect but Law 42/2007 does not contain a precise mandate to this end. Therefore, a protected area may host zones free from human intervention alongside other areas subject to diverse uses, such as agriculture, forestry, as well as different forms of infrastructure (mainly roads).

Another problem with the triple classification of areas set out in Law 42/2007 is the unequal application of certain mechanisms designed to protect the integrity of the sites. Protected areas (the first group mentioned above) enjoy a series of instruments not applicable to the other areas, unless the Autonomous Communities so decide. This is the case for, inter alia, the establishment of buffer zones designed to avoid external impacts, the declaration of public interest justifying compulsory purchases of property rights, and prohibiting the transformation of the physical or biological features of a site.

The criteria for the designation of Natura 2000 sites are laid down in the relevant EU directives and ECJ case law. The Spanish authorities have mainly relied on existing national categories to comply with the mandate of the Habitats Directive, including the adoption of conservation measures.

The third group (i.e., areas of international origin) relates to areas designated under conventions ratified by Spain,[52] and international instruments that lack legal binding effect, such as the Statutory Framework regarding biosphere reserves, adopted in 1995. International areas could also encompass so-called transboundary protected areas.[53]

Based on the above discussions, it may be concluded that the Spanish categories of protected areas are useful to provide protection for wilderness, or at least for certain qualities of this concept. However, they do not guarantee *per se* that some basic features, e.g., sufficient size and, in particular, lack of human intervention, will be respected.

### *4.4 Connectivity of sites and wilderness protection*

The duty to connect sites challenges traditional views of protected areas as nature sanctuaries confined within discrete boundaries. This matter is mentioned twice in Law 42/2007 requiring the Autonomous Communities to envisage mechanisms to connect, in particular, Natura 2000 sites and other sites relevant for biodiversity.[54] In Spain there are still ample locations with a low degree of fragmentation, such as mountain areas: the Picos de Europa national park and the Pyrenees mountain

[52] For instance, the Cooperation Agreement between Spain and Portugal concerning the creation of Tajo International Park (9 May 2012).

[53] Law 42/2007, Article 41. As regards management difficulties in the case of these areas see A. García Ureta, I. Lasagabaster Herrarte and I. Lazcano Brotóns, 'The Pyrenees: Missing a Convention?' in P. Quillacq and M. Onida, *Environmental Protection and Mountains. Is Environmental Law Adapted to the Challenges Faced by Mountain Areas?* (Innsbruck: Permanent Secretariat of the Alpine Convention, 2011), 128–145; www.alpconv.org/en/publications/alpine/Documents/legal_publication.pdf.

[54] Article 21.

range extending for approximately 450 km from the Bay of Biscay to the Mediterranean Sea. Corridors are probably best represented by livestock trails (*cañadas*), which cover more than 450,000 ha (one per cent of Spain's territory). They are essentially used by farmers as routes for sending livestock to markets or to pastures and they enjoy the *prima facie* reinforced status of a public domain.[55] However, they are very much affected by other infrastructures and uses since they are regularly narrow stretches of land. For instance, livestock trails cannot exceed 75 metres in width.

Connecting corridors have to proceed through a series of obstacles.[56] For instance, existing infrastructures may constrain (or affect) the number of corridors as well as their spatial reach. Furthermore, there is a tendency to identify corridors with purposes other than wilderness protection, such as recreational purposes which are used in respect of the so-called green ways (the result of the abandonment of railway tracks). Extra challenges are faced in establishing connectivity for species with large distribution areas, such as Cantabrian bears (approximately 5,000 $km^2$).[57] Although examples of restoring connectivity exist, for instance in the case of the Guadiamar Green Corridor in Doñana national park after a mineral waste spill in 1998, these difficulties make it doubtful as to whether the notion of connectivity may be able to reinstate large areas with relatively high wilderness qualities.

## 5 Practical implementation: conflicting matters

### *5.1 Wilderness and the weaknesses of environmental impact assessment*

As indicated above, the continuous human occupation of the land causes relentless damage to wilderness values. Dams, linear infrastructures, energy installations, mining operations and housing developments may be regarded as the most damaging in terms of loss of wilderness.[58] Environmental impact assessment (EIA) provides certain safeguards

[55] Livestock Trail Law 3/1995.

[56] M. Gurrutxaga San Vicente, 'La gestión de la conectividad ecológica del territorio en España: Iniciativas y retos', *Boletín de la Asociación de Geógrafos Españoles* 225 (2011), 225–244.

[57] See www.fundacionosopardo.org/wp-content/uploads/2013/02/Layman-Report1.pdf.

[58] See the case of the *Iberian lynx*; A. García Ureta, 'Do All Roads Lead to Doñana? Legal Protection of Proposed Sites of Community Importance under the Habitats Directive Case C-308/08', *Commission* v. *Spain*, Judgment of the ECJ (Fourth Chamber) 20 May 2010, *Environmental Liability* 2 (2010), 67–74.

regarding the analysis of the foreseeable effects of such projects; however, EIA is essentially a procedural requisite. It does not *per se* impede the execution of a plan or project embracing substantial harmful effects. This certainly applies to impacts on wilderness. Moreover, there is a current perception that procedural guarantees represent a heavy administrative burden on development projects. Furthermore, a public authority (e.g., an Autonomous Community or ministry) may be entitled to authorize a project while it also carries out the corresponding EIA.[59] This state of affairs does not sufficiently detach the assessment from the subject-matter of the project. It is for this reason that in practice a significant proportion of assessments endorse a conclusion that a particular project or plan may be executed.

It is also important to note that studies usually predetermine the scope and consequently the reach of foreseeable impacts, the environmental features to be assessed and, ultimately, the completeness of the study. In addition, the public authorities do not always have the capacity to assess the environmental studies submitted by private actors. In these cases consultants may be employed to perform such analyses, calling into question the impartiality of the procedure.[60] However, under the new environmental assessment Law 21/2013 the department in charge of the assessment is now empowered to terminate the procedure if it considers that the relevant environmental information is either incomplete or insufficient. It remains to be seen whether and how this provision will be applied in practice.

### 5.2 *Wilderness, infrastructures and courts*

In terms of the legal debate, much attention has been focused on who has oversight powers over the environment. As a result, the Constitutional Court has been called upon to judge many cases concerning the allocation of competences concerning the environment[61] and conservation areas.[62] For instance, the Autonomous Communities cannot adopt a management plan affecting military installations, even if such installations are located within Natura 2000 sites.[63] This may affect the

[59] CCJ 13/1998.

[60] In a similar fashion, the preparatory steps for the designation of SACs have also been subcontracted.

[61] For instance CCJ 111/2013 (environmental assessments in Natura 2000 areas).

[62] CCJ 102/1995; CCJ 87/2013.

[63] CCJ 82/2012 (Bardenas natural park).

effectiveness of such plans with regard to aspects such as wilderness protection.

However, there have also been more substantial judicial battles to stop infrastructure projects affecting wilderness areas and there are examples of well-organized successful interventions.[64] This was the case in respect of Fuentes Carrionas natural park (Autonomous Community of Castilla-León) and the proposed establishment of a ski resort by modifying the rules of the park's management plan to ban this type of development. This prospective project mobilized the local community and academics to protest in order to halt the development. The courts held, inter alia, that economic interests could not override clear-cut rules prohibiting such projects.[65] There were no data, analyses, reports or technical or scientific studies showing (a) a change in the environmental and socio-economic circumstances since the management plan was developed, and (b) assessing the impact of the development on the protection, conservation, improvement and rational use of the space.

The courts also held that the amendment to the management plan had changed its original objectives, namely the protection, conservation and improvement of the area. The overriding objective was to preserve wilderness values, biodiversity and ecosystems. Even though the promotion of socio-economic development of the local community was regarded as a general objective in the management plan, it could not take priority over the former (main) objective.

Similarly, the widening or upgrading of the M-501 road in the Madrid region was quashed by Spanish courts due to an incomplete assessment of its effects on Natura 2000 sites, a conclusion also based on a previous ECJ judgment.[66] Other cases have concerned attempts to exclude certain areas from the network of protected sites by resorting to arbitrary mechanisms. The Constitutional Court quashed a law adopted by the Autonomous Community of Murcia adjusting the dimensions of the regional categories of protected sites to those of sites of Community importance (which were much smaller). As a result, more than

[64] The Spanish Supreme Court quashed the amendment to the management plan; SCJ (Administrative Law Chamber) of 25 January 2012 (appeal 1169/2008).

[65] Judgment of the High Court of Castilla-León (Administrative Law Chamber) of 8 January 2008, appeal 858/2006; SCJ (Administrative Law Chamber) of 25 January 2012, appeal 1169/2008.

[66] Case C-560/08, *Commission* v. *Spain*; SCJ (Administrative Law Chamber) of 24 May 2012, appeal 4853/2009; SCJ (Administrative Law Chamber) of 14 February 2011, appeal 1511/2008.

11,000 ha of the regional network of protected sites were left unprotected, paving the way, inter alia, for the development of a valued coastal area (Marina de Cope). The development plan for the project (consisting of hotels, commercial areas, dwellings, several golf courses and a pier) was subsequently quashed by the regional High Court.[67]

However, a different outcome occurred in the case of a jail built in the Basque Country, occupying a surface of approximately 40 ha for a population of more than 720 inmates plus personnel. The project was located near a Site of Community Importance listed by the European Commission and containing priority habitats and species, such as the region's only population of European mink. Interestingly, this species was the object of an EU LIFE project (which had also been funded by the Spanish Government) to guarantee its survival.[68] Despite the apparent lack of a proper environment assessment, the Supreme Court concluded that a report roughly devoting four pages to the situation of the site and the foreseeable effects of the project was sufficient for the purposes of the appropriate environmental assessment as required by the Habitats Directive.[69] That is not the first time that the Spanish Supreme Court has sidestepped the Habitats Directive, and based on this case law it may be concluded that the judiciary sometimes conducts a marginal assessment of the projects without examining in detail the data and information before them. This position contradicts the case law of the ECJ that has expressly clarified that environmental statements must be as complete as possible and be based on the best scientific knowledge.[70]

On many occasions, the length of judicial procedures and the difficulties in obtaining interim measures favour the approval of projects, although such authorization may be quashed at a later stage (normally once the projects or their primary phases have been finalized). This has often proved the case for Natura 2000 sites. For instance, in 2011 the regional High Court quashed a plan permitting the development of a residential resort in the Autonomous Community of Extremadura, but it was not until 2014 that the Supreme Court definitively confirmed that

[67] Judgment of the High Court of Murcia (Administrative Law Chamber) of 31 May 2013, appeal 983/2004.

[68] LIFE 00NAT/E/7335. The total amount of the Project was 38,302,600 euros. The Commission granted fifty per cent (19,151,300 euros). The Spanish Government granted 9,575,630 euros. However, the Commission did not contest the project, paying lip service to its supervisory duty under TFEU.

[69] A. García Ureta, 'Habitats Directive and Jails: Why the Spanish Supreme Court Has Got It Wrong', *Environmental Liability* 3 (2011), 53–62.

[70] Case C-304/05, *Commission* v. *Italy*, at paras 61–69.

judgment.[71] By that time the first section of the project, comprising, inter alia, 180 dwellings (out of 550), a golf course and a hotel had already been erected. In addition, the regional government argued that it could not comply with the ruling because the demolition would cause far greater damage than the initial construction. In contrast, the courts have halted projects affecting the habitats of emblematic species (such as imperial eagle or brown bears), for instance quashing plans to build a ski resort or more than 1,000 houses and a golf course in a Natura 2000 site; however, this position is not widespread. In the previously mentioned case concerning the construction of a jail, the Supreme Court rejected an application for interim measures because suspension of the project would have resolved the subject-matter of the case (i.e., whether an assessment was compulsory), a conclusion that was not permitted at that stage of the process under the court's procedural rules.[72] Nevertheless, this outcome is arguably inconsistent with the Habitats Directive.

Another matter concerns the validation by law of projects that have already been declared incompatible with nature protection legislation by the courts. This evident violation of the separation of powers has been used as a means of avoiding legal challenges, since laws can only be appealed before the Constitutional Court yet citizens lack standing in such cases. One of the landmark examples was the construction of Itoiz dam in the Autonomous Community of Navarre. After a lengthy judicial process the Supreme Court quashed the project by ruling that the dam could not reach the maximum storage level planned as this would cause unacceptable effects upon three existing nature reserves. As a result, the storage level had to be reduced from 418 $hm^3$ to only 9.7 $hm^3$, which called the feasibility of the project into question.[73] However, the regional government modified the applicable nature conservation law by reducing the span of the nature reserves. Both the Spanish Constitutional Court and the ECHR accepted this outcome.[74] This standpoint paved the way for the adoption as recently as 2010 of over five laws to, inter alia, declassify protected habitats to facilitate the construction of a harbour, modify a nature protected site to allow the construction of a ski resort that had been previously prohibited, permit the establishment of a leisure resort, and to legalize an important number of constructions affecting the maritime domain. However, this trend has been dramatically reversed

[71] SCJ (Administrative Law Chamber) of 29 January 2014, appeal 2419/2011.

[72] Law 29/1998 on the jurisdiction of administrative law courts.

[73] SCJ of 14 July 1997, appeal 208/1996.

[74] CCJ 73/200; *Gorraiz Lizarraga* v. *Spain*, judgment of the ECHR of 27 April 2004.

following the ruling of the ECJ in the *Boxus* case, delivered in the light of the Aarhus Convention and finally by the Constitutional Court in its ruling 129/2013.

### 5.3 *Wilderness, property rights and the myth of the public domain*

Property rights are not absolute. Rather, they must be taken into account in relation to their role in society.[75] Even though the designation of a protected site in Spain does not *per se* alter property rights, e.g., by transforming them into the public domain, the authorities can impose restrictions on ownership rights provided they pursue objectives of general interest and do not constitute a disproportionate and intolerable intervention affecting the very essence of the rights so guaranteed.[76]

The deprivation of property rights requires compensation, as stated in Article 33(3) of the Spanish Constitution. However, the exercise of property rights may be regulated and restricted without compensation. As a result, different types of activities (e.g., agriculture or forestry exploitation) may be subject to limitations, for instance in relation to the methods employed, in order to protect habitats and species. These requirements would not automatically give rise to a need to pay compensation, provided the core element of the property rights in question is maintained. According to the Constitutional Court, the dividing line between the notion of deprivation and of regulation in cases concerning the designation of protected areas is usually the preservation of pre-existing traditional activities. If the rules on designation ban any of those activities, then compensation must be granted to holders of such rights.[77] The case law has already contemplated a number of situations in which the applicable management rules have prohibited the exercise of hunting rights or the exploitation of certain types of resources, such as wood, thus giving rise to a requirement to compensate.[78] Likewise, restrictions imposed to facilitate the recovery of a species are regarded

[75] Article 128(1) of the Spanish Constitution reads: 'All the Wealth of the Country in Its Distinct Forms Regardless of Its Ownership Is Subordinated to the General Interest.'

[76] Neither the Wild Birds Directive nor the Habitats Directive prohibits the carrying out of activities in protected areas but public authorities are not precluded from doing so. Case C-2/10, *Azienda Agro-Zootecnica Franchini Sarl, Eolica di Altamura Srl* v. *Regione Puglia.*

[77] CCJ 170/1989.

[78] SCJ (Administrative Law Chamber) of 20 September 2012, appeal 7089/2010.

as deprivation (e.g., prohibition of use of machinery).[79] However, the case law consistently requires owners to ascertain that (i) the uses did in fact previously exist,[80] and (ii) were undertaken in practice before the restrictions were imposed.[81] Mere expectations cannot be upheld, such as an alleged reduction in the value of an estate owing to the impossibility to exploit plots as irrigated lands.[82]

Public authorities may designate certain natural resources as falling within the public domain, a legal category that precludes the exercise of private property rights. Those goods remain inalienable and non-attributable and cannot be subject to attachment or encumbrance. The Spanish Constitution expressly includes into the public domain the off-shore zone, the beaches, the territorial sea and the natural resources of the economic zone and the continental shelf.[83] Other resources, such as continental water, or the livestock trails mentioned above, enjoy the same status. Protected natural areas under Law 42/2007 are not regarded as lying within the public domain, even though they frequently contain portions of land that are subject to this legal category and contribute to the connectivity of sites (e.g., watercourses).

However, there is an ongoing debate as to whether the public domain is truly capable of protecting wilderness, bearing in mind the example of Spanish coasts, especially after the approval of Coasts Law 29/1998. This piece of legislation was designed to end the constant degradation of the coastline and relied heavily on the might of the public domain doctrine.[84] The Law broadened the scope of the maritime-terrestrial public domain

[79] SCJ (Administrative Law Chamber) of 20 September 2012, appeal 7089/2010; SCJ (Administrative Law Chamber) of 24 June 2009, appeal 1182/2005; SCJ (Administrative Law Chamber) of 21 October 2003, appeal 10867/1998; SCJ (Administrative Law Chamber) of 30 April 2009, appeal 1949/2005.

[80] Judgment of Audiencia Nacional (Administrative Law Chamber) of 14 September 2001, appeal 54/2001 (alleged ecotourism activities in Doñana national Park); Judgment of the High Court of Catalonia (Administrative Law Chamber) of 9 March 2011, appeal 217/2010 (alleged use of intensive agriculture with plastics or irrigation).

[81] SCJ (Administrative Law Chamber) of 24 May 2013, appeal 2134/2010; Judgment of the High Court of the Autonomous Community of Castilla-La Mancha (Administrative Law Chamber) of 20 May 2002, appeal 279/2002; Judgment of the High Court of the Autonomous Community of Valencia (Administrative Law Chamber) of 13 January 2005, appeal 1138/2003.

[82] Judgment of the High Court of Castilla-La Mancha (Administrative Law Chamber) of 26 July 2010, appeal 400/2007.

[83] Article 132 of the Spanish Constitution.

[84] I. Lazkano Brotóns, and A. García Ureta, 'The 2013 Reform of Spanish Coastal Legislation: A Further Step towards Diminishing Environmental Protection', *Environmental Liability* 6 (2014), 1–10.

(MTPD) by amending the traditional notions of foreshore and beaches. This amendment aimed to preserve the integrity of maritime areas that have traditionally been subject to intense anthropogenic pressures in previous decades. The Law imposed *prima facie* strict conditions to the development of private properties and set out specially protected zones, notably an area of 100 metres from the demarcation line (*deslinde*) to the foreshore, separating the MTPD from private ownership (an easement of protection). The law also established a so-called zone or area of influence with at least 500 metres from the inner boundary of the seashore, where the erection of architectural screens or the accumulation of buildings was to be avoided. However, these safeguards did not halt the relentless degradation of the coasts and of wilderness areas. Approximately fifty per cent of beaches and seventy per cent of dunes on the Spanish coast have been degraded or profoundly altered, while more than sixty per cent of the immediate surroundings of the beaches of the Southern Mediterranean, Atlantic coasts and archipelagos have been urbanized. If the rhythms of human occupation experienced in the last sixty years continue (a period including three instances of economic recession), by 2030 the entirety of the Spanish coast will have been affected by human activities.[85]

Reforms were introduced in 2013, advancing a series of important changes to the areas forming part of the so-called banks of the sea (*ribera del mar*), although a number of acute current problems were neglected in this process. Prior to 2013 dunes were always included within the concept of beach 'with or without vegetation, formed by the action of the sea or the sea wind, or other natural causes'. Following the 2013 reforms dunes 'will be included *to the extent necessary* to ensure the stability of the beach and coastal defence', thus conferring a wide margin of discretion upon the pertinent authorities.[86] In addition, public ownership does not necessarily preclude private intervention on the coasts since franchises may be granted by the State for a period that has been extended to seventy-five years in the 2013 amendment (prior to this a majority of the existing franchises were due to expire by 2019).

Among the different cases that may illustrate the current state of affairs the Algarrobico hotel in the province of Almería (Autonomous Community of Andalusia) reflects the difficulties of enforcing basic protection provisions to maintain the integrity of Spanish coasts. Occupying some 75,000 $m^3$, the hotel was built in a protected nature

[85] M.A. Losada, 'La destrucción de las playas españolas', *El País* (20 August 2010), 21.

[86] The Constitutional Court has upheld this wording by CCJ 233/2015.

area and at 28 metres from the seashore with the acquiescence of the regional and local authorities, and with scant control from the Spanish Government until the damage was in effect done. Although the project was halted in 2005 (with ninety-four per cent of the construction already concluded), it was not until 2012 that the Supreme Court definitively ruled that the hotel had breached the Coasts Law. At the time of writing the hotel had nonetheless yet to be demolished.

Finally, it should be noted that, despite the strict provisions in coastal legislation, they can only preserve certain stretches of the coast and require the support of nature conservation rules to achieve a more effective degree of protection for these areas.

## 6 Concluding remarks

Wilderness may be regarded as a broad concept under Spanish law. It is usually equated to 'nature', as opposed to areas subject to human intervention. Whilst Natura 2000 status has been conferred upon approximately twenty-seven per cent of Spanish territory, the relevant areas offer varying degrees of protection to relatively unspoilt nature. Recent decades have experienced an on going tug of war between the protection of unspoilt areas and a steady invasion of man-made infrastructure. Generally, natural sites and species have received limited protection due to a lax application of town and country planning requirements, coastal protection and even nature conservation laws. This conflict is far from having been resolved, as reflected in successive judicial clashes.

The classification of sites highlights the number and, in particular, the quality of natural resources in Spain. The mere designation of sites is just the first step in guaranteeing their effective protection. The devil is in the detail of the respective management plans that (a) are being adopted at a slow pace (at present only fifteen per cent of Spain's Natura 2000 sites enjoy a management plan); or (b) fail to prioritize the true conservation of nature over human intervention. In addition, protected sites are exposed to a variety of pressures, including activities conducted along their boundaries, notwithstanding the existence of buffer zones that are theoretically designed to lessen such burdens. For instance, the illegal exploitation of water resources in Tablas de Daimiel national park prompted UNESCO in 2008 to threaten its potential withdrawal from the official list of biosphere reserves. In June 2014 the same institution recommended that the Spanish government prohibited the dredging of the Guadalquivir River, which would affect Doñana national park, and expressed its deep concern in relation to water management in the park. The question remains as to whether nature protection has achieved the position it deserves among the wide range of other pressing policies that may have direct bearing on its quality and integrity, including transport, energy, agriculture and housing. In practice, intervention by the public authorities in favour of development projects affecting nature at the central and regional levels is unlikely to decrease. They may be the first custodians of nature but, paradoxically, they also represent one of its primary threats given the number of projects that they have authorized so as to implement diverse public policies.

Indeed, one of the main challenges faced by wilderness areas in Spain is the need to ensure the simple but forceful application of the legal commitments set out in European and Spanish laws, a criticism that is also applicable to the national judiciary. In other words, whilst legal instruments to guarantee long-term favourable evolution of wilderness areas are already in place, their timely and effective application is currently less than ideal.

# 21

# Wilderness protection in Sweden

FILIPPO VALGUARNERA

## 1 Introduction

Sweden is most certainly an interesting legal system when considering the protection of wilderness, both for its well-rooted tradition in the field of environmental law and for the sheer quantity of untouched natural areas present in such a large country, which is inhabited by a mere nine million people. Moreover, as we will soon observe, the three main interests involved in the protection of wilderness – property/ production, recreation/outdoor life and conservation – have in Sweden a rather peculiar configuration. This is due to the ideological weakness of ownership (which, however, is being reinforced) in the Swedish legal tradition and to the existence of a legal institute such as the '*allemansrätt*' (literally 'every man's right'), protected by the Constitution, which allows the public to enter on private land in order to enjoy nature.

Before we go further, a few introductory remarks on the Swedish legal system as a whole are called for. The Swedish legal system shares with its continental cousins the centrality of statute law, as well as most of the techniques used to interpret legislation. Nonetheless, a few important differences must be taken into account. First, while the historical continuity in legal systems such as France, Germany and Italy has been interrupted by the codification movement – to the extent that one could sensibly divide the legal history of these countries into two large periods: before and after the Code – Sweden shares with the common law an extraordinary lack of clear-cut breaks. However, while the historical continuity of the English tradition is due to the work of the courts, in Sweden it is rather determined by a longstanding legislative tradition whose roots can be traced back to the old provincial laws of the thirteenth century. The codification movement has never taken root in Sweden.

The closest thing to a code is the Law of the Kingdom of Sweden (Sveriges Rikes Lag) of the year 1734 (of which only a few provisions have survived to this day), which was divided into partitions called 'balkar' (an ancient term that literally means 'beam'). To this day, as a symbol of continuity, many of the statutes deemed as central to a certain legal field are also called 'balkar'. There is, therefore, for instance, a 'brottsbalk' (criminal 'balk') and a 'rättegångsbalk' (procedural 'balk'). Some of the 'balkar' are more mysterious for the continental lawyer: for instance there is a 'byggningabalk' (literally 'balk' on the constructions, which contain some of the original provisions of the 1734 Law) and a 'jordabalk' (literally 'balk on the earth', containing mainly land law provisions). These are the result of a systematic organization of the law that is quite foreign to lawyers accustomed to the French Code Civil or the German Bürgerliches Gesetzbuch. Since 1998 there is also a 'miljöbalk', a 'balk' for the environmental law, which signals the importance that this branch of the law has over time acquired in the eyes of the legislature (hereafter, for reasons of simplicity, we will call it Environmental Code).

To summarize these first remarks, we could say that, to the extent that taxonomies are relevant, Sweden (together with Finland, Denmark, Norway and Iceland) belongs to a Nordic or Scandinavian legal family rather than to the civil law. It can be useful to keep this aspect in mind when exploring some of the features of the Swedish legal system that directly concern the protection of wilderness. The reader should not automatically assume that features common to most continental jurisdictions (such as the centrality of the notion of ownership) are present in Sweden as well.

This chapter is divided into six sections. The introduction is followed by a brief discussion of the main interests involved in the protection of wilderness in the Swedish setting. Section 3 is dedicated to a historical background of the protection of wilderness from the first national park legislation in 1909 to the Environmental Code in 1998. Section 4 describes the main legal devices for the protection of wilderness present in the Swedish legal system. Section 5 discusses a few operational issues in the protection of wilderness, focusing in particular on the role of environmental NGOs. Section 6 closes the chapter with a few concluding remarks.

## 2 Main interests involved in the protection of wilderness

In general terms, the protection of wilderness can be said to encompass the interaction (and potential friction) between three main interests: those of conservation, those related to ownership (including economic productivity) and those pertaining to recreational outdoor activities. Before we immerse ourselves in the more specific rules pertaining to the protection of wilderness, it is useful to assess how these three interests are dealt with in the Swedish legal tradition.

### *2.1 Property*

Property occupies, at least since the bourgeoisie became the hegemonic social class during the nineteenth century, a central position in the continental legal tradition. No provision could express this in a more poetic way than Article 544 of the French Civil Code:

> La propriété est le droit de jouir et disposer des choses de la manière la plus absolue, pourvu qu'on n'en fasse pas un usage prohibé par les lois ou par les règlements.[1]

A similar observation could be made about the English legal tradition. In that context, the poetic emphasis is not given by legislation but by a scholar, William Blackstone, who could arguably be considered one of the most influential minds in the history of common law (also by virtue of his deep impact on the American legal culture). Blackstone in his *Commentaries on the Laws of England* has this to say about property:

> There is nothing which so generally strikes the imagination, and engages the affections of mankind, as the right of property; or that sole and despotic dominion which one man claims and exercises over the external things of the world, in total exclusion of the right of any other individual in the universe.[2]

These powerful lines are among the most often quoted in the whole Anglo-Saxon legal literature. Although Blackstone himself was aware of the many limitations to private property, and especially land property, he managed to express an ideal, which was shared by the vast majority of the

[1] 'Ownership is the right to enjoy and dispose of things in the most absolute manner, provided they are not used in a way prohibited by statutes or regulations.' Art. 544 *Code Civil*, translation in English by G. Rouhette and A. Rouhette-Berton, 2006, www.legifrance.gouv.fr/content/download/1950/13681/version/3/file/Code_22.pdf.

[2] W. Blackstone, *Commentaries on the Laws of England* (Oxford: Clarendon Press, 1765–1769), Book II, at 2.

English bourgeoisie.[3] This ideal migrated to the United States and was actively promoted by its federal judges.[4]

The contrast with the Swedish tradition could not be starker. A careful search for a definition of property, much less an emphatic one, in the country's constitution or ordinary legislation would be fruitless. Similarly, the legal scholarship has not devoted to property even a fraction of the many volumes to be found in a French or Italian library. The explanation for this striking difference is mainly that in Sweden property never reached the status of an ideological fetish. This can be partly traced back to the relatively late industrialization of the country and the consequent late rise of the bourgeoisie as a dominant social group. The bourgeois values, which started to develop during the sixteenth century in England and France, peaking with the French Revolution, did not manage to influence in depth the core of Swedish law. Another part of the explanation is that the strong tensions about land ownership, which dominated English and French history, were comparatively weak in Sweden and tended to be solved through institutional channels rather than through a pattern of periodic revolts.[5] It can be interesting to remember that Swedish peasants very early on were represented as a state in the Swedish parliament (alongside the aristocracy, the bourgeoisie, and the clergy). The relative lack of tensions about ownership kept the notion of property on a neutral ideological ground.

From the ideological weakness of property in Sweden stemmed far-reaching consequences. Some of these are strictly technical, as brilliantly shown by Claes Martinson in a recent contribution.[6] Other consequences have broader policy implications. In particular, the relative weakness of property made it easier to restrict the landowners' powers for the public good and to implement the redistributive policies of the Social Democratic Party, which dominated the Swedish political scene during the twentieth century. This does not automatically mean that property was always sacrificed to the interest of conservation. We shall see that, at the beginning of the twentieth century, individual property rights were

[3] C.M. Rose, 'Canons of property talk, or, Blackstone's anxiety', *Yale Law Journal*, 108 (1998–1999), 601–632, at 603–604.

[4] E.T. Freyfogle, 'The enclosure of America', *Illinois Public Law and Legal Theory Research Paper Series No. 7* (10 October 2007), 1–54, at 41–48.

[5] O. Löfgren, 'Historical perspectives on Scandinavia peasantries', *Annual Review of Anthropology*, 9 (1980), 187–215, at 196–198.

[6] C. Martinson, *Ejendomsrettens overgang - Norden kontra verden*, 38:e nordiska juristmötet i Köpenhamn, The 38th Nordic Law Meeting (Copenhagen, 2008), http://jura.ku.dk/njm/39/823-844-bilaga-1.pdf/, pp. 823–843.

indeed taken into account in Europe's first legislation on national parks (1909). Such development, however, is a sign of the weakness of conservation interests vis-á-vis other public interests (such as production) during that era rather than a manifestation of the strength of individual property rights.

In more recent times, with the weakening of the social-democratic influence over Swedish politics and of the welfare ideal, the tendency has been to reinforce property both on a constitutional level – by reforming Chapter 2, paragraph 18 (nowadays paragraph 15) of the Form of Government, the main Swedish constitutional document, in 1994 and 2010 – and in the ordinary legislation – by changing the Expropriation Act (SFS 1972:719) in 2010 in favour of the landowner.

### 2.2 *Recreational outdoor activities*

The relative weakness of property rights in the Swedish legal tradition has brought about a rather peculiar legal institute called the *allemansrätt*. The term means literally 'every man's right', and it refers to the right of the public to enter on private land, even against the will of the owner, plant a tent, roam freely and even pick a reasonable amount of wild berries and mushrooms. The *allemansrätt* is often depicted as a very ancient institution in most Swedish and foreign descriptions. While this is by no means a false statement, it needs to be qualified. The truth of the statement lies in the fact that people in Sweden have always felt free to roam on uncultivated land and in areas distant from the owner's habitation. This freedom was confirmed in the statute law as early on as in the medieval provincial laws. However, it was not considered, nor described, as a positive right of the public, but rather as a grey unregulated area of no practical importance to the owner. The word *allemansrätt* appears in fact relatively late in legal literature (the first work mentioning the term is apparently a book on water rights by Adolf Åström published in 1899).[7]

The scenario changed rapidly during the twentieth century. Not only did the term *allemansrätt* penetrate common and legal parlance, but the social-democratic governments (which dominated Swedish politics starting in the 1930s) made it an integral part of their redistributive policies. The point was now to allow the working class to have access to the beautiful Swedish nature as a source of entertainment. This development was, of course, stimulated by the rapid economic growth of the

[7] A. Åström, *Svensk vattenrätt* (Stockholm: Norstedt, 1899), at 126.

country following World War II and by the increasing well-being of Swedish workers thanks to the construction of a generous welfare state. The result was not only that the *allemansrätt* ended up being considered a positive right, but also that it received constitutional protection. In 1994, Chapter 2, paragraph 18 (nowadays paragraph 15) of the Form of Government was changed in order to not only reinforce the protection of property, but also to acknowledge that 'everyone has a right of accessing nature in accordance with the allemansrätt (. . .)'.

The relevance of the *allemansrätt* for the protection of wilderness should not be underestimated: where in Part I of this volume the recreational use was identified as one of the values of wilderness, the *allemansrätt* makes this value the subject of a right of members of the public. This indirectly also touches upon the issue of protecting wilderness. While recreation and personal enjoyment is not the only reason to protect wilderness, it is true that people who have a personal relationship with nature have less difficulty accepting and supporting public policies aimed at protecting it against human aggression.[8] The other side of the coin, however, is that the *allemansrätt*, by promoting human interaction with the environment, may in some situations result in damage to flora, in disturbance to fauna or in impacts on wilderness qualities (e.g., through the establishment of pathways due to high visitor numbers).

### *2.3 Conservation*

Sweden has a relatively old tradition of serving the interest of natural conservation, starting in 1909 with the first legislation on national parks in Europe. Of particular interest is the relationship of conservation to the other two interests already examined. The friction between conservation and property/production seems obvious. In practice, the most pressing issue has been the matter of compensation for the landowners whose usage of their land has been limited, as it has a direct impact on the costs of conservation.

The weak political and constitutional status of property in Sweden allowed the legislature to serve the interest of conservation by acting on the rules pertaining to expropriation. Of particular interest is the reform carried out in 1972, which was explicitly aimed at reducing the costs for

[8] S. Strife and L. Downey, 'Childhood development and access to nature: a new direction for environmental inequality research', *Organization and Environment*, 22 (2009), 99–122, at 109–110.

compensation by affirming the principle that the owner should not be compensated for increases in the value of the land that he had not contributed to. Moreover, compensation was only granted to a landowner for 'significant' intrusions in his right, which meant that public authorities could refuse to grant him the permission to build close to the shores without granting him compensation.[9] However, more recently the expropriation rules have undergone significant changes in favour of the landowners under the impulse of the former right wing government. The result is that compensation must be paid when even a small part of the real estate is concerned and that compensation is now upgraded to one hundred and twenty-five per cent (!) of the market value.[10] Thus, conservation has become increasingly difficult to realize through the traditional legal tools due to rising costs for the treasury.

## 3 The notion of wilderness in Sweden: a historical background

The interests of property, recreation and environmental production are intimately related to the idea of 'wilderness' and to the functions that wilderness should serve according to the cultural trend and political ideology predominating in any given historical period. It is therefore useful to describe, although briefly and schematically, the different historical permutations that the notion of wilderness has undergone in the Swedish national culture.

Unsurprisingly, various authors point out that the roots of the protection of wilderness in Sweden can be traced back to the nineteenth century, an era culturally dominated by the Romantic Movement, with its focus on national heritage and on the beauty of untamed nature. While wilderness, until the rise of romanticism, had been considered in negative terms by the ruling class,[11] as the lack of civilization and inherently dangerous, the fast industrialization of Europe and the rapid growth of the urban population prompted the discovery of nature as a locus of recreation and spiritual restoration.

[9] G. Michanek and C. Zetterberg, *Den svenska miljörätten*, 3rd edn. (Uppsala: Iustus, 2012), at 68.

[10] *Ibid.*, at 436–437. See Expropriation Act 1972:719 Chapter 4, paragraph 1.

[11] See also Chapter 1. However, as already discussed with reference to the Czech Republic, one could make the case that nature was seen in a more positive light by the poor, who considered the forest as an important source of food. In fact, at the beginning of the twentieth century, a strong argument used by the legislature to continue supporting access to nature (*allemansrätt*) was the need of the poor to gather berries and mushrooms.

In Sweden, the enjoyment of wilderness was early on linked to its potential as a tool to educate the people to patriotic values. As pointed out by Klas Sandell and Sverker Sörlin, the rapid social and political changes between the nineteenth and twentieth centuries, stemming from the crisis of old social structures and the increasing political organization of the growing working class, brought about the need, in both conservative and liberal circles, to found a new set of common values, an idea of Fatherland which could unite the different social groups and prevent a more radical and violent social development. The exaltation of wilderness as the common heritage of all Swedes became part of such a cultural agenda.[12]

It should however be noted that Swedish legislation and preparatory works rarely use the term '*vildmark*' (the closest word to the English term 'wilderness'), preferring the much broader '*natur*'. This terminological choice – still in use in contemporary legislation – creates obvious difficulties with regard to the specific subject of this book, as we need to assess to what extent legal devices, created to protect nature in a broad sense, can also be used to protect 'wilderness'. A good example of this ambiguity is provided by the governmental inquiry on 'the measures required to protect nature and natural monuments in our country', delivered in 1907. The inquiry uses the term '*natur*' but, at least with regard to the proposal of instituting national parks, clearly refers to wilderness. The inquiry discusses the interest of creating large areas where 'natural life is allowed to develop without any cultural interference'.[13]

The inquiry of 1907 gives a clear picture of the main functions the protection of nature (and wilderness) was called to fulfil. First, the members of the commission underlined that protecting nature was going to serve the scientific community, allowing the study of plants and animals in an environment untouched by humankind.[14] From this perspective, the natural parks were compared to museums, botanic gardens and locations for field experiments. Second, the inquiry pointed out the importance of nature from an aesthetic point of view, meaning that untamed nature does contribute to the beauty of a location. Third,

[12] K. Sandell and S. Sörlin, 'Naturen som ungdomsfostrare' in K. Sandell and S. Sörlin (eds.), *Friluftshistoria - Från "härdande friluftsliv" till ekoturism och miljöpedagogik*, 2nd edn. (Malmö: Carlsson Bokförlag, 2008), 27–46, at 31–34.

[13] *Betänkande rörande åtgärder till skydd för vårt lands natur och naturminnesmärke* (1907), at 47.

[14] See also Chapter 3, where Mark Fisher discusses the role of science in evaluating wilderness in Europe.

the inquiry stressed that certain natural elements could be linked to folklore, fables or historical events. Protecting nature was therefore a way of securing the national heritage.[15] As a result of the inquiry the Parliament enacted the act on national parks and the act for the protection of natural monuments, both in 1909.

The statute concerning national parks (1909:56) established that only areas owned by the crown could be declared a national park (paragraph 1). In such an area all kinds of economic activities were forbidden (damaging living plants, mineral excavation, farming, hunting, etc.). Two exceptions are of interest. The first one stated that the prohibitions were not to limit individual rights, which suggests that in this period the interest of property, albeit weaker than in the rest of Europe, still outweighed conservation. The second exception concerned the Sami population (called the Lapps in the legislative language of the time), whose customary right to hunt, fish and deal with reindeer husbandry continued to be allowed even in the national parks (paragraph 2).

The contrast with the Yellowstone National Park, established in Wyoming in 1872, is strong. In the American 'mother of all national parks', the army (which controlled the park until 1916) forcibly removed the Native American population, creating an area untouched by humans,[16] an artificial environment able to satisfy the romantic appetite for untouched wilderness. This attitude, however, overlooks that humans themselves can very well be an integral part of an ecosystem and that removing them from an area can actually do more damage than good. In that sense, the Swedish attitude seems extraordinarily modern, especially as the open-air museum model inaugurated in Yellowstone was destined to become an internationally leading paradigm for many decades.[17] In fact, the Swedish legislature observed that the rights exercised by the Sami population did not influence the natural environment in any noticeable way and that the Sami were 'so intimately united with the natural environment that they, so to speak, complete it'.[18] However, as suggested by Anna Zachrisson, it is possible to interpret this policy in a less benevolent way, as a sign of a prejudice against the Sami as less evolved

[15] *Betänkande rörande åtgärder till skydd för vårt lands natur och naturminnesmärke* (1907), at 5–8.

[16] See also Chapter 1.

[17] A. Zachrisson, *Co-Management of Natural Resources - Paradigm Shifts, Key Concepts and Cases* (Umeå: Mountain Mistra Programme, 2004), at 21. See also Chapter 1.

[18] *Betänkande rörande åtgärder till skydd för vårt lands natur och naturminnesmärke* (1907), at 49.

and civilized and therefore well fitting in a national park.[19] Nonetheless, it is quite remarkable that the state even compensated the reindeers killed by bears or lynxes in the national parks, as the Sami were not allowed to protect their stock by hunting these animals.

The second statute issued in 1909, the act for the protection of natural monuments (1909:56), is of lesser importance for the protection of wilderness as defined in this book, as it was designed to protect particular areas or particular elements of the natural world, such as a rare geological formations, of interest for understanding the natural history of the country or because of their rarity. The statute also contained provisions directed at protecting endangered animal species and plants. Also in this case the interest of ownership seemed to prevail over that of conservation, as proceeding to put a natural monument under protection required the consent of the owner.

These first attempts to protect nature (and wilderness) had a few noticeable weaknesses. Two are of particular interest. First, the fact that private property still was considered a stronger interest than natural conservation, combined with rather unclear guidelines about what areas needed to be protected, led to a lack of coherence in the implementation of the law. Second, the administrative organization in charge of managing the parks was rather meagre, consisting mainly in the Academy of Science (a fact that further underlines that the interest of conservation was mainly seen as a way of securing specimens for scientific research).[20] This led Rutger Sernander, Professor at Uppsala University and special expert charged by the government to conduct an inquiry in 1935, to state that the existing administrative organization was not any longer capable of satisfying the needs of protecting nature, including wilderness (in fact, Sernander explicitly used the term 'vildmark' with regard to national parks).[21]

Sernander mentioned the rapid 'material development' as a cause for the quick obsolescence of the administrative framework.[22] Social and technological changes were indeed destined to accelerate. In Sweden, two main forces were at play. First, as already mentioned, Swedish political life during the twentieth century was dominated by the social-democratic

[19] A. Zachrisson, *Commons Protected For or From the People – Co-Management in the Swedish Mountain Region?* (Umeå: Department of Political Science, 2009), at 30.

[20] *Ibid.*, at 31.

[21] Statens Offentliga Utredningar ('SOU', Swedish Government Official Reports) 1935:26, at 147–148.

[22] *Ibid.*, at 199.

party (the first social-democratic government was formed in 1921 and the party controlled Parliament, by itself or in a coalition, almost uninterruptedly between 1932 and 1976), which carried through forceful redistributive policies, resulting in a very generous welfare system. Second, Swedish neutrality during the two world wars (Sweden was in fact the only Scandinavian country lucky enough not to be invaded by either Germany or the Soviet Union), combined with its export of steel to the German war machine, greatly contributed to the industrial development of the country.

The combined effect of these two factors was, on the one hand, an increasing pressure on wilderness due to urban and industrial development and, on the other hand, an increasing demand for uncontaminated green areas where the working class could spend their increasing free time and their vacations (a benefit of social-democratic politics) using the growing public transportations network, or even buying a car. These rapid social developments brought about a stronger interest for the wilderness as a means for leisure rather than as a collection of scientific specimens. This change in the balance of power between the different interests involved in the protection of wilderness is well demonstrated by a few motions submitted to the Swedish Parliament during the 1930s. For instance, Fredrik Ström in 1936 submitted a motion (n. 294) to the first chamber asking whether the interests of the public to enjoy outdoor life should be taken into account when considering the issue of selling land belonging to the Crown.[23]

These stimuli, in 1937, lead the government to start an 'inquiry on leisure' (*fritidsutredningen*) that brought about two reports: one about the regulation of constructions close to the shores (Statens Offentliga Utredningar (SOU) 1938:45), and the other on the creation of 'recreational reserves' (*fritidsreservat*) for the urban population (SOU 1940:12). It is of interest to observe that this second report contained, as an appendix, a note by the court of appeal judge Gunnar Carlesjö about the *allemansrätt*. In a sense, it can be said that this was the first attempt by the Swedish state to promote the *allemansrätt* as a means to ensure that everybody, and not only the landowning upper-class, had free access to nature.

As anticipated, the enlargement of the notion of wilderness to encompass also an aesthetic and a social dimension – now considered as important as the scientific perspective – did put the old administrative framework under pressure. For instance, it occurred to the Academy of

[23] SOU 1951:5, at 52–53.

Science itself that the increasing complexity of the interests involved in the protection of wilderness and the ever more difficult balance between the needs of production and those of conservation called for much greater investments.[24] The need for a more robust legal infrastructure brought about a more organic legislation, namely the act on the protection of nature of 1952 (*naturskyddslagen* – SFS 1952:688).

The new legislation, among other things, introduced the so-called natural parks (*naturparker*) in order to secure natural areas mainly for the purpose of recreation. Another statute, also in 1952 (SFS 1952:382), introduced special rules concerning the protection of shores, which can easily be understood considering that in the years following World War II the pressure on the coasts, both from landowners intending to build cabins and from the general public intending to use them for bathing, peaked. The protection boiled down to a severe restriction on building close to the shores (up to 300 metres from the waterline). Oddly, the 1952 reforms did not heed the call of the state inquiry (SOU 1951:5) for a new public authority specifically in charge of the protection of nature. The organizational structure continued therefore to be affected by coordination difficulties. This fact was pointed out in a report by a 1962 state inquiry that lamented the fact that the protection of wilderness had to a great extent relied upon private non-profit organizations rather than on the state.[25] As a consequence, the government in 1963 created the State Conservation Board (*Statens naturvårdsnämnd*), which in 1967 was reorganized into today's Environmental Protection Agency (*Naturvårdsverket*).

The aforementioned inquiry led also to another organic reform, namely the conservation act of 1964 (*naturvårdlagen* – SFS 1964:822), which introduced natural reserves, a tool intended to favour both conservation and recreation, substituting natural parks. The rules of the conservation act ended up, to a great extent and with few modifications, in the Environmental Code of 1998, which integrated and reorganized the quite fragmented environmental legislation concerning pollution as well as the protection of natural areas. The Environmental Code will be considered in the next section.

## 4 Legal tools for the protection of wilderness areas

The main legislation concerning not only the protection of wilderness, but more in general environmental law is the *miljöbalk*, which can be

[24] *Ibid.*, at 57–58.
[25] SOU 1962:36, at 372–373.

translated – somewhat imprecisely – as the Environmental Code. For our purposes, the most relevant parts of the legislation are Chapters 3 and 4, which contain the so-called husbandry rules, and Chapter 7, which contains legal tools to protect natural areas.[26] It should be noted that about twelve per cent of the Swedish territory is included in a Natura 2000 area. However, most of these zones overlap areas protected under domestic law. I will here focus on the latter.

### *4.1 General 'husbandry rules'*

The first group of rules, which is of interest for the protection of wilderness, consists of the so-called husbandry rules. These are rules contained in Chapters 3 and 4 of the Environmental Code and give a general indication about the usage of land and aquatic areas. These rules are mainly applied by public authorities in charge of spatial planning and zoning and of granting permits for economic activities with a potential impact on the environment.

The rule that most directly addresses wilderness, in the sense of pristine natural areas unsoiled by human infrastructure, is Chapter 3, paragraph 2:

> Large land and aquatic areas that are not at all, or just marginally, impacted by economic exploitation or by other interventions in the environment are to be protected, as far as possible, from actions which may significantly influence the areas' characteristics.

In order to understand how far the duty of Swedish authorities to protect such pristine areas goes one must assess the meaning of the rather vague expressions 'as far as possible' and 'significantly influence'. According to the preparatory works of the Environmental Code, 'as far as possible' refers to the necessity of balancing the interests of conservation with practical and economic considerations such as occupation and regional planning. Mere economic interests, however, cannot prevail on the protection of wilderness, unless a broad assessment of all the relevant factors shows that allowing human activities in those areas would, from a general point of view, foster good husbandry of resources. 'Significantly influence' means that trivial occurrences are excluded from the scope of

[26] For a review of these rules see Michanek and Zetterberg, *Den svenska miljörätten, supra* note 9, at 136–155 and 199–241.

the rule. The norm refers to human activities that have a prolonged or a very profound, albeit only temporary, impact on nature.[27]

Certain areas, called areas of national interest, enjoy a special degree of protection as these 'are to be protected', without weakening the provision with the expression 'as far as possible'. In other words, the characteristic for which the area is of national interest cannot be sacrificed in order to accommodate other types of needs (such as occupation and regional planning). The Environmental Code (Chapter 3, paragraphs 5–9) enumerates several features that may render an area 'of national interest', for instance its particular importance for reindeer husbandry, the fishing industry, national defence but also cultural conservation, natural conservation and the outdoor life. The last two interests seem of immediate relevance for the protection of the wilderness.

The preparatory works state that an area can be deemed to be of national interest for natural conservation because it illustrates important stages in the development of the Swedish natural landscape or because 'it is pristine and contains a great variety of natural habitats and biotopes'.[28] While the term 'wilderness', is not used, it is quite clear from this statement that the features associated with wilderness can confer to an area a particular kind of protection which is even stronger than that granted by Chapter 3, paragraph 2.

To summarize, one should distinguish between areas characterized by 'ordinary' wilderness (a type of wilderness which is not particularly rare or unique) and areas where the wilderness has a certain amount of uniqueness that makes them particularly worthy of protection. One should observe that, while there is no exhaustive list of 'areas of national interest', some particularly large areas are specifically mentioned in Chapter 4 of the Environmental Code. For instance, Chapter 4, paragraph 5 states:

> In the mountain areas of Långfjället-Rogen, Sylarna-Helags, Skäcker, Burvattnet, Hotagsfjällen, Frostviken-Borgafjällen, Marsfjällen-Vardofjällen, Artfjället, Tärna-Vindelfjällen, Sarek-Mavas, Kebnekaise-Sjaunja, Rostu and Pessinki can habitations and facilities be built only if it is necessary for reindeer husbandry, for the needs of the resident population, for conducting scientific research or to facilitate outdoor life. Other interventions can only take place if they can be carried out without impacting the characteristics of the areas.

[27] Proposition 1997/98:45, part 2, at 30 and Michanek and Zetterberg, *Den svenska miljörätten*, *supra* note 9, at 139–155.

[28] Proposition 1997/98:45, part 2, at 33.

It should be noted that the density of the population in those areas is extremely low, so while the provision does not entail a strict protection against all tangible signs of human activity, it significantly contributes to keeping most of these areas in a pristine and untouched state.

### *4.2 Protection of natural areas*

The most radical of the legal tools created to protect natural areas are undoubtedly the national parks. There are at the moment twenty-nine national parks in Sweden, covering a total of 632,253 ha of land. A high percentage (eighty-two per cent) of the land included in national parks is located in the mountain area in the northern county of Norrbotten.[29]

According to Chapter 7, paragraph 2 a 'large and cohesive' area can be declared a national park by the Government, with the consent of Parliament, with the purpose of conserving said area in its 'natural condition'. While the legislation does not explicitly use the term 'wilderness', it is quite clear that the primary purpose of this legal institute is to maintain large natural areas in a pristine condition. To enter national parks for leisure is by no means excluded but the interest of recreation clearly plays second fiddle to that of protection.

Chapter 7, paragraph 3 authorizes the Government to issue regulations in order to limit and regulate the use of land and water resources in the parks. Such power can be delegated to a public authority. A governmental regulation issued in 1987 (1987:938) establishes that the County Administrative Boards (*länstyrelser*) are in charge of the administration of the parks. Moreover, the Environmental Protection Agency (*Naturvårdsverket*) has been given the power to issue detailed regulations about the usage of the parks (requiring, however, that the CAB, the municipality and the Sea and Water Authority must be heard).

It must be observed that, in line with the very first statute on national parks (1909), it is still the case that only land owned by the state can be declared to be a national park. The reasons are constitutional, as the grave limitations on the usage and enjoyment of land that a national park brings about would constitute a de facto expropriation. By this limitation, if the state wants to include privately owned land in a national park, it must first start a proper and lawful expropriation procedure. Such a limitation should be discussed in the context of the development of expropriation rules in Sweden. While the original constitutional

[29] Statistics Sweden (*Statistiska Centralbyrån*, SCB), *Skyddad natur*, 31 December 2013, at 9.

guarantees were very faint, and the levels of monetary compensation rather low, the last two decades have witnessed a strong advancement of the landowners' rights (this aspect will be discussed in Section 5).

Of particular interest when discussing national parks are the rights of the Sami population. We saw, while dealing with the historical background, that the first Swedish legislation on national parks considered the Sami to be in such a perfect harmony with nature that they were allowed to continue to use the parks for reindeer husbandry. This possibility was progressively restricted to the point that the Environmental Code does not accord the Sami any particular status in relation to national parks. However, the EPA in its regulations regarding the national parks in northern Sweden authorizes Sami reindeer husbandry and even allows the Sami to use motor scooters in the parks. Moreover, a 2011 governmental regulation (2011:840) has authorized the CAB of Norrbotten to delegate to a non-profit organization called Laponiatjuottjudus and formed by Sami villages, the CAB of Norrbotten, the EPA, and the municipalities of Gällivare kommun and Jokkmokk the administration of the Laponian area; therefore opening up the area to a co-management solution between the state, the local authorities and the indigenous population.

A second tool of interest for the protection of wilderness goes under the label 'natural reserve' (*naturreservat*) and is mainly regulated in Chapter 7, paragraphs 4-8 of the Environmental Code. As of 31 December 2013, there are as many as 4042 natural reserves in Sweden, covering a surface of 4.5 million ha. About seventy-five per cent of the reserves are located in the northern mountain regions of the country.[30] A few important differences between these areas and the national parks must be observed. The first is that, while the government creates national parks, the creation of natural reserves is left to the local authorities (the CAB or the municipality). Second, while national parks can only be created on state-owned land, natural reserves can even encompass land owned by private individuals. The owner will be entitled to compensation if his usage of the land is significantly restricted. Third, Chapter 7, paragraph 4 states that a natural reserve can be created in order to 'preserve biological diversity, take care or preserve important natural environments or to secure areas for recreational outdoor activities'. The provision signals that, contrary to what we saw in the case of national

[30] Statistics Sweden, *Skyddad natur*, 31 December 2013, at 10 and Naturvårdsverket, *Naturreservat i Sverige*, 2010.

parks, the interest of conservation, while still very important, competes with the interest of recreation. This aspect is also very clearly illustrated in Chapter 7, paragraph 6, where it says that the authority that establishes the natural reserve can also, in order to facilitate the realization of the interests for which the reserve has been created, impose a series of intrusions on the rights of the owner. The statute mentions, among others, the construction of roads, paths, cabins, sanitary facilities, bathing areas and the opening of areas to the public where these are not already accessible according to the *allemansrätt*. These rules, as well as the rules limiting the usage of the land, must be attached to the decision to establish the reserve (Chapter 7, paragraph 5). The local authorities can introduce temporary exceptions, for instance to accommodate for a sport competition on the land. However, a condition for this is that 'the intrusion in the environment is, to a reasonable extent, compensated for in the reserve itself or in an other area' (Chapter 7, paragraph 7). It should be observed that 'compensation' does not mean financial compensation, but rather an extension of the environmental protection. This rule has been introduced in order for Sweden to respect the Ramsar Convention on the protection of wetlands, the Birds Directive (79/409/EEC) and the Habitat Directive (92/43/EEC). Finally, it is interesting to notice that Chapter 7, paragraph 9 grants the possibility to also declare a cultural landscape of particular interest a cultural reserve, governed by the same provisions that apply to natural reserves.

The fact that natural reserves are meant to serve potentially conflicting interests, and that most of the regulatory power is in the hand of local authorities, means that their value for the protection of wilderness can in practice vary significantly. It might be useful to provide a couple of concrete examples. The natural reserve of Bredåsen, in the municipality of Älvdalen, was instituted by the CAB of Dalarna with the explicit purpose of protecting wilderness. The total surface of the natural reserve is 1140 ha of which 982 ha is woodland. The purpose of instituting the natural reserve is to preserve biologic diversity, to facilitate outdoor life and to make it possible to conduct scientific research. The CAB aims at realizing these objectives by prohibiting forestry and other types of exploitation, by allowing natural processes and by 'preserving the area's wilderness'.[31] The natural reserve of Stendörren, instituted in 1971 by the CAB of Södermanland, serves instead primarily the interest of allowing outdoor tourism. The area covers 923 ha containing both water and

[31] Länsstyrelsen Dalarnas län, Decision 2012-12-17 in matter nr. 511-3920-2012.

islands. The reserve was instituted with the explicit purpose of facilitating recreational activities. The CAB's webpage tells us that the reserve is visited every year by about 200,000 persons and that the area is equipped with fireplaces, toilets and trash bins. Motor traffic is allowed on some of the roads. The human presence in the areas makes it difficult to speak about 'wilderness' in the true sense of the word, nor can the term be found in any of the relevant documents.[32]

A third type of protection for natural areas is granted in the form of 'biotope protection areas' (*biotopskyddsområde*), defined by Chapter 7, paragraph 11 as 'small land or water areas which, because of their peculiar characteristics, are the habitat of endangered animal species or plants, or are otherwise of particular value'. As of December 2013, there were as many as 7000 biotope protection areas covering about 24,000 ha.[33] The function of this type of instrument is manifestly conservation rather than recreation. In fact, the area involved should not be wider than what is necessary for the purpose of conservation. At the same time it is difficult to argue that this type of device is aimed at protecting 'wilderness', as the protected areas can very well be the product of human activity (for instance, old stone walls important for preserving certain types of animals). The protection can be granted in two different ways. First, the government can declare that all areas of a certain, easily recognizable, type in the whole country or in part of it should be protected. These types of areas – such as, for instance, avenues with at least five trees and wetlands not bigger than one hectare – are listed in annex 1 to the 'decree on the protection of natural areas according to the environmental code' (1998:1252). Second, the government can grant a municipality or a public authority, such as the EPA or the Forest Authority (*Skogsstyrelsen*), the power to protect specific areas. In a biotope protection area there is a general prohibition against activities that can damage the natural environment. Exemption from the prohibition can be granted, but such a power must be used parsimoniously.

Of great importance both for the interest of recreation and for the interest of conservation are the so-called 'areas for the protection of the shores' (*strandskyddsområde*), now regulated by Chapter 7, paragraph 13 and following of the Environmental Code, but, as we have seen, part of the Swedish legal systems since as early as 1952. The specific importance

[32] See www.lansstyrelsen.se/sodermanland/sv/djur-och-natur/skyddad-natur/naturreservat/nykoping/stendorren/Pages/index.aspx.

[33] Statistics Sweden, *Skyddad natur*, 31 December 2013, at 11.

of the shores as areas where the interests of property, conservation and recreation are most likely to collide is not difficult to comprehend: the beautiful Swedish coasts are obviously attractive to people wanting to build mansions and cabins close to the sea but also, and for the same reasons, to the larger group of people who, without owning land close to the sea, want nonetheless to have access to the shores. The landowners' interest in using the land, perhaps improving it with additional cabins, trampolines and other structures have therefore the potential to restrict the public's access to nature according to the *allemansrätt*.

The protection of the shores, according to Chapter 7, paragraph 13, pertains, as a general rule, to all areas in proximity of the sea, of lakes and of watercourses in order to protect access to the beaches by the public according to the *allemansrätt* and to 'conserve the conditions for the life of animals and plants on land and in the water'. This last function has been added to the legislation as late as in 1994. The reason must be searched for not so much in an underestimation of the interest of conservation by the legislature, but probably in a rather naïve idea that access to nature and conservation were two sides of the same coin and that protecting one implicitly meant protecting the other as well. That the protection of the shores nowadays is explicitly directed towards both interests is one of several signs that the Swedish legislature has realized that access to nature and conservation sometimes can come into conflict.

The protected area stretches from 100 metres on land to 100 in the water, measured from the shoreline during mean water level. The CAB can further extend the area to 300 metres if it is necessary to protect the interests of access to nature or conservation. In the protected area it is prohibited to erect buildings, to modify existing buildings or to build any other facilities (if the effect is to impede access by the public or to dissuade the public from entering the area), and to undertake other actions that significantly changes the conditions for the life of plants and animals. An important exception to these rules is prescribed by Chapter 7, paragraph 16 for the construction of facilities that are not used for housing and that are necessary for farming, fishing, forestry and reindeer husbandry as long as they cannot be placed outside the shore protection area without losing their function. The CAB can grant exemptions from the prohibition in various cases, for instance when it is evident (a very high standard) that the area is of no importance for the interests of conservation or access to nature.

Finally, the government can create an 'environmental protection area' (*miljöskyddsområde*) on a large water or land area if special rules are necessary because of pollution or because of other violations of environmental norms. The special rules to be applied in these areas are issued by the government or by a public authority to which the power has been delegated by the government.[34] Currently there are very few environmental protection areas. Their primary goal seems not to be the protection of wilderness, but rather to introduce special measures designed to improve the quality of the environment in areas where it has been compromised because of human activity.

## 5 The protection of the wilderness from an operational perspective

The legal instruments that have been described above offer a quite complex picture. While the term 'wilderness' is not encountered in Swedish legislation, one could argue that the legal system still provides for a good measure of protection for large, relatively pristine areas characterized by a high degree of naturalness and free of permanent human facilities. This is the case, in particular, with the vast, mountainous area in the North, where some of the country's largest national parks and most national reserves are concentrated. The effectiveness of the protection granted by legislation is, however, negatively influenced by two factors that must be taken into account.

The first element that in recent years has harmed the protection of wilderness is political. I mentioned earlier that the Swedish tradition is characterized by a relatively limited interest for property as an ideological fetish. This has historically resulted in inexpensive expropriation procedures and low monetary compensations for landowners whose land was impacted by the designation of a natural reserve, with all the following limitations on its usage. International pressures (mainly from the European Court of Human Rights[35]) and the political rise of the liberal parties – which in the 1990s broke the political hegemony of the social democratic party – resulted in stronger constitutional guarantees for private ownership and much more generous rules concerning economic compensation to the landowner in case of expropriation. The most radical change in the Expropriation Act was introduced in 2010. According to the new rules, the landowner is not only entitled to full compensation, but actually to one hundred and twenty-five per cent of

[34] Environmental Code, Chapter 7 paras 19–20.
[35] *Sporrong and Lönnroth* v. *Sweden*, 1982, series A, n. 98.

the market value.[36] The preparatory works justifies the added twenty-five per cent by referring to the fact that the expropriation violates the right of the owner to dispose of the land according to his or her own wishes. In other words, it can be seen as a compensation for the violation of the landowner's moral rights.[37] The Environmental Code refers to the rules contained in the Expropriation Act in order to determine, for instance, the compensation given to a landowner when a natural reserve is instituted. This obviously means that the cost sustained by the treasury in order to expand the protection of wilderness or to impose new obligations on the landowners has significantly increased, diminishing the practical applicability of the tools we have discussed in this chapter.

The second element has deeper historical roots and concerns the administrative structure in charge of granting permits and exemptions for activities to be carried out in the protected areas. As is to be expected in the case of such a diversity of interests, involving both the national and the local sphere, the decisions pertaining to the wilderness are taken by a variety of different institutional subjects, including municipalities (in charge, for instance, of issuing detailed zoning plans and of granting exemptions from the rules protecting the shores), the CABs (in charge, for example, of the administration of natural parks) and the EPA (which, among other things, issues regulations concerning activities in the national parks). An obvious weakness in this system is the risk that political actors entangled in local politics end up unduly putting other interests in front of the conservation of pristine natural areas. Mårten Wallberg, vice-president of the Society for Nature Conservation, expressed this thought in a particularly colourful way: 'to put municipalities in charge [of granting exemptions from regulations protecting the shores] is like letting a billy-goat work as a gardener'. Municipalities in the Stockholm area have been criticized, for instance, for the large number of exemptions granted for constructions close to the shore.[38] Given the concrete risk that political considerations may trump environmental protection – including the protection of wilderness – much of the Swedish debate surrounding environmental procedure has focused on the role played by NGOs.[39]

[36] Expropriation Act Chapter 4, para. 1 (par. 1–2).

[37] Proposition 2009/10:162, at 65–70.

[38] *Dagens Nyheter* (5 July 2013) http://www.dn.se/sthlm/kommuner-frikostiga-att-ge-dispens-fran-strandskyddet/ (last visited on 30 September 2014).

[39] For an enlightening account, on which I rely here, see J. Darpö, 'Biological diversity and the public interest', in *De lege 2009* (Uppsala: Iustus, 2009), at 201–236.

In an early stage (1952), the Swedish legislature granted three large NGOs[40] the right to appeal decisions taken according to environmental legislation. This policy, however, was reverted as soon as the Environmental Protection Agency (EPA) was established in 1967. The new agency acquired monopoly over the legal defence of public interests in environmental cases. This did not completely eliminate the influence of NGOs, as they could still play an important role in the decision-making process, but they were stripped of the right to appeal environmental decisions.

This restrictive policy was partially reversed in the 1999 Environmental Code. The new Code allowed non-profit NGOs to appeal decisions about permits, approvals and exemptions taken in accordance with the Code itself. Standing, however, was only granted to quite large NGOs (at least 2000 members), established since at least three years and with a history of active interest in environmental issues.[41] In practice, this meant that only two NGOs – the Swedish Society for Nature Conservation and the Swedish Ornithological Society – had access to environmental justice.[42]

The harsh conditions imposed on NGOs came under scrutiny of the European Court of Justice (ECJ) in 2009. The case concerned the right of a rather small Swedish environmental NGO (Djurgården-Lilla Värtans Miljöskyddsförening) to appeal against a decision of the Environmental Chamber (miljödomstolen) of the District Court of Stockholm that allowed an electricity company, under contract with the municipality of Stockholm, to construct a one-kilometre long tunnel. One of the questions was whether denying standing to NGOs with less than 2000 members violates Article 10a of Directive 85/337, as amended by Directive 2003/35. This directive implements the Aarhus convention. The Court ruled that:

> (. . .) [I]t is conceivable that the condition that an environmental protec tion association must have a minimum number of members may be relevant in order to ensure that it does in fact exist and that it is active. However, the number of members required cannot be fixed by national law at such a level that it runs counter to the objectives of Directive 85/337

[40] *Ibid.*, at 203: The Society for Nature Conservation, the Royal Academy of Sciences and the Local Heritage Movement.

[41] Chapter 16, para. 13.

[42] J. Darpö, K. Kuusiniemi and P. Vihervuori, 'Miljöprövningen i vågskålen – Landskampen mellan Sverige och Finland', in *Förvaltningsrättslig tidskrift*, 3 (2009), 323–361, at 354.

> and in particular the objective of facilitating judicial review of projects which fall within its scope.[43]

The conditions to grant NGOs standing were modified as a direct consequence of the 2009 decision. The number of members required by the Environmental Code was reduced to 100, while the type of NGOs was expanded from a single form of non-profit organization to also include, for instance, foundations.

While the 2009 decision and its aftermath significantly improved the possibilities for the public to challenge decisions concerning Swedish wilderness (such as permits and exemptions), the system still contained significant gaps that continued to put the Swedish legal system in tension with the Aarhus Convention. For instance, the NGOs had no legal standing in matters falling outside the scope of Chapter 16, paragraph 13 of the Environmental Code (in other words, decisions about permits, approvals and exemptions taken in accordance with legislation other than the Environmental Code). This was the case with the Forestry Act, which among other things regulates deforestation (this, of course, makes the statute very relevant for the protection of wilderness in a country like Sweden). Harvesting of trees requires simply a communication to the Swedish Forest Agency, unless it occurs in woods in the mountain area, where harvesting requires a permit. Until recently, NGOs had no way of challenging administrative decisions adverse to the interests of conservation.

The situation changed in February 2014. This time the agent of change was, somewhat unexpectedly, a domestic court, and more precisely the Supreme Administrative Court.[44] The case concerned the right of the Society for Nature Conservation to appeal a decision by the Swedish Forestry Agency to authorize harvesting of trees in a forest located in the Änok delta, an area in northern Sweden close to the mountains, which the Court describes as 'a roadless uninterrupted area of wilderness, of national interest[45] for the aims of conservation and outdoor life'. The Court reasoned that the facts of the case fell under the scope of Article 9.3 of the Aarhus convention according to which '(...) each Party shall ensure that, where they meet the criteria, if any, laid down in its national

[43] Djurgården-Lilla Värtans Miljöskyddsförening C-263/08, paras 47.

[44] Supreme Administrative Court (Högsta förvaltningsdomstolen) case nr. 5962–12. For an analysis of the case see J. Darpö, 'Med lagstiftaren på åskådarplats - Om implementeringen av Århuskonventionen genom rättspraxis', in *Infotorg Juridik - Rättsbanken* (5 March 2014), 1–8.

[45] See Section 4 for a definition of 'areas of national interest'.

law, members of the public have access to administrative or judicial procedures to challenge acts and omissions by private persons and public authorities which contravene provisions of its national law relating to the environment'. The Court continued by referring to the Slovak Brown Bear case by the ECJ,[46] which stated that a provision of the Convention that can be applied to situations concerning domestic law as well as EU-law has to be applied uniformly. The Supreme Administrative Court therefore concluded that the procedural law had to be interpreted as conferring an NGO, such as the Swedish Society for Nature Conservation, standing in the case at hand.

The most obvious effect of the Änok case is to extend the procedural range of environmental NGOs to matters regulated outside the Environmental Code, as long as Article 9.3 of the Aarhus Convention is applicable. As Jan Darpö points out, however, the Änok case does not have a direct impact on situations where the right to appeal has been limited by the legislature. Some of these special limitations cover matters of obvious importance for the protection of wilderness. This is the case with decisions taken by the CABs concerning, for instance, the hunting of wolves. The legislature has determined that this type of decision can only be appealed to the Environmental Protection Agency, therefore excluding the possibility that NGOs could take the case to an administrative court.[47] These remarks should, however, not detract from the importance of the case. While the business-friendly political majority that has governed Sweden from 2006 to 2014 has been quite passive with regard to wilderness protection, the legal developments brought about by the courts open the door to interesting possibilities for environmental organizations seeking to represent the interests of wilderness conservation.

## 6 Concluding remarks

It is not easy to make predictions about the future development of the protection of wilderness in Sweden. The Swedish legal system as a whole has entered a turbulent, and very interesting, phase that has a direct impact on the subject of this book.

This new phase has an ideological component and a component that we can call, in a broad sense, constitutional. The ideological element is

[46] ECJ C-240/09.

[47] Darpö, 'Med lagstiftaren på åskådarplats – Om implementeringen av Århuskonventionen genom rättspraxis', *supra* note 44, at 4.

particularly evident in the attempts by the legislature to protect private property, especially in the case of expropriations. Time will tell whether these attempts have long-lasting consequences or whether they, as seems likely, will be erased by a different parliamentary majority. The constitutional element, however, seems to be more stable in nature. It is not possible, in this context, to discuss these aspects in detail. It suffices to say that that it can be argued that Sweden is leaving behind a system strongly based on the will of the majority expressed in Parliament (the so-called principle of popular sovereignty) and approaching a model more similar to the American 'checks and balances'. Moreover, the strong sense of trust felt by the Swedish public towards the government and the political system as a whole is slowly but steadily declining. This has an immediate impact on the role played by public authorities and courts. The former are rapidly losing their status as sole representatives of the public interest in favour of NGOs, while the latter are entering into a period of unprecedented judicial policymaking,[48] compensating for the passive stance of the legislature, as we saw with regard to the Änok case. Both these factors, and the interactions between them, will play a decisive role in shaping legal protection of wilderness in the years to come.

[48] For a broader discussion of these aspects see F. Valguarnera, 'Judicial Policymaking in Sweden: A Comparative Perspective', in Scandinavian Studies in Law, 61 (2015), 185–216.

# 22

## Wilderness protection in the United Kingdom

SIMON BOYLE AND NICOLA WHEELER*

### 1 Introduction

While the UK has no pristine wilderness, there are areas of undeveloped land, especially in Scotland, that retain wilderness characteristics. In the UK, these areas are usually termed 'wild land' or 'wild areas', and therefore we reference these terms here.[1] Wild land attributes fall within the characteristics of wilderness, as discussed in this book, in their naturalness; absence of infrastructure and modern human society; and relatively large sizes. Such wild lands have high value for wildlife and humans. However, they are being rapidly lost, as wild land in itself receives no specific legal protection. In fact, of the top ten per cent wildest land in Scotland, only half is protected by any form of designation. Therefore, if we wish to retain the UK's wild land, it is essential that we act quickly before it is lost.

The UK (England, Scotland, Wales and Northern Ireland)[2] has a population of approximately 64 million and a total land area of 241,930 square km,[3] equating to a population density of 259.4 per square km.[4] After the last Ice Age approximately 12,000 years ago, the British Isles was primarily covered by heterogeneous woodland comprising thirty-three

* The authors wish to acknowledge the following individuals who contributed to this chapter: Sir Crispin Agnew QC, Jade Cantos, Dr Steve Carver, Ruth Chambers, Ben Christman, Ian Cowan, Johnny Dawes, Jack Ellerby, Vicki Elcoate, Angus Evers, Sheila George, John Hunt, Emma Ireland, Aidan Lonergan, Helen McDade, Angus Middleton, Mel Nicoll, Dr Romola Parish, Anne Robinson, Colin Robertson, Nick Ryden, Professor Adrian Phillips, Kirsty Schneeberger MBE, Stephen Sykes and Sheila Wren.

1 See, for example, Scottish Natural Heritage (SNH), Policy Statement No 02/03, 'Wildness in Scotland's Countryside', www.snh.gov.uk/docs/A150654.pdf, 2002, para. 5 and SNH, 'Core Areas of Wild Land 2013 Map', consultation paper, 2013. www.snh.gov.uk/docs/A1104206.pdf, para. 2.2.

2 The UK does not include the Isle of Man or the Republic of Ireland. The geographical term 'the British Isles' covers the UK, the Isle of Man and the Republic of Ireland.

3 World Bank Open Data, http://data.worldbank.org/.

4 *Ibid.*

tree species. However, once farming began around 5000 BC, wilderness was steadily eroded. This decline accelerated in the eighteenth century as the demand for timber in shipbuilding grew. Consequently, by the end of the nineteenth century, woodland cover in England was less than five per cent.[5] Further losses of woodland occurred during both World Wars, although since World War I (1914–1918) there has been an effort to re-instate the UK's woodland.[6] By the start of the twenty-first century, the estimated woodland cover across England had increased to eight point four per cent.[7] In contrast, woodland in Northern Ireland has decreased by thirteen per cent since the 1960s. Today, Northern Ireland has the lowest total woodland cover and ancient woodland cover in the UK, at just seven per cent and 0.08 per cent of the total land area respectively.[8] Generally, as discussed in Chapter 2, there is an altitudinal effect of wild land, with most areas of this nature being in the Scottish Highlands and Islands. However, a number of low areas with relatively high wilderness qualities, such as Rannoch Moor, exist.

The loss of wild land as an important policy issue has risen recently, due to conifer plantations, agriculture, urbanization, industrialization and power generation.[9] The focus of this chapter will be to discuss the extent to which wilderness areas (in UK terminology, wild lands) are protected by the UK's legal system and to assess policy and legislation. However, first, a brief explanation of the relevance of wilderness in UK society is provided.

## 2 Relevance of wilderness in society

Many rural communities identify strongly with their local environment. Wade Davis wrote that 'landscape defines character' and that 'culture springs from a spirit of place'.[10] This is evident in the Scottish Highlands, where Gaelic is still spoken and an entire genre of Gaelic poems and songs celebrating the land still exist. Recognition of the unique beauty of

[5] Steve Smith, *The National Inventory of Woodland and Trees – England* (Edinburgh: Forestry Commission, 2001), www.forestry.gov.uk/pdf/frnationalinventory0001.pdf /$file/frnationalinventory0001.pdf.

[6] The Forestry Commission was established in 1919.

[7] Smith, *The National Inventory of Woodland and Trees – England, supra* note 5.

[8] See the website of the Woodland Trust, www.woodlandtrust.org.uk/our-story/where-we-work/northern-ireland/.

[9] See Scottish Natural Heritage Policy Statement No 02/03, 'Wildness in Scotland's Countryside', *supra* note 1, paras 19–28.

[10] W. Davis, *The Wayfinders. Why Ancient Wisdom Matters in the Modern World* (Toronto: House of Anansi Press, 2009).

the UK's wild landscapes has long been appreciated by British writers, poets and painters, but is perhaps especially associated with the Romantic Movement of the eighteenth and early nineteenth centuries. Among the most notable champions of wilderness and nature was the poet William Wordsworth (1770–1850). Wordsworth lived most of his life in the English Lake District and many of his poems show his deep affinity with the natural world. The Scottish born John Muir (1838–1914) is widely regarded as the father of the modern environmental movement. In 1892 he was one of the founding members of the Sierra Club (now the largest environmental charity in the US) and its first president. Muir was largely responsible for preventing the development of the Yosemite Valley.[11]

Although the qualities of wild land have historically helped to define a number of cultures across the UK, as society has changed so too has our relationship and appreciation of wild land. From 1945 to 2000 there was an incremental reduction in wild land in Scotland,[12] reflecting prevailing policy, economy and/or technology of the time. The main drivers were hydro-electric developments (from the late 1940s to the early 1960s), afforestation (from 1960s to 1980s), private estate roads and ski developments.[13]

Since 2000, mapping by the Scottish Natural Heritage (hereinafter SNH) demonstrates an increase in land development. In Scotland, there has been a diminution of landscape with no visual human impact from forty-one per cent in 2002 to thirty-one per cent in 2008.[14] An SNH study of 2012 showed that Scotland's built environment had increased from sixty-five per cent in 2008 to seventy-one per cent in 2012.[15] SNH identifies that the most significant cause of this decline is wind farms.[16] The impacts of onshore wind energy developments on natural spaces are physical, as well as visual, including loss of peat lands, clean water sources and flood prevention capability.

There are two main reasons for building the UK's capacity for renewable energy generation. First, the need to reduce greenhouses gas (GHG)

[11] D. Worster, *A Passion for Nature: The Life of John Muir* (Oxford University Press, 2008), pp. 319–331.

[12] SNH Policy Statement 'Wildness in Scotland's Countryside', *supra* note 1, para. 19.

[13] *Ibid.*, paras 19–26.

[14] SNH, Scientific Advisory Committee, 'Natural Heritage Indicators', Section 5, 'Visual influence of built development and land use change'(SAC/2008/10/123), 2008.

[15] SNH, Scientific Advisory Committee, 'Natural Heritage Indicators', September 2013, www.snh.gov.uk/docs/A1064015.pdf.

[16] See Scottish Natural Heritage, Map N – 'Core wild land areas 2013 with search areas of wild land 2002, National Park, NSAs and wind farms', available through http://www.snh.gov.uk/docs/A938299.pdf.

emissions to mitigate the impacts of climate change. Second, to secure the UK's energy supply. Consequently, the UK government has set a target to increase renewable energy generation to fifteen per cent by 2020 (in 2011 three point eight per cent of energy was produced by renewable sources).[17] The Scottish government has set higher targets to produce one hundred per cent of gross annual electricity from renewable sources by 2020.[18]

However, the recent loss of wild areas attributable to onshore wind farms has led to a number of charities and other non-governmental organizations (NGOs) running campaigns to restrict these and other developments. For example, in June 2012 the Mountaineering Council of Scotland (MCofS) launched its manifesto (endorsed by the British Mountaineering Council and others) regarding onshore wind developments, arguing for more stringent controls and bans in wild land.[19]

Unconditional support for any renewable energy scheme without consideration of the wider environmental and social implications is not necessarily always warranted. For example, building a wind farm on peat lands may result in no net saving of carbon because of resulting damage to peat, which is a major UK carbon sink; there is more carbon stored in the UK's peat lands than there is in all of the forests of both the UK and France combined.[20]

As the necessity arises to balance the needs of protecting the UK's natural spaces with demand for renewable energy to prevent climate change, an 'eco-eco battle' has erupted in the UK. As an EU Member State, the UK is obliged to contribute to the EU 20-20-20 target, of reducing carbon emissions by twenty per cent compared with 1990 levels by 2020,[21] and a national eighty per cent reduction by 2050 under the Climate Change

[17] Department of Energy and Climate Change, *UK Energy Roadmap Update 2012* (London: Department of Energy and Climate Change). See also the EU Renewable Energy Directive 2009, The Climate Change (Scotland) Act 2009, NI Planning Policy Statement 18 (Renewable Energy) and 'Strategic Energy Framework for Northern Ireland 2010'.

[18] See Scottish Government, *2020 Routemap for Renewable Energy in Scotland* (Edinburgh: Scottish Government, 2011), www.scotland.gov.uk/Resource/Doc/917/0118802.pdf, at 9: 'We are now committed to generating an equivalent of one hundred per cent of electricity demand from renewable sources by 2020, along with at least eleven per cent renewable heat.'

[19] The Mountaineering Council of Scotland, 'Manifesto on Onshore Wind Farms: Protecting our Mountains – The MCofS manifesto on onshore wind farms', 6 June 2012, www.mcofs.org.uk/lps.asp.

[20] Environment Agency, *Valuing peat lands as a carbon store: Peatscapes, North Pennines*, 2013

[21] European Commission (2014) http://ec.europa.eu/clima/policies/package/index_en.htm.

Act 2008.[22] One of the key reasons such targets are necessary is to minimise the impacts of climate change from damaging natural spaces and species.

Biodiversity in the UK is declining. The State of Nature (2013)[23] measured the well-being of 155 species in the UK and found that numbers had declined by seventy-seven per cent over the last 40 years. Common causes for this decline are identified as the loss or fragmentation of habitat; inappropriate conifer plantations; and agriculture. It is argued that climate change will become increasingly dominant and 'the overall impact is likely to be negative'.[24]

Whilst there is a need to increase renewable energy resources, there is growing awareness that biodiversity should not be disregarded in this cause. However, seeing the matter as one of renewable energy versus wilderness is misunderstanding the real issue of how much energy we need and what should we take, bearing in mind that there are always environmental costs for this energy.

In the UK, there are a number of charities working towards the protection of wild land, for example, the National Trust and John Muir Trust. Such charities have strong public support, with nearly 4 million people paying to be a member of the National Trust in 2013.[25] A poll by Loch Lomond & the Trossachs National Park Authority, the Cairngorms National Park Authority and SNH found that eighty-six per cent of people believe further action is needed to preserve wild land in Scotland.[26]

## 3 Mapping wild lands and wild land policy

### *3.1 Mapping wild land in the UK as a basis for policy making*

#### Mapping and the Wild Land Quality Index

In order to inform and build robust policy and legislation to protect wild land, such areas need to first be identified. In the UK, this has been done

22 Department of Energy and Climate Change, *Reducing the UK's Greenhouse Gas Emissions by eighty per cent by 2050* (London: Department of Energy and Climate Change, 2013), www.gov.uk/government/policies/reducing-the-uk-s-greenhouse-gas-emissions-by-80-by-2050.

23 Royal Society for the Protection of Birds, *The State of Nature* (Bedfordshire: RSPB, 2013), http://www.rspb.org.uk/Images/stateofnature_tcm9–345839.pdf, at 6.

24 *Ibid.*

25 National Trust, *Annual Report 2012/2013* (Wiltshire: National Trust, 2013), www.nationaltrust.org.uk/document-1355802006974/.

26 Elaine Wilson Smith, Jon Crockett and Shirley McCoard, *Public Perception Survey of Wildness in Scotland*, Report for Loch Lomond and The Trossachs National Park Authority, Cairngorms National Park Authority & Scottish Natural Heritage, in Association with Research Now (Edinburgh: MVA Consultancy, 2012), www.snh.gov.uk/docs/A769658.pdf.

through detailed mapping of wild land. The absence of any pristine wilderness makes the mapping of the UK's wild land complex and so, as discussed by Steve Carver in Chapter 2, clear criteria are needed to enable wild land or wilderness maps to be drawn.

Wild land mapping by Carver and his colleagues at Leeds University is based upon the Australian National Wilderness Inventory (NWI) with its four basic spatial attributes to describe wilderness qualities. In the context of UK mapping, this approach, termed the Wild Land Quality Index (WQI), enables 'degrees' of wilderness to be mapped where wilderness is shown as a progressive continuum from the pristine to the urbanized. Such an approach led to the initial Wilderness Quality Index Map in 2002[27] and later the John Muir Trust map 2008.[28]

The national picture the WQI reveals is one of minimal wild land in the south-east of the UK with a gradual increase in wildness spreading north, with the highest levels being in Scotland. However, pockets of wild land are present in some of the National Parks in England and Wales, especially Dartmoor, Exmoor, the Lake District, Snowdonia, the Yorkshire Dales and the Peak District.[29]

### Scottish Natural Heritage: Wilderness maps

Scottish Natural Heritage (SNH) is the Scottish government's statutory advisor on various environmental issues including nature conservation and landscape management. On behalf of SNH, Mark Wrightham and John Mackay (Cyclists' Touring Club [CTC], Scotland) built an initial 'Search Areas for Wild Land' map to identify the most significant and valued areas of wild land in Scotland. SNH then digitized this map to produce the 2002 Search Areas for Wild Land Map[30] and it was included in SNH's 2002 policy statement, Wildness in Scotland's Countryside.

[27] S. Carver, A.J. Evans and S. Fritz, 'Wilderness attribute mapping in the United Kingdom', *International Journal of Wilderness*, 8(1) (2002), 24–29, http://eprints.whiterose.ac.uk /934/1/evansaj7.pdf.

[28] Map 'Wild Land in Britain. Top ten per cent wildest lands', produced by Steve Carver for the John Muir Trust, 2008.

[29] Carver et al., 'Wilderness attribute mapping in the United Kingdom', *supra* note 27.

[30] SNH, 'Search Areas for Wild Land', Map 3 attached to the Scottish Natural Heritage (SNH), Policy Statement No 02/03, 'Wildness in Scotland's Countryside', *supra* note 1. The map is available at www.snh.gov.uk/docs/A1101771.pdf. The SNH document states: 'The map presents 'a preliminary search map for areas of wild land. Its purpose is not to delimit wild land, but to act as a starting point for review of where the main resource of wild land is most likely to be found.'

SNH used this as the basis for its 'Wilderness Continuum Map', which was carried out in three phases. Phase I[31] involved the relative wildness for all of Scotland using four key physical attributes: perceived naturalness; rugged or challenging terrain; remoteness from public roads; and visible lack of built development and other modern artefacts. The resulting map, 'Relative Wildness throughout Scotland', was completed in January 2013. Phase II used the scores of relative wildness identified in Phase I and applied mathematical formula to arrive at a map based on these scores. Phase III used informed judgment, based upon GIS analysis, to provide a map showing the selected wild land areas. This map was published by SNH in April 2013 and is known as the 'Core Areas of Wild Land Map'.[32] There are forty such Core Areas identified on the map. A number of wild land maps A-N were then produced by SNH (see in particular Map N Core Wild Land Areas 2013 with Search Areas of Wild Land 2002, National Parks, NSAs and Wind Farms).[33]

The 'Core Areas of Wild Land Map' was referred to in a consultation draft of the Scottish Planning Policy of April 2013,[34] and in November 2013 SNH published the 'SNH Core Areas of Wild Land 2013 Map Consultation Paper.'[35] The consultation period ran from November to December 2013, with 410 submissions received during this time, of which 300 supported the wild land map. In June 2014 SNH published its 'Wild Land Areas Map'.[36]

Accurate and robust mapping of wild land is an essential prerequisite in protecting wild land. Indeed, a three-stage approach can be seen; mapping wild land; having policy that acknowledges such maps and sets policy objectives towards it; and finally providing statutory protection for wild land.

[31] Based on S.J. Carver, A. Comber, R. McMorran and S. Nutter, 'A GIS model for mapping spatial patterns and distribution of wild land in Scotland', *Landscape and Urban Planning*, 104(3–4) (2012), 395–409.

[32] SNH, 'Core Areas of Wild Land 2013 Map', *supra* note 1.

[33] SNH, 'Wild Land maps prepared for Phase II and III', www.snh.gov.uk/docs/A938299.pdf. See Map N 'Core Wild Land Areas 2013' with 'Search Areas of Wild Land 2002, National Parks, NSAs and Wind Farms'. *supra* note 16.

[34] Scottish Government, 'Scottish Planning Policy. Consultation Draft', April 2013, www.scotland.gov.uk/Resource/0042/00421076.pdf.

[35] SNH Core Areas of Wild Land 2013 Map Consultation Paper, www.snh.gov.uk/docs/A1104206.pdf.

[36] SNH, 'Wild Land Areas', www.snh.gov.uk/docs/A1323225.pdf.

### 3.2 *Wild land protection in UK planning policy*

The extent to which landscape is protected from development is largely a matter of policy set out by the executive and has to be considered separately for England, Scotland, Wales and Northern Ireland.[37] The conflict between economic development and protection of natural landscapes has always been at the heart of planning policy and the balance between these objectives is weighted according to political circumstances.

#### Planning policy in England and Wales

For England, the 'National Planning Policy Framework' (NPPF) was adopted in March 2012 and is the most significant and recent wholesale reworking of English planning policy,[38] led by a 'presumption in favour of sustainable development'.[39] The NPPF feeds into the plans of local councils and must be taken into account in all planning decisions. It expressly states that the presumption cannot override the protection offered by greenbelts and other designations (for example, Sites of Special Scientific Interest). Furthermore, it recognizes the intrinsic value and beauty of the countryside, designated or not. The NPPF makes no reference to wild land.[40]

In Wales there is the 'Planning Policy Wales', adopted in July 2014.[41] The word 'wild' may be found twenty-nine times in the document, but it only refers to 'wildlife' (wild flora and fauna), not to 'wild land'; however, the protection of 'landscape' receives much attention (ninety-seven times mentioned), particularly through Chapter 5 on 'Conserving and Improving Natural Heritage and the Coast'.

This contrasts with planning policy in Scotland. Although there is still no specific legislation protecting wilderness or wild land, in Scotland there have been important policy developments to ensure explicit attention to wild land, due partly to sustained pressure from NGOs and public opinion.

[37] For example, for Scotland under the Scotland Act 1998, the environment is one of the devolved matters.

[38] Department for Communities and Local Government, 'National Planning Policy Framework', March 2012, www.gov.uk/government/uploads/system/uploads/attachment_data/file/6077/2116950.pdf.

[39] *Department for Communities and Local Government, National Planning Policy Framework, 2012 Ibid.*, at 3–4.

[40] *Ibid.*

[41] Welsh Government, 'Planning Policy Wales', July 2014, http://wales.gov.uk/docs/desh/publications/140731planning-policy-wales-edition-7-en.pdf.

### Planning policy in Scotland

The National Planning Policy Guideline 14 (NPPG) on Natural Heritage, adopted in 1999, was the first national planning guide to reference wild land and it provided the first official definition of wild land: 'uninhabited and often relatively inaccessible countryside where the influence of human activity on the character and quality of the environment has been minimal'.[42] The document recognizes the unique character and diversity of the Highlands and Islands, and that its 'mountain and coastal landscapes are valued nationally and internationally for their quality, extensiveness and wild land character'.[43] It also recognized that there should be no or limited development in wild areas and that 'such areas are very sensitive to any form of development or intrusive human activity and planning authorities should take great care to safeguard their wild land character'.[44] This obligation has been worked out by requiring structure plans to 'include policies for protecting and enhancing the character of landscapes of regional importance, including any areas of importance for their wild land character'.[45] Furthermore, 'within the strategic framework established by the structure plan, local plans should: [. . .] include policies for the conservation and/or enhancement of landscape character, including, where appropriate, wild land character'.[46]

In response to the NPPG of 1999, in 2002 Scottish Natural Heritage produced the above-mentioned 'Policy Statement on Wildness in Scotland's Countryside'.[47] This document recognized the importance of wild lands in Scotland and noted how these were under threat, but it was written before the impact of wind farms. It advocated the use of existing designations, such as National Scenic Areas; however, it did not consider it appropriate to have a special designation for wild land.[48]

The NPPG of 1999 was replaced by the Scottish Planning Policy in 2010. Again, the importance and sensitivity of wild lands were recognized, but it made clear that the responsibility to take concrete action lies in the hands of planning authorities:

[42] Scottish Government, *National Planning Policy Guideline 14 (NPPG) on Natural Heritage* (Edinburgh: Scottish Government, 1999), www.scotland.gov.uk/Publications /1999/01/ nppg14, 'glossary of term'.
[43] *Ibid.*, para. 11.
[44] *Ibid.*, para. 16.
[45] *Ibid.*, para. 69.
[46] *Ibid.*, para. 71.
[47] See Scottish Natural Heritage Policy Statement No 02/03, 'Wildness in Scotland's Countryside', *supra* note 1.
[48] *Ibid.*, para. 35.

> The most sensitive landscapes may have little or no capacity to accept new development. Areas of wild land character in some of Scotland's remoter upland, mountain and coastal areas are very sensitive to any form of development or intrusive human activity and planning authorities should safeguard the character of these areas in the development plan.[49]

Following a draft document for consultation that was published in April 2013, on 23 June 2014 'Scotland's Third National Planning Framework' was laid before the Scottish Parliament.[50] The document provides a framework for the long-term development of Scotland as a whole. The overriding objective in NPF3 is:

> To create a more successful country, with opportunities for all of Scotland to flourish, through increasing sustainable economic growth. To achieve this, the Government Economic Strategy aims to share the benefits of growth by encouraging economic activity and investment across all of Scotland's communities, whilst protecting our natural and cultural assets.[51]

Paragraph 4.4 of the document notes that 'Scotland's landscapes are spectacular, contributing to our quality of life, our national identity and the visitor economy. [...] National Scenic Areas and National Parks attract many visitors and reinforce our international image. We also want to continue our strong protection for our wildest landscapes – wild land is a nationally important asset.'[52]

The 'Scottish Planning Policy' sits alongside the National Planning Framework and outlines the Scottish government's policy on nationally important land use. The current version was published in June 2014.[53] It

[49] The Scottish Government, *The Scottish Planning Policy* (Edinburgh: Scottish Government, 2010), www.scotland.gov.uk/Resource/Doc/300760/0093908.pdf, para. 128.

[50] Scottish Government, *Ambition – Opportunity – Place. Scotland's Third National Planning Framework* (Edinburgh: Scottish Government, 2014), www.scotland.gov.uk /Resource/0045/00453683.pdf.

[51] *Ibid.*, para. 1.1.

[52] The draft document for consultation in fact provided more detail that unfortunately was omitted from the final document of June 2014. Paras 2.18 to 2.21 of the draft for consultation dealt specifically with scenic and wild land and included a map showing the two National Parks and the forty National Scenic Areas. Four key points were identified: no wind farms should be developed in the two National Parks or National Scenic Areas. SNH has consistently advised against wind farm developments in wild land and uses the 'search areas for wild land' map to aid decision making; SNH has updated its wild land mapping to identify 'core' areas; and there is no intention to create a wild land statutory designation since it can be protected through existing planning controls.

[53] The Scottish Government, *Scottish Planning Policy* (Edinburgh: Scottish Government, 2014), www.scotland.gov.uk/Resource/0045/00453827.pdf.

echoes the NPF3 by stating that the planning policy should play a vital role in 'creating a more successful country, with opportunities for all of Scotland to flourish, through increasing sustainable economic growth'.[54] The document also includes a section on 'Valuing the Natural Environment' that also pays explicit attention to wild lands:

> Wild land character is displayed in some of Scotland's remoter upland, mountain and coastal areas, which are very sensitive to any form of intrusive human activity and have little or no capacity to accept new development. Plans should identify and safeguard the character of areas of wild land as identified on the 2014 SNH map of wild land areas.[55]

Thus, whilst the policy recognizes the importance of wild land and a connection has now been established between mapping of wild lands and planning policy, the Scottish planning policy continues to take a strong anthropocentric approach and does not ensure firm protection of wild lands. For instance, development in wild lands is not excluded:

> In areas of wild land [. . .] development may be appropriate in some circumstances. Further consideration will be required to demonstrate that any significant effects on the qualities of these areas can be substantially overcome by siting, design or other mitigation.[56]

Whether wind turbines can be built in the two National Parks in Scotland may well depend on the National Park Plan. For example, 'The Loch Lomond and Trossachs National Park Partnership Plan' states that 'large-scale commercial wind turbines are incompatible with the special qualities of the National Park';[57] 'large-scale commercial wind turbines' means 'more than one wind turbine and over 30m in height'.[58] Therefore, single

[54] *Ibid.*, para. 1.

[55] *Ibid.*, para. 200.

[56] *Ibid.*, para. 215. This approach can be contrasted to what was in the draft Planning Policy that was published for consultation in April 2013. Para 218 of that draft document set out areas where wind farms were either not permitted (Group 1) or restricted (Group 2). Group I were to be those 'areas where wind farms will not be acceptable' (National Parks and National Scenic Areas). Group 2 would be 'areas of significant protection', including 'core areas of wild land as shown in the SNH map', alongside World Heritage Sites, Natura 2000 and Ramsar sites, Sites of Special Scientific Interest and National Nature Reserves. However, inclusion in Group 2 would not have imposed a 'blanket restriction on wind farm development'.

[57] Loch Lomond and Trossachs National Park Authority, *National Park Partnership Plan 2012–2017*, www.lochlomond-trossachs.org/images/stories/Looking%20After/PDF/NP%20Plan/NPPPlan2012_final3.pdf, Rural Development Policy 5: Renewable Energy, at 45.

[58] *Ibid.*, at 47 (footnote 1).

turbines of less than 30 metres high could still be built in this National Park.

An additional consideration is the evolution of the Wild Land Areas map, in that as the boundaries of wild land change, it becomes harder to accurately monitor the loss of such areas through development. For example, the final Wild Land Areas map (published 23 June 2014) removed part of the Monadhliath Mountains, owing to the permission granted for the development of the Stronelairg wind farm. As this area now does not lie within an area identified as wild land, as per the 2014 map, any loss of this wild land would be hidden.

## 4 Legislation and wild land protection

While there is no special legal designation of wilderness or wild land in the UK, the law can provide incidental safeguard of wild lands through the protection of protected areas, habitats and species. The designations of protected areas in the UK fall into two main categories. First, those designations which aim to preserve or enhance landscape (Subsection 4.1). Second, designations aimed to protect wildlife and its habitats (Subsection 4.2).

### *4.1 Designated areas to protect landscapes and their relevance for wild lands*

Protected areas will generally have legislative protection although the extent of this protection against development may be fairly limited in the face of economic pressures. The main categories to protect landscape in the UK are listed in Table 1 below.

#### National parks legislation

There are currently fifteen National Parks in the UK, all of which are recognized internationally by the International Union for Conservation of Nature (IUCN) as Category V Protected Landscapes.[59] There are generally stricter planning controls within National Parks and each authority has its own strategic National Park Management Plan and Local Plan identifying planning, economic, social and environmental objectives and policies.

[59] See Nigel Dudley (ed.), *Guidelines for Applying Protected Area Management Categories* (Gland: World Conservation Union/IUCN, 2008), http://cmsdata.iucn.org/downloads/iucn_assignment_1.pdf; Category V relates to Protected Landscape/Seascape.

Table 1 *Landscape designations*

| Designation Type | Legislation | Designating Body | Total Number/ Land Area |
|---|---|---|---|
| National Parks- (England and Wales) | National Parks and Access to the Countryside Act 1949 | Natural England (implementing order by Secretary of State) Natural Resources Wales | 10 England (9.3% of land area) 3 Wales (19.9% of land area) |
| National Parks (Scotland) | National Parks Scotland Act 2000 | Designated by Scottish Ministers (Scottish Statutory Instrument 2002 No 201) | 2 (7.2% of land area of Scotland) |
| Areas of Outstanding Natural Beauty (England) | National Parks and Access to the Countryside Act 1949 | Natural England (under Countryside and Rights of Way Act 2000) | 33 (15% of land area of England) (Plus Wye Valley part England, part Wales) |
| Areas of Outstanding Natural Beauty (Wales) | National Parks and Access to the Countryside Act 1949 | Natural Resources Wales (prior to April 2013: Countryside Council for Wales) | 5 (plus Wye Valley) (4% total land area) |
| National Scenic Areas (Scotland) Note equivalent of AONBs in England | Town and Country Planning (Scotland) Act 1997 (as amended by Planning (Scotland) Act 2006) | Scottish Natural Heritage | 40 (13% of land area of Scotland) |
| AONBs in Northern Ireland | Nature Conservation and Amenity Lands (NI) Order 1985 and the Amenity Lands (NI) Act 1965 | Northern Ireland Environment Agency | 8 |

The National Parks and Access to the Countryside Act 1949[60] was passed to enable and promote public access to natural areas and to increase the preservation of natural beauty. The latter principle was strengthened in 1974 when the National Parks Policy Review Committee recommended that 'where irreconcilable conflicts exist between conservation and public enjoyment, then conservation interest should take priority'.[61] This is now known as the Sandford Principle and plays a key role in protecting National Parks from development. This principle has also been codified in Part III on National Parks of the Environment Act of 1995,[62] which act made amendments to the 1949 Act. However, most English National Parks contain little or no wild land as identified by WQI mapping and many of the UK's wild lands (primarily in mid-Wales and Scotland) are also outside National Parks. So, whilst National Parks legislation plays a vital role in the protection of the natural environment, it was never designed with the objective of protecting wild land and indeed the term 'wild land' does not appear in the legislation.

In Scotland, it was long considered that the landscape did not require the additional protection afforded by National Park status, partly because so much of the country was in a relatively wild state.[63] The National Parks Scotland Act 2000 allowed for the creation of National Parks in Scotland and led to the formations of the Loch Lomond and Trossachs National Park (2002) and the Cairngorms National Park (2003).[64] These both, but particularly Cairngorm, contain substantial areas of wild land.

There are currently no National Parks in Northern Ireland. However, in 2011 the Department of the Environment, Northern Ireland (DOE), published a White Paper on Enabling Legislation for National Parks,[65] followed by a public consultation document looking at governance options and issues with National Park development.[66] The Mourne Mountains, the Causeway Coast and Glens of Antrim, and the

60 National Parks and Access to the Countryside Act 1949, www.legislation.gov.uk/ukpga/Geo6/12-13-14/97.

61 *Report of the National Parks Policy Review Committee 1974* (Sandford report 1974), (London: Department of the Environment, 1974). See also the website of the National Parks of the UK, www.nationalparks.gov.uk/learningabout/whatisanationalpark/aimsandpurposesofnationalparks/sandfordprinciple.

62 Environment Act 1995, Section 62(2), www.legislation.gov.uk/ukpga/1995/25/contents.

63 Scottish Natural Heritage, *A Park System and Scenic Conservation in Scotland*, 1988.

64 Sections 109–125 of NPPF are relevant to National Parks in Scotland

65 Department of Environment, *Consultation Document of Enabling Legislation for National Parks*, August 2011.

66 *Ibid.*

Fermanagh Lakelands have been identified as potential candidate areas for designation. The Mourne Mountains is most likely to be the first national park in Northern Ireland[67] but the proposal has been highly controversial, with many local farmers objecting, and there is no definite timetable to set up a national park.

The fact that land is within a National Park does not mean that it cannot be developed, nor does the designation itself permit public access or ensure that the land is managed so as to conserve its conservation interest. However, large areas of national parks have been designated as Public Open Space and/or are owned by landowners, such as the National Trust, who permit public access.[68]

### Areas of Outstanding Natural Beauty (AONBs) – England, Wales and Northern Ireland

AONBs are regarded as having the same quality of landscape as National Parks.[69] However, unlike National Parks, AONBs do not have their own authorities with special planning controls and this therefore falls to local authorities. Each local planning authority with an AONB must prepare a management plan for it, but there is generally a lack of consistency and cohesion in the management and protection of AONBs.[70] It is only Northern Ireland that has AONBs that contains any real wild land – and principally the Mourne Mountains. This of course is a consequence of Northern Ireland not having any National Parks.

### National Scenic Areas (NSAs) Scotland

NSAs are the Scottish equivalent of AONBs. Originally, this was a non-statutory designation recognized within the Scottish planning system and NSAs were 'identified' by the Countryside Commission for Scotland (SNH's predecessor). The designation was finally put on a statutory footing by the Planning etc. (Scotland) Act 2006,[71] and the forty existing

[67] See www.npapa.org.uk/national-parks-of-northern-ireland.html.

[68] See National Parks (Scotland) Act 2000, Section 1 and Section 9(6).

[69] House of Lords Debate on 3rd April 2008: *Environmental Importance of Areas of Outstanding Natural Beauty*, E. Shepherd, pp. 1–3.

[70] Campaign to Protect Rural England, *Threats to Areas of Outstanding Natural Beauty*, 'A map showing proposed new developments that would be in Areas of Outstanding Natural Beauty across England' (Cheltenham: The countryside Agency 2006, 2011), www.cpre.org.uk/resources/countryside/landscapes/item/2360-threats-to-areas-of-outstanding-natural-beauty.

[71] Planning etc. (Scotland) Act 2006 (asp 17), Section 263A, www.legislation.gov.uk/asp/2006/17/pdfs/asp_20060017_en.pdf.

NSAs were formally designated by the Scottish Ministers in 2010, which together account for thirteen per cent of the land area of Scotland.[72]

A comprehensive review of all NSAs is set out in a SNH report (2010).[73] This report discusses 'special qualities' of NSAs, which are defined in the report as 'the characteristics that, individually or combined, give rise to an area's outstanding scenery'.[74] This definition relates to landscape qualities[75] and is based on the legal criterion of '[o]utstanding scenic value in a national context' in Section 263A of the Planning etc. (Scotland) Act 2006 for designating NSAs. Identification of 'special qualities' is not just based on objective descriptions, but also takes into account perceptions and emotions of people.[76] Consequently, when identifying NSAs there is space to pay attention to the subjective component of wilderness discussed in Chapter 1. This is also explicitly reflected in the SNH report: while wildness is not an explicit criterion for designation as an NSA in the Act, the checklist for making NSA inventories includes as one of the elements: 'Emotional response such as perceptions of remoteness, secrecy, wildness, exhilaration, safety, shelter, etc.'[77] And indeed, many of the descriptions in this report of existing individual NSAs mention wild land or wildness amongst the special qualities of the area.

Some of the NSAs form part of the two Scottish National Parks; however, many others, especially those in the Highlands and Islands, (for example Knoydart, the Cullin Hills and Wester Ross) contain some of the highest quality wild land in the UK. Consequently, for much of Scotland's wild land its NSA designation is the only statutory protection (other than incidental wildlife protection) that it has.

### Open Access Land

The Countryside and Rights of Way Act 2000 (CROW) in England and Wales enables the public to enjoy 'open-air recreation' on Open Access Land without having to keep to paths.[78] Open Access Land is shown on

[72] For a map of all NSAs, see 'Scottish Natural Heritage, National Scenic Areas, 2013', www.snh.gov.uk/docs/B691407.pdf.

[73] Scottish Natural Heritage, *The Special Qualities of the National Scenic Areas*. Commissioned Report No.374 (Inverness: SNH, 2012), www.snh.gov.uk/docs/B695223.pdf.

[74] *Ibid.*

[75] *Ibid.*, subsection 2.1.

[76] Scottish Natural Heritage, *The Special Qualities of the National Scenic Areas, supra* note 73, para. 1.2.

[77] *Ibid.*, para. 2.2.

[78] The Countryside and Rights of Way Act 2000, www.legislation.gov.uk/ukpga/2000/37/contents.

definitive maps that were prepared by the Countryside Council for Wales[79] (now Natural Resources Wales) and by Natural England.[80] The legislation came into effect once the definitive maps had been completed (May 2005 in Wales and 31 October 2005 in England).

The total area of Open Access Land in England is approximately 865,000 hectares, whilst in Wales one-fifth of the total area is Open Access Land.[81] Much Open Access Land is within National Parks and provides additional safeguarding of such areas from development, not least because of public objections to develop on such land. This also applies to Scotland, where people have a 'right to roam', based on the Land Reform (Scotland) Act 2003.[82] The area in England with the greatest extent of wild land is in the Lake District National Park and here Open Access Land covers nearly fifty-five per cent (approximately 500 square miles) of the National Park.[83] The vast majority of wild land within the Lake District National Park is Open Access Land.

### 4.2 *Designated areas to protect wildlife and their relevance for wild lands*

These designations can be divided into two categories; those based on UK and those based on EU legislation. In practice many sites will receive protection under both.[84]

#### UK Derived Legislation: Sites of Special Scientific Interest (SSSI), Areas of Special Scientific Interest (ASSI) and National Nature Reserves (NNRs)

Part III of the National Parks and Access to the Countryside Act 1949 introduced the legal categories of SSSIs, applying to Scotland, England and Wales. These designations were subsequently strengthened by the Wildlife and Countryside Act 1981. In Northern Ireland, the equivalent is

[79] See the website of the Countryside Council for Wales, www.ccgc.gov.uk/enjoying-the-country/open-access-land/open-access-maps.aspx.

[80] For an overview of rights of way maps of 85 authorities in England, see www.rowmaps.com.

[81] See the website of the Countryside Council for Wales, www.ccgc.gov.uk/enjoying-the-country/open-access-land.aspx.

[82] The Land Reform (Scotland) Act 2003, www.legislation.gov.uk/asp/2003/2/pdfs/asp_20030002_en.pdf.

[83] http://www.lakedistrict.gov.uk/visiting/thingstodo/walking/openaccess_and_crow.

[84] Because designated areas to protect wildlife are less important for wild land protection compared to the areas discussed in Subsection 4.1, a separate table is not included.

Areas of Special Scientific Interest (ASSIs). SSSIs provide the building blocks for the protection of nature in the UK and are managed by the owner of the land, subject to the restrictions imposed by the UK regulators. SSSIs are divided into two categories, biological SSSIs and geological SSSIs, and the majority are quite small.

SSSIs which are deemed to have particularly important natural terrestrial/coastal ecology, geology or wildlife, may be additionally designated as National Nature Reserves (NNRs), which provide additional protection. NNRs are managed by Natural England, Scottish Natural Heritage, Natural Resources Wales and Northern Ireland Environment Agency (NIEA)[85] for England, Scotland, Wales and Northern Ireland, respectively. Together these will be referred to in this section as the UK regulators.

Many NNRs are located in National Parks, for example, Loch Lomond (Scotland), Kinder Scout (Peak District, England) and Cwm Idwal (Snowdonia, Wales). Whilst some NNRs are owned by a UK regulator, most are privately owned. The quality of their management therefore depends on the terms of the NNR Agreement and the resources available to the UK regulator. Whilst SSSIs, ASSIs and NNRs are established in order to protect (often rare) species and habitats, they have played an important role in protecting some wild land areas.

### EU-derived legislation on wildlife protection

The Conservation of Wild Birds Directive 2009/47/EC (originally 79/409/EEC) (the 'Birds Directive') and the Habitats Directive (92/43/EEC) (The 'Habitats Directive') are the principal EU Directives that protect wildlife and habitats.[86] The Habitats Directive provides for the creation of Special Areas of Conservation (SACs) and the Birds Directive for Special Protection Areas (SPAs). Together SACs and SPAs form the network of ecological sites known as Natura 2000. These designations are powerful labels in helping to protect these sites, which may additionally be wild land.

The Habitats Directive aims to minimize the damage to natural areas across Europe. It has been of fundamental importance to nature protection in the UK, not least because it allows sites to be protected solely for their ecological value. The directive identifies two types of SAC site (Annex I encompasses habitat types and Annex II species types). In

[85] NNRs in Northern Ireland are defined in Part V of the Nature Conservation and Amenity Lands Order 1985.

[86] See Chapter 8.

accordance with the Bird Directive, SPAs are classified for rare and vulnerable birds (as listed in Annex I) and for regularly occurring migratory species. By 14 September 2011 there were a total of 269 SPAs in the UK.[87]

The directives have been transposed in England, Wales and Scotland by the Conservation (Natural Habitats &c.) Regulations 1994.[88] The directives have proved to be resilient legislation, having been used to prevent many environmentally destructive planning developments from proceeding. The reason it has proved so effective is largely due to the drafting of Article 6 of the Habitat Directive that applies to SACs as well as to SPAs. Some UK lawyers believe that the regime can prevent major developments, as it is often not possible to properly compensate for a lost habitat; for example, an essential feeding ground for migrating birds.[89]

### Natura 2000 and Ecological Networks

Natura 2000 was established by the EU to provide a European network of nature conservation sites; all SPAs and SACs are automatically Natura sites. In 2010, Professor Sir John Lawton's report 'Making Space for Nature' was produced for the Department for Environment Food & Rural Affairs (Defra), which stressed the urgency for resilient ecological networks. Defra adopted this approach in its 2011 'Natural Environment White Paper'. It concluded that to halt the further decline of biodiversity, additional wildlife corridors are required and furthermore that SSSIs and NNRs provide the key 'hubs' for this. In addition, this approach could be linked to biodiversity offsetting, as recommended recently by the Ecosystems Markets Task Force, sponsored by Defra,[90] where developers would be able to offset the ecological loss from the development by creating or improving a wildlife corridor. As the Natura 2000 designations can fall within areas of wild land, Natura 2000 sites can provide significant protection to wild land across the UK.[91] In Scotland there are a total of 392 Natura 2000 sites (239 SACs and 153 SPAs) and many of

[87] Joint Nature Conservation Committee, *Special Protection Areas: UK*, 2013.

[88] See Conservation of Habitats and Species Regs 2010. (The 1994 Regs still apply for Scotland.)

[89] D. Hart, 'Floods, Habitats and People: Wild Law in Action', *Environmental Law & Management* 23 (2011), 3–6. For a judicial assessment of the links between the Birds Directive and the Habitats Directive, see Supreme Court, *Sustainable Shetland* v. *The Scottish Ministers* [2015] UKSC 4 paras 19–20.

[90] See the Defra webpage on the 'Ecosystem Markets Task Force', www.defra.gov.uk/ecosystem-markets/.

[91] See Chapter 8.

these are in wild land areas. Although the purpose of the designation of a Natura site is to protect nature and generally prevent development they do incidentally help to protect wild land areas.[92]

## 5 Practical implementation, supervision and enforcement

### 5.1 *Monadhliath Mountains*

The Monadhliath Mountains, comprising 700 square miles of land to the south-east of Loch Ness, is an example of an area of wild land which is at risk of being developed, as most of this area of wild land lies outside the boundaries of a protected area. Four major wind farms have been built or approved in the Monadhliaths (at Farr, Corriegarth, Dunmaglass and Stronelairg) and a decision is being awaited from the Scottish Government regarding the application for the project at Allt Duine (thirty-one turbines). Despite objections by SNH[93] and several non-governmental organizations,[94] the Highland Council South Planning Committee approved the Stronelairg development, a decision which was upheld on 6 June 2014 by the Scottish Energy Minister, although conceding that the development would have 'a significant impact on the wilderness qualities' of the Monadhliath wild land area.[95] According to the Energy Minister Fergus Ewing,

> [t]he Stronelairg wind farm will create jobs both in its construction, and during its lifetime' and the Minister is also of the view that the project plays 'an important part in helping Scotland reach its target of the equivalent of 100 per cent of electricity demand generated from renewables.[96]

[92] See www.snh.gov.uk/docs/C248050.pdf. See page 18 for map showing Natura 2000 sites in Scotland.

[93] For a summary of SNH's objections, see Ian Bray, 'Objection to Stronelairg windfarm, southeast of Fort Augustus', SNH document SNH/12/11/Info1, 29 October 2012, www.snh.gov.uk/docs/B1164804.pdf.

[94] For the nine reasons why the John Muir Trust has taken legal action against the project, see the news article (no author mentioned) 'Stronelairg – the background to our challenge', *John Muir Trust Journal*, Autumn 2014, www.jmt.org/assets/jmt_journal_aut_14-stronelairg%20update.pdf, at 6.

[95] Scottish Government, 'Consent under s36 of the electricity act 1989 and deemed planning permission under s57(2) of the Town and Country Planning (Scotland) act 1997 for the stronelairg wind powered electricity generating station in the council area of the highlands', 6 June 2014, www.scotland.gov.uk/Resource/0045/00452641.pdf, at 5.

[96] See the webpage on 'decisions on new projects' of the Scottish Government, 'Stronelairg wind farm approved and Newfield wind farm refused' (6 June 2014), www.scotland.gov.uk/Topics/Business-Industry/Energy/Infrastructure/Energy-Consents/Whatsnew.

The John Muir Trust has stated that the area 'is arguably the wildest place in the UK where an industrial wind development has been approved'.[97] The area in question was in the draft Wild Land Areas Map published by SNH; however, the site was excluded from the final map of Wild Land Areas published on 23 June 2014, due to the consented wind farm. The John Muir Trust submitted a Freedom of Information Request to SNH; this response shows that the Scottish government asked SNH to revise this area in the final WLAs map due to Stronelairg so that the area would not be shown as wild land in the final Wild Land Areas map. Stronelairg is currently the largest wind farm ever approved in the Highland Council area, and each of the sixty-seven turbines will be up to 135 metres high. The John Muir Trust made an application for a Judicial Review of the decision and in November 2014 this application was supported by the National Trust for Scotland. The Outer House judgment was given on 4 December 2015, with Lord Jones holding that the Scottish Ministers had acted unreasonably; they did not 'take into account SNH's objection in principle to any windfarm development at Stronelairg, because mitigation was not possible' at para 264 of [2015] CSOH 163, 23 December 2015).

### 5.2 *The Shetland windfarm case*

The tensions between national energy demands and landscape and wildlife protection are also demonstrated in the Scottish case of *Sustainable Shetland* v. *Scottish Ministers.*[98] The case concerns an application for a Judicial Review by Sustainable Shetland against the decision of Scottish Ministers to permit the construction of Viking Windfarm, comprising 103 turbines of 145 metres in height across 50 square miles of central Shetland and disturbing up to 919,310 cubic metres of peat. This area has no protective landscape designation, despite parts of it having wild land character. SNH, the Scottish government's official adviser on the environmental impact of the project, opposed the scheme due to its potential effect on whimbrel and the landscape.[99]

[97] John Muir Trust, 'Stronelairg – the background to our challenge', *supra* note 94.

[98] Supreme Court, *Sustainable Shetland* v. *The Scottish Ministers* [2015] UKSC 4 on appeal from [2014] CSIH 60, P698/12, 9 July 2014, www.bailii.org/scot/cases/ScotCS/2014/2014CSIH60.html.

[99] SNH letter, 'Proposed Viking wind farm, Shetland the electricity works (Environmental Impact Assessment) (Scotland) Regulations 2000)', 24 July 2009, www.scotland.gov.uk/Resource/Doc/917/0084796.pdf.

It had been hoped that some protection against development might have been afforded by the operation of the Birds Directive,[100] as a result of the potential impact on whimbrel, a rare wading bird with ninety-five per cent of the UK population breeding in Shetland. SNH advised that there was a 'high likelihood of a significant adverse effect on the favourable conservation status of whimbrel at a national level' (para 1.7) due to construction disturbance, operational disturbance and collision mortality.[101] Although there are no SPAs on or close to the site, which would provide protection under the Birds Directive, whimbrel are protected under Article 4(2) of the Birds Directive, as a regularly occurring migratory species. In addition, they are listed in Schedule 1 of the Wildlife and Countryside Act 1981.

Despite SNH's objections on landscape and ornithological grounds and the Scottish Ministers' acceptance 'that the proposals would lead to significant changes to the landscape character for a considerable area of Shetland', on 4 April 2012 the Ministers granted the application.[102] In their view, any concerns would be outweighed by the economic benefits to the Shetland Islands. They also accepted that there would be an adverse effect on whimbrel, but concluded this would be 'outweighed by the benefits of the project, including the very substantial renewable energy generation'.[103] Surprisingly, given the issues, the Decision Letter made no reference to the Birds Directive.

The judgment, at first instance in the Outer House, was given by Lady Clark of Calton.[104] She held that she could not comment in relation to landscape issues because it was not within her remit in a Judicial Review to question matters of policy, which were at the discretion of the Scottish Ministers.[105] Whether Lady Clark was correct not to enquire on such policy matters is an important question. Arguably, having ministers with wide and unchallengeable discretionary powers is contrary to the Aarhus

[100] Directive 2009/147/EC of the European Parliament and of the Council of 30 November 2009 on the conservation of wild birds.

[101] SNH letter of 24 July 2009, Annex III.

[102] Scottish Government Decision letter on the 'Application for consent and deemed planning permission for the construction and operation of the Viking wind farm, in Central mainland, Shetland', 4 April 2012, www.scotland.gov.uk/Resource/0039/00391076.pdf.

[103] *Ibid.*, at 10.

[104] Outer House, Court of Session, Opinion of Lady Clark of Calton [2013] CSOH 158.

[105] Para. 217: 'In relation to landscape, the [Scottish Ministers] were entitled to make value judgments about landscape and come to a conclusion that however bad the landscape impact, in their opinion, other considerations and other values outweighed that.'

Convention in failing to provide information, enable public participation or provide access to justice.

In this Outer House decision Sustainable Shetland was more successful in relation to the whimbrel and the application of Article 2 of the Birds Directive. This requires Member States to maintain bird populations at a level corresponding to ecological, scientific and cultural requirements while taking account of 'economic and recreational requirements'.[106] The argument centred on whether this allowed for a balancing exercise between the maintenance of the whimbrel population against economic interests.

Following the opinion of Advocate General Fennelly in the Lappel Bank case,[107] Lady Clark held that Article 2 required a purposive interpretation. She stated that 'it imposes an obligation "to maintain the population of the species" at a level as specified in Article 2 [...] to maintain the population of species or to adapt to the level is the obligation' (para. 265). The judge stated that the Birds Directive was part of the 'essential legal framework' for the Scottish Ministers, who had 'not properly engaged with the Directive in any meaningful way' and she therefore found in favour of Sustainable Shetland on this point.

The case was appealed by the Scottish Ministers to the Inner House. Lord Brodie, who delivered the Opinion, took a much more restricted view of the Court's remit in a judicial review:

> The question which should have been the focus of the Lord Ordinary's attention was whether the grant of consent by the Scottish Ministers had been a lawful decision, once due account was taken of, inter alia, the Wild Birds Directive. Instead, the Lord Ordinary applied herself to the rather different question as to whether the Scottish Ministers, in their decision letter, had demonstrated that they had fully understood and complied with their on-going obligations under the Directive in respect of the United Kingdom population of whimbrel, irrespective of the likely effect on it of a consent to the development.[108]

The Inner House was satisfied that the Ministers had properly exercised their powers and complied with the obligations required by the Birds Directive. They had considered the assessment of SNH but were not bound by these views and were quite entitled to prefer the more positive

[106] David Hart, 'Wind farms, birds, and the rule of law' (Case Commentaries), *Environmental Liability* 21(4) (2013), 154.

[107] *R. v. Secretary of State for Environment exp RSPB* [1996] ECR 1-3805.

[108] Scottish Appeal Court, *Sustainable Shetland .v. Scottish Ministers, supra* note 98, para. 26.

effect of the development on the whimbrel as set out in the Habitats Management Plan prepared by consultants acting for the developer.[109] Nor was there any requirement for the Ministers to specifically refer to the Birds Directive in the Decision letter;[110] it was sufficient for the decision-maker to show that 'in substance' he had complied with his duties. In this case the Ministers had written eight paragraphs on the whimbrel[111] and therefore had paid proper regard to the issue.

Sustainable Shetland appealed against this decision to the Supreme Court. Counsel for Sustainable Shetland, Sir Crispin Agnew QC, argued that whilst the Scottish Ministers had considered the impact of the windfarm on the whimbrel they had failed to consider the impact of the development on their obligations under the Birds Directive, which includes the obligation under Article 2 to 'maintain the population of the species' as well as the requirement under Article 4 to take 'special conservation measures' in order to ensure the survival and reproduction of the species. The Inner House had correctly identified that the Scottish Ministers were required to comply with the obligation of the Birds Directive but had then failed to properly assess whether the Scottish Ministers had in fact discharged those obligations. In particular, the statement made in the Decision Letter that any impact on the whimbrel would be 'outweighed by the benefits of the project, including the very substantial renewable energy generation the development would bring' was wrong in law. Articles 2 and 4 do not permit a balancing exercise that allows economic requirements and/or climate change issues to override the strict obligations set out in those Articles.

In the Supreme Court, Lord Carnwath, who gave the court's judgment, compared the two approaches taken by the Outer House and the Inner House and held 'the Inner House was clearly right' (para 30). The Ministers were not required to establish the 'precise scope of the duties imposed by article 2' but rather 'to determine to grant consent to a particular development proposal, taking account of all material considerations for or against, of which the directive formed part' (para 32). Lord Carnwath acknowledged (para 38) that there was still debate on the relevance of economic factors referred to in Article 2 and that 'the need for a further reference [to the ECJ] may arise in an appropriate case'; however, this was not such a case.

[109] *Ibid.*, para. 28.
[110] *Ibid.*, at para. 29.
[111] Scottish Government Decision Letter, *supra* note 102, at 10–11.

This decision has therefore clarified that the UK courts will take a restricted view on the application of Article 2 of the Birds Directive and probably also of the Habitats Directive, thereby allowing the Executive wide discretion on whether to permit a development.

This means that wildlife legislation is going to do very little, if anything, to prevent the loss of wild land in the UK and so increases the urgency for the need for the statutory protection of wild land in its own right. Lady Clark indicated some sympathy for the landscape argument put forward by Sustainable Shetland that the wind farm would have a deleterious effect on the landscape but she judged that this was purely a policy matter on which the court could not interfere.[112] Under the current regime, without any landscape statutory protection (principally the National Parks legislation) wild land remains in a highly vulnerable position. Given the plight of UK biodiversity generally not only must existing wildlife legislation be properly upheld, but now is the time for the law to change its current focus on components of landscape, such as a species, to the wider view which looks at whole ecosystems. Such a shift of perspective would make an important contribution to the recovery of biodiversity in the UK.

### 5.3 *Recent cases*

There have been a number of recent cases where applications for the development of wind farms on wild land has been refused. These give considerable optimism that the Core Areas map is being taken seriously. The most notable are:

- Beinn Mhor, Glen Affric
  The application was for six turbines by a German developer. The application was refused by the Scottish Government Reporter on 9 July 2015. In his Decision the Reporter made twenty-eight references to wild land and concluded that '[t]he safeguarding of wild land is a significant national objective'.[113]
- Talladh-a-Bheithe, Rannoch Moor
  The proposal was for six turbines by a Netherlands based developer. It was identified that at the date the application was made, the developer had not been incorporated under the Companies Act 2006 and the Scottish Ministers returned the application as not competent.

[112] See at 219: 'that does not mean that I support the decision of the planning authority'.

[113] Directorate for Planning and Environmental Appeals, Decision by R. Hickman, a Reporter appointed by the Scottish Ministers, Planning appeal reference PPA-270-2120, 9 July 2015, www.dpea.scotland.gov.uk/CaseDetails.aspx?id=115638&T=20, para. 148.

- Carn Gorm, near Ben Wyvis
  The application was for a fourteen turbine wind farm near Ben Wyvis in Wild Land Area 29. It was refused by the Scottish Government Reporter on 9 November 2015,[114] following a Public Local Enquiry. As with Beinn Mhor (above) the Decision considered wild land issues in detail: 'Wild land' (paras 54–71) and 'Landscape impacts considered in relation to policy-wild land' (paras 72–87). The Reporter noted his agreement to the comments by the landscape witness for SNH and states: 'if the proposed wind farm were to be constructed, two of the perceptual responses – "sanctuary or solitude" and "arresting/inspiring qualities, sense of awe– prospect" would no longer be present in the vicinity of Little Wyvis and would be adversely affected across parts of the wider Ben Wyvis massif.'

## 6 The future of wilderness protection

The UK's wild lands are at a critical juncture; over the next two decades they can either be saved or lost forever. The authors consider that two complimentary alternatives should receive serious consideration: re-wilding and wild law.

### Re-wilding

Despite many areas of UK wild land having impoverished soils and limited biodiversity, they still have ecological value as they are relatively wild and have vast potential for 're-wilding'.[115] 'Re-wilding' is restoring the ecology of an area with the emphasis of either planting indigenous tree species or letting the land re-wild naturally.[116] This helps to enrich wild land and increases the likelihood of land being given statutory protection. Additionally, vegetation absorbs carbon dioxide and thus provides an alternative to relying on renewable energy to reduce UK carbon emissions.

One such project is the Carrifran Wildwood project (Southern Scotland). The 670 ha valley was afforested through assessing pollen records from 5000 years ago to restore the area to its former natural

[114] Directorate for Planning and Environmental Appeals, Decision by R. W. Maslin, a Reporter appointed by the Scottish Ministers, Planning appeal reference: PPA-270-2117, 9 November 2015, www.dpea.scotland.gov.uk/CaseDetails.aspx?id=115459&T=20, para. 67.

[115] Scottish Natural Heritage Policy Statement No 02/03, 'Wildness in Scotland's Countryside', *supra* note 1, para. 16.

[116] G. Monbiot, *Feral. Searching for Enchantment on the Frontiers of Rewilding* (London: Allen Lane, 2013), pp. 62–89.

state.[117] The Millennium Forest for Scotland initiative and Trees for Life are two other examples of re-wilding projects in the UK.[118] The latter is a charity established in 1989 to restore the Caledonian Pine Forest (originally 2600km$^2$). The long-term aim of the charity is to recreate the Caledonian Forest and re-introduce fauna. To date, Trees for Life has planted a million trees within the Glen Affric area and in 2008 purchased a 4000 hectare estate to implement an afforestation scheme.[119]

Re-wilding initiatives are also being undertaken at a national level. For example, the UK Peatland Carbon Code was introduced by Defra to re-establish peatland across the UK.[120] Peatland acts as a source of drinking water, a wildlife habitat and a setting for recreational activities. In addition, peatland is the UK's largest carbon store; in sequestering carbon, it an important mitigator against global warming. However, when damaged, peatland can gas rapidly[121] and current estimates are that eighty per cent of UK peatland is damaged.[122] Dartmoor and Exmoor have housed the first trials of peatland re-wilding in England, with positive results and additional benefits, including flood mitigation.[123] The RSPB is also carrying out extensive peatland restoration in Caithness.[124]

The UK government's first approved carbon certification scheme was the Woodland Carbon Code (2011).[125] The scheme allows businesses to reduce their carbon footprint by creating woodlands. Presently, the Woodland Carbon Code has enabled the planting of woodland that will, over its lifetime, absorb over 1 million tonnes of carbon dioxide.[126] The hope is that the UK Peatland Carbon Code will deliver similar success and that both codes will be integrated into a wider carbon market.[127]

117 M. Ashmole and P. Ashmole, *The Carrifran Wildwood Story: Ecological Restoration from the Grass Roots* (Ancrum: Borders Forest Trust, 2009), at 9–15.

118 Trees for Life, 'Restoring the Caledonian Forest', www.treesforlife.org.uk/.

119 *Ibid.*

120 Defra, *UK Peatland Carbon Code: A Defra Payment for Ecosystem Service Pilot Project* (London: Defra, 2012).

121 *Ibid.*

122 International Union for the Conservation of Nature, *Commissions of Inquiry on Peatlands* (Gland: IUCN, 2011).

123 Defra, *UK Peatland Carbon Code, supra* note 120.

124 Royal Society for the Protection of Birds, *Bringing the Bogs Back to Life* (Bedfordshire: RSPB, 2012).

125 For more information, see the webpage on the Carbon Code, established by the Forestry Commission, www.forestry.gov.uk/carboncode.

126 See the forest carbon website, www.forestcarbon.co.uk/.

127 Defra, *UK Peatland Carbon Code, supra* note 120.

## Wild law

Re-wilding appears to be promising; however, if legal protection of wild lands in the UK continues to be weak, long-term success of re-wilding projects may not be guaranteed. In thinking about strengthening legal protection of wild lands, the concept of 'Wild Law' could provide inspiration. Wild Law (Earth Jurisprudence) offers an eco-centred legal system. In the US Supreme Court case *Sierra Club* v. *Morton* (1972),[128] Douglas J's judgment drew largely on 'Should Trees Have Standing' by Christopher Stone.[129] Douglas J stated that the wilderness area known as Mineral King Valley, which was under threat of development into a leisure complex, ought to have standing allowing lawyers to 'speak for the valley'. This ultimately led to this area being included within the Sequoia National Park.

Recently, the South African lawyer and writer, Cormac Cullinan, has re-energized this debate in his book *Wild Law*,[130] arguing that the destruction of the natural environment is the result of a systemic failure to recognize man's true relationship with the natural world. Western society has developed to consider *Homo sapiens* as superior to all other species and this has resulted in a profound disconnect with nature and corresponding destructive behaviour.[131]

Wild Law considers wilderness to be essential not only from the perspective of humans, but from that of all species. Much of the language that we have encountered in this chapter would be anachronistic to 'wild lawyers', as these labels reflect the idea of selecting areas for the protection that we consider to be useful or interesting. With the steady reduction in biodiversity, perhaps the time has come to start putting nature first, beyond economic 'imperatives'.[132]

[128] *Sierra Club* v. *Morton*, 405 U.S. 727 (1972), https://supreme.justia.com/cases/federal/us/405/727/case.html.

[129] C.D. Stone, *Should Trees Have Standing? And other essays on law, morals and the environment* (Oxford University Press, 1996).

[130] C. Cullinan, *Wild Law: A Manifesto for Earth Justice*, 2nd Edition (Cambridge: Green Books, 2011).

[131] *Ibid.* See also Chapter 1.

[132] In the Supreme Court case of *Walton* v. *Scottish Ministers* [2012] UKSC 44, Lord Hope, considered the types of environmental cases where private rights had not been obviously disturbed and which might therefore be difficult to pursue through the courts. To illustrate the point he took an example of an osprey whose flight would be disturbed by a windfarm. In such circumstances the osprey and indeed all wild creatures should have their interests protected 'someone has to be allowed to speak up on its behalf.'

## 7 Conclusions

Almost all land in the UK has been affected by man, resulting in no remaining pristine wilderness. However, the UK does still have large areas of wild land that are of great value both for wildlife and for people. In the last decade or so, the loss of wild land and the threat of loosing the remaining wild land has become particularly acute, primarily due to onshore wind farm developments on what little wild land is left from previous exploitations of these areas. As we noted in section 3.1 the protection of wild land involves a three-stage approach: mapping the land, establishing sound policy and implementing legislation specifically designed to protect wild land. In Scotland, with the publication of the Wild Land Areas map this first task has been achieved. On policy, Scotland has made some progress by having national planning policy that refers to wild land – although the wording could be far stronger. The next task is to bring in legislation whose specific purpose is to protect wild land. If this does not happen then, as illustrated by the two cases discussed in Section 4, wild land areas with no statutory protection in the form of National Parks or National Scenic Areas are highly vulnerable to development.

In the UK we are fortunate that we do still have large areas of wild land that help define our national characters. Many of us have taken for granted that such wild areas have always been there and always will be. Unfortunately, they are at great risk of being lost forever, and therefore the time to bring in wild land legislation has become urgent.

# PART IV

# Conclusions

# 23

# Conclusions

## The Role of international, European and national law in protecting European wilderness: many options, good examples, but no guarantees

KEES BASTMEIJER[1]

### 1 Introduction

Within the preceding twenty-two chapters, thirty committed experts have shared comprehensive information and knowledge on the history, geographical distribution, values and legal protection of wilderness in Europe. This chapter aims to further connect all these contributions by summarizing the most important findings, identifying the main similarities and differences between wilderness protection under the various international, European and domestic legal systems, and, more specifically, by providing answers to the central questions of this book.

As a follow-up to the introductory chapter, Section 2 discusses the history of nature conservation and wilderness protection, with a specific focus on the European dimension. Section 3 provides an answer to the first central research question posed by this book: What does 'wilderness' mean in a European context, where may wilderness areas in Europe be found and what values do these areas represent? Next, this chapter proceeds to discuss the second research question and main topic of this book:

> What is the role of international, European and domestic law in protecting wilderness areas and their distinguishing qualities in Europe?

[1] The author would like to thank each of the contributors to this book for their helpful comments on an earlier draft of this chapter and for their rich and comprehensive chapters upon which this concluding chapter draws, as well as Frans Schepers (managing director of Rewilding Europe) for his valuable insights, which were of further assistance in developing this final chapter.

a. To what extent are European wilderness areas subject to protection under international and regional conventions and European law? (Section 4)
b. To what extent are European wilderness areas subject to protection under domestic law? (Section 5)

Based on Part II and Part III of the book and the analyses in Sections 4 and 5, several hurdles for effective legal wilderness protection can be identified (Section 6). Taking into account the threats posed to European wilderness and the lessons and best practice outlined in the preceding chapters, the final section considers whether and how the legal protection of wilderness can be further advanced in Europe (Section 7).

## 2 Wilderness in Europe: a historical perspective

### *2.1 Wilderness as frightening wastelands and a source of food and spirituality*

Clear parallels exist between the general international historical developments in relation to the concept of wilderness, discussed in the introductory chapter, and the specific developments in Europe as discussed in this book. Several authors explain that, prior to the Romantic Period in particular, wild nature was considered by many as a dangerous place, meant to be civilized by mankind. Zdeňka Křenová and Jiří Zicha[2] note that this attitude may not only have been linked to the Judeo-Christian tradition, but was already reflected in the Epic of Gilgamesh,[3] an epic poem from ancient Mesopotamia written over four thousand years ago: 'One aspect addressed in this epic work is the change in our external environment from nature to city, which closely reflects the internal change from a savage to a civilized person.'[4] Steve Carver refers to the perception of wilderness in the 'Age of Discovery' during which time, 'Europeans often bestowed upon them the idea, or at least the perception, of them being ungodly places; the home of wild animals that needed to be tamed and the land made otherwise fruitful.'[5] Carver explains:

[2] The authors refer to T. Sedlacek, *Economics of Good and Evil: The Quest for Economic Meaning from Gilgamesh to Wall Street* (Oxford University Press, 2011), p. 19.
[3] Andrew R. George, *The Epic of Gilgamesh: A New Translation* (London: Penguin Classics, 2000).
[4] Chapter 12.
[5] Chapter 2.

> Maps of this period were often illustrated with dragons and other fanciful creatures suggesting wild and dangerous beasts inhabited the uncharted corners of the world. Some maps contain the Latin phrase 'HC SVNT DRACONES' or 'here be dragons' further indicating that these lands were yet to be civilized.[6]

This resonates clearly with the original meaning of the word wilderness as 'place of wild beasts'.[7] Also Zdeňka Křenová and Jiří Zicha explain that 'the word "wilderness" has been translated into Czech – and, with some minor variations into most Slavic languages – as "divočina" or "pustina", which means a desolate, wild and unpopulated part of the world', and which 'is understood as a dangerous and unfriendly place where large predators and many strange creatures are considered to live'.[8]

However, it is interesting to note that conversely in the ancient Mesopotamian epic of Gilgamesh, the wilderness also received a degree of positive appreciation or admiration.[9] With reference to this epic, David G. Henderson stresses that '[p]eople have always found delight and fear mixed in the inhospitable beauty of the wilderness'.[10] He criticizes the view that there was a 'homogenously damning opinion of wilderness throughout all prior history'.[11] Henderson states: 'Rather I suggest that there is in wilderness much to love, much to fear and some that is lovely in its very fearsomeness. People in all times and places have responded to wilderness with both appreciation and apprehension.'[12]

One aspect of this positive side of wilderness, also forthcoming before the Romantic Period, will have been the important role played by wild nature in providing food for people. This is explicitly reflected in the original meaning of the word *erämaa* in Finland. Kai Kokko and Markku Oksanen explain: '*Erämaa* refers to an uninhabited area for hunting, fishing, berry-picking and, in some regions, burn-beating for cultivation. In short, *erämaa* is a place in which to acquire one's share of nature's bounty.'[13]

6 *Ibid.*

7 See Steve Carver, Chapter 2 and David Graham Henderson, *Wilderness: The History, Significance and Promise of an American Value*, dissertation (College Station: Texas A&M University, 2008), at 8–9.

8 Chapter 12.

9 Henderson, *Wilderness: The History, Significance and Promise of an American Value, supra* note 7, at 4–5.

10 *Ibid.*, at 2.

11 *Ibid.*, at 7.

12 *Ibid.*, at 8.

13 Chapter 14. The authors explain that 'the recent discussion in Finland about wilderness led to harmonization of the classification of Finnish nature protection areas with the

The historic importance of wild nature as a source of food and subsistence is also discussed in other chapters. Zdeňka Křenová and Jiří Zicha explain: 'People were afraid of the wilderness, but for many of them it was the only available refuge in times of war or when they were desperate for food or needed to hide from the authorities.'[14] Furthermore, appreciation of wild nature was also interrelated with spiritual and religious beliefs: 'For centuries, various fairy tales, myths and legends have saved many old religions from becoming extinct and have nurtured feelings and respect for wild nature.'[15]

### 2.2 *Motivations for the first European protected areas*

Despite these positive connotations of wilderness, it is fair to state that until at least the nineteenth century, the dominant view was that wild nature was meant to serve humankind. In many European countries this overarching conviction, alongside the emergence of the legal foundations of sovereignty and private property as well as various practical factors, such as increases in the human population and its demand for natural resources, have resulted in an intensive process of wilderness cultivation. For instance, Simon Boyle and Nicola Wheeler explain that due to a long process of increasing farming and, in particular, a growing demand for timber for shipbuilding in the eighteenth century, 'woodland cover in England was less than five per cent by the end of the nineteenth century.'[16]

However, as Carver explains, certain areas were simply not well suited for human settlement and farming, which is one of the reasons as to why wilderness can still be found in Europe. After identifying the most important remaining wilderness areas in Europe, Carver explains that '[m]uch of these patterns are driven by climate and topography with the most extreme and least readily farmed landscapes appearing the wildest in these maps'.[17] A second important factor that ensured that some parts of the land were not subjected to intensive transformation processes is that – as a consequence of the more positive attitude towards nature that

IUCN Protected Areas Categories System, which emphasizes wilderness as a place free from human influence.'

[14] Chapter 12.

[15] *Ibid.* For a comprehensive discussion on the relationship between human–nature attitudes and religion, see Eric Jorink, *Reading the Book of Nature in the Dutch Golden Age, 1575–1715* (Leiden: Brill, 2010) and Keith Thomas, *Man and the Natural World, Changing Attitudes in England (1500–1800)* (London: Penguin Books, 1984), Chapter VI.

[16] Chapter 22.

[17] *Ibid.*

developed during the nineteenth century[18] – natural areas began to be designated as protected areas across all parts of Europe.

As in other regions of the world, by the turn of the twentieth century it was often influential individuals in society who played an important role in this process. Sergiusz Urban explains for Poland that '[a]t the beginning of the twentieth century, several patriotic landowners transformed parts of their properties into nature reserves, giving the origin and inspiration for further protection of these areas'.[19] Zdeňka Křenová and Jiří Zicha explain that 'artists were [. . .] the first to call for the protection of nature' and that 'only a few fragments of primeval forest survived in the most remote areas or in the domains of enlightened owners, who issued private decrees that they should be protected'.[20] As examples, they mention Žofín and Hojná Voda primeval forests (1838) and the Boubín primeval forest (1858).[21] Richard Caddell explains that the private lease of the Vaika Islands in 1909 by the local lighthouse keeper Artur Toom 'to secure nesting and hatching sites from human intrusion' enabled formal legal protection of these islands as the first natural reserve in Estonia in 1910.[22] In the literature, similar developments have been described with regard to other European countries, in particular during the first decades of the twentieth century.[23]

The discussions in this book illustrate that the first National Parks in the US[24] inspired the establishment of the first (modern) protected areas across Europe. The reasons for designating National Parks were often multiple and included, in particular in the early twentieth century, also nationalistic motives.[25] As explained in Chapter 1, in the US, Australia

[18] See Steve Carver, Chapter 2: 'Only with the Romantic Period in the nineteenth century did Europeans begin to value wilderness as a source of artistic inspiration and spiritual refreshment rather than purely as a source of material resources and of land to be tamed.' See also Chapter 1.

[19] Chapter 18.

[20] Chapter 12.

[21] *Ibid.* The authors refer to M. Šíp. *Boubínský prales: Národní přírodní rezervace a její dějiny*. (Oldenburg: Ed. Sagitta, 2006), at 127 (also available in German).

[22] Chapter 13. The author refers to R. Caddell, 'Nature conservation in Estonia: from Soviet Union to European Union', *Journal of Baltic Studies* 40 (2009), 307–332.

[23] On the important role of inspiring individuals, particularly scientists, for the development of the *zapovednik* system, see Feliks Shtilmark, *History of the Russian Zapovedniks 1895–1999* (Edinburgh: Russian Nature Press, 2003), pp. 10–28.

[24] See Chapters 1, 2 and 3. The establishment of National Parks in the US was also inspired by Americans who had visited Europe. See, e.g., Mark Fisher (Chapter 3), who refers to the visits of the American botanist Harvey Hall to the Swiss National Park.

[25] See, for instance, Bernhard Gissibl, Sabine Hohler and Patrick Kupper, 'Introduction. towards a global history of national parks', in Bernhard Gissibl, Sabine Hohler and Patrick

and other parts of the world, the need to set aside significant tracts of nature to ensure recreational possibilities proved to be one of the central motivations in designating protected areas, particularly in the context of National Parks. In Europe, this motivation has played a role as well. For instance, Kai Kokko and Markku Oksanen explain that parliamentary documentation relating to the first Nature Conservation Act of 1923 in Finland expressly observed that National Parks 'are to be fun and a source of enjoyment for all the friends of free nature, sightseers and artists and all who admire land, air, water and animals'.[26] Meanwhile, in relation to neighbouring Sweden, with reference to a 1907 governmental inquiry entitled 'The measures required to protect nature and natural monuments in our country', Filippo Valguarnera explains that aesthetic considerations (the beauty of untamed nature) and the protection of natural history (e.g., the connections of nature with 'folklore, fables or historical events') constituted further motives for nature protection.[27]

However, in contrast to developments in the US, the setting aside of relatively undisturbed nature for the conduct of scientific research played a more important role in the early policies regarding protected areas in most European countries. As Mark Fisher explains in relation to the establishment of the first National Park in Switzerland: 'Undisturbed nature as a long term, open air laboratory, was [...] at the heart of a speech to the Swiss National Council, given in 1914 by Dr Walter Bissegger in support of the resolution to establish the Swiss National Park.'[28] With regard to Poland, Sergiusz Urban explains that, '[a]fter regaining its independence in 1918, Poland took up the duty of protecting its nature [...], inspired mainly by scientific motivations', an approach that was implemented through the work of the 1919 Temporary State Commission for the Nature Conservation and its successor, the 1926 National Council for

Kupper (eds.), *Civilizing Nature: National Parks in Global Historical Perspective* (New York: Berghahn Books, 2012), pp. 1–26, at 16: 'Imperialism, internationalism and nationalism all provided frameworks and opportunity structures for the global transfer and local appropriation of the national park idea.'

[26] Chapter 14. The citation is from the 'Report of the Legal Affairs and Commerce Committee of Parliament', 1922.

[27] See Chapter 21. Valguarnera refers to the governmental inquiry *Betänkande rörande åtgärder till skydd för vårt lands natur och naturminnesmärke* (1907), at 5–8.

[28] Chapter 3. See also Anna-Katharina Wöbse, who explains that Switzerland, when establishing the first National Park in 1914 'emphasized the scientific rather than the touristic aspect of the national park and restricted public access': Anna-Katharina Wöbse, 'Framing the heritage of mankind. National parks on the international agenda', in Gissibl, Hohler and Kupper (eds.), *Civilizing Nature: National Parks in Global Historical Perspective*, *supra* note 25, pp. 140–156, at 143.

Nature Conservation.[29] According to Filippo Valguarnera scientific research was also one of the important motives for setting aside natural areas in Sweden. In relation to the 1907 governmental inquiry he explains: 'the members of the commission underlined that protecting nature was going to serve the scientific community, allowing the study of plants and animals in an environment untouched by humankind'.[30] Scientific research constituted an even more central motivation for the establishment of the *zapovedniki* in Russia. Feliks Shtilmark quotes Professor Grigory Kozhevnikov from his 1909 report *The necessity of setting up zapovedny areas for protecting Russian nature*: 'For us to have the opportunity of studying nature, we must attempt to preserve the more typical formations in their original inviolability.'[31]

As exemplified by the Swedish sentiments, the relatively strong focus on scientific research brought certain early initiatives in natural area protection in Europe very close to the concept of wilderness protection. Filippo Valguarnera is convinced that this was the intention of the 1907-inquiry:

> The inquiry uses the term '*natur*' but, at least with regard to the proposal of instituting national parks, clearly refers to wilderness. The inquiry discusses the interest of creating large areas where 'natural life is allowed to develop without any cultural interference'.[32]

Similar conclusions may be drawn in relation to certain other early protected area initiatives, such as the first *zapovedniki* in Estonia and Russia and the Swiss National Park.[33] In respect of the latter, Mark Fisher states: 'The first article of the Decree [of 3 April 1914 on the establishment of a Swiss National Park] stated that a Swiss National Park is established in which the entire animal and plant life would be left to its free and natural development, protected from any human influence.'[34]

Despite these early initiatives to protect wilderness, the cultivation of European nature for the benefit of agriculture, industry, transport and

29 Chapter 18.

30 See Chapter 21. Valguarnera refers to the governmental inquiry, *supra* note 27, at 5–8.

31 Shtilmark, *History of the Russian Zapovedniks 1895–1999*, *supra* note 23, at 17. Shtilmark explains that in the early twentieth century – in particular motivated by the over-exploitation of sable – also a second type of *zapovedniki* was advocated and developed, namely 'game *zapovedniki*', in Shtilmark's words 'a very ancient method of restricting the exploitation of nature' (at 22).

32 See Chapter 21. Valguarnera refers to the governmental inquiry, *supra* note 27, at 47.

33 See Chapters 13 and 19.

34 *Ibid.* Fisher refers to Art. 1 of the 'Bundesbeschluss betreffend die Errichtung eines Schweizerischen Nationalparkes im Unterengadin' (BS 4 259), Nationalrat 3, April 1914.

other social and economic interests continued in all parts of Europe. For instance, Agustín García-Ureta explains that at the beginning of the twentieth century, wetlands in Spain were still 'conceived as little more than an indication of poverty, a source of infection (malaria) and an obstacle for the development of extensive agricultural exploitations', and that 'under a 1918 Law (not formally repealed until Water Law 29/1985) many wetlands [. . .] were intensively drained, providing new areas for extensive agriculture'.[35] He also explains that 'there was also an undeclared interest in gaining property titles through wetlands drainage'.[36] Likewise there has been a substantial decrease of wilderness in other parts of Europe since the turn of the twentieth century. For instance, in relation to Norway Ole Kristian Fauchald explains: 'The area of wilderness has been estimated at forty-eight per cent of the total land area of mainland Norway in 1900, thirty-four per cent in 1940, twelve point two per cent in 1988, eleven point seven per cent in 2008 and eleven point six per cent in 2013.'[37]

Even within many of the recent international conventions and other legal instruments for nature conservation in Europe, this concern regarding the continued degradation of nature has been expressly articulated. For instance, the preamble of the Nature Conservation Protocol to the Alpine Convention states: 'aware that, in huge areas, the ways and intensity of using the Alpine territory in recent decades have caused, and will continue to cause if perpetuated, irrecoverable losses of elements of the landscape, biotopes and species worth preserving'.[38]

This brings us to the question as to where wilderness has endured in Europe and what values these areas represent.

## 3 Defining, mapping and valuing wilderness in Europe

### *3.1 Working definition and mapping remaining wilderness in Europe*

As noted in the first two chapters of this book, there has been a rich international debate on the meaning of the term 'wilderness'. Approaches include descriptions of wilderness as a 'real place' with certain tangible or even measurable characteristics, or as a more subjective, imaginary or

[35] Chapter 20.
[36] *Ibid.*
[37] Chapter 17.
[38] Preamble of the Nature Conservation Protocol to the Alpine Convention.

philosophical concept.[39] Although the latter approach is often taken in poetry and literature, the 'real-place approach' is clearly dominant in policy, law and protected areas management, with the definitions prescribed in the US Wilderness Act 1964 and by the IUCN's representing perhaps the best-known examples internationally. More recently, the approach of defining wilderness as a 'real place' has also been embraced by the EU Commission:

> A wilderness is an area governed by natural processes. It is composed of native habitats and species, and large enough for the effective ecological functioning of natural processes. It is unmodified or only slightly modified and without intrusive or extractive human activity, settlements, infrastructure or visual disturbance.[40]

This definition was also adopted as the working definition of wilderness for this book. The three main qualities of wilderness areas identified in the European Commission's Guidelines, which are also clearly recognizable in the internationally prevalent definition of wilderness by the IUCN, have received particular attention throughout this book:

- *Naturalness:* native species and ecosystem and free functioning natural processes;
- *Undevelopedness:* The absence of roads, buildings, bridges, tracks, cables or other proof evidence of the modern human society, as well as a minimum distance from such facilities and development;
- *Relatively large size (scale):* often indicated by means of acres or hectares, the time needed to cross the area, or related to the effective ecological functioning.[41]

This enhanced understanding of the essential characteristics of 'wilderness' also enables a discussion on where the wilderness may still be found in Europe and much work has been done to map remaining areas of wilderness in Europe.[42] The Wildland Research Institute of the

[39] See Chapter 1.
[40] European Commission, 'Guidelines on Wilderness in Natura 2000. Management of terrestrial wilderness and wild areas within the Natura 2000 Network' (hereinafter Guidelines on Wilderness in Natura 2000), Technical Report - 2013 – 069, prepared with the assistance of Alterra, PAN Parks Foundation and Eurosite (Brussels: European Union, 2013), http://ec.europa.eu/environment/nature/natura2000/wilderness/pdf/WildernessGuidelines.pdf, at 10.
[41] To prevent unnecessary complexity, the quality of 'undisturbedness' is not adopted as a separate wilderness quality for the purpose of this book. See Chapter 1, note 165.
[42] See Chapter 2.

University of Leeds has been particularly active in this field and by taking a 'wilderness continuum' approach[43] it is possible to not only map the most pristine areas that remain in Europe, but also natural areas that exhibit a relatively high 'degree' of residual wilderness qualities. The research of this institute shows that there are still a considerable number of areas with relatively advanced wilderness qualities left in Europe. As explained by Steve Carver in Chapter 2, high latitude and high altitude appear to be two important factors as most wilderness areas can be found 'in the Scandinavian countries of Iceland, Norway, Sweden, Finland' and 'in mountainous regions of the Alps, the Pyrenees, the Highlands of Scotland and the Carpathians'.[44] 'One or two locations buck this trend with key lowland and coastal landscapes standing out including the Danube delta, Doñana National Park and the island, lake/forest/bog communities of southern Finland and Estonia.'[45]

In several other chapters of this book, the remaining wilderness areas in Europe have been addressed in greater detail within individual appraisals of the selected countries or regions. For instance, Harald Egerer et al. observe that 'about 225 virgin forests with areas larger than 10 ha have been identified in the Carpathians',[46] with a total surface of more than 300,000 ha.[47] Carver explains that recently a 'European Wilderness Register' has been developed that indicates all remaining wilderness areas in the EEA member countries.[48] He states: 'This provides improved data on wilderness at the level of countries all over Europe, and makes it possible for countries to set their own priorities for maintenance and improvement of wilderness quality within their national territory.'[49] He further considers that '[i]n the long run the wilderness register should give support on prioritizing areas for protection within the Natura 2000 and Emerald networks across Europe.'[50]

43 See Chapters 1 and 2.
44 Chapter 2.
45 *Ibid.*
46 Chapter 10. The authors refer to M. Samec, *The Carpathians 'Existing Instruments and Programmes and a Carpathian Sector Analysis'* (Vienna: United Nations Environment Programme 2002), at 36.
47 Chapter 10. The authors refer to University of Padova, Dept TeSAF, *Report on Current State of Forest Resources in the Carpathians* (Legnaro: University of Padova, 2008), at 13.
48 Chapter 2.
49 *Ibid.*
50 *Ibid.*

### *3.2 A critical review of the working definition in the light of the international, European and domestic legal systems*

#### Countries with 'wilderness' definitions

As the term 'working definition' reflects, the authors have critically compared this definition with the terminology used in the relevant international regime (Part II) and in domestic cultures and legal systems (Part III). These discussions showcase that of all the European countries that have been studied, only a handful explicitly use the term 'wilderness' in domestic law and policy-making: namely Iceland, Finland and Norway.[51] Although the Russian protected area category of *zapovednik* certainly facilitates the strict protection of areas with high wilderness qualities, the term 'wilderness' is nevertheless not used in this context. Austria gets close to explicit 'wilderness legislation' in the Province of Styria through a law establishing the Austrian National Park 'Gesäuse', for which, as Volker Mauerhofer explains, this province 'lists in its annex I all the current six IUCN protected areas categories, including "Wilderness Area".'[52]

Of those countries that explicitly refer to wilderness in law and/or policy, the Icelandic definition appears to connect best with the working definition employed in this book. The 2013 Act on Nature Conservation, that entered into force on 15 November 2015, defines wilderness as 'an area of uninhabited land usually at least 25 km$^2$ in size and at least 5 km away from man-made structures and other evidence of technology, such as power lines, power stations, reservoirs and main roads'.[53] Aðalheiður Jóhannsdóttir explains that naturalness was more explicitly reflected in the definition of the previous act, the 1999 Act Nature Conservation; however, she further observes that under the 2013 act this quality of naturalness is clearly included in the substantive provision on wilderness

[51] For 'mainland Norway', discussions in Chapter 17 show that the term is particularly based in policy and soft-law, but the term is explicitly used in the legislation addressing Spitsbergen/Svalbard. It must be noted that for this book not all European countries have been studied. For instance, Germany has adopted an explicit policy on wilderness as part of its National Biodiversity Strategy, defining wilderness ('Wildnisgebiete') as 'ausreichend große, (weitgehend) unzerschnittene, nutzungsfreie Gebiete, die dazu dienen, einen vom Menschen unbeeinflusst Ablauf natürlicher Prozesse dauerhaft zu gewährleisten.' See Subsection 5.3, and https://www.bfn.de/0311_wildnis.html.

[52] Chapter 11. Volker Mauerhofer refers to: Gesetz vom 12. März 2002 über den Nationalpark Gesäuse (Nationalparkgesetz Gesäuse, Stmk. NPG) Provincial Law Gazette – Landesgesetzblatt (short LGBl.) No. 61/2002.

[53] Chapter 16. The definition is included in Article 5(19) of the 2013 Act on Nature Conservation.

protection – Article 46 of the 2013 Act: 'Large land areas wherein human influences are minimal and where nature can evolve without the pressure from human activities can be formally protected as uninhabited wilderness.'[54]

The Finnish Act on Wilderness Reserves illustrates that, in a rare context in which the term 'wilderness' is used explicitly in the legislation in Europe, it is also important to assess to what extent the legislation ultimately aims to protect the wilderness qualities described above. According to Kai Kokko and Markku Oksanen, the understanding of wilderness (*erämaa*) as 'a place in which to acquire one's share of nature's bounty'[55] has also received explicit recognition in Section 1(1) of the Finnish Wilderness Act, with areas established pursuant to the statute to expressly 'preserve the wilderness character (*erämaaluonne*) of the areas, to safeguard Sámi culture and natural sources of livelihood and to improve multiple use of nature and the prerequisites for such use'.[56] Consequently, the Act does not only relate to the protection of wilderness qualities as described in Chapter 1, it is further concerned with balancing 'the protection of wilderness characteristics with human use of nature as a source of livelihood or based on Sámi culture'.[57] This balancing of interests may well result in the approval of activities that would not be allowed in the strictly protected zones of National Parks or natural reserves.

Ole Kristian Fauchald outlines that in Norway a 'definition of "wilderness" was developed in the 1970s by Statistics Norway for a committee established to propose reforms to the country's nature protection policy'.[58] He explains that wilderness 'applied to areas located more than five kilometres from significant infrastructure', while an exhaustive list of 'types of technical infrastructure' clarified what infrastructure 'would prevent an area from qualifying as "wilderness"'.[59] The definition became a 'decision-making tool for other policy and administrative decisions', and was more recently supplemented by the concept of 'interference-free areas' (*inngrepsfrie områder*), signifying 'areas that are between three and five km ('zone 1') and between one and three km ('zone 2') from

[54] *Ibid.*
[55] Chapter 14 and Subsection 2.1.
[56] *Ibid.* Unofficial translation by the authors.
[57] *Ibid.*
[58] Chapter 17. The author refers to literature in which it is stated that the Norwegian wilderness concept was inspired by the 1964 US Wilderness Act.
[59] *Ibid.* The author refers to Statistics Norway, *Natural Resources and the Environment 2007: Norway* (Oslo, 2008), at 131.

significant technical infrastructure'.[60] Although this terminology connects well with certain wilderness qualities, Fauchald explains that it is unclear as to the thresholds of anthropogenic influence necessary for an ecosystem to cease to qualify as wilderness or as an interference-free area and that such areas still may include permanent infrastructures that are not listed (e.g., private cabins).

### The absence of the term 'wilderness' in most legal systems

The comparison between the working definition of wilderness and the international, regional or domestic legal system proved to be challenging for many authors, since in most systems the term 'wilderness' is completely absent. For instance, Agustín García-Ureta explains that the terms used in Spanish nature conservation law include 'natural patrimony' and 'biodiversity', but not 'wilderness' or 'wild nature'.[61] A similar situation is apparent in most other European countries, even for those in which the concept of wilderness protection has become a topic of intensive public debate. For instance, Zdeňka Křenová and Jiří Zicha state: 'Currently, there is still no official definition of the term "wilderness" in the Czech Republic, despite many discussions on this topic in recent years.'[62] Richard Caddell draws a similar conclusion for Estonia: 'Although Estonia can be generally considered a jurisdiction within which wilderness values have received a strong measure of protection, the notion of "wilderness" itself is paradoxically absent from national legislation.'[63] In fact, even in the language of several European countries, the term 'wilderness' does not exist or is difficult to translate. For instance, Sergiusz Urban explains that for Poland, 'probably closest to the term wilderness is the phrase "wild nature": *dzika przyroda*'.[64]

However, as noted by Cyril Kormos and Harvey Locke, 'a law need not use the word *wilderness* to protect wilderness values. It is the substance, not the form, that matters most'.[65] The discussions in this book reflect this truism in a European context. Although the term 'wilderness' itself is not used in most of the international, regional and domestic law systems that

[60] *Ibid.* The author refers to www.miljødirektoratet.no/no/Tema/Miljoovervakning/Inngrepsfrie-naturomrader-i-Norge-/Hva-er-INON/.

[61] Chapter 20.

[62] Chapter 12.

[63] Chapter 13.

[64] Chapter 18.

[65] See Cyril F. Kormos and Harvey Locke, 'Introduction', in Cyril F. Kormos (ed.), *A Handbook on International Wilderness Law and Policy* (Golden: Fulcrum Publishing 2008), at 23.

were considered in this book, the respective analyses – as summarized in Sections 4 and 5 – nonetheless reveal that natural areas with relatively high wilderness qualities may receive substantial legal protection under existing nature protection law at the European and domestic level.

Coming back to the working definition as used in this book, the discussions in previous chapters give cause to revisit the question considered in the introductory chapter of how 'wild' (and more specifically how large) an area must be to qualify as 'wilderness'. Taking note of the discussions on social values of European wilderness, one could also question whether the social perspective of wilderness should receive explicit recognition in the European wilderness definition.

### How 'wild' should an area be to qualify as 'wilderness'?

In the earlier appraisal of this question in the introductory chapter, it was considered useful to adopt an approach based on a 'wilderness continuum',[66] which, in the words of Nash, comprised 'a spectrum of conditions or environments ranging from the purely wild on the one end to the purely civilized on the other – from the primeval to the paved'.[67] The discussions in the preceding chapters confirm that this is a useful approach for Europe. Most authors emphasize that the term 'pristine wilderness' in a European context would be problematic due to the high level of historical and, indeed, continuing human disturbance of nature throughout Europe. Further factors, notably, the pernicious influences of climate change and the spread of non-native species, might ultimately ensure that no real pristine nature will be left in the continent. While there are good arguments for paying special attention to the relatively few European natural areas that still are close to a state of pristine wilderness, there are many areas that are now considered to be 'wild' but which are in fact restored (secondary) wilderness areas.[68] These areas may well have the values discussed in Chapters 3 to 5 (see Subsection 3.3). If we assume that these values are considered important, it is not helpful to restrict the discussion of the legal protection of wilderness to these few (almost) pristine areas only. Thus, accepting the concept of a spectrum of wilderness:

[66] M. Fisher, S. Carver, Z. Kun, R. McMorran, K. Arrell and G. Mitchell, 'Review of Status and Conservation of Wild Land in Europe', Project commissioned by the Scottish Government (Edinburgh, Scottish Government, 2010), www.scotland.gov.uk/Resource/Doc/1051/0109251.pdf.

[67] See R.F. Nash, *Wilderness & the American Mind* (4th edn.) (New Haven: Yale University Press, 2001), at 6.

[68] See Chapter 3.

- acknowledges that wilderness may be restored and therefore does not consider wilderness as something that will eventually become extinct;
- enables the protection of wilderness qualities and related values for those areas that are not in the highest (most wild) level of the wilderness continuum as well;
- still permits the attribution of stricter legal protection to those areas that are closer to a state of pristine wilderness (e.g., old-growth forests), compared with natural areas in which human influences are more pronounced.

The consequence of this approach is that governments and stakeholders may take different positions in relation to the question of what level of 'wilderness' protection is desirable in law. The discussions by Aðalheiður Jóhannsdóttir illustrate that within a country these views may also develop over time. She explains that the definition of wilderness in the 1999 Act on Nature Conservation of Iceland was revised because it was 'considered unnecessarily strict'[69] and, moreover, 'the highly specific wording of the size requirements precludes some valuable wilderness areas in Iceland – essentially uninhabited areas that are not located in the traditional highlands'.[70]

It should however be noted that 'flexibility' in the constitution of wilderness may also have unintended adverse consequences for wilderness protection: efforts to protect wilderness may be frustrated because more open and flexible definitions of wilderness may be used as arguments for leaving more space for human disturbance in relatively pristine wilderness areas.

## The wilderness quality of 'large size'

Of the three main qualities of wilderness the quality of 'relatively large size' has received the most critical reflections. For instance, in some European countries this quality is not part of the national understanding of what wilderness is. Sergiusz Urban explains, for instance, that in Poland the term 'wild nature' (*dzika przyroda*) 'means natural ecosystems, not affected, or only slightly affected by human civilization (e.g., buildings and roads) – although not necessarily very large in size'.[71] Taking an even more critical view, various authors highlight that

[69] Chapter 16.

[70] *Ibid.* The author explains that insertion of the word 'usually' in the new definition makes it also possible to designate areas as 'wilderness' that are smaller than 25 km$^2$.

[71] Chapter 18.

sometimes relatively small natural areas may score so highly in relation to the other two wilderness qualities that the large size-quality should not prevent these areas from being recognized as wilderness. For instance, Ole Kristian Fauchald states in relation to the distance requirements (related to large size) that form part of the Norwegian understanding of wilderness:

> the definition is based on distance from significant infrastructure. This means that certain important areas that have wilderness characteristics – in particular, virgin and old forests in southern Norway – fall outside the scope of the concept since they do not fulfil the distance criterion.[72]

This discussion connects well with the above discussed revision of the Icelandic definition of wilderness as well as with the discussions by Simon Marsden, who considers Surtsey Island (Southern Iceland) as a genuine 'wilderness', despite its small size.[73] Thus, in the European context, there might be reasons to consider the quality of size as less crucial than the other two wilderness qualities.

Nonetheless, an important contra-argument is that also in Europe the large size of certain natural areas clearly contributes to their 'wildness' as perceived by people. 'Large size' makes wilderness special and scarce, in particular in Europe. Furthermore, the large size is often important in ensuring self-functioning ecosystems and is therefore related to the quality of 'naturalness'. Dropping this wilderness quality from the working definition appears therefore not to be a good idea, also because the 'continuum of wilderness approach' may prevent an overly rigid application of the large size quality.

## Including the social perspective in the European wilderness definition?

The approach of defining wilderness as a 'real place', i.e., a place characterized by certain tangible or measurable qualities, aims to address the often expressed criticism against prospective wilderness legislation that it is merely a subjective or philosophical concept that cannot constitute a discernible foundation for regulating human activities. However, the discussions on the social values of Europe's wilderness in Chapter 4 and Part III chapters beg the question of whether the social values of wilderness should be more explicitly reflected in the definition of wilderness.

[72] Chapter 17.
[73] Chapter 6.

An argument against this approach might be that the definition as such should focus on what constitutes wilderness rather than the values it represents. However, one could also argue that certain social perceptions towards wilderness are in fact 'characteristic qualities' of wilderness, which may determine whether or not an area should be considered a wilderness. Furthermore, Cyril Kormos et al. demonstrate that several jurisdictions outside Europe have included the social aspect in the definition in addition to 'real place' qualities.[74] For instance, the definition in the Wilderness Act of 1987 of New South Wales in Australia includes the phrase: 'the area is capable of providing opportunities for solitude and appropriate self-reliant recreation'.[75] A similar formulation might be added to the European wilderness definition, although one should acknowledge that, as Nicole Bauer explains, 'wilderness' may be perceived and valued differently by people in different countries throughout Europe (and even by those within a single country).[76]

### The working definition as a useful basis for Europe-wide discussions

The definition developed by the European Commission's Guidelines and addressed in this book appears to work well, although the acceptance of the concept of a spectrum (continuum) of wilderness is important, especially in Europe. While the last true wilderness (complying strongly with the components of the working definition) requires special attention and may be subject to stricter protection, the wilderness spectrum approach facilitates recognition of wilderness restoration and the protection of wilderness qualities and related values in areas that do not meet all components of the definition, but are still relatively 'wild'. Furthermore, one should acknowledge that the definition does not aim to exclude humans from wilderness[77] and that people from different European countries (and even within a country) may value the 'real place' wilderness quite differently. It should also be emphasized that in many European countries the term 'wilderness' is not explicitly used. However, as long as people are aware of

[74] See Kormos and Locke, 'Introduction', *supra* note 65, at 21–23 and 33–37.

[75] *Ibid.*, at 33.

[76] The working definition of 'rewilding' used by Rewilding Europe in their Annual Review 2014 (Nijmegen: Ecoprint, 2015, at 3) reflects also the opportunities of rewilding 'for modern society to reconnect with such wilder places for the benefit of all life'.

[77] Kormos and Locke, 'Introduction', *supra* note 65 at 23: Kormos and Locke state: '[. . .] wilderness protected by law is not a place whose reason for being is to exclude people, but rather a formally designated place where only certain human uses are allowed in order to maintain its wild character'.

these issues, the working definition constitutes a valuable basis for productive pan-European comparison and evaluation.

### 3.3 *Values of European wilderness*

The historical perspectives of wilderness in Europe advanced in this volume already reveal numerous values that have been attributed to wilderness. For millennia wild nature may have invoked fear, but it has also been valued as a place to find food and shelter, to connect with the spiritual world and to observe and experience the beauty and power of supernatural spirits and Gods. In more recent times, wilderness has been increasingly valued as a place to escape the busy city life and find spiritual and physical satisfaction. As in other parts of the world, in many European countries these values have been depicted in works of literature and art. Although nature has been an inspiration for scientific research for centuries, the notion of protecting undisturbed nature as a reference point for science became particularly popular since the beginning of the twentieth century.

It is questionable whether certain attitudes towards wilderness have been completely displaced by other attitudes over time. For instance, in the current era, Nicole Bauer concludes that '[i]n general, Europeans are found to have a nature friendly attitude', but that 'reasons for a relatively negative evaluation of wilderness'[78] are still forthcoming. These reasons 'are often either aesthetic reasons or feelings of fear and loss of control, or a perceived loss of familiar landscapes'.[79] Volker Mauerhofer notes that in Austria the German word for wilderness, *Wildnis*, still often carries negative connotations.[80] So, long-entrenched ideas about wilderness continue to colour societal debates. However, in general it is clear that the shift towards a more positive appreciation of wild nature over the last two centuries, as in North America and Australia, also applies to Europe and to some extent even began here. Bauer expects that this trend will continue: 'in Europe we notice indications of a change in the attitudes towards wilderness or wilderness-related phenomena, meaning that we can expect the attitudes towards wilderness to be more positive in the future'.[81]

In view of this trend towards a more positive appreciation of wilderness, combined with the diminution of such areas, we might expect wilderness to represent an increasingly relevant concept in economics,

[78] Chapter 4.
[79] *Ibid.*
[80] Chapter 11.
[81] *Ibid.*

given 'the science of scarcity', which 'is based on the fact that there is less available than people want'.[82] However, Nele Lienhoop and Bernd Hansjürgens consider this to be more nuanced:

> Nature and its services are often public goods in the sense that there is non-rivalry in consumption (if A enjoys wilderness, B's benefits are not reduced) and non-excludability (it is impossible, or very expensive, to exclude a person from enjoying wilderness). [. . .] [I]f markets for these "goods" do not exist, it follows that there is also no (market) mechanism that reflects scarcity.[83]

Hence 'the decline of wilderness areas can be explained economically: there are no markets, scarcity is not made explicit, and people use wilderness areas for free.'[84]

However, Lienhoop and Hansjürgens also convincingly show that 'value that society attaches to wilderness provides an indication of its scarcity' and that 'the foremost role of economics in wilderness protection is to make the values of wilderness' explicit.[85] This may be achieved by economic valuation techniques that make it possible 'to express these values in monetary terms'.[86] Although these techniques are anthropocentric, based on human preferences, an economic valuation of wilderness facilitates consideration of the loss of wilderness values in decision-making processes regarding projects, such as new roads and hydropower installations. 'Economics makes transparent that every decision we take is inevitably connected with opportunity costs: if we choose an option, we lose other options.'[87] This could modify the current 'profit-oriented business perspective' in which economic arguments are only used in favour of 'short-term economic interests, such as logging and hydropower generation'.[88]

Interestingly, economic values of wilderness are not limited to 'use values'. Lienhoop and Hansjürgens consider that in relation to the concept of economic valuation it 'is much broader than is often stated:'[89]

[82] Chapter 5.

[83] *Ibid.* Lienhoop and Hansjürgens refer to, among others, P. Morton, 'Wildland Economics: Theory and Practice', in F. S. McCool, D. N. Cole, W. T. Borrie and J. O'Loughlin (eds.), *Wilderness science in a time of change conference – Volume 2: Wilderness within the context of larger systems* (Missoula: USDA Forest Service – RMRS, 2000), pp. 238–250.

[84] Chapter 5.

[85] *Ibid.*

[86] *Ibid.*

[87] *Ibid.*

[88] *Ibid.*

[89] *Ibid.*

> It does not only include direct values or indirect values for humans (e.g. regulating services provided by wilderness areas), but also 'non-use values' (i.e. values derived from wilderness areas without using these areas directly or indirectly). Such non-use values are those derived from the existence of wilderness areas (existence value), or the benefits provided for other people of the same generation or future generations (altruistic value), or the benefits obtained from the possibility to use wilderness in the future (option value).[90]

Consequently, at least in theory, the shift towards more positive attitudes towards wilderness, increasing social values attributed to wilderness and an advancing knowledge base of its economic values might ensure that wilderness receives more explicit recognition in modern decision-making processes. This is, of course, dependent upon the ability of these systems and the political context to facilitate opportunities for this shift.

In contrast to these strong anthropocentric social and economic considerations towards valuing wilderness, Mark Fisher emphasizes the importance of wilderness for species other than humans. Fisher explains that '[t]he greatest possible dynamic interaction in natural processes comes when the functional or trophic diversity is greatest, when species are present in all trophic levels of a natural system, such as top predators, middle (meso) predators, plant eaters, plants, carrion and detritus feeders'.[91] Accordingly, for Fisher a considerable part of Europe's biodiversity depends heavily upon areas with high wilderness qualities. In discussing this 'wilderness dependency of species in Europe', Fisher notes that the survival of certain species 'has a strong linkage to specific natural processes, while others are only able to survive in areas with sufficient space and access to certain trophic functions of wild nature':[92]

> An example of the first group are those species dependant on the dead and decaying wood that is characteristic of ancient forests, such as lichens, fungi and invertebrates, as well as the forest specialist woodpeckers that prey on those invertebrates and which, along with some owls and bats, find nesting homes in that dead wood. The second group comprise the herbivores and carnivores in need of areas with sufficient home range and with elements of the trophic assemblies that are needed to support them.[93]

[90] *Ibid.*

[91] Chapter 3.

[92] *Ibid.* Fisher refers to Edit Borza and Vlado Vancura, 'Last of the wild: overview of status and monitoring of some wilderness related species in the Natura 2000 network' (Budapest: PAN Parks Foundation/Kenguruprint, 2009; reprinted in 2011), www.europarc.org/uploaded/documents/1271.pdf. See also Chapters 7 and 8.

[93] *Ibid.*

Fisher addresses both groups in more detail, providing several concrete examples of species that have become threatened due to the decrease of wilderness areas in Europe. For instance, in parts of Sweden:

> [t]here is very little deciduous forest older than 30 years [. . .], particularly of aspen (*Populus tremula*) and birch (*Betula spp.)* and this has been accompanied by a gradual, natural overgrowth with spruce, resulting in a decline of the white-backed woodpecker by eighty per cent over the last 20 years, so that it has now become assessed as Critically Endangered.[94]

Meanwhile, in respect of the second group, '[i]nsufficient suitable home range, coupled with persistent illegal killing, predominantly by hunters, has led to the [Brown] bear population of the Central Apennines in Italy being assessed as Critically Endangered'.[95] Arie Trouwborst further observes that, although many populations of large carnivores 'have adapted themselves to a variety of modified landscapes with different levels of human influences', it is also clear that 'all five species of large carnivore seem to prosper most in large, relatively undisturbed and non-fragmented areas'.[96] Moreover '[f]ood, denning and other ecological conditions tend to be favourable in such areas', while '[g]enerally, fewer roads also mean less habitat fragmentation and less traffic mortality', and 'in areas with little human activity, human-carnivore conflict levels – and by extension legal and illegal killing – tend to be low'.[97] Furthermore, Trouwborst states that certain species, such as the wolverine, simply 'like to keep a safe distance between their den sites and human infrastructure such as roads'.[98] Consequently, in Fisher's view, it is no coincidence that 'areas with the highest number of predator species and with intact large carnivore guilds are likely to be indicative of locations for exploring and conserving wilderness qualities'.[99] Fisher also explains that the human-driven extinction of large carnivores in many parts of Europe has resulted in excessive populations of herbivores and ultimately in fewer free-functioning ecosystems

[94] *Ibid.* Fisher refers to Vitryggig hackspett (*Dendrocopos leucotos*) Rödlistan, ArtDatabanken, Sveriges lantbruksuniversitet, www.artfakta.se/Artfaktablad/Dendro copos_Leucotos_100046.pdf.

[95] *Ibid.* Fisher refers to 'Orso bruno marsicano (Ursus arctos ssp. marsicanus)', in *Liste Rosse italiane* (IUCN Comitato Italiano), www.iucn.it/scheda.php?id=539974414.

[96] Chapter 7.

[97] *Ibid.*

[98] *Ibid.* Trouwborst refers to R. May et al., 'Habitat characteristics associated with wolverine den sites in Norwegian multiple-use landscapes', *Journal of Zoology* 287(2012), 195.

[99] Chapter 3.

and species-rich natural areas.[100] Thus, large carnivores need wilderness areas, but wilderness areas also need large carnivores.

Furthermore, the discussions by Fisher show that the group of wilderness-dependant species does not only consist of the well-known mammal predators. For instance, he notes that the Greater Spotted Eagle (*Aquila clanga*) needs 'extensive territories of large wet, deciduous forests in the lowlands that border wetlands, bogs and marshes' during the breeding season.[101] The species 'is very intolerant of permanent human presence in its breeding area or hunting range and consequently birds abandon their territories once people start to live and work nearby'.[102] Due to increased human developments, the species 'has become extinct or almost extinct in Finland, Latvia, Lithuania, Hungary, Romania, so that it is assessed as Vulnerable'.[103]

## 4 The role of international law and EU law in protecting wilderness in Europe

### *4.1 Little attention for wilderness: sustainable development and biodiversity conservation as leading objectives*

The discussions in Part II make clear that neither the selected international and regional conventions nor the EU directives on nature protection explicitly refer to the concept of wilderness. The protection of wilderness as defined herein is not an explicit objective of these conventions and directives, although the protection of virgin forests as an important pillar of the Carpathian Convention may be considered as an exception.

As discussed above, the desire to set aside relatively untouched natural areas for scientific research generated early domestic initiatives in protected area legislation that bore a close resemblance to wilderness protection; however, many of the international and regional nature protection agreements that have been adopted since the Stockholm Declaration of 1972 strongly focus on sustainable development, the conservation of 'biological diversity' and the 'sustainable', 'rational' or 'wise' use of biodiversity. This is also true of the international and regional conventions discussed in Part II. For instance, Article 4 of the Carpathian

[100] *Ibid.*
[101] *Ibid.*
[102] *Ibid.*
[103] *Ibid.* Fisher refers to BirdLife International, *Aquila clanga*, in IUCN Red List of Threatened Species, version 2013.2 (2013), www.iucnredlist.org/details/full/22696027/0.

Convention obliges the Contracting Parties to 'pursue policies aiming at conservation, sustainable use and restoration of biological and landscape diversity throughout the Carpathians'.[104] Volker Mauerhofer, Ewald Galle and Marco Onida characterize the Alpine Convention as 'an international legal instrument for sustainable development', which 'is based on the awareness that environment and development have close interlinkages'.[105] Moreover, while sustainable development is not mentioned in the 1972 World Heritage Convention itself, the ideal has been introduced into its working practices through numerous decisions, declarations and the Operational Guidelines.[106] For instance, in the Budapest Declaration of 2002, the World Heritage Committee recognizes heritage 'as an instrument for the sustainable development of all societies through dialogue and mutual understanding'[107] and states that it will:

> **seek to ensure** an appropriate and equitable balance between conservation, sustainability and development, so that World Heritage properties can be protected through appropriate activities contributing to the social and economic development and the quality of life of our communities.[108]

Likewise, many of the more specific regulations under these legal regimes focus on sustainable development and biodiversity conservation. For instance, the objective of the Tourism Protocol to the Alpine Convention 'is to contribute to sustainable development in the Alpine region [. . .] by encouraging environmentally-friendly tourism through specific measures and recommendations which take the interests of both the local population and tourists into account'.[109] This perspective of balancing interests to encourage sustainable development is even more prominent in the Protocol on Spatial Planning and Sustainable Development to the Alpine Convention:

> aware that protection of the environment, social and cultural promotion and economic development of the Alpine territory are all objectives of

104 Chapter 10.
105 Chapter 9.
106 For an overview of the introduction and development of the sustainability concept into the system of the World Heritage Convention, see the webpage 'World Heritage and Sustainable Development', http://whc.unesco.org/en/sustainabledevelopment.
107 World Heritage Convention, 'Budapest Declaration on World Heritage', Decision of the World Heritage Committee, Document WHC-02/CONF.202/25, Paris, 1 August 2002, http://whc.unesco.org/en/decisions/1217/, para. 1.
108 *Ibid.*, para. 3(c).
109 Art. 1 of the Tourism Protocol to the Alpine Convention.

> equal importance, and that therefore it is necessary to find an appropriate, durable balance among them.[110]

It should be stressed that the ideals of sustainability and biodiversity conservation are extremely important. However, the balancing of interests incumbent in these approaches may render wilderness protection a sensitive issue and too ambitious objective.

In theory, the biodiversity perspective might also result in a tendency to limit nature conservation efforts to the level of preventing specific threatened species and habitat types from becoming extinct, but the authors of Part II show that the ambitions regarding nature protection within the international legal systems appraised nevertheless exceed the level of 'deathbed conservation'.[111] It is true that the EU legislation appears to focus strongly on specific species and habitats; however, to maintain or restore such species and populations to a favourable conservation status and to ensure their effective long-term protection, a broader ecosystem approach is often needed. The international and regional conventions discussed in Part II place more explicit emphasis upon ecosystem protection as an essential condition for biodiversity conservation. Furthermore, several of these conventions also have the objective of protecting other natural values, such as landscape or natural beauty.

This relatively broad scope of protection is particularly clear within the World Heritage Convention. The discussion by Simon Marsden specifies that while natural heritage may play an important role in the conservation of threatened species of animals and plants, it also extends to geological and physiographical formations and 'natural sites or precisely delineated natural areas of outstanding universal value from the point of view of science, conservation or natural beauty'.[112] Similar provisions may be found in the other conventions, such as the Nature Conservation Protocol to the Alpine Convention: 'Alps are one of the largest continual natural spaces in Europe, set apart for its unique beauty, ecological diversity and extremely sensitive ecosystems [. . .].'[113]

110 Preamble of the Spatial Planning and Sustainable Development Protocol to the Alpine Convention.

111 This term characterizes laws that aim to protect species that already have a very poor conservation status. See, for instance, A. Trouwborst, 'Seabird bycatch – deathbed conservation or a precautionary and holistic approach?', *Journal of International Wildlife Law & Policy* 11(4) (2008), 293–333.

112 Art. 2 of the World Heritage Convention; see Chapter 6.

113 Preamble of the Nature Conservation Protocol to the Alpine Convention.

Thus, on the one hand the focus on sustainability and biodiversity is likely to be one of the reasons underpinning the lack of direct attention for the wilderness concept in the selected international and regional legal instruments. On the other hand, this focus has not prevented the systems from being – at least in theory – ambitious in respect of nature protection generally, which may present considerable opportunities for protecting wilderness in Europe.

To fully appreciate these opportunities – the 'legal tools' for European wilderness protection – the authors of Part II studied the legal systems in detail, paying special attention to the three main wilderness qualities as discussed in Chapter 1. The following subsections provide an overview of these outcomes, noting also concrete examples of wilderness protection under these international and EU instruments.

### *4.2 European wilderness protection through international conventions and European law*

The lack of a definition of or direct reference to the term 'wilderness' implies that these regimes do not include a general obligation to designate and protect such areas. One provision of the Carpathian Convention system gets very close, however: while the term wilderness is not used, Article 7(5) specifically seeks to protect 'virgin forests', undisputedly an important category of European wilderness. According to this provision, 'Parties shall pursue policies aiming at designating protected areas in natural, especially virgin forests in sufficient size and number, with the purpose to restrict or adapt their use according to the objectives of conservation to be achieved.'[114] As explained by Harald Egerer et al., this provision has been operationalized in the Protocol on Sustainable Forest Management of 2011, which entered into force in November 2013. The Protocol defines 'virgin forests' as 'natural forests which have not been influenced directly by human activities in their development'[115] and states in Article 10(1):

> Each Party shall take measures in its national territory aimed at identifying and protecting natural, especially virgin forests of the Carpathians, by

[114] Art. 7(5) of the Framework Convention on the Protection and Sustainable Development of the Carpathians (The Carpathian Convention). See Chapter 10.

[115] Art. 7(k) of the Protocol on Sustainable Forest Management to the Framework Convention on the Protection and Sustainable Development of the Carpathians. See Chapter 10.

> establishing Protected Areas in sufficient size and number and implementing other specific measures of protection.[116]

The convention and its protocols also contain several other provisions that connect well with one or more wilderness qualities. For instance, for the quality of 'naturalness' it is relevant to note that Article 4(3) of the Carpathian Convention obliges the Parties to 'pursue policies aiming at the prevention of introduction of alien invasive species and release of genetically modified organisms threatening ecosystems, habitats or species, their control or eradication'.[117] Measures must also be taken to 'improve and ensure continuity and connectivity of natural and semi-natural habitats in the Carpathians'[118] and to ensure the recovery of large carnivores.[119] With regard to the wilderness quality of an absence of permanent facilities and infrastructure, one of the relevant provisions is the obligation to 'promote revitalisation and upgrading of existing tourist, recreational and sport infrastructure objects rather than the construction of new ones in the Carpathians'.[120]

The Alpine Convention system also pays attention to the protection of forests with a high degree of naturalness. Volker Mauerhofer, Ewald Galle and Marco Onida explain that the Mountain Forest Protocol to the Alpine Convention does not use terms like 'old-growth', 'pristine' or 'virgin', but that emphasis is put on the degree of naturalness of the forest ecosystem: Article 10(1) on 'Natural forest reserves', states:

> The Contracting Parties undertake to mark off natural forest reserves in a sufficient number and size, and also to keep them in a way that protects their natural dynamics for the purpose of research, with the intention of generally suspending any form of exploitation or to adapt it to the purposes of the reserve. The areas are to be selected so as to obtain a representative sample of, if possible, all the mountain forest ecosystems.

Mauerhofer, Galle and Onida explain that the other Protocols to the Alpine Convention also contain obligations to protect Alpine areas. Although the wilderness concept has received little explicit attention, the authors clearly show that many prohibitions and obligations in the protocols to protect certain Alpine areas are highly compatible with one

116 *Ibid.*, Art. 10(1). See Chapter 10.

117 See Chapter 10.

118 Art. 9(1) of the Protocol on Conservation and Sustainable Use of Biological and Landscape Diversity to the Carpathian Convention.

119 *Ibid.*, Art. 12(2).

120 Art. 16(6) of the Protocol on Sustainable Tourism to the Carpathian Convention. See Chapter 10.

or two of the main components of wilderness as described in Chapter 1. For instance, as far as the 'naturalness' is concerned, Article 11(3) of the Nature Conservation Protocol to the Alpine Convention obliges the Parties to protect areas to safeguard undisturbed ecological processes:

> They shall set aside areas of respect and tranquillity that ensure giving priority to the wild animal and plant species over other interests. They shall ensure that, in these areas, there is the peace necessary for the ecological process typical of the species to take place undisturbed, and shall reduce or prohibit any form of use incompatible with the ecological processes of these areas.[121]

Particularly relevant for the second main wilderness quality – the absence of permanent proof of modern society (e.g., buildings and roads) – is Article 9 (4) of the Spatial Planning and Sustainable Development Protocol under the Alpine Convention. This provision requires that 'spatial and sustainable development plans and/or programmes include' [. . .] 'delimiting of tranquil areas and areas in which construction of buildings and infrastructures is restrained or prohibited, as are other damaging activities'.[122] The authors explain that most of the other Protocols also contain obligations that may directly result in protection of this wilderness quality in certain areas. For instance, the Parties are obliged to 'undertake, in accordance with their laws and ecological criteria, to establish designated quiet areas where no tourist facilities will be developed' (Article 10 of the Tourism Protocol).

Besides these protected area provisions, the Alpine Convention also contains concrete obligations or prohibitions that are more generally applicable and are relevant for protecting wilderness. For instance, the authors explain that the Nature Conservation Protocol under the Alpine Convention 'contains some very specific obligations and prohibitions that directly promote "naturalness"',[123] such as the obligation for Parties 'to implement a fishing and hunting ban for specific animal species (Art. 15), ensure the recovery of endemic species (Art. 16) and prevent the settlement of animal and plant species which do not belong to the natural habitat (Art. 17)'.[124] Furthermore, Article 13(2) of the Protocol on Soil Conservation obliges the Parties to ensure that 'forest shall be used and maintained in such a way that soil erosion and harmful soil compaction are avoided'.

121 Art. 11(3) of the Nature Conservation Protocol. See Chapter 9.
122 See Chapter 9.
123 *Ibid.*
124 *Ibid.*

Article 15(2) of the Tourism Protocol to the Alpine Convention is particularly relevant for the wilderness quality of the absence of permanent proof of modern society: 'The Contracting Parties undertake to limit as much as possible, and if necessary prohibit, sporting activities using motorised vehicles outside areas designated by competent bodies.'[125] This provision mirrors the off-road driving prohibition in Icelandic legislation.[126] The same protocol contains also an interesting example of an obligation that enables wilderness restoration, again particularly relevant for the second wilderness quality. Article 12(2) states: 'Both new authorisations to operate ski lifts and concessions will be subject to disused ski lifts being dismantled and removed, and areas no longer in use being returned to nature, giving priority to plant species native to the area.'

In respect of the World Heritage Convention, Simon Marsden also concludes that the three identified main wilderness qualities connect well with several important components of the convention: 'The definitions of OUV, the natural properties and the criteria for listing them are, as will be seen below, similar to the definitions of the wilderness qualities canvassed in the Introduction of this book.'[127] The author explains that the wilderness quality of 'naturalness' is reflected in several criteria for listing a natural site as a world heritage site, such as the criterion of 'outstanding examples representing significant on-going ecological and biological processes in the evolution and development of terrestrial, fresh water, coastal and marine ecosystems and communities of plants and animals'.[128] As far as the second wilderness quality is concerned, Marsden explains that the presence of modern permanent facilities and infrastructure may well make it impossible to prove the 'outstanding universal value' of a natural site or to demonstrate its 'wholeness and intactness' (as requirements of integrity).[129]

Likewise, the World Heritage Operational Guidelines explicitly provide that a natural site does not have to be pristine to qualify as world heritage: 'For all properties nominated under criteria (vii) - (x), biophysical processes and landform features should be relatively intact. However, it is recognized that no area is totally pristine and that all natural areas are in a dynamic state, and to some extent involve contact with people.'[130] This approach accords with defining and mapping

[125] *Ibid.*
[126] See Art. 17(1) of the Icelandic Act on Nature Conservation 1999 and Chapter 16.
[127] Chapter 6.
[128] *Ibid.*
[129] *Ibid.*
[130] *Ibid.* Marsden refers to para. 90 of the World Heritage Operational Guidelines.

wilderness on the basis of a continuum approach. Furthermore, similarly to the wilderness concept, the Operational Guidelines also explicitly accept that '[h]uman activities, including those of traditional societies and local communities, often occur in natural areas' and that '[t]hese activities may be consistent with the Outstanding Universal Value of the area where they are ecologically sustainable'.[131]

Marsden explains that the third wilderness quality of 'relatively large size' has been addressed specifically as a component of 'integrity': 'Any property listed under the Convention must be of "adequate size" because integrity is a crucial determinant of OUV.'[132]

Thus, the three main qualities of wilderness areas connect well with criteria for determining Outstanding Universal Values under the WHC. This does not in itself oblige the Contracting Parties to designate wilderness areas as heritage sites; however, the convention certainly provides the option to do so. Marsden explains that Australia has taken this approach towards the Tasmanian Wilderness and Heard Island, while also in Europe the WHC has been applied to protect a number of important wildernesses. Among nearly forty European natural WHC sites, there are several areas exhibiting relatively high wilderness qualities, such as the Białowieża Forest (Poland and Belarus), the Virgin Komi forests (Russia), Teide National Parks (Spain) and Pirin National Park (Bulgaria).[133] However, Marsden also stresses that in implementing the WHC, 'natural properties [are] under-represented' and that 'within this category marine and Arctic properties are currently also very limited',[134] which underlines the potential of the WHC to play an even greater role in wilderness protection in Europe.

Compared to the above discussed conventions, the Bern Convention and the EU Birds directive and Habitats directive are characterized by a far stronger focus on the protection of wild species of plants and animals and natural habitats. Arie Trouwborst explains that wilderness protection is not part of the aims of the Bern Convention aims and is not 'addressed in so many words in any of the other provisions of the Convention';[135] however, his discussions show that it may play a role in protecting wilderness in Europe. For instance, he explains that for both pillars of the

[131] *Ibid.*
[132] *Ibid.* Marsden refers to examples in paras 92–95 of the World Heritage Operational Guidelines.
[133] *Ibid.*
[134] *Ibid.*
[135] Chapter 7.

convention – the species protection provisions and the provisions on habitat protection – those species listed in the appendices require special attention and that Appendix II in particular may 'include many species that appear to be associated with, or even dependent on, areas with wilderness qualities'.[136] Besides large carnivores (see Subsection 3.3),[137] Trouwborst refers to the 'black stork (*Ciconia nigra*), white-tailed eagle (*Haliaeetus albicilla*), bearded vulture (*Gypaetus barbatus*), gyrfalcon (*Falco rusticolus*), capercaillie (*Tetrao urogallus*), European bison (*Bison bonasus*), [and the] Eurasian beaver (*Castor fiber*)'.[138] According to Trouwborst, achieving the conservation of such species at 'levels corresponding to ecological requirements' [Art. 2] 'will entail the protection of large, undisturbed areas'.[139] Consequently, he concludes that:

> a faithful implementation of the Bern Convention by its contracting parties is likely to further the protection of wilderness (qualities), as a consequence of the close links between the latter and a number of species and habitats protected under the Convention.

Similar conclusions were drawn in relation to the EU Natura 2000 regime. The criteria for the selection of Natura 2000 sites do not refer to the concept of wilderness and wilderness protection is not an explicit aim of the Natura 2000 regime; however, Article 6 of the Habitats Directive may result in strict legal protection of wilderness qualities if such qualities are important for maintaining or restoring the favourable conservation status of Natura 2000 species and habitat types. The European Commission has also been shown to be receptive to wilderness approaches to Natura 2000 sites, which may result in more space for linking biodiversity conservation and wilderness protection. Furthermore, as noted in Chapter 8, the EU directives explicitly allow Member States to adopt stricter approaches than required under the directives, which is illustrated by the ECJ case on the Italian prohibition of wind turbines in Natura 2000 sites.

136 *Ibid.*

137 *Ibid.* Trouwborst explains that the brown bear, wolf, wolverine and Iberian (or pardel) lynx are listed in Appendix II of the convention, while the Eurasian lynx is listed in Appendix III.

138 *Ibid.* Trouwborst refers to the European Commission's *Guidelines on Wilderness in Natura 2000, supra* note 40, at 88–91, which lists these species as species with 'wilderness values'. See also Chapter 8.

139 Chapter 7.

### 4.3 *Examples of wilderness protection under the conventions and EU directives*

Although not an exhaustive account, the examples of implementation and practical use of the selected conventions and EU directives clearly illustrate their value for wilderness protection in Europe. In relation to the Carpathian Convention, Harald Egerer et al. show that specific transboundary projects, such as the BioREGIO Carpathians Project, facilitate a clear interpretation and implementation of the provisions of the Convention. The authors explain that this project, even if wilderness protection was not an explicit aim, resulted in several concrete recommendations with a high 'wilderness-relevance'.[140] The recommendation to '[i]dentify and protect all near-natural, old growth and virgin forests', to '[e]stablish non-intervention zones in all large forest protected areas', to '[m]aintain different structural elements in forests: deadwood, hollow trees, microhabitats, rare tree species', to '[a]dopt non-intervention management for alpine and remote subalpine grasslands', and – for wetlands – to '[a]dopt passive (minimal intervention) management for suitable sites (e.g., wetland forests, raised bogs, swamps)', are among the important examples.[141]

Using examples from the southern hemisphere, Simon Marsden illustrates the role of the World Heritage Convention 'in the protection of wilderness'.[142] In relation to the Tasmanian Wilderness, he discusses *Commonwealth* v. *Tasmania*, a 1983 Australian High Court case that 'prevented the completion of a hydro-electric dam' based on the judgment that Articles 4 and 5 of the Convention 'imposed an international obligation on Australia to take appropriate measures to preserve the World Heritage Area'.[143] The two European examples discussed by Marsden – Surtsey (Iceland) and Svalbard (Norway) – indicate that the convention may play a similar role in wilderness protection in Europe.[144]

The discussions by Mauerhofer, Galle and Onida show that the more specific regulations of the Protocols under the Alpine Convention in particular have the potential to protect wilderness areas from large infrastructure developments and that clear examples of this application

[140] Chapter 10.

[141] *Ibid.*, Recommendations F1, F2 and F3, G1 and W1.

[142] Chapter 6.

[143] *Ibid.* Marsden refers to *Commonwealth of Australia and Another v State of Tasmania and Others* (Judgment of 1 July 1983, 68 ILR 266, and T.C. Atherton and T. Atherton, 'The power and the glory: national sovereignty and the World Heritage Convention', *Australian Law Journal*, 69 (1995), 631.

[144] *Ibid.*

exist.[145] For instance, in Austria, in 2004 'the independent Environmental Senate (Umweltsenat) based its refusal to authorize the expansion of a skiing area on Article 14(1) of the Protocol on Soil Conservation' because the project 'could significantly affect highly dynamic, natural alpine slopes'.[146] The authors note that this 'opinion of the Environmental Senate was subsequently confirmed by the Administrative Court of Austria'.[147]

### *4.4 Protection of European wilderness under international and EU law: many options, good examples but no guarantees*

To what extent are European wilderness areas the subject of protection under international and regional conventions and European law? It is clear that wilderness protection is not an explicit aim of the conventions and EU directives discussed above; nevertheless, these evaluations show that they contain various legal tools that may be used to protect or restore wilderness in Europe. Of these, the most powerful relate to area protection; however, species protection provisions and other general obligations and prohibitions may also result in the protection of one or more of the main wilderness qualities. Concrete examples of the application of these tools further illustrate that these are not merely theoretical options: there are examples of their actual use, resulting in the protection of some of Europe's most impressive wildernesses.

Notwithstanding these examples of 'best practice', it must be concluded that none of the legal instruments provide real guarantees that wilderness in Europe will actually be protected at the macro level. Since wilderness protection is not an explicit objective of these instruments, these tools are merely 'options' and their actual use in a wilderness context is heavily dependent upon awareness and political will. Furthermore, *if* governments decide to actually apply these mechanisms, there is no guarantee that they will specifically address all of the main wilderness qualities under these auspices. The central lesson from these case-studies is that, while many of these instruments are of particular relevance for one wilderness quality, if they only serve to address a single quality the wilderness character of an area may still be compromised.

This raises the important question of whether the Contracting Parties and institutional bodies of the systems are aware of the wilderness

[145] Chapter 9.
[146] *Ibid.* The authors refer to Decision US 6B/2003/8-57 *(Case Mutterer Alm)*, 22 March 2004.
[147] *Ibid.* The authors refer to VwGH 8 June 2005, 2004/03/0116.

concept and the values represented by it, and whether they might adopt an explicit policy to protect and restore wilderness in Europe. Without such a commitment, wilderness protection under these systems will mainly be coincidental and therefore unlikely to be comprehensive. As wilderness protection is not an explicit aim of these systems, their willingness to adopt clear wilderness policies will depend upon persuading such bodies that wilderness conservation has a clear resonance for the discharge of their respective mandates.

The European Commission has paid substantial attention to the question of how the implementation of Natura 2000 may dovetail with wilderness protection.[148] Elsewhere, however, there has been little discussion of the correlation between wilderness protection and the overarching aims of other regimes. In part this may be caused by a lack of awareness, but may also be indicative that multilateral actors are concerned about socio-economic tensions. For instance, in relation to the Alpine Convention, Mauerhofer, Galle and Onida explain that the serious social and economic challenges in those areas with greatest wilderness potential are likely to make an explicit wilderness policy difficult to accept. Simon Marsden observes that wilderness is gaining increasing importance for the World Heritage Convention: 'Wilderness protection has become more important over the history of the Convention given the decrease in the number, size and integrity of wilderness areas globally, and its prioritized objective to represent the range of outstanding natural areas worldwide.'[149] However, also under this system, no explicit wilderness policy has yet been developed. This also applies to the Carpathian and Bern Conventions. For the latter, Trouwborst concludes that '[c]lear potential [. . .] exists for cross-fertilization between the Convention's objectives and obligations on the one hand, and the protection of wilderness on the other hand', but that a 'further clarification of the relationship between the Bern Convention and wilderness protection is clearly desirable'.[150] For this purpose, the author advocates 'the development and adoption of a Standing Committee Recommendation, containing express guidance on the role of the conservation and restoration of "naturalness" and other wilderness (qualities) in the implementation of the Convention by its contracting parties'.[151]

148 Chapter 8.
149 Chapter 6.
150 Chapter 7.
151 *Ibid.*

## 5 The role of domestic law in protecting wilderness in Europe

### *5.1 Little attention for wilderness: sustainable development and biodiversity conservation as leading objectives*

The discussions in the chapters in Part III make clear that few countries have developed explicit laws and policies to protect wilderness. In part this may be explained by the limited attention to the wilderness concept in international and EU law discussed above:[152] the implementation of these standards does not automatically require explicit attention to wilderness values in domestic law and policy. Furthermore, the discussions in Part III give the impression that the relatively strong focus of EU standards in particular has facilitated a strong impulse for Member States to shift regulatory attention from a broader concept of nature protection towards more specific components of biodiversity and their sustainable use. As discussed above and in Chapter 8, the EU directives are particularly characterized by a strong focus on specific (and mostly listed) species and habitat types.

For instance, Zdeňka Křenová and Jiří Zicha state that '[i]n 2005, shortly after the accession of the Republic to the European Union, the government adopted a National Biodiversity Strategy' and the authors explain that neither this policy document, nor its later amendments 'deal directly with the term "wilderness" or "wild nature", its conservation or restoration'.[153] Sergiusz Urban explains that in Poland nature protection policy also focuses strongly on biodiversity conservation and the sustainable or rational use of biodiversity, which 'appears to be the effect of the strong influence of international and European nature conservation law on Polish domestic policy and law making'.[154] Kai Kokko and Markku Oksanen conclude that also in Finland 'the emphasis has been less specifically on wilderness conservation (*erämaasuojelu*) and more on the promotion and conservation of biodiversity and its sustainable utilization'.[155]

Despite the lack of explicit attention to the wilderness concept in most European countries, the discussions in Part III show that the domestic legal systems nevertheless provide many tools to protect European areas exhibiting relatively high wilderness qualities. The following subsections provide an overview of these mechanisms and an indication of their actual value in facilitating wilderness protection.

[152] See Subsection 4.1.
[153] Chapter 12.
[154] Chapter 18.
[155] Chapter 14.

### 5.2 *The role of constitutions and general environmental law in protecting wilderness*

Constitutions and the general environmental laws of the selected countries do not explicitly refer to wilderness, but some of the components of these laws may still be relevant to wilderness protection. For instance, the Polish legislature 'establishes the duty for the public authorities to protect the environment (Art. 74(2)) and to prevent the degradation of the environment (Art. 68(4))', and to 'pursue policies ensuring the ecological security of current and future generations (Art. 74(1))'.[156] Article 9(1) of the 1993 Constitution of the Russian Federation (*Konstitutsiia Rossiiskoi Federatsii*) states that '[l]and and other natural resources shall be utilised and protected in the Russian Federation as the basis of life and activity of the people living in the corresponding territories'.[157] For Iceland, Aðalheiður Jóhannsdóttir refers to the potential functions of overarching environmental principles (e.g., the precautionary principle) that have been codified in Articles 8–11of the Icelandic Act on Nature Conservation 2013: 'Although these environmental principles are rather general, they should nonetheless enhance environmental decision making and, as such, could contribute to the conservation of wilderness qualities.'[158]

Some of these more general provisions of environmental law correlate more explicitly with one or more of the main wilderness qualities. For instance, Article 4(2) of the Russian Federal Law 'On protection of the environment' provides: 'The following shall be subject to priority protection: the natural ecological systems, natural landscapes and natural complexes which have not been exposed to man-made effects.'[159] Agustín García-Ureta explains that the Spanish 'Criminal Code punishes a series of activities affecting "the balance of the natural systems", thus reflecting the importance of at least one wilderness quality, i.e., that of relatively intact natural processes.'[160] Meanwhile, the 'husbandry rules' in relation to land and water, as laid down in the Swedish Environmental

[156] *Ibid.* See also Section 20 of the Constitution of Finland, 731/1999, 11 June 1999: 'Nature and its biodiversity, the environment and the national heritage are the responsibility of everyone. [. . .].'

[157] Chapter 19. The authors refer to the Constitution of The Russian Federation (Konstitutsiia Rossiiskoi Federatsii), Art. 9(1) as well as to Art. 58: 'Everyone shall be obliged to preserve nature and the environment, treat and carefully the riches of nature.'

[158] Chapter 16.

[159] Chapter 19. The authors refer to Federal Law on Environmental Protection, No. 7-FZ of January 10, 2002.

[160] Chapter 20. Agustín García-Ureta refers to Art. 325 of the Spanish Criminal Code.

Code, advance various general obligations and prohibitions that support the wilderness concept and which must be taken into account in, for instance, spatial planning. Filippo Valguarnera refers to Chapter 3, paragraph 2, of the Code that states:

> Large land and aquatic areas that are not at all, or just marginally, impacted by economic exploitation or by other interventions in the environment are to be protected, as far as possible, from actions which may significantly influence the areas' characteristics.[161]

Under these husbandry rules, 'areas of national interest', which may include 'areas of national interest for the purposes of nature conservation', require even stricter protection.[162] Valguarnera explains that, according to the preparatory works of this legal instrument 'an area can be deemed to be of national interest for natural conservation because it illustrates important stages in the development of the Swedish natural landscape or because "it is pristine and contains a great variety of natural habitats and biotopes"'.[163]

In theory, wilderness may indeed profit from the efforts of governments to ensure general environmental protection; however, their specific value in relation to wilderness may often be indirect. For most countries such general provisions appear to establish a legal framework that is worked out in more detail by specific provisions with a more direct relevance for wilderness protection, such as protected area systems.

### 5.3 *Explicit 'wilderness' legislation in Europe*

The discussions in Part III show that each of the surveyed jurisdictions have adopted nature conservation laws that elaborate regulatory competences to designate and protect various categories of protected areas. These categories have been often derived from a rich history of domestic nature conservation efforts. As discussed in Section 2, the motives for developing the first protected areas (particularly National Parks and *Zapovedniki*) reflect values that are today attributed to wilderness, even if wilderness has never been recognized as a separate category of protected area in many European counties. Moreover, while categories of domestic protected areas correlate well with the categories distinguished

[161] Chapter 21.
[162] *Ibid.* See the Swedish Environmental Code, Chapter 3, para. 6.
[163] *Ibid.* The author's quotation originates from: Proposition 1997/98:45, part 2, at 33.

in the 2008 IUCN Guidelines on protected areas categories,[164] wilderness has received explicit legal attention in only a very few European jurisdictions.

As described by Aðalheiður Jóhannsdóttir, Article 38(1) and Article 46 of the Icelandic Act on Nature Conservation of 2013 provide the Minister for the Environment and Natural Resources the competence to designate and formally protect 'uninhabited wilderness': 'large land areas wherein human influences are minimal and where nature can evolve without the pressure from human activities'.[165] The aim of this protection strongly reflects the main qualities and values of wilderness, as discussed in Part I of this book:

> The protection should aim to safeguard the characteristics of the areas, e.g., to maintain diverse and unusual landscapes, panoramas and/or conserve complete large ecosystems, and ensure that present and future generations can enjoy therein solitude and nature without disturbance from man-made infrastructures or traffic from motor vehicles.[166]

It is clear that this system does not 'create rights or duties unless a wilderness area has been formally designated and protected', but according to Jóhannsdóttir there are better prospects for this instrument to be used compared to the 1999 Act.

The other example of explicit wilderness legislation is the Finnish Act on Wilderness Reserves, although as noted above, Kai Kokko and Markku Oksanen explain that the Act does not only relate to the protection of wilderness qualities but rather aims to establish a balance between 'the protection of wilderness characteristics' and 'human use of nature as a source of livelihood or based on Sámi culture',[167] a balancing of interests that may well lead to the acceptance of activities that would not otherwise be allowed in strict protected zones of National Parks or natural reserves. Kokko and Oksanen make clear that forestry, mining and road constructions may be permitted under strict conditions and are therefore activities

[164] Nigel Dudley (ed.), *Guidelines for Applying Protected Area Management Categories* (Gland: World Conservation Union/IUCN, 2008), http://cmsdata.iucn.org/downloads/iucn_assignment_1.pdf.

[165] Chapter 16. The author also refers to the definition of uninhabited wilderness in Article 5 (19) of the Act.

[166] Translation from the Icelandic act by Aðalheiður Jóhannsdóttir; see Chapter 16. Aðalheiður Jóhannsdóttir explains that '[t]hese objectives shall be elaborated further in a subsequent officially published regulation, which will have a general legal effect and be applicable to the designated wilderness area in question'.

[167] Chapter 14. The authors explain that 'the basis of Sámi culture lies in its livelihoods – reindeer herding, fishing and hunting – which are also protected under Section 17.3 of the Finnish Constitution'.

that are not completely banned.[168] For instance, the 'Government may grant a permit for the construction of a permanent road that clearly serves the public good or provides a natural source of income in the area.'[169] Thus, while the twelve designated wilderness areas cover large tracts of wilderness, the legal regime does not fully guarantee the protection of each of the main wilderness qualities. In fact, the authors explain that 'the legal protection of ecological values in the reserves and, indirectly also the wilderness character, has become stronger' 'after the main parts of the wilderness reserves were included in the Natura 2000 network'.[170] Furthermore, the authors explain that 'there are areas in Finland that may be considered wilderness as defined in Chapter 1 of this book, but have not been designated as wilderness reserves under the AWR [Act on Wilderness Reserves], for instance because safeguarding subsistence life-styles was not among the primary aims of protecting these areas'.[171]

The discussions in Part III also suggest that, in theory at least, one option might be to designate and protect an important individual wilderness area through a separate 'wilderness act' or administrative regulation. The Icelandic Act on Vatnajökull National Park of 2007 is suggestive of this approach, even if this provision does not relate to an explicit wilderness designation but to the designation of a large area with high wilderness qualities as a National Park. Another example is discussed by Volker Mauerhofer, Edward Galle and Marco Onida in relation to the Alpine region of Austria, where in 2002 the province of Lower Austria designated the 'Wilderness Dürrenstein'.[172] While this example is also based on another category of protected area (as Natura 2000 site and already previously as Nature Conservation Area), the IUCN listing of this area as wilderness area (category Ib) reaffirms the wilderness qualities and wilderness-oriented management of the area.[173]

Finally, it must be noted that some European countries have adopted explicit policies (but not laws) on wilderness protection, often as part of broader approaches to nature conservation and spatial planning. Discussions in Chapter 17 show that this is the case for Norway. Germany has also adopted an explicit wilderness objective as part of its National Biodiversity Strategy: 'By the year 2020, throughout two per cent of

[168] *Ibid.*
[169] *Ibid.* The authors refer to Section 5.2 of the Finnish Act on Wilderness Reserves.
[170] *Ibid.*
[171] *Ibid.*
[172] Chapter 9.
[173] *Ibid.*

Germany's territory, Mother Nature is once again able to develop undisturbed in accordance with her own laws, and areas of wilderness are able to evolve.'[174] The explanatory note to this objective states: 'In order to reactivate the natural processes of habitat momentum, a certain proportion of Germany's territory must be exempted from human influence.'[175]

An explicit and quantitative objective for wilderness was also considered by Austria; however, Volker Mauerhofer explains that in the Austrian National Biodiversity Strategy an alternative approach is taken. He states: 'goal 10 (entitled "Species and Habitat types have to be maintained") of that strategy lists as one of the sixteen measures the elaboration of options for the designation of natural sites (areas without intervention with wilderness character) within the frame of existing conservation site concepts by means of conservation contracts.'[176] Mauerhofer explains that this measure also aims to support other strategy goals, such as the goal to adapt wildlife and fish stock to natural conditions.[177]

### 5.4 *Wilderness protection through other categories of protected areas: National Parks, Natural Reserves and* Zapovedniki

The discussions in Part III show that the nature conservation legislation of most European countries enables the designation of various categories of protected areas. For various historical and political reasons, countries often use different categories with differing names and conservation objectives, although in many respects these correlate well with the IUCN categories.[178] Spatial constraints preclude a full appraisal of each such category here, although attention is merited for three specific categories that – in the absence of explicit wilderness areas – may generally be considered as most relevant for protecting areas with relatively

174 Nationale Strategie zur biologischen Vielfalt, Bundesministerium für Umwelt, Naturschutz und Reaktorsicherheit (BMU), (Berlin: BMU, 2007), www.biologischevielfalt.de/fileadmin/NBS/documents/broschuere_biolog_vielfalt_strategie_bf.pdf, at 2 (in German; citation from the English version, https://www.cbd.int/doc/world/de/de-nbsap-01-en.doc, at 36).

175 *Ibid.* (English version), at 53.

176 Chapter 11. The author refers to the Biodiverstäts-Strategie Österreich 2020+ (Vienna, Umweltbundesamt, 2014), at 23 (translation by Volker Mauerhofer from the German original).

177 *Ibid*, goal 4, at 14: 'Wildtierbestand und Fischbestand sind an die naturräumlichen Verhältnisse angepasst.'

178 Dudley (ed.), *Guidelines for Applying Protected Area Management Categories, supra* note 164, at 15.

high wilderness qualities: namely National Parks, Nature Reserves and *Zapovedniki*.

## National Parks

In many European countries, the definitions of National Parks and/or the criteria for designating areas as National Parks cover at least two of the three main wilderness qualities identified in Chapter 1: the requirement of a relatively large size (with a specific minimum size often set) and a high degree of 'naturalness'. This is in fact very much in line with the IUCN definition of National Parks:

> large natural or near natural areas set aside to protect large-scale ecological processes, along with the complement of species and ecosystems characteristic of the area, which also provide a foundation for environmentally and culturally compatible spiritual, scientific, educational, recreational and visitor opportunities.[179]

For instance, Filippo Valguarnera explains that in Sweden, 'a "large and cohesive" area can be declared a national park by the Government, with the consent of Parliament, with the purpose of conserving said area in its "natural condition"'.[180] The author explains that '[w]hile the legislation does not explicitly use the term "wilderness", it is quite clear that the primary purpose of this legal institute is to maintain large natural areas in a pristine condition'.[181] Sandor Fulop observes that in Hungary '[t]he national parks [. . .] are defined as large territories, having valuable natural traits that are not yet changed significantly'.[182] In the Czech Republic, National Parks have been defined 'as extensive areas, that are unique nationally or internationally, a considerable part of which is covered by natural ecosystems or ecosystems that are little affected by human activities, where plants, animals and abiotic nature are of exceptional scientific and educational importance'.[183] Similarly, in Spain, National Parks must have a minimum size and 'must span a continuous and non-fragmented area that is sufficiently large to permit their natural evolution, without or with minimal human intervention, to maintain their physical and biological characteristics, and to ensure the functioning of natural processes'.[184]

179 *Ibid.*, at 16.
180 Chapter 21. The author refers to Chapter 7, para. 2 of the Environmental Code.
181 *Ibid.*
182 Chapter 15. Sandor Fulop refers to Act LXIII of 1996 on Nature Protection, Art. 28(2).
183 Chapter 12. Zdeňka Křenová and Jiří Zicha refer to Art. 15 of the Act on Nature and Landscape Protection.
184 Chapter 20.

Other domestic systems characterize National Parks as relatively large areas with a high degree of free-functioning ecosystems (naturalness), while some definitions also include more explicitly the social or recreational value of such areas. For instance, Sergiusz Urban explains that Article 8(1) of the 2004 Act on Nature Protection describes a 'national park (park narodowy)' in Poland as 'an area of outstanding natural, scientific, social, cultural and educational values, with the surface area of not less than 1000 ha, in which the entire nature as well as the landscape is subject to protection'.[185] For some countries the criteria to designate National Parks even appears to include all three main wilderness qualities. For instance, Ole Kristian Fauchald notes in relation to Norway that according to 'Section 35 of the Nature Diversity Act, national parks may be established only on "[l]arge areas of natural habitat [. . .] where there is no major infrastructure".'[186]

In view of these clear connections between the wilderness concept and the criteria for National Parks it is not surprising that in many European countries National Parks indeed include natural areas with relatively high wilderness qualities. For Norway, Fauchald explains that '[t]he core protection of wilderness and interference-free areas takes place through the establishment of national parks and nature reserves'.[187] Fulop states that in Hungary 'the core zones of national parks and the parts of the national parks that were designated as biosphere reserves are very close to the wilderness as defined in Chapter 1'.[188] In Finland many National Parks (areas not designated under the Act on Wilderness Reserves) include large wilderness areas:

> These parks and reserves include areas with almost no influence from modern human society and have relatively high wilderness qualities. Furthermore, wilderness protection is sometimes explicitly acknowledged as a management objective. For example, one of the specific purposes of Urho Kekkonen National Park, a large area located in several municipalities (Savukoski, Sodankylä and Inari) is wilderness protection.[189]

[185] Chapter 18.

[186] Chapter 17. The author explains that '[t]he preparatory works indicate that Section 35 should be read as referring only to the original list of infrastructure'.

[187] Chapter 17. Nonetheless, the author explains that 'Norwegian national parks have generally been categorized as IUCN category II (national parks) and not as IUCN category Ib (wilderness areas).'

[188] Chapter 15.

[189] Chapter 14.

Other authors also confirm that many existing National Parks include areas with relatively high wilderness qualities. Jóhannsdóttir explains that the Icelandic Act on Vatnajökull National Park:

> protects a spacious, uninhabited and, to a large extent, a wilderness area, comprising thirteen per cent of Icelandic territory – including Europe's largest glacier, Vatnajökull, which spans 8000 $km^2$ – endowing it with a unique governance system and a legal framework of protective measures.[190]

As far as the legal protection of National Parks is concerned, the system differs from country to country; however, the relatively strong focus on large size and naturalness discussed above indicates that the main weakness of the National Park regimes for wilderness protection may particularly relate to the third quality: the regimes may have fewer guarantees to prevent infrastructural works, such as roads, buildings (e.g., to support tourism), bridges, tracks, or other permanent facilities that are typical for modern human society. Generally, the legal regimes will prohibit such plans and projects, but exceptions to these prohibitions are often forthcoming. For instance, Fauchald states that in National Parks in Norway '[n]o activity that has a lasting impact on the natural environment [. . .] is permitted [. . .] unless such impact is essential to achieving the purpose of protection';[191] moreover, he also explains that 'Section 48 of the Act permits local management boards to "grant exemption" from the protected area regulation and from Section 35 of the Act[192] if "important public interests make it necessary".'[193] National Park regimes in other countries also still leave scope for the development of infrastructure or other permanent facilities for human uses (e.g., Czech Republic, Estonia, Poland and Spain).

As indicated by the above IUCN definition, in many countries the social (e.g., recreational and educational) values of nature are particularly important for the category of National Parks. As Kokko and Oksanen explain for Finland, 'strict nature reserves are mainly protected for scientific purposes and national parks are fairly open outdoor areas'.[194] For Estonia, Richard Caddell explains: 'National parks are [. . .] intended [. . .] to operate as multi-use sites, wherein wilderness objectives are to be reconciled with recreational uses and cultural heritage considerations.'[195]

[190] Chapter 16. Aðalheiður Jóhannsdóttir refers to Act No 60/2007 on Vatnajökull National Park and Regulation No 608/2008 on Vatnajökull National Park with amendments.

[191] Chapter 17. The author quotes Section 35 of the Norwegian Nature Diversity Act.

[192] *Ibid.*

[193] *Ibid.*

[194] Chapter 14.

[195] Chapter 13.

In fact, according to the IUCN, the designation of sites for human use and related permanent infrastructure distinguishes the typical category II areas (National Parks) from the category Ib areas (wilderness areas):

> Category Ib and II protected areas are often similar in size and in their aim to protect functioning ecosystems. But whereas II usually includes (or plans to include) use by visitors, including supporting infrastructure, in Ib visitor use is more limited and confined to those with the skills and equipment to survive unaided.[196]

This difference weakens the role of National Park regimes for wilderness protection. Generally, however, this weakness may be addressed through a 'zoning' approach: dividing the large National Parks into various zones that are characterized by different management aims with different sets of regulations applied thereto. Zoning regimes often provide for the option (or requirement) to designate 'core zones' with high wilderness qualities that enjoy the highest level of protection against human disturbance. The IUCN Guidelines explicitly refer to this option: 'Category II protected areas will often have core zones where numbers of visitors are strictly controlled, which may more closely resemble category Ib.'[197] Depending on the domestic legal system, this 'zoning approach' may be executed in different ways, for instance by formal regulations relating to the National Park, by according certain areas within the National Park the status of a strict nature reserve (see below), through soft-law approaches (e.g., zoning in management plans) or a combination of these different tools.[198]

Several authors explain that this approach to zoning within National Parks has been applied in domestic legal systems in Europe and that wilderness receives far-reaching protection in the zones that receive the strictest protection. For instance, Urban explains that twenty-one per cent of the surface of the twenty-three national parks in Poland 'is protected under the severe regime of "strict protection" (*ochrona ścisła*)', which protection 'implies a total and permanent abandonment

[196] Dudley (ed.), *Guidelines for Applying Protected Area Management Categories*, *supra* note 164, at 15. See also at 17: 'Visitation in category II will probably be quite different from in wilderness areas, with more attendant infrastructure (trails, roads, lodges etc.) and therefore probably a greater number of visitors.'

[197] *Ibid.*, at 17.

[198] See, for instance, Chapter 13; Caddell explains that the zoning approach in the Soomaa national park (Estonia) is executed through a combination of formal zoning (e.g., designation of a strict nature reserve and conservation zones) and 'further zoning [. . .] under the Management Plan developed for the site, establishing four clear zones of activity'.

of human interference with ecosystems and their natural components'.[199] A similar system of zoning in National Parks is in force in Estonia. Caddell states that in the past some six to eight per cent of the National Park Lahemaa 'was [. . .] withdrawn specifically to preserve its wilderness character, while a further two-thirds of the park was available only to the most passive forms of recreation'.[200] He explains that '[t]his broad practice has endured within the current legislative framework':

> Three distinct types of zones are envisaged within national parks, namely 'strict nature reserves' (*loodusreservaat*), 'conservation zones' (*sihtkaitsevöönd*) and 'limited management zones' (*piiranguvöönd*). Of these, strict nature reserves and conservation zones present the clearest mechanisms for the protection of wilderness values within nationally protected areas.[201]

National Parks are also zoned in the Czech Republic. Zdeňka Křenová and Jiří Zicha explain that in the so-called first zone of a National Park stricter regulations apply, such as the prohibition 'to construct new buildings', to 'leave marked pathways without the approval of a nature protection authority', or 'to alter the existing composition and area of plant cultures'.[202] The authors conclude:

> the first zones, which are delimited in all four Czech national parks, are the most relevant parts of national parks for wilderness protection. The qualities of large size and naturalness receive attention for the whole area of national parks, but the absence of permanent infrastructure is a special and important requirement established by the law for especially these first zones.[203]

Thus, while most domestic National Park regimes reflect two main wilderness qualities, the third one may well be covered by a zoning approach; however, as will be discussed in Subsections 6.2 and 6.3, there are several recent developments that may make wilderness protection through National Parks more difficult.

[199] Chapter 15. The author refers to Article 5(9) of the Nature Protection Act 2004 and to www.mos.gov.pl/artykul/2236_parki_narodowe/311_parki_narodowe.html.
[200] Chapter 13. The author refers to P.R. Pryde, *Environmental Management in the Soviet Union* (Cambridge: Cambridge University Press, 1991), at 162.
[201] *Ibid.* The author refers to Section 26(3) of the Estonian Nature Conservation Act 2004.
[202] Chapter 12.
[203] *Ibid.*

## Nature reserves

In many European countries the protected area category of (strict) nature reserves[204] may also play a role in protecting wilderness. Again, most definitions and criteria for designation as described by the authors correlate well with the IUCN's definition of strict nature reserves: 'strictly protected areas set aside to protect biodiversity and also possibly geological / geomorphological features, where human visitation, use and impacts are strictly controlled and limited to ensure protection of the conservation values'.[205] The authors emphasize that the wilderness quality of a 'relatively large size' is often not met by these reserves[206] and that the aims of protection generally focus on the protection of specific rare species, habitats or ecosystems and on scientific research. As Křenová and Zicha explain for the Czech Republic, the 109 national nature reserves are 'smaller areas of exceptional natural value, with important and unique ecosystems from a national or international point of view'.[207] In Spain, the Autonomous Communities describe nature reserves as 'a space of moderate dimension that, owing to its fragility and scientific importance, must be preserved in an integral way with all its biotic and abiotic elements and natural ecological processes, while human occupation is considered incompatible with that objective'.[208] Meanwhile, Caddell states that in Estonia a nature reserve is 'prescribed for the preservation, protection, restoration, research and introduction of the natural environment'.[209] The biodiversity focus and scientific importance of nature reserves are also emphasized in the Polish definition of nature reserve: 'natural reserve (*rezerwat przyrody*) "encompasses areas preserved in their natural state, as well as habitats of plants, animals and fungus, elements of inanimate nature of outstanding natural, scientific or landscape values"

[204] Fisher and Carver explain that the titles of strict protected nature reserves differ substantially among European countries; see Mark Fisher and Steve Carver, 'European wilderness as revealed by strict protection in nature conservation and forest legislation', presentation at WILD 10, 4–10 October 2013, Salamanca (Spain), www.wildlandresearch.org/media/uploads/MF_science_section.pdf.

[205] Dudley (ed.), *Guidelines for Applying Protected Area Management Categories, supra* note 164, at 13.

[206] *Ibid.*, at 15: Strict nature reserves 'are often (but not always) relatively small, in contrast to Ib'.

[207] Chapter 12.

[208] Chapter 20. The author refers to Art. 14(2)(a) of Law 5/2005 of the Autonomous Community of the Balearic Islands.

[209] Chapter 13. The author refers to Section 27(1) of the Estonia Nature Conservation Act 2004.

(Art. 13.1)'.[210] Urban explains that also for nature reserves in Poland 'there is no minimum size threshold and in practice these areas are often relatively small (the smallest occupies as little as 0.1 ha.)'.[211]

In view of the main aims of nature reserves, their constituent legal regimes generally contain strict regulations in relation to the two qualities of naturalness and absence of permanent facilities and infrastructure. For instance, Křenová and Zicha consider that the Czech legislation 'establishes a prohibition on altering or damaging these areas, and that their utilization is contingent upon preserving or improving the existing state of the natural environment'.[212] They also explain that '[f]orests in national nature reserves cannot be categorized as timber forests' and that '[r]estrictions also apply to deviating from marked paths without the approval of a nature protection authority, collecting plants or catching animals, camping and outdoor activities such as climbing'.[213] For Norway, Fauchald observes that '[a]ccording to Section 37 of the Nature Diversity Act, within a *nature reserve* no activity is allowed that "reduces the conservation value of the area as described in the purpose of protection", and according to the same provision, nature reserves "may be given absolute protection from all activity, projects and access or passage"'.[214] Although similar strict regimes are applied in other European countries, the differences between domestic systems should again be taken into account. For instance, these characterizations – which are in line with the IUCN category of strict nature reserve – do not fully apply to Swedish nature reserves, since such areas may also be designated to 'secure areas for recreational outdoor activities'.[215]

The discussions in Part III also establish that in practice the 'tool' of a nature reserve is actually applied for the benefit of European wilderness protection. Notwithstanding the small size of most nature reserves and the fact that wilderness protection is not the main objective underpinning this designation, many nature reserves meet the other two main wilderness qualities: nature reserves are generally characterized by a high degree of naturalness and very low level of human influences. Nature reserves are

[210] Chapter 18.
[211] *Ibid.* See also Chapter 17: '[n]ature reserves tend to be small (average size: 2.75 km$^2$)'.
[212] Chapter 12.
[213] *Ibid.*
[214] Chapter 17.
[215] Chapter 21. Valguarnera refers to Chapter 7 §4 of the Environmental Code. With a reference to Chapter 7 §6 he further observes that this aim may also result in the realization of facilities to support recreation in nature reserves.

sometimes located close to human settlements and infrastructure,[216] but many nature reserves are situated in the relatively wilder parts of a country. For instance, Valguarnera explains that '[a]s of 31 December 2013, there are as many as 4042 natural reserves in Sweden, covering a surface of 4,5 million ha.' and that '[a]bout seventy-five per cent of the reserves are located in the northern mountain regions of the country'.[217]

The relatively 'wild character' of certain nature reserves may also be explained by their location within other protected areas, particularly National Parks. For instance, for the United Kingdom, Simon Boyle and Nicola Wheeler explain that '[m]any NNRs [National Nature Reserves] are located in National Parks, for example, Loch Lomond (Scotland), Kinder Scout (Peak District, England) and Cwm Idwal (Snowdonia, Wales)'.[218] Also, in Norway '[s]ome nature reserves are located within national parks or protected landscapes' and Fauchald explains that '[e]specially where they are located within national parks, nature reserves can be assumed to cover areas with a high degree of wilderness'.[219] Křenová and Zicha note that in the Czech Republic 'smaller protected areas, usually strictly protected nature reserves, can occur inside the confines of national parks',[220] particularly if older nature reserves retain their status after they have been incorporated into a National Park. For instance, in 1991 the nature reserve Trojmezná became part of the Šumava NP, but that – when several years later the 'first zone' of the National Park 'was fragmented and opened for cutting the bark beetle infected trees' – 'the original status of the nature reserve (supported by civil blockade organized by NGOs) helped to protect the most valuable parts of this area against logging and the degradation of ecosystems'.[221]

Nature reserves may also be subjected to a zoning approach themselves. For instance, Caddell states that in Estonia 'as with national parks, a nature reserve [. . .] may also comprise a series of strict nature reserves,

[216] See, for instance, Chapter 17. Ole Kristian Fauchald explains: 'Section 37 of the Nature Diversity Act has extended nature reserves so that they may be established also in areas with significant human interference, and where the purpose of the protected area is dependent on continued human interference.'

[217] Chapter 21. The author refers to Statistics Sweden, *Skyddad natur*, 31 December 2013, at 10.

[218] Chapter 22.

[219] Chapter 17. Ole Kristian Fauchald refers to the three nature reserves Kattuglehøi, Mesætermyre and Veslehjerkinntjønnin, all located in Dovre National Park.

[220] Chapter 12.

[221] *Ibid.* The authors refer to Z. Křenová and J. Hruška, 'Proper zonation – an essential tool for the future conservation of the Šumava National Park', *European Journal of Environmental Sciences*, 2(1) (2012), 62–72.

conservation zones and limited management zones'.[222] The author explains that in Estonia '[p]rotected wilderness sites are most prevalent within nature reserves: three per cent of the net territory of these zones has been designated as strict nature reserves and forty-three per cent as WCZs' (Wilderness Conservation Zones).[223]

### *Zapovedniki*

According to Caddell '[i]n principle, *zapovednost* – the conceptual foundation of the *zapovednik* system – remains arguably the most explicit legal mechanism for the protection of wilderness values to have been applied in Europe'.[224] Indeed, experts like Professor Grigory Kozhevnikov advocated in 1908 nature reserves in which '[n]othing should be eliminated, added, or improved' and in which '[o]ne should leave nature to itself and observe the results'.[225] In 1910, in accordance with these ideas the first *zapovednik* was established in the region that is now Estonia (Vaika Islands Bird Sanctuary).[226] As discussed in Chapters 13 and 20 political support for *zapovedniki* has changed substantially over time, but today the instrument still holds a strong position in nature conservation law in Russia and a number of other former soviet countries.[227] Caddell and Natalia Danilina et al. explain that in many such areas human influences have increased, e.g., through increased access for tourism, biodiversity measures or climate change, but numerous *zapovedniki* are still characterized as areas with high wilderness qualities.

[222] Chapter 13. The author refers to Section 27(2) of the Estonia Nature Conservation Act 2004. For Estonia it is therefore important to distinguish nature reserves (a category of protected areas) from strict nature reserves (a strictly regulated zone within protected areas).

[223] *Ibid.*, at 41.

[224] Chapter 13.

[225] Quoted in Chapter 19. Quotations are from Grigory Kozhevnikov, 'On the Necessity for Setting up Preserved Areas for the Protection of Russian Nature', in Proceedings of the All-Russian Acclimatization Anniversary Congress in 1908 in Moscow. B.1, MA, 1909, http://ecoethics.ru/on-the-necessity-for-setting-up-preserved-areas-for-the-protection-of-russian-nature/. See also Shtilmark, *History of the Russian Zapovedniks 1895–1999*, *supra* note 23, pp. 1–26, in particular at 17.

[226] Chapter 13.

[227] According to Richard Caddell, 'Baltic States eradicated the *zapovednik* system shortly after independence towards a more Natura 2000-orientated approach to makes themselves attractive accession candidates.' Personal communication, 21 May 2015.

## 5.5 *Protection of wilderness under other legislation: spatial planning, forestry and EIA*

Apart from protected area regimes, other domestic legal instruments may also play a role in protecting wilderness in Europe. Many of these instruments, such as the prohibition of off-road driving in Iceland, apply both in and outside protected areas. Again, the summary below does not aim to be exhaustive; attention is focused on four important fields of law with significant wilderness protection potential: spatial planning, forestry, environmental impact assessment (EIA) and private property rights.

### Protection of wilderness under spatial planning law

As the term wilderness is not used in most nature conservation regimes, it is no surprise that it is also alien to most domestic spatial planning systems. Nevertheless, in a small number of exceptional systems spatial planning instruments and wilderness are interconnected. In Iceland, one of the principal objectives of the Act No 123/2010 on Spatial Planning is 'landscape and nature protection and the prevention of environmental damage and overuse in the light of sustainable development',[228] and as Jóhannsdóttir explains, the term 'landscape' 'includes, inter alia, urban areas, rural areas, virgin wilderness, rivers, lakes and marine areas'.[229] This provides options for governments with spatial planning competences (e.g., the seventy-four municipalities) to attribute legal protection to areas with wilderness qualities through, for instance, spatial plans (particularly master plans and zoning plans).[230] As in most spatial planning systems, such plans must be respected in making particular decisions on building plans. Likewise, in Norway, '[w]ilderness areas may be identified in municipal plans and thus be afforded protection against specific projects'.[231] For this purpose, the term 'interference-free areas' (*inngrepsfrie områder*) may be used,[232] although Fauchald considers that '[t]he use of the revised definition as a basis for land-use planning has been controversial'.[233] The author explains:

[228] Chapter 16. The author refers to Art. 1(b) of the Act No 123/2010 on Spatial Planning.
[229] *Ibid.*, Art. 2(13).
[230] *Ibid.*
[231] Chapter 17. The author refers to Chapters 11 and 12 of the Planning and Building Act, in particular Sections 11-8, 11-9, 12-5 and 12-7.
[232] See Chapter 17 and Subsection 3.2.
[233] Chapter 17.

> One argument has been that the definition means that minor projects may lead to highly significant loss of wilderness and interference-free areas. Another argument has been that the informal introduction of the concepts into public administrative practices lacks political legitimacy. It has also been held that there is a weak connection between the concepts and officially endorsed environmental objectives such as biodiversity and recreation.[234]

According to Fauchald, the 'government that took office in October 2013 promised to discontinue the use of "interference-free areas" as a tool in land-use planning',[235] although it is unclear what this would mean for the options of municipalities to protect relatively wild areas through their spatial plans.

Also, in many other spatial planning systems governments at various levels have opportunities to protect areas with relatively high wilderness qualities, but most of these systems will not explicitly use terms like 'wilderness' or 'interference-free areas'. In some legal systems, attention to such areas in spatial planning may also be required through general obligations, such as the 'husbandry rules' in the Environmental Code of Sweden.[236]

### Forestry legislation

Various authors also discuss the interrelationships between forestry legislation and wilderness protection. It is clear from these examples that forestry legislation has been strongly influenced by commercial interests and that this has resulted in much loss of wilderness. For instance, García-Ureta explains that '[d]eforestation steadily (but stubbornly) continued to invade large portions of Spain, thereby heavily affecting the naturalness of areas and limiting the total amount of relatively wild areas'.[237] He considers that '[l]ocal species of trees were replaced by fast-growing ones, like eucalyptus, providing swift economic benefits at the expense of diversity and soil quality'.[238] Discernible tensions between forestry interests and wilderness protection are apparent in a number of jurisdictions, notably Finland, although conversely several authors also stress the positive role that forestry legislation may play in wilderness protection in Europe. For instance, Sandor Fulop explains that the 2009 Forestry Act[239] in

234 *Ibid.*

235 *Ibid.* The author refers to 'Politisk plattform for en regjering utgått av Høyre og Fremskrittspartiet, Sarbuvollen', 7 October 2013, at 60 and Parliamentary Document 8:37 S (2009–2010).

236 Chapter 21. See also Subsection 5.2.

237 Chapter 20.

238 *Ibid.*

239 Act XXXVII of 2009 on the forests, on the protection of them and on forestry.

Hungary distinguishes six categories of forests and observes that in preparing district forestry plans 'natural forests (undisturbed, their content, structure and dynamics are natural, with no alien or invasive species)' and 'natural-like forests (similar to natural forests, but alien species can be found up to twenty per cent, with no invasive species)' 'shall be preferred and maintained to the maximum extent possible'.[240] Financial incentives also play an important role in the protection of the most pristine forest areas: 'Where forests are transformed into other uses, the forest protection fee will be increased fourfold in the case of natural and natural like forests than in the case of other ones.'[241]

The role of forestry legislation for wilderness protection appears even more prominent in Estonia. Richard Caddell explains that the 'Forest Act presents particular scope to assist in wilderness conservation through the establishment of a network of Woodland Key Habitats (WKHs)',[242] in which '[e]conomic activities may be restricted or even prohibited entirely'.[243] The establishment of this network has even impacted on private property rights through 'compulsory leases'.[244] Caddell also explains that 'forest resources are [...] subject to an overarching development plan to be concluded on a ten-yearly basis', which plan 'includes provision for the withdrawal of a certain volume of forestry from economic use and its preservation as a *de facto* wilderness area'.[245] Based on all these tools and their actual usage, Caddell concludes that the forestry legislation in Estonia 'established a legal guarantee that a substantial volume of the national mainland is to remain carpeted by pristine endemic woodland for the long-term future'.[246]

## Environmental Impact Assessment

Environmental Impact Assessment (EIA) and wilderness protection have a troublesome relationship. For instance, experiences with EIA in Antarctica demonstrate that, although EIAs should take into account impacts on

[240] Chapter 15. The author refers to Art. 34(2)(a) of the Forestry Act.
[241] *Ibid.* The author refers to Art. 81(2) (ba),(bb) and 82(4) of the Forestry Act.
[242] Chapter 13. Caddell refers to Article 23(1) of the Estonia Forest Act 2006.
[243] *Ibid.* Caddell refers to Article 26(6).
[244] *Ibid.* Caddell refers to P. Põllumäe, H. Korjus and T. Paluots, 'Management motivations of Estonian forest owners', *Forest Policy and Economics* 42 (2014), 8–14, at 11.
[245] *Ibid.* Caddell states: 'The latest Forest Development Programme, concluded in 2010, mandates the strict protection of at least ten per cent of the total area of Estonian forestry.'
[246] *Ibid.*

wilderness, such assessments are problematic.[247] In Europe this is compounded by the problem that in most countries wilderness protection is not an explicit aim of law and policy, which will often serve to keep considerations of wilderness impacts outside the scope of the EIA process. *Vice versa*, it is unsurprising that the examples of explicit attention for wilderness in EIA regulations can be found in Norway and Iceland.

Fauchald explains that 'Section 4(b) of the Regulation on Environmental Impact Assessment requires that environmental impact assessments be conducted where planning or project decisions concern activities that "are located in or are in conflict with important interference-free areas".'[248] In such situations it must be assumed that the EIA should also include the impacts on interference-free areas;[249] however, the author states that the regulations are not explicit on this and he doubts in view of existing EIA case-law whether this will be enforced by Norwegian courts.[250]

Jóhannsdóttir explains that under the Icelandic EIA act, 'wilderness' must be considered to be part of the term 'landscape',[251] and since landscape impacts must be part of the EIA process the 'question as to whether wilderness is likely to be affected by an individual project should [...] be taken into account'.[252] Despite this requirement, the author explains that '[c]urrent practice indicates that direct references to wilderness values in EIA reports or in the NPA EIA decisions are rather scarce, although some examples can be found'.[253] She also states that in particular 'large scale energy resources utilization and related installations' and 'the construction of new roads' 'are likely to affect wilderness

247 For discussions on the problematic assessment of wilderness impacts as part of EIAs for plans and projects in Antarctica, see Kees Bastmeijer and Ricardo Roura, 'Environmental Impact Assessment in Antarctica', in: Kees Bastmeijer and Timo Koivurova (eds.), *Theory and Practice of Transboundary Environmental Impact Assessment* Leiden, Brill/ Martinus Nijhoff Publishers, 2008, pp. 175–219.

248 Chapter 17. The author refers to Forskrift om konsekvensutredninger, FOR 2009–06–26 no. 855.

249 For Spitsbergen/Svalbard, the EIA regulations refer explicitly to wilderness and require the assessment of impacts on wilderness as part of the process: see the Regulations relating to environmental impact assessment and delimitation of the land-use planning areas in Svalbard, https://www.regjeringen.no/en/dokumenter/regulations-relating-to-environmental-im/id512069/.

250 Chapter 17.

251 Chapter 16. The author refers to the definition of landscape in Art. 2(13) of the Act No 123/2010 on Spatial Planning, which provision makes clear that '[l]andscape includes, inter alia, urban areas, rural areas, virgin wilderness, rivers, lakes and marine areas'.

252 *Ibid.* The author refers to Art. 3 of the EIA Act. See also Art. 2(iv)(e) of Annex III to this act.

253 *Ibid.*

values' if these are situated in the Icelandic Highlands; however, she concludes that '[a]s yet, it appears that no such projects have been cancelled due to their effects on wilderness qualities'.[254]

The discussions in relation to Austria demonstrate that wilderness qualities may receive attention in EIA practice, although the term wilderness is not used in EIA legislation. Mauerhofer explains that in an administrative procedure on the question of whether an EIA was needed for an alpine ropeway construction project, an official expert emphasized that 'this glacier area is a part of a landscape unmodified by humans, and that those wilderness areas have particular importance because of their inherent uniqueness'.[255] Based on this judgment, it was concluded that an EIA was indeed necessary; it is as yet unclear what role will be played by the EIA in the final decision-making process.

This weak protection accorded by EIA to wilderness, as reflected in various chapters, may in part be explained by more general characteristics and concerns in relation to EIA. For instance, Agustín García-Ureta observes that 'EIA is essentially a procedural requisite' that 'does not *per se* impede the execution of a plan or project embracing substantial harmful effects'.[256] He further notes that the actor responsible for conducting the EIA often has direct interests in the project, which results in a situation that 'in practice a significant proportion of assessments endorse a conclusion that a particular project or plan may be executed.'[257] This concern may be replicated in many European countries.

### 5.7 *Protection of wilderness and property rights*

As noted in the introductory chapter, in recent centuries private property rights over natural components (e.g., land) have become more absolute and exclusive. Subsection 6.6 discusses that this may constitute an obstacle to wilderness protection; however, discussions in Part III show that this process has been less extreme in some parts of Europe. For instance, Valguarnera provides historical explanations for the fact that 'in Sweden property never reached the status of an ideological fetish'.[258] For instance, compared to many other West European countries, private property on land in Sweden has always been less absolute and exclusive,

[254] *Ibid.*
[255] Chapter 11; Volker Mauerhofer's translation of the expert's opinion in German.
[256] Chapter 20.
[257] *Ibid.*
[258] Chapter 21.

which also leaves space for the 'every man's right' (*allemansrätt*).[259] This right is also part of the legal system of other Scandinavian countries and, as Richard Caddell explains, also 'Estonia has retained the Nordic tradition of the "everyman's right" (*igameheõigus*), prescribing a customary privilege to freely roam the land between sunrise and sunset.'[260] For Spain, Agustín García-Ureta explains that in case law the right to appropriate nature as exclusive and absolute private property has been substantially limited: 'species, habitats and areas with high wilderness qualities cannot be conceived as freely available resources', and the author explains that '[i]n this sense, the Supreme Court has held in a case concerning the bear hunting that the animal was a legal good relevant for society as a whole due to its ecological value'.[261]

Such limitations to exclusive appropriation may help to keep wild nature out of the 'wrong hands', although it may also make wilderness protection more difficult for landowners that aim to protect wilderness. For instance, managers of wilderness areas in the Nordic countries may experience problems with certain tourist activities that threaten wilderness qualities, while the organizers of such activities base their right to conduct these activities on the *allemansrätt*. Caddell explains that in Estonia, the 'exercise of the *igameheõigus* is a residual freedom, contingent upon the permission of the owner of the land – whether public or private – which is deemed to have been granted "if the owner has not fenced the plot or marked it in a manner that demonstrates the intent to restrict strangers' stay on the plot"'.[262] In this way, the 'everyman's right' requires land owners with strict wilderness objectives to take measures that in fact have adverse impacts on the wilderness quality of 'undevelopedness'.[263]

This illustrates the difficulty of the relationship between wilderness and private property: whether property rights are good for wilderness values depends very much on the individual situation, the specific rules that apply and – probably most important – the objectives of the owner. Property rights may constitute an obstacle to wilderness protection (see

[259] *Ibid.*
[260] Chapter 13.
[261] Chapter 20. The author refers to Supreme Court Judgment (Criminal Law chamber), 1 April 1993, appeal 594/1990.
[262] *Ibid.* Caddell quotes Section 32(2) of the Nature Conservation Act 2004 (NCA).
[263] Caddell explains that since an amendment of Section 32(2) NCA of 3 March 2015, the 'general presumption' that permission is granted if the area is not fenced or marked does not apply to 'power-driven or off-road vehicles'.

below), but may also promote strong wilderness protection if the owner is motivated to do so. Examples include the National Trust in the United Kingdom,[264] Rewilding Europe,[265] the European Wilderness Society[266] and IUCN's international Land Purchase for Conservation initiative.[267]

The appropriation of wilderness areas with the aim of safeguarding protection may also arise from public protests against specific threats. For instance, in relation to the plan to build a dam in the Danube wetlands in Austria, Volker Mauerhofer explains that '[s]ome years after the escalation of the conflict a NGO started a national campaign which culminated in a fundraising evening', which 'provided the NGO with the financial means to buy more than 400 hectares of forests [. . .] on the southern bank of the Danube River'.[268] The author explains that in 1996 '[t]his land area was later included as part of the core zones of the Danube Wetlands National Park'.[269]

Finally, in most domestic administrative law systems private ownership ensures access to judicial procedures, while engaged citizens are often denied such access. Again, depending on the situation and the ambitions of the land-owners, this may constitute a blessing or a curse for wilderness protection. For instance, in the Icelandic 'Brekka land-case' the landowners used their *locus standi* to challenge the authorization of a road construction.[270]

### *5.8 Human access to wilderness*

In relation to North America, David G. Henderson has stated that 'wilderness is not the absence of people, even though it may often have no people in it'.[271] In his view '[t]he American West was wilderness, not because there were no people, but because there were wolves and grizzly

264 Chapter 22.

265 'Rewilding Europe', http://www.rewildingeurope.com.

266 See the Society's objective 10 for the period 2015–2020: 'Identify wilderness areas which can be protected by leasing or buying strategic lots of property', http://wilderness-society.org/objectives-2015–2020/.

267 See IUCN, *Land Purchase for Conservation, An Effective Strategy for Biodiversity Conservation* (Amsterdam: IUCN, 2009), at 11: 'Some of the fragments of the forests remaining in places such as the Atlantic Rainforest in Brazil, are now critical for the survival of endemic species, and by buying these remaining fragments and getting legal protection for them, the NGOs are in a unique position to make conservation history.'

268 Chapter 11.

269 *Ibid.*

270 Chapter 16.

271 Henderson, *Wilderness: The History, Significance and Promise of an American Value*, *supra* note 7, at 4–5.

bears'.[272] Aside from the grizzly bears, this comment appears also to reflect the common view of wilderness in Europe. Discussions in this book illustrate that also in Europe people have generally always had access to protected areas. Although this access may be very limited for *zapovedniki*, strict protected zones in National Parks or strict nature reserves (e.g., only scientific research), in most European protected areas with relatively high wilderness qualities various forms of human activities are allowed. From a wilderness perspective, this need not be a concern; however, as stressed by Kormos, Martin and Barr,[273] it is important to ensure that human uses do not affect the main characteristics and values of the wilderness area.[274]

In Europe this fundamental standard for wilderness protection is difficult to enforce due to the absence of explicit policy towards wilderness under most international, European and domestic legal systems. Public permission for activities that are connected to wilderness qualities, such as hiking, small-scale camping and kayaking, is generally considered acceptable or – from an educational perspective – even desirable; however, because protection of wilderness is not an explicit aim, most regulations on human activities also leave scope for activities that adversely affect wilderness qualities. This is illustrated by many examples discussed in this book, such as the allocation of tourism facilities in National Parks, the conditional option to allow roads or wind turbines in Natura 2000 sites and the toleration of summer houses in 'interference-free areas' in Norway.

Tensions also arise in the relationship between wilderness protection and indigenous people.[275] On the one hand, the modern conviction is that wilderness protection and the protection of the rights and traditions of indigenous people should go hand in hand.[276] The 2008 IUCN

[272] *Ibid.*

[273] C.F. Kormos, V.G. Martin and B. Barr, 'New Directions in Wilderness Designation', in: Kormos, *A Handbook on International Wilderness Law and Policy, supra* note 65.

[274] This standard is also reflected in explicit wilderness legislation in other parts of the world. See, for instance, Art. 4(a) of the Wilderness and Ecological Reserves Act of Labrador and Newfoundland (www.assembly.nl.ca/legislation/sr/statutes/w09.htm#4_), which provides that the wilderness reserves designated under the Act 'are subject to no or little human activity [. . .] to provide for the continued existence of those areas as large wilderness areas'. For a comprehensive analysis of the activities that may or may not be undertaken in wilderness areas under current domestic wilderness legislation, see Kormos and Locke, 'Introduction', *supra* note 65.

[275] See the discussion on forced relocation of indigenous people as a consequence of National Park designations in the past, Chapter 1, Subsection 3.2.

[276] See Kormos, Martin and Barr, 'New Directions in Wilderness Designation', *supra* note 273.

Guidelines on protected areas categories also explicitly states that IUCN opposes the use of the 'categories as an excuse for expelling people from their traditional lands'.[277] Valguarnera explains that this view is recognizable in early nature protection practices in Sweden: in the early twentieth century 'the Swedish legislature observed that the rights exercised by the Sámi population did not influence the natural environment in any noticeable way and that the Sámi in fact were "so intimately united with the natural environment that they, so to speak, complete it"'.[278] Even today, some Sámi still live according to old traditions and – as Westerners might consider – 'close to nature'.

However, on the other hand, certain current practices of indigenous people are conducted on a scale (e.g., because of population growth or market opportunities) or in a form (e.g., through the use of modern technology) that clearly has adverse impacts for wilderness qualities (e.g., disturbance by motorized vehicles, impacts on naturalness).[279] Examples discussed in this book include impacts on biodiversity due to large-scale reindeer herding,[280] the use of motorized transport means for reindeer herding[281] and the (illegal) killing of carnivores to protect reindeer.[282] Many of these tensions are not currently addressed by existing legal systems. For instance, Kokko and Oksanen explain that '[f]rom a biodiversity perspective, it has been observed that the AWR [Act on Wilderness Reserves] has not been successful in balancing intensive reindeer herding and biodiversity protection in wilderness areas'.[283] Meanwhile Valguarnera explains that the regulations for the National Parks in Northern Sweden 'allow[s] the Sámi to use motor scooters in the parks'.[284] Consequently, if wilderness protection is strived for, it is necessary to continue a constructive dialogue as to how such tensions

277 Nigel Dudley (ed.), *Guidelines for Applying Protected Area Management Categories*, *supra* note 164, at 6.

278 Chapter 21. The quote used by the author is from *Betänkande rörande åtgärder till skydd för vårt lands natur och naturminnesmärke* (1907), at 49.

279 See, e.g., Marcus Colchester, 'This park is no longer your land', *UNESCO Courier*, 2001/07, at 14: 'many indigenous peoples have adopted new ways of farming their lands, harvesting timbers and other natural resources. Many now hunt with new weapons and use industrial technologies to process and transport crops. Customary systems of regulating access to these resources now need rethinking if they are to be effective.'

280 Chapters 14 and 17.

281 Chapter 21.

282 Chapter 14.

283 *Ibid.*

284 Chapter 21.

may be mitigated, while taking into account the wilderness concept as well as the rights and traditions of indigenous people.

### 5.9 *Protection of European wilderness domestic law: many options, good examples but no guarantees*

To what extent are European wilderness areas the subject of protection under domestic law? It can be seen that very few European countries have adopted explicit wilderness laws and policies and the main components of these systems were discussed. The Icelandic legislation, in particular, connects closely to the wilderness concept as defined in the introductory chapter, although the effectiveness of this legislation remains difficult to assess. Despite a lack of explicit attention for the wilderness concept in other European countries, various legal tools are available to protect European areas with relatively high wilderness qualities. Constitutional provisions and general provisions of environmental law may provide a certain basic protection for wilderness, although most such instruments are relatively general; the protection is thereby often indirect. Spatial planning law and EIA legislation provide further options for wilderness protection, although in most countries the strength of these tools for wilderness protection is limited: spatial planning systems are strongly characterized by decision-making based on the balancing of interests, which generally work in favour of short-term socio-economic interests than long-term wilderness protection (see below). Similarly, EIA legislation applies specifically to wilderness values in only a small number of countries. Even where it does, the objectivity of the EIA is not always guaranteed, EIA impacts may be difficult to 'measure' and even if wilderness impacts are identified, such information may have limited influence on decision-making concerning large economic plans and projects. Forestry law and private property rights may also play a role in wilderness protection but both categories have a 'love-hate relationship' with wilderness: depending on the content of the legislation and the particular situation, the application of these norms may have positive or negative implications for wilderness protection.

This brings us to the instruments that currently appear to be most important for wilderness protection in Europe: National Parks (particularly the more strictly protected core zones in such parks), nature reserves and *zapovedniki*. In most European countries, the definitions and legal protection regimes for these categories correlate closely with at least two of the three main wilderness qualities and the chapters provide numerous examples whereby these instruments are actively used to protect important European wilderness areas.

Notwithstanding this broad mix of legal tools for wilderness protection, a broadly similar picture emerges at the domestic level as to the transnational level: few legal guarantees exist for wilderness protection in Europe. Explicit national wilderness policies are few and far between and, since these mechanisms are facultative 'options', political will remains the determining factor in their application. This realty is indicative of a series of obstacles facing the ability of the identified tools to effectively protect Europe's wilderness.

## 6 Obstacles to wilderness protection in Europe

The above discussions show that a major hurdle for wilderness protection in Europe is that the actual use of the above-identified legal options for the protection of European wilderness is unsure due to the facultative character of the available tools and the absence of an explicit aim to protect wilderness in most international, European and domestic legal systems. From the discussions in Part II and III also a series of other core obstacles to wilderness protection are apparent, across all tiers of governance.

### 6.1 *The weak position of wilderness in 'balancing interests-systems'*

The discussions in Parts II and III confirm the trend, discussed in the introductory chapter, that nature conservation law has focused strongly on the conservation of 'biological diversity' (biodiversity) and the 'sustainable', 'rational' or 'wise' use of biodiversity and less on relatively undisturbed natural areas.[285] In Chapter 1 this development was in part explained by the importance that was attributed to specific natural values (e.g., threatened species and habitats), but also by the scope left by these concepts for balancing social and economic interests with nature conservation. 'Setting aside relatively untouched natural places is simply more difficult in a world society where human interests have the central focus.'[286] Or as Sarkar has put it: 'Biodiversity conservation can avoid contentious political issues while simultaneously promoting long-term conservation by maintaining independence and distance from wilderness preservation.'[287]

285 Chapter 1.
286 *Ibid.*
287 Sahotra Sarkar, 'Wilderness preservation and biodiversity conservation. Keeping divergent goals distinct', *BioScience* 49, 5 (1999), 405–412, at 410. See Chapter 1.

Many legal systems discussed in this book do indeed appear to enable or even promote this balancing of interests, including the option to prioritize social and economic interests. For instance, the Nature Conservation Protocol of the Alpine Convention states in Article 9(2):

> In accordance with national law, unavoidable impairments must be offset by measures for conservation of nature and the countryside, while the impairments that cannot be compensated may only be allowed on condition that, having evaluated all the interests, the needs for nature and countryside conservation are not dominant. However, even in these cases, measures must still be taken to conserve nature and the countryside.[288]

Considerable scope for balancing interests also exists in National Park regimes, where domestic legislation often makes it possible to authorize activities as exceptions to the general prohibitions.[289] In principle, there is little obvious objection to the balance of interests approach. Indeed, Ross noted some 25 years ago that conservation biologists preferred this path:

> The wilderness idea has fallen on hard times of late. Not only does industry fight it at every turn, but even conservation biologists now shun wilderness in favor of the more moderate notion of sustainable management of natural resources. Sustainability is being hailed as a new paradigm for conservation [. . .]; it seems to represent the perfect middle ground in resource conflicts.[290]

However, in the practice of nature conservation there are many examples that illustrate that while balancing of interests and searching for the 'middle ground' in resource conflicts may result in effective nature conservation in general, this is certainly not reflected in wilderness protection. Without strict boundaries for human ambition, in decision-making on plans and projects there appears to be a general tendency to emphasize the short-term (often economic interests). One of the specific examples discussed in this book concerns the project to build sixty-seven wind turbines of about 135 metres in height in the Scottish Monadhliath Mountains, discussed by Boyle and Wheeler.[291] The consent letter of the Scottish government for this project states:

[288] See also Chapter 9 and Subsection 4.1.

[289] See Subsection 5.4.

[290] Reed F. Noss, 'Sustainability and wilderness', in J. Baird Callicott and Michael P. Nelson (eds.), *The Great New Wilderness Debate. An Expansive Collection of Writings Defining Wilderness from John Muir to Gary Snyder* (Athens: University of Georgia Press, 1998), pp. 408–413, at 408.

[291] Chapter 22.

> The design of the windfarm has gone to considerable lengths to safeguard the area's wild land character insofar as possible, and the impacts that remain have been weighed against the benefits of the development. Fundamentally, Ministers are of the view that on balance the very significant renewable energy benefits of this development and their contribution to sustainable economic growth mean that the development is broadly supported by policy.[292]

### *6.2 Changing politics: the tendency to create more scope for anthropogenic activities in wilderness areas*

Changing domestic and local politics may constitute an additional hurdle for long-term wilderness protection. This has, for instance, been illustrated by the historical developments of the *zapovednik* regimes in Estonia and Russia,[293] but this topic is relevant in all parts of Europe, certainly so in more recent eras. Such changing politics may, for instance, relate to weakening the legal protection of areas with high wilderness qualities to create more space for commercial activities. For instance, Fauchald explains that in 2003 the Norwegian 'government and the Parliament adopted a policy of more extensive recreational and commercial use of national parks'.[294] Kokko and Oksanen also recognize these challenges in Finland: 'The expansion of tourism, with the cross-country and snowmobile traffic it involves, windmill parks and the role of the extractive industries (mining) are quite new, emerging issues.'[295] Meanwhile in Estonia, 'the more recent trend is for conservation designations to be established as managed zones, which remain under protection but with a clear toleration for socio-economic activities'.[296] Richard Caddell states: 'there appears to be discernible pressure to renew the protection rules for existing conservation areas in favour of a softer management regime within particular sites'.[297]

[292] Scottish Government, 'Consent under s36 of the Electricity Act 1989 and deemed planning permission under s57(2) of the Town and Country Planning (Scotland) Act 1997 for the Stronelairg wind powered electricity generating station in the council area of the highlands', 6 June 2014, www.scotland.gov.uk/Resource/0045/00452641.pdf, at 5. See also at p. 10: 'Ministers are of the view that the impact on wild land does not on this occasion warrant refusal of consent.'

[293] See Chapters 13 and 19.

[294] Chapter 17.

[295] Chapter 14.

[296] Chapter 13.

[297] The author refers to personal communication with Uudo Timm; see Chapter 13, notes 86 and 102.

### 6.3 *Decentralization of competences*

Changing politics that may affect wilderness protection may also relate to the division of competences between various levels of governments. The discussions in Part III indicate that in many countries, competences regarding the establishment and protection of nature protection areas have to a certain degree been decentralized or are in the process of becoming so. For instance, in Poland local authorities have a veto in respect of proposals for new National Parks or extending existing National Parks.[298] In 2009 in Norway, 'a local management reform was introduced, to extend to all national parks: decision-making power will be moved from regional government agencies (county governors) to local management boards composed of municipal, county and, where relevant, Sámi politicians'.[299] The position of local governments towards nature has not been specifically studied for the purpose of this book project, but the discussions in various chapters indicate that – because of fear over limitations upon economic development – local governments often oppose the establishment of nature reserves. For instance, research discussed by Urban shows that '[i]n the case of Natura 2000, opposition was expressed mainly by the local governments of those municipalities where new protected areas were designated'.[300] Fulop explains for Hungary that '[w]hile at the national level the spatial planning policy of the country is seemingly quite supportive of nature protection, the major stresses on wilderness area are exerted by the local spatial plans where the social and economic pressure for development is at its strongest'.[301] In a similar vein, Valguarnera also notes in Sweden, 'the decisions pertaining to the wilderness are taken by a variety of different institutional subjects, including municipalities' and that '[a]n obvious weakness in this system is the risk that political actors entangled in local politics end up unduly putting other interests in front of the conservation of pristine natural areas'.[302]

[298] Chapter 18.

[299] Chapter 17. The author refers to O.K. Fauchald and L.H. Gulbrandsen, 'The Norwegian reform of protected area management: a grand experiment with delegation of authority?' *Local Environment: The International Journal of Justice and Sustainability*, 17:2 (2012), 203–222.

[300] See Chapter 18. Quotation is from Malgorzata Grodzinska-Jurczak and Joanna Cent, 'Expansion of nature conservation areas: Problems with Natura 2000 implementation in Poland?', *Environmental Management*, 47(1) (2011), 11–27, at 14.

[301] Chapter 15.

[302] Chapter 21. As an example, Valguarnera states that '[m]unicipalities in the Stockholm area have been criticized [. . .] for the large number of exemptions granted for constructions close to the shore'.

## 6.4 *Decreasing support of the general public*

The general public may stimulate the protection of wilderness in a country in several ways, particularly by voting for the political parties that appreciate nature and by taking public action against projects that constitute concrete threats to wilderness. This may take the form of direct protest or influencing the media, but may also be more indirect by supporting non-governmental pressure groups that take action on behalf of the general public. Several authors discussed 'success stories' of wilderness protection whereby the general public and NGOs played a decisive role. For instance, Volker Mauerhofer discussed how in 1985 a peaceful occupation action prevented the construction of a hydropower dam in the largest Austrian lowland wetlands alongside the Danube River.[303] Other examples include public protests 'against the construction of a hydroelectric power station in the Katun River' (Russia, 1980s),[304] and against road constructions at Mount St. Anna (Poland, 1998), and the Rospuda valley (Poland, 2007).[305]

However, in several countries it appears that public support for nature, or more specifically wilderness, has decreased over the last decade. As explained by Urban, in Poland the general public appears to take the view that 'habitat fragmentation is inevitable and that projects, such as road constructions, should in most cases be considered acceptable as these projects represent prevailing public interest'.[306] He also explains that the support for environmental NGOs is limited, which substantially weakens the position of these groups in public discussions on plans and projects that may compromise wilderness values.

Similar developments were reflected in other countries. García-Ureta explains that for Spain 'the environment is not perceived as a problem'[307] and that 'green political parties obtained less than 0.5 per cent of the votes in the general elections held in 2011'.[308] He considers that 'only NGOs can be regarded as the bulwark pressing for better and improved nature protection' but, according to the author, 'they lack a large number of affiliates to sustain their activities'.[309]

303 Chapter 11.
304 Chapter 19.
305 Chapter 18.
306 *Ibid.*
307 Chapter 20, Agustín García-Ureta refers to the July 2014 barometer of the Centre for Sociological Surveys (CIS); www.cis.es/cis/export/sites/default/-Archivos/Indicadores/documentos_html/TresProblemas.html.
308 *Ibid.*
309 *Ibid.*

On the positive side it should, however, be noted that in particular since 2009 several NGOs (e.g., the Wild Europe Initiative, the European Wilderness Society and Rewilding Europe) have been focusing their work on the protection of wilderness or 'rewilding' in Europe. The joint organization of workshops and the adoption of 'A Vision for a Wilder Europe' are among the initiatives that reflect the strengthened collaboration between these NGOs.[310]

### 6.5 *Challenges related to climate change*

Wilderness protection, particularly the protection of the high level of naturalness, is threatened by climate change. For instance, Kokko and Oksanen explain:

> Because wilderness reserves and other nature protection areas are mainly located in the northerly areas of the country and sometimes at high altitudes, the flora and the fauna there are very susceptible to the effects of global climate change. Some of the species populations are the southernmost to be found and the sea constitutes an obstacle to their moving northwards. Even where an area may remain otherwise unmodified by virtue of a wilderness protection policy, the habitats are subject to change.[311]

### 6.6 *Private property rights*

As noted above, wilderness protection and property rights have a complicated relationship that may have positive or negative implications for wilderness. Property rights may provide a strong legal tool to protect wilderness if the owner seeks to protect wilderness (see above). However, private property rights may also constitute a hurdle for wilderness protection. For instance, in many domestic systems discussed in Part II natural areas can in principle only be designated as National Park if the areas are state-owned. Also, Article 46 of the Icelandic Nature Conservation Act 2013 makes clear that 'uninhabited wilderness' 'should be owned by the state unless particular reasons justify other arrangement based on an agreement between the Minister and the land owner'.[312] In each of these domestic systems expropriation of privately owned lands is

[310] Magnus Sylvén and Staffan Widstrand, *A Vision for a Wilder Europe, January 2015* (2nd edn.), e-publication, www.rewildingeurope.com/wp-content/uploads/2015/03/WILD10-Vison-for-a-Wilder-Europe-2015.pdf.
[311] Chapter 14.
[312] Chapter 16.

possible but politically this is often very sensitive. Valguarnera explains that in 2010 in Sweden this hurdle was raised by changing the Expropriation Act:

> According to the new rules, the landowner is not only entitled to full compensation, but actually to one hundred and twenty-five per cent of the market value. The preparatory works justifies the added twenty-five per cent by referring to the fact that the expropriation violates the right of the owner to dispose of the land according to his or her own wishes.[313]

Wilderness protection may also be limited when after designation of wild areas as protected area, existing land-use rights are respected. For instance, Kokko and Oksanen explain that '[i]f a private owner had a right to build a road before the AWR was enacted (e.g., in the form of an easement or a usufruct or as part of a full private property right on the land), this right is usually respected'.[314]

## 6.7 *Factors that are weakening implementation and compliance*

At the international level, Mauerhofer, Galle and Onida explain that the effectiveness of the protocols to the Alpine Convention is severely limited due to the fact that Switzerland still has not yet ratified any of these Protocols.[315] The application of international agreements may also be hindered by 'reservations' by the Contracting Parties. For instance, Arie Trouwborst notes that thirteen parties entered reservations to the (level of) protection of large carnivores (particularly the bear and wolf) under the Bern Convention.[316] Taking into account the vast and often transboundary habitats of these large carnivores and their role in ensuring a high degree of naturalness in wilderness areas,[317] such reservations directly affect wilderness qualities in Europe. Several other weaknesses of the international regimes that may also limit the role of these instruments in wilderness protection have received attention, such as the lack of a 'non-compliance procedure' under the World Heritage Conventions.[318]

Various authors also discussed factors that may weaken compliance at the domestic level. To a certain degree, several of the hurdles discussed above (e.g., focus on economic interests, decentralization and a

313 Chapter 21. The author refers to the Expropriation Act, Chapter 4, para. 1(1)(2).
314 Chapter 14.
315 Apart from the Monaco Protocol; see Chapter 9.
316 Chapter 7.
317 Chapters 3 and 7.
318 Chapter 6.

decrease of the general public's 'activism') may already weaken the application and enforcement of the legal instruments that are available for wilderness protection; however, these concerns are amplified by certain additional compliance issues. An example is the concern of insufficient budgets for management and qualified staff, a concern afflicting Russian *zapovedniki* as well as many other large protected areas in Europe.[319]

## 7 Conclusions: options for strengthening wilderness protection in Europe

### 7.1 *Many options, good examples, but no guarantees*

In Europe, a loss of wilderness has occurred due to an intensive process of cultivation, attributable to the conviction that wild nature was meant to serve humankind, the legal emphasis upon sovereignty and private property as well as various practical factors, such as the increase of the human population, technology innovation and commercialization. Since the turn of the twentieth century, however, initiatives have been taken across Europe – often driven by inspiring and influential individuals – to protect the last remaining relatively undisturbed natural areas. Besides recreational objectives, particular scientific research interests constituted important motivations for the protection of such land, which brought many of the early protected area initiatives close to the modern concept of wilderness protection. Nonetheless, until the last two decades the term 'wilderness' was rarely used in the context of European law or policy. The various case-studies in this book show that even today 'wilderness' receives very little explicit attention in international, European and domestic instruments that are relevant for nature protection in Europe.

Notwithstanding this very limited legal attention for wilderness in Europe, the concept of protecting relatively large, ecologically intact and undeveloped natural areas has received increasing attention over the last decade. Stimulated by the Resolution of the European Parliament, European NGOs, universities, governments and individuals have invested substantial efforts in developing a definition for wilderness in a European context, inventorying the remaining wilderness in Europe and promoting the protection of these areas.[320] As discussed in Part I, knowledge and awareness of the values of European wilderness have also

[319] Chapter 19. See also Chapter 18.
[320] See Chapters 1 and 2 and Section 2 and Subsections 3.1 and 3.2.

substantially increased.[321] This renders it both possible and important to evaluate the role of international, European and domestic law in protecting wilderness areas and their distinguishing qualities in Europe.

The answers to the first three main research questions of this book have already been summarized above. Section 3 discussed the working definition of 'wilderness' in a European context, where wilderness areas in Europe still may be found, and the values that these areas represent. Section 4 considered the extent to which European wilderness areas receive protection under international and regional conventions and European law, while the state of wilderness protection under domestic law was summarized in Section 5. These outcomes show that wilderness protection is not an explicit aim of the conventions and EU directives discussed in this book, while very few European jurisdictions have adopted explicit wilderness protection legislation. On a positive note, the legal frameworks provide many tools to protect areas with relatively high wilderness qualities without necessarily making explicit reference to the term 'wilderness'. Within each of these systems, protected area legislation is clearly the most pertinent mechanism for wilderness protection in Europe, although areas with relatively high wilderness qualities may also receive protection through other legislation, such as general environmental law, spatial planning law, forestry law, environmental impact assessment law and property law.

The discussions also illustrate the effective practical use of these tools. These include a series of developments across all tiers of governance. On an international level, the protection of wilderness areas as World Heritage Sites provides one potentially effective avenue to promote wilderness values. Regionally, the Bern Convention and its application to the habitats of large carnivores may also offer scope for the protection of large tracts of wilderness-quality land. Specific obligations and policies are forthcoming under the auspices of the Alps Convention and the Carpathian Convention, respectively, and at the EU level initiatives have been pursued to promote a degree of confluence between biodiversity protection established under Natura 2000 and the protection of wilderness. On a national level, notable developments towards a wider set of 'best practices' include wilderness protection through National Parks or nature reserves regimes and/or by zoning approaches within such protected areas, transboundary wilderness protection such as Europe's Wild Heart

[321] See Chapters 3, 4 and 5 and Subsection 3.3.

project,[322] the protection of Russian wilderness under the century-old *zapovednik* system, wilderness protection under forestry legislation through the establishment of a 'network of Woodland Key Habitats',[323] a separate act to protect wilderness in the Icelandic highlands, explicit wilderness protection at the municipal level (e.g., natural reserve Bredåsen in the Swedish municipality of Älvdalen)[324] and general prohibitions on off-road use of motorized vehicles.[325]

These are positive developments for the protection of wilderness in Europe. Clearly, international treaties, EU directives and domestic legislation play a much more substantive role in protecting wilderness in Europe than one would expect from a preliminary assessment of the relevant legal instruments.

However, this positive message on the many options and good examples of legal wilderness protection in Europe should not hide the clear and, unfortunately, more negative overall conclusion from this study: in the case of almost all the legal tools identified herein, their actual use for the benefit of wilderness protection in Europe is uncertain and heavily dependent upon public awareness and political will. Most legal instruments are facultative, and none of the legal instruments, in isolation or combination, provide real legal guarantees that wilderness in Europe will be protected at a larger scale. Moreover, the position of wilderness is further weakened in European societies that are strongly focused on economic growth, where systems are based on 'balancing interests' and increasing decentralization, and where (at least in a number of countries) the general public appears to have limited interest in joint action against developments with an impact upon wilderness.

### *7.2 Options for strengthening wilderness protection in Europe*

Taking into account all the previous discussions, this chapter now turns to the question of whether there is a need to strengthen the legal protection of wilderness areas in Europe, and, if so, what are the options to do so?

Whether the legal framework requires strengthening depends of course in the first place on whether the values of European wilderness are considered sufficiently important to ensure they receive adequate

[322] See Chapter 12.
[323] Chapter 13.
[324] Chapter 21.
[325] Chapter 16.

protection, an issue that has received intensified European-wide attention since 2006.[326] This debate and the arguments thereto used cannot be comprehensively summarized here, but as already reflected in Section 4 of the introductory chapter, there are many strong voices among academic experts, governments, NGOs, as well as the European Parliament in favour of enhanced protection for the remaining wilderness areas in Europe, as well as to promote initiatives to restore or 're-wild' natural areas in Europe. Many chapters of this volume have also paid substantial attention to the reasons underpinning why wilderness protection must be considered important: notably the possible benefits of wilderness protection in attaining the primary aims of existing legal systems, the values of European wilderness for the recovery of threatened species of wild plants and animals, and the cultural, social and economic values for not only current generations of people, but also the value of wilderness protection for future generations. For instance, Fulop explains that without adequate wilderness protection, we cannot be considered to have discharged our equitable commitments to future generations.[327] The essence of this discussion is well captured by Norton's consideration:

> suppose that our generation converts all wilderness areas and natural communities into productive mines, farmlands, production forests, or shopping centres, and suppose that we do so efficiently and that we are careful to save a portion of the benefits, and invest them wisely, leaving the future far more wealthy than we are. Does it not make sense to claim that, in doing so, we harmed future people, not economically, but in the sense that we seriously and irreversibly narrowed their range of choices and experiences? A whole range of human experience would have been obliterated; the future will have been (...) impoverished.[328]

[326] See Chapter 1, Section 4.

[327] Chapter 15.

[328] B. Norton, 'Ecology and opportunity. Intergenerational equity and sustainable options', in: A. Dobson (ed.), *Fairness and Futurity. Essays in Environmental Sustainability and Social Justice* (Oxford University Press, 1999): 118–150, at 130–131. See also Hicham-Stéphane Afeissa, 'The transformative value of ecological pragmatism: an introduction to the work of Bryan G. Norton', 1, *Surveys and Perspectives Integrating Environment and Society* (SAPIENS), 1 (2008): 51–57, 53. See also Kees Bastmeijer, 'Intergenerational equity and the Antarctic Treaty System: Continued efforts to prevent "mastery"', in: Gudmundur Alfredsson, Timo Koivurova (eds. in chief) and Kamrul Hossain (special ed. Volume 3), 3 *The Yearbook of Polar Law* (Boston/Leiden: Brill/Martinus Nijhoff Publishers, 2011), 635–682.

If we could agree on the desirability or need to ensure adequate protection for European wilderness, the discussions in this book show that – as explained above – the legal protection indeed requires strengthening.

Recommendations for Strengthening Wilderness Protection in Europe

(a) **Consider the development of explicit policies for wilderness protection under the various existing international, European and domestic legal systems**
Since most of the legal regimes discussed herein (international, European or domestic) have primary objectives other than wilderness protection, the application of these tools in real terms to protect wilderness is uncertain. The current examples of wilderness protection under most legal systems appear not to be based on explicit wilderness policies and therefore have an overly 'coincidental' character. Therefore, in the various international, European and domestic legal systems it is important to:
- increase awareness about the wilderness concept;
- increase awareness of the values of wilderness;
- study the relationship between wilderness protection and the existing primary objectives (particularly biodiversity conservation and sustainable use of natural resources) of the legal system:[329]
  - study how wilderness protection and the primary objectives of the legal systems may strengthen each other;
  - identify potential contradictions between the primary objectives of legal systems and wilderness protection and develop ideas how such contradictions may be prevented/addressed;
- develop explicit policies on wilderness protection.[330]

(b) **Distinguish between areas with different degrees of wilderness qualities when identifying values, developing wilderness policy and strengthening legal protection. While the last most intact wilderness areas require the strictest levels of protection, protection of all the main wilderness qualities of other areas is crucial for**

[329] See also Subsection 4.4.

[330] According to the Wild Europe Initiative, a 'growing number of countries are now adopting national strategies for restoration of large-scale natural ecosystems, amid increased awareness of their benefit to conservation objectives and society in general'; see http://www.wildeurope.org/index.php/restoration/national-strategies/a-wind-of-change-in-western-europe.

**wilderness restoration and rewilding and – ultimately – for facilitating greater wilderness coverage in Europe in the future**

In creating awareness in relation to wilderness, in getting a better understanding of its values, as well as in establishing policy and legal protection, the 'wilderness continuum approach' makes it possible to distinguish between various degrees of wilderness. In terms of legal protection, it is particularly important to ensure the strictest protection for the last remaining areas that are close to pristine wilderness (approximately one per cent of the terrestrial territory, e.g., old-growth forests and relatively undisturbed natural wetlands).[331] In respect to these areas, the continuum approach should not be used to argue that lowering the degree of wildness is not problematic. Rather, the continuum approach makes it possible not only to focus on the last percentile of near pristine wilderness, but also to value and protect wilderness qualities and related values of less pristine areas and of areas with high potential for wilderness restoration or rewilding.[332] This is particularly important to ensure that Europe may have more wilderness in the future and to prevent an approach that does not go beyond the level of 'deathbed conservation' of the real last wildernesses.

(c) **Ensure improvement and effective use of existing legal tools to protect all the main qualities of wilderness and/or consider the adoption of explicit wilderness protection law**

For each legal system, the adequacy of the available legal instruments to implement subsequent wilderness protection policies (see under (a) and (b)), should be assessed. As concluded above, many of the legal tools in international, European and domestic law connect only with one or two of the main wilderness qualities, while complete and effective wilderness protection entails the protection of all of these qualities. For this reason, it may be necessary to adjust the way in which these instruments are applied in practice or even these instruments themselves. Effective wilderness

[331] The Wild Europe Initiative stresses that there is 'a need to secure effective strategy for protection of remaining areas of old growth forest'; see 'Options for building a strategy for old growth forest protection in Europe', http://www.wildeurope.org/index.php/wild-areas/old-growth-forest-protection-strategy.

[332] Definitions of rewilding often particularly reflect the wilderness quality of naturalness with a focus on free-functioning ecosystems. See, for instance, Henrique M. Pereira and Laetitia M. Navarro (eds.), *Rewilding European Landscapes* (Dordrecht: Springer, 2015), at 11. See also the working definition used by Rewilding Europe in their Annual Review 2014, *supra* note 76, at 3.

protection often requires the application of a mixture of instruments, but wilderness protection through strict area protection (e. g., through strict protected zones in National Parks or strict protected nature reserves with attention to all three main wilderness qualities) appears to be most promising.

If existing legal instruments are considered insufficient to ensure adequate protection and adjustments are not made to address these concerns, the development of new instruments, explicitly aimed at securing wilderness protection, should be considered. The legislation of Iceland connects best with the working definition of European wilderness and may constitute an inspiring example.

(d) **Consider the establishment of minimum legal requirements at the international or European levels to set a minimum standard for wilderness protection in Europe**

Even if at the domestic level discernible wilderness policies are developed and legal mechanisms to protect wilderness are available, the factors discussed in Section 6 and elsewhere in this book may frustrate effective wilderness protection. There may simply be too little political will to implement and enforce long-term wilderness protection due to a combination of factors, such as the current strong focus on biodiversity and sustainable use of natural resources, the tendency to prioritize socio-economic interests in decision-making processes that are based on balancing interests, a trend of decentralization of nature protection competences and the diminishing enthusiasm of the general public in various European countries to protest against plans and projects that may impact adversely upon wilderness values.

Therefore, initiatives under (a), (b) and (c) above at various governance levels could be made less dependent on voluntary action by establishing minimum standards on wilderness protection and restoration at the European level.[333] Such minimum standards could, for instance, include:

i. An obligation to ensure strict protection of the areas that are close to the status of 'pristine' wilderness (the last remaining true wilderness areas; see (b) above);

[333] See, e.g., Chapter 18. Sergiusz Urban states: 'Most likely, if wilderness is to be better protected and enforced in Poland, there is a need for external inspiration, coming from international and regional (for example the European Union or the Council of Europe) legislation.'

ii. An obligatory strict target for restoring/rewilding natural areas, e.g., as a percentage of the total territory and linked to a concrete date.[334]

The minimum standards could be set through, for instance:

- The adoption of an explicit wilderness protection strategy in the European Union to integrate the successful implementation of the Natura 2000 system with wilderness restoration and protection (only relevant for EU Member States);
- The adoption of a separate Convention on the Protection of Wilderness in Europe,[335] for instance under the umbrella of the Council of Europe;
- The adoption of a Memorandum of Understanding between the Secretariats of existing conventions and the European Commission, focused on the achievement of clear and measurable wilderness objectives through these existing international and European legal instruments.

While minimum European standards would primarily aim to protect and restore wilderness and related values, efforts to meet these standards may also strongly support the achievement of international and European nature policy objectives and the implementation of obligations under existing international and European nature conservation law. For example, as explained in Part II, wilderness may contribute to certain biodiversity objectives of the EU directives and the Bern Convention, as well as the protection of universal outstanding natural values under the World Heritage Convention and may further support the implementation of various obligations of the Alpine and Carpathian convention. And as M. Navarro and Henrique M. Pereira explain, rewilding could also contribute to the implementation of the targets regarding the 'restoration of degraded ecosystems' and several other objectives under the Convention on Biological Diversity (Aichi Targets 14 and 15) and the 2020 EU

[334] An example of a European country that has adopted an explicit 'rewilding' objective is Germany. To meet the two per cent wilderness objective (see Subsection 5.3), rewilding is considered necessary: see the Nationale Strategie zur biologischen Vielfalt, *supra* note 174 (English version; https://www.cbd.int/doc/world/de/de-nbsap-01-en.doc), at 53. See also Max Rossberg's report on the 'Wilderness Workshop in Vilm' (Germany), available through the website of the European Wilderness Society, http://wilderness-society.org/wilderness-workshop-vilm-germany/.

[335] Mark Fisher and Steve Carver have advocated a European Wilderness Convention in their presentation 'European wilderness as revealed by strict protection in nature conservation and forest legislation', *supra* note 204. At WILD 10, Resolution 17, 'A Wilderness Convention for Europe' was adopted, http://resolutions.wild10.org/wp-content/uploads/2013/10/res17_wilderness-convention-europe_final.pdf.

biodiversity strategy.[336] These and many other experts also emphasize the social and economic benefits of wilderness protection and rewilding.[337] This three-pronged approach – wilderness protection as an independent objective, as a strategy to implement existing conventions and EU law, and as a strategy to strengthen ecosystem services – may constitute a strong foundation for attaining consensus on legal wilderness standards for Europe.

[336] Laetitia M. Navarro and Henrique M. Pereira, 'Towards a European Policy for Rewilding', in Pereira and Navarro (eds.), *Rewilding European Landscapes, supra* note 332, 205–223, at 217.

[337] *Ibid.* See also Chapters 4 and 5 as well as Sylvén and Widstrand, *A Vision for a Wilder Europe, supra* note 310, action point 5.

# INDEX

Printed in the United States
By Bookmasters